D1343759

DK
SPACE
Encyclopedia

SPACE
Encyclopedia

Heather Couper and Nigel Henbest

A Dorling Kindersley Book

TO DADDY, CAPTAIN G. C. E. COUPER ESQ. (1921–98)
YOU'LL ALWAYS BE MISSION CONTROL

LONDON, NEW YORK, MUNICH,
MELBOURNE, and DELHI

PARKES RADIO TELESCOPE, NEW SOUTH WALES, AUSTRALIA

Senior Editor
Jackie Wilson

Senior Art Editor
Miranda Kennedy

Editors
Emma Johnson, Isabel Moore, Steve Setford, Giles Sparrow, Marek Walisiewicz

Designers
Sarah Crouch, Kelly Flynn, Martyn Foote, Rebecca Johns, Jim Marks

Contributors
Helen Gavaghan BSc, David Hughes BSc DPhil FRAS FInstP CPhys,
Tony Jones BSc PhD CPhys MInstP, Ian Ridpath FRAS, Robin Scagell FRAS,
Giles Sparrow BSc MSc, Carole Stott BA FRAS

Managing Editor Jayne Parsons
Managing Art Editor Gill Shaw
DTP designer Nomazwe Madonko
Picture research Liz Moore
Production Lisa Moss

Hardback edition first published in Great Britain in 1999.
This edition published in Great Britain in 2003
by Dorling Kindersley Limited,
80 Strand, London WC2R 0RL

2 4 6 8 10 9 7 5 3 1

Copyright © 1999, © 2003, Dorling Kindersley Limited, London
A Penguin Company

All rights reserved. No part of this publication may be reproduced,
stored in a retrieval system, or transmitted by any means, electronic,
mechanical, photocopying, recording, or otherwise, without the
prior permission of the copyright owner.

A CIP catalogue record for this book is available
from the British Library.
ISBN 1-4053-0109-0

Reproduced in Italy by G.R.B. Editrice, Verona
Printed and bound in Spain by Artes Graficas Toledo S.A.

See our complete catalogue at
www.dk.com
D.L.TO:285-2003

DUMBBELL NEBULA

CONTENTS

VERY LARGE ARRAY RADIO TELESCOPE, NEW MEXICO, USA

CENTRAL PART OF OUR GALAXY, THE MILKY WAY

HOW TO USE THIS BOOK

THE DK SPACE ENCYCLOPEDIA contains detailed information on every aspect of astronomy, space, and the Universe. Entries are grouped into sections, so that all the information about planets, stars, galaxies, or spacecraft can be found together. Within each section are main entries. Each entry opens with an introduction to the subject, then goes into more detail in separate, easy-to-manage topics that use photos and artwork to illustrate the facts. To find information on a particular subject, the index will guide you to all the entries on that topic.

PAGE LAYOUT
The information on each page is presented in a way that makes it easy to understand what is going on. Start reading the introduction, move on to the sub-entries, and then read the annotations.

Introduction: Each main entry starts with an introduction that provides an overview of the subject. After reading this, you should have a good idea of what the page is all about.

Sub-entries provide important additional information and expand on points in the introduction.

ABBREVIATIONS

km = kilometre
m = metre
cm = centimetre
mm = millimetre (tenth of 1 centimetre)
nm = nanometre (millionth of 1 millimetre)

km/h = kilometres per hour
km/s = kilometres per second
kg = kilogram
g = gram
s = second
m = minute
d = day
y = year

°C = degrees Centigrade
° = degrees (angle)
g = acceleration due to gravity
ly = light year
AU = astronomical unit

billion = thousand million
trillion = thousand billion
quadrillion = thousand trillion
quintillion = thousand quadrillion

PLANETARY NEBULAS

LIKE A FLOWER BURSTING INTO BLOOM, a planetary nebula unfolds into space. Another swollen red giant has died and puffed off its outer layers in an expanding cloud that will shine for tens of thousands of years. All stars with a mass up to eight times that of the Sun will end their lives in this way, their material spread out into delicate glowing rings and shells. The nebula will gradually fade and disappear, but at its heart is a white dwarf – the hot, dense remains of the star's core that, over billions of years, will cool and disappear.

Outer lobes of older gas

Inner shell of recently ejected gas

Hydrogen makes up most of material in the nebula. In this Space Telescope photograph, it is shown in red.

Heavy oxyge... up as...

CAT'S EYE NEBULA
When a red giant has no more helium fuel to burn, its core shrinks and the star expands once again. But this time the expansion is so sudden that the outer layers of the star lift off and blow away into space. The intensely hot core lights up the departing gas and creates a planetary nebula (given its name by William Herschel, who thought that the disc-like clouds looked like planets). Planetary nebulas last a few thousand years, and so are quite rare – only about 1,500 are known in the Milky Way Galaxy. The Cat's Eye Nebula is one of the most complex. It is about 1,000 years old.

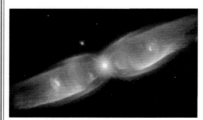

CAT'S EYE NEBULA

White dwarf lies at the centre. It is the burned-out core of a red giant, which astronomers think may be part of a double star system.

BUTTERFLY NEBULA
One of the most beautiful planetary nebulas is Minkowski 2-9, an example of a butterfly nebula. Astronomers believe that the white dwarf at its centre is pulling material off a larger companion star, creating a swirling disc of gas and dust. When the red giant blew off its outer layers, the disc deflected the material into two jets, streaming out at more than 300 km/s. The nebula lies about 2,100 light years from Earth in the constellation of Ophiuchus, and is about 1,200 years old.

👁 SPOTTING PLANETARY NEBULAS
Planetary nebulas are faint and often cannot be seen without a telescope. One of the easiest to find is the Ring Nebula in Lyra, to the southeast of Vega and east of Sheliak. It looks like a small, faint smoke ring and can be seen through a small telescope on a dark, moonless night.

RING NEBULA AND NEARBY STARS

NOTABLE PLA...

Name	Constel...
Helix	Aquari...
Dumbbell	Vulpecu...
Owl	Ursa M...
Bug	Scorpi...
Ring	Lyra
Saturn	Aquari...
Clown	Gemini...
Blinking Planetary	Cygnus...
Little Dumbbell	Perseus...
Cat's Eye	Draco

FIND...
PROPERTIES OF STA...
SUPERNOVAS 184 • NEUTR...

👁 PRACTICAL TOPICS
An eye symbol next to an entry indicates that it gives information about an object that you can see for yourself. Wherever possible, these are stars and other objects that can be seen with the naked eye. The final section of the book is also devoted to Practical Stargazing and contains useful information on finding your way around the night sky, star maps, and tips on stargazing.

DATA BOXES
Many pages have a data file box that gives facts and figures about key objects featured in the entry. For example, this box contains information about some of the most prominent planetary nebulas in the Milky Way Galaxy, such as their names, distance from Earth, and size.

Distances given for planets, stars, galaxies, and other objects are always the distance from Earth.

COLOUR BORDERS
Each of the six sections of the book has a different colour border to help you locate the section easily. This page on planetary nebulas has a blue border because it is within "The Stars" section.

1983 INFRARED ASTRONOMY
The first infrared astronomy satellite, IRAS, is launched. It must be cooled to extremely low temperatures with liquid helium, and after a period of 300 days its supply of helium is exhausted. During this time it completes an infrared survey of 98% of the sky.

TIMELINE
The Reference Section at the end of the Encyclopedia includes a Timeline. This charts the key developments in astronomy and space exploration from the earliest times to the present day.

VENUS AT A GLANCE
Venus is a rocky planet with a structure and size similar to Earth's. Its atmosphere helps to make it the hottest planet of all. It spins slowly, in the opposite direction to most planets.

TILT, SPIN, AND ORBIT — Orbits Sun in 224.7 days.

Axis tilts from the vertical by 2.7°.

Spins on its axis once every 243 days.

ATMOSPHERE

Nitrogen 3.5% and trace gases

Carbon dioxide 96.5%

STRUCTURE — Iron and nickel core — Rocky mantle — Silicate crust

SCALE — Venus is a little smaller than the Earth.

Sun — Venus is the second planet from the Sun.

LOCATER

WHITE DWARFS
At the centre of every planetary nebula is a tiny, hot star called a white dwarf. This is the burned-out core of the original red giant, rich in carbon and oxygen produced by the star's helium-burning reactions, and exposed now the outer layers have been removed. Because they are no longer producing energy, white dwarfs have collapsed down to a very small volume – a typical white dwarf has the mass of the Sun compressed into a volume about the size of the Earth. About 10% of all the stars in the Galaxy may be white dwarfs, but they are so faint that only the nearest ones can be seen.

Sirius B is the closest white dwarf to the Sun. It is a tiny star in orbit around the bright star Sirius.

EVOLUTION OF WHITE DWARFS
When a red giant puffs off its outer layers, the exposed core is seen as the bright central star in a planetary nebula, on the far left of the Hertzsprung-Russell diagram. The core is extremely hot, and appears as a bright point of light with a temperature as high as 100,000°C. As the core cools, it moves into the bottom left of the diagram as a white dwarf. It has no more nuclear fuel to burn and gradually cools, moving down to the right as it fades away.

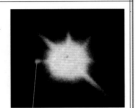

Planetary nebula phase

Supergiants

Red giants

Temperature

Absolute magnitude

MAIN SEQUENCE

Visual luminosity

White dwarf phase

Spectral type O B A F G K M

Exposed core moves rapidly across diagram to become a white dwarf.

Planetary nebula forms as outer layers of star are lost.

DENSITY OF A WHITE DWARF
White dwarf material is a million times more dense than water. This means that the gravitational field around a white dwarf is intense. A person standing on a white dwarf would weigh about 600 tonnes. A matchbox of white dwarf material would weigh as much as an elephant.

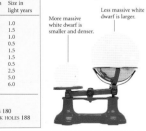

Less massive white dwarf is larger.

More massive white dwarf is smaller and denser.

CHANDRASEKHAR LIMIT
No white dwarf can have a mass greater than 1.4 times the mass of the Sun. This surprising discovery was made in 1930 by Subrahmanyan Chandrasekhar, who showed that the more massive a white dwarf is, the more it is crushed under its own gravity, and the smaller it is. If the core of the burnt-out star is heavier than 1.4 solar masses (the Chandrasekhar limit), it collapses to form a neutron star or a black hole.

[partially visible table, left edge:]

EBULAS

...e in ...ars	Size in light years
	1.0
	1.5
	1.0
	0.5
	1.5
	1.5
	0.5
	2.5
	5.0
	6.0

NTS 180
...ACK HOLES 188

...nebula is made of
...off the star
...red giant phase.
...not by the white
...he middle.

PLANETS AT A GLANCE
In the "Planets and Moons" section, there is an "At a glance" box for each planet and for Earth's Moon. These boxes give information on the individual characteristics, making it easy to compare the features of planets.

LANDMARK BOXES
Many pages have a box (with a tinted background) that gives historical information. Most give landmarks of achievement, either in astronomers' understanding of the Universe or the technology used for studying and exploring space, in date order.

Index and glossary: if you come across a term that you do not understand – such as Hertzsprung-Russell diagram – look it up in the glossary or index. The glossary defines about 200 terms. In the index, a bold page number indicates a major entry.

People: the nationality and dates of birth and death are given in the text for most people. However, for individuals that appear in the biography pages in the Reference Section, this information is given there.

FIND OUT MORE
There is a Find Out More box for each entry. This box lists other entries in the Space Encyclopedia where you can find out more about a particular subject. For example, this page on planetary nebulas gives four entries that tell you more about the death of stars and one entry that helps you to understand how stars change between birth and death.

GALILEO GALILEI
1564–1642

Italian mathematician, physicist, and astronomer who was the first to turn a telescope toward the heavens

As professor of mathematics at the Universities of Pisa and Padua, Galileo did much to disprove ancient Greek theories of physics. On learning of the invention of the telescope, he built one in 1609 and discovered that the Sun spun around every 25 days, the Moon was mountainous, Jupiter had four satellites, and Venus showed Moon-like phases. The Venus observations helped prove that the Sun and not Earth was at the centre of the Solar System. These revolutionary ideas, coupled with his belligerent nature and love of publicity, got him into trouble with the Church, and late in life he was tried by the Inquisition in Rome and placed under house arrest.

LORD OF THE RINGS

- In 1610 Galileo Galilei looked at Saturn through his primitive telescope, but mistook the planet's rings for two moons. Galileo called these "moons" ears.

GALILEO'S DRAWINGS OF THE EARS

- Christiaan Huygens recognized Saturn's rings in 1655.

- In 1675, Giovanni Cassini discovered the gap between rings A and B (now known as the Cassini Division).

BIOGRAPHIES
Pages 280–289 contain details on 75 people who have made key contributions to our knowledge of space. The biographies tell you about their lives, when they lived, and what they did.

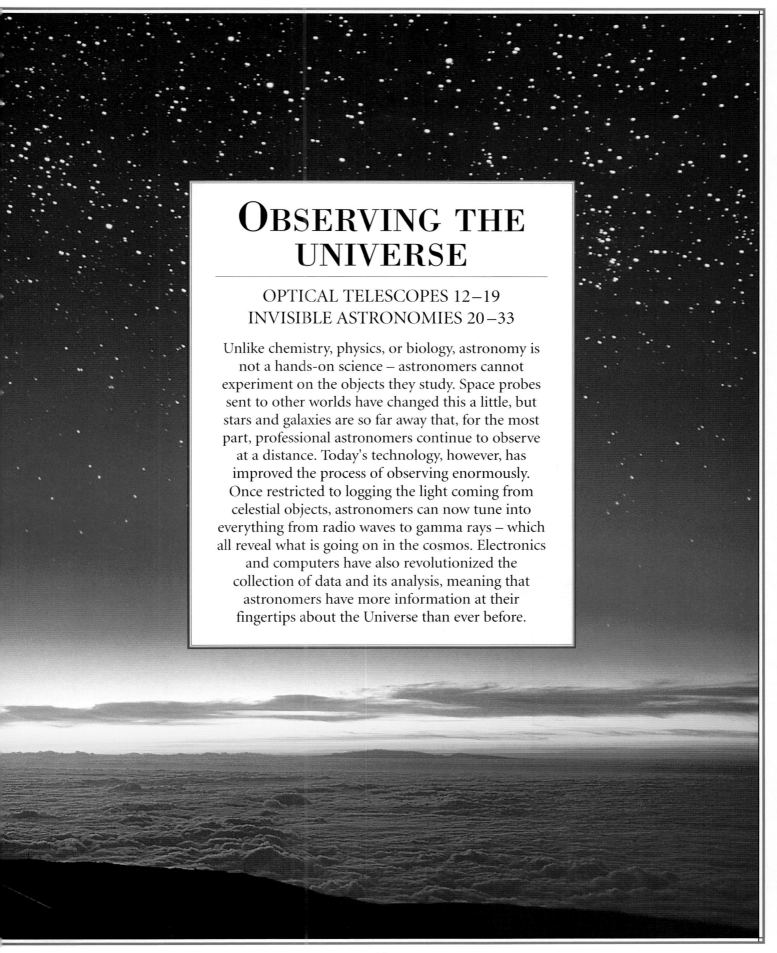

OBSERVING THE UNIVERSE

Unlike chemistry, physics, or biology, astronomy is not a hands-on science – astronomers cannot experiment on the objects they study. Space probes sent to other worlds have changed this a little, but stars and galaxies are so far away that, for the most part, professional astronomers continue to observe at a distance. Today's technology, however, has improved the process of observing enormously. Once restricted to logging the light coming from celestial objects, astronomers can now tune into everything from radio waves to gamma rays – which all reveal what is going on in the cosmos. Electronics and computers have also revolutionized the collection of data and its analysis, meaning that astronomers have more information at their fingertips about the Universe than ever before.

HUBBLE SPACE TELESCOPE

THE ULTIMATE TELESCOPE for astronomers seeking pin-sharp views of the depths of the Universe is the Hubble Space Telescope. Launched in 1990 after decades of planning, Hubble is an unmanned observatory in orbit far above the clouds and atmospheric haze that block the view of Earth-based telescopes. Astronomers from dozens of countries use Hubble, operating it by remote control. The human observer at the eyepiece has been replaced by sensitive light detectors, while electronic cameras record exquisite views of the cosmos.

HOW HUBBLE WORKS

The heart of Hubble is a reflecting telescope – much like telescopes on Earth. In space, however, it must operate without mains electricity, a mounting to swivel it around, or cables linking it to control computers. Instead, Hubble carries the type of equipment found on many satellites: solar panels to provide power, reaction wheels for pointing, and radio antennas for communicating with Earth.

RECEIVING A HUBBLE IMAGE OF THE TARANTULA NEBULA

GROUND CONTROL

Mission control for Hubble is at NASA's Goddard Space Flight Center, in Maryland, USA. All signals to and from Hubble pass through this centre, where engineers constantly monitor the spacecraft's health. The engineers act as a link between the orbiting telescope and the Hubble astronomers, working at the nearby Space Telescope Science Institute in Baltimore, who control the telescope's observing schedule.

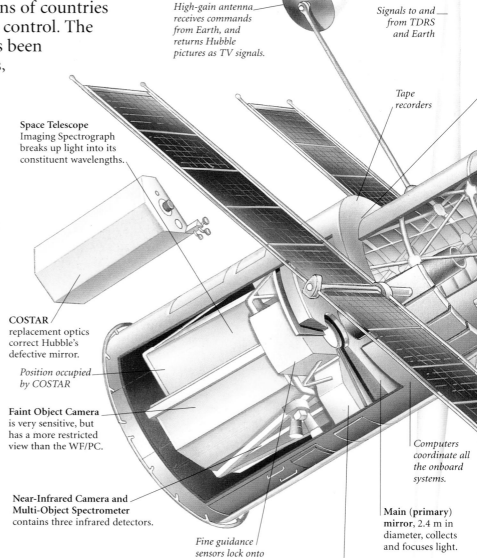

Tracking and Data Relay Satellite (TDRS) acts as a go-between for Hubble's radio messages. From its high orbit, it can keep both Hubble and ground control in sight.

High-gain antenna receives commands from Earth, and returns Hubble pictures as TV signals.

Signals to and from TDRS and Earth

Tape recorders

Space Telescope Imaging Spectrograph breaks up light into its constituent wavelengths.

COSTAR replacement optics correct Hubble's defective mirror.

Position occupied by COSTAR

Faint Object Camera is very sensitive, but has a more restricted view than the WF/PC.

Near-Infrared Camera and Multi-Object Spectrometer contains three infrared detectors.

Fine guidance sensors lock onto bright stars, to ensure that the telescope is steady and the images are not blurred.

Computers coordinate all the onboard systems.

Main (primary) mirror, 2.4 m in diameter, collects and focuses light.

Wide Field and Planetary Camera (WF/PC) is the main electronic camera.

TDRS ground station in New Mexico, USA, relays signals to and from Hubble and the Goddard Space Flight Center.

HUBBLE DATA	
Launched	25 April 1990
Main mirror	2.4-m diameter
Secondary mirror	0.34-m diameter
Length	13.1 m
Diameter	4.3 m
Solar panels	12.1 x 2.4 m
Mass	11.6 tonnes
Height of orbit	610 km
Period of orbit	95 minutes
Speed	27,700 km/h
Intended lifetime	15 years (may be extended)
Cost (at launch)	$1.5 billion

DEFECTIVE MIRROR

The first pictures astronomers received from Hubble were out of focus, though still better than any ground-based telescope. NASA realized that the mirror had been made in slightly the wrong shape, 0.002 mm too shallow at the outer edge.

Reaction wheels point Hubble at stars and other targets in space.

Sunshade protected the telescope at launch, and helps to prevent bright sunlight spoiling images.

Magnetometer senses Hubble's movement through the Earth's magnetic field.

Handrail for astronauts

Secondary mirror is supported within the telescope tube.

Light is reflected from the main mirror to the secondary, and then to the cameras and other detectors behind the main mirror.

Solar arrays provide power by converting sunlight into electricity.

Second high-gain antenna

BEST GROUND-BASED VIEW OF GALAXY M100

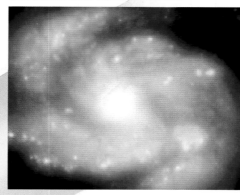

HUBBLE'S IMAGE OF GALAXY M100

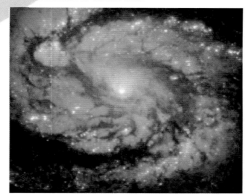

ADVANTAGES OF HUBBLE

Telescopes viewing the Universe from Earth must look upwards through our turbulent atmosphere, which constantly shifts and distorts the light from stars and galaxies – rather like looking through the swirling water in a busy swimming pool. That's why stars seem to twinkle. From its perch above the atmosphere, Hubble has a clear view of everything in the Universe, from planets to quasars billions of light years away.

SERVICING MISSIONS

With Hubble firmly in the grip of Space Shuttle Discovery, astronauts Steven Smith and Mark Lee service the orbiting telescope. Like any other vehicle, Hubble needs regular servicing. Shuttle astronauts replace equipment such as computers and tape recorders and update the telescope by installing new cameras and detectors for light and infrared radiation. On the first servicing mission in 1993, they installed "contact lenses" to correct the focus because of a fault on the main mirror that blurred Hubble's view.

HUBBLE'S SECOND SERVICING MISSION IN 1997

HUBBLE HISTORY

• American astronomer Lyman Spitzer (1914–) first proposed an extraterrestrial observatory in 1946.

• In 1977, NASA began to build Hubble.

• The Space Shuttle launched Hubble in 1990. Astronomers soon found the main mirror was slightly the wrong shape, but computers could help compensate for the fault.

• In 1992, Hubble found evidence for a massive black hole in the galaxy M87.

• Servicing mission in 1993 corrected Hubble's vision.

• In 1994, Hubble recorded Comet Shoemaker-Levy 9's impact with Jupiter.

• In 1995, Hubble photographed starbirth in the Eagle Nebula. Hubble also produced a view of the most distant galaxies, up to 10 billion light years away.

• An infrared camera was added to Hubble in 1997. Later it checked landing sites for Mars Pathfinder and monitored dust storms on Mars.

• In 1999, Hubble detected the galaxy containing an energetic gamma-ray burster – the most powerful explosion ever observed.

How telescopes work

Gathering light from the sky is still astronomers' main source of information about the Universe. With the exception of the Sun, most celestial bodies are far away and appear relatively dim. A telescope captures as much light as possible – the more light it collects, the more information it provides. There are two types of telescope. Reflectors capture light using a mirror, and refractors use a lens. Most modern professional telescopes are reflectors with mirrors many metres across, situated on mountain tops above the distortions caused by air moving in the lower atmosphere.

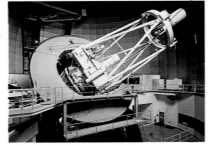

Cage for observer

AAT ON ITS HORSESHOE MOUNTING

AAT REFLECTOR
Located in Australia's Warrambungle Mountains, the Anglo-Australian Telescope (AAT) has a mirror 3.9 m in diameter. The secondary mirror can be replaced by a cage where an astronomer can sit to take photographs.

GEMINI 8-M REFLECTOR
The twin Gemini telescopes, sited in Hawaii and Chile, are run by astronomers from seven countries.

Main mirror is 8 m in diameter, and captures light from objects 500 million times fainter than can be seen by the naked eye.

Data-recording equipment is placed behind the main mirror or on the observing platform.

Mirror cell

Axle for tilting telescope up and down

Observing platform

Whole telescope mounting swings around horizontally.

REFLECTING TELESCOPES

Reflectors, such as the Gemini Telescope, capture light with a huge curved mirror, after which the image can be reflected towards any part of the telescope by secondary mirrors. This means the data-recording equipment does not have to be a part of the moving telescope. Reflectors have two key advantages over refractors. They collect light with a mirror, so there is no colour fringing. And, because a mirror can be supported at the back, there is no limit to the size of telescope.

REFRACTING TELESCOPES

Refractors capture light with a lens, which focuses the image onto a photographic plate or electronic light detector. The image is upside down, but in astronomy this does not matter. Refractors are robust and useful for viewing bright objects, but the thick glass of the lens absorbs precious light from fainter objects. The lens will also focus different colours of light at different points, giving rise to colour fringing. Lenses are also heavy: a lens more than 1 m across will bend under its own weight.

CORRECTING COLOUR FRINGING

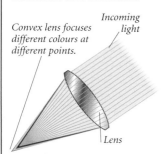

Convex lens focuses different colours at different points.

Incoming light

Lens

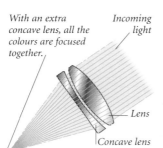

With an extra concave lens, all the colours are focused together.

Incoming light

Lens

Concave lens

MIRRORS

Telescope mirrors are made of low-expansion glass ceramic, polished for over a year, and coated with a thin film of aluminium. They must be absolutely smooth or the incoming light will be distorted and the images blurred. The mirror surface on the Gemini Telescope is polished to an accuracy of 16 billionths of a metre.

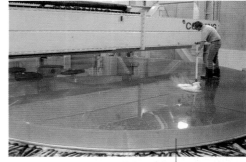

Gemini mirror is so smooth that if the 8-m mirror were the diameter of Earth, the largest bump would be only 30 cm high.

The telescope can be pointed to any part of the sky, and then "locked" on to the chosen object as it moves across the sky. Long exposures produce the best data for analysis.

Secondary mirror

Open frame lessens weight.

Schmidt photo of the Orion region covers an area of the sky 12 moonwidths across.

Conventional reflector sees an area of sky 1 moonwidth across. Two moonwidths is equivalent to 1° of sky, and from the horizon to directly overhead is 90°.

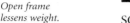

SCHMIDT TELESCOPE

A Schmidt telescope is a combination of reflector and refractor. Its mirror reflects starlight onto a curved photographic plate. The curved plate gives it a wide-angle view, but it needs a lens to eliminate distortions. The Schmidt can image large areas of sky – useful for carrying out sky surveys and tracking down objects for large reflectors to home in on.

LIGHT PATH IN REFLECTOR

Convex secondary mirror

Concave main mirror

Incoming light from objects in space, is collected by the main mirror.

Light is reflected from the main mirror towards secondary mirror.

Light reflected from secondary mirror passes through hole in the main mirror.

Light is focused onto a battery of instruments waiting to record the data.

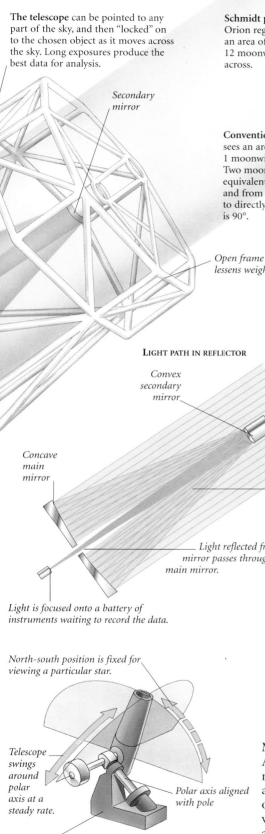

North-south position is fixed for viewing a particular star.

Telescope swings around polar axis at a steady rate.

Polar axis aligned with pole

Equatorial mounting has axis of the mount pointing at the celestial pole (north or south, depending on the hemisphere). The telescope swivels around the axis to follow the stars as they circle the pole.

Telescope tilts up and down.

Telescope swings around horizontally.

Altazimuth mounting allows big telescopes to be mounted horizontally, able to tilt up or down (in "altitude") and swing around (in "azimuth") to follow the stars.

MOUNTINGS

A telescope's mounting is almost as important as its mirror. It has to support the weight of the telescope and to swing it around as Earth spins on its axis, otherwise the objects being observed would drift out of view. There are two main types of mounting: equatorial and altazimuth. The altazimuth is the mainstay of today's professional telescopes. Continuous computer control allows giant telescopes such as Gemini to follow the paths of objects as they move across the sky.

FIRST REFRACTOR

• **Galileo** did not invent the telescope, but in 1609 he was the first to realize that a combination of lenses could be used to magnify the heavens. His telescopes were no more powerful than toys, but with them he discovered craters on the Moon, four moons of Jupiter, and the stars of the Milky Way.

Main lens

Telescope mounting

Eyepiece

FIRST REFLECTOR

• **Isaac Newton**, who pioneered so many areas of science, also made a study of how light was split up by a lens. He concluded that lenses would always form images with coloured fringes, and so set about designing a telescope that collected light with mirrors instead. His reflecting telescope, built in 1668, had a solid metal mirror made of copper, tin, and arsenic.

Mirror

Eyepiece

Telescope mounting

FIND OUT MORE

NEW DESIGNS 16
ANALYSING LIGHT 18
RADIATIONS FROM SPACE 20
SPINNING EARTH 242
REFRACTING TELESCOPES 270
REFLECTING TELESCOPES 272

New Designs

THE BIGGER THE MIRROR in a telescope, the more light it can collect and the more detail that can be seen. But mirrors more than 8 metres in diameter have limitations. One is the atmosphere: even an enormous mirror will still have its vision blurred by constantly moving pockets of air in the atmosphere. The other is size: the bigger the mirror, the more difficult it is to transport and handle. The latest ground-based telescopes use ingenious solutions to get around these limitations.

KECK TELESCOPES

The twin Keck Telescopes are situated on the 4,200-m summit of Mauna Kea in Hawaii, high above the cloud and water vapour in the lower atmosphere. The telescope mirrors measure 10 m across – giving them a light-collecting area half the size of a tennis court. A single mirror this size would bend under its own weight, so instead each mirror is made of 36 six-sided segments. Each segment weighs 400 kg and is 1.8 m wide and 7.7 cm thick.

Domes, 30 m high, protect the Keck Telescopes. The telescopes themselves weigh 270 tonnes and stand eight storeys tall. They are mounted on lightweight frames that provide strength while minimizing weight and cost.

Keck mirror has a total light-collecting area 17 times greater than the Hubble Space Telescope. Hubble can see more clearly, but the Keck Telescopes can see farther.

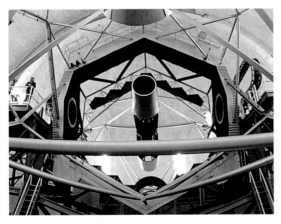

ACTIVE OPTICS

The first segmented mirror in the world is on the Keck 1 Telescope, completed in 1992. Both Keck Telescopes use active optics systems to counteract distortions caused by the weight of the mirrors or the wind. A computer controls the mirrors, adjusting each segment twice a second to an accuracy that is a thousand times finer than a human hair. As a result, the 36 segments behave as a single unchanging sheet of glass.

WORLD'S MOST POWERFUL TELESCOPES

Name	Diameter	Location	Comments
Very Large Telescope	4 x 8.2 m	Chile	Equivalent to 16.4 m
Large Binocular Telescope	2 x 8.4 m	USA	Equivalent to 11.9 m
Hobby-Eberly	11 m	USA	Not steerable
Keck I	10 m	Hawaii	First segmented mirror
Keck II	10 m	Hawaii	Twin of Keck I
Subaru	8.3 m	Hawaii	Japanese
Gemini North	8.1 m	Hawaii	International
Gemini South	8.1 m	Chile	International
Multiple Mirror Telescope	6.5 m	USA	Formerly had 6 mirrors
Zelenchukskaya	6.0 m	Russia	First large altazimuth
Hale	5.0 m	USA	"200-inch telescope"
William Herschel	4.2 m	Canary Islands	British-led
Cerro Tololo	4.0 m	Chile	Interamerican
Anglo-Australian	3.9 m	Australia	British/Australian
Mayall	3.8 m	USA	American

Buildings housing the VLT telescopes rotate along with the instruments, compensating for the Earth's rotation.

VERY LARGE TELESCOPE

The biggest telescope in the world is the European Southern Observatory's Very Large Telescope (VLT) in Chile. It consists of four 8.2-m telescopes – each a billion times more powerful than the naked eye. Linked together by a powerful computer, the VLT telescopes can scoop up as much light as a single mirror 16.4 m across. When combined with three other 1.8-m telescopes on the site, they have the power to see very fine detail – enough to spot an astronaut walking on the Moon.

OPTICAL SYNTHESIS

Five small telescopes, each with a 40-cm mirror, make up the Cambridge Optical Aperture Synthesis Telescope (COAST). Based on radio astronomy techniques, light from the five telescopes, spaced 100 m apart, is combined to mimic the image from a telescope with a 100-m mirror. Although it cannot gather as much light, COAST has extremely good resolution – it could read a car number plate at 1,000 km.

CAMBRIDGE OPTICAL APERTURE SYNTHESIS TELESCOPE

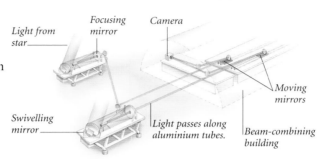

Light from star

Focusing mirror

Camera

Moving mirrors

Swivelling mirror

Light passes along aluminium tubes.

Beam-combining building

Swivelling mirror gathers light.

Beam-combining building

Fixed telescope mirror focuses light.

Small mirror reflects light into aluminium tubes.

ADAPTIVE OPTICS

With the atmosphere constantly moving, our view of the stars is blurred. In adaptive optics, a powerful laser creates an artificial star high in the atmosphere near the star under observation. A computer works out how the light from the artificial star is distorted as it travels through the atmosphere. It then shapes a constantly moving flexible mirror to focus the light back into a point, thus sharpening all the images that the telescope is seeing.

LASERS SHOOT INTO THE NEW MEXICO SKY

BIGGEST TELESCOPES

• In 1948, the USA completed the 5-m Hale Telescope on Palomar Mountain in California, superseding the Mount Wilson "100-inch" built in 1917. Hale collected data on photographic plates.

• From 1975 to the late 1980s, several 4-m class telescopes were constructed. Although smaller than Hale they used more sensitive electronic detectors.

• In 1976, Russia built the 6-m Zelenchukskaya Astrophysical Observatory telescope in the Caucasus Mountains. It was the first large telescope in the world with an altazimuth mount, but the telescope itself had poor optics.

• The 10-m Keck Telescope was completed in 1992. It is the first in the 10-m class of telescopes, which use huge apertures to exploit the efficiency of modern electronic detectors.

• The Very Large Telescope – equivalent to a 16.4-m telescope – will become fully operational in 2001.

FIND OUT MORE

HUBBLE SPACE TELESCOPE 12
HOW A TELESCOPE WORKS 14
ANALYSING LIGHT 18
RADIO ASTRONOMY 24

ANALYSING LIGHT

PROFESSIONAL ASTRONOMERS RARELY LOOK directly through telescopes. The human eye is simply not a good enough light detector. Instead, telescopes capture light from objects such as stars, nebulas, or galaxies with sensitive electronic cameras that build up an exposure over minutes or even hours if the object is very faint. Spectrographs split up light by its wavelengths to reveal the strength of each; computers analyse the results to show how hot the object is and what it is made of. Together, these two instruments can wring the last drop of information out of the light from a planet, star, or galaxy.

LIGHT-SENSITIVE CHIPS

Stunning pictures of galaxies look like photos, but are built up from a grid of squares, or pixels, like the image on a TV screen. They are taken with electronic cameras built around a light-sensitive computer chip called a charge-coupled device (CCD). CCDs are more sensitive than photographic plates: a 2-minute CCD exposure can show details as faint as a 1-hour photographic exposure.

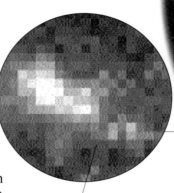

A **magnified CCD image** breaks up into coloured squares, or pixels, showing that it is a digital image.

CCD IMAGE OF SPIRAL GALAXY NGC **5457**

CCD from a big telescope, containing 524,288 pixels on a surface the size of a postage stamp

Spider mount

CHARGE-COUPLED DEVICE (CCD)

The CCD forms the heart of home camcorders and many TV cameras. It is a thin silicon chip with a light-sensitive surface divided into thousands or millions of square pixels (picture elements). When light falls on a pixel, an electric charge builds up: the more light, the larger the charge. At the end of the exposure, circuits built into the chip read off the patterns of charges, row by row, and feed them into a computer where they are stored as a digital image.

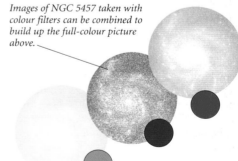

Images of NGC 5457 taken with colour filters can be combined to build up the full-colour picture above.

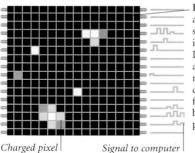

Pixels in a CCD are silicon squares separated by thin insulating walls. Light hitting a pixel ejects negatively charged electrons from the silicon, building up a positive charge.

Charged pixel *Signal to computer*

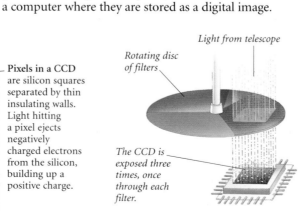

Rotating disc of filters

Light from telescope

The CCD is exposed three times, once through each filter.

SEEING IN COLOUR

A CCD can only see in black and white, but colour reveals vital information such as the temperature of stars. To obtain a full-colour image, astronomers take the same view several times, passing the light through filters and combining the images. All astronomers use the same colour filters – green, blue, and red – making it easier to compare images taken by different telescopes.

NGC 5457 is so faint that the human eye at the telescope eyepiece can see only the brightest regions.

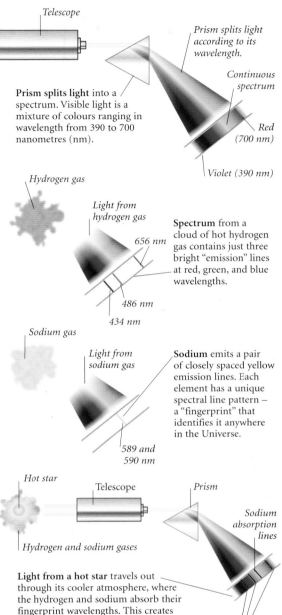

SPECTROSCOPY

Light is a mixture of different wavelengths, each corresponding to a different colour. The shortest wavelengths are violet and the longest red. In spectroscopy, astronomers use a prism or a diffraction grating (a glass plate etched with thousands of closely spaced lines) to spread out light into a spectrum of colours. The spectrum is crossed by bright or dark lines at different wavelengths. The power of spectroscopy lies in analysing these lines to reveal the elements that are present in the object and how hot it is.

Hot star

Telescope

Prism splits light according to its wavelength.

Prism splits light into a spectrum. Visible light is a mixture of colours ranging in wavelength from 390 to 700 nanometres (nm).

Continuous spectrum

Red (700 nm)

Violet (390 nm)

Hydrogen gas

Light from hydrogen gas

656 nm

Spectrum from a cloud of hot hydrogen gas contains just three bright "emission" lines at red, green, and blue wavelengths.

486 nm

434 nm

Sodium gas

Light from sodium gas

Sodium emits a pair of closely spaced yellow emission lines. Each element has a unique spectral line pattern – a "fingerprint" that identifies it anywhere in the Universe.

589 and 590 nm

COMPUTERS IN ASTRONOMY

Computers have taken over astronomical data handling. Most data – for instance, the output from CCDs and spectrographs – now comes in digital form, and it is a simple task to use computers to analyse it or to manipulate the images so as to emphasise the features of interest. Computers can also scan photographic plates, saving astronomers many hours of work.

Hot star

Telescope

Prism

Sodium absorption lines

Light from a hot star travels out through its cooler atmosphere, where the hydrogen and sodium absorb their fingerprint wavelengths. This creates dark absorption lines on the spectrum.

Hydrogen and sodium gases

Hydrogen absorption lines

PHOTOGRAPHIC PLATES

Before CCDs, astronomers relied on black-and-white photographic plates. Plates are still essential for some purposes. A wide-angle Schmidt telescope, for example, can record millions of stars and galaxies in a single exposure, but it needs a curved light detector more than 300 mm wide – far larger than any CCD. A large photographic plate can be bent to fit the focus of a Schmidt telescope.

The Anglo-Australian Telescope is one of the few big modern telescopes that can take photographic plates.

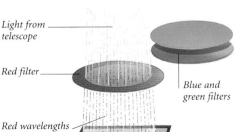

Light from telescope

Red filter

Blue and green filters

Red wavelengths pass through filter to expose photographic plate.

Colour separation technique: three black-and-white photographic plates are exposed through filters. They are then printed through the same filters onto a single sheet of paper, producing a full-colour image.

SPECTRAL LINES OF ELEMENTS

Element	Wavelengths (nanometres)		
Aluminium	394	–	–
Calcium	393	397	–
Helium	467	588	–
Hydrogen	434	486	656
Iron	373	375	382
Magnesium	383	384	518
Nitrogen	655	658	–
Oxygen	501	630	–
Silicon	390	–	–
Sodium	589	590	–

FIND OUT MORE

HOW TELESCOPES WORK 14
RADIATIONS FROM SPACE 20
MEASURE OF THE STARS 162 • PROPERTIES OF STARS 168

RADIATIONS FROM SPACE

A N INNOVATION AS CRUCIAL as the invention of the telescope swept astronomy in the late 20th century. New technology enabled astronomers to tune in to all the radiation coming from objects in space – and not simply light. Capturing light tells only part of the story. It is like hearing a single note from a melody: to experience the music fully you need to listen to all the notes, from the highest to the lowest. Light forms just one part of a whole range of electromagnetic radiation. Tuning in to invisible waves of energy, such as radio waves and X-rays, reveals a startlingly different picture of the Universe.

BEYOND OUR ATMOSPHERE

Stars, galaxies, and other objects in space all give off electromagnetic radiation. Whether it is in the form of light or radio waves, it consists of a stream of vibrating electric and magnetic fields spreading outwards. Travelling at 300,000 km/s (the speed of light), this radiation may travel thousands or even millions of light years towards us, but most is then absorbed by Earth's atmosphere. Invisible astronomy has only come of age since scientists have been able to intercept radiation in space.

Core of quasar (gamma rays)

Cluster of galaxies (X-rays)

HIGH-ENERGY SOURCES

Energetic regions of the Universe emit short-wavelength radiation. Gamma rays may come from electrons and antimatter annihilating each other. Very hot gas in clusters of galaxies emits X-rays, while hot atmospheres around stars pour out ultraviolet radiation.

Compton Gamma Ray Observatory

Rosat (X-ray)

Skylab Solar Telescope (extreme ultraviolet)

ORBITAL OBSERVATORIES

Most wavelengths are absorbed by gases in Earth's atmosphere, and are best studied by satellites which intercept radiation directly from space. The Hubble Space Telescope also flies in space for sharper views, unaffected by air movements in the lower atmosphere.

Height at which atmosphere has absorbed all radiation

Balloon carrying gamma ray and X-ray detectors

Spectrum has no end, but gamma rays with shorter and shorter wavelengths (and higher energies) are increasingly rare in the Universe.

Wavelengths within the light blue areas are unobservable from Earth's surface.

ELECTROMAGNETIC SPECTRUM

All radiation moves like a wave at sea, and the distance between the crests of the waves is known as the wavelength. Different radiations are distinguished by different wavelengths: those with the shortest wavelengths have the highest frequencies (number of waves per second) and carry the most energy.

	GAMMA RAYS					X-RAYS		
0.000,001 nm	0.000,01 nm	0.000,1 nm	0.001 nm	0.01 nm	0.1 nm	1 nm

Gamma rays have the shortest wavelengths – less than 0.01 nanometres (billionths of a metre). They are the most energetic form of radiation. Sources include the enigmatic gamma-ray bursters, which may be distant superpowerful exploding stars.

X-rays are emitted by hot gas between 1 million and 100 million °C – as found between galaxies and near black holes. X-ray detectors resemble Geiger counters more than telescopes. X-rays are absorbed in the upper atmosphere.

Ultraviolet radiation: the hottest stars emit most of their energy at these wavelengths. Earth's ozone layer protects us from the worst of the Sun's damaging ultraviolet radiation, but obstructs the astronomer's view of the ultraviolet Universe.

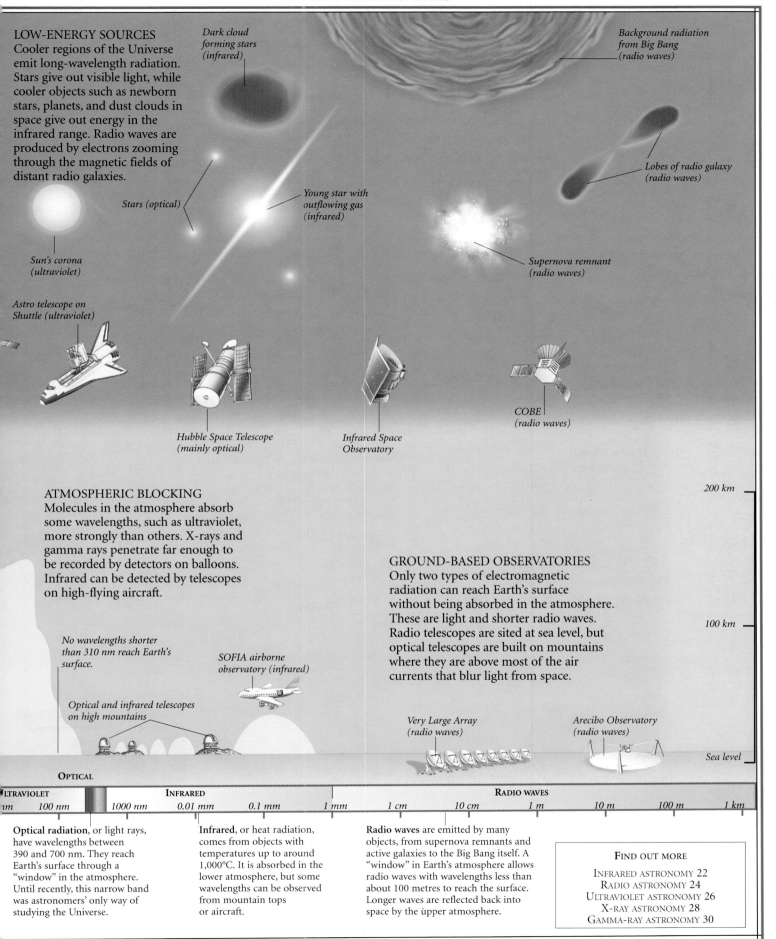

LOW-ENERGY SOURCES
Cooler regions of the Universe emit long-wavelength radiation. Stars give out visible light, while cooler objects such as newborn stars, planets, and dust clouds in space give out energy in the infrared range. Radio waves are produced by electrons zooming through the magnetic fields of distant radio galaxies.

Dark cloud forming stars (infrared)

Background radiation from Big Bang (radio waves)

Stars (optical)

Young star with outflowing gas (infrared)

Lobes of radio galaxy (radio waves)

Sun's corona (ultraviolet)

Supernova remnant (radio waves)

Astro telescope on Shuttle (ultraviolet)

Hubble Space Telescope (mainly optical)

Infrared Space Observatory

COBE (radio waves)

200 km

ATMOSPHERIC BLOCKING
Molecules in the atmosphere absorb some wavelengths, such as ultraviolet, more strongly than others. X-rays and gamma rays penetrate far enough to be recorded by detectors on balloons. Infrared can be detected by telescopes on high-flying aircraft.

GROUND-BASED OBSERVATORIES
Only two types of electromagnetic radiation can reach Earth's surface without being absorbed in the atmosphere. These are light and shorter radio waves. Radio telescopes are sited at sea level, but optical telescopes are built on mountains where they are above most of the air currents that blur light from space.

No wavelengths shorter than 310 nm reach Earth's surface.

SOFIA airborne observatory (infrared)

100 km

Optical and infrared telescopes on high mountains

Very Large Array (radio waves)

Arecibo Observatory (radio waves)

Sea level

OPTICAL

ULTRAVIOLET | **INFRARED** | **RADIO WAVES**

| 1 nm | 100 nm | 1000 nm | 0.01 mm | 0.1 mm | 1 mm | 1 cm | 10 cm | 1 m | 10 m | 100 m | 1 km |

Optical radiation, or light rays, have wavelengths between 390 and 700 nm. They reach Earth's surface through a "window" in the atmosphere. Until recently, this narrow band was astronomers' only way of studying the Universe.

Infrared, or heat radiation, comes from objects with temperatures up to around 1,000°C. It is absorbed in the lower atmosphere, but some wavelengths can be observed from mountain tops or aircraft.

Radio waves are emitted by many objects, from supernova remnants and active galaxies to the Big Bang itself. A "window" in Earth's atmosphere allows radio waves with wavelengths less than about 100 metres to reach the surface. Longer waves are reflected back into space by the upper atmosphere.

FIND OUT MORE

INFRARED ASTRONOMY

IF OUR EYES WERE SENSITIVE to infrared, or heat, radiation the night sky would appear quite different. It would be filled with glowing cosmic clouds and scattered, distant galaxies ablaze with newborn stars. We would be able to pick out young stars and the centre of our Galaxy, which are normally hidden by tiny grains of dust in space – infrared can travel straight through interstellar dust. Everything in the Universe cooler than normal stars (around 3,000°C) emits infrared. By using infrared telescopes, astronomers can reveal information invisible to the optical telescope.

INFRARED WAVELENGTHS

As its name suggests, infrared lies just beyond the red end of the visible spectrum. It covers a much wider part of the electromagnetic spectrum than visible light: from 700 nanometres (billionths of a millimetre) to 1 millimetre, where radio waves begin. Astronomers divide infrared into four bands: near, mid-, and far infrared, and submillimetre waves. Observing infrared radiation is always a struggle within Earth's atmosphere, where carbon dioxide and water vapour absorb infrared. Some of the shorter and longer wavelengths, though, do reach mountain tops.

HEAT DIFFERENCES

Detectors can pick up variations in heat from an object: an infrared view of an elephant shows temperature differences of around 1°C. Using infrared, astronomers can observe a much wider temperature range, from stars at 3,000°C to very cold dust clouds at –250°C. In a Universe where gas clouds can be as hot as a million degrees, these are the cool objects.

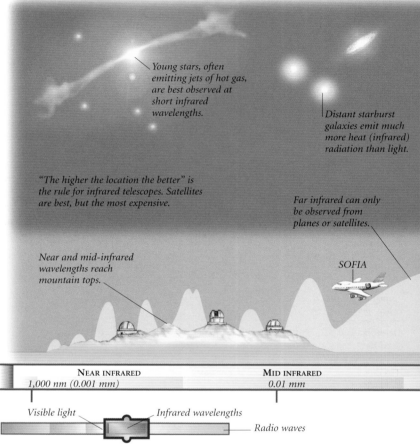

Young stars, often emitting jets of hot gas, are best observed at short infrared wavelengths.

Distant starburst galaxies emit much more heat (infrared) radiation than light.

"The higher the location the better" is the rule for infrared telescopes. Satellites are best, but the most expensive.

Far infrared can only be observed from planes or satellites.

Near and mid-infrared wavelengths reach mountain tops.

SOFIA

NEAR INFRARED	MID INFRARED
1,000 nm (0.001 mm)	0.01 mm

ELECTROMAGNETIC SPECTRUM LOCATER

Visible light — *Infrared wavelengths* — Radio waves

KEY INFRARED TELESCOPES					
Name	Mirror diameter	Location	Height in km	Dates	
UK Infrared Telescope	3.8 m	Hawaii	4.2	1979–	
NASA Infrared Telescope Facility	3.0 m	Hawaii	4.2	1979–	
Caltech Submillimeter	10 m	Hawaii	4.2	1987–	
James Clerk Maxwell	15 m	Hawaii	4.2	1987–	
Kuiper Airborne Observatory	0.9 m	Lockheed C141	12.5	1974–95	
SOFIA	2.5 m	Boeing 747SP	13	2001–	
IRAS	0.6 m	Polar orbit	900	1983	
ISO	0.6 m	Elliptical orbit	1,000	1995–98	
Space Infrared Telescope Facility	0.85 m	Solar orbit	50 million	2001–	

EARTH-BASED TELESCOPES

Infrared telescopes resemble optical telescopes: in fact, the latest big reflectors are designed to observe both infrared and visible light. An infrared camera, however, must have a cooling system so that any heat it gives off does not overwhelm the faint infrared from space.

Liquid helium poured into an infrared camera keeps it chilled to –270°C.

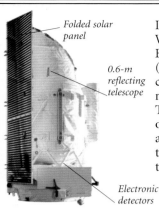

Folded solar panel

0.6-m reflecting telescope

Electronic detectors

IN ORBIT
Well above Earth's atmosphere, the European Infrared Space Observatory (ISO) satellite has shed new light on colliding galaxies, hidden star nurseries, and interstellar clouds. To minimize interference from its own heat, the telescope was enclosed in a giant flask, cooled to –270°C. When the liquid helium coolant ran out after three years, ISO had to stop observing.

The constellation of Orion is dominated at optical wavelengths by seven stars making the hunter's outline.

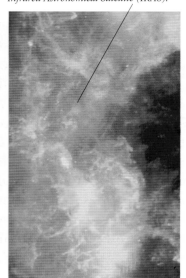

Immense, cool dust clouds dominate the same region in this image captured by the Infrared Astronomical Satellite (IRAS).

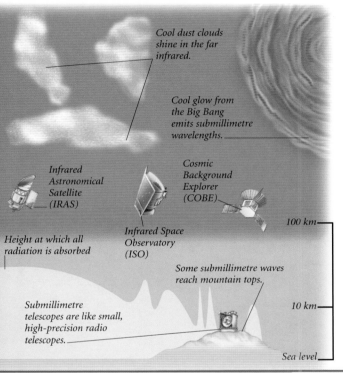

Cool dust clouds shine in the far infrared.

Cool glow from the Big Bang emits submillimetre wavelengths.

Infrared Astronomical Satellite (IRAS)

Cosmic Background Explorer (COBE)

Infrared Space Observatory (ISO)

Height at which all radiation is absorbed

Some submillimetre waves reach mountain tops.

100 km

Submillimetre telescopes are like small, high-precision radio telescopes.

10 km

Sea level

FAR INFRARED	SUBMILLIMETRE	RADIO
0.1mm	1 mm	

INTERSTELLAR CLOUDS IN ORION
Infrared telescopes are sensitive to lukewarm and cool material, including vast clouds of dust and gas stretching hundreds of light years across the constellation of Orion. Generally, they have temperatures of about –200°C (red in the IRAS image). In the denser regions, the heat from newborn stars warms the dust and gas to around 1,000°C (white areas). To optical telescopes, these clouds are visible only as dark silhouettes. In contrast, most of the stars seen at optical wavelengths are too hot to show up in infrared.

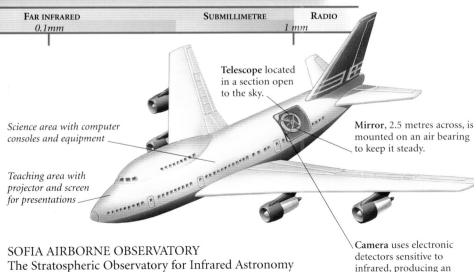

Telescope located in a section open to the sky.

Mirror, 2.5 metres across, is mounted on an air bearing to keep it steady.

Science area with computer consoles and equipment

Teaching area with projector and screen for presentations

Camera uses electronic detectors sensitive to infrared, producing an image made up of pixels.

SOFIA AIRBORNE OBSERVATORY
The Stratospheric Observatory for Infrared Astronomy (SOFIA) is a Boeing 747SP which carries an infrared telescope above most of Earth's absorbing atmosphere. It is cheaper and more flexible than a satellite, and can carry a bigger telescope. Its 2.5-m mirror is far larger than ISO's.

INFRARED LANDMARKS
• In 1800, Sir William Herschel found that a thermometer registered heat when placed beyond the red end of the Sun's spectrum. He called this invisible radiation infrared.

• The first ground-based infrared sky survey, in 1969, identified 5,612 cool stars.

• IRAS, launched in 1983, discovered 250,000 cosmic infrared sources. These included starburst galaxies, which emit far more heat than light as they give birth to many thousands of stars.

• Infrared telescopes revealed superheated 3,000-km plumes of gas when Comet Shoemaker-Levy 9 hit Jupiter in 1994.

• In 1998, the Infrared Space Observatory discovered that water is widespread in space, from moons to interstellar clouds.

FIND OUT MORE
HOW TELESCOPES WORK 14 • ANALYSING LIGHT 18
RADIATIONS FROM SPACE 20
LIFECYCLE OF STARS 170
INTERSTELLAR MEDIUM 196

RADIO ASTRONOMY

BY TUNING IN TO RADIO WAVES from space, astronomers have discovered many of the most energetic objects and most explosive events in the Universe. These include the remains of supernovas, magnetic whirlpools around supermassive black holes, and even the radiation from the Big Bang in which the Universe was born. Radio telescopes can also track down molecules in space, the raw material of new planets and life. No one is allowed to broadcast at the wavelengths used to study the Universe. Even so, radio telescopes increasingly suffer from radio pollution – from mobile phones, for example.

RADIO SPECTRUM

Radio waves have the longest wavelengths of any electromagnetic radiation, covering all wavelengths longer than 1 millimetre. Most radio waves can penetrate the atmosphere down to the Earth's surface, although radio waves longer than 100 m are reflected back into space by the ionosphere, a layer at the top of the atmosphere. Scientists often refer to radio waves by frequency – the number of waves that pass every second. The shorter the wavelength, the higher the frequency.

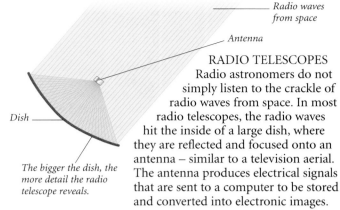

Radio waves from space

Antenna

Dish

The bigger the dish, the more detail the radio telescope reveals.

RADIO TELESCOPES
Radio astronomers do not simply listen to the crackle of radio waves from space. In most radio telescopes, the radio waves hit the inside of a large dish, where they are reflected and focused onto an antenna – similar to a television aerial. The antenna produces electrical signals that are sent to a computer to be stored and converted into electronic images.

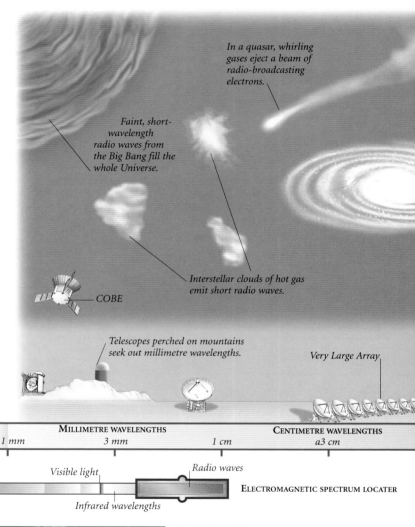

In a quasar, whirling gases eject a beam of radio-broadcasting electrons.

Faint, short-wavelength radio waves from the Big Bang fill the whole Universe.

Interstellar clouds of hot gas emit short radio waves.

COBE

Telescopes perched on mountains seek out millimetre wavelengths.

Very Large Array

MILLIMETRE WAVELENGTHS			CENTIMETRE WAVELENGTHS	
1 mm	3 mm	1 cm	a3 cm	

Visible light

Radio waves

Infrared wavelengths

ELECTROMAGNETIC SPECTRUM LOCATER

KEY RADIO TELESCOPES

Name	Size	Location
Single dish		
Arecibo	305 m (fixed)	Puerto Rico
Greenbank	110 x 100 m	USA
Effelsberg	100 m	Germany
Jodrell Bank	76 m	UK
Parkes	64 m	Australia
Nobeyama	45 m	Japan
IRAM	30 m	Spain
James Clerk Maxwell	15 m	Hawaii
Swedish-ESO	15 m	Chile
Kitt Peak Millimeter Wave Telescope	11 m	USA
Arrays		
Very Long Baseline Array	8,000 km/10 dishes	Across USA
Australia Telescope	320 km/8 dishes	Australia
MERLIN	230 km/7 dishes	UK
Very Large Array	36 km/27 dishes	USA
BIMA	2 km/10 dishes	USA
Plateau de Bure	0.4 km/5 dishes	France
Submillimeter Array	0.5 km/8 dishes	Hawaii

RADIO DISH
The large radio telescope at the Nobeyama Radio Observatory in Japan has a curved dish 45 metres in diameter, more than 10 times the area of a tennis court. Yet its surface is smooth and accurately shaped to less than the width of a blade of grass. This precision surface allows the dish to focus radiation of millimetre wavelengths from molecules of gas in the space between stars.

TELESCOPE ARRAYS

Radio telescopes have a fuzzier view than optical telescopes, because radio waves are much longer than light waves. To reveal more detail, astronomers mimic, or synthesize, a bigger telescope by connecting several small telescopes. The 27 dishes of the Very Large Array can be moved along three railway tracks to a maximum distance of 36 km apart. The Very Long Baseline Array stretches across the USA, and provides a sharper view than the Hubble Space Telescope.

VERY LARGE ARRAY IN NEW MEXICO

RADIO MILESTONES

JANSKY'S RADIO TELESCOPE ANTENNA

• Radio astronomy began in 1932, when Karl Jansky discovered radio "static" coming from the Milky Way.

• In 1942, British scientist Stanley Hey (1909–) found strong radio outbursts from the Sun.

• In 1949, Australian radio astronomers identified the first radio sources outside the Solar System.

• In 1951, scientists at Harvard picked out the 21-cm signal emitted by hydrogen in the Milky Way.

• The first quasar, 3C 273, was identified in 1963: it was a powerful radio source. Meanwhile, the first interstellar molecule (hydroxyl) was discovered by its radiation at 18 cm.

• In 1965, Arno Penzias and Robert Wilson discovered the faint echo of heat from the Big Bang – the cosmic background radiation.

• In 1967, Tony Hewish and Jocelyn Bell Burnell found the first pulsar, PSR 1919+21.

• In 1992, the Cosmic Background Explorer satellite measured ripples in the cosmic background radiation – the first signs of galaxy formation.

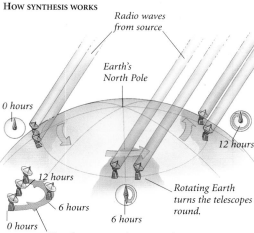

The two lobes of a distant radio galaxy are visible only to a radio telescope.

Hydrogen in the Milky Way and other galaxies emits radio waves at a wavelength of 21 cm.

The ghostly remains of a star that exploded long ago live on, as a radio-emitting supernova remnant.

Most radio telescopes observe waves shorter than 1 metre.

Jodrell Bank   Arecibo

300 km
150 km
Sea level

METRE WAVELENGTHS
30 cm   1 m

EARTH-ROTATION SYNTHESIS

A single line of telescopes – or even the Y-shape of the Very Large Array – leaves gaps in the synthesized large mirror which can distort the final radio picture. In the 1950s, Martin Ryle suggested a solution. Instead of taking a snapshot view full of holes, the telescopes observe the same radio source for 12 hours. As the Earth rotates, it carries each telescope around the others in a slow half-circle, synthesizing parts of a much larger telescope.

HOW SYNTHESIS WORKS

Radio waves from source

Earth's North Pole

0 hours

12 hours

12 hours

6 hours

0 hours

6 hours

Rotating Earth turns the telescopes round.

View from space: the green telescope appears to make a half-circle around the red telescope over 12 hours. Without moving the telescopes, this method has filled in part of a much larger "dish".

SYNCHROTRON RADIATION

In many radio sources, from supernova remnants to galaxies, the radio waves are created by high-speed electrons trapped in magnetic fields. They produce radio waves of a type called synchrotron radiation, which is strongest at the longer wavelengths. In this image of galaxy Fornax A, the radio-emitting lobes show where electrons are whizzing through tangled magnetic fields.

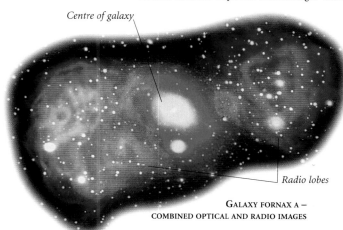

Centre of galaxy

Radio lobes

GALAXY FORNAX A –
COMBINED OPTICAL AND RADIO IMAGES

ULTRAVIOLET ASTRONOMY

T O TRACK DOWN THE HOTTEST STARS – 50 times hotter than the Sun – astronomers must use ultraviolet radiation. A star that is hotter than 10,000°C shines most brightly at ultraviolet wavelengths. Ultraviolet can also reveal what is in the hot, invisible gas clouds between the stars. Ozone in Earth's atmosphere, however, makes observing difficult. In everyday life, the ozone layer protects us from the Sun's ultraviolet radiation, and we worry about the ozone hole, but the ozone layer blocks astronomers' view of sources of ultraviolet radiation in the Universe.

ULTRAVIOLET WAVELENGTHS

Ultraviolet radiation has shorter wavelengths than visible light, stretching from the violet end of the visible spectrum (390 nanometres) down to the start of the X-ray region (10 nm). Wavelengths between 10 and 91 nm are called extreme ultraviolet. Ultraviolet telescopes must fly above Earth's atmosphere. Atoms of oxygen and nitrogen at high altitudes block out the shorter ultraviolet wavelengths, while the ozone layer, between 10 and 50 km up, blocks the remaining wavelengths.

HYDROGEN FOG

Many atoms in space are very efficient at absorbing ultraviolet radiation. Hydrogen, the most common element in space, absorbs the extreme ultraviolet wavelengths so strongly that it acts as a fog which hides most of the distant Universe.

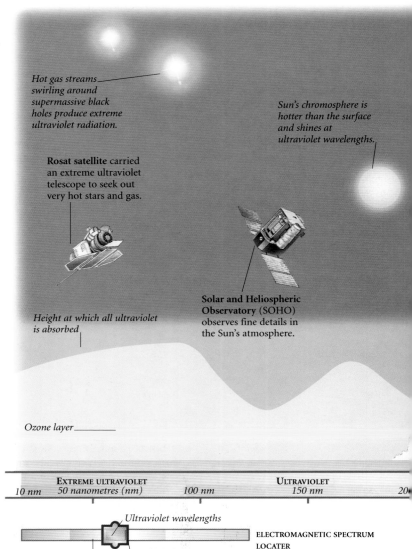

Hot gas streams swirling around supermassive black holes produce extreme ultraviolet radiation.

Sun's chromosphere is hotter than the surface and shines at ultraviolet wavelengths.

Rosat satellite carried an extreme ultraviolet telescope to seek out very hot stars and gas.

Solar and Heliospheric Observatory (SOHO) observes fine details in the Sun's atmosphere.

Height at which all ultraviolet is absorbed

Ozone layer

EXTREME ULTRAVIOLET		ULTRAVIOLET	
10 nm	50 nanometres (nm)	100 nm	150 nm	20

Ultraviolet wavelengths

X-rays   Visible light

ELECTROMAGNETIC SPECTRUM LOCATER

ASTRO ULTRAVIOLET OBSERVATORY

Small telescopes point Astro to target.

Large ultraviolet telescope

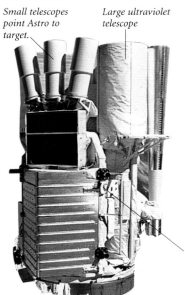

Base is mounted in Shuttle payload bay.

ORBITING TELESCOPES

Most ultraviolet telescopes are on satellites operated remotely from control centres on Earth. The first was the Copernicus satellite, launched in 1972. The Astro ultraviolet observatory, however, flies in the Space Shuttle, and is operated by astronauts. Astro returns to Earth with the Shuttle, and can be refurbished between flights.

Astro ultraviolet observatory has three telescopes which all look at the same star or galaxy. It simultaneously takes an ultraviolet picture and studies the spectrum at ultraviolet wavelengths.

KEY ULTRAVIOLET TELESCOPES

Name	Mirror size	Orbit	Dates
Copernicus	0.80 m	Low Earth	1972–81
International Ultraviolet Explorer	0.45 m	Geostationary	1978–96
Astro	0.38 m	Low Earth	1990, 1995
Rosat	0.58 m	Low Earth	1990–98
Extreme Ultraviolet Explorer	2 x 0.40 m	Low Earth	1992–
SOHO	0.12 m	1.5 million km	1995–

GLOWING GASES IN SOLAR ATMOSPHERE

An extreme ultraviolet image of the Sun reveals a thin, patchy shell of glowing gas – colour-coded to show different brightnesses – surrounding a black globe. The Sun's visible surface, at 5,500°C, is too cool to emit extreme ultraviolet, and appears dark. Above the surface, in the chromosphere, the gas reaches temperatures of 100,000°C and shines brightly in ultraviolet. The temperature and density of gas varies with changes in the Sun's magnetic field.

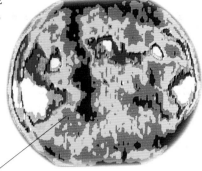

Red is the faintest gas in ultraviolet, and white the brightest.

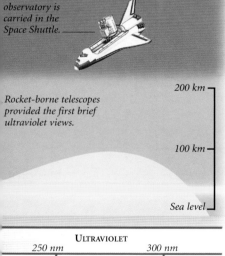

The hottest stars in our Galaxy, at 200,000°C, shine most brilliantly in the ultraviolet.

Distant galaxies glitter with hot, young, ultraviolet-bright stars.

Astro ultraviolet observatory is carried in the Space Shuttle.

200 km

Rocket-borne telescopes provided the first brief ultraviolet views.

100 km

Sea level

ULTRAVIOLET

250 nm   300 nm

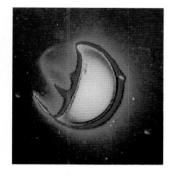

EARTH'S HALO

When viewed with an ultraviolet telescope, Earth is surrounded by a glowing halo. Atoms in the upper atmosphere are heated by charged particles from the Solar wind. On Earth's dark side (left), bright bands correspond with auroras.

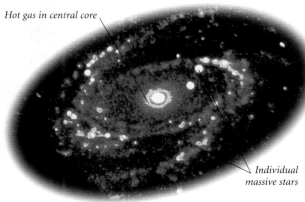

Hot gas in central core

Individual massive stars

HOT STARS IN GALAXIES

Spiral galaxies appear at their most spectacular in the ultraviolet, which reveals only the hottest stars. Here, the Astro telescope has viewed the galaxy M81, which lies 12 million light years away in the constellation Ursa Major. The bright spots are clusters of massive stars, 10 times hotter than the Sun, that will quickly burn away.

STARBURST GALAXY

M94 is a galaxy where a large number of stars have recently burst into life. Viewed through an optical telescope, however, only a bright central bulge composed mainly of old, cool stars, is visible. An ultraviolet image, taken by the Astro ultraviolet observatory, shows a completely different structure. Instead of the central bulge; there is a giant ring of hot young stars formed within the past 10 million years.

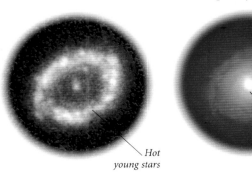

Hot young stars

Old cool stars

ULTRAVIOLET IMAGE OF M94   **OPTICAL IMAGE OF M94**

ULTRAVIOLET MILESTONES

• In 1801, German physicist Johann Ritter (1776–1810) discovered that the light-sensitive chemical silver chloride is blackened by invisible radiation lying beyond the violet end of the Sun's spectrum.

• The first ultraviolet spectrum of the Sun was taken in 1946 from a German V-2 rocket.

• The Apollo 16 crew set up an ultraviolet observatory on the Moon in 1972, observing the Earth and hot stars.

• In 1973, the Copernicus satellite measured deuterium (heavy hydrogen) left over from the Big Bang. Meanwhile, Skylab discovered the Sun's atmosphere is blotchy, with empty "coronal holes".

• Extreme ultraviolet rays from space were discovered in 1975 by the Apollo-Soyuz space mission.

• In 1978, the International Ultraviolet Explorer satellite discovered large amounts of nitrogen in the exploding star Nova Cygni 1978.

• In 1987, the International Ultraviolet Explorer monitored the radiation outburst from Supernova 1987A, providing a precise distance to the supernova, and so to its host galaxy, the Large Magellanic Cloud.

• The Rosat survey in 1990 discovered over 1,000 very hot stars, emitting extreme ultraviolet.

X-RAY ASTRONOMY

At x-ray wavelengths, the sky looks totally alien, filled with large glowing pools of gas and strange fluctuating X-ray stars. X-rays are a very short-wavelength, high-energy type of radiation, only given out by objects hotter than a million degrees – they show up the Universe's hot spots. The atmospheres of the Sun and similar stars shine only faintly in X-rays. Supernova remnants and the gas around pulsars and black holes, where temperatures may reach 100 million °C, are much more powerful X-ray sources.

X-RAY SPECTRUM

X-rays are high-energy electromagnetic radiation with wavelengths between 0.01 and 10 nanometres, much shorter than visible light. The shortest X-rays carry the most energy. X-rays may be extremely penetrating on Earth – doctors use them to show the body's interior – but the upper atmosphere absorbs all the X-rays from space. So X-ray detectors must be carried beyond the atmosphere on rockets or satellites.

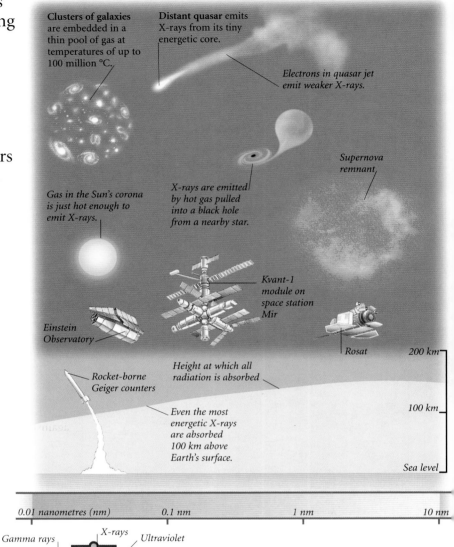

Clusters of galaxies are embedded in a thin pool of gas at temperatures of up to 100 million °C.

Distant quasar emits X-rays from its tiny energetic core.

Electrons in quasar jet emit weaker X-rays.

Gas in the Sun's corona is just hot enough to emit X-rays.

X-rays are emitted by hot gas pulled into a black hole from a nearby star.

Supernova remnant

Kvant-1 module on space station Mir

Einstein Observatory

Rosat

Rocket-borne Geiger counters

Height at which all radiation is absorbed

Even the most energetic X-rays are absorbed 100 km above Earth's surface.

200 km

100 km

Sea level

| 0.01 nanometres (nm) | 0.1 nm | 1 nm | 10 nm |

Gamma rays   X-rays   Ultraviolet

Visible light

ELECTROMAGNETIC SPECTRUM LOCATER

X-RAY TELESCOPES

X-rays are very difficult to focus because they are absorbed by traditional curved mirrors. They can be reflected only if they hit a metal surface at a very shallow angle, grazing it like a bullet ricocheting off a wall. X-ray telescopes use highly polished tapering metal cylinders, called grazing incidence mirrors, to focus radiation.

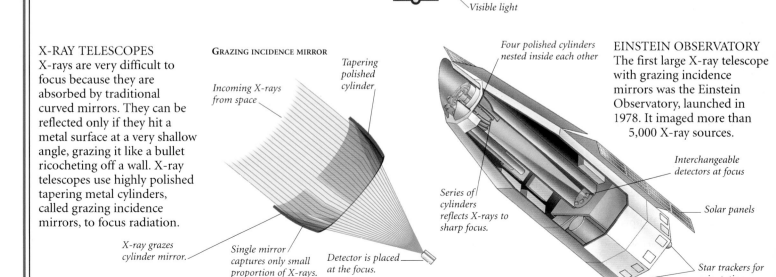

GRAZING INCIDENCE MIRROR

Tapering polished cylinder

Incoming X-rays from space

X-ray grazes cylinder mirror.

Single mirror captures only small proportion of X-rays.

Detector is placed at the focus.

Four polished cylinders nested inside each other

Series of cylinders reflects X-rays to sharp focus.

EINSTEIN OBSERVATORY

The first large X-ray telescope with grazing incidence mirrors was the Einstein Observatory, launched in 1978. It imaged more than 5,000 X-ray sources.

Interchangeable detectors at focus

Solar panels

Star trackers for orientation

KEY X-RAY SATELLITES

Name metres	Size in	Dates	Country
Uhuru	0.28	1970–73	USA
Ariel V	0.17	1974–80	UK
HEAO-1	1.00	1977–79	USA
Einstein Observatory	0.58	1978–81	USA
Exosat	2 x 0.3	1983–86	European
Ginga	0.63	1987–91	Japan
Kvant-1	0.25	1987–99	Russia
Rosat	0.8	1990–99	USA/Germany
Chandra X-ray Observatory	1.2	1999–	USA
X-ray Multi-Mirror Mission	3 x 0.7	2000–	European

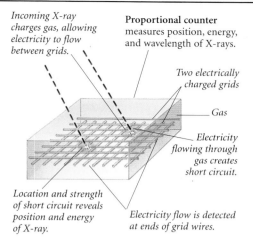

Incoming X-ray charges gas, allowing electricity to flow between grids.

Proportional counter measures position, energy, and wavelength of X-rays.

Two electrically charged grids

Gas

Electricity flowing through gas creates short circuit.

Location and strength of short circuit reveals position and energy of X-ray.

Electricity flow is detected at ends of grid wires.

DETECTING X-RAYS

Astronomers use two types of detectors at the focus of an X-ray telescope. The CCD is an electronic detector used in most optical telescopes and simply records the number of X-rays striking it. The proportional counter, a sophisticated version of the Geiger counter used to detect radiation on Earth, creates the X-ray equivalent of a colour image.

MIR TELESCOPE

The manned space station Mir also acted as an orbiting observatory. Its Kvant-1 scientific module carried an X-ray telescope, which sharpened its view using a coded mask. Observing Supernova 1987A, it discovered emission lines in the X-ray spectrum that proved the exploding star had created radioactive elements.

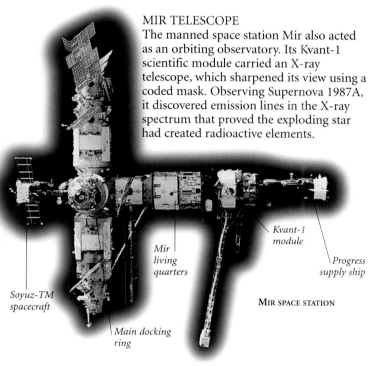

Soyuz-TM spacecraft

Mir living quarters

Main docking ring

Kvant-1 module

Progress supply ship

MIR SPACE STATION

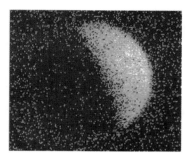

ROSAT VIEWS THE MOON

In this ghostly view, the right side of the Moon glows as it is illuminated by the Sun's X-rays. The dark side is silhouetted against the scattered dots of an X-ray background that comes from distant galaxies: each dot is an individual X-ray hit. (The bright dots on the Moon's dark side are electronic noise in the X-ray detector.)

X-RAY MILESTONES

- X-rays from the Sun were first discovered in 1949.

- In 1962, a rocket-borne X-ray detector found the first X-ray source beyond the Solar System, Scorpius X-1.

- In 1971, the Uhuru satellite discovered the first evidence for black holes: X-rays from Cygnus X-1. It also found X-rays from gas in distant galaxy clusters.

- The Einstein Observatory, launched in 1978, found that quasars and some young stars emit X-rays.

- In 1987, the X-ray telescope on the Mir space station detected X-rays from a supernova.

- Rosat, launched in 1990, discovered 100,000 X-ray sources.

ROSAT X-RAY TELESCOPE

FIND OUT MORE

SUPERNOVA REMNANTS

About 11,000 years ago a supernova exploded in the constellation Vela, 1,500 light years away from Earth. At its brightest, it must have outshone the full Moon, but all that is left now is a huge bubble of hot gas, 140 light years across. Optical telescopes can barely detect it, but Rosat's sensitive X-ray telescope revealed the gas which, in places, is still 8 million °C. Rosat also detected a much smaller and more distant supernova remnant, Puppis A.

ROSAT IMAGE OF VELA SUPERNOVA REMNANT

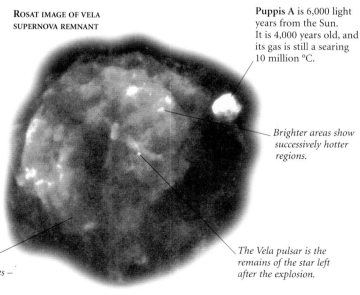

Puppis A is 6,000 light years from the Sun. It is 4,000 years old, and its gas is still a searing 10 million °C.

Brighter areas show successively hotter regions.

Faint areas show cooler gas temperatures – about 1 million °C.

The Vela pulsar is the remains of the star left after the explosion.

GAMMA-RAY ASTRONOMY

GAMMA RAYS expose the most violent corners of the Universe, including pulsars, quasars, and black holes. They are radiation with the shortest wavelengths, and highest energies, of all. No star or gas cloud is hot enough to shine at these wavelengths. Instead, gamma rays are generated by radioactive atoms in space, by particles colliding at almost the speed of light, and by matter and antimatter annihilating each other. Gamma-ray astronomy is still in its infancy, and astronomers have yet to identify many sources of this high-energy radiation.

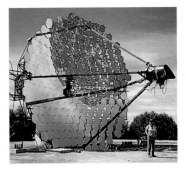

CERENKOV DETECTOR SITED IN ARIZONA

CERENKOV DETECTOR
Gamma rays from space never reach Earth, but ground-based instruments can still detect them. A Cerenkov detector collects light like an ordinary telescope, but is on the lookout for flashes of light in Earth's atmosphere. Each flash lasts only a few billionths of a second and is caused by a gamma ray smashing into atoms of gas.

GAMMA-RAY SPECTRUM
Even the longest gamma rays, bordering on X-rays, have wavelengths that are smaller than an atom. There is no lower limit to gamma-ray wavelengths: the shortest ever detected is a million billion times shorter than ordinary light. Such short-wavelength gamma rays are uncommon, because objects with the energy to create them are extremely rare in the Universe. All gamma rays from space are absorbed by Earth's atmosphere.

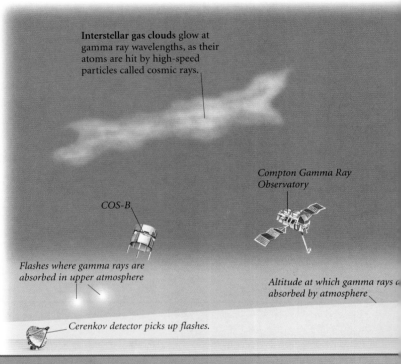

Interstellar gas clouds glow at gamma ray wavelengths, as their atoms are hit by high-speed particles called cosmic rays.

COS-B

Compton Gamma Ray Observatory

Flashes where gamma rays are absorbed in upper atmosphere

Altitude at which gamma rays a absorbed by atmosphere

Cerenkov detector picks up flashes.

0.000,000,000,1 nm   0.000,000,01 nm   0.000,001 n

Gamma rays   X-rays

Visible light

ELECTROMAGNETIC SPECTRUM LOCATER

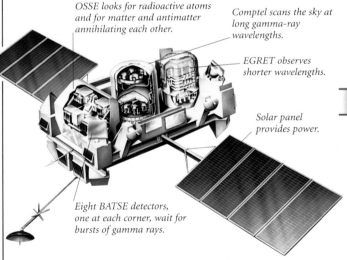

OSSE looks for radioactive atoms and for matter and antimatter annihilating each other.

Comptel scans the sky at long gamma-ray wavelengths.

EGRET observes shorter wavelengths.

Solar panel provides power.

Eight BATSE detectors, one at each corner, wait for bursts of gamma rays.

COMPTON GAMMA RAY OBSERVATORY
The 17-tonne Compton Gamma Ray Observatory is the most massive observatory ever launched, and the second of NASA's "Great Observatories" (the Hubble Space Telescope was the first). The satellite carries four detectors. It uses a variety of methods to form images of the gamma-ray sky at two different wavelengths and to study gamma-ray spectra and bursts.

DETECTING GAMMA RAYS
Gamma rays pass straight through a mirror or lens, so detectors use indirect methods to form images. In EGRET, gamma rays pass through thin layers of the metal tungsten, and produce two particles – an electron and a positron – when they hit a tungsten atom. The paths of these particles are measured by a stack of spark chambers that work like the counters used in X-ray detectors.

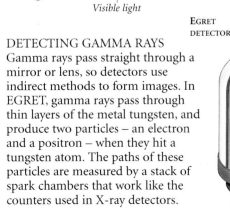

EGRET DETECTOR

Incoming gamma ray

Thin tungsten sheets

Spark chambers

Sparks triggered by electron and positron

Energy detector absorbs particles to measure gamma-ray energy.

SKY IN GAMMA RAYS

The sky looks very different when viewed at gamma-ray wavelengths. We see none of the usual stars and constellations. Instead, huge glowing clouds of gas stretch across the view. Among them are bright points, flashing on and off. Some are pulsars, with a regular period to their flashing. Others, called gamma-ray bursters, flare brilliantly for just a few seconds, outshining everything else in the gamma-ray sky.

Clouds of gas in the Milky Way, bombarded by high-speed electrons

Unidentified source

Cygnus X-1: gas swirling around a black hole

Quasar 3C 279: a distant galaxy with a massive central black hole

Centre of the Milky Way Galaxy

Crab Pulsar flashes 30 times a second.

Vela Pulsar flashes 13 times a second.

Large Magellanic Cloud contains many pulsars and black holes.

Whole sky map from the Compton satellite. Red shows the strongest gamma-ray sources, and yellow and green less intense regions.

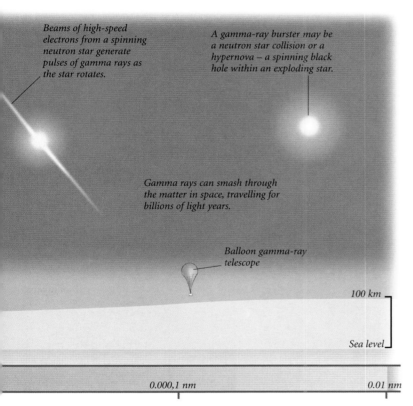

Beams of high-speed electrons from a spinning neutron star generate pulses of gamma rays as the star rotates.

A gamma-ray burster may be a neutron star collision or a hypernova – a spinning black hole within an exploding star.

Gamma rays can smash through the matter in space, travelling for billions of light years.

Balloon gamma-ray telescope

100 km

Sea level

0.000,1 nm   0.01 nm

GAMMA RAY MILESTONES

• The first gamma-ray astronomy experiments were carried on board rockets and NASA's Orbiting Solar Observatory satellites in the 1960s.

• Gamma-ray bursts were discovered in 1969 by American Vela military satellites designed to monitor nuclear testing on Earth.

• The SAS-2 satellite detected gamma-ray pulses from the Crab and Vela Pulsars in 1972.

• In 1977, Geminga was discovered. The third strongest gamma ray source, but almost undetectable at other wavelengths, Geminga is the nearest neutron star.

• In 1978, the COS-B satellite identified gamma rays from a quasar (3C 273) for the first time.

• A balloon-borne experiment in 1979 discovered gamma rays from annihilation of matter and antimatter near the centre of the Milky Way.

• In 1998. using data gathered by the Compton Gamma Ray Observatory, astronomers identified gamma-ray bursts as explosions in very distant galaxies.

CODED MASKS

Gamma rays cannot be focused, but coded masks offer one way of creating a high-resolution gamma-ray image. The mask is a grid of gamma-absorbing material with a distinctive pattern, positioned above a spark chamber. When exposed to a gamma-ray source, the mask casts a shadow where no gamma rays are detected. The position of this shadow can show the position of the gamma-ray source very accurately.

CODED MASK GAMMA-RAY DETECTOR

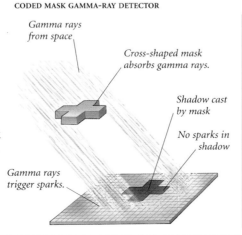

Gamma rays from space

Cross-shaped mask absorbs gamma rays.

Shadow cast by mask

No sparks in shadow

Gamma rays trigger sparks.

KEY GAMMA-RAY TELESCOPES

Name	Orbit	Dates
Vela 5A, 5B	High Earth	1969–79
SAS-2	Low Earth	1972–73
COS-B	Elliptical	1975–82
HEAO-3	Low Earth	1979–81
Granat/Sigma	Elliptical	1989–
Compton Gamma Ray Observatory	Low Earth	1991–
Integral	Elliptical	2001–

FIND OUT MORE

RADIATIONS FROM SPACE 20 • X-RAY ASTRONOMY 28
NEUTRON STARS 186 • BLACK HOLES 188 • ACTIVE GALAXIES 216

UNUSUAL TELESCOPES

Almost all our knowledge of the distant Universe has come from studying radiation – light, radio waves, infrared, ultraviolet, X-rays, and gamma rays – from space. But more exotic messengers are also crisscrossing the cosmos, carrying information about the most violent events of all. Astronomers have studied cosmic rays (actually high-energy particles) for many decades, and more recently have detected elusive neutrinos. Other messengers are predicted by theory, but have yet to be detected. They include particles of dark matter, which may make up most of the mass of the Universe, and gravitational waves, shudders in the fabric of space itself.

VIOLENT BEGINNINGS

Way out in space, a mighty explosion erupts. It may be a star dying as a supernova, two neutron stars crashing together, or superhot gas making the one-way trip into a black hole. Such explosions generate all kinds of radiation, including light, radio waves, and gamma rays. But they also spew into space a range of more exotic particles and waves that carry unique information about this astrophysical chaos.

COSMIC RAYS

Despite their name, cosmic rays are not a kind of radiation: they are fragments of atoms smashed up in high-energy explosions and whizzing through space at almost the speed of light. Most are nuclei of hydrogen (protons), with a sprinkling of nuclei of heavier elements and electrons. The most energetic cosmic rays come from the centres of quasars. Others are sent speeding through space by supernova explosions.

COSMIC AIR SHOWER

After its long journey through space, a cosmic ray particle is destroyed when it hits an atom in Earth's upper atmosphere. Energy from the collision creates several lower-energy particles, which still have enough energy to create more particles in turn as they crash into other atoms lower in the atmosphere. The result is a shower of particles, raining down over several square kilometres.

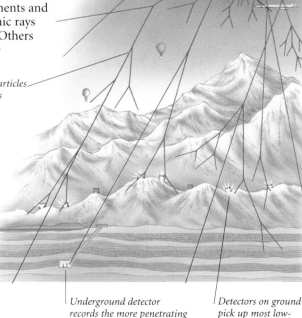

Incoming cosmic ray

Collision with atom in air

Airborne detectors

Lower-energy particles include electrons and neutrinos.

Underground detector records the more penetrating particles.

Detectors on ground pick up most low-energy particles.

DETECTING COSMIC RAYS

Cosmic ray particles are so rare that a single detector in space would intercept very few. Instead, astronomers try to detect the air shower of lower-energy particles as they reach the ground, using arrays of particle detectors like these at La Palma in the Canary Islands. If the cosmic ray is heading vertically downward, the air shower is circular. Otherwise the air shower has an oval shape that reveals the original direction of the cosmic ray.

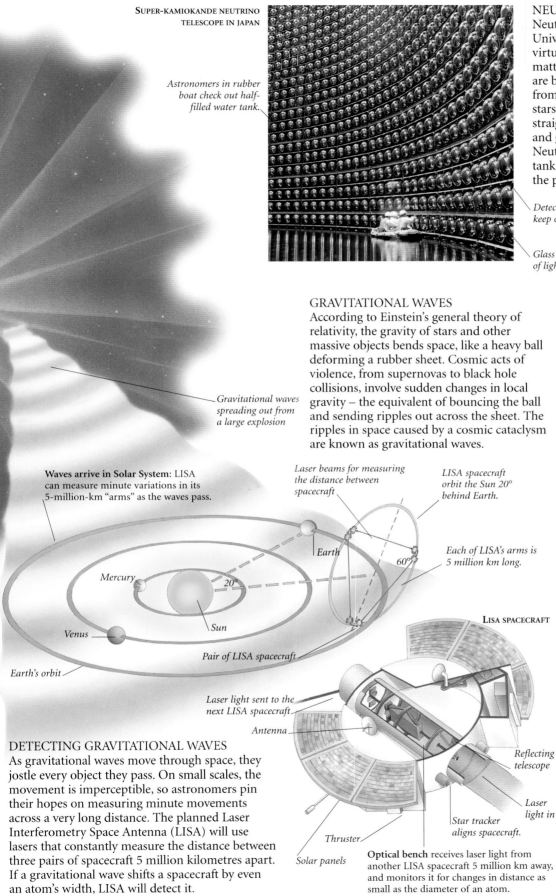

SUPER-KAMIOKANDE NEUTRINO
TELESCOPE IN JAPAN

Astronomers in rubber
boat check out half-
filled water tank.

NEUTRINOS

Neutrinos are the ghost particles of the
Universe. With no electric charge and
virtually no mass, they pass through
matter almost unscathed. Neutrinos
are born in the hottest places of all,
from the Big Bang to the centres of
stars and supernovas. They can travel
straight through a star's outer layers,
and give a unique insight into its core.
Neutrino telescopes often use a huge
tank of water to trap a tiny fraction of
the particles passing through.

Detector is sited underground to
keep out other types of particle.

Glass "bulbs" act as detectors that record a flash
of light when a neutrino passes through the tank.

GRAVITATIONAL WAVES

According to Einstein's general theory of
relativity, the gravity of stars and other
massive objects bends space, like a heavy ball
deforming a rubber sheet. Cosmic acts of
violence, from supernovas to black hole
collisions, involve sudden changes in local
gravity – the equivalent of bouncing the ball
and sending ripples out across the sheet. The
ripples in space caused by a cosmic cataclysm
are known as gravitational waves.

Gravitational waves
spreading out from
a large explosion

Waves arrive in Solar System: LISA
can measure minute variations in its
5-million-km "arms" as the waves pass.

Laser beams for measuring
the distance between
spacecraft

LISA spacecraft
orbit the Sun 20°
behind Earth.

Earth

60°

Each of LISA's arms is
5 million km long.

Mercury

20°

Venus

Sun

Pair of LISA spacecraft

Earth's orbit

LISA SPACECRAFT

Laser light sent to the
next LISA spacecraft

Antenna

DETECTING GRAVITATIONAL WAVES

As gravitational waves move through space, they
jostle every object they pass. On small scales, the
movement is imperceptible, so astronomers pin
their hopes on measuring minute movements
across a very long distance. The planned Laser
Interferometry Space Antenna (LISA) will use
lasers that constantly measure the distance between
three pairs of spacecraft 5 million kilometres apart.
If a gravitational wave shifts a spacecraft by even
an atom's width, LISA will detect it.

Reflecting
telescope

Laser
light in

Star tracker
aligns spacecraft.

Thruster

Solar panels

Optical bench receives laser light from
another LISA spacecraft 5 million km away,
and monitors it for changes in distance as
small as the diameter of an atom.

EXOTIC DETECTORS

● In 1912, Austrian
physicist Victor Hess
(1883–1964) launched
balloons that discovered
cosmic rays from space.

● Albert Einstein predicted
gravitational waves in 1916.

● French scientist Pierre
Auger (1899–1993)
discovered air showers in
1938, revealing the existence
of high-energy cosmic rays.

● In 1969, Solar neutrinos
were detected at Homestake
Mine, South Dakota, USA.

● The discovery in 1974 of
the first binary pulsar (two
neutron stars spiralling
together and losing
gravitational energy)
provided indirect evidence
for gravitational waves.

● In 1987, the first
neutrinos from beyond the
Solar System – released by
the explosion of Supernova
1987A – were picked up by
underground detectors in
Japan and the USA.

FIND OUT MORE

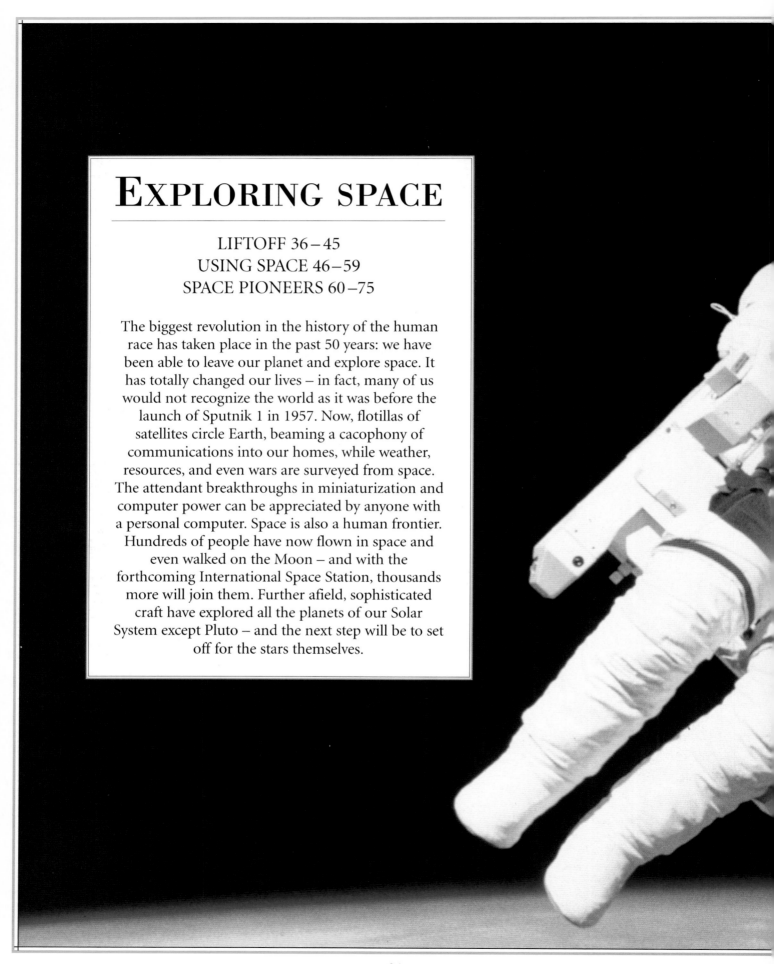

Exploring Space

LIFTOFF 36–45
USING SPACE 46–59
SPACE PIONEERS 60–75

The biggest revolution in the history of the human race has taken place in the past 50 years: we have been able to leave our planet and explore space. It has totally changed our lives – in fact, many of us would not recognize the world as it was before the launch of Sputnik 1 in 1957. Now, flotillas of satellites circle Earth, beaming a cacophony of communications into our homes, while weather, resources, and even wars are surveyed from space. The attendant breakthroughs in miniaturization and computer power can be appreciated by anyone with a personal computer. Space is also a human frontier. Hundreds of people have now flown in space and even walked on the Moon – and with the forthcoming International Space Station, thousands more will join them. Further afield, sophisticated craft have explored all the planets of our Solar System except Pluto – and the next step will be to set off for the stars themselves.

HOW ROCKETS WORK

A ROARING INFERNO LIFTED the Apollo astronauts towards their historic encounter of 20 July 1969, when Neil Armstrong became the first man to walk on the Moon. Every second for the first 120 seconds of their journey, almost 3 tonnes of kerosene surged into the combustion chambers of the five F1 engines of the Saturn V rocket. These engines produced a thrust at liftoff equivalent to 32 Boeing 747s at takeoff. Today, mighty chemical reactions still power rockets. Computers monitor the launcher's climb, correcting the angle of ascent. The whole event is governed by the laws of physics, in particular Newton's three laws of motion.

MASS AND WEIGHT
The mass of an object is a measure of how much matter it consists of. Mass is the same everywhere. The weight of an object is the result of the force of gravity acting on the object's mass. Gravity (and therefore weight) decrease with distance from Earth.

— Rocket at rest

Gravity —

THRUST AND ACCELERATION
A launcher needs sufficient thrust to lift its own mass and to overcome gravity. As fuel burns during the ascent, mass is reduced. With increased distance from the Earth, both mass and the pull of gravity lessen, and the rocket picks up speed and accelerates to space.

Thrust —

— Gravity

ACTION AND REACTION
The thrust that lifts the launcher comes from burning fuel in its combustion chamber. If the chamber were sealed, it would explode. Gases are allowed to escape through a nozzle. Because they cannot escape upwards, the gases exert an upward force (reaction) that is equal and opposite to the force (action) of the escaping exhaust.

— Thrust

— Combustion chamber

Liftoff

ARIANE 5
Ariane rockets launch about half the world's large commercial satellites. Ariane 5's thrust at liftoff comes from a main engine and two boosters, which together produce a thrust equal to the weight of 1,200 tonnes. The mass of the rocket on the ground is 740 tonnes. The extra 460 tonnes of thrust available allows the launcher to lift off. After about 2 minutes, the boosters run out of fuel and are discarded; then the main engine burns out and falls away. Finally, a small engine releases the satellite into orbit.

ARIANE 5

MAIN STAGE

ARIANE 5 LAUNCHERS
Ariane can launch one, two, or multiple satellites. How many depends on the satellites' weight on the ground and the orbit they are designed for.

Fuel pipe delivers liquid oxygen to main engine combustion chamber, where it combines with liquid hydrogen.

Liquid helium pressurizes the fuel tanks.

Main engine burns for 570 seconds.

Exhaust nozzle of main engine swivels to steer rocket.

Main engine combustion chamber

Exhaust nozzle of booster is at a fixed angle.

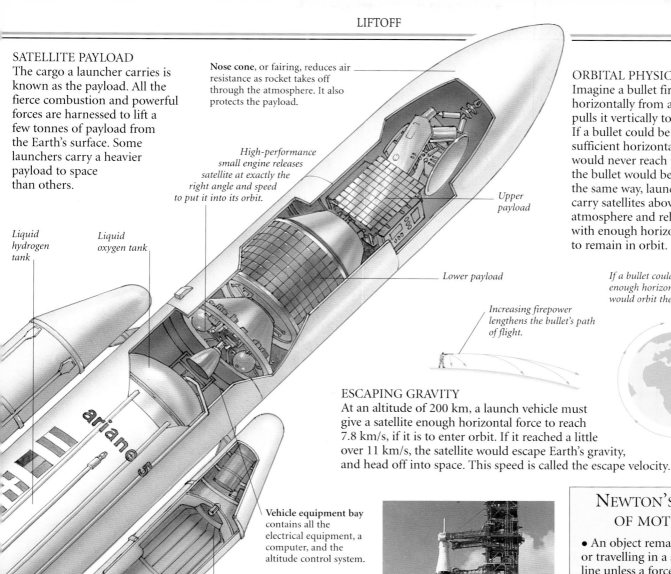

SATELLITE PAYLOAD
The cargo a launcher carries is known as the payload. All the fierce combustion and powerful forces are harnessed to lift a few tonnes of payload from the Earth's surface. Some launchers carry a heavier payload to space than others.

Nose cone, or fairing, reduces air resistance as rocket takes off through the atmosphere. It also protects the payload.

High-performance small engine releases satellite at exactly the right angle and speed to put it into its orbit.

Upper payload

Lower payload

Liquid hydrogen tank

Liquid oxygen tank

Vehicle equipment bay contains all the electrical equipment, a computer, and the altitude control system.

Igniter starts the solid fuel burn.

Solid fuel propellant in three segments inside the casing

Solid fuel boosters have a burn time of 130 seconds.

Before liftoff, the main engine ignites. If it operates correctly, the solid fuel boosters are ignited.

ORBITAL PHYSICS
Imagine a bullet fired horizontally from a gun. Gravity pulls it vertically towards Earth. If a bullet could be fired with sufficient horizontal force, it would never reach the ground: the bullet would be in orbit. In the same way, launch vehicles carry satellites above the atmosphere and release them with enough horizontal force to remain in orbit.

If a bullet could be fired with enough horizontal force, it would orbit the Earth.

Increasing firepower lengthens the bullet's path of flight.

ESCAPING GRAVITY
At an altitude of 200 km, a launch vehicle must give a satellite enough horizontal force to reach 7.8 km/s, if it is to enter orbit. If it reached a little over 11 km/s, the satellite would escape Earth's gravity, and head off into space. This speed is called the escape velocity.

NEWTON'S LAWS OF MOTION

- An object remains at rest or travelling in a straight line unless a force acts upon it. For a satellite, the main forces are gravity and the horizontal force of the launch vehicle.

- The acceleration of an object is equal to the overall force acting upon it divided by its mass. For a rocket, the two main forces are thrust upwards and gravity downwards.

- For every action, there is an equal and opposite reaction. The action of releasing high pressure gas from combustion has a reaction that gives liftoff.

STAGES TO ORBIT
Maximum thrust is needed in the lower atmosphere. Rockets achieve this in different ways. Ariane 5 has a main stage boosted by two solid fuel rockets. After two minutes, these fall away and the main engine completes the journey to space with a lighter load. But in the giant Saturn V launcher, when the fuel was spent the first stage fell away, leaving the second stage to fire and take over, followed by a third.

Saturn V was built to send astronauts to the Moon.

FIND OUT MORE
ROCKET PROPULSION 38
SPACE LAUNCHERS 40
COUNTDOWN 44
SATELLITES AND ORBITS 58
FLYING TO SPACE 60

ARIANE 5 LIFTOFF DATA

Fact	Rocket boosters	Main engine
Length	30 m each	30.5 m
Propellant	237 tonnes each	Liquid oxygen 130 tonnes, liquid hydrogen 225 tonnes
Mass	270 tonnes each	170 tonnes
Maximum thrust	630 tonnes each	Thrust in vacuum 120 tonnes

ROCKET PROPULSION

AT THE START OF THE SPACE AGE, rockets were more likely to end up as a ball of fire or to veer off course than to reach the correct orbit. Now, they are more reliable as rocket scientists have learnt the best way to make, combine, and supply the propellant. The propellant contains fuel and the oxidant fuel needs to burn and release energy. Rockets carry their own oxidant into space, unlike aircraft which use oxygen from the atmosphere. Fuel and oxidants can be solid or liquid: liquid fuels produce more thrust for every second than solid propellant.

SPACE SHUTTLE FUEL

At liftoff, propellant accounts for nearly 90 per cent of the weight of the Space Shuttle system. Both solid and liquid propellants are used. The external tank carries liquid hydrogen and, separately, the liquid oxygen needed for combustion. About 470 kg of propellant are delivered to each of the three main engines every second. The solid fuel is in the boosters on either side of the orbiter. Each booster weighs 83 tonnes, and can hold 504 tonnes of propellant.

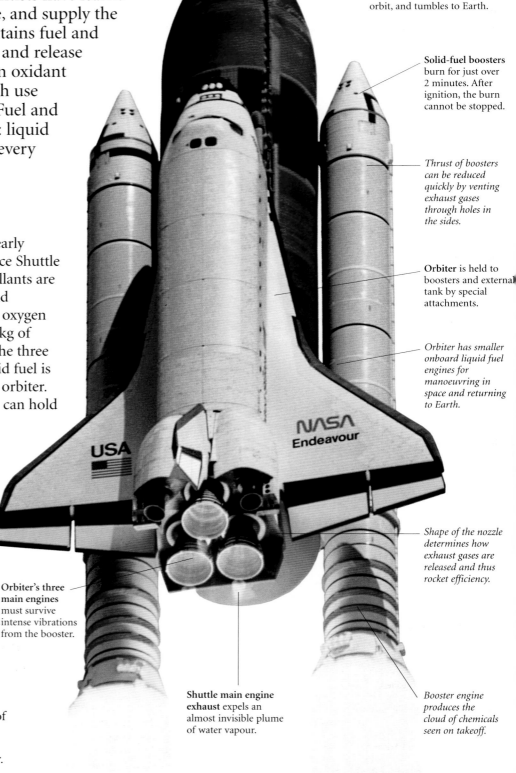

SPACE SHUTTLE

External fuel tank separates from orbiter when nearly in orbit, and tumbles to Earth.

Solid-fuel boosters burn for just over 2 minutes. After ignition, the burn cannot be stopped.

Thrust of boosters can be reduced quickly by venting exhaust gases through holes in the sides.

Orbiter is held to boosters and external tank by special attachments.

Orbiter has smaller onboard liquid fuel engines for manoeuvring in space and returning to Earth.

Shape of the nozzle determines how exhaust gases are released and thus rocket efficiency.

Orbiter's three main engines must survive intense vibrations from the booster.

Shuttle main engine exhaust expels an almost invisible plume of water vapour.

Booster engine produces the cloud of chemicals seen on takeoff.

ASTRONAUT ON FLIGHT DECK OF SHUTTLE

SPACE LAUNCHES

The Shuttle provides a gentler ride to orbit for astronauts than earlier launchers. The maximum acceleration is three times that of gravity (3 g). It occurs briefly before the boosters fall away and for 5 minutes before the external tank separates from the orbiter.

SOLID ROCKET FUEL

The propellant in solid-fuel rockets is shaped into pellets that contain both oxidant and a fuel. The pellets also contain substances to prevent them decomposing in storage. The way the propellant is packed into the casing determines how the energy is released. If it is packed so that the surface burns at a constant rate (neutral burn), it provides an even thrust. If the pellets are packed so that the surface area where burning occurs increases gradually, thrust increases gradually (progressive burn). If the burning surface area decreases, the thrust decreases gradually (regressive burn).

NEUTRAL BURN

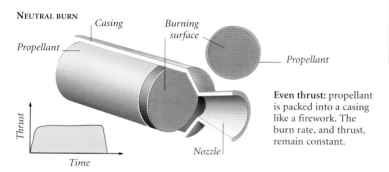

Even thrust: propellant is packed into a casing like a firework. The burn rate, and thrust, remain constant.

PROGRESSIVE BURN

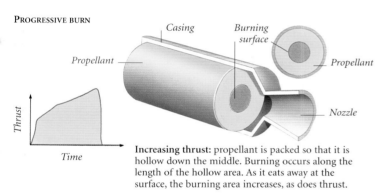

Increasing thrust: propellant is packed so that it is hollow down the middle. Burning occurs along the length of the hollow area. As it eats away at the surface, the burning area increases, as does thrust.

REGRESSIVE BURN

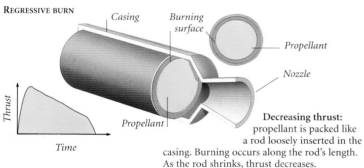

Decreasing thrust: propellant is packed like a rod loosely inserted in the casing. Burning occurs along the rod's length. As the rod shrinks, thrust decreases.

ROCKETS THEN AND NOW

	Goddard's rocket	Space Shuttle
First test flight	12 March 1926	12–14 April 1981
Length	3.4 m	55.4 m
Mass at liftoff	2.7 kg	1.9 million kg
Propellant mass	2 kg	1.7 million kg
Flight time	2.5 s	Up to 16 days
Height	12.5 m	1,000 km (maximum altitude)
Distance	56 m	Orbits the Earth
Speed	96 km/h	30,000 km/h
Thrust at liftoff	40 newtons*	35 meganewtons**

* A newton is the unit of force that causes a mass of 1 kg to move with an acceleration of 1 m per second per second.

** A meganewton is 1 million newtons.

LIQUID ROCKET FUEL

Liquid oxygen needed to burn the fuel.

Liquid hydrogen stored separately from liquid oxygen.

Liquid hydrogen and liquid oxygen mix and burn in combustion chamber.

LIQUID ROCKET FUEL

The boiling point of liquid oxygen is −183°C, cold enough to crack metal or shatter rubber. Liquid hydrogen boils at −253°C. Such low temperatures make both difficult to handle, but they make an efficient propellant.

SPECIFIC IMPULSE DATA

Propellant	Specific impulse
Solid fuel (used in Space Shuttle)	262 seconds
Liquid nitrogen tetroxide/UDMH* fuel (used in Russian Proton)	360 seconds
Liquid oxygen/kerosene (used in Saturn V)	363 seconds
Liquid oxygen/liquid hydrogen (used in Shuttle and Ariane 5)	462 seconds

* UDMH – unsymmetrical dimethylhydrazine

SPECIFIC IMPULSE

The efficiency of a propellant, known as specific impulse, is defined as the time for which 1 kg of propellant can deliver 1 kg of thrust. So, 1 kg of propellant with a specific impulse of 262 seconds, such as that in the Space Shuttle's solid rocket boosters, can produce 1 kg of thrust for 262 seconds. The higher the specific impulse, the more effective the mix. Liquid propellants have higher specific impulses than solid fuels have.

ROCKET MILESTONES

• The Chinese made gunpowder from saltpetre, charcoal, and sulphur in the 10th century. It was the first solid rocket fuel.

• American pioneer Robert Goddard made history on 26 March 1926 when he launched the first liquid-fuelled rocket.

GODDARD WITH HIS ROCKET

• Wernher von Braun developed the V-2 during World War II. His work later contributed to the first US space launcher.

• The Soviet Union launched the world's first satellite on 4 October 1957. It was lifted off by a launcher first developed as a missile.

FIND OUT MORE

HOW ROCKETS WORK 36
SPACE LAUNCHERS 40
COUNTDOWN 44
SPACE SHUTTLE 62

SPACE LAUNCHERS

N O ONE WOULD BUY A ROLLS ROYCE for the school run, and nor would anyone build a mighty Saturn V to launch a satellite the size of a basket into an orbit close to Earth. One of the main decisions facing spacecraft owners is which launch vehicle should place their craft into orbit. Reliability, cost, and technical capability are all important. Like car manufacturers, launch companies offer a variety of models. The heavy-lift launchers are favoured for sending space probes on interplanetary journeys or satellites into a high geostationary orbit above Earth. Air launch rockets, the "minis" of space, are well suited to placing small payloads in low-Earth orbit.

DELTA II

Delta rockets ferry large satellites, such as the Thor III communications satellite, to orbit.

HEAVY-LIFT ROCKETS

The Russian Proton rocket and Europe's Ariane 5 can be thought of as rockets with muscle. They can place 20 tonnes – the equivalent of 20 cars – into low-Earth orbit. For such launches, Proton has three stages. There is a four-stage version for launching spacecraft on interplanetary journeys.

WORKHORSE OF ROCKETRY

The Delta family has launched satellites since 1960 and Delta II since 1989. Delta II can launch 1.8 tonnes into a transfer orbit for geostationary orbit. Delta II's record of reliability contributed to the Delta family being called the "workhorse" of rocketry. Delta III is the latest addition to the family and can place 8 tonnes in low-Earth orbit, or 4 tonnes in a transfer orbit to geostationary orbit.

Proton launches large satellites, such as the Asiasat HSG-1, to low-Earth orbit. Asiasat beams television and telephone signals to Asia and the Pacific.

The Proton family of launchers has placed large satellites in orbit since 1965.

L1011 AIRCRAFT WITH PEGASUS ROCKET UNDERNEATH

AIR LAUNCH ROCKETS

An L1011 Stargazer aircraft carries the Pegasus rocket to an altitude of 12.2 km. The aircraft releases the rocket above open ocean. The rocket's wings provide aerodynamic lift, keeping the Pegasus in flight. After five seconds, the first of three rocket stages ignites. Ten minutes later, the payload is in orbit. Pegasus can launch 500 kg into a low-Earth orbit.

Pegasus can launch multiple small satellites. This is crucial for launching the new fleets of mobile communications satellites.

H-II launchers are the centrepiece of Japan's space programme.

H-II can launch the HOPE space plane intended to ferry goods to and from the International Space Station.

ROCKET CAPABILITIES

Name	Destination of payloads			Length in metres
	Low-Earth	Geostationary	Planets	
Ariane 5	Yes	Yes	Yes	51
Atlas family	Yes	Yes	Yes	28–53
Delta family	Yes	Yes	Yes	39 (Delta II)
H-II	Yes	Yes	Yes	48
Long March family	Yes	Yes	Yes	28–52
Pegasus	Yes	Yes	Yes	15.5
Proton family	Yes	Yes	Yes	50–60
Polar Satellite Launch Vehicle	Yes	No	No	44
R7	Yes	No	No	29
Saturn V	Designed for Apollo Moon missions			110
Titan family	Yes	Yes	Yes	Up to 65

ROCKETS FOR SPACE STATIONS

The US Space Shuttle and Russian Proton lifted heavy International Space Station elements to orbit. Other launchers provide back-up. Europe plans to use Ariane 5 to launch the Automated Transfer Vehicle, which will carry fuel for station manoeuvres and also provide supplies, while Japan plans to provide its H-II launcher to lift the HOPE space plane to the Space Station.

ROCKET CHALLENGERS

Spacecraft are complicated, and one tiny mistake can destroy a multimillion dollar mission. Nearly all orders for launchers go to companies (usually in the USA, Russia, Europe, or Japan) with the most experience of manufacturing space technology. Other countries launch their own rockets, but find it hard to sell them to others. China is now making an effort to sell its rockets abroad.

CHINESE LONG MARCH ROCKET

Long March rockets have carried small satellites, like the Asia-Pacific Mobile Tele-communications system, to orbit.

Nose cone

The Earth resources satellite ERS-2 fitted inside Ariane 5.

FAMOUS LAUNCHERS

• The R7 Soviet launch vehicle was made up of a central rocket and boosters. It placed the first satellite, Sputnik, in orbit in 1957.

• Saturn V, the rocket which lifted the Apollo missions from Earth, made its last flight on 14 May 1973, when it launched the Skylab Space Station.

• In 1974, NASA combined a Titan rocket with the upper stage of a Centaur rocket. The combination sent the Voyager spacecraft on their historic tour of the outer Solar System.

SATURN V

First flight: 9 November 1967

Lifted Apollo on its way to the first Moon landing: 16 July 1969

Made its 11th and final flight: 14 May 1973

MATCHING LAUNCHERS AND PAYLOADS

The most important question the satellite owner asks when choosing a launch vehicle is, "How much can it lift"? Even if the launcher has the lift capacity, the nose cone must be the right shape for the satellite to fit inside. The satellite must also be able to withstand the forces exerted on the payload during liftoff. Each rocket behaves in a different way, imposing different forces on the payload.

LAUNCH CENTRES

LAUNCH CENTRES ARE THE GATEWAYS TO SPACE. They can be small sites, or vast, expensive complexes sprawling over many hectares. The world's largest spaceports have many launchpads. In the weeks before launch, engineers assemble the launch vehicle in multistorey buildings. Then giant platforms lumber to the pad carrying the assembled launcher. Scattered around the site are the control room from which mission specialists oversee the final countdown, huge tanks for the propellant, weather stations that check conditions at the site on the day of launch, and tracking stations to monitor the early part of the ascent to space.

KENNEDY SPACE CENTER
The 56.600 hectares of the Kennedy Space Center at Cape Canaveral is NASA's launch site for the Space Shuttle. There is a 4.5-km runway, which the staff checks for stray alligators and bobcats prior to a landing.

WORLD LAUNCH SITES

Launch site	Location	Owner
Alcantara	Brazil	Brazil
Baikonur	Kazakhstan	Russia
Jiuquan	China	China
Kagoshima	Japan	Japan
Kapustin Yar	Russia	Russia
Kennedy	Florida	USA
Kourou	French Guiana	France
Plesetsk	Russia	Russia
San Marco	Italy	Italy
Sriharikota	Andhra Pradesh	India
Tanegashima	Japan	Japan
Vandenberg	California	USA
Xichang	Sichuan	China
Zenit	At sea	Business consortium

KOUROU SPACE CENTRE
Kourou is where Arianespace (responsible for more than half the world's large commercial satellites) and the European Space Agency launch satellites. It is close to the Equator and therefore favourable for placing satellites into the geostationary orbit directly above the Equator.

Alcantara launch centre in Brazil is the newest one in the world.

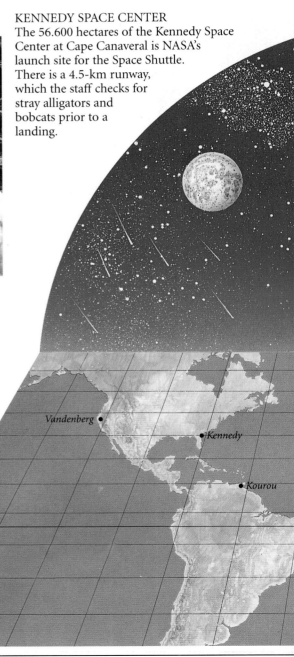

Vandenberg

Kennedy

Kourou

Equator

BAIKONUR COSMODROME
Baikonur, in Kazakhstan, is the world's largest space centre and one of the oldest – American spy planes recorded construction there in 1955. The very first satellite, Sputnik, was launched from Baikonur in 1957. Russian rockets supplying the International Space Station are launched from there.

LAUNCH LOCATIONS

Several factors influence the choice of launch site. During the first 40 years of the space age, terrible accidents showed how important it is to keep launches away from populated areas. However, the site must be accessible because of the heavy equipment needed for a launch. The USA and Europe resolved these problems by locating sites in accessible coastal areas and by launching over oceans. Geography is also important. Launches to the east, for example, are preferable because they benefit from Earth's eastward rotation. It is also best to have a site close to the Equator, where that rotation is greatest.

LAUNCH SITE PROFILES

Launch site	First launch	Payloads
Alcantara	1999	Commercial, science
Baikonur	4 November 1957	Crewed, science, commercial
Jiuquan	26 July 1975	Commercial
Kagoshima	11 February 1970	Commercial, science
Kapustin Yar	16 March 1962	Science
Kennedy	9 November 1967	Crewed, commercial, science
Kourou	10 March 1970	Commercial, science
Plesetsk	17 March 1966	Military, applications
San Marco	26 April 1967	Rockets
Sriharikota	18 July 1980	Science, applications
Tanegashima	11 February 1975	Science, commercial
Vandenberg	28 February 1959	Military
Xichang	29 January 1984	Science, applications
Zenit Sea Platform	27 March 1999	Commercial

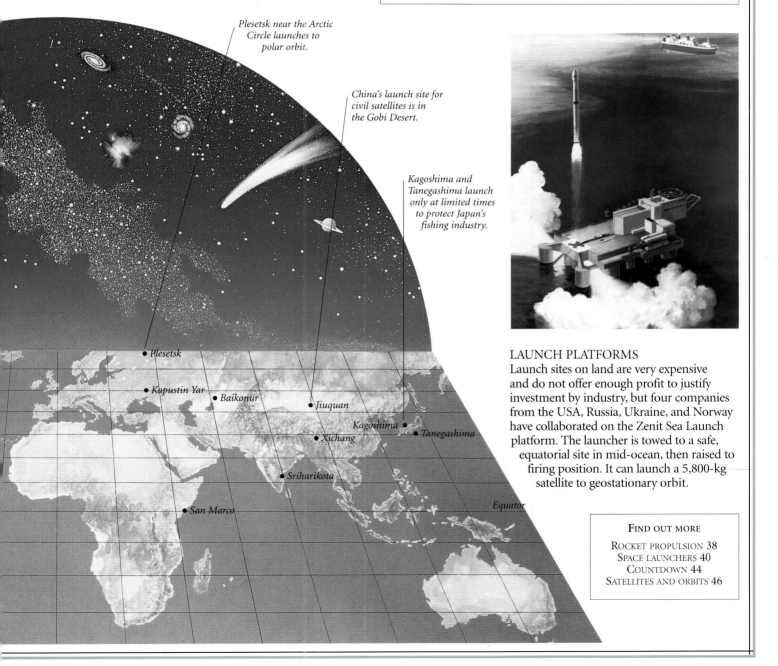

Plesetsk near the Arctic Circle launches to polar orbit.

China's launch site for civil satellites is in the Gobi Desert.

Kagoshima and Tanegashima launch only at limited times to protect Japan's fishing industry.

- Plesetsk
- Kapustin Yar
- Baikonur
- Jiuquan
- Kagoshima
- Xichang
- Tanegashima
- Sriharikota
- San Marco

Equator

LAUNCH PLATFORMS

Launch sites on land are very expensive and do not offer enough profit to justify investment by industry, but four companies from the USA, Russia, Ukraine, and Norway have collaborated on the Zenit Sea Launch platform. The launcher is towed to a safe, equatorial site in mid-ocean, then raised to firing position. It can launch a 5,800-kg satellite to geostationary orbit.

FIND OUT MORE

ROCKET PROPULSION 38
SPACE LAUNCHERS 40
COUNTDOWN 44
SATELLITES AND ORBITS 46

COUNTDOWN

THE FINAL PART OF EVERY LAUNCH CAMPAIGN begins when all the separate components arrive at the launch centre to be assembled into the launch vehicle. The launch campaign for Ariane 5, for example, begins 21 days before the scheduled liftoff, and the countdown itself begins six hours before. During this final countdown, engineers make the site ready for launch, and personnel are evacuated from the area. About an hour before liftoff, preparations begin for the synchronized sequence of events that leads to those famous words: "Ten, nine, eight..."

ROCKET TRANSPORTATION
The ship carrying the parts of the Ariane 5 rocket to French Guiana begins its journey in Bremen, Germany, where the upper stage is loaded. Other components are shipped along Europe's rivers to Rotterdam in Holland or to Le Havre in France, where they join the ship for Kourou. The crossing from Le Havre to Kourou takes 11 days.

MISSION CONTROL
The Jupiter control room in Kourou, French Guiana, directs the Ariane 5 liftoff. Three teams monitor the status of the launcher, payload, and the tracking stations that will follow its ascent, while weather and safety teams work elsewhere. When all report status *green*, the director of operations authorizes the final stage of countdown.

Observation lounge of Jupiter control room

PAYLOAD INTEGRATION
For a launch on Ariane 5, satellites and their protective nose cone are mounted on the launcher in the final assembly building about eight days before liftoff. The satellite is linked via Ariane 5 to the Jupiter control room so that the payload can be monitored during the final countdown.

Communications satellite being prepared for Ariane 5.

JUPITER CONTROL ROOM DURING AN ARIANE LAUNCH

Leader of tracking team monitors launcher's path with radar.

Mission controllers monitor launch support equipment at and near the launchpad.

Screen displays trajectory of launch.

Telecoms link with stations that track the launcher's ascent.

Payload team monitors satellite's status and ensures owner's tracking stations are ready to receive signals once satellite is in orbit.

Four computers in the foreground are reserved for senior personnel from the French and European Space Agencies, the satellite owner, and Arianespace.

Director of operations (DDO) authorizes final countdown: "To everyone from DDO, attention ... start of synchronized sequence."

Launch team leader filters information about launcher status to DDO.

Deputy launch team leader acts as backup to DDO.

TO THE LAUNCHPAD

An 870-tonne launch table supports the launcher during assembly. The day before liftoff, a truck tows the launcher and table along rail tracks to the launchpad. Together the truck and table weigh 1,500 tonnes (the equivalent of 1,500 cars). Propellant (fuel and oxidant) is piped into the launcher at the pad.

A service unit on the launch table keeps Ariane 5 cool during its trip to the launchpad.

ON THE LAUNCHPAD

There are three trenches at the launch area through which flames from the boosters and main engine escape during liftoff. A tower supplies water at the rate of 30 cubic metres per second during launch to reduce noise and to cool the trenches and launch table. Without the water, vibrations from the noise could damage the launcher and its payload.

COUNTDOWN TO LIFTOFF	
–360 seconds	Synchronized sequence leading to main ignition begins
–30 seconds	Valves open to flood flame trenches with water
–13 seconds	Onboard computers authorized to take over
Main ignition	Main engine ignition sequence begins and its operation is checked. Finally both of the solid rocket boosters are ignited.
Main ignition + 7 seconds	We have liftoff!

LIFTOFF

Six hours before liftoff, the launch area is readied. The flight program is loaded into the two onboard computers and the program initiated to check radio links between the launcher and the ground. Five hours before launch, the main stage tanks are filled with propellant. Six minutes before liftoff, the synchronized sequence leading to liftoff begins.

FIND OUT MORE

How rockets work 36
Rocket propulsion 38
Space launchers 40
Launch centres 42

SATELLITES AND ORBITS

ANYTHING IN ORBIT AROUND another object can be called a satellite. The Moon, for example, is a natural satellite of Earth. Since 1957, hundreds of artificial satellites have been launched into orbit around Earth. They come in many shapes and sizes, and occupy different types of orbit, depending on what they are designed to do. Many communications satellites occupy geostationary orbit, for example, while many weather satellites are in polar orbit. Whichever orbit they follow, satellites must remain stable so that their instruments always point in the right directions.

STABILIZING SATELLITES

If a satellite is not stable – if it swings about in an unpredictable way – it cannot do its job. For example, the dish of a communications satellite must always point towards its receiving station, or towards the right country if it is transmitting television signals. Two techniques commonly used to maintain stability are spin and three-axis stabilization.

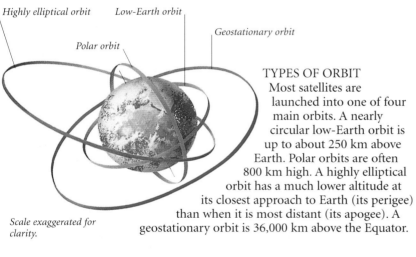

Highly elliptical orbit *Low-Earth orbit*

Polar orbit

Geostationary orbit

Scale exaggerated for clarity.

HS 376 SPIN-STABILIZED COMMUNICATIONS SATELLITE

Antenna for telemetry and command

Antenna dish does not spin.

Antenna feed radiates radio signals that reflect off the dish.

Equipment is designed to fit into the satellite's cylindrical shape.

If sensors detect a wobble in the satellite, thrusters correct spin and restore stability.

Outer panels slip down in orbit to uncover solar panels beneath. This increases the power available to the satellite.

Solar cell panels

TYPES OF ORBIT

Most satellites are launched into one of four main orbits. A nearly circular low-Earth orbit is up to about 250 km above Earth. Polar orbits are often 800 km high. A highly elliptical orbit has a much lower altitude at its closest approach to Earth (its perigee) than when it is most distant (its apogee). A geostationary orbit is 36,000 km above the Equator.

TELEMETRY, TRACKING, AND COMMAND

Telemetry – literally, measuring from far away – allows people on the ground to receive measurements from satellites in orbit. The measurements, sent as radio signals, might include information that allows operators to pinpoint the satellite's position. This allows people to track the satellite, and to send command signals that can change its position. Telemetry also includes data that allow ground controllers to check that the satellite is operating correctly.

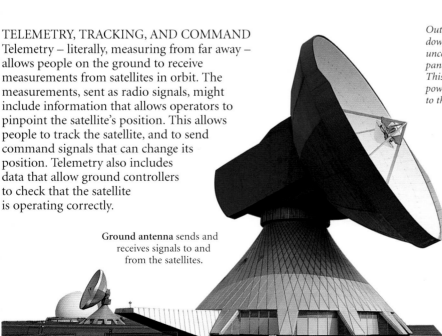

Ground antenna sends and receives signals to and from the satellites.

SPIN STABILIZATION

Things that spin are naturally stable. A spinning top remains stable if it is spun fast enough, and the turning of its wheels helps to keep a bicycle upright. In the early days of satellites, designers decided to exploit this principle. The result is spin-stabilized satellites. These are often cylindrical in shape, and make about one revolution every second. The antenna dish must always point to Earth, so it does not spin. Designers must take care that the dish does not destabilize the satellite.

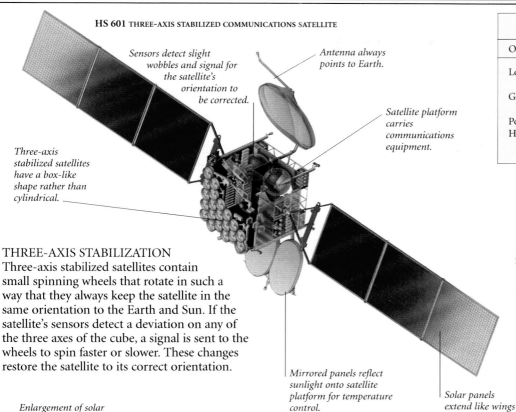

HS 601 THREE-AXIS STABILIZED COMMUNICATIONS SATELLITE

Sensors detect slight wobbles and signal for the satellite's orientation to be corrected.

Antenna always points to Earth.

Satellite platform carries communications equipment.

Three-axis stabilized satellites have a box-like shape rather than cylindrical.

SATELLITE ORBITAL DATA

Orbit	Typical payload
Low-Earth	Mobile communications, reconnaissance
Geostationary	Weather, communications, navigation
Polar	Weather, navigation
Highly elliptical	Communications at northern latitudes

OTHER STABILIZING METHODS

The forces exerted on a satellite can be used to maintain stability in space. For example, large satellites can exploit gravity to align themselves so that their instruments always point to Earth. Others interact with Earth's magnetic field to gain stability. The method of stabilization depends on the job the satellite has to do and the orbit it occupies.

THREE-AXIS STABILIZATION

Three-axis stabilized satellites contain small spinning wheels that rotate in such a way that they always keep the satellite in the same orientation to the Earth and Sun. If the satellite's sensors detect a deviation on any of the three axes of the cube, a signal is sent to the wheels to spin faster or slower. These changes restore the satellite to its correct orientation.

Mirrored panels reflect sunlight onto satellite platform for temperature control.

Solar panels extend like wings and always face the Sun.

Enlargement of solar cells in a panel

FIRST SATELLITES

- The Soviet Sputnik 1 (launched 4 October 1957) was the first satellite. It sent no telemetry.

- Explorer 1 (launched 1 February 1958) was the first US satellite. It found hints of the Van Allen radiation belts.

- The US Explorer 7 (launched 7 August 1959) carried the first instruments to study climate.

- The US Transit 1B (launched 13 April 1960) was the world's first navigation satellite.

- The first weather satellite was US TIROS 1 (launched 1 April 1960). It sent pictures to Earth for two months.

- Intelsat's Early Bird (launched 6 April 1965) was the first commercially operated communications satellite.

SOLAR CELLS

Solar cells produce electrical power when light falls on them. On satellites, the cells are arranged into solar panels, sometimes called arrays. They provide satellites with the power they need to do their job. In addition, the cells provide the power needed to keep the satellite and its payload in orbit.

WESTAR SATELLITE RESCUE

In 1984, Westar 6's telemetry showed that the satellite had failed to reach its correct orbit after launch.

HOUSEKEEPING DATA

Information about a satellite's health is called housekeeping data. These data alert ground control when something is wrong – if the satellite is becoming unstable, for instance. Ground-based operators can often send a command to solve the problem, or organize a rescue mission.

Space Shuttle astronaut retrieves the Westar satellite to bring it back to Earth for repair.

FIND OUT MORE

COMMUNICATIONS SATELLITES

TELEPHONE CALLS, TELEVISION BROADCASTS, and the Internet can all be relayed by communications satellites. These satellites connect distant places and make communication possible with remote areas. Many are in geostationary orbit (GEO), but so great is the demand for communications that this orbit has become crowded. Since the 1990s, fleets of satellites have been launched into low-Earth orbit (below GEO) to carry signals for the growing number of mobile phones.

TRANSPONDERS

Devices called transponders are at the heart of communications satellites. They contain a chain of electronic components. These components clean up radio signals, which can be distorted after travelling through the atmosphere, and convert them to the frequency necessary for transmission back to Earth. They also amplify the signals before retransmitting them.

COMMUNICATIONS SATELLITE TRANSPONDER

INTELSAT V SATELLITE

GEOSTATIONARY SATELLITES

Satellites in GEO above the Equator always seem to stay over the same spot on Earth. They appear stationary because a satellite 36,000 km above Earth takes the same time to complete one orbit as Earth takes to spin on its axis. They remain in sight of the same Earth station.

Three satellites, spaced evenly apart in GEO, can view the entire planet, except the polar regions.

Science fiction author Arthur C. Clarke first suggested GEO for communications satellites in 1945.

COMMUNICATIONS LINK

Antennas on the ground and on satellites send and receive radio waves that carry telephone calls, television signals, or data. A telephone call from Europe to the USA, for example, might pass through the public telephone network to a nearby Earth station, which transmits the radio waves to a satellite in GEO. The satellite would then amplify and retransmit the radio waves to an antenna in the USA, where the signal is routed over the telephone network to its destination.

Thanks to communications satellites, telephone calls are possible between plane and ground.

Radio signals lose strength as they travel through space.

EARTH STATIONS

The antennas and other equipment needed on the ground to transmit and receive signals to and from satellites are known as the Earth station. Earth stations can be housed in large buildings. Their antennas act as a gateway through which, for example, thousands of telephone calls are transmitted to and from a satellite. Earth stations can also be small units, designed to fit on ships or planes.

Antennas transmit and receive signals. They are key to an Earth station's operation, regardless of whether the station is on land, sea, or in the air.

SATELLITE FOOTPRINT

Just as the beams of spotlights have different shapes and sizes, so radio waves transmitted by a satellite fall on Earth with a particular pattern. This pattern is known as the satellite footprint. Antennas within the footprint can transmit and receive signals to and from the satellite.

Satellite footprint might cover a whole continent or one small country.

SATELLITE ANTENNAS

Early antennas used to spill their signals in all directions, wasting the satellite's limited power. Now they are more sophisticated and can transmit high-powered narrow beams at a specific area of the Earth. These antennas are often too large to fit the nose cone of the launch rocket, so the antenna is unfurled or deployed in orbit.

EVOLVING CAPACITY

Satellite	First launched	Transmission capability		
		TV channels		Voice circuits
Early Bird	1965	1	or	240
Intelsat III	1968	4	or	1,500
Intelsat V	1980	2	and	12,000
Intelsat VIII	1997	3	and	22,500

COMMUNICATIONS MILESTONES

• In 1954, the US Navy sent a message from Washington DC to Hawaii by bouncing a signal off the Moon's surface.

ECHO

• In 1960, NASA and Bell Telephone launched an aluminized balloon called Echo that reflected signals across North America.

• The world's first geostationary satellite for commercial traffic was Early Bird (Intelsat I), launched in April 1965.

Intelsat satellites have provided international communications systems for more than three decades.

Antenna can focus signals to a specific region on Earth.

SATELLITE CONSTELLATIONS

In the late 1990s, constellations or fleets of satellites, such as Globalstar and Iridium, were launched into low-Earth orbits (LEO). These satellites are much closer to Earth than GEO satellites, and so need smaller, cheaper equipment for relaying messages. Communications satellites in LEO can be cheaper for applications, such as mobile phones, than a system based on GEO satellites.

Iridium constellation has 66 satellites.

Globalstar constellation has 48 satellites.

Communications downlink

Antenna dish sends and receives signals.

Transponder is located inside the satellite.

Communications downlink

Half-circuit is a two-way communications link between one Earth station and a satellite.

Uplink and downlink use different frequencies.

The white circles are satellite footprints. The satellites themselves are in green and occupy orbits shown in red. Footprints overlap one another to provide global coverage.

Iridium satellites can pass signals between one another, which gives them great flexibility as a mobile communications system.

Communications uplink

FREQUENCY

Radio waves are part of the electromagnetic spectrum. Communications satellites transmit radio waves at frequencies that pass through the atmosphere without being absorbed by water vapour.

Full circuit is a two-way communications link by satellite between two Earth stations.

Channel is a one-way communications link between an Earth station and satellite.

MOBILE PHONE

Communications ...link

Ships can stay in constant communication with land by using satellites.

NAVIGATION SATELLITES

To STEER AN ACCURATE COURSE between two places, a navigator needs to know his or her exact position. For thousands of years, sailors calculated their positions using the Moon, stars, and Sun. When clouds obscure the sky, however, it is easy to go far off course. Satellite navigation systems have solved this problem. Satellites transmit radio waves that can be detected on Earth even when it is cloudy. As a result, navigation is now possible in any weather. By the late 1990s, the Global Positioning System (GPS) developed in the USA had become the most reliable and accurate navigation system ever.

HOW GPS WORKS

GPS consists of 24 satellites as well as equipment on the ground. The satellites broadcast their positions and the time. They are spaced in orbits so that a receiver anywhere on Earth can always receive signals from at least four satellites. The GPS receiver knows precisely when the signal was sent and when it arrived, and so can calculate the distance between itself and each of the satellites. With this information, it works out its own position, including altitude.

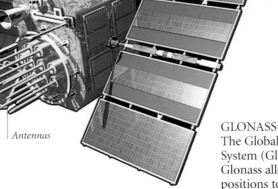

ARTIST'S IMPRESSION
OF GPS ORBITS

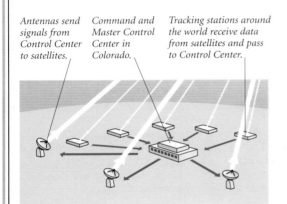

Antennas send signals from Control Center to satellites.

Command and Master Control Center in Colorado.

Tracking stations around the world receive data from satellites and pass to Control Center.

GPS SATELLITE

Each GPS satellite has a mass of 844 kg, about the same as a small car. When the solar panels are fully open, the satellites are 5.3 m wide. Each satellite carries atomic clocks to give time accurately. The satellites are designed to last for seven and a half years, and their orbit is at an altitude of 20,200 km.

GPS GROUND CONTROL

The US Air Force monitors the speed, position, and altitude of GPS satellites. Tracking stations send this information to the Master Control Center. Using this, the centre predicts the satellites' positions in orbit for the next 12 hours. Ground antennas transmit these positions to the satellites for broadcasting to Earth. The tracking data enable the Control Center to update constantly predictions of the satellites' positions.

Thrusters keep the satellite orientated correctly towards Earth.

GLONASS SATELLITE

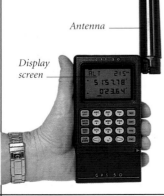

Antenna

Display screen

GPS receivers can be as small as mobile phones.

Antennas

GPS RECEIVERS

Early receivers displayed the user's position as latitude and longitude, which had to be plotted on a map. Modern ones will display a map marking the user's position to within a few metres. As well as position, the receivers calculate speed and direction of travel.

GLONASS

The Global Orbiting Navigation Satellite System (Glonass) is owned by Russia. Glonass allows users to work out their positions to between 20 m and 100 m. When needed, special techniques permit greater precision. Glonass satellites give worldwide coverage. The European Space Agency is improving coverage of Europe by building equipment designed to receive signals from both Glonass and GPS.

NAVIGATION SYSTEMS DATA

	GPS	Glonass
Number of satellites	24	24
Number of orbits	6	3
Altitude	20,200 km	19,000 km
System complete	March 1994	January 1996

There are four satellites in each GPS orbit.

Satellites were launched into six different circular orbits to give global coverage.

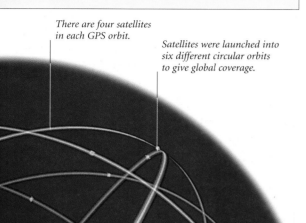

ATOMIC CLOCKS

Atomic clocks keep time with spectacular accuracy: Caesium clocks lose only a second every million years. Smaller atomic clocks on GPS and Glonass satellites keep time to within 1 second every 300,000 years, enabling accurate time signals to be transmitted to Earth.

CAESIUM ATOMIC CLOCK

IN-CAR NAVIGATION ROUTE MAP

CAR NAVIGATION

Manufacturers of cars from France to Japan are installing GPS receivers to aid route planning – more than half a million Japanese cars are already equipped with the system. Some emergency vehicles also use GPS signals to pinpoint their locations. By linking the GPS receiver with a computer map, paramedics, police, or fire fighters can quickly see the fastest route to the scene of an emergency.

AIRCRAFT SPRAYING CROPS

AIR NAVIGATION

Until the early 1990s, pilots of locust-spraying aircraft in the Sahara desert had only a map and compass to guide them. Given that the Sahara has few oustanding features visible, navigating was difficult. By 1991, small GPS receivers were available, and pest-spraying aircraft could pinpoint their positions to within 30 m.

NAVIGATION MILESTONES

POLARIS SUBMARINE MISSILE

● Transit was the first satellite navigation system. The USA launched it in January 1964 to improve position location of Polaris nuclear submarines.

● The US Navy made Transit available to civilian users in July 1967.

● In October 1978, the US Air Force launched the first satellite that it acknowledged to be a GPS satellite.

● More GPS and Glonass satellites were launched in the 1980s and 1990s, increasing the number of places at which signals could be received at every minute of the day.

● In the late 1990s, the European Space Agency tested equipment that could receive both GPS and Glonass signals.

FIND OUT MORE

METEOROLOGY SATELLITES

THE WAY WEATHER SYSTEMS DEVELOP and move around the globe can be seen by meteorology satellites. They record the images that appear nightly on our television screens, show cloud cover, and monitor hurricanes growing and moving across the oceans. Meteorology satellites also carry instruments that take readings, which are converted to the temperatures, pressures, and humidities needed for weather forecasting. These, together with information from sources such as weather buoys, balloons, and ships, help forecasters to improve their predictions.

HURRICANE CENTRE
During the tropical storm season between May and November, the US National Hurricane Center in Miami keeps a 24-hour watch of all satellite data. As storms develop, satellites track their paths across the oceans. The centre distributes storm and hurricane warnings for the Caribbean, all the coasts of the USA, and the Gulf of Mexico.

HURRICANE FORECASTING
Before weather satellites existed, hurricanes would develop unseen over oceans and strike land with very little warning. One notorious hurricane killed 6,000 people in Texas in 1906. Hurricanes are extreme tropical storms with wind speeds persistently in excess of 120 km/h. In tropical storms, winds circle a calm eye of low air pressure. Now weather satellites constantly view the oceans where such storms gather strength. People need no longer die for lack of warning.

HURRICANE FRAN IN 1996

SCANNING THE GLOBE
Geostationary satellites scan the region beneath them every 30 minutes. If a tropical storm develops, they scan that region in more detail every 15 minutes. The satellites also measure temperature, which helps forecasters predict hurricane strength.

HOMING IN
As the tropical storm becomes a hurricane and nears land, the US Air Force scrambles its Weather Squadron – the Hurricane Hunters – which flies into the storm and adds its measurements to those of coastal radar and satellites.

Hurricane eye

HURRICANE ALLEN IN 1980

HURRICANE FLORENCE IN 1994

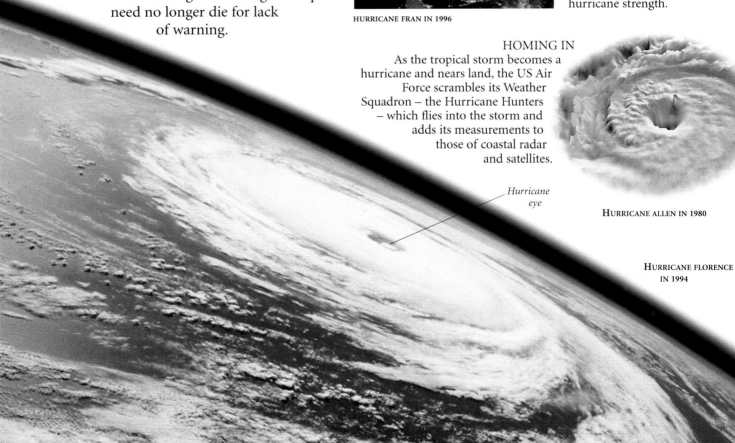

METEOSAT SATELLITE

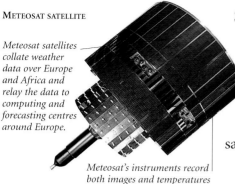

Meteosat satellites collate weather data over Europe and Africa and relay the data to computing and forecasting centres around Europe.

Meteosat's instruments record both images and temperatures in the atmosphere.

SATELLITES AND COMPUTING

Computers are essential for scientists to turn satellite measurements into the temperatures, pressures, humidities, and wind speeds needed for a weather report. The computers also combine data from radar, ships, buoys, planes, and satellites to give timely and accurate forecasts.

WEATHER ORBITS
Weather satellites occupy geostationary and polar orbits. Geostationary satellites, such as GOES, stay above the same place on the Equator and record changes continually. Each one can see a third of the globe, but they have a poor view of northern regions. Polar orbit satellites, such as NOAA 10, do not have a constant view of the same region, but they do see the poles and more detail than is possible from geostationary orbit.

GOES satellites are positioned in geostationary orbit to observe the USA and either the Atlantic or Pacific Ocean.

GOES SATELLITE

Satellites in geostationary orbit 36,000 km above Earth can keep a constant watch on a wide area.

NOAA 10 SATELLITE

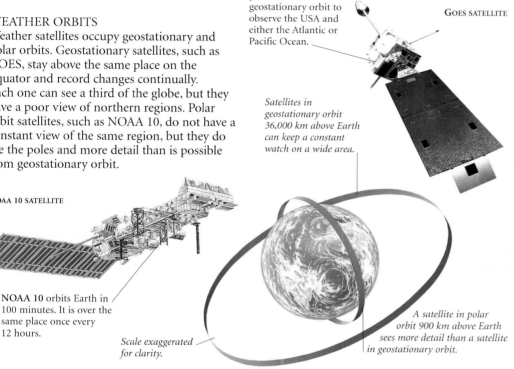

NOAA 10 orbits Earth in 100 minutes. It is over the same place once every 12 hours.

Scale exaggerated for clarity.

A satellite in polar orbit 900 km above Earth sees more detail than a satellite in geostationary orbit.

WEATHER MILESTONES

• A meteorology experiment in space was carried out from a US satellite launched in 1959. It measured solar radiation reaching Earth and reflected back to space. Earth's radiation balance is important because it drives the world's climate.

• The US launched TIROS, the first weather satellite, in 1960. It recorded 23,000 cloud images from a 750-km orbit, including the first images from space of clouds moving.

• The Soviet Union placed Cosmos 122, its first weather satellite, in orbit in 1966.

• In April 1970, NASA launched Nimbus 4, which carried the first instrument for measuring temperature at different altitudes in the atmosphere.

• The US launched the first geostationary weather satellite in 1974.

• Europe's first Meteosat satellite was launched into geostationary orbit in 1977. With its Japanese and US counterparts, it provided the first global view of Earth's weather from geostationary orbit.

Japan

HURRICANE NEARING JAPAN

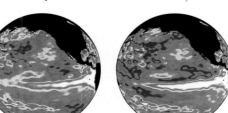

EL NIÑO DEVELOPING IN 1997

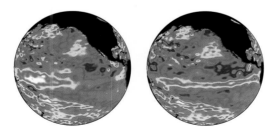

25 April

25 May

25 June

25 September

EL NINO
During El Niño, warm water replaces the usually cold water off South America, which appears to affect weather throughout the world. These satellite pictures show the warm current as a red/white area, moving eastwards near the Equator. Black areas are land while other colours represent cooler water surrounding the warm current. By analysing such images, scientists hope to understand the links between El Niño and changes in the world's weather.

PREDICTING LANDFALL
It is very difficult to predict the track of a hurricane, but for each year during the past 20 years satellites have contributed to improvements of between 0.5 and 1 per cent in the accuracy of forecasts. The place where a hurricane will make land – known as landfall – can now be predicted to within less than 160 km.

EARTH RESOURCES SATELLITES

SATELLITES THAT HELP SCIENTISTS to study Earth's surface are called Earth resources satellites. They can show whether crops are failing or ice caps are melting, and can pinpoint resources such as metal ores or coal. This is possible because the satellites' instruments analyse light and other radiation reflected and emitted from surface features. Each feature – a forest or building, for instance – has a different signature of reflected and emitted radiation. Satellites pass regularly over the whole globe, allowing scientists to produce maps that trace how a particular area changes over time.

OCEAN SURVEILLANCE

Oceans cover more than two-thirds of the globe. So to understand the Earth and its climate, it is important to know what happens in and above the oceans – where currents are, for example, and the levels of temperatures and winds. Aircraft and ships cannot keep a constant watch over all the Earth's vast watery regions, but satellites can. One of the first satellites designed for ocean surveillance was ERS-1.

ERS-1 carried instruments to measure infrared and microwave radiation, which are the wavelength bands that give the most information about ocean and atmospheric conditions.

ERS-1

THEMATIC MAPPER

Different types of radiation have different wavelengths: blue light has a shorter wavelength than red, for example. The thematic mapper is an instrument aboard Landsat satellites that measures the intensity of radiation in seven different wavelength bands, including four in the infrared region of the electro-magnetic spectrum. By assigning a different colour to each band, scientists can build up a map of a particular area.

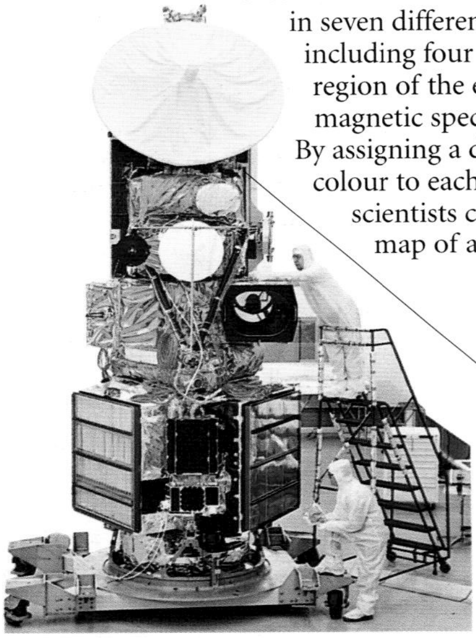

Thematic mapper

Infrared instrument, below the satellite pointing to Earth, measured sea-surface and cloud temperature.

Radar altimeter on ERS-1 recorded wave height and shape of ocean surface, allowing wind speed to be deduced.

LANDSAT 4 SATELLITE

WHAT THE MAPPER REVEALS

Each of a thematic mapper's wavelength bands reveals something different about the Earth. Band five, for example, detects the range of infrared wavelengths that shows moisture content in vegetation. If the intensity of this band is low, the plants might be on the verge of failing, even if the crop looks green to the eye.

MONITORING CROPS IN CALIFORNIA, USA

TOPEX-POSEIDON OCEANOGRAPHIC RESEARCH SATELLITE

Topex-Poseidon helped scientists study in detail how currents and tides change.

THEMATIC MAPPER DATA

Band	Wavelengths in nanometres	Applications
1	450–520 (blue/green)	Maps coastal water; differentiates between soil and vegetation
2	520–600 (green/yellow)	Reflects healthy vegetation
3	630–690 (red)	Helps identify plants
4	760–900 (infrared)	Outlines bodies of water
5	1,550–1,750 (infrared)	Measures moisture of plants
6	10,400–12,500 (infrared)	Measures heat stress of plants
7	2,080–2,350 (infrared)	Maps sources of hot water

OCEAN RESEARCH

A basic measurement for ocean and climate research is ocean height, which gives scientists information about currents and tides. From its 1,330-km high orbit, Topex-Poseidon made measurements to within an accuracy of 4.3 cm. It collected more data in a month than all research ships had in the previous hundred years.

Radar worked with two types of antennas to give a microwave image of ocean and coastal areas and to show the choppiness (and so winds) of the ocean.

Antennas monitored the choppiness of the ocean.

Antennas collected data for a microwave image of the ocean and coastal areas.

MULTISPECTRAL SCANNER

SPECTRAL RESOLUTION

The multispectral scanner (MSS) on Landsat 1 was the first satellite instrument to record radiation intensity in different wavelength bands (red, green, and two infrared ranges). Like the thematic mapper, the MSS uses a range of wavelengths to gather information about different aspects of the Earth's surface.

DEFORESTATION

A Landsat image shows forests in the Ivory Coast in Africa. The colours identify different types of surface: red is forest and pale blue is soil, while brown indicates crops. Successive images taken over months or years showed that the red area is decreasing because trees are being cut down.

SATELLITE VIEW OF IVORY COAST

MINERAL DEPOSITS IN CHILE

FALSE COLOURS

People cannot see infrared, so when scientists map it, they give each infrared wavelength band an identifying colour. Such maps are called false colour images. In this false colour photograph, the volcanic soil is shown as brown, vegetation is red, and water dark blue, while the white colour indicates the presence of mineral deposits.

RESOURCES MILESTONES

Antenna for beaming data to Earth, and the antenna mast

LANDSAT 1

● In 1972, Landsat 1 was launched by the USA. It took the first combined visible and infrared image of Earth's surface.

● In 1978, the US Seasat satellite made the first valuable measurements of oceans with radar.

● In 1986, France launched SPOT 1. This was the first Earth resources satellite to detect radiation using small silicon chips.

● In September 1992, the Topex-Poseidon mission began collecting ocean data in unprecedented detail.

● Over 30 new satellites are now being planned, some carrying instruments to detect 32 to 256 different wavelength bands.

MILITARY SATELLITES

MANY OF THE EARLIEST SATELLITES – developed by the USA or the Soviet Union – were made for the armed services. Military satellites are widely used today. From the safety of orbit, satellites can gather information about battlefields, take pictures so detailed they can show where a person is standing, locate missing troops, and provide secure communications. Some satellites monitor the globe, watching for signs of the launch of a nuclear missile or a nuclear explosion.

MILITARY NAVIGATION

The Global Positioning System (GPS), now so popular with commercial users, was originally developed for the US military. Using a hand-held device which receives signals from four GPS satellites, people can find their positions – latitude, longitude, and altitude – to within a few metres. During the Gulf War in 1991, GPS helped Allied troops find their way across the huge, empty Arabian desert.

Solar panels supply power to transmit navigation signals.

GPS SATELLITE

High-resolution telescope

HELIOS 1 SATELLITE

Antennas and sensors are used for specifically military purposes. These include detection of nuclear explosions.

SATELLITES AND DEFENCE

The USA has been launching Defense Support Program (DSP) satellites into geostationary orbit since the 1970s. Each satellite can monitor large sections of the Earth's surface. They carry sensors to detect the launch of ballistic missiles and can send a warning to Earth within seconds of a missile igniting. These satellites, and similar ones launched by Russia, have reduced the advantage of a surprise attack.

DSP SATELLITE

Lasers allow communication between individual satellites in the DSP fleet.

Infrared sensors detect the heat from the exhaust of a missile launch.

SATELLITE SURVEILLANCE

Several nations have sophisticated spy satellites. The French Helios satellite is fairly typical: from its low-Earth orbit it can spot an object on the Earth as small as a bicycle. Not much is known about satellites that carry out military surveillance – most information about spy satellites is, not surprisingly, top secret.

SEARCH AND RESCUE

In June 1995, Serbian forces shot down US Air Force Captain Scott O'Grady over Bosnia. Using his GPS receiver, O'Grady worked out his position on the ground and signalled the coordinates to F16 aeroplanes overhead. He was rescued by marines.

CAPTAIN O'GRADY

By detecting ballistic missile launches so quickly, DSP satellites could provide sufficient time for a retaliatory strike in the event of an attack.

INTERCONTINENTAL BALLISTIC MISSILE

MILITARY SATELLITES

Application	Payload
Navigation	Navigation beacons, time signal, and nuclear explosion sensors
Early warning	Sensors to detect ballistic missiles and radiations from nuclear explosions
Reconnaissance	Cameras, telescopes, and sensors
Communications	Equipment and antennas able to scramble or jam signals

SBIRS SATELLITES

At the end of the 1990s, the US government began a 10-year programme to replace the DSP satellites with a fleet of satellites called the Space-Based Infrared System (SBIRS). Like DSP, the SBIRS satellites carry sensors to detect missile launches. When complete, SBIRS will also carry out reconnaissance.

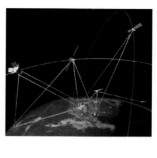

Artist's impression of how SBIRS satellites could work together in three different orbits by 2007.

SBIRS PROFILE

- SBIRS satellites detect and track missiles, and trigger the firing of the defensive missiles intended to destroy incoming targets.

- The US Defense Department plans to launch the first SBIRS satellites into geostationary and highly elliptical orbits. Together these orbits will give coverage of the whole Earth.

- SBIRS satellites in low-Earth orbit will work with satellites in the higher orbits to improve missile warning, and in addition will collect detailed surveillance of battlefields.

- Sensors able to detect three bands of frequencies within infrared and visible radiation can track a missile through all stages of its flight.

The second generation of GPS satellites, like the DSP satellites, is part of the Nuclear Detonation Detection System.

SKYNET 4

Antennas extending on either side of the satellite transmit the navigation signals used by both military and civilian missions.

Military communication satellites, such as the British-owned Skynet 4, provide a secure communication system for the armed forces.

Antenna designed to transmit at military frequencies. Military antennas and frequencies are different from those used on civilian communications satellites.

Solar panels supply 1,200 watts of electrical power, less than many electric hairdryers.

NUCLEAR EXPLOSIONS

Many nations have signed treaties, such as the Nuclear Weapons Nonproliferation Treaty, agreeing to limit the development and testing of nuclear weapons. Sensors on different types of satellites help check whether any treaty members are cheating. GPS and DSP satellites, for example, carry sensors that can detect the visible light, X-rays, and electromagnetic pulses given off by nuclear explosions.

SECURE COMMUNICATION

Armed forces need reliable communications links between ships, aircraft, and small mobile receivers on land. During battles or training exercises, these links will be busy with communications traffic, but they will be much quieter at other times. Unlike military communications satellites, commercial ones carry high volumes of traffic at all times. Military communications are encrypted (transmitted in code) to prevent eavesdroppers from listening in.

US troops setting up a mobile phone system.

SPACE DEBRIS

Anything in orbit that has no use is called space debris. This includes discarded rockets and obsolete satellites that could stay in orbit for millions of years, as well as fragments from satellites that exploded or were destroyed. Half a century after the first satellite, more than 90 per cent of the objects orbiting Earth are space junk. Each break-up adds to the rubbish and increases the risk of an orbiting spacecraft being hit by a piece of debris. Even a collision with a fleck of paint could put a spacecraft out of action. Space nations have begun to examine how they can reduce the junk left in space.

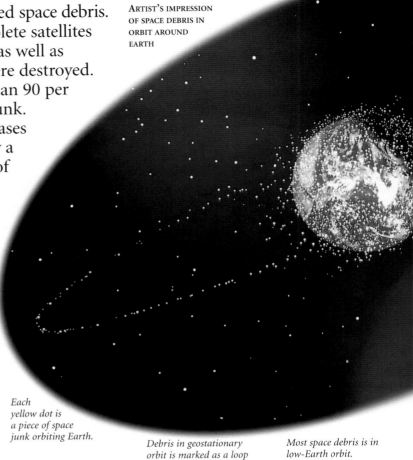

ARTIST'S IMPRESSION OF SPACE DEBRIS IN ORBIT AROUND EARTH

HAZARDS IN SPACE

There are an estimated 8,500 items of space debris bigger than 10 cm in orbit around Earth. The rubbish is created at many stages of a space operation, such as during separation when the nose cone is discarded once a satellite is released to orbit. Space junk accumulates most quickly in those orbits that are used most often. Satellites and debris could collide at speeds of up to 40,000 km/h, causing serious damage.

Each yellow dot is a piece of space junk orbiting Earth.

Debris in geostationary orbit is marked as a loop around Earth.

Most space debris is in low-Earth orbit.

TRACKING DEBRIS
The worldwide radar network of the North American Aerospace Defense Command (NORAD) monitors objects in orbit. Items as small as a tennis ball are routinely detected in low-Earth orbit, while 1-m objects can be observed in geostationary orbit. Computers use this information to predict the likelihood of a collision with spacecraft.

Screens at NORAD headquarters display information about the location of space debris.

TOO SMALL TO TRACK
The smallest piece of debris that NORAD routinely tracks is about the size of the finger of an astronaut's glove. Debris smaller than that – say the size of a cherry pip – colliding with a spacecraft at speeds of between 30,000 and 45,000 km/h, would still deliver the force of a hand grenade.

ASTRONAUT'S GLOVE

CLEANING UP SPACE
Scientists have some novel ideas for removing debris from space. One suggestion is that a robot could loiter in orbit and capture old spacecraft as they drifted by. A solar-powered laser would slice the satellites into smaller pieces, which could be taken to the International Space Station for recycling.

DEBRIS IN ORBIT			
Object size	Number	% of total	% of mass
Over 10 cm	8,500	0.02	99.93
1–10 cm	110,000	0.31	0.035
0.1–1 cm	35 million	99.67	0.035

Of the 8,500 observable space objects larger than 10 cm, only about 500 are operational spacecraft.

HYPERVELOCITY IMPACT TEST CHAMBER

NORAD cannot reliably detect debris between 10 and 30 cm in size.

DEBRIS IMPACT

Debris can hit a spacecraft at high speeds, known as hypervelocities. The force of impact depends on whether the collision is head-on, from the side, or from behind. Space agencies use special test chambers to examine what damage hypervelocity impacts cause to different materials. Ultra-highspeed cameras record the damage when guns fire bullets at 25,000 km/h. In space, objects could hit at even higher speeds.

The effect of a steel ball the size of a pea hitting a steel plate at 15,000 km/h.

MEEP MODULE ON MIR SPACE STATION

DAMAGE CONTROL

The best form of damage control is not to be hit in the first place, so the International Space Station (ISS) is designed to move out of the path of large chunks of debris. Experiments such as the Mir environmental effects payload (MEEP) provided data on the risks the ISS faces. The goal is to move the ISS no more than six times per year.

DEBRIS DAMAGE

● Damage can be caused by naturally occurring particles. In 1982, a speck of dust pitted a porthole on the Salyut Space Station.

● The smallest marking on a ruler is 1 mm. A speck of paint one-fifth that size made a 4 mm crater in the window of the Space Shuttle in 1983.

● In June 1996, the upper stage of a Pegasus rocket broke up. This event created 700 objects larger than 10 cm and 300,000 of 4 mm to 10 cm in size.

PAINT FLAKE CRATER ON SPACE SHUTTLE

PROTECTION

One way to protect sensitive areas of a spacecraft is to wrap it in layers of lightweight ceramic fibre. Each layer disperses the energy of a particle, which disintegrates before it hits the spacecraft wall. These ceramic bumpers are being used on the ISS to prevent the type of damage recorded in hypervelocity test chambers.

INTERNATONAL SPACE STATION

APOLLO 12 AFTER SPLASHDOWN FROM ORBIT

RE-ENTRY

Satellites return to Earth slowly. Friction with the air heats them when they re-enter Earth's atmosphere. Some disintegrate, while others survive and hit the ground or sea. In future, owners may have to control the end of their satellite's life so that it is removed from orbit and does not remain as debris.

FLYING TO SPACE

IT IS HARD TO IMAGINE A TIME without spaceflight. Yet in 1956, when Tom Hanks, star of the film *Apollo 13* was born, most people considered satellites and spaceflight to be science fiction – an impossible dream. Not everyone agreed. A few scientists and engineers around the world believed that the technology would soon exist to launch satellites and people into space. Military authorities in the USA and the Soviet Union had a strong interest in rocket development because rockets could launch both missiles and satellites. In the autumn of 1957, those believing in space exploration were proved right.

US CREWED SPACE PROGRAMME

The US crewed space programme got under way less than a month after Gagarin's historic flight, when Alan Shepard reached an altitude of 180 km and returned to Earth. His suborbital flight was part of the Mercury programme (1958–63). The aim of Mercury was to put an astronaut in space, observe his reaction, and return him safely to Earth.

5 MAY 1961

25 MAY 1961

SPACE AGE DAWNS

Fascination, excitement, and fear dominated people's emotions when they learnt that the Soviet Union had launched the first ever artificial satellite. Named Sputnik, the satellite was the brainchild of Sergei Korolev, architect of the Soviet space programme. Sputnik transmitted a tracking signal for 21 days.

RECOVERY

Two dogs – Belka and Strelka – were carried into space by Sputnik 5. Ground controllers signalled the satellite back to Earth after a day in orbit. The dogs became the first creatures to survive the weightlessness of space and the forces of re-entry.

20 AUGUST 1960

4 OCTOBER 1957

3 NOVEMBER 1957

FIRST ANIMAL IN SPACE

When Sputnik 2 was launched, the attention of the world was fixed on the dog, Laika, who was aboard. She was the first living creature in space. Laika suffered no ill effects during launch, but died when the oxygen ran out in orbit.

12 APRIL 1961

FIRST PERSON IN SPACE

Yuri Gagarin was the first person in space. He flew in a spherical Vostok spaceship, seated in an ejector seat on rails. Gagarin's successful flight followed two disasters for the Soviet space programme. One of these killed many people and showed the importance of locating launch centres in remote, unpopulated areas.

CHALLENGE FOR THE MOON

President John F. Kennedy boosted America's ambitions in space when he launched the Apollo lunar exploration programme. Later that year he told students: "We choose to go to the Moon in this decade not because it is easy but because it is hard." The Apollo programme was one of the most technically complex projects of the 20th century.

SPACEWALK

Soviet cosmonaut Alexei Leonov made the first spacewalk from the Voskhod 2 spacecraft. During the spacewalk, Leonov's spacesuit expanded, so when he tried to get back in through the airlock he had to struggle to close the outer hatch. When Leonov eventually re-entered Voskhod 2, he had spent 20 minutes in space.

18 MARCH 1965

SOYUZ SPACECRAFT

Soviet cosmonaut Vladimir Komorov became the first person to die in space when he was killed aboard his Soyuz 1 spacecraft. Four months earlier three American astronauts had died in a fire on the launchpad while testing Apollo 1. All four were victims of the race to be first to land on the Moon.

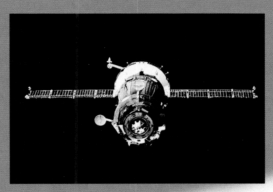

24 APRIL 1967

SPACE STATIONS

The Soviet Union developed space stations to provide an orbiting laboratory for experiments in space. The first of these, Salyut 1, was 14.4 m long and had an engine so that it could change orbit and a docking unit. Two spacecraft – Soyuz 10 and Soyuz 11 – visited Salyut. The crew of Soyuz 11 died when a seal failed on their descent module as they returned to Earth. Nevertheless, the Soyuz missions showed that technology could be developed to ferry people between Earth and space.

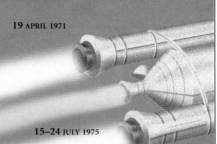

19 APRIL 1971

15–24 JULY 1975

20 JULY 1969

4–18 DECEMBER 1965

GEMINI 7

Gemini 7 logged 14 days in space – the first spaceflight to last more than a few days. The US Gemini programme was the stepping stone from Mercury to Apollo. The spacecraft included a cockpit for two astronauts and a resource module containing fuel, oxygen, and food. Gemini's aim was to demonstrate the feasibility of long-duration spaceflight and of rendezvous and docking. All were necessary for lunar exploration.

APOLLO-SOYUZ LINK

In the midst of the Cold War, the USA and Soviet Union achieved one cooperative space mission – the Apollo-Soyuz rendezvous. The two crews manoeuvred their craft together and docked. For a few days they worked on science experiments in each other's spacecraft, and then completed their missions independently.

RENDEZVOUS

Gemini 6 and 7 became the first spacecraft to rendezvous. At an altitude of 260 km and speeds of about 30,000 km/h, they came within 30 cm of each other – little more than the height of this book.

MOON LANDING

With the words "The Eagle has landed", Neil Armstrong, Commander of US Apollo 11, marked the arrival of people on a world other than Earth. Armstrong and Buzz Aldrin guided Eagle, the lunar module, to the surface of the Moon while Michael Collins remained in control of the command module. Armstrong and Aldrin spent 22 hours on the surface, and two and a half hours outside the Eagle Module. They collected 22 kg of rock and dust samples.

FIND OUT MORE

SPACE LAUNCHERS 40
SATELLITES AND ORBITS 46
LIVING IN SPACE 64
SCIENCE IN SPACE 66
INTERPLANETARY TRAVEL 72
PROBES TO THE PLANETS 80
EXPLORING THE MOON 98

SPACE SHUTTLE

THE FIRST TEST FLIGHT of the Space Transportation System (STS) was in 1981. STS, usually referred to as Space Shuttle, is made up of an orbiter with three main engines, an external tank, and two solid rocket boosters. Cargo is carried to space in the orbiter's payload bay. Propellant for the main engines is supplied from the external tank. After each mission the orbiter returns to Earth, gliding to a landing on a very long runway. The STS launches satellites and space probes, carried the Spacelab space station, and provides a platform for construction and repairs in space.

THERMAL PROTECTION

When an orbiter re-enters Earth's atmosphere, friction heats the outside of it to between 300°C and 1,500°C. A protective coating is therefore needed to prevent the orbiter from melting. Different types of protection shield the different parts. The edge of the wings and nose tip are the hottest. About 70% of the surface is covered with tiles that absorb heat between 370°C and 1,260°C. These tiles transfer heat so slowly it does not reach the orbiter.

☐ *Felt protects the top of the orbiter, where heat does not exceed 370°C.*

■ *Reinforced carbon-carbon insulation protects the hottest (above 1,260°C) parts of the orbiter.*

SHUTTLE ORBITER

An orbiter is a space plane. The STS carries one orbiter, but has a choice of four: Discovery, Atlantis, Columbia, and Endeavour. Each orbiter can carry seven crew members and stay in orbit for at least 10 days. The orbiters' cabins have three decks – flight deck, mid-deck, and a lower deck that houses life-support equipment.

Ladder to mid-deck, which has sleeping bunks, washroom, galley, and airlock allowing access to space.

Payload bay

SHUTTLE ORBITER

Flight deck where pilot and commander sit.

Lower deck houses equipment to maintain a habitable environment for the flight crew in the orbiter.

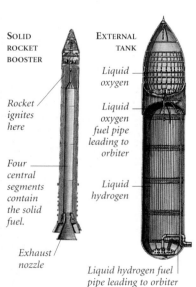

SOLID ROCKET BOOSTER

Rocket ignites here

Four central segments contain the solid fuel.

Exhaust nozzle

EXTERNAL TANK

External tank

Solid rocket booster

Liquid oxygen

Liquid oxygen fuel pipe leading to orbiter

Liquid hydrogen

Liquid hydrogen fuel pipe leading to orbiter

EXTERNAL TANK

The external tank connects the orbiter and boosters during the ascent to orbit, and it carries the liquid hydrogen fuel and liquid oxygen. The tank is discarded after each flight.

SOLID ROCKET BOOSTERS

The solid rocket boosters propel the orbiter to an altitude of 45 km and are designed to last for 20 flights. After each flight, they are recovered from the ocean and prepared for the next one. The boosters support the weight of the entire STS on the ground.

FLIGHT PROFILE

3. External tank released.

4. Orbiter reaches low-Earth orbit.

5. Orbiter stays in space for 10–16 days.

Fuel tank falls back to Earth.

2. Boosters discarded.

6. Orbiter positions itself ready to return to Earth.

Parachutes open as boosters fall back to Earth.

7. Orbiter re-enters Earth's atmosphere.

1. Space Shuttle blasts off.

Ships recover the rockets.

9. Orbiter glides in to land on 4.5 km runway.

Space Shuttle assembly building

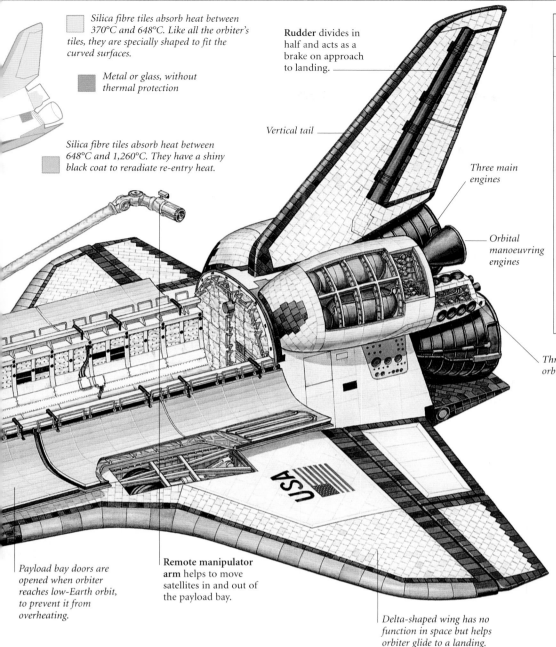

Silica fibre tiles absorb heat between 370°C and 648°C. Like all the orbiter's tiles, they are specially shaped to fit the curved surfaces.

Metal or glass, without thermal protection

Silica fibre tiles absorb heat between 648°C and 1,260°C. They have a shiny black coat to reradiate re-entry heat.

Rudder divides in half and acts as a brake on approach to landing.

Vertical tail

Three main engines

Orbital manoeuvring engines

Thrusters for small orbital adjustments

Payload bay doors are opened when orbiter reaches low-Earth orbit, to prevent it from overheating.

Remote manipulator arm helps to move satellites in and out of the payload bay.

Delta-shaped wing has no function in space but helps orbiter glide to a landing.

ORBITAL SPECIFICATIONS

Orbiter length
37.24 m

Orbiter height
17.27 m

Wingspan
29.79 m

Payload bay
18.3 x 4.6 m

Orbit speed
28,800 km/h

Withstands temperatures up to 1,500°C

Altitude in orbit between 185 and 1,000 km

Mission duration between 10 and 16 days

CHALLENGER EXPLOSION

The Challenger orbiter exploded on 28 January 1986 killing everyone on board. A joint between two segments of one of the boosters had failed. Hot gases burned through the booster casing and hit the external tank. The tank split. Liquid hydrogen burned fiercely in the air and the vehicle broke up within 15 seconds.

LAUNCH TO LANDING

The three main engines start at 0.12-second intervals, followed by the solid rocket boosters. Bolts holding down the STS are released for liftoff. The orbital manoeuvring system (OMS) places the orbiter into the correct orbit once the boosters and tank are discarded. One hour before landing, the OMS and thrusters position the orbiter for re-entry.

8. Orbiter gets ready for high-speed glide onto runway.

KEY SHUTTLE MISSIONS

• The first Shuttle flight, with the orbiter Columbia, was on 12–14 April 1981.

• The next three flights, all with Columbia, were between November 1981 and July 1982, and tested the Shuttle's remote manipulator arm.

• Between 6 and 13 April 1984, the Challenger crew launched a platform to learn how materials and biological samples are affected during long exposures to space.

• Crew of the orbiter Atlantis deployed the Galileo probe. An upper stage boosted the probe on its path to Jupiter.

• The orbiter Discovery carried the Hubble Space Telescope to orbit on its 24 –29 April 1990 mission .

LIVING IN SPACE

ENGINEERS DESIGN SPACE STATIONS so that astronauts can live for long periods in the hostile environment of space, where there is no oxygen, no soil in which to grow food, no water, and no air pressure. Life support systems on board must provide oxygen and filter the carbon dioxide that people breathe out. The air also has to be pressurized to levels close to those on Earth and temperature maintained at comfortable levels. In future, food may be grown in space, but to date crews have had to be supplied with food and water.

MIR ABOVE THE PACIFIC OCEAN

MIR SPACE STATION

Mir is the longest surviving space station. It consists of a core module, with six additional modules added over the first 10 years of its life. The space station has been staffed continuously since 1987, some cosmonauts remaining on board for more than a year at a time. Solar panels and batteries supply the modules with power. Each day an alarm awakens the crew at 8 a.m. Moscow time, and mission control sends the cosmonauts their work schedule. Mir can contact ground controllers only once every 90 minutes when it passes over a receiving station.

PERSONAL HYGIENE

Mir has a shower for its astronauts, but showers are not always successful in space because water can escape. On Space Shuttle, astronauts take a sponge bath. For male astronauts, shaving with an electric razor is a bad idea, because whiskers escape and get into the eyes. Shaving with foam is better, and growing a beard is easiest of all.

Mir can carry a crew of up to six cosmonauts.

Astronaut shaving on board the Space Shuttle.

DAMAGE TO SPEKTR MODULE

Solar panels on each module supply power for research and life support.

There are 76 square metres of solar panels on the whole of Mir.

DANGERS

On 25 June 1997, the Progress ship carrying supplies to Mir crashed into the Spektr science module, severing power lines. US astronaut Mike Foale and his Russian colleagues battled for hours to save power and avoid catastrophe.

MIR MILESTONES

• The core module of Mir was launched in February 1986.

• In July 1987, the Kvant 1 module docked with the core. In December 1987, it was joined by Kvant 2, carrying equipment for biological experiments.

• In July 1990, the Kristall module was launched. It had a port for docking with the Space Shuttle, and carried equipment

for microgravity research on the properties of materials.

• The Spektr module docked with Mir in May 1995, carrying equipment for observing Earth. In June 1995, a docking module was added to make it easier for the Shuttle to dock with Mir.

• The Priroda module was launched on 26 April 1996. It observed Earth from space.

SPACE FOOD

One astronaut smuggled a ham sandwich aboard after John Glenn, the first American to orbit Earth in 1962, told him how bad the food was. All food is ferried from Earth, so it must be lightweight. Bits of food float away, so chunks are sometimes covered in edible gelatin to prevent crumbs. Usually, however, food is dried and water added to it when needed. Supply ships carry 10-litre containers of water to Mir but the Space Shuttle produces some of its own.

SPACE MENU	
BREAKFAST	Fruit or cereal, beef pasty or scrambled eggs, cocoa, fruit drink
LUNCH	Turkey pasta or hot dogs, bread, bananas or almond crunch bar, fruit drink
DINNER	Soup or fruit cocktail, rice pilaff or steak, broccoli au gratin, pudding, fruit drink

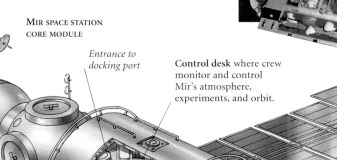

MIR SPACE STATION CORE MODULE

Entrance to docking port

Control desk where crew monitor and control Mir's atmosphere, experiments, and orbit.

Rendezvous antenna at tip of solar panels guides spacecraft to dock.

Small antenna communicates with craft about to dock.

Large antenna relays messages to satellites.

Walls, floor, and ceiling are different colours to help crew orientate themselves.

Cosmonauts use the station exercise bike to keep fit.

Cabins contain a wash basin and sleep area.

Target for docking spacecraft

SPACE TOILET

Restraints hold an astronaut in place while he or she uses the toilet. A vacuum is switched on to ensure a good seal between body and the seat. On the Space Shuttle, solid waste is dried and treated to prevent bacterial growth, then stored. Urine is stored with waste water, and periodically dumped.

Operating handle

Seat

Handhold

Control panel

Foot restraint

Control to shut off vacuum

Waist strap

SAFE SLEEP

If astronauts just went to sleep anywhere, they would float about the cabin and get in everybody's way. To prevent this, sleeping areas are designed with a waist strap that holds the sleeper in place. Astronauts also use eyeshades to help them sleep because the Sun rises and sets every hour and a half on a spacecraft in near-Earth orbit. They may need ear muffs, too, if other crew members are working nearby.

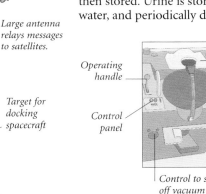

Special straps keep astronaut attached to the walkway.

Using a moving walkway is one way an astronaut can keep fit.

KEEPING FIT

In space the body does not have to work as hard as it does on Earth because there is so little gravity acting on it. This means that muscles waste away. All crews in space must follow a careful exercise plan to keep their muscles strong, and every space station must carry keep fit equipment, such as an exercise bike.

SCIENCE IN SPACE

GRAVITY KEEPS PEOPLE'S FEET on the ground and influences the way a plant's roots sink into the soil or how two fluids mix. The force of gravity cannot be changed on Earth, so scientists go into orbit to carry out gravity experiments. In orbit, bodies do not escape the effects of Earth's gravity, but if an astronaut drops a pencil it will float. This is because the spacecraft, the astronaut, and the pencil are all in free fall towards Earth (even though they will never get there). All are experiencing weightlessness, also known as microgravity. Microgravity provides conditions in which scientists can explore the effects of gravity on physical and biological processes.

SPACELAB

The European Space Agency designed the Spacelab space station to be carried in the payload bay of the Space Shuttle. It was made up of two pressurized laboratories, where astronauts carried out microgravity experiments, and three unpressurized laboratories, or external pallets, for experiments that needed to be exposed to space. Sometimes Spacelab carried pressurized modules, sometimes external pallets, sometimes a combination of the two. First launched in 1983, the last Spacelab mission flew in 1997.

Skylab was used by three teams of astronauts between May 1973 and February 1974.

SKYLAB

Skylab, the first US space station, was launched in 1973 (the first space station was the Russian Salyut 1 launched in 1971). It studied how people behave if they live in space for extended periods of time. Skylab scientists also learnt a great deal about solar flares, huge eruptions of matter and energy on the Sun that affect space around the Earth.

INSIDE SPACELAB

The crew slept in the Shuttle orbiter and floated through the access tunnel to work in Spacelab's pressurized modules. Experiments were contained in specially designed units, called racks, that carried equipment for a range of studies from investigating crystal growth to observing cell development. The racks were specially outfitted for each mission. Some racks were designed for particular types of experiment, such as cell biology.

In orbit, the payload bay housing Spacelab remained open.

Spacelab sat inside the Space Shuttle payload bay.

Pressurized modules were 4 m wide. One was 7 m in length, the other 4.3 m.

SPACELAB

Spacelab was designed to look as though it had a roof, floor, and walls.

Access tunnel between Spacelab and orbiter

Shuttle orbiter

Footholds helped to keep the astronauts upright while they worked.

MIR

ASTRONOMY FROM MIR

Mir space station had one module, Kvant 1, dedicated to studying galaxies, quasars, and neutron stars. Kvant 1 was about 6 m long and 4 m wide. One telescope observed objects emitting ultraviolet radiation and three others detected X-ray emissions. The telescopes could all make observations over a long period without affecting other work on Mir.

BIORACK AND ANTHRORACK
On several missions, the Spacelab carried a Biorack, which had incubators for hundreds of samples of cells and microorganisms. Scientists studied how microgravity affected their development and behaviour. Another rack, Anthrorack, carried equipment to investigate microgravity's effect on the human body.

BIORACK EXPERIMENTS UNIT IN SPACELAB

MICROGRAVITY EXPERIMENTS

• Russian scientists studied how hearts and lungs behave during long stays on space stations, and whether the rate of processes such as digestion varies.

• Mir crews have grown wheat seeds to find out how the seeds would mature in microgravity.

• Seeing combustion in microgravity has given Russian and American scientists information that will help in the design of jet engines.

• Crystal growth experiments on Mir and Spacelab allowed researchers to test more efficient ways of producing semiconductors for computers.

This Spacelab flight consisted of one pressurized module plus two external pallets.

Each pallet had its own electrical power and cooling system.

External pallets were 3 m wide and could support 3 tonnes of equipment.

Infrared telescope

Instrument to investigate Earth's magnetic field.

EXTERNAL PALLET
Some instruments for observing Earth or radiation in space, such as telescopes, needed to be exposed to space. These were fitted to external pallets. Control equipment was normally housed in the pressurized module: if Spacelab was in a pallet-only mode, this was put in a cylindrical container at the front of the first pallet.

Single external pallet

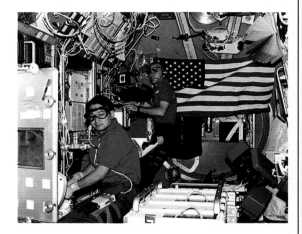

INTERNATIONAL MICROGRAVITY LAB
Spacelab undertook two international microgravity laboratory missions. Scientists around the world designed experiments for microgravity, and the Shuttle and Spacelab crews carried them out. Projects included discovering the effect of microgravity on the human nervous system, and on the development of shrimp eggs, lentil seedlings, and bacteria. Results were sent to the scientists on Earth for analysis.

BIOLOGY IN MICROGRAVITY
Biologists want to know what influences the way fertilized eggs develop. In 1996, Shannon Lucid, a visiting NASA astronaut, put eggs into Mir's incubator, and each day removed one, which stopped development. The eggs were compared with eggs at a similar stage of development on Earth. The Mir eggs had more abnormalities, but this may have been due to radiation rather than weightlessness.

ASTRONAUT SHANNON LUCID AT WORK IN MIR

SPACE STATIONS

Name	Nationality	Launch year
Salyut 1	Soviet Union	1971
Skylab	USA	1973
Spacelab	Europe	1983
Mir	Russia	1986
International Space Station	International	1998

FIND OUT MORE

INTERNATIONAL SPACE STATION

THE USA AND RUSSIA LAUNCHED the first parts of the International Space Station (ISS) in 1998: Brazil, Canada, the European Space Agency, and Japan have also contributed elements. It is scheduled to be fully assembled by 2004 and, when complete, the ISS will have a wingspan of 110 m, a length of 80 m, and a mass of nearly 500 tonnes. The ISS carries a permanent crew, starting with the arrival of the first three crew members in January 2000. Astronauts from many nations carry out a wide-ranging programme of research while on board.

STATION ELEMENTS

The International Space Station is made up of more than 100 elements. The biggest contribution – including a connecting node, solar panels, habitation module, an unpressurized module, and two laboratories – is from the USA. A core module, providing living quarters for the first few years, comes from Russia. Canada is providing a robot arm. Two connecting nodes originate in Europe. Most of the participating space agencies will help to transport supplies to the station.

INTERNATIONAL SPACE STATION

ISS is one of the brightest objects in the night sky – second only to Venus.

EUROPEAN LABORATORY

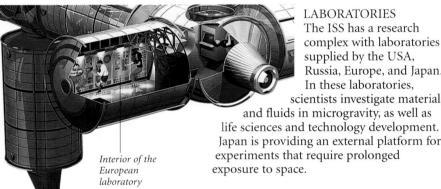

Interior of the European laboratory

LABORATORIES

The ISS has a research complex with laboratories supplied by the USA, Russia, Europe, and Japan. In these laboratories, scientists investigate materials and fluids in microgravity, as well as life sciences and technology development. Japan is providing an external platform for experiments that require prolonged exposure to space.

ISS will be the size of a football pitch when complete.

Solar panels convert the Sun's energy into electricity for powering the station.

HARDWARE INTEGRATION

The process of bringing all the equipment together for a space station is called hardware integration. Many services, such as electrical cabling, needed by the different modules in the ISS are installed by engineers while the modules are still on the ground. Experimental racks and other scientific equipment for the laboratories are fitted in orbit.

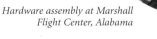

Hardware assembly at Marshall Flight Center, Alabama

Station gym

Astronauts relax around the table.

ISS RESEARCH

Scientists plan to use the microgravity environment of the ISS to investigate how gravity affects many processes. The shape of a flame in space is a good example of the consequences of microgravity. The flame on the left looks unusual because microgravity reduces convection currents that cause warm air to rise and cool air to sink.

Upper deck

HABITATION MODULE

When the US habitation module is added, probably in 2004, the ISS will reach its onboard crew capacity of seven. The module will be more than 8 m long and 4 m wide, and will contain sleep stations, a toilet, galley, shower, and medical facility.

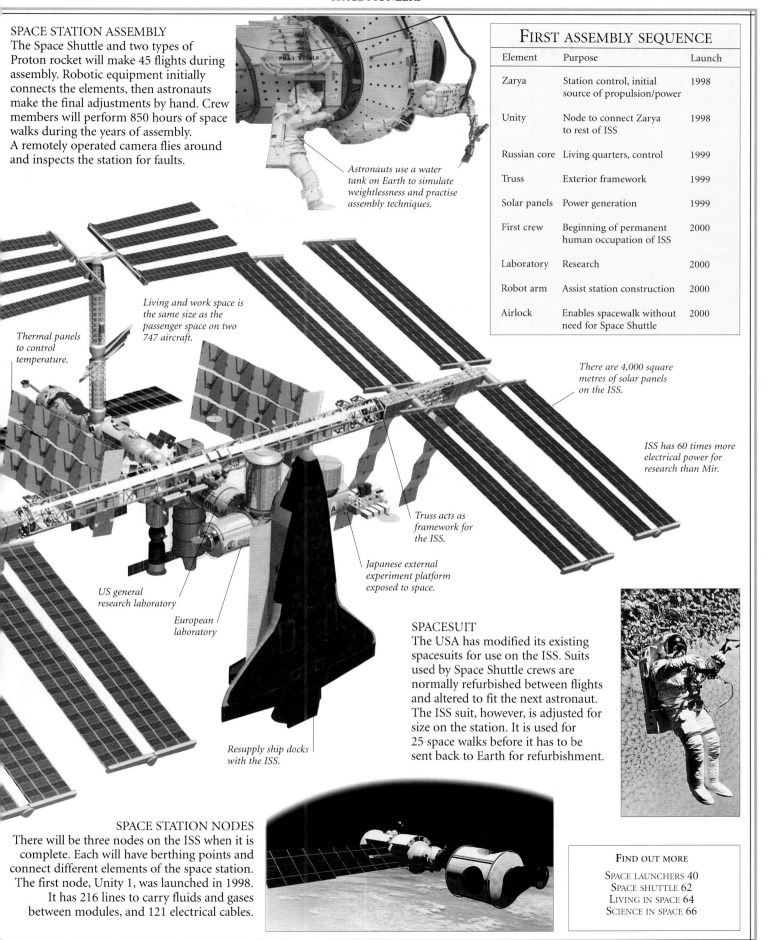

SPACE STATION ASSEMBLY

The Space Shuttle and two types of Proton rocket will make 45 flights during assembly. Robotic equipment initially connects the elements, then astronauts make the final adjustments by hand. Crew members will perform 850 hours of space walks during the years of assembly. A remotely operated camera flies around and inspects the station for faults.

Astronauts use a water tank on Earth to simulate weightlessness and practise assembly techniques.

FIRST ASSEMBLY SEQUENCE

Element	Purpose	Launch
Zarya	Station control, initial source of propulsion/power	1998
Unity	Node to connect Zarya to rest of ISS	1998
Russian core	Living quarters, control	1999
Truss	Exterior framework	1999
Solar panels	Power generation	1999
First crew	Beginning of permanent human occupation of ISS	2000
Laboratory	Research	2000
Robot arm	Assist station construction	2000
Airlock	Enables spacewalk without need for Space Shuttle	2000

Thermal panels to control temperature.

Living and work space is the same size as the passenger space on two 747 aircraft.

There are 4,000 square metres of solar panels on the ISS.

ISS has 60 times more electrical power for research than Mir.

Truss acts as framework for the ISS.

Japanese external experiment platform exposed to space.

US general research laboratory

European laboratory

Resupply ship docks with the ISS.

SPACESUIT

The USA has modified its existing spacesuits for use on the ISS. Suits used by Space Shuttle crews are normally refurbished between flights and altered to fit the next astronaut. The ISS suit, however, is adjusted for size on the station. It is used for 25 space walks before it has to be sent back to Earth for refurbishment.

SPACE STATION NODES

There will be three nodes on the ISS when it is complete. Each will have berthing points and connect different elements of the space station. The first node, Unity 1, was launched in 1998. It has 216 lines to carry fluids and gases between modules, and 121 electrical cables.

FIND OUT MORE

SPACE LAUNCHERS 40
SPACE SHUTTLE 62
LIVING IN SPACE 64
SCIENCE IN SPACE 66

FUTURE SPACEPLANES

GETTING INTO SPACE IS EXPENSIVE. It typically costs more than £10,000 ($20,000) for each kilogram of payload carried. Huge amounts of money are wasted when using a multistage rocket to reach orbit, because much of the spacecraft is simply lost. One way to reduce costs is to use vehicles that reach orbit in just one stage. Single-stage-to-orbit (SSTO) spacecraft are an obvious way of getting around the problem. Modern technologies, such as light but strong materials and new engine designs, are making SSTO a reality. A single-stage reusable spaceplane called X-33 began final testing in 1999, but NASA's spacecraft designers are already looking ahead.

VENTURESTAR (X-33)

An ingenious wedge shape gives NASA's VentureStar, or X-33, a distinctive look but also helps it to fly: it has a "lifting body" design. The X-33 takes off vertically but glides to a landing. It is a prototype for an SSTO spaceplane that may take over the role of the Space Shuttle. Uncrewed flights within the atmosphere will help NASA decide whether to scale up the prototype.

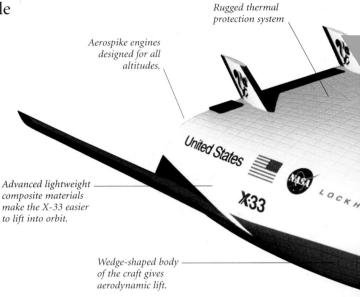

Rugged thermal protection system

Aerospike engines designed for all altitudes.

Advanced lightweight composite materials make the X-33 easier to lift into orbit.

Wedge-shaped body of the craft gives aerodynamic lift.

CLIPPER GRAHAM (DC-XA)

Clipper Graham was a test vehicle for future spaceplane technologies. It was made from advanced, lightweight composite materials and operated at temperatures and pressures an SSTO spaceplane will meet. In 1996, after four flights, the vehicle crashed.

DC-XA was a subsonic test vehicle.

CLIPPER GRAHAM
(DC-XA)

TEST FLIGHT OF X-34

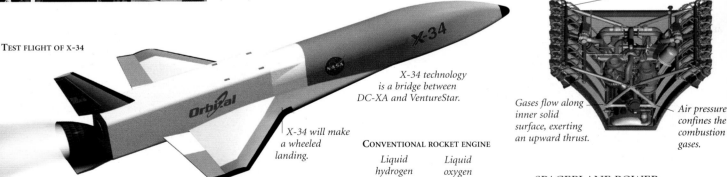

X-34 technology is a bridge between DC-XA and VentureStar.

X-34 will make a wheeled landing.

AEROSPIKE ENGINE

Combustion gases are expelled from tiny nozzles.

Gases flow along inner solid surface, exerting an upward thrust.

Air pressure confines the combustion gases.

X-34 PROTOTYPE

In 1999, the X-34 began testing the lightweight materials, thermal protection, and landing systems needed for SSTO. Compared with VentureStar (X-33), the rocket is small and is designed to be launched from the air, beneath an aeroplane. The 27 test flights were planned to be increasingly tough, culminating in a suborbital flight at eight times the speed of sound (Mach 8).

CONVENTIONAL ROCKET ENGINE

Liquid hydrogen

Liquid oxygen

Nozzle

Escaping exhaust gases provide thrust.

SPACEPLANE POWER

Conventional rocket engines do not work at their best most of the time. This is because the shape of the nozzle, through which exhaust gases leave the engine, does not change. To work efficiently, the nozzle would need to change shape as the rocket climbs into the atmosphere.

X-37 AND X-38

Scientists are following up the VentureStar and the X-34 with designs for future spaceplanes called X-37. NASA has laid down one rule for any designs that are put forward: the craft must be fully reusable. X-38 is the name given to a vehicle that could be used to return crew from the International Space Station.

JAPANESE SPACEPLANE

Short wings

DEVELOPING SPACEPLANES

- In 1944, Eugen Sänger (1905–64) put forward ideas for an aircraft that would be boosted to orbit by rockets and glide back to Earth.

- The USA's first test vehicle for spaceplanes was X-15. It flew 199 times from 1959 to 1968, reaching Mach 6.7.

- Lessons from the X-15 and US Air Force's Dyna-Soar (X-20A) programmes helped engineers design the Space Shuttle in the 1970s.

- In the mid-1970s, the US Air Force developed the lifting body principle as part of the X-24A project.

HOPE

Japanese engineers designed the H-II Orbiting Plane (HOPE) to carry supplies to the International Space Station and return cargo to Earth. HOPE flies without a crew. The first test flight, in 1999, allowed scientists to study how well the vehicle could withstand re-entry when it returned to Earth.

VentureStar is designed to reach speeds of Mach 13 to 15.

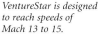
VentureStar™

ROTON

One radical idea developed to make rockets light enough for SSTO launches is to design them without the heavy equipment that pumps propellant. With the Roton rocket, a motor on the launchpad would spin its engine so that propellant is thrown into the combustion chambers. For stability during re-entry, and for a soft landing, rotor blades similar to those on a helicopter are deployed.

PROPOSED ROTOR-BLADED SSTO SPACEPLANE

AEROSPIKE ENGINE TEST FLIGHT

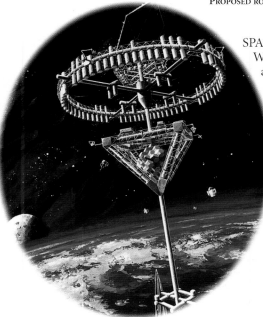

SPACE TOURISM

When access to space becomes cheap and easy enough, many people's dreams of travelling to space might be realized. One idea is a hotel in a 1,200-km orbit. A tether, nearly 1,000 km long, would be suspended from the hotel to a space dock 250 km above Earth. People would travel to the dock in reusable, suborbital planes, and catch an elevator to the hotel.

AEROSPIKE ENGINE

Peak performance is possible all the way to orbit with an aerospike engine. The conventional bell-shaped nozzle is turned inside out to give an inner solid surface. The "outer" surface is simply air pressure and, as air pressure decreases with altitude, the nozzle shape changes as the rocket ascends.

INTERPLANETARY TRAVEL

THE PLANETS ARE VERY FAR AWAY. A spacecraft travelling at 100 km/h – a typical speed of a car on a motorway – would take about 60 years to reach Mars. Fortunately, rockets travel much faster than this. The Voyager probes sped from the Earth at 52,000 km/h. But even at this speed, travel to the planets takes a long time. Space scientists are using today's probes to test the technologies critical for future interplanetary travel. They are also working out how to grow crops in space and to live for long periods with limited resources. This will help interplanetary travellers to be self-sufficient: essential for spending years in space.

DEEP SPACE 1

Automatic navigation system guided DS1 to within less than 10 km of asteroid 1992 KD.

DEEP SPACE 1

A new series of small NASA spacecraft, known as deep space probes, are testing risky technologies that have never been used in space before. The first of these, Deep Space 1 (DS1), was launched in 1998. The spacecraft guided itself to the asteroid 1992 KD with an automated navigation system. DS1 also tested more efficient solar cells and a new type of rocket known as an ion drive.

DS1 made the closest ever fly-by of any celestial body.

DS1 travelled 188 million km to rendezvous with asteroid 1992 KD.

ION ENGINE

ION DRIVE
An ion is an electrically charged atom. Inside an ion drive, a gas consisting of ions is pulled towards a charged grid and expelled at high speed. This pushes the spacecraft in the opposite direction. Spacecraft with ion drives could reach 10 times the speed of Voyager. However, they may take months to reach this speed.

LEAVING EARTH
An interplanetary space probe is initially put into orbit around Earth. Mission controllers fire rockets that cause the probe to leave Earth orbit and go into orbit around the Sun. The probe's solar orbit is carefully calculated so that it crosses the orbit of its target planet. Mission controllers time the probe's injection into solar orbit so that the probe and planet will arrive at the same place at the same time.

Sun

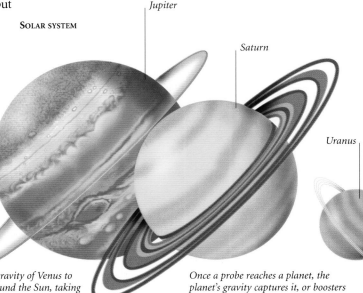

SOLAR SYSTEM

Jupiter

Saturn

Uranus

Mercury   *Venus*   *Earth*   *Mars*

To reach Mercury and Venus, a probe accelerates away from Earth in the opposite direction to Earth's motion.

Mariner 10 used the gravity of Venus to swing it into orbit around the Sun, taking it close to Mercury every 176 days.

Once a probe reaches a planet, the planet's gravity captures it, or boosters fire to manoeuvre the probe into orbit.

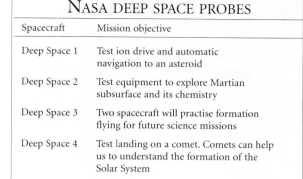

Advanced high efficiency solar panels generated electricity to power the ion drive.

NASA DEEP SPACE PROBES

Spacecraft	Mission objective
Deep Space 1	Test ion drive and automatic navigation to an asteroid
Deep Space 2	Test equipment to explore Martian subsurface and its chemistry
Deep Space 3	Two spacecraft will practise formation flying for future science missions
Deep Space 4	Test landing on a comet. Comets can help us to understand the formation of the Solar System

SPACE VISIONARIES

- Jules Verne (1828–1905) was the first to write as though space travel were a technical reality.

- H. G. Wells (1866–1946) imagined interplanetary travellers invading Earth from Mars in his book, *The War of the Worlds*.

- Arthur C. Clarke's books routinely include interplanetary travel. In *Songs of Distant Earth*, people have long since abandoned Earth.

- Gene Roddenbury (1921–91), creator of the *Star Trek* TV series, looked beyond interplanetary travel and imagined routine journeys among the stars.

INTERPLANETARY TRAVEL RISKS

The Earth's atmosphere and magnetic field shield people and electronic equipment from damaging high energy radiation. It is important, therefore, that space scientists find shielding as effective as Earth's natural protection for future crewed interplanetary missions. Spacecraft will also have to withstand micrometeorite impacts that could punch holes in their sides and so kill astronauts in the craft.

SELF-SUFFICIENCY IN SPACE

Future space colonies will have to be self-sufficient, growing their own food and recycling the atmosphere as well as plant, animal, and human waste. Such total recycling is very difficult to achieve, as eight people found in 1991–93, when they tried to live in a self-contained artificial environment as part of the Biosphere II project in Arizona, USA.

BIOSPHERE II, ARIZONA

Scientists experiment with ecosystems in Biosphere II, which is sealed from its surroundings.

PSYCHOLOGY AND SPACE EXPLORATION

If space colonies are to succeed, psychologists need to understand more about how people in small groups interact when they are isolated from everyone and everything. The people sealed in Biosphere II in 1991 found this seclusion difficult. The Biosphere crew members were luckier than space explorers, because they could have broken the seal. Space colonists would have no such option.

To reach Mars and the planets beyond, a probe accelerates away from Earth in the same direction as Earth's orbit around the Sun.

Cosmonauts on Mir successfully grew mung beans in space.

CREATING FUEL ON MARS

Unless colonists can make their own fuel on Mars, they will be unable to return home. One idea for achieving this is to export a fuel manufacturing plant from Earth to Mars. This would compress carbon dioxide from the Martian atmosphere, and mix it with hydrogen shipped from Earth to give water and methane. The water would be split into hydrogen and oxygen. Methane and oxygen could then be used as fuel and oxidant for visits to Earth.

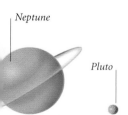

Neptune

Pluto

SPACE AGRICULTURE

Scientists on the Mir space station made a modest attempt to grow plants. Successful space colonies will need to be much more ambitious. Cultivating plants will be vital to colonies because plants not only produce oxygen to breathe, they also supply food for people and livestock. Plants are important, too, because greenery enhances mental well-being and would help colonists cope with stress.

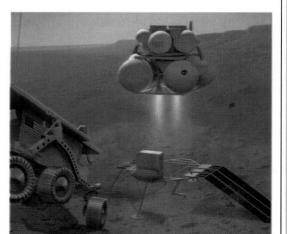

With a crew of six, it could take 30 tonnes of oxygen and methane to lift off from Mars.

ARTIST'S IMPRESSION OF CREATING FUEL

FIND OUT MORE

SCIENCE IN SPACE 66
INTERNATIONAL SPACE STATION 68
FUTURE SPACEPLANES 70

FUTURISTIC STARSHIPS

Beyond the solar system, the Earth's nearest neighbour, the alpha Centauri star system, is about 40 trillion km away. Using the fastest current technology, it would take spacecraft about 10,000 years to get there, even if it were possible to carry enough propellant to complete the journey. Light, the fastest thing known in the Universe, could reach alpha Centauri in a little over four years. For routine interstellar exploration such as that aboard *Star Trek*'s USS Enterprise, the spaceship would need to travel faster than light. No one yet knows whether this would be possible.

SPEED LIMITATIONS

In 1905, Albert Einstein published the first of his two great theories – that of special relativity. The theory shows that travel at the speed of light is impossible. For example, the faster an object moves, the heavier it becomes. So spacecraft travelling at the speed of light would have infinite mass. In Einstein's theory, only electromagnetic radiation – which has no mass – can travel at the speed of light (300,000 km/s).

LIMITS OF CONVENTIONAL ROCKETS

The Voyager spacecraft left the Solar System travelling at nearly 60,000 km/h. At that speed it would take Voyager 80,000 years to reach alpha Centauri. There would also not be enough mass in the Universe to provide propellant for a conventional chemical rocket to reach alpha Centauri.

MILKY WAY

Solar System and alpha Centauri are 4.4 light years apart in the Orion Arm, 25,000 light years from the centre of the Milky Way.

PROPELLANT LIMITATIONS

Rockets have to carry all their fuel and oxidant with them. No matter how efficient the rocket is, it is impossible to carry enough propellant for interstellar travel. NASA estimates that even an ion engine, which can reach speeds of 10 times that of Voyager 2, would need 500 supertankers of propellant to reach alpha Centauri within a century.

SUPERTANKER

VOYAGER 2

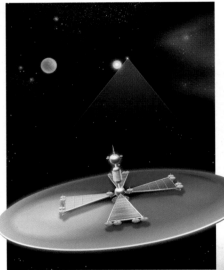

FORWARD'S PROPOSED STELLAR PROBE

LASER DRIVES

Lasers could eliminate the need for propellant. American scientist Robert Forward (1932–) was the first to come up with ideas for laser-driven spacecraft. One concept is to launch a spacecraft carrying a laser into Earth orbit. The laser light would beam at sails attached to a stellar probe. Pressure from the laser light would drive the probe to 20% of the speed of light.

COMING HOME
Reaching a star is only part of the story. Crew need to slow the probe to explore. Forward's probe would use three nested sails. The outer separates on approach and laser light from Earth reflects off it back onto the two inner sails, stopping the probe. After, another burst of light pressure would accelerate the innermost sail back to Earth.

Forwar arrangeme of solar sai

ARTIST'S IMPRESSION OF ANTIMATTER SPACECRAFT

WARP DRIVE

In 1915, Einstein published his theory of general relativity, which deals with how space and time are distorted or "warped" near massive objects. *Star Trek*'s USS Enterprise travelled faster than light, but wrongly imagined antimatter engines driving the starship. Nevertheless, *Star Trek* inspired Mexican physicist Miguel Alcubierre (1964–) to investigate whether it might be possible to build a warp drive.

Andromeda is the nearest spiral galaxy to the Milky Way.

Andromeda is 2.5 million light years away from Earth.

ANTIMATTER ENGINES

The TV series *Star Trek* made antimatter engines famous. They power the warp drive that propels the Enterprise at speeds faster than light. Antimatter exists and releases huge amounts of energy when it collides with matter. Indeed, matter-antimatter engines may one day power spaceships – but not at speeds faster than light.

ARTIST'S IMPRESSION OF WARP TRAVEL

ALCUBIERRE'S DRIVE

Alcubierre's warp engine would contract space in front of a starship, and expand it behind. A starship with a warp drive would be travelling slower than the speed of light within its own space, but the contraction and expansion of space itself would be sweeping along faster than the speed of light.

USS ENTERPRISE

NEGATIVE MASS

Warp drive would need negative mass to expand space behind a starship, and equal amounts of positive mass to contract space in front of it. Quantum physics suggests negative mass might exist, but no one knows.

Star Trek writers first coined the phrase warp drive for travelling faster than light.

WORMHOLES

American physicist Kip Thorne (1940–) put forward the idea of wormholes. These might provide a shortcut through space and time. A wormhole is a bit like a tunnel drilled through a mountain: the problem is that wormholes would be chance events and short-lived, likely to close and crush anyone passing through. Physicists suggest that negative energy, which is associated with negative mass, could keep wormholes open. Then all an interstellar, or even intergalactic, traveller need worry about is that the wormhole ends in the right part of space – and time!

ARTIST'S IMPRESSION OF A WORMHOLE

EN ROUTE TO STAR TRAVEL

● In 1960, American physicist Robert Bussard suggested that a magnetic field 3,200 km wide could guide hydrogen from interstellar space to power a nuclear fusion rocket.

● In the early 1960s, US space enthusiasts proposed propelling a starship by exploding nuclear bombs behind it. They called it Project Orion.

● In 1970, the British Project Daedalus updated the Orion idea. It proposed minibombs to propel a spacecraft to Barnard's Star, 5.9 light years from Earth.

IMPRESSION OF PROJECT DAEDALUS

FIND OUT MORE

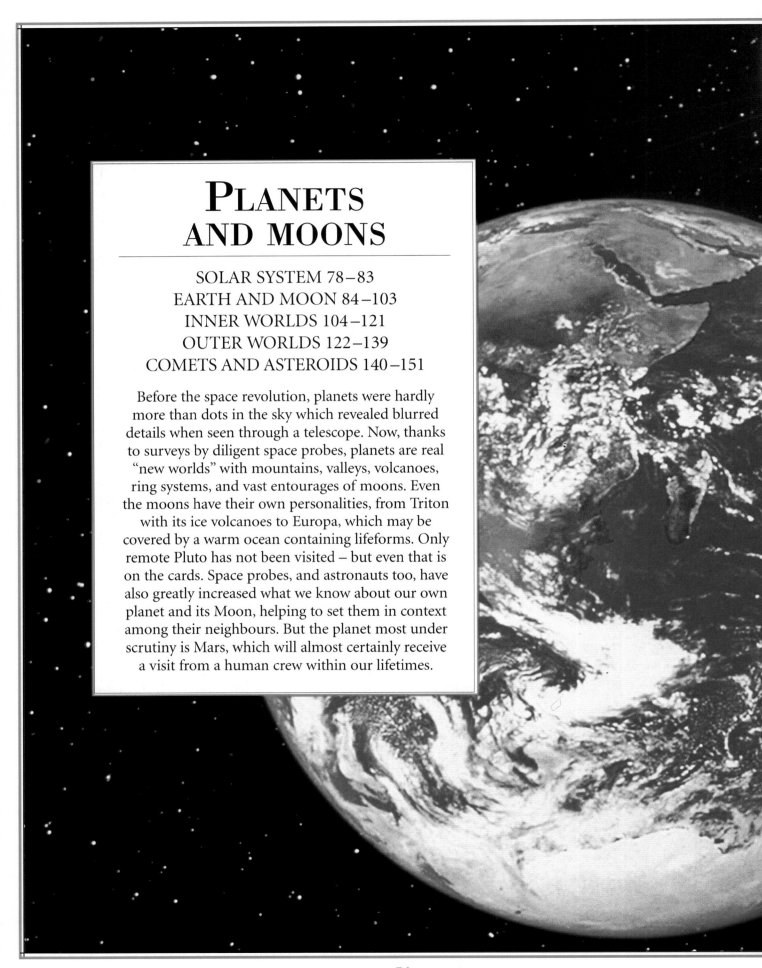

PLANETS AND MOONS

Before the space revolution, planets were hardly more than dots in the sky which revealed blurred details when seen through a telescope. Now, thanks to surveys by diligent space probes, planets are real "new worlds" with mountains, valleys, volcanoes, ring systems, and vast entourages of moons. Even the moons have their own personalities, from Triton with its ice volcanoes to Europa, which may be covered by a warm ocean containing lifeforms. Only remote Pluto has not been visited – but even that is on the cards. Space probes, and astronauts too, have also greatly increased what we know about our own planet and its Moon, helping to set them in context among their neighbours. But the planet most under scrutiny is Mars, which will almost certainly receive a visit from a human crew within our lifetimes.

SOLAR SYSTEM

HURTLING AROUND OUR SUN are nine planets, more than 60 moons, millions of asteroids and other rocky objects, and countless comets. Together, they make up the Solar System, which fills a volume of space 15 trillion kilometres in diameter. Closest to the Sun is the disc-shaped part of the system that contains the planets. Way beyond, in the outer reaches of the Solar System, is the Oort Cloud, a sphere-shaped region of comets.

Viewed from above the Sun's north pole, the planets would be seen to orbit in an anti-clockwise direction.

Pluto, the most distant planet, has the most elongated orbit.

OUTER PLANETS
Jupiter, Saturn, Uranus, Neptune, and Pluto are the outer planets. The first four are often called gas giants, because these vast planets are mostly made of gas. They each have a ring system and a family of moons. Pluto is different in size, structure, and composition from the others.

Uranus, and its rings and moons, orbits the Sun on its side. It is tilted over by 98°.

PLANETARY ORBITS
The planets do not move around the Sun in circular paths but in ellipses. One complete circuit of the Sun is an orbit. The length of the orbit and the time to complete one orbit (a planet's orbital period, or year) increases with successively distant planets. The planets form two distinct groups – the inner and the outer planets – separated by the Asteroid Belt, which contains billions of smaller space rocks.

INNER PLANETS
The closest planets to the Sun – Mercury, Venus, Earth, and Mars – are known as the inner planets. They are made of rock and are smaller than the outer planets. Only Earth and Mars have moons.

Mars is colder than Earth. In general, the farther a planet is from the Sun, the cooler it is.

Venus is almost identical in size to the Earth. It has the hottest surface temperature of all the planets.

Sun contains more than 99 per cent of the Solar System's mass. The pull of its gravity holds the system together.

Mercury, the planet closest to the Sun, has the shortest and fastest orbit around the Sun.

Earth is the only planet known to have liquid water and life.

HOW FAR FROM THE SUN?
The distance of each planet from the Sun varies as it moves around its orbit, because it follows an elliptical path. Pluto, for example, is nearly 3 billion kilometres nearer to the Sun at its closest point, or perihelion, than at its farthest point, or aphelion. The scale below gives the average distances of the planets from the Sun in astronomical units (AU).

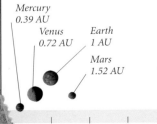

Mercury 0.39 AU

Venus 0.72 AU

Earth 1 AU

Mars 1.52 AU

Jupiter 5.20 AU

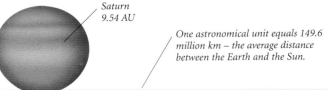

Saturn 9.54 AU

One astronomical unit equals 149.6 million km – the average distance between the Earth and the Sun.

Uranus 19.19 AU

| 1 | 2 | 3 | 4 | 5 | 6 | 7 | 8 | 9 | 10 | 11 | 12 | 13 | 14 | 15 | 16 | 17 | 18 | 19 |

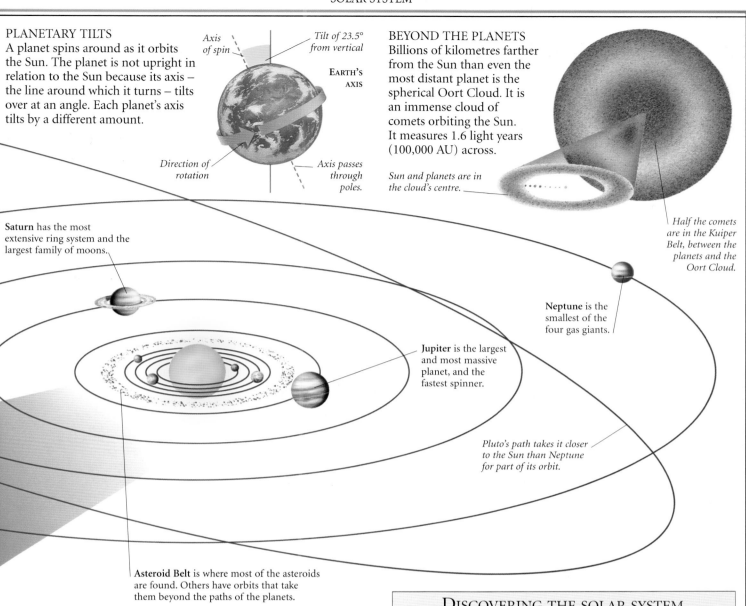

PLANETARY TILTS

A planet spins around as it orbits the Sun. The planet is not upright in relation to the Sun because its axis – the line around which it turns – tilts over at an angle. Each planet's axis tilts by a different amount.

Axis of spin

Tilt of 23.5° from vertical

EARTH'S AXIS

Direction of rotation

Axis passes through poles.

BEYOND THE PLANETS

Billions of kilometres farther from the Sun than even the most distant planet is the spherical Oort Cloud. It is an immense cloud of comets orbiting the Sun. It measures 1.6 light years (100,000 AU) across.

Sun and planets are in the cloud's centre.

Half the comets are in the Kuiper Belt, between the planets and the Oort Cloud.

Saturn has the most extensive ring system and the largest family of moons.

Neptune is the smallest of the four gas giants.

Jupiter is the largest and most massive planet, and the fastest spinner.

Pluto's path takes it closer to the Sun than Neptune for part of its orbit.

Asteroid Belt is where most of the asteroids are found. Others have orbits that take them beyond the paths of the planets.

VITAL STATISTICS

Planet	Diameter in km	Time for one spin on axis	Time for one orbit	Minimum distance from Sun in km	Maximum distance from Sun in km
Mercury	4,880	58.65 d	87.97 d	46.0 million	69.8 million
Venus	12,104	243 d	224.70 d	107.5 million	108.9 million
Earth	12,756	23.93 h	365.26 d	147.1 million	152.1 million
Mars	6,794	24.62 h	686.98 d	206.6 million	249.2 million
Jupiter	142,984	9.93 h	11.86 y	740.6 million	816.0 million
Saturn	120,536	10.66 h	29.46 y	1.35 billion	1.51 billion
Uranus	51,118	17.24 h	84.01 y	2.73 billion	3.01 billion
Neptune	49,532	16.11 h	164.79 y	4.46 billion	4.54 billion
Pluto	2,274	6.39 d	247.68 y	4.45 billion	7.38 billion

DISCOVERING THE SOLAR SYSTEM

- Mercury, Venus, Earth, Mars, Jupiter, Saturn, and the Moon were known in ancient times. The Earth was believed to be at the centre of the Solar System.

- In the 16th century, Nicolaus Copernicus proposed that the planets revolve around the Sun.

EARTH-CENTRED SOLAR SYSTEM MAP

- Uranus was discovered in 1781, Neptune in 1846, and Pluto in 1930.

- The existence of a cloud of comets surrounding the planetary part of the Solar System was first suggested in 1932.

FIND OUT MORE

PROBES TO THE PLANETS 80 • BIRTH OF THE SOLAR SYSTEM 82
MINOR MEMBERS 140 • OTHER SOLAR SYSTEMS 178

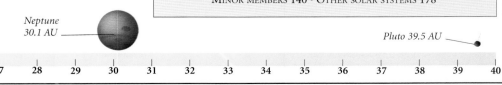

Neptune 30.1 AU

Pluto 39.5 AU

21 22 23 24 25 26 27 28 29 30 31 32 33 34 35 36 37 38 39 40

PROBES TO THE PLANETS

ONCE THE FIRST ROCKETS had successfully reached space, a new investigative tool – the space probe – became available to space scientists and astronomers. Space probes are car-sized robot craft launched by rockets. They travel to a predetermined target and investigate it using their on-board instruments. Probes have given us close-up views of all but one of the planets, many moons, a comet, and even asteroids. They have taught us much about the Solar System.

Ulysses used gravity assist from Jupiter in 1992 in order to fly under the Sun in 1994.

ULYSSES

GRAVITY ASSIST
A rocket or the Space Shuttle starts a space probe on its path towards its target. If a probe needs extra help to reach its goal, it can use a technique called gravity assist. This involves following a flight path that takes it close to another planet. The probe makes use of the planet's gravity to speed up and change direction.

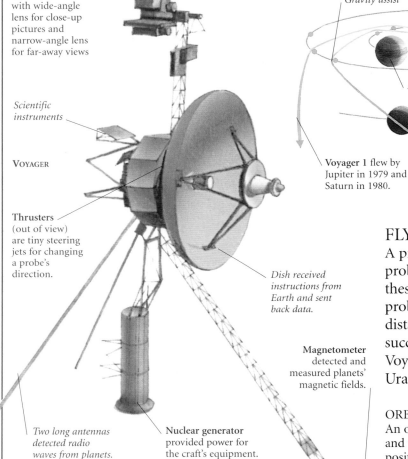

Camera platform with wide-angle lens for close-up pictures and narrow-angle lens for far-away views

Scientific instruments

VOYAGER

Thrusters (out of view) are tiny steering jets for changing a probe's direction.

Two long antennas detected radio waves from planets.

Nuclear generator provided power for the craft's equipment.

Dish received instructions from Earth and sent back data.

Magnetometer detected and measured planets' magnetic fields.

Gravity assist

Earth

Jupiter

Saturn

Uranus

VOYAGERS 1 AND 2 FLIGHT PATHS

Voyager 1 flew by Jupiter in 1979 and Saturn in 1980.

Neptune

Voyager 2 flew by Jupiter, Saturn, Uranus, and Neptune between July 1979 and August 1989.

FLY-BY PROBES
A probe may fly by a target, orbit it, or land on it. Some probes follow a course that involves more than one of these methods and more than one target. A fly-by probe surveys its target as it flies past, often at a distance of several thousand kilometres. The most successful fly-by probes to date were two identical craft, Voyagers 1 and 2, that investigated Jupiter, Saturn, Uranus, and Neptune between 1979 and 1989.

ORBITERS
An orbiter probe travels to a planet or moon and then moves into orbit around it. Once in position, its sensitive instruments are turned on and the probe starts investigating its target.

MAGELLAN

LANDERS
Probes have landed on the Moon, Venus, and Mars. Each of the two Viking probes that visited Mars combined an orbiter and a lander. Once in orbit, the lander separated from the rest of the probe. It used parachute-braking and retro-rockets to make a smooth touch down. The one-piece Pathfinder landed on Mars in 1997 without first going into orbit. On the surface it released Sojourner, a robot rover vehicle.

VIKING

Vikings 1 and 2 landed on Mars in July and September 1976.

Orbit of Mars

Magellan orbited Venus in August 1990.

Sun

Orbit of Venus

Orbit of Earth

Magellan launched in May 1989.

Vikings 1 and 2 launched in August and September 1975.

VIKING AND MAGELLAN FLIGHT PATHS

EQUIPMENT AND EXPERIMENTS

A probe may receive instructions from Earth on what tasks to carry out and when; otherwise it follows a mission programmed into its on-board computers. It is powered by electricity generated by solar panels or a nuclear generator. On board are the control systems that operate the probe and its scientific equipment. The Cassini orbiter, launched in 1997, carries a lander probe, Huygens, that will investigate the atmosphere and surface of Titan, Saturn's largest moon.

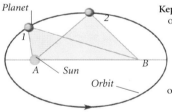

Antenna dish allows probes to stay in touch with Earth.

Heat-resistant shield to stop Huygens from burning up in Titan's atmosphere

Cassini will reach Saturn in 2004 and will orbit the planet and its moons for 4 years.

Huygens, carried here, will be released by Cassini to investigate Titan.

Experiment platform holds the equipment Huygens will use to test Titan's surface and atmosphere.

Surface science package, the size and shape of a top hat, contains a number of separate experiments.

This device will be the first part of Huygens to touch Titan's surface. No one knows whether Huygens will touch down on land or ocean.

If Huygens lands in an ocean, this piece of equipment will test the water's depth.

By sending beeping sounds to each other, these instruments will help to measure the density, composition, and temperature of Titan's atmosphere and surface.

BEFORE THE PROBES

Until the invention of space probes, astronomers had to rely on the human eye and telescopes. To the naked eye, the planets look little more than bright stars. The eye's view can be improved with a telescope, but even the best Earth-based instruments show the surface of only one rocky planet, Mars. Very little detail of the extensive moon and ring systems of the large outer planets can be seen.

Jupiter / *Venus*

KEPLER'S LAWS OF PLANETARY MOTION

Space scientists use these laws, devised by Johannes Kepler in the 17th century, to calculate the paths of space probes and to ensure that they reach the right planet at the right time.

Planet

1 *2* *A* *Sun* *B*

Orbit

Kepler's first law states that a planet orbits the Sun in a path called an ellipse, with the Sun at one focus. There are two focuses within an ellipse (A or B). The distance from one focus (A) to any point on the ellipse (1 or 2) and back to the other focus (B) is always the same.

Kepler's second law describes a planet's speed – fastest when close to the Sun and slower when farther away. Mathematically it says: draw a line from the planet to the Sun and another line after a certain time, say 100 days, and the area enclosed will always be the same.

Area is the same each time.

100 days *100 days* *Sun* *100 days*

Orbital path

Motion of Mars, Jupiter, and Saturn during one Earth orbit

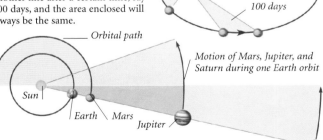

Sun *Earth* *Mars* *Jupiter* *Saturn*

Kepler's third law states that the farther a planet is from the Sun, the slower it travels and the more time it takes to complete one orbit. The relationship between distance and orbital period is fixed, so astronomers need only find a planet's speed to calculate its distance from the Sun.

KEY SPACE PROBES

Probe	Type	Target	Encounter	Achievements
Pioneer 10	Fly-by	Jupiter	1973	First to cross Asteroid Belt; took close-ups of Jupiter
Mariner 10	Fly-by	Mercury	1974–5	Only probe to Mercury
Venera 9	Orbiter/lander	Venus	1975	First views of Venusian surface
Vikings 1 and 2	Orbiter/lander	Mars	1976	Photographed Martian surface; searched for life
Pioneer 11	Fly-by	Saturn	1979	First detailed Saturn views
Giotto	Fly-by	Comet Halley	1986	First view of the nucleus of a comet
Voyagers 1 and 2	Fly-by	Jupiter	1979	Details of all four planetary systems;
		Saturn	1980–81	Voyager 2 was first probe
		Uranus	1986	to Uranus and Neptune
		Neptune	1989	
Galileo	Fly-by/orbiter	Gaspra	1991	First fly-by of an asteroid;
		Jupiter	1995	first orbit of Jupiter

FIND OUT MORE

HOW ROCKETS WORK 36 • SPACE LAUNCHERS 40 • SOLAR SYSTEM 78
VENUSIAN SURFACE 112 • MARS: SEARCH FOR LIFE 116 • SATURN'S MOONS 132

BIRTH OF THE SOLAR SYSTEM

MOST ASTRONOMERS BELIEVE that all the members of the Solar System, from the giant Sun to the smallest asteroid, were born out of a vast, spinning cloud of gas and dust – the solar nebula. The process began 5 billion years ago with the formation of the Sun. The planets and other objects formed from unused material. When the Solar System was nearly complete, 500 million years later, just 0.002 per cent of the solar nebula's original mass remained. The rest had been blown away or pushed out into space.

1 A giant, spinning cloud of gas and dust collected in space to form the solar nebula. This was the material from which the Solar System would eventually be created.

2 The Sun formed as gravity caused the solar nebula to contract, leaving a spinning outer disc of material.

Sun   Disc

Dust and gas particles in the disc clumped together to form larger, grain-like particles.

SOLAR NEBULA

As the vast cloud spun and cooled, material was drawn into the centre. The centre became denser and hotter, and began generating energy by nuclear fusion – the Sun was born. At the same time, the rest of the solar nebula formed into a disc consisting mainly of hydrogen and helium gas, with some dust, rock, metal, and snow. Rocky and metallic material near the Sun came together to form the inner planets. In the cooler, outer regions, snow combined with rock, metal, and gas to form the outer planets.

3 The newborn Sun blew off excess material. Rings formed in the disc of material surrounding the Sun as it, too, contracted. Planetesimals – large, rocky objects – formed within the rings.

Grains collided to form ever larger, rocky particles, eventually producing planetesimals.

Gravity pulls the star's core in with such force that it sends a shock wave through space.

PLANETARY FORMATION

Planet	Made from	Mass of ring (Earth = 1)	Planet's present mass (Earth = 1)	Time to form in yrs
Mercury	Rock, metal	30	0.06	80,000
Venus	Rock, metal	160	0.82	40,000
Earth	Rock, metal	200	1.00	110,000
Mars	Rock, metal	200	0.11	200,000
Jupiter	Rock, metal, snow, gas	4,000	318	1 million
Saturn	Rock, metal, snow, gas	400	95.16	9 million
Uranus	Rock, metal, snow, gas	80	14.54	300 million
Neptune	Rock, metal, snow, gas	100	17.15	1 billion
Pluto	Rock, metal, snow	—	0.002	1 billion

FIND OUT MORE

SUPERNOVA SHOCK WAVE

A massive star may explode as a supernova at the end of its life. In some supernovas, the star's core collapses in on itself and produces a powerful shock wave that travels out through space. Some astronomers believe that the contraction of the solar nebula may have been triggered by a shock wave from a supernova.

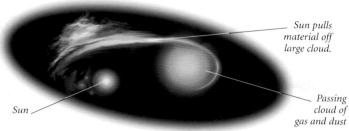

Sun pulls material off large cloud.

Sun

Passing cloud of gas and dust

CAPTURE THEORY

Not all astronomers agree that the planets and other bodies formed at the same time or from the same cloud of material as the Sun. The capture theory suggests that part of a giant cloud of gas and dust passing close to the young Sun was captured by the Sun's gravity. This eventually split into mini-clouds that contracted and formed the planets.

BIRTH OF THE PLANETS

The planets began to form about 4.6 billion years ago. Apart from Pluto, each planet came together from an initial, ring-shaped mass of material around the Sun. (Pluto was created from the leftovers.) As the planets formed, tiny particles stuck together to make grain-sized lumps, then pebbles and boulders, and eventually larger bodies called planetesimals. When they were a few kilometres across, the planetesimals' gravity was strong enough to attract more and more material.

OTHER SOLAR SYSTEMS

Since the 1980s, astronomers have found increasing numbers of other solar systems. Young stars surrounded by a disc of gas and dust, such as HR 4796A, are thought to be in the early stages of forming planets. Astronomers believe that there are other stars that are orbited by fully formed planets, although the planets themselves cannot be seen.

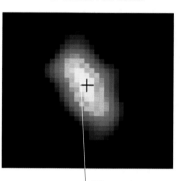

HR 4796A inside the disc.

ORIGIN THEORIES

• In 1796, Pierre de Laplace proposed the nebula theory: that the Solar System formed as a rotating nebula flattened out. The Sun was created first, and leftover material formed the planets.

• In the 19th century, there were several encounter theories. One suggested that a comet knocked planetary material out of the Sun, and another that the solar nebula formed as two stars collided.

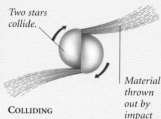

Two stars collide.

Material thrown out by impact

COLLIDING STARS THEORY

• In 1917–18, English astronomers James Jeans (1877–1946) and Harold Jeffreys (1891–1989) both proposed the tidal theory: that the planets formed from material pulled out of the Sun by a passing star. It was accepted for many years.

Rings produced planets.

Rocky planets, such as Mercury, were molten when young. They each developed a metallic core beneath a rock exterior.

Rock and metal between Mars and Jupiter failed to create a planet, but instead formed the Asteroid Belt.

Solar System debris consisted mainly of space rocks known as asteroids and chunks of snow and dust called comets.

4 Planetesimals joined to form larger bodies called protoplanets. These, in turn, came together to form the rocky planets: Mercury, Venus, Earth, and Mars.

5 Protoplanets also formed in the outer regions of the disc. As they grew larger, their gravity attracted vast amounts of gas, creating the gas giants: Jupiter, Saturn, Uranus, and Neptune.

Gas giants, such as Saturn, first formed a solid core and then captured a huge atmosphere.

6 Pluto formed from material not used in the gas giants. Remaining chunks of dust, rock, and snow were drawn into the Sun and destroyed or thrown out of the planetary Solar System. Many formed the Oort Cloud of comets.

EARTH

AN ALIEN VISITING THE SOLAR SYSTEM would have a wonderful choice of worlds to explore, from the rings of Saturn to the volcanic Hell of Venus. The third planet from the Sun, however, would most intrigue an interstellar visitor. It combines many of the features of other planets with some that are all its own. Earth has volcanoes as on Venus and Mars, craters as found on Mercury, and swirling weather systems similar to those on Jupiter and Neptune. However, it is the only planet that has both liquid water and frozen ice, the only planet with an atmosphere rich in oxygen, and the only one – as far as we know – where life exists.

DOUBLE PLANET
The third planet from the Sun appears to be almost a double planet, as shown in this Galileo space probe image. Earth's Moon is one-quarter its size, larger in proportion to its planet than any other apart from Pluto and its moon Charon. The two worlds are very different – Earth is bright and bustling while the Moon is dull and lifeless.

BLUE PLANET
From space, Earth stands out as a blue gem, its colour coming from the vast expanses of water on its surface. Earth is the only planet with a surface temperature between 0°C and 100°C, where water can be liquid at the surface. On Mercury and Venus, closer to the Sun, water would boil away, while on more distant Mars it is frozen.

SIGNS OF LIFE
Seen from space, Earth is the only planet with strong signs of life. The evidence ranges from plants that change with the seasons and oxygen in the atmosphere, to artificial radio signals and lights at night. Artificial structures – even the Great Wall of China – are not easily seen from space.

Streetlights in cities

Burning gas at oil wells

EARTH AT NIGHT

Campfires in Africa

Fishing fleets off coast of Japan

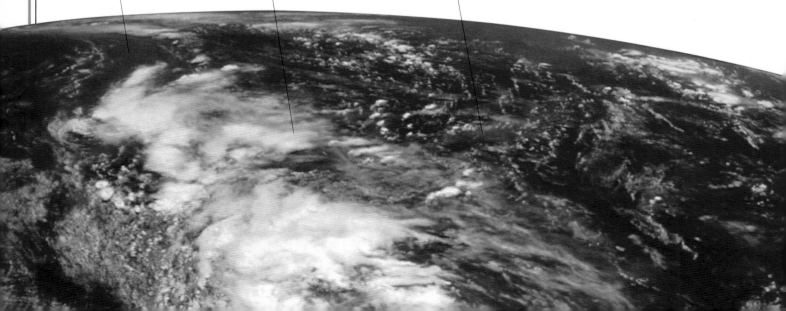

Oceans and seas cover 71% of the Earth's surface.

Clouds condense from water vapour that has evaporated from the oceans.

Rain from clouds returns water to the oceans, completing what is called the water cycle.

EARTH AT A GLANCE

Earth is the largest of the rocky planets. It is the only planet with a crust split into moving plates, oxygen in its atmosphere, and liquid water and life on its surface.

TILT, SPIN AND ORBIT

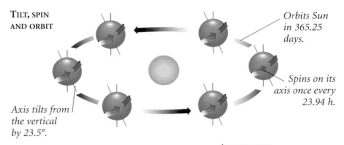

Orbits Sun in 365.25 days.

Spins on its axis once every 23.94 h.

Axis tilts from the vertical by 23.5°.

ATMOSPHERE

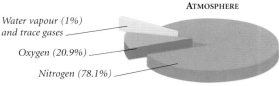

Water vapour (1%) and trace gases

Oxygen (20.9%)

Nitrogen (78.1%)

STRUCTURE

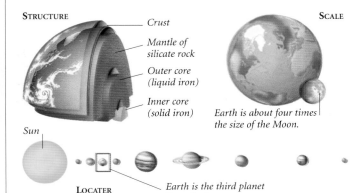

Crust

Mantle of silicate rock

Outer core (liquid iron)

Inner core (solid iron)

SCALE

Earth is about four times the size of the Moon.

Sun

LOCATER

Earth is the third planet from the Sun.

EARTH AS A MAGNET

For its size, Earth has the strongest magnetic field of any planet. The magnetism arises in its core, where swirling currents of molten iron generate electric and magnetic fields. The magnetism changes direction as time passes, causing the magnetic poles to wander. At present, the magnetic poles are about 2,000 km from the North and South Poles.

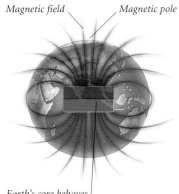

Magnetic field   *Magnetic pole*

Earth's core behaves like a bar magnet at its centre.

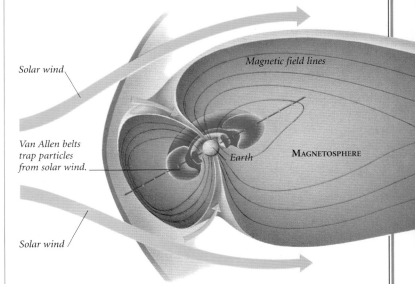

Magnetic field lines

Solar wind

Van Allen belts trap particles from solar wind.

Earth   **MAGNETOSPHERE**

Solar wind

MAGNETOSPHERE

Earth's magnetism extends far into space to form a huge "magnetic bubble" surrounding Earth. This magnetosphere protects Earth from the effects of the solar wind – electrified particles that sweep outwards from the Sun at high speeds. Some particles are trapped in two regions near Earth, called the Van Allen belts. Others stream down to the magnetic poles, lighting up the atmosphere as auroras.

ICE

More than a tenth of Earth's surface is covered in ice, mostly in the ice caps at the poles. Other planets, including Mars, have polar ice caps, but only on Earth do ice and water exist together. The ice caps grow in winter and shrink in summer, when giant icebergs break off into the surrounding ocean.

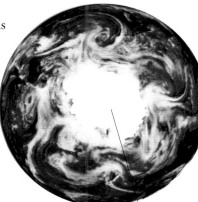

Antarctic ice cap, seen from space

VITAL STATISTICS

Diameter	12,756 km
Average distance from Sun	149.6 million km
Orbital speed around Sun	27.79 km/s
Sunrise to sunrise	24 hours
Mass (Earth=1)	1
Volume (Earth=1)	1
Average density (water=1)	5.52
Surface gravity (Earth=1)	1
Average surface temperature	15°C
Number of moons	1

FIND OUT MORE

SOLAR SYSTEM 78 • MOON 92 • MERCURY 104
VENUS 108 • MARS 114 • SPINNING EARTH 242
EARTH'S ORBIT 244 • AURORAS AND HALOES 264

EARTH'S SURFACE

SHAPED BY GEOLOGICAL FORCES that are found on no other planet, Earth's surface is unique. The crust (outer shell) is split into huge sections called plates, which are always on the move so that today's map of Earth is only a snapshot of a changing world. The moving plates float on a partially molten layer of rock. As they collide or move apart, the surface rocks are destroyed or renewed. These forces continually replace Earth's rocks, so most parts of the surface are younger than 200 million years old.

SEDIMENTARY ROCK
Silt washed down by the River Ganges will be compressed under the sea into solid rock, which may be pushed up again as mountains. Such sedimentary rocks result from erosion by rivers, glaciers, wind or waves.

GANGES DELTA

PLATE TECTONICS

Strip away the oceans and a strange planet emerges. Earth's surface is shaped by plate tectonics, the forces caused by the moving plates. There are eight large plates and many smaller ones. Some consist only of ocean floor, while others include continents. The edges of the plates are marked by long cracks, winding ridges, strings of volcanoes, and earthquake zones.

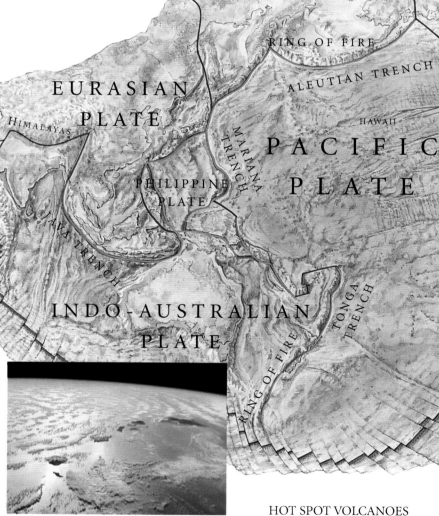

RING OF FIRE
EURASIAN PLATE
ALEUTIAN TRENCH
HIMALAYAS
HAWAII
MARIANA TRENCH
PACIFIC PLATE
PHILIPPINE PLATE
JAVA TRENCH
INDO-AUSTRALIAN PLATE
TONGA TRENCH
RING OF FIRE

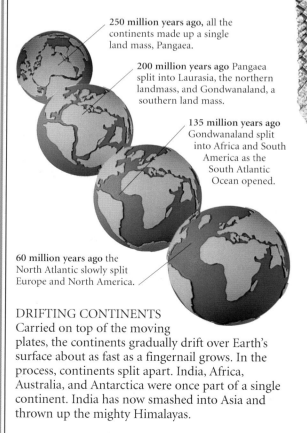

250 million years ago, all the continents made up a single land mass, Pangaea.

200 million years ago Pangaea split into Laurasia, the northern landmass, and Gondwanaland, a southern land mass.

135 million years ago Gondwanaland split into Africa and South America as the South Atlantic Ocean opened.

60 million years ago the North Atlantic slowly split Europe and North America.

DRIFTING CONTINENTS
Carried on top of the moving plates, the continents gradually drift over Earth's surface about as fast as a fingernail grows. In the process, continents split apart. India, Africa, Australia, and Antarctica were once part of a single continent. India has now smashed into Asia and thrown up the mighty Himalayas.

HAWAIIAN ISLANDS

Plate movement
Volcano
Rising lava in hot spot

HOT SPOT VOLCANOES
Hawaiian volcanic islands come from a hot stream of lava that rises deep within the Earth and emerges at a "hot spot". The moving Pacific Plate carries the island away, so the hot spot must break through the crust again and build up a new volcano.

The natural arch of Durdle Door, in the UK, formed when waves eroded soft rocks.

DURDLE DOOR

WHERE PLATES MOVE APART

Where two plates move apart, fresh lava wells up from below to form a winding mountain range, known as a mid-ocean ridge because the join between the plates forms part of the ocean floor. The Mid-Atlantic Ridge is the longest mountain range on Earth. Its highest peaks emerge as islands such as Iceland, Ascension Island, and Tristan da Cunha.

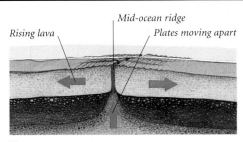

Rising lava *Mid-ocean ridge* *Plates moving apart*

MID-OCEAN RIDGE

SWISS ALPS

ICELAND

EURASIAN PLATE

NORTH AMERICAN PLATE

ALPS

MID-ATLANTIC RIDGE

ARABIAN PLATE

CARIBBEAN PLATE

COCOS PLATE

ANDES

AFRICAN PLATE

EAST PACIFIC RISE

NAZCA PLATE

SOUTH AMERICAN PLATE

RING OF FIRE

MID-ATLANTIC RIDGE

TRISTAN DA CHUNA

ANTARCTIC PLATE

SCOTIA PLATE

COLLIDING CONTINENTS

The Alps are the result of a smash-up between two continents. As the African Plate pushes northwards, it crumples up the Eurasian Plate to form a string of mountains.

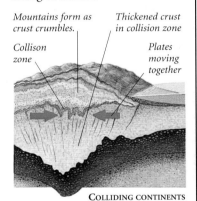

Mountains form as crust crumbles. *Thickened crust in collision zone*

Collison zone *Plates moving together*

COLLIDING CONTINENTS

SPREADING WORLD

- In 1924, German meteorologist Alfred Wegener (1880–1930) suggested that continents were drifting apart.

- In 1960, American geologist Harry Hess (1906–69) proposed plate tectonic theory, confirmed in 1963 by the expansion of the Indian Ocean floor.

FIND OUT MORE

BIRTH OF SOLAR SYSTEM 82
JUPITER'S MOONS 126

VOLCANIC POOLS IN THE ANDES

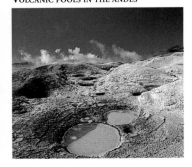

WHERE PLATES MEET

The Andes are part of a volcanic chain – the Ring of Fire – that extends around the Pacific Ocean. As South America moves west, it rides up over the Nazca Plate. This process, known as subduction, forces ocean-floor rocks under the continent, where they are melted by Earth's heat and erupt as volcanoes.

SUBDUCTION

Pacific Ocean floor forced under South America.

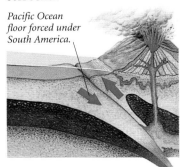

EARTH'S ATMOSPHERE

Planet earth is surrounded by a thin layer of gas called the atmosphere, which protects its surface from the harshness of space. Compared with the size of Earth, the atmosphere is no thicker than the skin of an apple, but it is a busy place. Heated unevenly by the Sun and spun around by the Earth, the air is forced into ever-changing swirling patterns. Earth's atmosphere is the most complex and unpredictable in the Solar System. The atmosphere is also an essential blanket for life on Earth, keeping the planet at a comfortable temperature and protecting the surface from dangerous radiation.

STRUCTURE OF THE ATMOSPHERE

The atmosphere is a mixture of gases (mainly nitrogen and oxygen), water, and dust. It is about 500 km deep, but has no real boundary, fading into space as it gets thinner. At ground level, the circulating atmosphere produces strong winds, blowing in a pattern caused by the Sun's heat and the Earth's rotation. Between the main wind systems there are swirling ovals of high pressure (anticyclones) and low pressure (depressions).

MIR SPACE STATION
Earth's atmosphere has no top, but thins out into space, so satellites such as Mir actually orbit within Earth's atmosphere. The air slows them down, so they eventually fall out of orbit and burn up.

Low pressure region (a depression)

Troposphere, containing most of the clouds and stormy weather, is 8 km high at the poles, 18 km over the Equator.

Stratosphere, from tropopause (between troposphere and stratosphere) to 50-km altitude, contains the ozone layer.

Mesosphere, 50–90 km above ground, is the coldest region, at –100°C.

Thermosphere, at an altitude of 90–500 km, is heated to 1,000°C by the Sun's X-rays.

Exosphere, more than 500 km above Earth, where gases boil away into space.

Thunderstorms, where moist air is rising and condensing rapidly

LAYERS OF ATMOSPHERE

Take a vertical slice of Earth's atmosphere and it forms several distinct layers: troposphere, stratosphere, mesosphere, thermosphere, and exosphere. As height increases, the air gets thinner, but temperature is more variable. In the troposphere, the temperature decreases with height, because rising air expands and cools. The stratosphere is warmer as it absorbs ultraviolet from the Sun. The thermosphere is heated by the Sun's X-rays.

GREENHOUSE EFFECT

Without the atmosphere, Earth would be 30°C colder – below freezing almost everywhere. The air traps heat like a greenhouse: sunlight can shine down on the ground, warming it up, but not all the resulting infrared (heat radiation) can escape back through the atmosphere.

High pressure region (an anticyclone)

Gases in atmosphere

Sunlight

Clear skies

Heat from Earth

Heat radiated back to Earth

OZONE HOLE

In the stratosphere is the ozone layer – a band of gas that protects Earth from the Sun's harmful ultraviolet rays. This layer has thinned above Antarctica (violet and blue areas on this false-colour satellite image). The ozone holes around both poles are thought to be caused by chlorofluorocarbons (CFCs), found in some aerosol sprays and packaging.

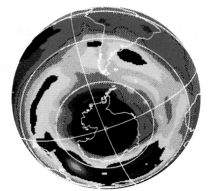

CHANGING CLIMATE

The world's temperature in the troposphere (red is hotter in this image) is monitored by satellites. The Earth is warming up by about 0.02°C per year, probably because extra carbon dioxide enhances the greenhouse effect. This increase comes from burning coal and oil and the destruction of rainforests, which absorb the gas.

CHANGING ICE COVER

Earth sometimes cools to freezing, despite the blanketing effect of the atmosphere. These ice ages may be caused by Earth's axis wobbling so that seasons become more and then less extreme. The most recent ice age ended 10,000 years ago. At present, Earth is warmer, but it will not last.

Maximum ice cover 18,000 years ago

Ice cover today

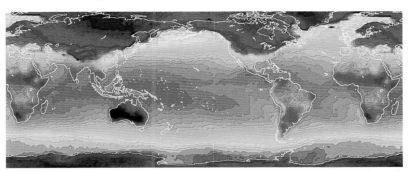

Line of clouds marks a weather front.

WIND CIRCULATION

Winds move around the Earth in a distinctive pattern. At the Equator, warm air rises, moves north and south, then descends and flows back at sea level. At each pole, cold air sinks and spreads. Then it warms up and rises to flow back at high altitude. Caught between these circulating currents, air at middle latitudes circulates the opposite way.

Winds in northern hemisphere are twisted to the right by Earth's rotation.

Sea level winds

Equator

Earth's rotation

North Pole

Polar easterlies

Westerlies

Northeast trade winds

Southeast trade winds

Westerlies

Cold polar air sinks and spreads to warmer areas.

High altitude winds

Winds in southern hemisphere are twisted to the left by Earth's rotation.

South Pole

UP IN THE AIR

• In 1643, Italian physicist Evangelista Torricelli (1608–47) invented the barometer for measuring atmospheric pressure.

• Edmond Halley published the first map of winds over the Earth in 1686. George Hadley (1685–1768) explained how tropical trade winds are generated.

• In 1848, balloonist James Glaisher (1809–1903) measured atmospheric temperature above ground – the first weather reports.

• In 1990 a committee of world scientists reported that carbon dioxide from human activities increases the greenhouse effect.

FIND OUT MORE

RADIATIONS FROM SPACE 20
VENUSIAN ATMOSPHERE 110
EARTH'S ORBIT 244

LIVING PLANET

IN 1990, THE GALILEO SPACE PROBE swept past a very strange world. Its instruments revealed a green covering over much of the land surface, a highly corrosive gas in the atmosphere, and some odd radio signals. As part of its route to Jupiter, Galileo was passing planet Earth. The green covering was biological material absorbing sunlight. In the process, it was constantly releasing the corrosive gas oxygen, which would otherwise disappear in chemical reactions. Earth has one special quality that sets it apart from every other object in the Universe: it is the only place where life is known to exist.

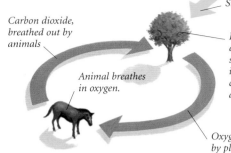

Carbon dioxide, breathed out by animals

Sunlight

Animal breathes in oxygen.

Plant absorbs carbon dioxide. Using sunlight, it incorporates the carbon into its leaves and releases oxygen.

Oxygen released by plant

OXYGEN CYCLE
All life on Earth is linked by cycles. Through the oxygen cycle, plants and animals depend on each other for survival. Animals use oxygen to release energy from food, breathing out carbon dioxide. Plants live on carbon dioxide, converting it back to oxygen.

LIFE ON EARTH
Earth is the only world with life, because it is a "Goldilocks planet". It is not too hot, so water does not boil away, and not too cold, so it does not freeze. It is not too small, so it can contain an atmosphere, and not too big, so it is not "all atmosphere" like the planet Jupiter.

EVOLUTION OF LIFE
Planet Earth is home to more than a million different species of living things, ranging from bacteria to giant trees and mammals. All have come about by the process of evolution – changes in successive generations as species adapt to their surroundings and competitors. For the first 3 billion years, the only life on Earth was in the form of single cells, living in the sea. They evolved into multicelled plants and animals 570 million years ago. Later, some of these ventured onto dry land.

2 Large shallow pools concentrated chemicals to make the first cells 4 billion years ago. The first simple plants arrived on dry land about 400 million years ago. Animals, including the first insects, followed the plants ashore.

3 In warm times, about 200 million years ago, giant tree ferns and dinosaurs flourished.

4 Today, life is still evolving. A new threat to all life is human activity, which is destroying hundreds of species every year.

BLACK SMOKERS
Not all life requires sunlight to survive. These worms live in darkness on the ocean floor, thousands of metres underwater. They exist on chemicals and energy produced by volcanic vents on the sea bed called black smokers. Similar creatures might live in the oceans of Jupiter's moon Europa.

BLACK SMOKER

COSMIC FORCES
Life on Earth is exposed to lethal forces from the surrounding universe. The impact of a comet or asteroid, powerful flares on the Sun, or the explosion of a nearby star can all cause "mass extinctions" on Earth, like the sudden death of the dinosaurs.

ORIGIN OF LIFE: LIGHTNING

According to one theory, life on Earth began when lightning flashed through Earth's early atmosphere, making the gases combine to form the molecules essential for life. Chemists imitate the process with an electric spark in a flask of gas.

ORIGIN OF LIFE: COMETS

A rival theory says that the molecules of life – or even living cells – were brought to Earth on comets. In 1986, the Giotto spacecraft discovered that the solid nucleus of Halley's Comet is covered with a dark crust, made of carbon-rich molecules similar to the substances making living cells.

LIVING CELLS

All life is made of microscopic cells. Some organisms consist of a single cell, while the human body has 100 billion cells. Cells differ in detail, depending on their function in the body, but all have the same basic parts.

SINGLE CELLS

Many species consist of a single cell. They include pond-dwelling algae and bacteria that spread diseases. Some live in boiling springs or deep underground. Sometimes single cells group together in colonies, such as the stony-looking stromatolites.

SIMPLE LIFE-FORMS

Some of the simpler life-forms have survived for hundreds of millions of years. Ferns were the first plants to colonize dry land, well before flowering plants evolved. Molluscs in the sea and insects on land have stayed the same for 350 million years.

COMPLEX SYSTEMS

Many plants and animals have evolved to become more complex. Flowering plants use insects to pollinate them. Birds and mammals are warm-blooded, so they can endure temperature changes. Dolphins and all apes – including humans – have large brains to help them survive.

1 In the beginning, volcanic activity and huge electrical storms may have provided the spark that started life on Earth.

Ribosome – where proteins are made

Nucleus – holding the cell's DNA

Mitochondrion – the cell's energy source

Stromatolites

Fern

Cockroach (insect)

Flowering plants use birds and other animals to disperse their seeds.

Humming bird

The most recent forms of plant and animal life have only evolved over the past 2 million years.

FIND OUT MORE

SEARCH FOR LIFE ON MARS 116
JUPITER'S MOONS 126
OTHER SOLAR SYSTEMS 178
LIFE ON OTHER WORLDS 236
ET INTELLIGENCE 238

MOON

THE MOON IS THE CLOSEST celestial object to the Earth. The pair waltzes through space together, with the Moon spinning around the Earth as the Earth itself orbits the Sun. The Moon is larger and brighter than any other object in the night sky. It has no light of its own but shines by reflecting sunlight. As it moves around our planet, we see changing amounts, or phases, of the Moon's sunlit side. Up to three times a year, the Moon's bright face is eclipsed as it passes through the Earth's shadow.

EARTH FROM MOON'S SURFACE

From the Moon, Earth's daytime side appears large in the lunar sky.

There is no lunar atmosphere to impede the view.

EARTH'S SATELLITE

The Moon is the Earth's only natural satellite. Most moons are much smaller than their parent planets, but our Moon is relatively large in comparison, with a diameter one-quarter that of the Earth. It is almost big enough for the Earth and Moon to be thought of as a double-planet system.

VITAL STATISTICS	
Diameter	3,476 km
Average distance from Earth	384,400 km
Orbital speed around Earth	1.02 km/s
New Moon to new Moon	29.53 days
Mass (Earth =1)	0.01
Volume (Earth = 1)	0.02
Average density (water = 1)	3.34
Surface gravity (Earth = 1)	0.17
Average surface temperature	−20°C

FIND OUT MORE

EARTH 84 • LUNAR INFLUENCES 94
MOON'S SURFACE 96 • ECLIPSES OF THE SUN 160

MOON AT A GLANCE

The Moon is a dusty, barren sphere of rock with no atmosphere or liquid water. It takes the same time to rotate on its axis as it does to orbit the Earth.

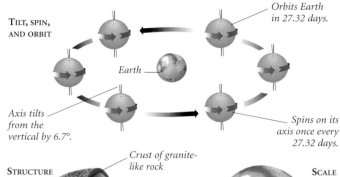

TILT, SPIN, AND ORBIT

Orbits Earth in 27.32 days.

Earth

Axis tilts from the vertical by 6.7°.

Spins on its axis once every 27.32 days.

STRUCTURE

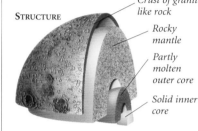

Crust of granite-like rock

Rocky mantle

Partly molten outer core

Solid inner core

SCALE

Moon is just over a quarter the diameter of Earth.

Apogee (farthest point from Earth)

Earth's equator

Moon's orbit

Perigee (nearest point to Earth)

ORBITAL PATH

The Moon's orbit around the Earth is not quite circular, so the distance between them varies. At its closest the Moon is 363,300 km from the centre of the Earth, and at its farthest it is 405,500 km away. The Moon's path is tilted at an angle to Earth's Equator.

SIDEREAL AND LUNAR MONTHS

The 27.32 days it takes for the Moon to orbit the Earth is called a sidereal month. But the Moon actually takes slightly longer – 29.53 days – to complete its cycle of phases, because the Earth is also moving around the Sun. This is the lunar or synodic month, and it is the basis of our calendar months.

Waning crescent: only a thin slice of the Moon's disappearing sunlit part is still visible.

Light from the Sun

New Moon: the Moon is between the Sun and Earth, so the sunlit part is facing away from us. The side facing Earth is in darkness and invisible.

Moon's orbit

LUNAR ECLIPSES

When the full Moon moves through the Earth's shadow, a lunar eclipse occurs. The Earth stops direct sunlight from reaching the Moon, and the Moon's face darkens or is reduced to a faint red disc. In a total eclipse, the entire Moon is in the umbra, the central, darkest part of the shadow. In a partial eclipse, some of the Moon is in the umbra and the rest is in the penumbra, the paler, outer part.

Eclipsed Moon looks red if Earth's atmosphere bends Sun's rays so that they fall on lunar surface.

Path of Moon

A total lunar eclipse can last for more than an hour.

TIME-LAPSE PHOTOGRAPH OF TOTAL LUNAR ECLIPSE

Earth

Umbra

Penumbra

Sunlight

HOW A LUNAR ECLIPSE OCCURS

Earth casts a conical shadow into the night sky.

Total eclipse occurs when all of Moon is in umbra.

Moon can take up to four hours to pass through Earth's shadow completely.

LUNAR ECLIPSES 2000–2010
If the Moon is above your horizon at night, the eclipse will be visible.
21 January 2000 (total)
16 July 2000 (total)
9 January 2001 (total)
5 July 2001 (partial)
16 May 2003 (total)
8–9 November 2003 (total)
4 May 2004 (total)
28 October 2004 (total)
17 October 2005 (partial)
7 September 2006 (partial)
3–4 March 2007 (total)
28 August 2007 (total)
21 February 2008 (total)
16 August 2008 (partial)
31 December 2009 (partial)
26 June 2010 (partial)
21 December 2010 (total)

Werewolves howling

PHASES OF THE MOON

Just like the Earth, one half of the Moon is always bathed in sunlight, while the other is shrouded in darkness. As the Moon circles the Earth, its shape seems to change as we see varying amounts, or phases, of its sunlit part. The phases follow a cycle, from new Moon, when the dark side is facing us, to full Moon, when we see all of the sunlit part, and back to new Moon.

MOON MYTHS

Old folk tales, myths, and superstitions attributed strange powers to the Moon. A full Moon was said to turn some people mad and others into vicious werewolves, and give extra powers to witches. For some people, the Moon's dark and light markings resembled the face of a man or the shape of a hare or rabbit.

Last quarter: we see half of the sunlit part of the Moon. A quarter of the cycle of phases remains to be completed.

Waning gibbous: we can see about three-quarters of the sunlit part, but it is steadily decreasing, or waning.

CYCLE OF THE MOON'S PHASES

Earth

Moon

Line of sight from Earth

Full Moon: the entire sunlit part is visible when the Moon is on the opposite side of the Earth to the Sun.

Waxing gibbous: the amount of the sunlit part we can see continues to increase. About three-quarters is now visible.

Waxing crescent: just a slice of the sunlit part is visible, but it is growing in size. The Moon is said to be waxing.

First quarter: half the sunlit part can be seen when the Moon completes the first quarter of its orbit.

LUNAR INFLUENCES

ALTHOUGH THE MOON IS MUCH SMALLER than the Earth, it still has an influence on its bigger companion. Just as the Earth's gravity pulls on the Moon, the gravity of the Moon pulls on the Earth, stretching it into a slight oval. This distortion barely affects the solid landmasses, but it makes the oceans bulge on either side of the planet, producing tides along the coastlines. The tides, in turn, affect the speed of the Earth's spin and the distance between the Earth and Moon.

TIDES

Twice each day the oceans rise in a high tide and then fall back in a low tide, as the Earth's surface sweeps in and out of the tidal bulges created by the Moon's gravity. This tidal cycle lasts 24 hours and 50 minutes, because the Moon's movement around the Earth means that it arrives above a given spot 50 minutes later each day. The actual height of the tides depends not only on the position of the Moon on its orbit, but also on local geography.

HIGH TIDE, SEVERN ESTUARY, ENGLAND

LOW TIDE, SEVERN ESTUARY, ENGLAND

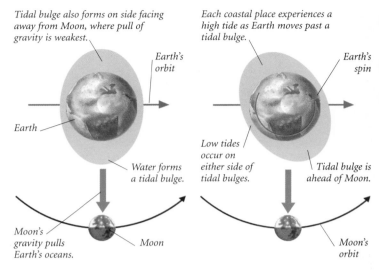

Tidal bulge also forms on side facing away from Moon, where pull of gravity is weakest.

Earth's orbit

Earth

Water forms a tidal bulge.

Moon's gravity pulls Earth's oceans.

Moon

Each coastal place experiences a high tide as Earth moves past a tidal bulge.

Earth's spin

Low tides occur on either side of tidal bulges.

Tidal bulge is ahead of Moon.

Moon's orbit

CAUSES OF TIDES

Water on the side of the Earth closest to the Moon feels the Moon's gravitational pull most strongly, while water on the opposite side of the Earth is least affected. Two bulges of tidal water form and follow the Moon as it orbits the Earth. The Earth's rotation causes the tidal bulges to be carried around slightly ahead of the Moon, rather than directly in line with it.

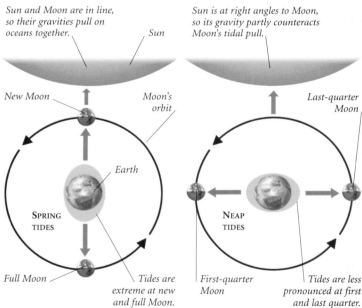

Sun and Moon are in line, so their gravities pull on oceans together.

Sun

New Moon

Moon's orbit

Earth

SPRING TIDES

Full Moon

Tides are extreme at new and full Moon.

Sun is at right angles to Moon, so its gravity partly counteracts Moon's tidal pull.

Last-quarter Moon

NEAP TIDES

First-quarter Moon

Tides are less pronounced at first and last quarter.

SPRING AND NEAP TIDES

At full Moon and new Moon, the Sun, Earth, and Moon are directly in line. The Sun's gravity and the Moon's tidal pull combine to produce the highest high tides and the lowest low tides. These are known as spring tides. When the Moon is at its first- and last-quarter phases, the Sun is at right angles to the Moon. The Sun's gravity partly counteracts the tidal pull of the Moon, resulting in neap tides. These are the lowest high tides and the highest low tides.

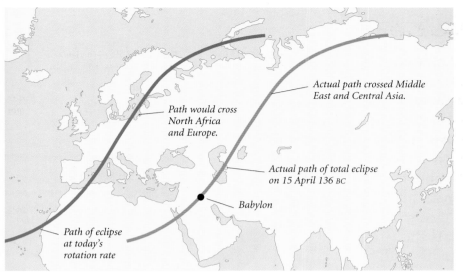

Path would cross
North Africa
and Europe.

Actual path crossed Middle
East and Central Asia.

Actual path of total eclipse
on 15 April 136 BC

Babylon

Path of eclipse
at today's
rotation rate

TOTAL SOLAR ECLIPSE OF 136 BC

TIDAL SLOWING

Friction between the Earth's surface and its tidal bulges is gradually slowing the planet's rotation, so that it is taking longer and longer to spin on its axis. Evidence for this comes from records of past total solar eclipses. The path of the total eclipse of 15 April 136 bc included the city of Babylon in Persia. If the Earth was spinning then at the same rate as it is today, the path of the eclipse would have been much farther west. Coral fossils also provide evidence. Their growth lines reveal that the Earth's day was about three hours shorter 350 million years ago.

FOSSILIZED
CORAL

LASER RANGING

Astronomers can monitor the distance between the Earth and Moon using laser ranging. A laser beam is fired at the Moon and reflects back to Earth. Astronomers know that light travels at about 300,000 km/s, so they calculate the Earth-Moon distance by halving the time taken for the beam to get there and back. The distance can be calculated to within a couple of centimetres.

Moon rotates
on axis while
orbiting.

Day 1

Earth

Day 7

Moon

Day 21

Moon's orbit

A point on the
Moon's nearside
will always face
towards the Earth.

Day 14

MOON'S FACE

The Moon takes the same time to orbit the Earth as it does to spin on its axis. As a result, the same side of the Moon, the nearside, always faces the Earth. The slowing of the Earth's rate of spin means that the Moon is gradually moving away from the Earth and spinning more slowly itself. If this continues, the length of the Earth's day and month would eventually be equal. The same side of the Earth would then always face the Moon.

Mare Orientale

👁 SEEING THE FARSIDE

The effect of libration is easy to see, especially with binoculars. This picture was taken when the maximum amount of the farside surface was visible at the Moon's western edge. Part of the Mare Orientale is visible at the lower left of the Moon's face.

LIBRATION

The Moon's orbit is not quite circular, causing its speed to vary. It moves faster when it is close to the Earth, and slower when farther away: this means that its rotation does not exactly match with its position around its orbit. As a result, we can sometimes see around the edge of the Moon. This effect, libration, helps us to see up to 9% of the Moon's farside, which is usually hidden.

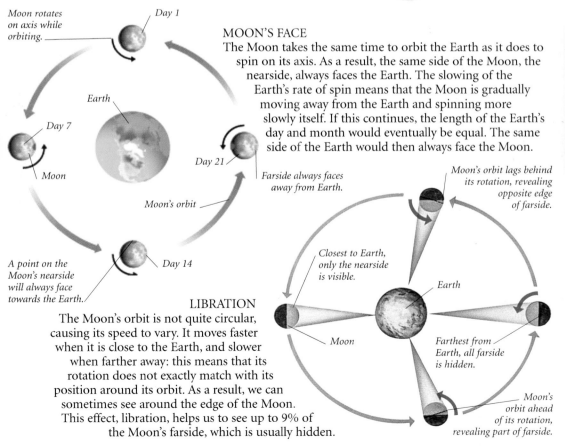

Farside always faces
away from Earth.

Moon's orbit lags behind
its rotation, revealing
opposite edge
of farside.

Closest to Earth,
only the nearside
is visible.

Earth

Moon

Farthest from
Earth, all farside
is hidden.

Moon's
orbit ahead
of its rotation,
revealing part of farside.

FIND OUT MORE

EARTH 84 • MOON 92
NEARSIDE OF THE MOON 100
FARSIDE OF THE MOON 102
SPINNING EARTH 242

MOON'S SURFACE

FROM EARTH, THE MOON LOOKS a very grey world, but even the variations in its greyness can tell us something about it. The lighter areas are older, higher land, covering about 85 per cent of the Moon, while the darker areas are younger, lowland plains. By studying the lunar surface with telescopes, and with the aid of photographs, measurements, and samples taken by space probes and astronauts, astronomers have managed to unravel the Moon's history. They can date the different stages of its development, from its birth 4.6 billion years ago right up to the present day.

Mars-sized body struck Earth a glancing blow.

Ejected material formed a ring around Earth, then clumped together to form the Moon.

ORIGIN OF THE MOON

No one is certain how the Moon was created. It may be that the Moon formed alongside the Earth, or that it was born elsewhere and then captured by the Earth's gravity. The most likely idea is the "big splash" theory, which suggests that a Mars-sized body travelling at high speed collided with the young Earth. Molten material from the two bodies splashed into space around the Earth. This material eventually formed the Moon.

Regolith is the surface layer of dust and rock created by meteorite bombardment.

Mare, which means sea in Latin, is the name given to a dark plain on the Moon.

Craters are bowl-shaped scars left by meteorites. Crater comes from the Greek word for bowl.

Rocky crust is 60–100 km thick.

Highlands, above the level of the maria, were the first parts of the crust to cool and solidify.

Only 7% of the light falling on the Moon is reflected by its surface.

Mountain ranges are uplifted areas of crust that ring some of the maria and large craters.

The largest craters, several hundred kilometres across, are called basins.

LUNAR LANDSCAPE

Two distinctive landscape forms are noticeable on the Moon: dark grey plains, or maria (singular: mare), and lighter highlands. Covered in a vast number of craters, the highlands are the oldest surviving parts of the Moon's crust. The smooth plains are large craters that were filled with lava. They often contain a few smaller, more recent craters, and are usually surrounded by mountains.

HISTORY OF THE MOON

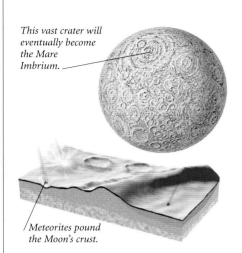

This vast crater will eventually become the Mare Imbrium.

Meteorites pound the Moon's crust.

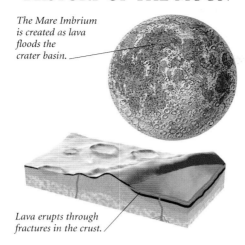

The Mare Imbrium is created as lava floods the crater basin.

Lava erupts through fractures in the crust.

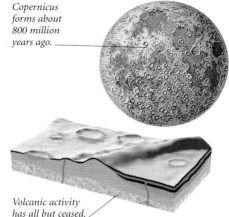

Copernicus forms about 800 million years ago.

Volcanic activity has all but ceased.

1 FOUR BILLION YEARS AGO During the first 750 million years of its life, the Moon went through a period of devastating bombardment by meteorites. Their impact punctured the crust and formed craters all over the surface.

2 THREE BILLION YEARS AGO The rate of bombardment slowed. A time of intense volcanic activity followed as large, deep craters filled with lava (molten rock) welling up from 100 km below the surface. The lava solidified to form the maria.

3 THE MOON TODAY The Moon's surface has changed little in the past 1.6 billion years. A few bright, young craters, such as Copernicus, stand out. Most of the original crust has been destroyed by cratering.

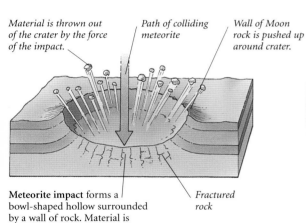

Material is thrown out of the crater by the force of the impact.

Path of colliding meteorite

Wall of Moon rock is pushed up around crater.

Meteorite impact forms a bowl-shaped hollow surrounded by a wall of rock. Material is ejected from the crater hollow.

Fractured rock

Path of ejecta (ejected material)

Secondary craters are formed by falling ejecta.

Secondary cratering occurs when the ejected material lands beyond the crater's edge and creates numerous smaller craters.

Loose debris on crater floor

SURFACE TEMPERATURES
The Moon experiences extremes of temperature. The lunar surface is −180°C at its coldest, but reaches a searing maximum of 110°C. The Moon's lack of atmosphere means that there is nothing to regulate the surface temperature. A sunlit part of the surface is exposed to the full heat of the Sun, but when shadow falls upon it the heat is lost.

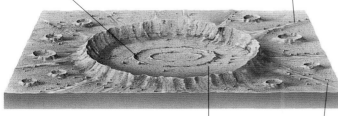

Rings of mountains form as floor of crater "bounces back" after impact.

A crater with rays of ejecta leading off it is known as a ray crater.

Fully formed crater may remain unchanged for millions of years unless it is damaged and reshaped by further impacts. There is no water or weather to wear it away. All craters form in a similar way, but they may have different features, from terraced walls and central peaks to rays and blankets of ejected material.

Blanket of ejecta covers area beyond crater walls.

CRATER FORMATION
The Moon's craters were formed by space rocks crashing into the lunar surface. Anything heading towards the Moon from space will reach the surface, because there is no protective atmosphere to burn it up. A space rock that strikes the surface is called a meteorite. The depth, diameter, and features of the crater will depend on the size and speed of the impacting meteorite.

FIND OUT MORE
NEARSIDE OF THE MOON 100
FARSIDE OF THE MOON 102
MERCURY 104 • ASTEROIDS 146
METEORITES 148

EXPLORING THE MOON

People have dreamed of exploring the moon for hundreds of years. The United States and Russia made the dream a reality in the middle of the 20th century. In 1959, Luna 1 – the first spacecraft to leave the Earth's gravity – was launched towards the Moon. A decade of intense space activity followed as Russian and American probes, robots, and crewed craft were sent to investigate and land on the lunar surface. Other planets and their moons then became the target of space missions, but in the 1990s spacecraft returned to the Moon. Scientists are now planning lunar bases, where astronauts will live and work for months at a time.

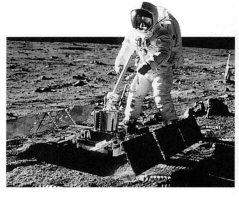

APOLLO SCIENTIFIC EXPERIMENTS
The astronauts left behind experiments, plus equipment to send the results back to Earth. They measured moonquakes (movements in the lunar crust), the soil temperature, the amount of dust in space, and the number of solar particles reaching the Moon.

8 Command Module enters atmosphere 120 km above Earth.

7 Approaching Earth, Command Module separates from Service Module.

3 The rest of the rocket is discarded, while the Command, Service, and Lunar Modules continue to Moon.

4 Lunar Module descends to Moon's surface.

1 Lift-off from Cape Canaveral.

5 Command and Service Modules orbit Moon, waiting for Lunar Module to return.

6 Astronauts link up and Lunar Module is abandoned.

2 Saturn V's engines fire to send the Apollo craft to the Moon.

9 Craft parachutes into ocean.

VOYAGE TO THE MOON
In July 1969, astronauts Neil Armstrong and Buzz Aldrin touched down on the Moon's nearside in the Lunar Module 102 hours and 45 minutes after their Saturn V rocket lifted off from Cape Canaveral, USA. The third crew member, Mike Collins, remained in orbit in the Command and Service Modules. The astronauts met up for the journey home.

APOLLO PROGRAMME
In 1961, the USA set up the Apollo programme, with the aim of sending astronauts to the Moon by the end of the decade. A powerful rocket, the Saturn V, was designed and built. The early Apollo missions tried it out on various parts of the intended journey. Starting with Apollo 11 in 1969, six missions landed on the Moon. Twelve astronauts explored and photographed its surface, and brought 388 kg of rock and soil back to Earth for analysis.

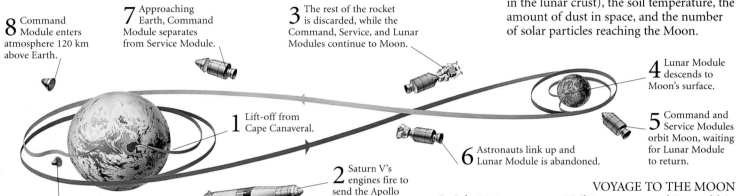

Apollo 15's Jim Irwin

Lunar Module was the astronauts' home on the Moon. The upper part blasted off for the journey back to Earth.

Lunar rover was a jeep-like electric car used by astronauts of Apollos 15, 16, and 17.

CREWED APOLLO MOON LANDINGS

Mission	Date of landing	Landing site	Activity	Time on Moon
Apollo 11	20 July 1969	Mare Tranquillitatis	First astronaut to set foot on Moon	22 hours
Apollo 12	19 November 1969	Oceanus Procellarum	First major scientific experiments set up	32 hours
Apollo 14	5 February 1971	Fra Mauro	First landing in lunar highlands	34 hours
Apollo 15	30 July 1971	Hadley-Apennines	First lunar rover excursions	67 hours
Apollo 16	21 April 1972	Descartes region	Explored highlands	71 hours
Apollo 17	11 December 1972	Taurus-Littrow	Longest and last stay on Moon	75 hours

ICE ON THE MOON

The space probes Clementine, launched in 1994, and Prospector, launched in 1998, found evidence that water ice is hidden in shadowed craters in the Moon's polar regions. The ice probably comes from comets that crashed into the Moon long ago. It could be either melted to supply a future Moon base with water, or broken down into oxygen for astronauts to breathe and into hydrogen for rocket fuel.

Prospector orbited 100 km above the Moon for most of 1998, before lowering to an altitude of just 10 km.

Antennas sent TV pictures back to Earth.

LUNAR PROBES

The Apollo missions are famous for taking astronauts to the Moon, but many remote-controlled craft, such as the US Ranger and Surveyor probes, also made the journey. The Russian Luna probes were the first to reach the Moon, orbit it, photograph its farside, and land on its surface. Lunokhod 1 and 2, two Russian robot vehicles, explored the Moon between 1970 and 1973.

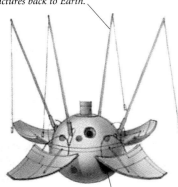

Luna 9 was the first probe to make a successful soft landing on the Moon in 1966.

"Petals" opened after landing to allow antennas to extend.

Lunokhod 1 was a radio-controlled vehicle that trundled 10 km over the Moon's surface in 1970 and 1971.

Radio antenna

Lid with solar cells for power

Cameras allowed scientists on Earth to direct the vehicle.

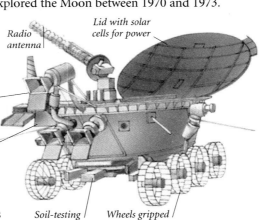

Soil-testing equipment

Wheels gripped soft lunar soil.

LUNAR FIRSTS

- Luna 2 became the first space probe to hit the Moon when it crash-landed on the surface in 1959. The next month, Luna 3 took the first photographs of the farside.

- Ranger 7 crashed on the Moon in 1964 and returned the first close-up images, taking 4,308 photographs.

- In 1966, Luna 9 sent back the first television pictures from the lunar surface.

MOON ROCK

- Apollo 8 carried the first astronauts around the Moon in 1968, making 10 orbits.

- In 1969, Neil Armstrong became the first person to walk on the Moon. His Apollo 11 mission brought back rock and soil samples.

- In 1970, Luna 16 made the first automated retrieval of Moon samples.

MOON BASES

Within 50 years, there may be permanent bases on the Moon, with telescopes for studying the stars, and mines for extracting the Moon's rich mineral resources. Such bases could also be stopping-off points for explorers travelling farther into the Solar System, or even unusual holiday destinations for space tourists.

Communication dishes relay messages to and from Earth.

Lunar cars carry inhabitants over the surface.

Solar panels provide the living quarters with power.

Living quarters buried under the soil protect Moon-dwellers from the extreme temperatures and bursts of solar radiation.

NEARSIDE OF THE MOON

THE DOMINANT FEATURES on the Moon's nearside – the side that always faces the Earth – are the dark maria, which early astronomers thought were seas. These lava-filled basins formed when molten rock seeped through the Moon's crust to fill depressions left by meteorite impacts. Even the largest – Oceanus Procellarum – is smaller than the Mediterranean Sea. Everywhere the surface is pockmarked by craters, including inside the maria and on the mountains that surround them. All the landings by spacecraft have been on the Moon's nearside.

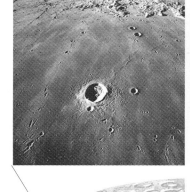

MARE IMBRIUM
This huge mare formed about 3.85 billion years ago, when a meteorite impact created a large basin, hurling material over much of the nearside. During the next billion years, it filled with lava from inside the Moon.

Aristarchus, a 37-km-diameter crater, is the brightest point on the entire Moon.

Oceanus Procellarum is a large mare, but not as well-preserved as the Mare Imbrium.

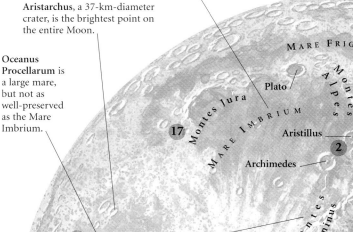

MONTES APENNINUS
The Montes Apenninus are one of the most impressive ranges of lunar mountains. Along with the Montes Carpatus, Caucasus, Jura, and Alpes, they make up the walls of the Mare Imbrium, as a broken ring of mountains around its edge. They formed as the meteorite that produced the mare struck the lunar surface, forcing up the surrounding land.

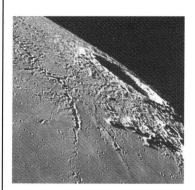

COPERNICUS
One of the best examples of a lunar ray crater is Copernicus. It is 107 km in diameter and nearly 4 km deep, with rays of bright rock fragments leading out from it. Young craters and central peaks lie inside it, and its edge is well defined by terraced walls. Analysis of ray material collected by the crew of Apollo 12 showed it to be 850 million years old.

NEARSIDE FEATURES
The extensive maria, the darkest of the nearside features, lie between 2 and 5 km below the usual surface level. The most recently formed features are the bright ray craters. The southern area – the roughest part of the nearside surface – is mainly high, cratered land with a handful of large, walled plains. Both polar regions are highland areas.

TYCHO
The ray crater Tycho, formed 100 million years ago, contains central mountain peaks and is ringed by high, terraced walls. Its rays are only visible under direct light around the time of full Moon.

Map labels
MARE FRIG
Montes Alpes
Plato
Montes Jura
MARE IMBRIUM
17
Aristillus
2
Archimedes
Montes Apenninus
13
Oceanus Procellarum
Montes Carpatus
Eratosthenes
Kepler
9
Encke
Hevelius
Flamsteed
1
12 3
6
14
Fra Mauro
Grimaldi
7
Ptolemaeus
9
MARE NUBIUM
Gassendi
MARE HUMORUM
MARE ORIENTALE
7
Schickard
Longomontanus
Clavius

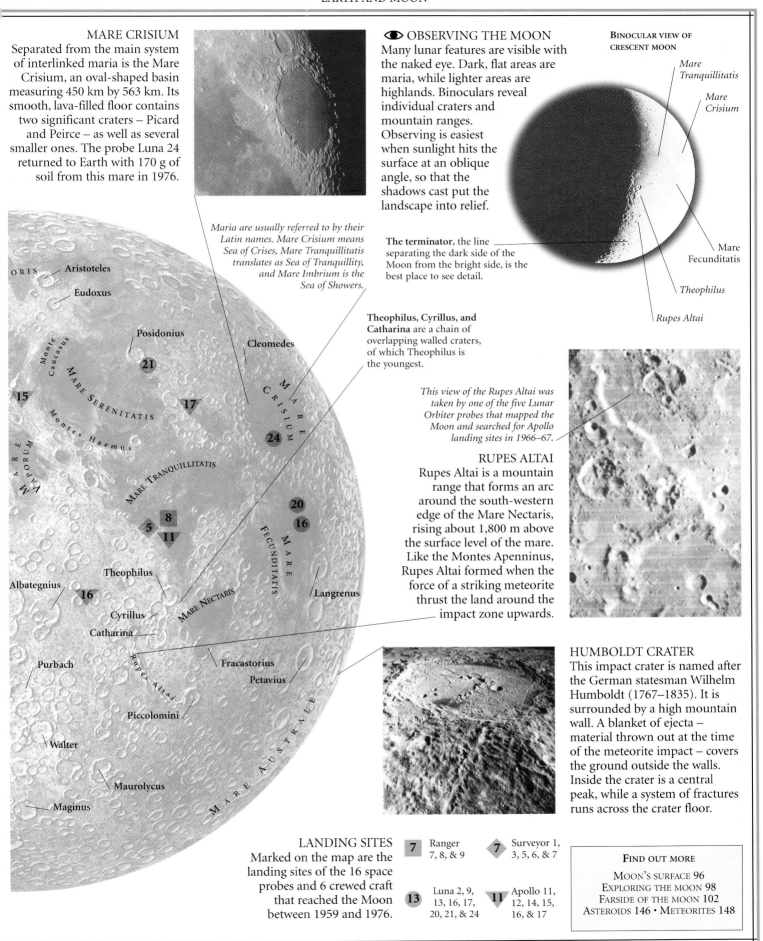

MARE CRISIUM

Separated from the main system of interlinked maria is the Mare Crisium, an oval-shaped basin measuring 450 km by 563 km. Its smooth, lava-filled floor contains two significant craters – Picard and Peirce – as well as several smaller ones. The probe Luna 24 returned to Earth with 170 g of soil from this mare in 1976.

Maria are usually referred to by their Latin names. Mare Crisium means Sea of Crises, Mare Tranquillitatis translates as Sea of Tranquillity, and Mare Imbrium is the Sea of Showers.

☉ OBSERVING THE MOON

Many lunar features are visible with the naked eye. Dark, flat areas are maria, while lighter areas are highlands. Binoculars reveal individual craters and mountain ranges. Observing is easiest when sunlight hits the surface at an oblique angle, so that the shadows cast put the landscape into relief.

The terminator, the line separating the dark side of the Moon from the bright side, is the best place to see detail.

BINOCULAR VIEW OF CRESCENT MOON

Mare Tranquillitatis

Mare Crisium

Mare Fecunditatis

Theophilus

Rupes Altai

Theophilus, Cyrillus, and Catharina are a chain of overlapping walled craters, of which Theophilus is the youngest.

This view of the Rupes Altai was taken by one of the five Lunar Orbiter probes that mapped the Moon and searched for Apollo landing sites in 1966–67.

RUPES ALTAI

Rupes Altai is a mountain range that forms an arc around the south-western edge of the Mare Nectaris, rising about 1,800 m above the surface level of the mare. Like the Montes Apenninus, Rupes Altai formed when the force of a striking meteorite thrust the land around the impact zone upwards.

HUMBOLDT CRATER

This impact crater is named after the German statesman Wilhelm Humboldt (1767–1835). It is surrounded by a high mountain wall. A blanket of ejecta – material thrown out at the time of the meteorite impact – covers the ground outside the walls. Inside the crater is a central peak, while a system of fractures runs across the crater floor.

LANDING SITES

Marked on the map are the landing sites of the 16 space probes and 6 crewed craft that reached the Moon between 1959 and 1976.

7 Ranger 7, 8, & 9

7 Surveyor 1, 3, 5, 6, & 7

13 Luna 2, 9, 13, 16, 17, 20, 21, & 24

11 Apollo 11, 12, 14, 15, 16, & 17

FIND OUT MORE

MOON'S SURFACE 96
EXPLORING THE MOON 98
FARSIDE OF THE MOON 102
ASTEROIDS 146 • METEORITES 148

Map labels: ORIS, Aristoteles, Eudoxus, Posidonius, Monte Caucasus, Cleomedes, MARE SERENITATIS, Montes Haemus, MARE VAPORUM, MARE TRANQUILLITATIS, MARE CRISIUM, MARE FECUNDITATIS, MARE NECTARIS, Langrenus, Theophilus, Cyrillus, Catharina, Albategnius, Rupes Altai, Fracastorius, Petavius, Purbach, Piccolomini, Walter, Maurolycus, Maginus, MARE AUSTRALE

FARSIDE OF THE MOON

THE FARSIDE OF THE MOON is always turned away from the Earth. Its appearance remained a mystery until 1959, when the Russian space probe Luna 3 was able to travel behind the Moon and send back the first photographs. Although the farside looks similar to the Moon's nearside, there are obvious differences. It has few maria, because the lunar crust is thicker than on the nearside, making it difficult for lava to seep through into the impact basins left by colliding space rocks. The farside is also more heavily cratered. Astronomers are puzzled as to why this should be.

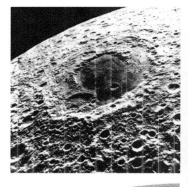

MARE MOSCOVIENSE
One of the few maria lying entirely on the farside, the 277-km diameter Mare Moscoviense is smaller than large farside crater basins such as Apollo. Its dark floor makes it stand out clearly against its surroundings.

Gagarin is a crater commemorating Yuri Gagarin, the first person to go into space.

TSIOLKOVSKY
A prominent farside feature is Tsiolkovsky, whose dark floor of solidified lava makes it halfway between a crater and a mare. It is 185 km across, with a large, mountain-like structure in its centre. The area close to Tsiolkovsky is heavily cratered. The surface material in this area is thought to be some of the oldest on the Moon.

VAN DE GRAAFF
This irregularly shaped crater is about 233 km in diameter and has several smaller craters inside it. Rather surprisingly for such a large crater, Van de Graaff is only 4 km deep. The basin has a stronger magnetism and is more radioactive than the land surrounding it, which may be because volcanic rock lies buried under the surface of the crater.

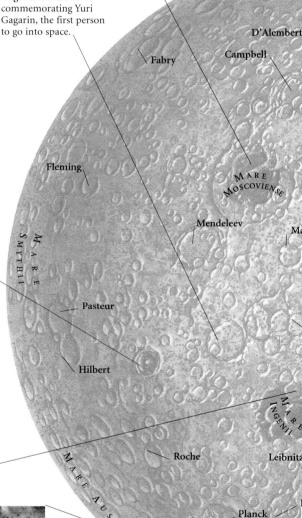

Schwarzschild
D'Alembert
Fabry
Campbell
Fleming
MARE MOSCOVIENSE
Mendeleev
Mandel'shtam
MARE SMYTHII
Pasteur
Heaviside
Aitken
Hilbert
MARE INGENII
Roche
Leibnitz
MARE AUSTRALE
Planck
Poincaré
Schrödinger

FARSIDE FEATURES
The two prominent maria on the farside are the Mare Orientale and Mare Moscoviense. Craters abound but they tend to be smaller and not as dark as those on the nearside. The most noticeable craters are the circular depressions such as Hertzsprung, Apollo, and Korolev. Hertzsprung's outer ring is broken by smaller craters.

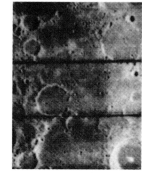

MARE AUSTRALE
This mare creeps into both nearside and farside views of the Moon. Its shape is poorly defined. It is probably an area of dark volcanic rock rather than a true impact basin.

KOROLEV

Measuring 437 km across, the Korolev Crater is among the largest ringed formations on the farside of the Moon. It is one of 10 craters on the farside that exceed 200 km in diameter. Many smaller craters lie inside Korolev. One of these, Krylov, has a central peak and measures about 50 km across.

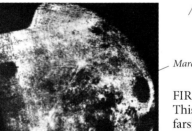

Krylov

Many of the farside craters are named after scientists and philosophers. Joule refers to the English physicist James Joule (1818–89).

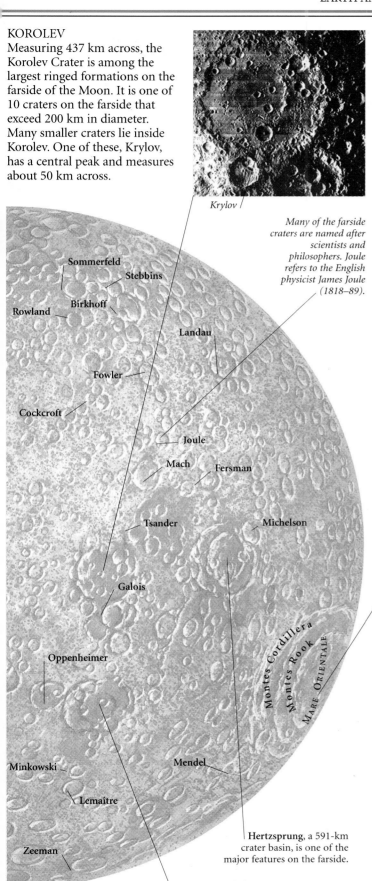

Sommerfeld
Stebbins
Birkhoff
Rowland
Landau
Fowler
Cockcroft
Joule
Mach
Fersman
Tsander
Michelson
Galois
Oppenheimer
Montes Cordillera
Montes Rook
MARE ORIENTALE
Minkowski
Mendel
Lemaitre
Zeeman

Hertzsprung, a 591-km crater basin, is one of the major features on the farside.

Apollo crater was named in honour of the Apollo missions to the Moon.

POLAR REGIONS

The north and south poles were the last parts of the Moon to be mapped. This was done by the space probe Clementine in 1994. Mosaic maps, made by assembling the thousands of images that Clementine sent back, suggest that some of the polar craters are permanently shadowed from the Sun's rays.

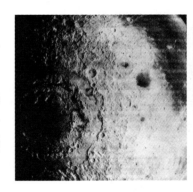

LUNAR SOUTH POLE

In permanently shadowed areas, ice exists in the soil.

Schrödinger Crater

Mare Moscoviense

FIRST FARSIDE VIEW

This photograph of the Moon's farside was taken in October 1959 by Luna 3. The image was not good by today's standards, but it was still clear enough for large features to be identified, including the Mare Moscoviense.

MARE ORIENTALE

This huge mare, the Moon's youngest, straddles the boundary between the farside and nearside. Measuring 327 km across, it is surrounded by concentric rings of mountains with a diameter of 900 km. Beyond them lies ejected material, which has covered earlier craters. Only the centre of the impact basin filled with lava.

MAPPING THE MOON

- In 1609, Englishman Thomas Harriot (1560–1621) drew a Moon map based on observations made with his telescope. A year later, Galileo's maps drew attention to the Moon's features.

- 18th-century astronomers, using new, improved telescopes, made progressively more detailed maps of the lunar surface.

LUNAR ORBITER SPACE PROBE

- The first photographs of the Moon were taken in 1840. Photographic Moon atlases were published in the late 19th century.

- Detailed images were sent back by US Lunar Orbiter probes in the 1960s, and by Clementine in 1994.

FIND OUT MORE

MOON'S SURFACE 96 • EXPLORING THE MOON 98
NEARSIDE OF THE MOON 100 • ASTEROIDS 146 • METEORITES 148

MERCURY

Scorched and blasted by solar radiation, Mercury is the planet closest to the Sun. This dry, rocky world has an atmosphere so thin that it barely exists. Of all the planets in the Solar System, Mercury travels around the Sun the fastest, but spins slowly on its axis. From the Earth, faint markings can be seen on the planet's surface, but our only close-up views date from the 1970s, when the space probe Mariner 10 flew by and revealed Mercury to be a heavily cratered world. Astronomers are puzzled as to why this small planet has such a vast iron core.

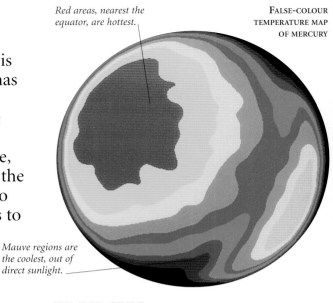

Red areas, nearest the equator, are hottest.

FALSE-COLOUR TEMPERATURE MAP OF MERCURY

Mauve regions are the coolest, out of direct sunlight.

SCARRED SURFACE

About 4 billion years ago, in the early history of the Solar System, the young Mercury's surface was punctured by meteorite impacts. Lava flooded out from the interior to form extensive plains, giving the planet an appearance that, at first glance, resembles the Moon. With no wind or water to shape its crater-scarred landscape, Mercury has remained virtually unchanged since then.

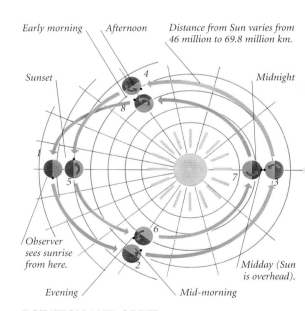

Craters vary from a few metres to hundreds of kilometres across.

Younger craters are surrounded by light-coloured streaks of ejected material.

Brontë crater

Craters are generally shallower than on the Moon. Material thrown out by impacts did not travel as far as it did on the Moon, because Mercury's gravity is stronger.

In this image taken by Mariner 10, ultraviolet light from the Sun causes the surface to look bleached.

TEMPERATURE

Roasted by its neighbour, the Sun, Mercury has the greatest variation in day and night temperatures of any planet. The average surface temperature is 167°C, but when the planet is closest to the Sun, the temperature can soar to above 450°C. At night, it cools quickly, since Mercury's atmosphere is too thin to retain the heat, and temperatures fall to as low as –180°C.

Early morning *Afternoon* *Distance from Sun varies from 46 million to 69.8 million km.*

Sunset *Midnight*

Midday (Sun is overhead).

Observer sees sunrise from here.

Evening *Mid-morning*

ROTATION AND ORBIT

Mercury turns slowly on its axis, taking nearly 59 days to complete one rotation, but it speeds along on its path around the Sun, making one orbit in just 88 days. For an observer standing on Mercury, these two motions would produce an interval of 176 days between one sunrise and the next. A person watching a sunrise from position 1 would have to wait to return to position 1 before seeing the Sun rise again. During this time, the planet would have completed two orbits of the Sun.

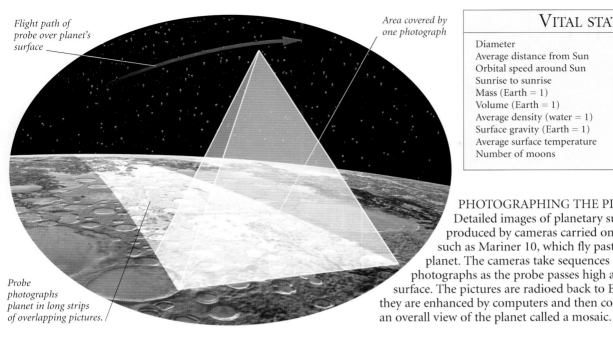

Flight path of probe over planet's surface

Area covered by one photograph

Probe photographs planet in long strips of overlapping pictures.

VITAL STATISTICS

Diameter	4,880 km
Average distance from Sun	57.9 million km
Orbital speed around Sun	47.87 km/s
Sunrise to sunrise	176 days
Mass (Earth = 1)	0.06
Volume (Earth = 1)	0.06
Average density (water = 1)	5.43
Surface gravity (Earth = 1)	0.38
Average surface temperature	167°C
Number of moons	0

PHOTOGRAPHING THE PLANETS

Detailed images of planetary surfaces are produced by cameras carried on space probes such as Mariner 10, which fly past or orbit a planet. The cameras take sequences of overlapping photographs as the probe passes high above the surface. The pictures are radioed back to Earth, where they are enhanced by computers and then combined to give an overall view of the planet called a mosaic.

MERCURY AT A GLANCE

A dense, fast-moving, rocky planet with a large metal core, Mercury has weak gravity and a thin atmosphere. It is the second smallest planet after Pluto.

TILT, SPIN, AND ORBIT

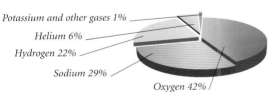

Orbits Sun in 87.97 days.

Spins on its axis once every 58.65 days.

Axis of rotation is almost vertical.

ATMOSPHERE

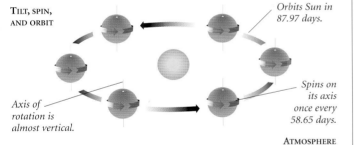

Potassium and other gases 1%
Helium 6%
Hydrogen 22%
Sodium 29%
Oxygen 42%

STRUCTURE

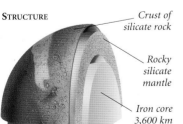

Crust of silicate rock

Rocky silicate mantle

Iron core 3,600 km in diameter

SCALE

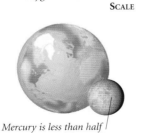

Mercury is less than half the diameter of the Earth.

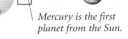

Sun

Mercury is the first planet from the Sun.

LOCATER

The area of space affected by a planet's magnetism is called the magnetosphere.

MAGNETIC CORE

Like the Earth, Mercury has a magnetic field, but it is very weak – only about 1% as strong as the Earth's. Mercury's magnetism is produced by its huge iron core, which stretches three-quarters of the way to the surface. Astronomers believe the core is made of solid iron, perhaps surrounded by a thin layer of liquid iron and sulphur.

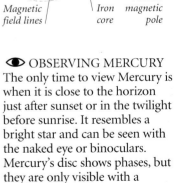

North magnetic pole

Axis of spin

Magnetic field lines

Iron core

South magnetic pole

OBSERVING MERCURY

The only time to view Mercury is when it is close to the horizon just after sunset or in the twilight before sunrise. It resembles a bright star and can be seen with the naked eye or binoculars. Mercury's disc shows phases, but they are only visible with a moderately powerful telescope.

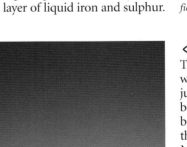

Mercury

FIND OUT MORE

PROBES TO THE PLANETS 80
BIRTH OF SOLAR SYSTEM 82
EARTH 84 · MOON'S SURFACE 96
IMPACTS 150

MERCURY'S SURFACE

MERCURY IS NEVER FAR FROM THE SUN in Earth's sky, so it is a difficult planet to observe. Even a space-based observatory, such as the Hubble Space Telescope, cannot provide views of Mercury's surface, since the Sun's rays would damage the telescope's sensitive instruments. With the aid of protective sunshields, the space probe Mariner 10 succeeded in producing detailed images of Mercury. Its flight path allowed it to photograph only part of the surface, leaving more than half still to be explored.

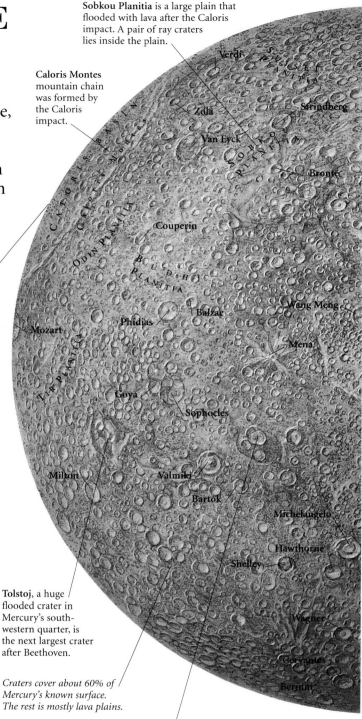

Sobkou Planitia is a large plain that flooded with lava after the Caloris impact. A pair of ray craters lies inside the plain.

Caloris Montes mountain chain was formed by the Caloris impact.

CALORIS BASIN

This enormous crater is about 1,300 km wide. It was formed about 3.6 billion years ago when an asteroid-sized space rock about 100 km across crashed into Mercury. Although the centre of the Caloris Basin has yet to be photographed, the rest of the crater floor is known to be dotted with smaller and more recent impact craters.

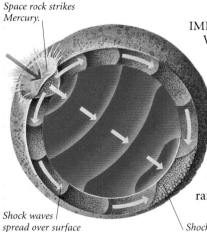

Space rock strikes Mercury.

IMPACT SHOCK WAVES

When the vast space rock that formed the Caloris Basin struck Mercury, the planet was still young. Its crust and upper mantle had not yet stabilized and were still cooling and compressing. The shock waves from the impact rippled through the planet, buckling the surface to form ranges of hills and mountains.

Shock waves spread over surface and through planet.

Shock waves converge and crumple surface opposite the impact site.

Tolstoj, a huge flooded crater in Mercury's south-western quarter, is the next largest crater after Beethoven.

Craters cover about 60% of Mercury's known surface. The rest is mostly lava plains.

CRATERED WORLD

Mercury is a cratered world, its surface battered and shaped by the impact of thousands of meteorites. One massive impact produced the Caloris Basin. Surrounding the Basin is a ring of mountains, the Caloris Montes. Beyond this are areas covered in rock ejected from the crater by the impact, and smooth, lava-flooded plains. Mercury's surface is also crossed by many wrinkles, ridges, and cracks formed as the young planet cooled and shrank.

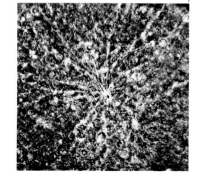

BEETHOVEN

The crater Beethoven is the second largest surface feature. Its 643-km-wide floor was flooded with volcanic material and pitted by later meteorite impacts. Many of Mercury's craters are named after men and women of the arts – in this case, the German composer Ludwig van Beethoven (1770–1827).

This part of Mercury and all of its opposite side are unmapped, because they were not photographed by Mariner 10.

Borealis Planitia
Monteverdi
Rubens
Vyasa
Stravinsky
Velázquez
Holbein
Al-Hamadhani
Praxiteles
Kuan Han-Ch'ing
Mussorgskij
Proust
Wren
Lermontov
Li Po
Glotto
Vivaldi
Yeats
Handel
Polygnotus
Homer
Machaut
Titian
Renoir
Repin
Matisse
Ibsen
Chekhov
Unkei
Bramante
Schubert
Coleridge
Discovery Rupes
Boccaccio

Solar panel

Magnetic sensor

MARINER 10

In 1974 and 1975, Mariner 10 made three fly-bys of Mercury, coming within 327 km of the surface. The images it sent back revealed features as small as 1.5 km across. It found that the planet has a magnetic field.

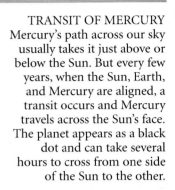

Mercury

TRANSIT OF MERCURY

Mercury's path across our sky usually takes it just above or below the Sun. But every few years, when the Sun, Earth, and Mercury are aligned, a transit occurs and Mercury travels across the Sun's face. The planet appears as a black dot and can take several hours to cross from one side of the Sun to the other.

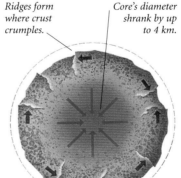

DISCOVERY RUPES

Towering up to 2 km above its surroundings, the Discovery Rupes is a vast ridge that stretches for about 500 km across Mercury's surface. So far, 16 similar features have been found, 8 of which lie in the south-eastern quarter of the planet.

Ridges form where crust crumples.

Core's diameter shrank by up to 4 km.

Petrarch is one of the younger craters on Mercury. Its smooth floor contains a few craters of more recent origin.

LIFE OF MERCURY

- Mercury was formed about 4.6 billion years ago. Over the next 700 million years, the surface became cratered by space rocks.

- By 500 million years later, the planet had cooled and shrunk to its present size.

- Mercury was known to people in ancient times. Observations in the 17th century showed that Mercury has phases.

- Mercury's 59-day rotation period was established in 1965 by bouncing radar waves off the surface.

- In 1974, Mariner 10 sent back the first detailed images of the planet's surface.

- In 1991, radar was used to study Mercury's unseen areas.

SOUTH POLAR REGION

Mercury's polar regions include areas that are always shaded from the Sun's heat. Scientists studying these regions by reflecting radar off them believe there may be water ice at Mercury's poles. The findings need to be confirmed because another substance, such as sulphur, could produce similar results.

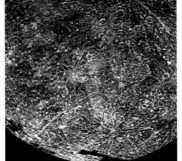

WRINKLES AND RIDGES

The young Mercury used to spin faster than it does today, and was hotter. Wrinkles formed on its surface as its spin slowed. And as Mercury cooled, it shrank. Great ridges formed as the crust crumpled up around the shrinking interior.

VENUS

CALLED AN INFERIOR PLANET because it orbits closer to the Sun than the Earth does, Venus is a sphere of rock similar in size to the Earth – but there the comparison ends. Venus is a dark, hostile world of volcanoes and suffocating atmosphere. Its average temperature is higher than that of any other planet. From Earth, we can see only the planet's cloud tops. Hidden under this thick blanket of gas is a landscape moulded by volcanic eruption.

CLOUD-TOP VIEW OF VENUS

Western elongation: Venus visible before sunrise.

Inferior conjunction: Venus lost in Sun's glare.

Venus

Sun

Earth

Superior conjunction: Venus lost in Sun's glare.

Eastern elongation: Venus visible after sunset.

ORBIT OF VENUS
Venus orbits closer to the Sun than Earth does, so it sometimes passes between Earth and the Sun. Around the time of this inferior conjunction, Venus is lost from view in the Sun's glare. Venus is brightest at its elongations, when it is farthest from the Sun in the sky. At these times, the planet is visible either after sunset or before sunrise.

SURFACE FEATURES
The Venusian surface has changed greatly during the planet's life. The present surface is only about half a billion years old. The rocky landscape we see now was formed by intense volcanic activity – a process that still continues today. Rolling volcanic plains with highland regions cover much of the planet. The most extensive region of highland is Aphrodite Terra, which has several large volcanoes, including Maat Mons.

Maat Mons, one of the largest volcanoes on Venus, rises 9 km from the surrounding land and measures 200 km across.

Computer-generated view using radar images from Magellan space probe.

Lava flows extend for hundreds of kilometres across the plains at the base of Maat Mons.

Pancake domes are volcanoes with flat tops and steep sides. These, in Alpha Regio, average 20 km in diameter and 750 m in height.

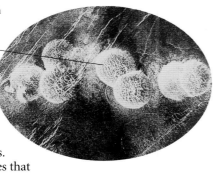

VOLCANOES

Volcanic activity is evident all over Venus. Its surface has long lava flows, volcanic craters, and dome- and shield-shaped volcanoes. There are 156 large volcanoes that measure more than 100 km across, nearly 300 with diameters of between 20 and 100 km, and at least 500 clusters of smaller volcanoes. Pancake dome and arachnoid volcanoes are notable for their unusual shapes.

Arachnoids are volcanoes with a spider-like appearance. This volcano, in Eistla Regio, is about 35 km across. Ridged slopes circle the rim of the concave summit.

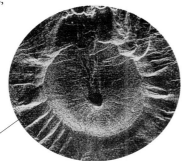

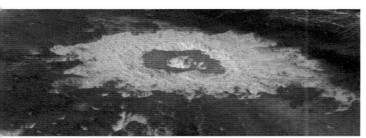

IMPACT CRATER IN LAVINIA PLANITIA

IMPACT CRATERS

Over 900 impact craters have so far been identified on Venus. They range in size from 1.5 to 280 km across. More than 60 per cent of these are undamaged and in their original condition. Their rings are sharply defined and they are still surrounded by material ejected by the meteorite impact. A handful of the remaining 40 per cent of craters have been damaged by volcanic lava. The rest have been altered by the cracking and movement of Venus's crust.

VITAL STATISTICS

Diameter	12,104 km
Average distance from Sun	108.2 million km
Orbital speed around Sun	35.02 km/s
Sunrise to sunrise	117 days
Mass (Earth = 1)	0.82
Volume (Earth = 1)	0.86
Average density (water = 1)	5.2
Surface gravity (Earth = 1)	0.9
Average surface temperature	464°C
Number of moons	0

FIND OUT MORE

SOLAR SYSTEM 78 • PROBES TO THE PLANETS 80
VENUSIAN ATMOSPHERE 110 • VENUSIAN SURFACE 112
MARS 114 • ASTEROIDS 146 • IMPACTS 150

VENUS AT A GLANCE

Venus is a rocky planet with a structure and size similar to Earth's. Its atmosphere helps to make it the hottest planet of all. It spins slowly, in the opposite direction to most planets.

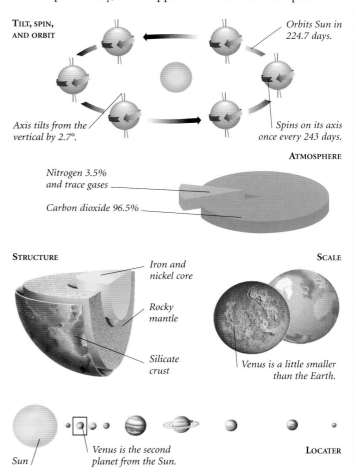

TILT, SPIN, AND ORBIT

Orbits Sun in 224.7 days.

Axis tilts from the vertical by 2.7°.

Spins on its axis once every 243 days.

ATMOSPHERE

Nitrogen 3.5% and trace gases

Carbon dioxide 96.5%

STRUCTURE

Iron and nickel core

Rocky mantle

Silicate crust

SCALE

Venus is a little smaller than the Earth.

Sun

Venus is the second planet from the Sun.

LOCATER

Belts of narrow ridges rise a few hundred metres and stretch for hundreds of kilometres across the plain.

VENUSIAN PLAINS

Over three-quarters of Venus is covered by plains that were largely formed by volcanic processes. The plains are marked by volcanic and impact craters, lava flows, and features sculpted by the Venusian wind.

Lavinia Planitia is one of the main plains of Venus.

VENUSIAN ATMOSPHERE

WHEN VENUS AND EARTH WERE YOUNG, some 4 billion years ago, their atmospheres were similar. Today, things are very different. The Venusian atmosphere, with a mass 100 times greater than the Earth's, is so thick that you would never see the stars from its surface. It is mainly carbon dioxide, but also includes sulphur dust and droplets of sulphuric acid from the planet's many volcanic eruptions. This hostile atmosphere makes Venus a hot, gloomy, suffocating world.

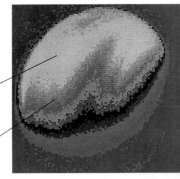

Orange shows the presence of sulphur dioxide.

Bands show pattern of cloud-top movement.

VENUS IN ULTRAVIOLET
The Pioneer Venus space probe took many ultraviolet pictures of the planet. These images showed the cloud patterns at the top of the atmosphere and helped scientists to understand its composition.

STRUCTURE OF THE ATMOSPHERE
Immediately above the Venusian surface is a clear region of atmosphere, stretching up to a height of 40 km or so. Above this is a thick, unbroken cloud layer rising a further 20 km. The clouds, which contain dust and sulphuric acid, stop direct sunlight from reaching the surface, making Venus permanently overcast. Finally, there is a clear, sparse layer of atmosphere stretching at least another 20 km.

INFRARED IMAGE OF CLOUDS OVER NORTH POLE

North pole

Blue collar is about 35°C cooler than surrounding clouds.

POLAR COLLAR
Pioneer's infrared images revealed large temperature variations in the clouds. This overhead view shows a collar of cool cloud (coloured blue) surrounding a warmer region of cloud centred on Venus's north pole.

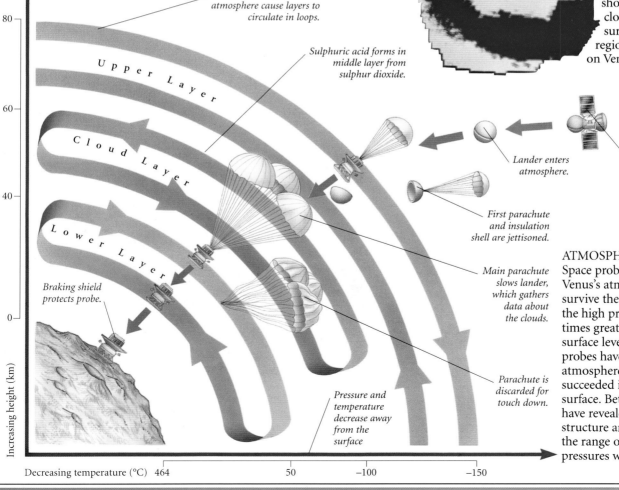

Temperature differences in atmosphere cause layers to circulate in loops.

Sulphuric acid forms in middle layer from sulphur dioxide.

Upper Layer

Cloud Layer

Lower Layer

Braking shield protects probe.

DESCENT OF RUSSIAN VENERA SPACE PROBE

Lander enters atmosphere.

The combined orbiter and lander circles the planet before separating.

First parachute and insulation shell are jettisoned.

Main parachute slows lander, which gathers data about the clouds.

ATMOSPHERIC STUDY
Space probes sent to fly through Venus's atmosphere have to survive the corrosive clouds and the high pressure, which is 90 times greater than the Earth's at surface level. A number of probes have entered the atmosphere, and some have succeeded in reaching the surface. Between them, they have revealed the atmosphere's structure and composition, and the range of temperatures and pressures within it.

Parachute is discarded for touch down.

Pressure and temperature decrease away from the surface

Increasing height (km)

80

60

40

0

Decreasing temperature (°C)   464   50   −100   −150

CLOUD-TOP PATTERNS

The atmosphere moves quickly around the rocky planet. Ultraviolet cloud-top images show that the clouds move in an east-to-west direction and circle the planet in about 4 days. The clouds move in the same direction as the planet spins, but 60 times faster, at up to 350 km/h. Lower down, atmospheric motion is much slower, and the surface winds barely reach 10 km/h.

These ultraviolet images were taken by Pioneer Venus orbiter in May and June 1980, from a distance of about 50,000 km.

2 MAY 1980
AT 7:19 PM

3 MAY 1980
AT 0:29 AM

Patterns change quickly as clouds speed over surface.

Hot gases from the equator spiral up to polar region.

CLOUD MOVEMENT

The Sun's heat drives the clouds around Venus. As gases in the equatorial part of the atmosphere are warmed by the Sun, they rise and move towards the cooler polar regions. The newly arrived gases sink to the lower cloud layer as they cool. They move back to the equator and the process starts again.

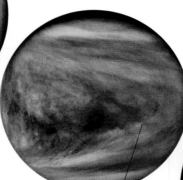

3 MAY 1980
AT 5:07 AM

Cloud-top movement forms Y- or V-shaped patterns.

◉ PHASES OF VENUS

Like the Moon, Venus has phases, which means that we see differing amounts of its sunlit side. We never see the full Venus, because when the whole of the sunlit side points towards the Earth, Venus is obscured by the Sun. As it moves around the Sun and gets closer, it grows larger in the Earth's sky, but we see less and less of its sunlit side.

Cloud tops move from right to left in these images.

7 JUNE 1980
AT 1:04 AM

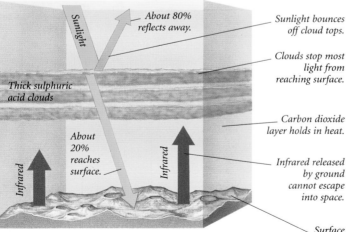

About 80% reflects away.

Sunlight

Sunlight bounces off cloud tops.

Clouds stop most light from reaching surface.

Thick sulphuric acid clouds

About 20% reaches surface.

Carbon dioxide layer holds in heat.

Infrared

Infrared

Infrared released by ground cannot escape into space.

Surface temperature is 464°C, about 400°C higher than it would be without an atmosphere.

GREENHOUSE EFFECT

Less than a quarter of the sunlight falling on Venus reaches the surface. Light that gets through the clouds warms the ground which, in turn, releases the heat in the form of infrared radiation. Like glass trapping heat in a greenhouse, the atmosphere traps the infrared radiation, so the temperature on Venus builds up and is always very hot.

PROBES TO VENUS

Name	Type	Arrived	Achievement
Mariner 2	Fly-by	Dec 1962	Found carbon dioxide in atmosphere
Venera 4	Atmosphere	Oct 1967	First data returned from atmosphere
Veneras 5 and 6	Atmosphere	May 1969	Tested atmosphere, assumed to have impacted with surface
Veneras 7 and 8	Lander	Dec 1970 July 1972	First landers to send data back from Venusian surface
Veneras 9 and 10	Orbiter/ lander	Oct 1975	Landers returned one image each of rock-strewn surface
Pioneer-Venus 1	Orbiter	Dec 1978	First global radar map
Pioneer-Venus 2	Multiprobe	Dec 1978	Five probes studied composition and structure of atmosphere
Veneras 11 and 12	Fly-by/ lander	Dec 1978	Landers reached surface, but television cameras failed
Veneras 13 and 14	Lander	Mar 1982	First colour pictures from surface; first soil samples analysed
Veneras 15 and 16	Orbiter	Oct 1983	Radar images of surface
Vegas 1 and 2	Atmosphere/ lander	June 1985	Balloon probes investigated atmosphere; landers tested surface
Magellan	Orbiter	Aug 1990	Radar imaging of surface

FIND OUT MORE

PROBES TO THE PLANETS 80 • EARTH'S ATMOSPHERE 88 • MOON 92
VENUS 108 • VENUSIAN SURFACE 112 • JUPITER'S ATMOSPHERE 124

VENUSIAN SURFACE

ALTHOUGH VENUS IS THE CLOSEST PLANET to the Earth, its surface is perpetually hidden by cloud. Only in the last 30 years have scientists succeeded in "seeing" through its cloud layers, using radar techniques similar to airport radar that can locate aircraft through cloud and fog. The data collected by Earth-based instruments and orbiting space probes have been combined to produce a global map of the planet. The most detailed data came from Magellan, the most recent and successful of the orbiters. As this view of one side of Venus shows, it is a planet of volcanic plains with some highland regions.

MAXWELL MONTES
In the middle of Ishtar Terra, a highland region about the size of Australia, is the steep Maxwell Montes mountain range – the highest part of the Venusian surface, rising up to 12,000 m.

Ishtar Terra is an elevated plateau encircled by narrow belts of mountains.

Lakshmi Planum is a smooth volcanic plain dominated by two large shield volcanoes, Colette and Sacajawea.

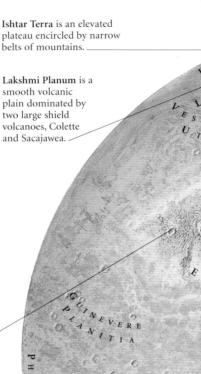

SIF MONS
The thousands of volcanoes spread randomly over the Venusian surface are outlets where the planet's internal heat can escape through the crust. Some of the largest volcanoes, such as Sif Mons, are found in Eistla Regio. Sif Mons stands approximately 2,000 m above the surrounding plain and has a diameter of about 300 km.

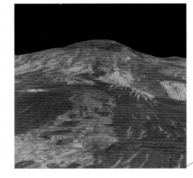

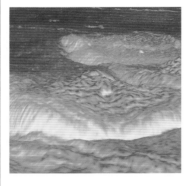

ALPHA REGIO
The first feature to be identified on the Venusian surface using Earth-based radar was Alpha Regio. Located in Venus' southern hemisphere, Alpha Regio is an area of volcanic highland measuring about 1,300 km across. It includes low, domed hills, intersecting ridges, and troughs and valleys.

SURFACE FEATURES
Venus is a largely smooth planet – about 90 per cent of it rises no higher than 3 km. Lowland volcanic plains, or planitia, cover 85 per cent of the surface. The remaining 15 per cent consists of a number of highland areas, named terra or regio, that were pushed up by movements in the planet's crust. Magellan identified individual features as small as 120 m across, and revealed dunes and streaks in the rock formed by the action of the wind.

Lavinia Planitia is a lava plain cut off from the rest of the Venusian lava plains by Alpha Regio.

Magellan's data added about 4,000 surface features to the global map of Venus. Many are named after famous women, such as the biblical figure Eve.

Map labels: ISHTAR TERRA, LAKSHMI PLANUM, Colette, VESTA RUPES, UT RUPES, Sacajawea, SEDNA PLANITIA, Gula Mons, Sappho Patera, EISTLA, GUINEVERE PLANITIA, PHOEBE REGIO, Navka Planitia, TINATIN PLANITIA, Innini Mons, Hathor Mons, ALPHA REGIO, Eve, LAVINIA PLANITIA, LADA

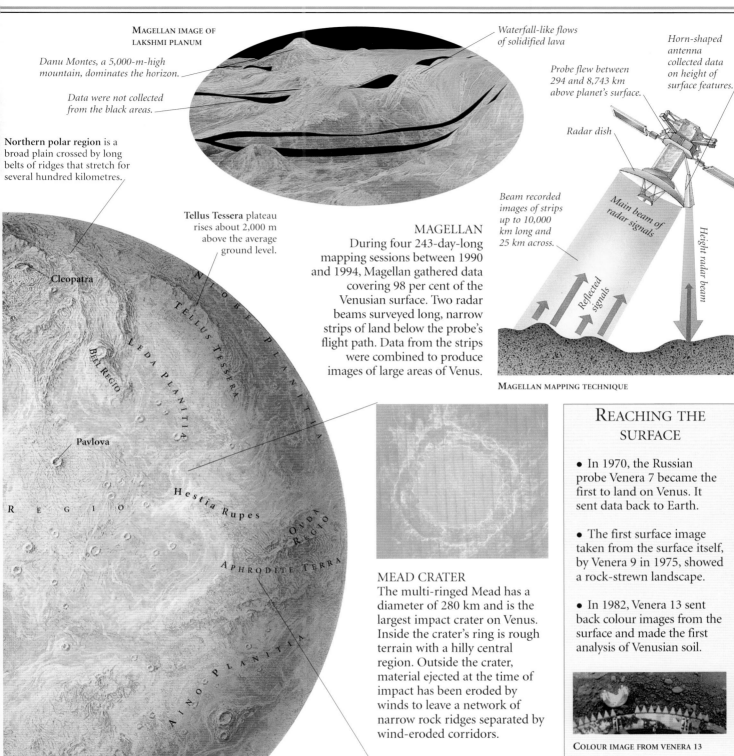

MAGELLAN IMAGE OF LAKSHMI PLANUM

Danu Montes, a 5,000-m-high mountain, dominates the horizon.

Data were not collected from the black areas.

Waterfall-like flows of solidified lava

Horn-shaped antenna collected data on height of surface features.

Probe flew between 294 and 8,743 km above planet's surface.

Radar dish

Beam recorded images of strips up to 10,000 km long and 25 km across.

Main beam of radar signals

Reflected signals

Height radar beam

MAGELLAN MAPPING TECHNIQUE

Northern polar region is a broad plain crossed by long belts of ridges that stretch for several hundred kilometres.

Tellus Tessera plateau rises about 2,000 m above the average ground level.

Cleopatra

NIOBE PLANITIA

TELLUS TESSERA

BELL REGIO

LEDA PLANITIA

Pavlova

REGIO

Hestia Rupes

OVDA REGIO

APHRODITE TERRA

AINO PLANITIA

Most highlands rise about 4,000–5,000 m above the lowland plains.

MAGELLAN
During four 243-day-long mapping sessions between 1990 and 1994, Magellan gathered data covering 98 per cent of the Venusian surface. Two radar beams surveyed long, narrow strips of land below the probe's flight path. Data from the strips were combined to produce images of large areas of Venus.

MEAD CRATER
The multi-ringed Mead has a diameter of 280 km and is the largest impact crater on Venus. Inside the crater's ring is rough terrain with a hilly central region. Outside the crater, material ejected at the time of impact has been eroded by winds to leave a network of narrow rock ridges separated by wind-eroded corridors.

APHRODITE TERRA
The most extensive highland region on Venus, Aphrodite Terra stretches for 6,000 km. The western part shows little evidence of volcanic activity, but the eastern part is occupied by Atla Regio, a large volcanic rise with rifts and volcanic peaks, such as Maat Mons.

REACHING THE SURFACE

● In 1970, the Russian probe Venera 7 became the first to land on Venus. It sent data back to Earth.

● The first surface image taken from the surface itself, by Venera 9 in 1975, showed a rock-strewn landscape.

● In 1982, Venera 13 sent back colour images from the surface and made the first analysis of Venusian soil.

COLOUR IMAGE FROM VENERA 13

● Small landers dropped by the Russian probes Vegas 1 and 2 in 1985 measured surface temperature and pressure, and analysed rock.

FIND OUT MORE

MARS

THE PLANET MARS WAS NAMED after the Roman god of war because of its angry red appearance. Sometimes known as the Red Planet, it is composed of dense, rocky material and, along with Mercury, Venus, and Earth, it is one of the four terrestrial – or Earth-like – planets of the inner Solar System. Mars is one and a half times more distant than the Earth from the Sun. In the late 1990s, scientists began to study the Red Planet in unprecedented detail. They may yet uncover fossils, or even show that primitive life exists there today.

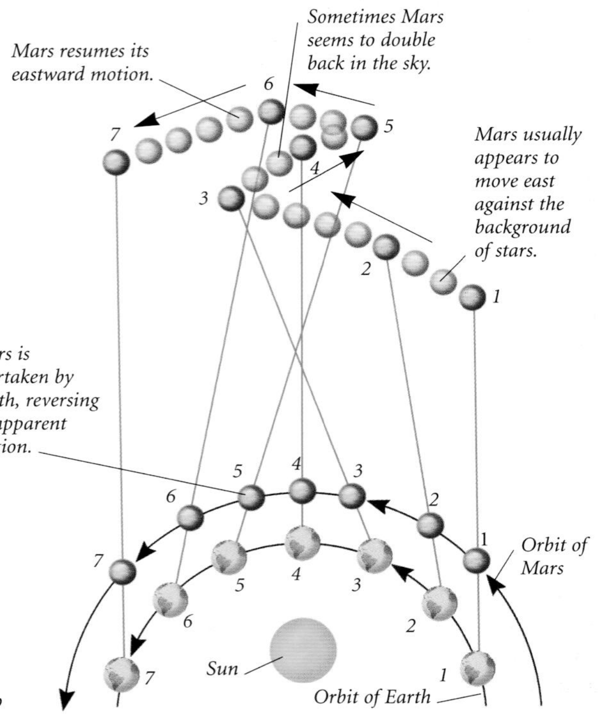

The smooth northern lowlands were formed after an intense period of meteorite bombardment.

The pale areas around the rims of impact craters are wind-blown dust deposits.

Dark areas are thought to correspond to regions of fine-grained rock formed from solidified lava.

Mars resumes its eastward motion.

Sometimes Mars seems to double back in the sky.

Mars usually appears to move east against the background of stars.

Mars is overtaken by Earth, reversing its apparent motion.

Orbit of Mars

Sun

Orbit of Earth

RETROGRADE MOTION

Planets beyond Earth, including Mars, sometimes seem to drift backwards in the sky. This is known as retrograde motion. The planet is still travelling forward, but it appears to fall behind as Earth, which orbits the Sun faster than Mars, overtakes it.

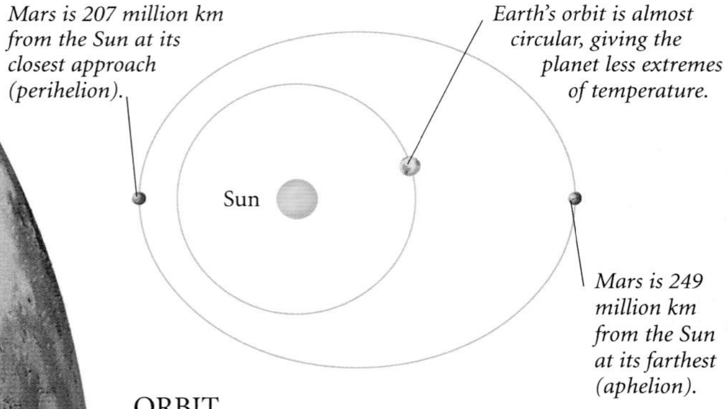

Mars is 207 million km from the Sun at its closest approach (perihelion).

Earth's orbit is almost circular, giving the planet less extremes of temperature.

Sun

Mars is 249 million km from the Sun at its farthest (aphelion).

ORBIT

Mars has a more elliptical orbit than Earth, so its distance from the Sun varies more. At its closest approach, Mars receives 45 per cent more solar radiation than when it is farthest. Temperatures on the surface can vary from −125°C to 22°C.

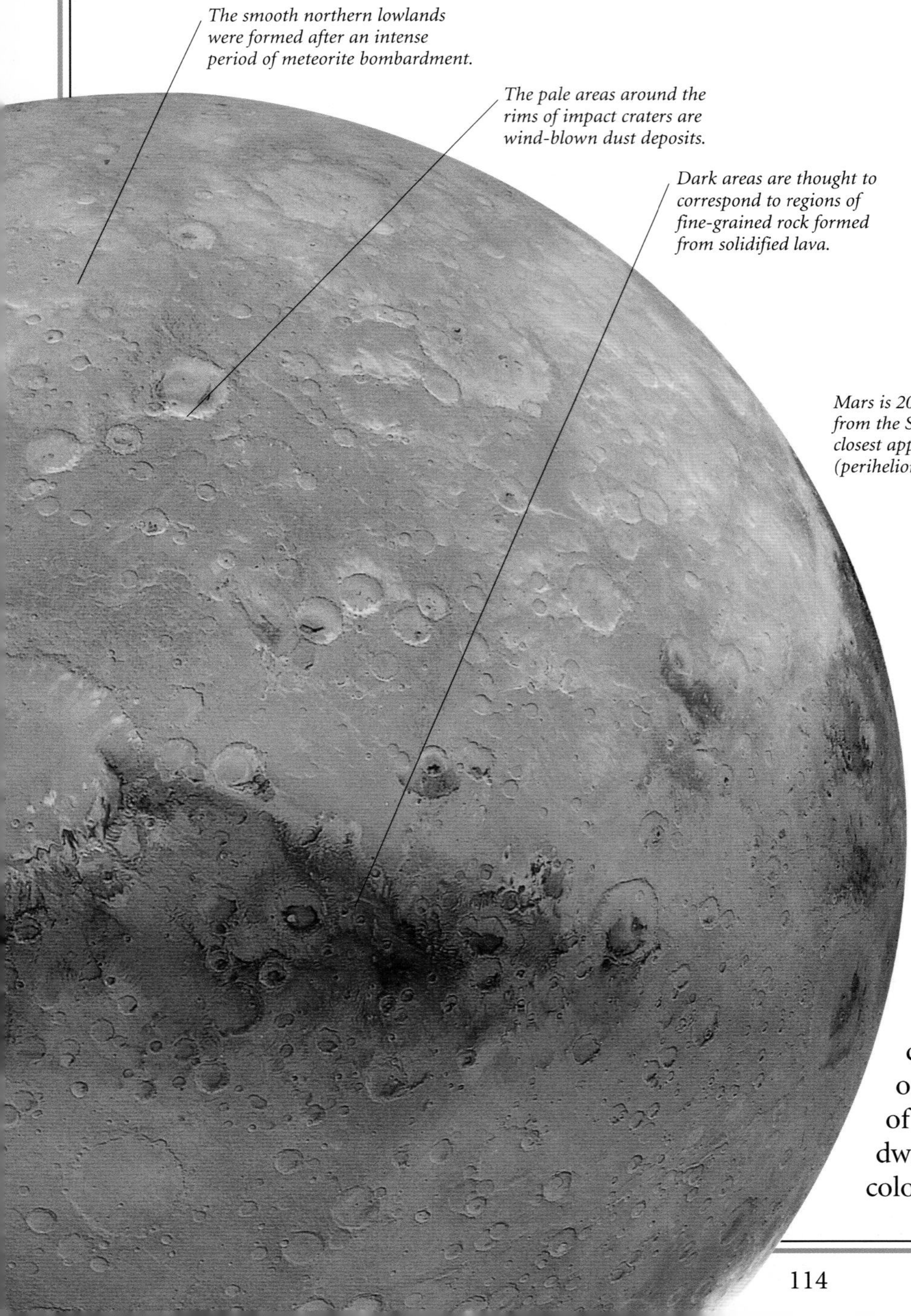

SURFACE FEATURES

Much of the Red Planet's surface is a frozen rock-strewn desert interrupted by dunes and craters. But Mars also has some of the most spectacular and diverse features of the Solar System. Its volcanos and canyons dwarf those found on Earth. The planet's red colour comes from soil rich in iron oxide (rust).

MOONS AND THEIR ORBITS

The Martian moons – Phobos and Deimos – were first observed in 1877. They are among the darkest objects in the Solar System because they reflect very little light. These small, lumpy satellites have a lower density than Mars and both are heavily cratered. The moons orbit the planet in an easterly direction. Phobos is 26 km in diameter and Deimos is just 16 km at its widest. Astronomers believe the moons to be asteroids captured by Mars's gravity.

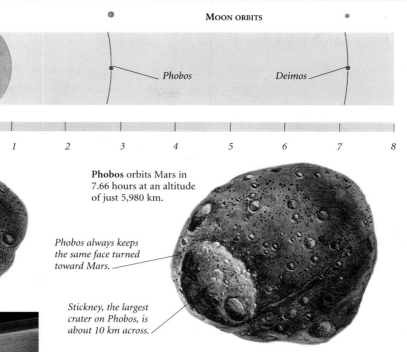

MOON ORBITS

Phobos

Deimos

Scale in radii of Mars 1 radius = 3,397 km   1   2   3   4   5   6   7   8

Phobos orbits Mars in 7.66 hours at an altitude of just 5,980 km.

Deimos orbits Mars in 30.3 hours at an altitude of 20,040 km.

The Martian moons are made of carbon-rich rock.

Phobos always keeps the same face turned toward Mars.

Stickney, the largest crater on Phobos, is about 10 km across.

ATMOSPHERE

Mars has clouds, weather, and prevailing winds. Its thin atmosphere is mainly carbon dioxide. At times, one-third of the atmosphere can be frozen at the poles. Each day solar winds sweeping at supersonic speeds from the Sun carry away a little more of the atmosphere.

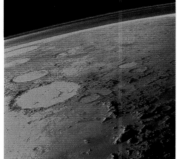

LAYERS IN THE MARTIAN ATMOSPHERE

◉ MARS IN THE SKY

Mars can be seen with the naked eye, especially at times of opposition (when the Earth lies between the Sun and Mars). Opposition occurs every 26 months, and at this time Mars is well-lit and at its closest to our planet. Mars is particularly close to Earth every 15–17 years. In this picture, it appears as the second brightest object in the sky, after the planet Jupiter.

VITAL STATISTICS

Diameter	6,794 km
Average distance from Sun	227.9 million km
Orbital speed around Sun	24.13 km/s
Sunrise to sunrise	24.63 hours
Mass (Earth = 1)	0.11
Volume (Earth = 1)	0.15
Average density (water = 1)	3.93
Surface gravity (Earth = 1)	0.38
Average surface temperature	−63°C
Number of moons	2

FIND OUT MORE

MARS AT A GLANCE

Mars is a rocky planet with an iron-rich core. It is about half the size of the Earth, and has a similar rotation time. Its atmosphere is thin, and pressure at the surface is 1 per cent of the Earth's.

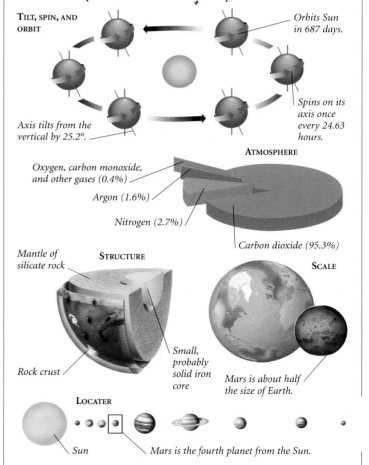

TILT, SPIN, AND ORBIT

Orbits Sun in 687 days.

Spins on its axis once every 24.63 hours.

Axis tilts from the vertical by 25.2°.

ATMOSPHERE

Oxygen, carbon monoxide, and other gases (0.4%)

Argon (1.6%)

Nitrogen (2.7%)

Carbon dioxide (95.3%)

STRUCTURE

Mantle of silicate rock

Small, probably solid iron core

Rock crust

SCALE

Mars is about half the size of Earth.

LOCATER

Sun

Mars is the fourth planet from the Sun.

SEARCH FOR LIFE ON MARS

IN THE LATE 18TH CENTURY, THE ASTRONOMER William Herschel observed dark areas on the surface of Mars. His theory that these were seas of water fuelled speculation that life existed on Mars. A century later, Giovanni Schiaparelli made detailed telescopic studies of the planet and reported seeing channels, which many interpreted as being canals dug by intelligent life forms. Hopes of finding life on the Red Planet were set back in July 1965, when the Mariner 4 probe sent back images of its barren surface. But life may have existed or even exist today in places not yet explored.

Mangala Vallis dried river bed photographed by the Viking Orbiter.

EVIDENCE OF A WATERY PAST

Life as known on Earth needs water. Although liquid water cannot exist on Mars in today's frozen conditions, surface features suggest that water must once have flowed on the planet. Probes have detected channels that can only have been carved by running water. And scientists believe that a huge block-strewn area of Mars – the chaotic region – may have formed when water locked in the ground escaped rapidly, causing the surface to fracture.

DRIED-UP CHANNELS ON MARS

This channel was formed when huge volumes of groundwater were released on to the Martian surface.

ORIGINS OF THE WATER

Liquid water was widespread in the early days of Mars. Intense meteorite bombardment and volcanic activity kept the planet warm, even at its great distance from the Sun. Life may have started then. Today, most of the water is locked up as ice in the soil – a permafrost layer. Pure sheets of ice occur at the poles.

The Martian surface probably had water 3 billion years ago.

CANALS ON MARS?

The channels first seen by Giovanni Schiaparelli were mapped in the 1890s by Percival Lowell from his observatory in Flagstaff, Arizona, USA. Lowell argued that they were canals that carried water from the Martian poles to arid equatorial regions, and converged at oases. The channels seen by both Lowell and Schiaparelli later proved to be an optical illusion.

Lowell's map shows canals that do not match the channels actually observed on Mars.

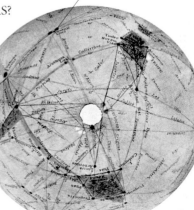

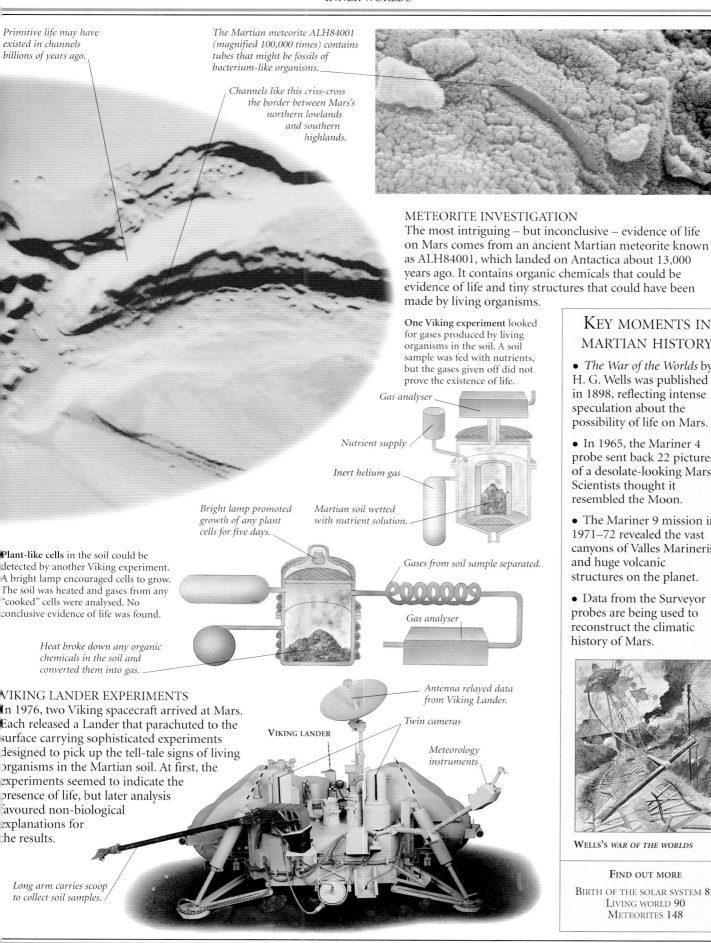

Primitive life may have existed in channels billions of years ago.

The Martian meteorite ALH84001 (magnified 100,000 times) contains tubes that might be fossils of bacterium-like organisms.

Channels like this criss-cross the border between Mars's northern lowlands and southern highlands.

METEORITE INVESTIGATION

The most intriguing – but inconclusive – evidence of life on Mars comes from an ancient Martian meteorite known as ALH84001, which landed on Antactica about 13,000 years ago. It contains organic chemicals that could be evidence of life and tiny structures that could have been made by living organisms.

One Viking experiment looked for gases produced by living organisms in the soil. A soil sample was fed with nutrients, but the gases given off did not prove the existence of life.

Gas analyser

Nutrient supply

Inert helium gas

Bright lamp promoted growth of any plant cells for five days.

Martian soil wetted with nutrient solution.

Plant-like cells in the soil could be detected by another Viking experiment. A bright lamp encouraged cells to grow. The soil was heated and gases from any "cooked" cells were analysed. No conclusive evidence of life was found.

Gases from soil sample separated.

Gas analyser

Heat broke down any organic chemicals in the soil and converted them into gas.

VIKING LANDER EXPERIMENTS

In 1976, two Viking spacecraft arrived at Mars. Each released a Lander that parachuted to the surface carrying sophisticated experiments designed to pick up the tell-tale signs of living organisms in the Martian soil. At first, the experiments seemed to indicate the presence of life, but later analysis favoured non-biological explanations for the results.

Antenna relayed data from Viking Lander.

VIKING LANDER

Twin cameras

Meteorology instruments

Long arm carries scoop to collect soil samples.

KEY MOMENTS IN MARTIAN HISTORY

• *The War of the Worlds* by H. G. Wells was published in 1898, reflecting intense speculation about the possibility of life on Mars.

• In 1965, the Mariner 4 probe sent back 22 pictures of a desolate-looking Mars. Scientists thought it resembled the Moon.

• The Mariner 9 mission in 1971–72 revealed the vast canyons of Valles Marineris and huge volcanic structures on the planet.

• Data from the Surveyor probes are being used to reconstruct the climatic history of Mars.

WELLS'S *WAR OF THE WORLDS*

FIND OUT MORE

BIRTH OF THE SOLAR SYSTEM 82
LIVING WORLD 90
METEORITES 148

MISSIONS TO MARS

SINCE 1996 A STREAM OF ROBOTIC SPACECRAFT has left Earth for Mars. More await launch, and still more are being built. Like determined detectives, these space probes seek answers to mysteries raised by the probes that explored Mars in the 1960s and 1970s. Was Mars once warm and wet? What happened to the water? How did the Martian atmosphere evolve? How might the surface have interacted with the atmosphere? The spacecraft investigating Mars aim to find out how geology and climate combine to tell the story of the planet, and whether primitive life might have existed there in the past. They will pave the way for human exploration and even colonization of the Red Planet.

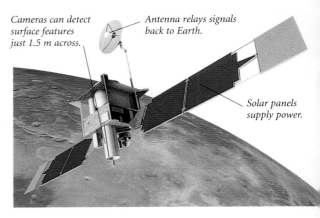

Cameras can detect surface features just 1.5 m across.

Antenna relays signals back to Earth.

Solar panels supply power.

GLOBAL SURVEYOR

Global Surveyor reached Mars in September 1997, and spent 18 months slowing down into a low orbit just 350 km above the surface. It carried cameras and spectrometers designed to map the planet in detail, and study its weather patterns and chemical composition.

EXPLORING THE SURFACE

NASA's lightweight Pathfinder spacecraft landed on the Martian surface on 4 July 1997 after a seven-month journey from Earth. Its landing site in Ares Vallis, a flood plain in the northern hemisphere, was chosen because of the variety of rocks and soil types scientists believed could be found there. Pathfinder was equipped with instruments including an advanced stereoscopic camera. It also carried the six-wheeled Sojourner Rover to explore its surroundings.

PATHFINDER

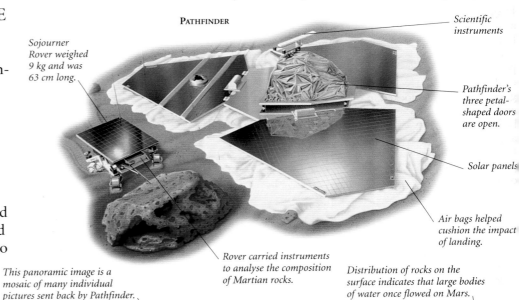

Sojourner Rover weighed 9 kg and was 63 cm long.

Scientific instruments

Pathfinder's three petal-shaped doors are open.

Solar panels

Air bags helped cushion the impact of landing.

Rover carried instruments to analyse the composition of Martian rocks.

Distribution of rocks on the surface indicates that large bodies of water once flowed on Mars.

PATHFINDER MARTIAN PANORAMA

This panoramic image is a mosaic of many individual pictures sent back by Pathfinder.

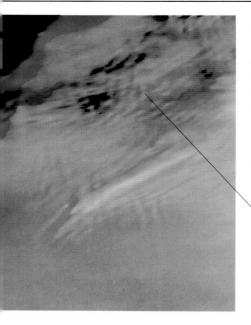

HOSTILE TO LIFE

There is no liquid water on Mars because it is too cold most of the time. There is no breathable oxygen and the surface is scoured by sometimes-violent winds carrying fine dust particles. And there is no ozone in the upper atmosphere to protect life from damaging ultraviolet radiation.

The Martian atmosphere is too thin to support life. Hazy clouds of water ice are sometimes observed.

WORKING IN BIOSPHERE II

COLONIES ON MARS

The first colonies on Mars are likely to be artificial structures built to contain a breathable atmosphere and exclude damaging radiation. The idea of humans living in self-contained air- and water-tight enclosures has been tested on Earth at the Biosphere II project in Tucson, Arizona.

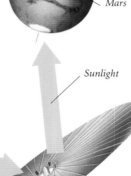

Mars

TERRAFORMING MARS

In theory, the Martian environment could be altered to make the planet habitable for humans. This task is known as terraforming. An important early step would be to warm the planet by inducing a greenhouse effect. This could be done by unfreezing the greenhouse gas carbon dioxide locked in the planet's rocks and polar ice caps. Many centuries would pass before temperature and pressure rose to the point at which plants could survive on the planet.

Sunlight

Sunlight

Giant mirrors orbiting Mars could reflect sunlight to evaporate frozen carbon dioxide in the southern ice cap.

PROBES TO MARS

Name	Year of arrival	Country	Type of probe
Mariner 4	1965	USA	Flyby
Mars 3	1971	Russia	Orbiter and lander
Viking 1	1976	USA	Orbiter and lander
Viking 2	1976	USA	Orbiter and lander
Global Surveyor	1997	USA	Orbiter
Pathfinder	1997	USA	Lander and rover
Climate Orbiter	1999	USA	Orbiter
Polar Lander	1999	USA	Lander
Nozomi	2004	Japan	Orbiter

FIND OUT MORE

INTERPLANETARY TRAVEL 72 • PROBES TO THE PLANETS 80
LIVING WORLD 90 • EXPLORING THE MOON 98
SEARCH FOR LIFE ON MARS 116
LIFE ON OTHER WORLDS 236

The depth of the Sojourner Rover's tracks showed that the soil is fine and powder-like.

The Rover samples a rock nicknamed "Yogi".

Pathfinder found that Martian airborne dust is magnetic.

SURFACE OF MARS

THE MARTIAN SURFACE IS A PLACE of geological extremes, shaped by volcanic activity, meteorite bombardment, floods, and winds. There is no vegetation and no water. Unlike Earth's crust, which is made of many moving plates, Mars's surface is probably just one piece. The lack of movement in the crust explains many of the planet's features, including its huge volcanos and volcanic flood plains. These can build up to great sizes because molten rock continues to pour out from the same spot on the surface for millions of years.

LAND STRUCTURES

Highlands dominate the planet's southern hemisphere, while vast lowland plains lie to the north. Long cliffs exist between the two regions. Craters formed by meteorite impacts scar the planet's southern regions, and are scattered across the north. Huge volcanos such as Olympus Mons, the Valles Marineris canyon system, and many ridges and fractures are found in or around Tharsis Rise, just north of the equator.

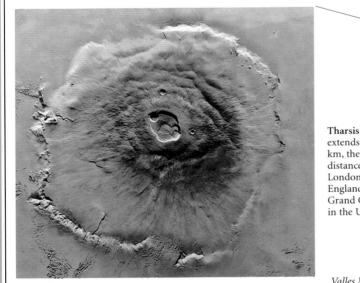

OLYMPUS MONS
The largest volcano on Mars – and indeed in the Solar System – is Olympus Mons. It rises 24,000 m above the surrounding plains of Tharsis Rise and has a 6,000-m high cliff at its base. The volcano is 600 km across, and the caldera (crater) is 90 km across. Its most recent eruption may have been just 25 million years ago.

ALBA PATERA
Located on the northern edge of Tharsis Rise, Alba Patera is a 1,600 m peak with a diameter of 464 km. It may be a volcano or a corona – a structure that forms when a bubble of hot magma pushes up the planet's crust.

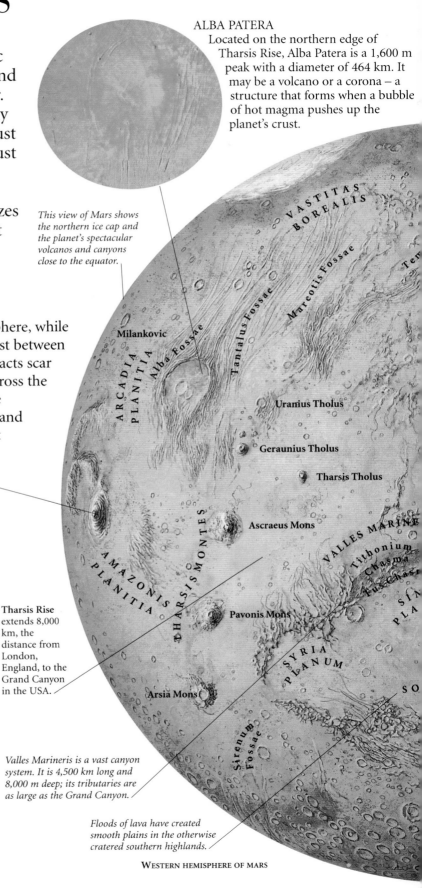

This view of Mars shows the northern ice cap and the planet's spectacular volcanos and canyons close to the equator.

Tharsis Rise extends 8,000 km, the distance from London, England, to the Grand Canyon in the USA.

Valles Marineris is a vast canyon system. It is 4,500 km long and 8,000 m deep; its tributaries are as large as the Grand Canyon.

Floods of lava have created smooth plains in the otherwise cratered southern highlands.

WESTERN HEMISPHERE OF MARS

Map labels: VASTITAS BOREALIS, Mareotis Fossae, Tantalus Fossae, Tem, Milankovic, ARCADIA PLANITIA, Alba Fossae, Uranius Tholus, Geraunius Tholus, Tharsis Tholus, Ascraeus Mons, VALLES MARINE, Tithonium Chasma, Tus Chas, THARSIS MONTES, AMAZONIS PLANITIA, Pavonis Mons, SÍN PLA, SYRIA PLANUM, Arsia Mons, Sirenum Fossae, SO

IMPACT CRATERS

Most of Mars's craters were formed by intense meteorite bombardment more than 3.8 billion years ago. One theory suggests that a particularly huge impact caused the difference between the highlands in the south and the northern lowlands.

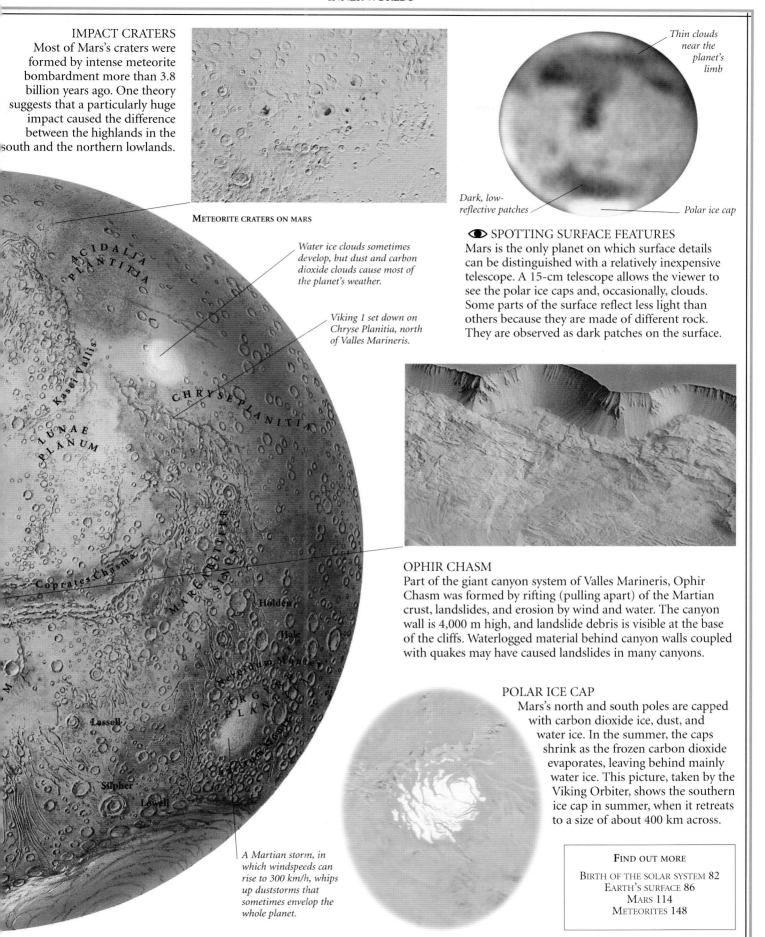

METEORITE CRATERS ON MARS

Thin clouds near the planet's limb

Water ice clouds sometimes develop, but dust and carbon dioxide clouds cause most of the planet's weather.

Viking 1 set down on Chryse Planitia, north of Valles Marineris.

Dark, low-reflective patches

Polar ice cap

👁 SPOTTING SURFACE FEATURES

Mars is the only planet on which surface details can be distinguished with a relatively inexpensive telescope. A 15-cm telescope allows the viewer to see the polar ice caps and, occasionally, clouds. Some parts of the surface reflect less light than others because they are made of different rock. They are observed as dark patches on the surface.

ACIDALIA PLANITIA

Kasei Vallis

CHRYSE PLANITIA

LUNAE PLANUM

Coprates Chasma

MARGARITIFER SINUS

Holden

Hale

Nereidum Montes

ARGYRE PLANITIA

Lassell

Silpher

Lowell

OPHIR CHASM

Part of the giant canyon system of Valles Marineris, Ophir Chasm was formed by rifting (pulling apart) of the Martian crust, landslides, and erosion by wind and water. The canyon wall is 4,000 m high, and landslide debris is visible at the base of the cliffs. Waterlogged material behind canyon walls coupled with quakes may have caused landslides in many canyons.

POLAR ICE CAP

Mars's north and south poles are capped with carbon dioxide ice, dust, and water ice. In the summer, the caps shrink as the frozen carbon dioxide evaporates, leaving behind mainly water ice. This picture, taken by the Viking Orbiter, shows the southern ice cap in summer, when it retreats to a size of about 400 km across.

A Martian storm, in which windspeeds can rise to 300 km/h, whips up duststorms that sometimes envelop the whole planet.

FIND OUT MORE
BIRTH OF THE SOLAR SYSTEM 82
EARTH'S SURFACE 86
MARS 114
METEORITES 148

JUPITER

THE FIFTH PLANET FROM THE SUN is very different from the terrestrial (Earth-like) planets. Jupiter is by far the largest planet in the Solar System – over 1,300 Earths would fit into its volume, and its mass is 2.5 times that of all the other planets combined. It exerts a huge gravitational pull, which has deflected comets that may otherwise have hit the Earth. Jupiter is a gas giant; unlike the small, rocky inner planets, it has no solid surface but is all gas and liquid except for a very small rocky core. All that is visible is the gas exterior. The planet has 16 moons and a dusty ring system.

STRUCTURE

Jupiter is a giant ball of hydrogen and helium, compressed into a liquid inside, and probably into a solid at the core. Knowledge of the core is limited, but it is likely to be 10–15 times more massive than the Earth's. Pressure and temperature 20,000 km below the cloud tops are so intense that hydrogen turns into a liquid that behaves like a metal. Ordinary liquid hydrogen lies above the metal. Hydrogen and helium gases form an atmosphere surrounding the planet.

RING SYSTEM

Jupiter's faint ring system was first seen in images sent back by the Voyager 1 space probe in 1979. Later images from the Voyager 2 and Galileo probes revealed details of its structure. There is a "cloudy" inner ring that extends towards the cloud tops, a flattened central ring, and an outer ring, which Galileo has shown to be one ring embedded within another. The rings are formed from dust knocked off Jupiter's four inner moons by meteorites.

1   4

9:42 p.m.

2   5

3   6

11:34 p.m.

ROTATION

Jupiter spins very rapidly, taking 9 hours 55 minutes to rotate on its axis, compared with the 24 hours the much smaller Earth takes. The forces resulting from its fast rotation flatten the planet, making it bulge at its equator. Jupiter is 7 per cent shorter from pole-to-pole than across the equator.

Jupiter's rapid spin can be observed with an Earth-based telescope. Over a period of 2 hours the Great Red Spot moves about one-quarter of the way round the planet. The planet appears upside-down in this telescope image.

If Jupiter had been 50 times more massive, its core would have been hot enough to fuse hydrogen, and Jupiter would have become a star.

Compounds including sulphur give Jupiter its multi-coloured appearance.

Jupiter is sometimes known as the banded planet because of its bands of different coloured clouds.

Spots, ovals, and streaks on cloud tops are weather disturbances.

JUPITER AT A GLANCE

Jupiter is a giant planet. It has no crust and its atmosphere is a 1,000 km-thick gaseous shell surrounding inner layers of liquid hydrogen, liquid metallic hydrogen, and a solid core.

TILT, SPIN, AND ORBIT

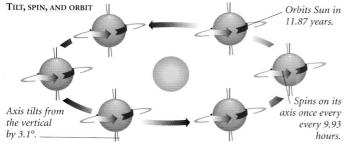

Orbits Sun in 11.87 years.

Spins on its axis once every every 9.93 hours.

Axis tilts from the vertical by 3.1°.

ATMOSPHERE

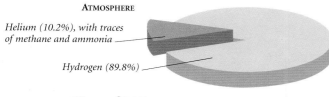

Helium (10.2%), with traces of methane and ammonia

Hydrogen (89.8%)

STRUCTURE

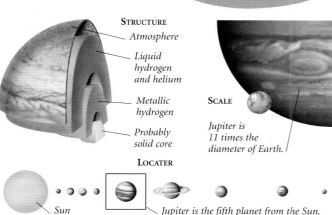

Atmosphere

Liquid hydrogen and helium

Metallic hydrogen

Probably solid core

SCALE

Jupiter is 11 times the diameter of Earth.

LOCATER

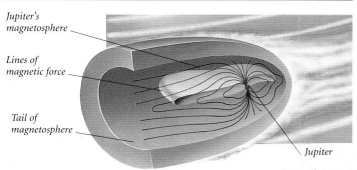

Sun

Jupiter is the fifth planet from the Sun.

MAGNETISM

Jupiter's magnetic field is 20,000 times stronger than the Earth's. Scientists think electric currents in the fast-spinning metallic hydrogen within the planet create the field. This reaches out into space, surrounding the planet in a huge magnetic bubble, or magnetosphere. Its tail extends 650 million km past the orbit of Saturn.

Jupiter's magnetosphere

Lines of magnetic force

Tail of magnetosphere

Jupiter

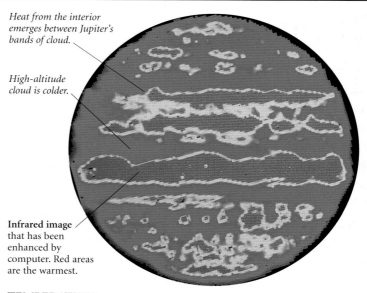

Heat from the interior emerges between Jupiter's bands of cloud.

High-altitude cloud is colder.

Infrared image that has been enhanced by computer. Red areas are the warmest.

TEMPERATURE

Jupiter gives out more heat than it receives from the Sun. The heat is generated by the planet as it contracts. Jupiter was once 700,000 km across – five times its present diameter. Great amounts of energy were released as the planet shrank, and it continues to contract by about 2 cm per year. The temperature at Jupiter's cloud tops is now −110°C, and is believed to increase by 0.3°C for every kilometre of depth, giving a core temperature of approximately 30,000°C.

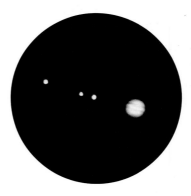

◑ OBSERVING JUPITER

Jupiter is the fourth brightest object in the sky. It can be seen by the naked eye, and details such as its banding can be seen with a 15-cm telescope.

DISCOVERY TIMELINE

- In 1610, German astronomer Simon Marius discovered and named the four largest moons of Jupiter; they were later studied by Galileo Galilei.

- Jupiter's Great Red Spot was first observed in the 17th century.

- Astronomers observed the planet's strong emissions of radio waves in 1955.

- Pioneer 10 was the first probe to reach Jupiter in 1973. It discovered Jupiter's unusually massive magnetic field.

- In 1995, Galileo arrived at Jupiter. Its orbiter and probe have revolutionised knowledge of the planet.

FIND OUT MORE

VITAL STATISTICS

Diameter (equatorial)	142,984 km
Diameter (polar)	133,708 km
Average distance from Sun	778.4 million km
Orbital speed around Sun	13.07 km/s
Sunrise to sunrise (at cloud tops)	9.84 hours
Mass (Earth = 1)	318
Volume (Earth = 1)	1,321
Average density (water = 1)	1.33
Gravity at cloud tops (Earth = 1)	2.36
Cloud-top temperature	−110°C
Number of moons	16

JUPITER'S ATMOSPHERE

THERE ARE FEW MORE TURBULENT ENVIRONMENTS in the Solar System than Jupiter's atmosphere. The planet's rapid rotation helps whip up winds that have been measured by the Galileo probe at 650 km/h. Huge swirling storm systems can be seen from the Earth, and giant superbolts of lightning have been detected by spacecraft sent to the planet. Jupiter formed from the same ancient gas cloud as the Sun, so studies of its deep atmosphere are giving scientists a better understanding of the earliest history of the Solar System.

North Polar Region

North Temperate Belt is bounded on its southern edge by red ovals.

CLOUD TOPS

Jupiter is a giant gas ball, which is compressed into a liquid, then a solid, with increasing depth. It does not have a solid surface, so astronomers often refer to properties such as temperature at the level in the atmosphere where the pressure is the same as Earth's atmospheric pressure at sea level: this coincides roughly with the level of the white clouds.

North Equatorial Belt has a twisted rope-like appearance caused by violent winds.

GREAT RED SPOT

A hurricane three times the size of Earth has raged in Jupiter's atmosphere for more than 300 years. Known as the Great Red Spot (GRS), it rotates anti-clockwise every six Earth days. The GRS, which towers about 8 km above neighbouring clouds, is thought to be made mainly of ammonia gas and ice clouds.

Damp air rises in the GRS and is whipped into a swirling spiral.

BOUNDARY BETWEEN ZONE AND BELT

ZONES AND BELTS

Bright bands (called zones) in the atmosphere are areas of rising gas, while dark bands (belts) are regions of falling gas. The tops of the belts are about 20 km lower than the tops of the zones. The colour of the belts may be caused by traces of sulphur or organic molecules.

Low pressure system

High pressure system

Rapid rotation of planet

ATMOSPHERIC CIRCULATION

Heat from Jupiter's interior, rather than the Sun, supplies most of the energy that drives the planet's weather. Rising heat combined with rapid rotation stretches high- and low-pressure systems all the way around the planet. Storms grow at the boundaries between the pressure systems.

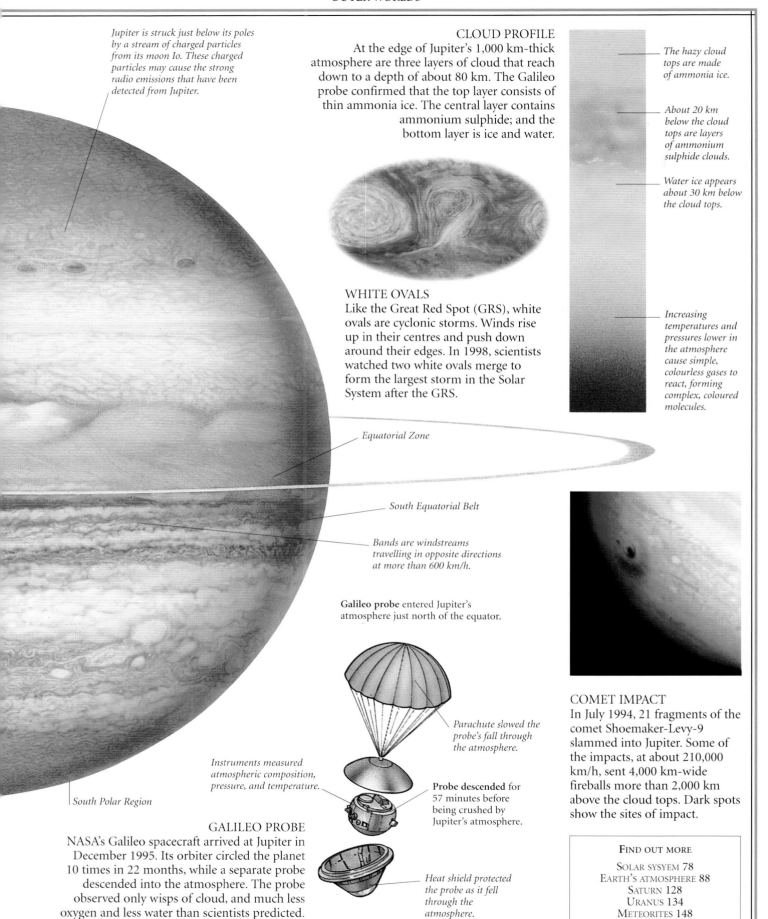

Jupiter is struck just below its poles by a stream of charged particles from its moon Io. These charged particles may cause the strong radio emissions that have been detected from Jupiter.

CLOUD PROFILE
At the edge of Jupiter's 1,000 km-thick atmosphere are three layers of cloud that reach down to a depth of about 80 km. The Galileo probe confirmed that the top layer consists of thin ammonia ice. The central layer contains ammonium sulphide; and the bottom layer is ice and water.

The hazy cloud tops are made of ammonia ice.

About 20 km below the cloud tops are layers of ammonium sulphide clouds.

Water ice appears about 30 km below the cloud tops.

Increasing temperatures and pressures lower in the atmosphere cause simple, colourless gases to react, forming complex, coloured molecules.

WHITE OVALS
Like the Great Red Spot (GRS), white ovals are cyclonic storms. Winds rise up in their centres and push down around their edges. In 1998, scientists watched two white ovals merge to form the largest storm in the Solar System after the GRS.

Equatorial Zone

South Equatorial Belt

Bands are windstreams travelling in opposite directions at more than 600 km/h.

Galileo probe entered Jupiter's atmosphere just north of the equator.

Parachute slowed the probe's fall through the atmosphere.

Instruments measured atmospheric composition, pressure, and temperature.

Probe descended for 57 minutes before being crushed by Jupiter's atmosphere.

South Polar Region

GALILEO PROBE
NASA's Galileo spacecraft arrived at Jupiter in December 1995. Its orbiter circled the planet 10 times in 22 months, while a separate probe descended into the atmosphere. The probe observed only wisps of cloud, and much less oxygen and less water than scientists predicted.

Heat shield protected the probe as it fell through the atmosphere.

COMET IMPACT
In July 1994, 21 fragments of the comet Shoemaker-Levy-9 slammed into Jupiter. Some of the impacts, at about 210,000 km/h, sent 4,000 km-wide fireballs more than 2,000 km above the cloud tops. Dark spots show the sites of impact.

FIND OUT MORE
SOLAR SYSYEM 78
EARTH'S ATMOSPHERE 88
SATURN 128
URANUS 134
METEORITES 148

JUPITER'S MOONS

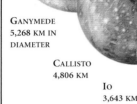

JUPITER AND ITS 16 KNOWN MOONS are often described as looking like a mini Solar System. They are extremely varied – some are rocky, some icy, and, tantalisingly, some may have had the conditions needed to foster primitive life. All the moons except one – Amalthea – are named after the lovers of Zeus, the equivalent in Greek mythology of the Roman god Jupiter. The four largest moons were first investigated by Galileo in 1610. Fittingly, it is a probe called Galileo that has revealed how the complex elements of the Jovian system work together and affect one another.

GANYMEDE
5,268 KM IN
DIAMETER

CALLISTO
4,806 KM

IO
3,643 KM

EUROPA
3,130 KM

GALILEAN MOONS

The four moons studied by Galileo are – with increasing distance from Jupiter – Io, Europa, Ganymede, and Callisto. They range between 0.9 and 1.5 times the size of our own Moon, and each has its own distinct personality. The Galilean moons orbit Jupiter in nearly circular paths almost exactly around the planet's equator.

EUROPA

The surface of Europa is smooth ice. Evidence from the Galileo probe points to the existence of a liquid ocean beneath the ice. Some scientists think aquatic life may have arisen in the warmer parts of the ocean. The Hubble Space Telescope has also detected a thin atmosphere of oxygen on Europa.

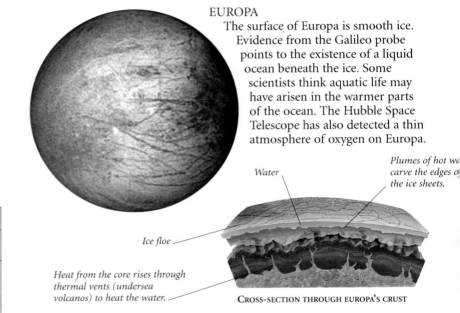

Water

Plumes of hot wa carve the edges o the ice sheets.

Ice floe

Heat from the core rises through thermal vents (undersea volcanos) to heat the water.

CROSS-SECTION THROUGH EUROPA'S CRUST

JUPITER'S MOONS

Name	Diameter in km	Distance to Jupiter (km)	Orbit in days	Year of discovery
Metis	40	127,960	0.29	1979
Adrastea	20	128,980	0.30	1979
Amalthea	200	181,300	0.50	1892
Thebe	100	221,900	0.67	1979
Io	3,643	421,600	1.77	1610
Europa	3,130	670,900	3.55	1610
Ganymede	5,268	1,070,000	7.15	1610
Callisto	4,806	1,883,000	16.69	1610
Leda	10	11,094,000	239	1974
Himalia	170	11,480,000	251	1904
Lysithea	24	11,720,000	259	1938
Elara	80	11,737,000	260	1905
Ananke	20	21,200,000	631	1951
Carme	30	22,600,000	692	1938
Pasiphae	36	23,500,000	735	1908
Sinope	28	23,700,000	758	1914

INNER MOONS

Of Jupiter's 12 smaller moons, four have orbits within Io's. They are constantly battered by meteorites, producing dust which replenishes the planet's rings. The innermost moons, Metis and Adrastea, will eventually spiral into the planet. The largest of the non-Galilean moons is the potato-shaped Amalthea. Sulphur from Io may give Amalthea its red colour.

AMALTHEA

MOONS AND THEIR ORBITS

The moons beyond the Galilean moons divide into two groups. Leda, Himalia, Lysithea, and Elara may be fragments of a shattered asteroid. The four most distant moons are likely to be captured asteroids. They orbit in the direction opposite to that of the inner moons.

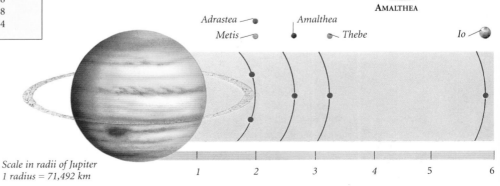

Adrastea

Metis

Amalthea

Thebe

Io

Scale in radii of Jupiter
1 radius = 71,492 km

1   2   3   4   5   6

PROBES TO JUPITER'S MOONS

Name	Date	Mission highlights
Voyager 1	Mar 79	Images of Galilean moons. Volcanism observed on Io.
Galileo	Dec 96	Ganymede's magnetosphere detected. Images show ice, volcanos, or geysers have shaped Europa's surface.
Galileo	Jun 97	Evidence of an ocean below Callisto's icy surface.

GANYMEDE

Jupiter's largest satellite is bigger than the planet Mercury. The Galileo probe discovered that Ganymede has its own magnetosphere, which made scientists revise their ideas about its structure. Previously they thought the moon had a rocky core surrounded by water with a crust of ice on the surface. They now think Ganymede's core is molten iron surrounded by a rocky mantle with an ice shell.

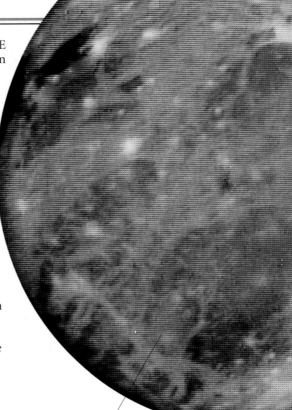

Ganymede's surface has faults similar to the San Andreas fault in California, USA, where grooves have slipped sideways.

CALLISTO

The surface of Callisto is completely covered with craters, dating from the birth of Jupiter's system. Callisto consists of about 60 per cent rock and iron and 40 per cent ice and water. The Galileo probe has detected variations in the magnetic field around the moon. Scientists think the variations may be caused by electric currents flowing in a salty ocean beneath Callisto's icy crust.

Io is covered with volcanoes, molten sulphur lakes, lava flows and mountains up to 8,000 m high.

Volcanos can send up plumes of gas 250 km high. Many giant volcanos are erupting on the moon at any one time.

IO

The gravities of Jupiter, Europa, and Ganymede tug and push at Io, bending the crust back and forth. The moon generates heat as molecules bump and grind against one another. As a result, Io is the most volcanically active body in the Solar System. It has a thin atmosphere of sulphur dioxide.

OBSERVING MOONS
It is possible to track the changing positions of the four Galilean moons over a few hours with a good pair of binoculars. The moons played a vital role in the history of astronomy; the fact that they orbited another planet showed that not everything revolved around the Earth.

Farthest moon: 23.7 million km from Jupiter

Europa   Ganymede   Callisto   Leda   Himalia   Lysithea   Elara   Ananke   Carme   Pasiphae   Sinope

10   20   30   150   160   170   290   300   310   320   330   340

SATURN

SATURN, THE SECOND LARGEST PLANET, is the easiest to recognize because of the bright rings around its equator. Like Jupiter, it is a large ball of gas and liquid topped by clouds. Nearly 10 times farther from the Sun than we are, Saturn was the most distant planet known before the invention of the telescope. To the naked eye it looks like a fairly bright, yellowish star, but you need a telescope to see the rings. Three space probes have flown past Saturn – Pioneer 11, and Voyagers 1 and 2 – and a fourth mission, Cassini, will arrive in 2004.

VOYAGER FLY-BY
In 1980, the space probe Voyager 1 flew past Saturn and its largest moon, Titan. Voyager 2 followed in 1981, before going on to Uranus and Neptune.

Saturn's cloud patterns are hidden by a haze of ammonia crystals.

Rings are made of particles and larger pieces of ice.

BUTTERSCOTCH PLANET
Saturn, like Jupiter, has a surface of clouds, drawn out into bands by the planet's spin. Saturn's clouds are calmer and less colourful than those on Jupiter. They are also lower in the atmosphere and colder (the white clouds at the top are –140°C). Above the clouds is a layer of haze, which gives Saturn its butterscotch colour and makes it look smoother than Jupiter.

ATMOSPHERE
Saturn has three main layers of clouds, composed of the same gases as Jupiter's clouds, but with a haze above them. The cloud layers are farther apart on Saturn because the planet's gravity is weaker than Jupiter's.

White clouds

Dark orange clouds

Blue clouds

Saturn is nine times wider than the Earth.

STORMS ON SATURN
Every 30 years or so, during summer in the northern hemisphere, storms break out on Saturn, producing large white spots near the equator. These pictures, taken by the Hubble Space Telescope, show a storm cloud that broke out in 1990 and spread right around the planet.

STORM STAGE 1

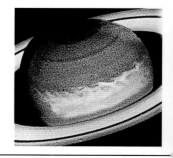

Clouds form bright belts and dark zones, like those on Jupiter.

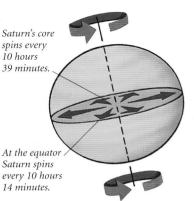

Saturn's core spins every 10 hours 39 minutes.

At the equator Saturn spins every 10 hours 14 minutes.

BULGING PLANET

Saturn spins every 10 hours 14 minutes at the equator, but takes nearly half an hour longer at the poles. Its low density, combined with its fast spin, mean that Saturn's equator bulges more than that of any other planet. Saturn is 11 per cent wider at the equator than at the poles.

PLANET DENSITY

Saturn is the least dense of the planets, with an average density only 70 per cent that of water (it is much denser than this at the centre, but less dense near the surface). An object with Saturn's low density would float in water.

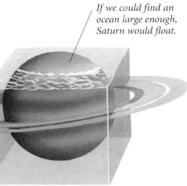

If we could find an ocean large enough, Saturn would float.

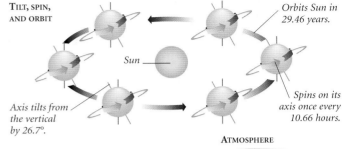
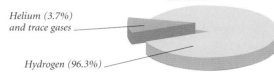

SATURN AT A GLANCE

Nine times the diameter of the Earth, Saturn has a rocky centre, with outer layers of liquid and gas. Bright rings of icy particles circle the planet's equator.

TILT, SPIN, AND ORBIT

Orbits Sun in 29.46 years.

Sun

Axis tilts from the vertical by 26.7°.

Spins on its axis once every 10.66 hours.

ATMOSPHERE

Helium (3.7%) and trace gases

Hydrogen (96.3%)

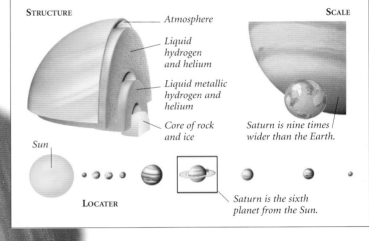

STRUCTURE

Atmosphere

Liquid hydrogen and helium

Liquid metallic hydrogen and helium

Core of rock and ice

Sun

SCALE

Saturn is nine times wider than the Earth.

LOCATER

Saturn is the sixth planet from the Sun.

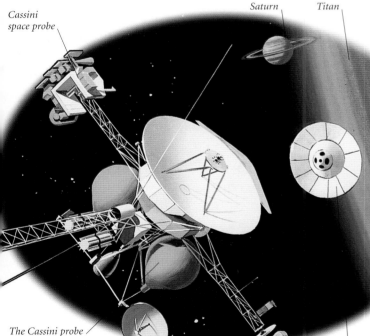

Cassini space probe

Saturn

Titan

The Cassini probe will arrive at Saturn in 2004.

Huygens space probe

CASSINI MISSION

The Cassini probe, launched in 1997, is a space mission to study Saturn, its rings, and its moons. Cassini will go into orbit around Saturn in 2004, and send back information for four years. It will drop a smaller probe, called Huygens, which will land on the surface of Saturn's largest moon, Titan.

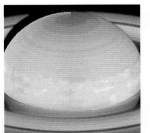

STORM STAGE 2

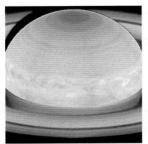

STORM STAGE 3

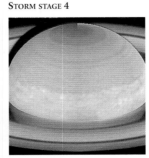

STORM STAGE 4

VITAL STATISTICS

Diameter (equatorial)	120,536 km
Diameter (polar)	108,728 km
Average distance from Sun	1.427 billion km
Orbital speed around Sun	9.66 km/h
Sunrise to sunrise (at cloud tops)	10.23 hours
Mass (Earth=1)	95
Volume (Earth=1)	763.59
Average density (water=1)	0.69
Gravity at cloud tops (Earth=1)	0.92
Cloud-top temperature	−140°C
Number of known moons	18

FIND OUT MORE

SATURN'S RINGS

FOUR PLANETS HAVE RINGS – Jupiter, Saturn, Uranus, and Neptune – but Saturn's are by far the brightest, a glorious sight through even small telescopes. The rings may look solid but they actually consist of chunks of ice and rock, ranging from specks of dust to icebergs larger than a house, orbiting Saturn's equator like a swarm of moonlets. Saturn's rings are probably the remains of one or more captured comets that have broken up, probably within the past few hundred million years.

GLORIOUS RINGS
This view of Saturn cannot be seen from Earth. It was taken by Voyager 2 in 1981, looking back as it left the planet on its way to more-distant Uranus and Neptune. The rings are lit up by sunlight shining through from behind. Saturn's globe shows through the inner part of the rings.

Shadow of rings on globe

Icy lumps make up the rings. They range from tiny particles to pieces a few metres across.

Spokes are dark smudges caused by dust hovering above the broad B ring.

Ring C is transparent.

Planet visible through Cassini Division

Ring D is so close to the planet that it almost touches it.

ANATOMY OF THE RINGS
Three main rings can be seen through telescopes from Earth: an outer A ring, the bright central B ring, and the transparent inner C ring (also called the Crepe ring). Space probes show that the particles in these main rings are arranged in thousands of closely packed ringlets. On either side of these three rings are fainter ones found by space probes. The D ring is closest of all to Saturn, with rings F, G, and E farther out.

D ring
C ring
B ring
Cassini Division
A ring
Encke Division
F ring

INNER RINGS
Ring B is the brightest ring, and the broadest of those visible from Earth. Cassini's Division, nearly 5,000 km wide, lies between it and the A ring. A narrower gap, the Encke Division, splits the A ring. Two other faint rings, G and E, which lie farther from Saturn, are not shown here.

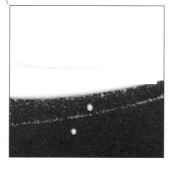

SHEPHERD MOONS
Two small moons, Pandora and Prometheus, orbit either side of the narrow F ring. They are known as shepherds because they prevent the ring particles from straying. The F ring was discovered by the Pioneer 11 probe in 1979, and the shepherd moons were seen by Voyager 1 a year later.

VOYAGER CLOSE-UP

Seen by the Voyager space probes in close-up, the rings of Saturn break up into countless narrow ringlets, looking like the grooves of an old-fashioned gramophone record. Ringlets were found even in the gaps such as the Cassini Division. This image shows the C ring and part of the B ring. The colours are not real, but are added by computer to highlight the differences in the rings.

LORD OF THE RINGS

• In 1610 Galileo Galilei looked at Saturn through his primitive telescope, but mistook the planet's rings for two moons. Galileo called these "moons" ears.

GALILEO'S DRAWINGS OF THE EARS

• Christiaan Huygens recognized Saturn's rings in 1655.

• In 1675, Giovanni Cassini discovered the gap between rings A and B (now known as the Cassini Division).

• Johann Encke (1791–1865) discovered the Encke Division in 1837.

• In 1895, US astrophysicist James Keeler (1857–1908) confirmed spectroscopically that the rings were a swarm of orbiting particles.

• Pioneer 11 discovered the F ring in 1979.

• In 1980 and 1981, Voyagers 1 and 2 discovered that the rings consist of thousands of ringlets.

• The Cassini probe will study Saturn's rings in 2004.

CASSINI MISSION FLYING OVER RINGS

Each particle is a satellite of Saturn.

Smaller particles are up to several centimetres in size.

Dust from the moon Enceladus may be found in the E ring, which is the farthest from Saturn.

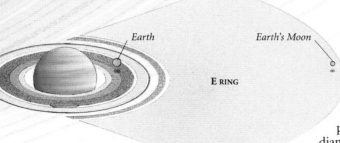

Earth

Earth's Moon

E RING

SIZE OF RINGS

Saturn's rings stretch farther than the rings of any other planet. The faint E ring goes out to 480,000 km, farther than the Moon is from Earth. Despite their great extent, Saturn's rings are only about 10 metres thick in places, so that in relation to their diameter they are much thinner than a sheet of tissue paper.

👁 PRACTICAL

Saturn's axis is tilted at 26.7 degrees, so we see the rings from various angles as the planet orbits the Sun. Twice during its 29.5-year orbit, the rings are edge-on to us. Being so thin, they then vanish from view in small telescopes. The rings will next be edge-on to us in September 2009.

Rings edge-on as seen from Earth

Viewed from Earth, with the naked eye, Saturn looks like a yellowish star. With a telescope you can see the rings.

2025

Sun

2003 2032

Earth

2017

2009

Saturn's orbit

Rings tilted at their maximum

Rings tilted at their maximum

It takes 14–15 years for the rings to get bigger and then appear to vanish.

Rings edge-on as seen from Earth

SATURN'S MOONS

Saturn's family of moons is larger than that of any other planet in the Solar System. At present we know of 18 for certain, ranging in size from Titan, the second largest moon in the Solar System, to tiny Pan, only about 20 km across, which lies in a gap in the A ring called the Encke Division. Some of Saturn's moons share the same orbits. All the moons have a low density and are thought to consist of a mixture of rock and frozen water. More small moons may exist, and the Cassini probe should find them when it arrives at Saturn in 2004.

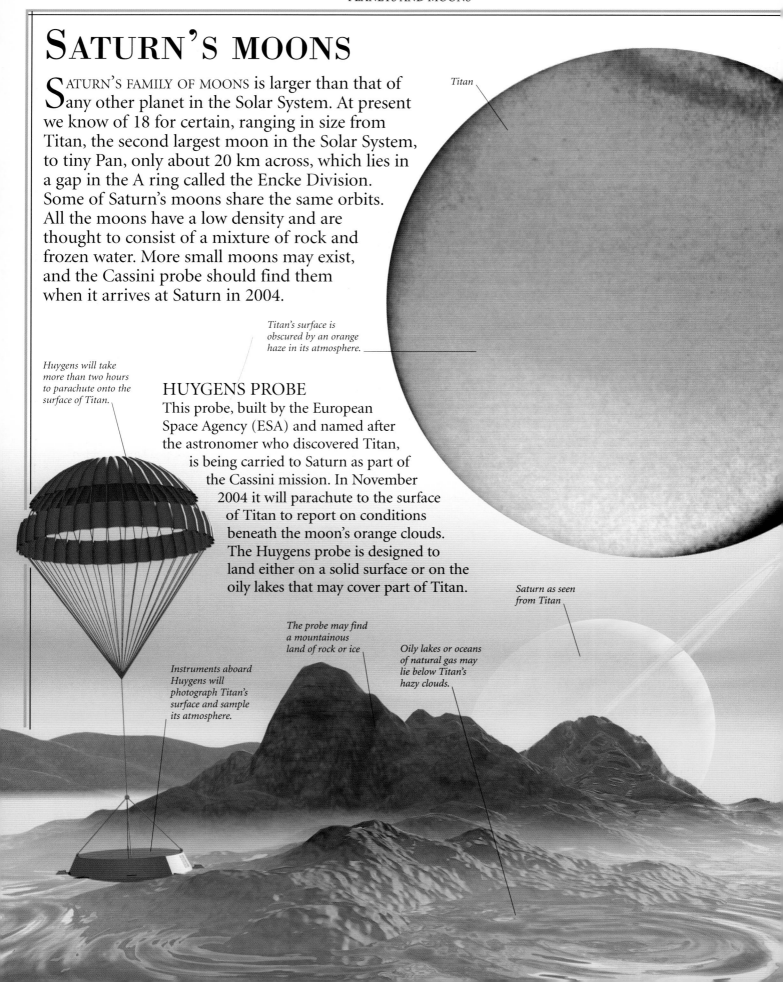

Titan

Titan's surface is obscured by an orange haze in its atmosphere.

Huygens will take more than two hours to parachute onto the surface of Titan.

HUYGENS PROBE
This probe, built by the European Space Agency (ESA) and named after the astronomer who discovered Titan, is being carried to Saturn as part of the Cassini mission. In November 2004 it will parachute to the surface of Titan to report on conditions beneath the moon's orange clouds. The Huygens probe is designed to land either on a solid surface or on the oily lakes that may cover part of Titan.

Saturn as seen from Titan

The probe may find a mountainous land of rock or ice

Oily lakes or oceans of natural gas may lie below Titan's hazy clouds.

Instruments aboard Huygens will photograph Titan's surface and sample its atmosphere.

TITAN

Bigger than the planet Mercury, Titan is the only moon in the Solar System with a thick atmosphere. In fact, its atmospheric pressure is 50 per cent greater than the pressure at sea level on Earth. Titan's main gas is nitrogen, as it is on Earth. The similarities end there, because Titan is in deep freeze, at a temperature of about −180°C. Smoggy orange clouds hide the moon's surface from view.

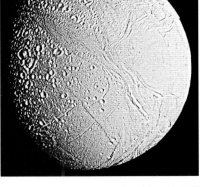

ENCELADUS

Parts of this moon's bright, icy surface are cratered, but other parts are so smooth they seem to have melted, wiping out any craters. Grooves on the surface of Enceladus are thought to be faults in the crust.

VITAL STATISTICS

Satellite	Diameter in km	Distance to Saturn (km)	Orbit (days)	Date of discovery
Pan	20	133,583	0.57	1990
Atlas	34	137,640	0.60	1980
Prometheus	100	139,350	0.61	1980
Pandora	88	141,700	0.63	1980
Epimetheus	110	151,422	0.69	1966
Janus	191	151,472	0.69	1966
Mimas	398	185,520	0.94	1789
Enceladus	498	238,020	1.37	1789
Tethys	1,060	294,660	1.89	1684
Telesto	25	294,660	1.89	1980
Calypso	16	294,660	1.89	1980
Dione	1,120	377,400	2.74	1684
Helene	32	377,400	2.74	1980
Rhea	1,528	527,040	4.52	1672
Titan	5,150	1,221,850	15.95	1655
Hyperion	280	1,481,100	21.28	1848
Iapetus	1,436	3,561,300	79.33	1671
Phoebe	220	12,952,000	550.48	1898

DIONE

Dione, the fourth largest moon of Saturn, has a varied surface. Parts are covered with craters 100 km or more in diameter, while other areas have few craters. Some of Dione's surface is streaked with white ice that has seeped out through cracks in the crust. Rhea, a slightly larger moon, looks similar to Dione.

Dione

MOON SEARCH

● In 1655 Christiaan Huygens discovered Titan, Saturn's largest moon.

● In 1671 Giovanni Cassini discovered Iapetus and in 1672 he located Rhea.

● Cassini discovered Tethys and Dione in 1684.

● In 1944 the atmosphere of Titan was discovered by Dutch-born astronomer Gerard Kuiper (1905–73).

● When Saturn's rings were edge-on in 1966, astronomers discovered Janus and Epimetheus.

● In 1980 Voyager 1 flew past Saturn, discovering the moons Atlas, Prometheus, and Pandora.

● The Hubble Space Telescope mapped the surface of Titan in 1994 using infrared wavelengths.

● Huygens probe is due to land on Titan in 2004.

EPIMETHEUS AND JANUS

Janus and Epimetheus are two small moons with orbits only 50 km apart near the edge of Saturn's rings. Every four years or so, when the inner moon overtakes the outer, the two swap orbits, one moving farther away from Saturn and the other dropping closer. Epimetheus and Janus may be halves of a former moon that broke apart.

Epimetheus

Janus

MOON'S ORBITS

Some of Saturn's moons suffer from orbital overcrowding – tiny Helene shares the orbit of Dione, always keeping about 60° ahead of it, while Tethys has to share its orbit with two small moons, one ahead of it (Telesto) and one behind (Calypso). Atlas marks the outer edge of the A ring. The outermost moon, Phoebe, orbits in the opposite direction to the others.

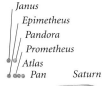
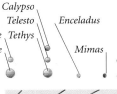
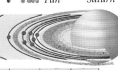

Phoebe *Iapetus* *Hyperion* *Titan* *Rhea* *Helene* *Tethys* *Dione* *Calypso* *Telesto* *Enceladus* *Mimas* *Janus* *Epimetheus* *Pandora* *Prometheus* *Atlas* *Pan* *Saturn*

|215 | |59 |24 |23 |22 |21 |20 |10 |6 |5 |4 |3 |2 |1 |

Scale in radii of Saturn (1 radius = 60,268 km)

FIND OUT MORE

EARTH'S ATMOSPHERE 88
MOON'S SURFACE 96
JUPITER'S MOONS 126

URANUS

URANUS, THE FIRST PLANET to be discovered through a telescope, was spotted on the night of 13 March 1781 by William Herschel. It is too faint to be easily seen with the naked eye, although you can find it with binoculars. Uranus is the third largest planet in the Solar System, but its most remarkable feature is that it appears to lie on its side, so that first one pole and then the other points to the Sun as it moves along its orbit. Perhaps Uranus was knocked over by another object while it was forming. Uranus has 17 known moons and a series of faint rings.

STRUCTURE AND COMPOSITION

Uranus has the least interesting appearance of any of the planets. Like Jupiter and Saturn it is covered in clouds, but its clouds are almost featureless, apart from a few brighter streaks that were photographed by the Voyager 2 space probe. The clouds of Uranus consist of methane ice crystals and appear blue-green because methane gas in the atmosphere above filters out other colours.

RINGS

Uranus has 11 known rings, which circle the planet's equator. The rings – and the equator – appear to be almost upright, because Uranus is tilted on its side. Being very dark, the rings are difficult to see from Earth. Two tiny moons, Cordelia and Ophelia, orbit either side of the outermost ring (the Epsilon ring), shepherding it into place.

VOYAGER 2 IMAGE OF THE RINGS

Uranus is tilted on its side and its narrow rings are made up of particles about 1 metre across.

Slight bulge at equator caused by rapid rotation.

Oberon is the second largest moon of Uranus. It is 1,523 km wide and, at 582,600 km, is the most distant moon.

Titania, at 1,578 km wide, is the largest moon of Uranus, and orbits it at a distance of 435,800 km.

Puck is the largest of the moons discovered by Voyager 2; even so this tiny moon is only 150 km across.

VITAL STATISTICS

Diameter	51,118 km
Average distance from Sun	2.871 billion km
Orbital speed around Sun	6.82 km/s
Sunrise to sunrise	17.24 hours
Mass (Earth=1)	14.5
Volume (Earth=1)	63.1
Average density (water=1)	1.32
Gravity at cloud tops (Earth=1)	0.89
Cloud-top temperature	−197°C
Number of known moons	17

MAGNETIC FIELD

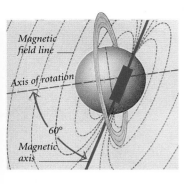

Uranus generates a magnetic field 50 times stronger than Earth's. However, the magnetic field is tilted at 60° to its axis rotation – which would be like Earth's north magnetic pole being in Morocco. Even more extraordinary, the magnetism is generated in the mantle rather than the core.

Magnetic field line

Axis of rotation

60°

Magnetic axis

MIRANDA

Miranda, the smallest of the five main moons (diameter 470 km), has a jumbled surface with a bright tick mark and grooves, shown in detail above. One theory is that Miranda broke apart and came together again.

URANUS' MOONS

Ten of Uranus' 17 moons were discovered by the Voyager 2 space probe in 1986. The moons are named after characters in the writings of William Shakespeare and Alexander Pope. The largest, Titania, is less than half the size of Earth's Moon. The two most distant moons (not shown below) were spotted from Earth in 1997. They are 10 times farther out than Oberon, and orbit Uranus in the opposite direction from all the other moons.

ARIEL AND UMBRIEL

These two moons are similar in size (about 1,160 km), but look very different. Ariel is the brightest of the major moons, while Umbriel is the darkest. Ariel is remarkable for the valleys on its surface, caused by its crust cracking.

Ariel

Umbriel

URANUS AT A GLANCE

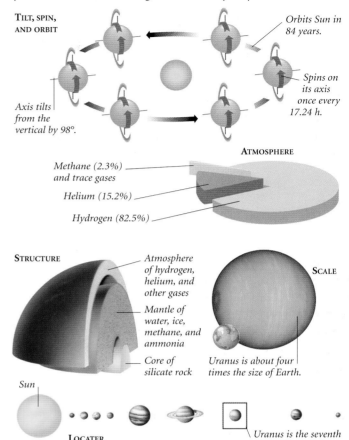

Uranus's extreme tilt gives it unusually long seasons. As the planet follows its 84-year orbit around the Sun, each pole has 42 years of continuous sunlight, followed by 42 years of darkness.

TILT, SPIN, AND ORBIT

Orbits Sun in 84 years.

Spins on its axis once every 17.24 h.

Axis tilts from the vertical by 98°.

ATMOSPHERE

Methane (2.3%) and trace gases

Helium (15.2%)

Hydrogen (82.5%)

STRUCTURE

Atmosphere of hydrogen, helium, and other gases

Mantle of water, ice, methane, and ammonia

Core of silicate rock

Sun

SCALE

Uranus is about four times the size of Earth.

LOCATER

Uranus is the seventh planet from the Sun.

DISCOVERING URANUS

- In 1781, William Herschel discovered Uranus while looking at the sky through his home-made telescope in Bath, England.

- The rings of Uranus were found in 1977 when the planet happened to be passing in front of a star.

- In 1986, Voyager 2 flew past Uranus and detected 10 new moons.

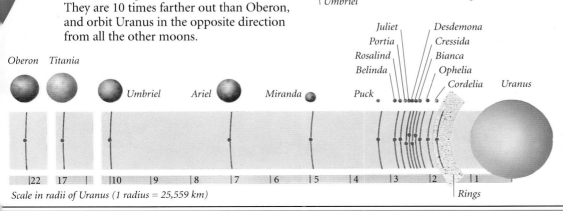

Oberon *Titania* *Umbriel* *Ariel* *Miranda* *Puck* *Juliet* *Portia* *Rosalind* *Belinda* *Desdemona* *Cressida* *Bianca* *Ophelia* *Cordelia* *Uranus*

Rings

Scale in radii of Uranus (1 radius = 25,559 km)

| |22| |17| |10| |9| |8| |7| |6| |5| |4| |3| |2| |1| |

NEPTUNE

THE MOST DISTANT OF THE FOUR GIANT PLANETS in the Solar System, Neptune is 30 times farther from the Sun than Earth. It was discovered by German astronomer Johann Galle in 1846, but its existence was predicted earlier, from the fact that its gravity was pulling Uranus off course. Eight moons are known, along with a faint set of rings. Through small telescopes and binoculars Neptune appears as a faint dot. In many ways, it is similar to Uranus.

Neptune's atmosphere has bright white clouds.

At least four rings surround the planet.

Great Dark Spot surrounded by bright clouds of methane ice.

NEPTUNE AT A GLANCE

Neptune is similar to Uranus in terms of size, rotation period, and internal structure. However, there is more activity in Neptune's clouds and its axis is not tilted at such a large angle.

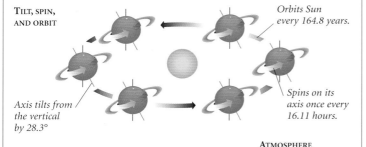

TILT, SPIN, AND ORBIT

Orbits Sun every 164.8 years.

Spins on its axis once every 16.11 hours.

Axis tilts from the vertical by 28.3°

ATMOSPHERE

Methane (about 1%) and trace gases

Helium (19%)

Hydrogen (80%)

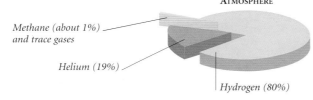

STRUCTURE

Atmosphere of hydrogen, helium, and methane gases

Mantle of icy water, methane, and ammonia

Core of silicate rock

SCALE

Neptune is four times wider than the Earth.

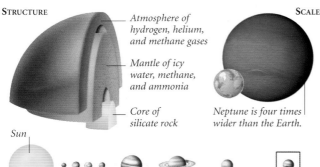

Sun

LOCATER

Neptune is the eighth planet from the Sun.

ATMOSPHERE

There is more methane gas in the highest levels of Neptune's atmosphere than there is on Uranus, and this makes Neptune's clouds appear bluer. Most of the gas in Neptune's atmosphere is hydrogen and helium. The clouds are stormier than those of Uranus because the inside of the planet is warmer, stirring up the gas to produce white and dark clouds that appear and disappear.

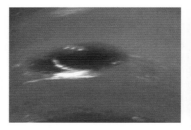

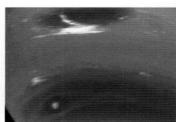

GREAT DARK SPOT
A large oval cloud, about the same size as Earth, was discovered by Voyager 2 in 1989, but had vanished when the Hubble Space Telescope looked at Neptune in 1994. Rotating anti-clockwise every 16 days, it was rimmed with brighter, higher clouds of methane .

SCOOTER
Voyager 2 photographed a bright feature in Neptune's southern hemisphere. It seemed to scoot around the planet more quickly than the Great Dark Spot and so was named the Scooter. Made up of bright streaks of cloud, it changed shape from day to day.

CLOUDS

Bright streaks of cloud, similar to cirrus clouds on Earth but made of methane, were photographed by Voyager 2. These cloud bands, thousands of kilometres long, cast shadows on the main deck of cloud 50–100 km beneath.

VITAL STATISTICS

Diameter	49,532 km
Average distance from Sun	4.498 billion km
Orbital speed around Sun	5.48 km/s
Sunrise to sunrise	16.11 h
Mass (Earth=1)	17.2
Volume (Earth=1)	57.74
Average density (water=1)	1.64
Gravity at cloud tops (Earth=1)	1.13
Cloud-top temperature	−200°C
Number of known moons	8

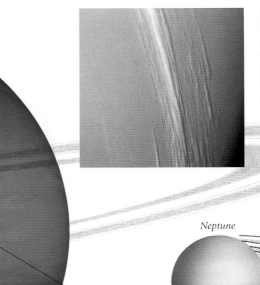

Blue colouring due to methane in the planet's atmosphere.

Thalassa · Despina · Galatea · Proteus · Triton

Neptune · Naiad · Larissa · Nereid

| 1 | 2 | 3 | 4 | 5 | 14 | 15 | 224 | 225 |

Scale of radiuses of Neptune

MOONS

Six of Neptune's eight moons were discovered by Voyager 2 in 1989. Triton (which orbits in the opposite direction to the other moons) and Nereid were first seen from Earth. The four closest moons orbit between the planet's rings, which are probably made of dust from the moons' surfaces.

South polar ice cap on Triton

Triton is 2,706 km across.

HURRICANE WINDS

Winds blowing from east to west at over 2,000 km/h were measured near the Great Dark Spot, making Neptune the windiest planet in the Solar System.

VOLCANO ON TRITON

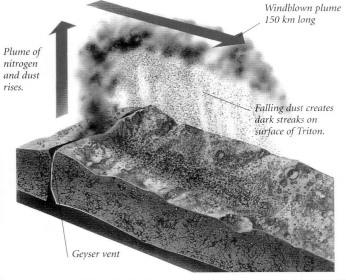

Windblown plume 150 km long

Plume of nitrogen and dust rises.

Falling dust creates dark streaks on surface of Triton.

Geyser vent

TRITON

The largest moon of Neptune, Triton is bigger than the planet Pluto. Probably Triton was once a separate body that was captured by Neptune's gravity. Triton has the coldest surface in the Solar System, −235°C, and is covered with frozen nitrogen and methane.

VOLCANOES OF ICE

Dark streaks on Triton, photographed by Voyager 2, are caused by pockets of nitrogen gas erupting like geysers. Gas and fine, dark dust rise 8 km above the surface and are then blown downwind for 150 km or so in Triton's thin atmosphere.

VIEWS OF NEPTUNE

● Johann Galle, a German astronomer, discovered Neptune in 1846. William Lassell (1799–1880) in England discovered Triton.

● Gerard Kuiper (1905–73), a Dutch-born US astronomer, discovered Nereid, the outermost moon, in 1949.

● In 1984, signs of rings around Neptune were detected from Earth.

● In 1989, Voyager 2 flew past Neptune, giving the first good view of its clouds, rings, and moons.

VOYAGER 2

FIND OUT MORE

SOLAR SYSTEM 78
JUPITER'S ATMOSPHERE 124
SATURN 128
URANUS 134

PLUTO

PLUTO IS THE SMALLEST PLANET OF ALL, and the most distant from the Sun. The astronomer Clyde Tombaugh discovered it in 1930. Pluto's orbit is the least circular of all the planets. Pluto is so small and unusual that some astronomers now wonder if it deserves to be regarded as a true planet at all, or simply the largest of a family of icy bodies, known as the Kuiper Belt, beyond Pluto.

Pluto's surface is covered in frozen nitrogen and methane.

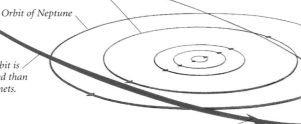

PHOTOGRAPH TAKEN 23 JANUARY 1930

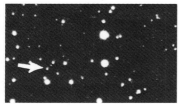

SEARCH FOR A PLANET
Pluto reveals itself as a tiny dot that has moved on these two photographs, taken six days apart. Clyde Tombaugh discovered Pluto at Lowell Observatory in Arizona, USA, in February 1930. He continued to search the sky for more planets, but did not find any.

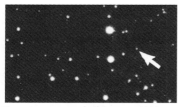

PHOTOGRAPH TAKEN 29 JANUARY 1930

MOST DISTANT PLANET
From Pluto's great distance, the Sun appears a thousand times fainter than it does from Earth but still much brighter than the stars. Pluto's temperature is about –220°C, but when it is closest to the Sun its surface warms up just enough for some of the ice to turn to gas and produce a thin atmosphere. As Pluto's orbit takes it away from the Sun, the gas freezes again and makes a new layer of ice on the surface.

ANATOMY OF PLUTO
Pluto is 2,274 km in diameter, smaller than Earth's Moon (as well as several of the moons of other planets). The Hubble Space Telescope can just make out bright markings, thought to be made by patches of ice, on its otherwise dark reddish surface. There may be craters on Pluto, caused by impacts of smaller objects, as shown in this artist's impression.

Elliptical and angled orbit of Pluto.

Orbit of Uranus

Orbit of Neptune

Pluto's orbit is more tilted than other planets.

For a time Pluto lost its title as the outermost planet, when it passed inside Neptune's orbit in 1979.

Sun

UNUSUAL ORBIT
Pluto's orbit is far from circular, taking it between 4.45 and 7.38 billion km from the Sun. On each 248-year orbit, Pluto comes closer to the Sun than Neptune for about 20 years (as it was between 1979 and 1999) but the two planets cannot collide. Pluto's orbit is tilted at 17° to the Earth's orbit, a greater slant than that of any other planet.

ARTIST'S IMPRESSION OF SUN FROM SURFACE OF PLUTO

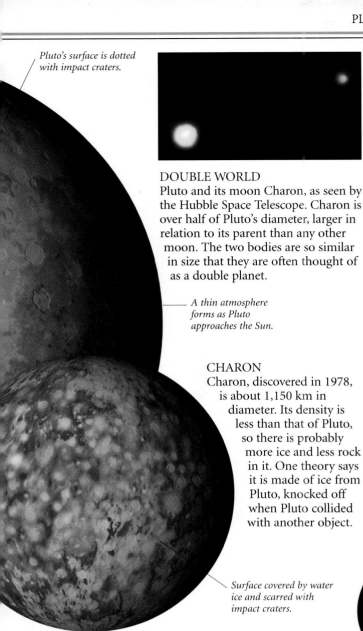

Pluto's surface is dotted with impact craters.

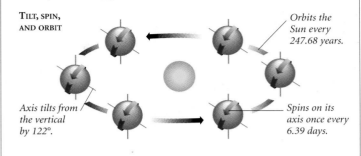

DOUBLE WORLD
Pluto and its moon Charon, as seen by the Hubble Space Telescope. Charon is over half of Pluto's diameter, larger in relation to its parent than any other moon. The two bodies are so similar in size that they are often thought of as a double planet.

A thin atmosphere forms as Pluto approaches the Sun.

CHARON
Charon, discovered in 1978, is about 1,150 km in diameter. Its density is less than that of Pluto, so there is probably more ice and less rock in it. One theory says it is made of ice from Pluto, knocked off when Pluto collided with another object.

Surface covered by water ice and scarred with impact craters.

PLUTO AT A GLANCE
Pluto is a tiny ball of ice and rock much smaller than the Earth. The tilt of its axis is greater than that of Uranus. The most likely theory is that a collision also knocked off ice to make Charon.

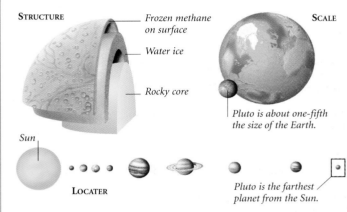

TILT, SPIN, AND ORBIT

Orbits the Sun every 247.68 years.

Axis tilts from the vertical by 122°.

Spins on its axis once every 6.39 days.

STRUCTURE

Frozen methane on surface

Water ice

Rocky core

Sun

SCALE

Pluto is about one-fifth the size of the Earth.

LOCATER

Pluto is the farthest planet from the Sun.

PLUTO EXPRESS
No space probes have been sent to Pluto. NASA is planning a mission called the Pluto-Kuiper Express. This space probe is to be launched in December 2004. It will fly past Pluto and Charon, photographing their surfaces, before passing into the Kuiper Belt beyond.

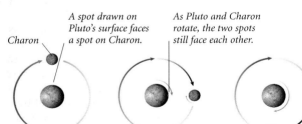

Charon

A spot drawn on Pluto's surface faces a spot on Charon.

As Pluto and Charon rotate, the two spots still face each other.

Charon is never visible from this side of Pluto.

SYNCHRONIZED ORBITS
Pluto and Charon keep the same sides facing each other as they turn – so if you were standing on one side of Pluto you would see Charon hanging in the sky, while someone on the other side of Pluto would not see Charon at all. Charon moves around Pluto every 6 days, 9 hours at a distance of 19,400 km.

VITAL STATISTICS

Diameter	2,274 km
Average distance from Sun	5.9 billion km
Orbital speed around Sun	4.75 km/s
Sunrise to sunrise	6.39 days
Mass (Earth=1)	0.002
Volume (Earth=1)	0.006
Average density (water=1)	2.05
Surface gravity (Earth=1)	0.067
Surface temperature	−223°C
Number of moons	1

FIND OUT MORE

SOLAR SYSTEM 78 • PROBES TO THE PLANETS 80
BIRTH OF SOLAR SYSTEM 82 • MINOR MEMBERS 140
ASTEROIDS 146 • IMPACTS 150

MINOR MEMBERS

NEARLY ALL THE MASS OF THE SOLAR SYSTEM is found in the Sun, planets, and their moons. The remaining, tiny proportion of the material is distributed among a huge number of small objects. These are the minor members of the Solar System. They are lumps of rock, or combinations of rock, dust, ice, and snow. The rocky bodies, the asteroids, are in the planetary region of the Solar System. The snow and dust objects, the comets, form the Oort Cloud on the outer edge. In between are the Kuiper Belt objects discovered at the end of the 20th century.

OUTER SOLAR SYSTEM

The Oort Cloud, named after the Dutch astronomer Jan Oort, marks the outer edge of the Solar System. The spherical cloud is made of orbiting comets that surround the planetary region of the Solar System out to an average distance of 0.8 light years. Between the Cloud and the planets, a ring, or belt of comet-like objects orbit the Sun. This is the Kuiper Belt, named after the astronomer Gerard Kuiper (1905–73).

Oort Cloud consists of about 10 trillion comets. They have been here since the creation of the Solar System 4.6 billion years ago. The Cloud is 1.6 light years (7.6 million million km) across.

It takes a comet on the edge of the Oort Cloud 10 million years to orbit the Sun. Comets cannot exist beyond the Oort Cloud because the Sun's gravity is not strong enough here to stop them being pulled away by a passing star.

The combined mass of all the comets in the Oort Cloud is equivalent to about three Earths.

The Oort Cloud extends a fifth of the distance to the nearest star.

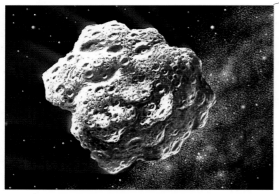

ARTIST'S IMPRESSION OF KUIPER BELT OBJECT

KUIPER BELT

At least 70,000 objects, with diameters of more than 100 km, are believed to exist in the Kuiper Belt. This region stretches from the orbit of Neptune into the outer Solar System. From Earth it is possible to see only those objects that lie close to the inner edge of the Belt. More than 80 of them have been discovered, although none has been seen close up. They are believed to be comet-like objects.

Kuiper Belt

INNER SOLAR SYSTEM

The majority of minor members in the planetary Solar System are asteroids, most of which orbit the Sun in a doughnut-shaped ring or belt between Mars and Jupiter. Others, such as the comet-like Centaurs, orbit further from the Sun. Minor members from the outer Solar System also pass through the planetary region. They follow orbits that bring them from the Oort Cloud and Kuiper Belt, close to the Sun and away again.

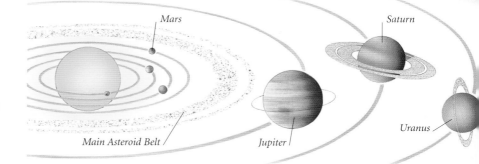

Mars

Saturn

Main Asteroid Belt

Jupiter

Uranus

SEARCHING FOR MINOR MEMBERS

Professional astronomers use the world's most powerful telescopes to search for distant minor members. They make detailed images of the sky using sensitive electronic detectors, called CCDs, which are capable of recording the faint light of objects in the Kuiper Belt. They then compare pictures taken at different times in the hope of finding minor members, whose movements show up against the starry background.

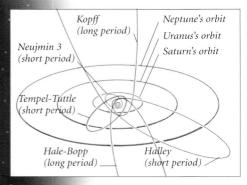

Kopff (long period)
Neujmin 3 (short period)
Neptune's orbit
Uranus's orbit
Saturn's orbit
Tempel-Tuttle (short period)
Hale-Bopp (long period)
Halley (short period)

PERIODIC COMETS

Comets can only become visible when they leave the Oort Cloud and travel towards the Sun. Some of these, known as periodic comets, follow paths that return them regularly to our skies. About 135 are short-period comets, which orbit the Sun in less than 200 years. Long-period comets may take thousands of years to return.

CENTAURS

A group of minor members called Centaurs follow paths between the orbits of Jupiter and Neptune. Astronomers believe that Centaurs follow these orbits for only a few million years. They could be Kuiper Belt objects on their way into the planetary system to become short-period comets.

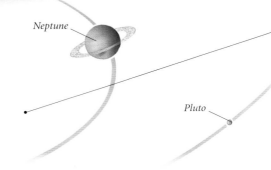

Neptune

Pluto

DISCOVERING THE MINOR MEMBERS

• The first asteroid was discovered in 1801. A century later nearly 500 had been discovered, but still nobody knew what they were made of.

• As recently as 1910 many people feared the return of Halley's Comet. They ate anti-comet pills and dreamed of travelling to the safety of the Moon.

FEAR OF COMETS, 1910

• In 1986, the Giotto space probe returned the first close-up view of the centre of a comet – its snowy nucleus.

• Astronomers continue to find new minor members. In particular, they are looking for Kuiper Belt objects and near-Earth asteroids.

COMETS

THERE ARE BILLIONS OF COMETS in the Solar System, living at the edge of it and forming the enormous spherical Oort Cloud. Individually, they are small, irregularly shaped lumps of snow and rocky dust, each following its own orbit around the Sun. Occasionally, one leaves the Cloud and travels into the inner Solar System. As it gets closer to the Sun this nucleus develops a huge head and two long tails. The comet is then large enough and bright enough to be seen in Earth's sky. About 750 comets have been seen and another 10 to 20 or so are added to the list each year.

Gas tail is characteristically blue and narrow.

COMET HALE-BOPP
Once every 10 years or so a spectacular comet, such as Hale-Bopp, is seen in the night sky. It was clearly visible by eye during much of 1997.

ANATOMY OF A COMET
Throughout its life, a comet consists of a nucleus – a loose collection of snow and rocky dust. Comets that travel through the inner Solar System, however, are changed by the Sun's heat, and for a short time the snow turns to gas and forms a glowing head – the coma. The solar wind and radiation also sweeps away gas and dust from the nucleus into two tails – one gas, the other dust.

Coma can grow to 100,000 km across.

Nucleus of snow and dust, usually only kilometres in size, is hidden from view inside the coma.

The camera was one of 10 instruments that analysed and took images of Halley's Comet.

Giotto space probe

NUCLEUS OF A COMET
The only solid part of a comet, the nucleus, was seen for the first time in March 1986. The space probe Giotto flew to Halley's Comet as it followed its path through the inner Solar System. Giotto gathered data for about 10 hours, photographing the nucleus from 600 km. It measured 16 km from end to end.

Cutaway shows snow and dust structure inside the comet's nucleus.

Bright side faces the Sun.

Gas and dust are released from the nucleus when its surface is heated by the Sun.

Impact crater

Crust of dark dust

Chain of hills on surface

SPACE PROBES TO COMETS
Astronomers are keen to study comets, as cometary material dates from the formation of the Solar System. The space probe Stardust will photograph Comet Wild 2 in January 2004 before returning to Earth with a sample of its dust and gas.

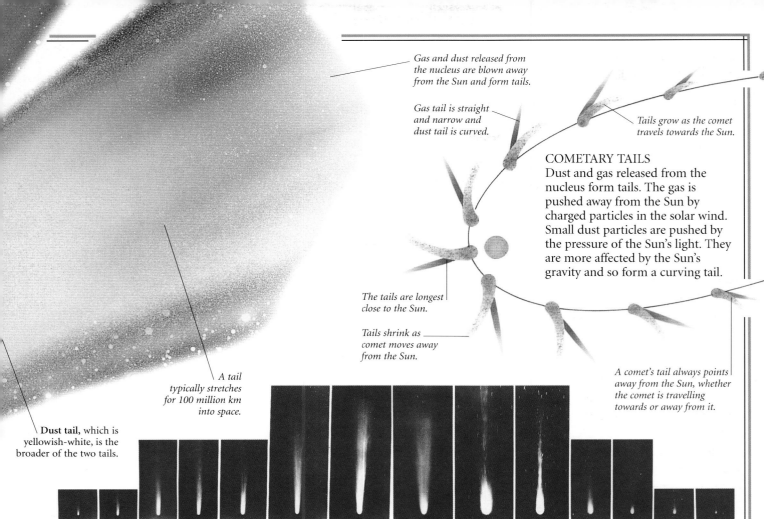

Gas and dust released from the nucleus are blown away from the Sun and form tails.

Gas tail is straight and narrow and dust tail is curved.

Tails grow as the comet travels towards the Sun.

COMETARY TAILS

Dust and gas released from the nucleus form tails. The gas is pushed away from the Sun by charged particles in the solar wind. Small dust particles are pushed by the pressure of the Sun's light. They are more affected by the Sun's gravity and so form a curving tail.

The tails are longest close to the Sun.

Tails shrink as comet moves away from the Sun.

A comet's tail always points away from the Sun, whether the comet is travelling towards or away from it.

A tail typically stretches for 100 million km into space.

Dust tail, which is yellowish-white, is the broader of the two tails.

HALLEY'S COMET, 26 APRIL–11 JUNE 1910

THE TAIL OF HALLEY'S COMET

A comet develops new tails each time it travels on the part of its orbit that takes it close to the Sun. The tails last for only a short time – about two months. These photographs show how the tails developed and decayed during the return of Halley's Comet in 1910. They cover the period from 26 April to 11 June (left to right) of that year.

COMETARY BREAKUP

Comets travelling through the inner Solar System average 100 orbits before losing all their gas and dust. However, if a comet is pulled off its path, it could die in a more spectacular way. Comets have been pulled into the Sun and one, Shoemaker-Levy-9, was pulled apart by Jupiter's gravity. Twenty-one pieces crashed into Jupiter's atmosphere in July 1994.

COMET SHOEMAKER-LEVY-9

COMETS TO LOOK OUT FOR

Comet	Constellation	Magnitude	Viewing date
Borrelly	Cancer	9.5	Sept 2001
Encke	Aquila	7	Dec 2003
Tempel 1	Virgo	9.5	June 2005
Chernykh	Cetus	10	Oct 2005
Schwassmann-Wachmann 3	Hercules	1.5	May 2006
Honda-Mrkos-Pajdusakova	Aries	10	June 2006
Faye	Pisces	10	Nov 2006
Tuttle	Pisces	5	Jan 2008
22P Kopff	Aquarius	9	July 2009
Wild 2	Virgo	8.5	March 2010

FIND OUT MORE

SOLAR SYSTEM 78 • PROBES TO THE PLANETS 80
BIRTH OF THE SOLAR SYSTEM 82 • MINOR MEMBERS 140
METEORS 144 • ASTEROIDS 146

☞ SPOTTING COMETS

Some comets are bright enough to see with the naked eye, others can only be picked out using binoculars or a telescope. Whatever the method, comets always look like fuzzy patches of light in the night sky. They travel at speed through the Solar System and, while you will not see one move, you should be able to chart its nightly progress.

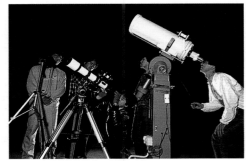

COMET WATCHING WITH TELESCOPES

METEORS

EVERY NIGHT, BRIGHT STREAKS OF LIGHT can be seen in Earth's sky. These are meteors, also known as shooting stars because of their appearance. They are caused by pieces of rock and dust – lost by comets or colliding asteroids – which burn up as they travel through Earth's atmosphere. These particles, meteoroids, are strewn throughout the Solar System. Each year, Earth sweeps up 200,000 tonnes of meteoroids. Particles burn up, appearing as random space meteors, or as part of a meteor shower.

RAINING METEORS
Meteors have been seen in Earth's sky since prehistoric times, but when this Leonid shower occurred in November 1799 it was known only that they were extraterrestrial. The link between comets and meteor showers was not made until the late 19th century.

LIFE OF A METEOR
Meteors come from short-period comets or asteroids. Comets lose material when they travel close to the Sun, and pieces of asteroid break off when asteroids collide. When a meteoroid enters Earth's atmosphere, it is heated by friction and evaporates, producing a trail of light – a meteor – along its path. Short-period comets leave a stream of meteoroids along their orbit. If Earth crosses the orbit of one of these comets, a shower of meteors is seen.

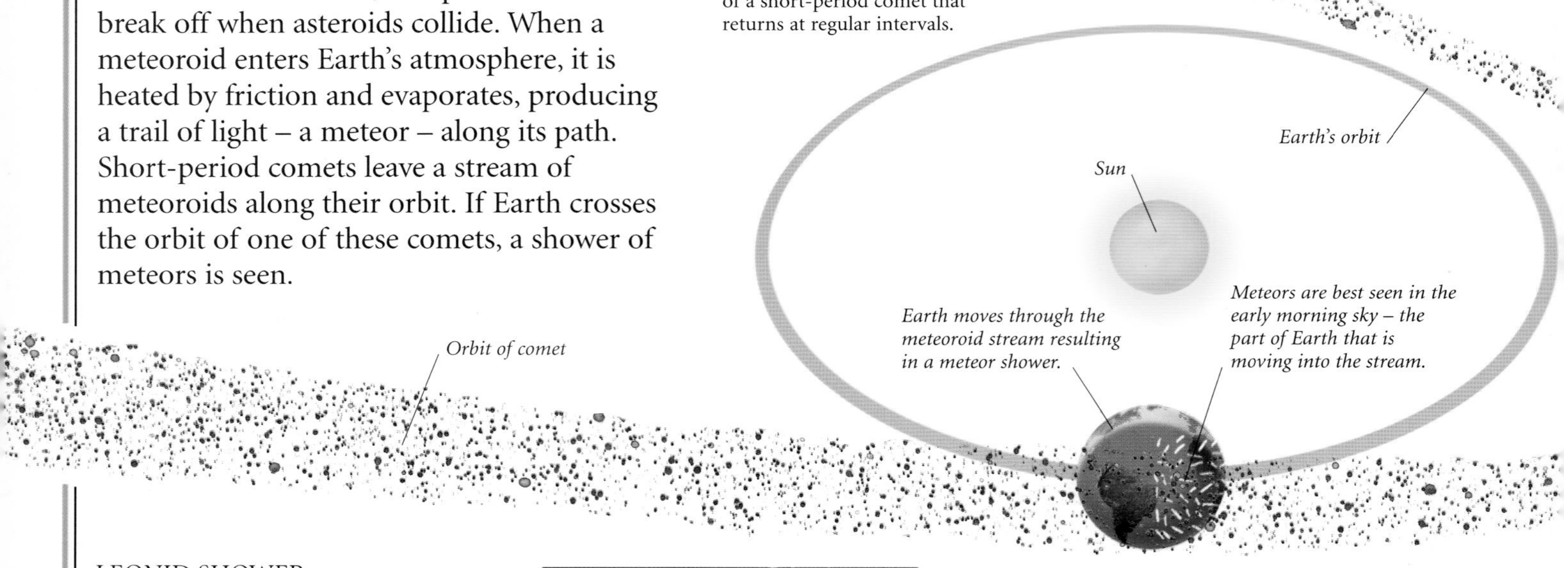

Meteoroid stream is a ring of dust scattered along the orbit of a short-period comet that returns at regular intervals.

Earth's orbit

Sun

Orbit of comet

Earth moves through the meteoroid stream resulting in a meteor shower.

Meteors are best seen in the early morning sky – the part of Earth that is moving into the stream.

LEONID SHOWER
This long-exposure photograph shows the stars as short trails of light. The longer trails in the foreground are meteors that fell as part of the Leonid meteor shower in November 1966. The trail of meteors in a shower such as the Leonids all seem to start from one point in the sky. This point is called the radiant.

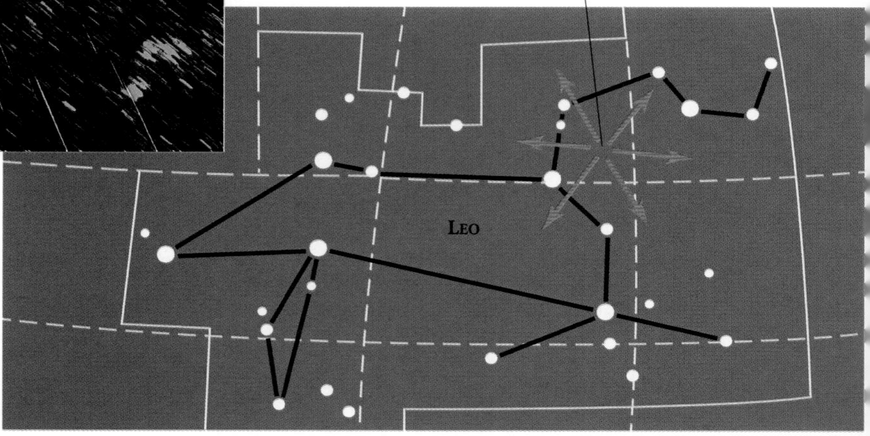

Leonid meteor shower appears to come from a point in the lion's mane. There are usually 10 meteors an hour during the Leonids.

LEO

METEOR SHOWER ORIGIN
Meteor showers are named after the constellation in which the radiant is found. The Leonids appear to start in the constellation Leo (the lion), for example. The Leonids occur each November, when Earth passes through the meteoroid stream left by Comet Tempel-Tuttle. They are one of several annual meteor showers.

FIREBALLS AND BOLIDES

The larger the meteoroid, the brighter the meteor. The brightest ones are known as fireballs, and have a magnitude of at least –5, brighter than the planet Venus. The meteoroid that created this fireball, seen in March 1933, did not burn up completely. Tens of thousands of fireballs occur in Earth's atmosphere each year. About 5,000 of them break up and explode – they are classified as bolides.

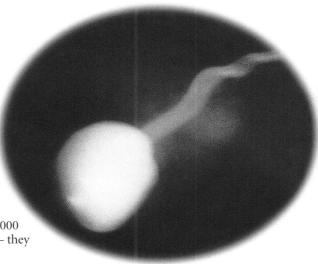

FROM METEOROID TO METEOR

The fate of a meteoroid entering the Earth's atmosphere depends on its size, speed, and how easily it breaks up. Small ones burn up in the higher part of the atmosphere. Larger or fast-moving meteoroids fall closer to Earth before they burn up. Very rarely, a large meteoroid, or fragment of one, survives the atmosphere and hits the surface; it is then known as a meteorite.

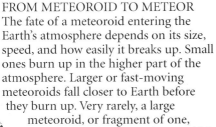

A meteoroid stream can take tens to hundreds of years to form.

Gel used on aircraft

COLLECTING METEOR DUST

Meteoroids range in size from tiny dust particles of one-millionth of a gram to 1-tonne space rocks. For the past 20 years, scientists have been collecting and studying the smaller particles. Aircraft with gel-covered panels cruise at altitudes of about 20 km. When the fast-moving particles collide with the gel they stick to it and can be studied later in the laboratory.

A meteoroid enters the atmosphere at between 11 and 74 km/s.

Meteors occur at between 120 and 80 km above the Earth.

Visible meteors have magnitudes in the range of 3.75 to 0.75.

Fireballs occur lower in the atmosphere and are brighter than normal meteors.

Meteoroid break-up usually occurs between 30 and 10 km above the ground.

Single rocks that slow down fall on the ground.

Large rocks that do not slow down cause explosion craters.

SINGLE METEOR

Meteors that are not part of a shower and fall on their own – single meteors – are seen throughout the year. About 10 an hour can be seen. The trail of a typical single meteor is about 1 metre across and 7–20 km long and usually lasts for less than a second.

◖ SPOTTING METEORS

The best time to go meteor watching is when Earth is travelling through a concentration of meteoroids and a meteor shower is expected. The best annual showers are listed below. No special equipment is needed. Let your eyes adapt to the darkness, look towards the shower's radiant, and wait. You will see the highest hourly rate of meteors at around 4 a.m., when you will be on the part of Earth that is heading into the dust stream.

METEOR SHOWERS

Name	Date	Constellation
Quadrantids	1–6 Jan	Boötes
April Lyrids	19–24 April	Lyra
Eta Aquarids	1–8 May	Aquarius
Delta Aquarids	15 July–15 Aug	Aquarius
Perseids	25 July–18 Aug	Perseus
Orionids	16–27 Oct	Orion
Taurids	20 Oct–30 Nov	Taurus
Leonids	15–20 Nov	Leo
Geminids	7–15 Dec	Gemini

FIND OUT MORE

MINOR MEMBERS 140 • COMETS 142
ASTEROIDS 146 • METEORITES 148
IMPACTS 150 • PHOTOGRAPHING THE NIGHT SKY 266

ASTEROIDS

Billions of space rocks, known as asteroids, orbit the Sun within the inner Solar System. The asteroids are sometimes called minor planets because each one follows its own orbit around the Sun, spinning as it travels. More than 90 per cent are in a doughnut-shaped region, the Asteroid Belt or Main Belt, which lies between the orbits of Mars and Jupiter. They take between three and six years to orbit the Sun. Asteroids range in size, shape, and colour. Only one, Vesta, is large and bright enough to be seen with the naked eye. Even those observed through the most powerful telescopes are seen as dots of light. Space probes flying past asteroids have revealed four close up.

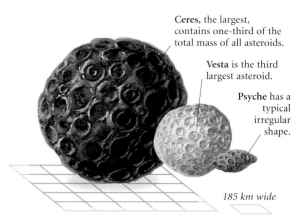

Ceres, the largest, contains one-third of the total mass of all asteroids.

Vesta is the third largest asteroid.

Psyche has a typical irregular shape.

185 km wide

SIZES OF ASTEROIDS
The first asteroid to be discovered – Ceres – is also the biggest, with a diameter of 932 km. However, Ceres is not typical. Only those asteroids that measure more than 300 km across are spherical, and as most asteroids are much smaller than this, they are irregular in shape. As few as 10 are larger than 250 km in diameter.

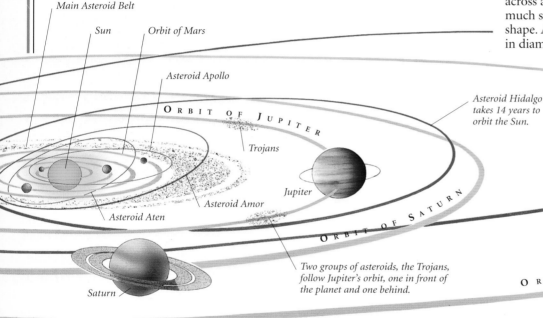

Main Asteroid Belt

Sun

Orbit of Mars

Asteroid Apollo

ORBIT OF JUPITER

Trojans

Jupiter

Asteroid Aten

Asteroid Amor

Asteroid Hidalgo takes 14 years to orbit the Sun.

Chiron, an asteroid discovered in 1977, has an unusually elliptical orbit and is now thought to be a comet.

ORBIT OF SATURN

Uranus

ORBIT OF URANUS

Saturn

Two groups of asteroids, the Trojans, follow Jupiter's orbit, one in front of the planet and one behind.

ASTEROID BELT
The Main Belt of asteroids stretches from about 254 million km to about 598 million km from the Sun. The belt contains billions of asteroids, all moving independently around the Sun. They travel in the same direction as the planets, spinning as they move. Many of the asteroids are tiny, only metres across, but about a billion are more than 1 km across. They are generally spaced thousands of kilometres apart.

If all the asteroids were put together, they would make only 15% of the Moon's mass.

ARTIST'S IMPRESSION OF NEAR-EARTH ASTEROID

NEAR EARTH ASTEROIDS
Some asteroids follow orbits that bring them close to Earth's orbit. These are members of the Apollo, Amor, and Aten groups. The name of each group comes from an individual asteroid. Members of a group follow a certain orbit. The Atens stay mainly inside Earth's orbit, the Apollos cross Earth's orbit, and the Amors follow orbits that take them between those of Mars and Earth.

MAPPING THE MAIN BELT

More than 9,000 asteroids have been identified and observed long enough for their orbits and rotation period to be calculated. The first asteroids to be discovered in the early 19th century, starting with Ceres in 1801, were seen through telescopes. The asteroids that astronomers find today are too faint to be seen through a telescope but can be picked out on photographs or by electronic detectors. The Main Belt has several gaps, known as Kirkwood Gaps, which are swept free of asteroids by Jupiter's gravity.

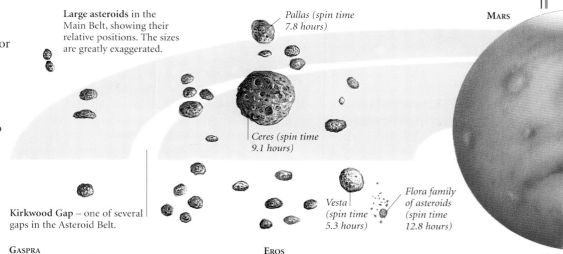

Large asteroids in the Main Belt, showing their relative positions. The sizes are greatly exaggerated.

Pallas (spin time 7.8 hours)

Mars

Ceres (spin time 9.1 hours)

Kirkwood Gap – one of several gaps in the Asteroid Belt.

Vesta (spin time 5.3 hours)

Flora family of asteroids (spin time 12.8 hours)

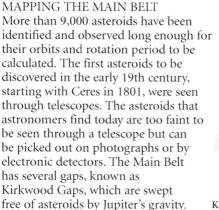

ORBIT OF PLUTO

Pluto

ORBIT OF NEPTUNE

Neptune

GASPRA

EROS

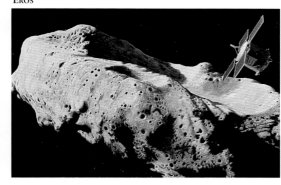

TYPES OF ASTEROIDS

There are three main types of asteroids – those made of rock, those made of metal, and those that are a mixture of the two. Gaspra is a rock asteroid, the first to be seen close up. It is about 19 km long, orbits the Sun every 3.3 years and was photographed by the Galileo space probe in October 1991.

SPACE PROBE

In June 1997, the Near Earth Asteroid Rendezvous (NEAR) space probe showed that the 66-km-long asteroid, Mathilde, is riddled with giant craters and has an interior full of holes. In December 1998, the probe flew past Eros, revealing a 33-km-long pock-marked body. To complete its survey, NEAR will go into orbit around Eros in February 2000.

When the impacting asteroid is less than 1/50,000th of the larger body, a crater forms.

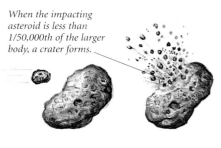

COLLISIONS BETWEEN ASTEROIDS

The Main Belt has not always looked as it does today. When the Solar System was forming it consisted of about 640 rocky balls, each larger than Ceres. These protoplanets collided and broke up and a large amount of material was lost. The remaining pieces of asteroid collided and formed the present-day Main Belt. There are three types of collisions, and they still occur today.

A FAILED PLANET

The Asteroid Belt is believed to be the leftovers of an unborn planet. Material in the Belt region formed more than 600 large, rocky balls – protoplanets – but failed to create one large body 4.6 billion years ago when the Solar System planets were forming. The gravity of the young planet Jupiter stirred up the protoplanets, which collided and broke up to form the large number of objects in the belt today.

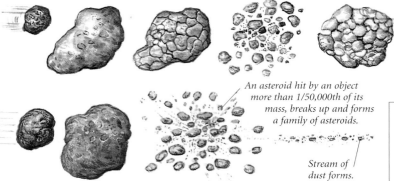

When the impacting body is 1/50,000th of the body it hits, the larger asteroid breaks up and forms a ball of rubble.

An asteroid hit by an object more than 1/50,000th of its mass, breaks up and forms a family of asteroids.

Stream of dust forms.

FIND OUT MORE
SOLAR SYSTEM 78
BIRTH OF SOLAR SYSTEM 82
MINOR MEMBERS 140
METEORS 144
METEORITES 148

METEORITES

Each year about 3,000 space rocks, weighing more than 1 kilogram and too big to burn up in Earth's atmosphere, land on Earth's surface. These rocks are called meteorites. Most fall in the sea, and are never found. Other meteorites are seen to fall on land and are quickly collected from the ground. Some arrive unnoticed and may be discovered years, or even centuries, later.

STONY METEORITE

Most of the meteorites found on Earth are lumps of stone. About 3,000 of these have been collected. They can be subdivided, based on their texture, into chondrites that contain "drops" of solidified rock, and achondrites that do not.

Dark fusion crust formed as meteorite fell through Earth's atmosphere.

METEORITE TYPES

Meteorites are usually made of materials commonly found on Earth, but in different proportions. They are believed to represent the material in the early Solar System. Meteorites are divided into three types.

Meteorite consists of iron-nickel alloy.

IRON METEORITE

The second most common meteorites consist mainly of iron-nickel metal with small amounts of other minerals. Most iron meteorites were originally molten and formed in the cores of asteroids.

Canyon Diablo meteorite, which collided with Earth 50,000 years ago.

This 6-cm stony-iron, found in Antarctica, is from an asteroid.

STONY-IRON METEORITE

The rarest meteorites are a mixture of stone and iron. Some were formed from molten iron-nickel and the stony mineral olivine, and others by impact and welding of metal and stony fragments.

Pale-green olivine crystals set in iron-nickel.

BARWELL STONY METEORITE

This example of a meteorite within a meteorite is made of rock from one asteroid, and melted fragments from another. It fell as part of a shower of rocks over Barwell, England, on 24 December 1965.

METEORITE ORIGINS

Most of the meteorites collected are from asteroids, but 17 came from the Moon, and 13 from Mars. A few may be from comets. Meteorites are also found on the Moon; most of these are believed to come from asteroids.

ASTRONAUT JACK SCHMITT INVESTIGATES THE SITE OF A METEORITE IMPACT ON THE MOON

METEORITE FINDS

The largest known meteorite was found in the ground in 1920. It is called Hoba West after its landing site in south-west Africa. The iron meteorite remains intact and embedded in the limestone ground where it fell. It is a national monument of Namibia.

Melted surface solidifies into a thin black crust.

Piece broken off reveals lighter original rock.

Molten rock flows away from direction of fall.

ANATOMY OF A METEORITE

Friction with the Earth's atmosphere causes the outer surface of a falling space rock to heat up and melt. Some meteorites have a uniform outer surface, while others have a front and a rear surface.

SEARCHING FOR METEORITES

Scientists find about 10 meteorites a year by searching undisturbed areas of the Earth, including Antarctica, the Sahara Desert, and deserts in Australia. It is easy to spot the dark meteorite falls against the snow and ice.

STUDYING METEORITES

Most meteorites are kept in museums or universities, where they are studied by scientists. Special equipment uses the principle of radioactive decay – the breaking down of elements to form other elements over time – to date meteorites and look at how they are formed.

UNDERSTANDING METEORITES

• Single falls, or showers of rocks from a fragmented meteorite, have been recorded since ancient Egyptian times.

ENSISHEIM METEORITE FALL

• The Donnerstein meteorite, which fell near Ensisheim, France, in 1492, is the earliest surviving example of a meteorite fall.

• A meteorite shower in Jilin, China on 8 March 1976 was the most widely observed fall in history.

NOTABLE METEORITES

Name and site	Tonnes	Year of fall or find
Iron meteorites		
Hoba West, Namibia	60	1920
Ahnighito, Greenland	30.4	1895
Bacuberito, Mexico	27	1871
Mbosi, Tanzania	26	1930
Stone meteorites		
Jilin, China	1.77	1976
Norton County, Kansas, USA	1	1948
Long Island, Kansas, USA	0.56	1891
Paragould, Arkansas, USA	0.4	1930
Bjurbole, Finland	0.3	1899
Recent finds		
Dar al Gani 400 (Moon)	1.4 kg	1998
Dar al Gani 476 (Mars)	2 kg	1998

FALLING METEORITES

Every year about six space rocks are seen or heard falling to Earth. On 5 May 1991, Arthur Pettifor heard a loud whining followed by a crash as a meteorite fell in his garden near Cambridge, England. The stony rock was still hot from its journey through the atmosphere.

FIND OUT MORE
MERCURY'S SURFACE 106
METEORS 144
IMPACTS 150

IMPACTS

When a meteorite collides with Earth it can form an impact crater – a bowl-shaped hollow in the Earth's surface. Space rocks have produced craters in this way throughout Earth's life, especially when the planet was young, about 4 billion years ago. Craters of between 1 m and more than 1,000 km wide exist in large numbers on planets and moons throughout the Solar System. About 150 have been found on Earth.

IMPACT ON MIMAS
All the rocky planets, and many planetary moons, have impact craters. The icy surface of Mimas, one of Saturn's moons, is covered in them. One huge crater, Herschel, is 130 km across – a third of Mimas' diameter. It was probably the largest impact that a moon of Mimas' size could withstand without breaking up.

HOW CRATERS ARE FORMED
All craters, whether on Earth or another planet or moon, are formed in much the same way. An impacting meteorite blasts surface material from the point of impact and produces a crater. The size of the crater depends on the size of the original rock. A 30-m space rock hitting Earth can produce a crater 1 km in diameter.

1 Meteorite breaks up and burns up as it meets the friction of the atmosphere.

2 Outer layer of rock is shattered as the meteorite impacts with Earth.

3 Shock waves move through the surface as the meteorite burrows into Earth.

4 An explosion, caused by heat and compression, blasts a crater in Earth's surface.

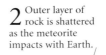

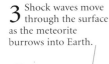

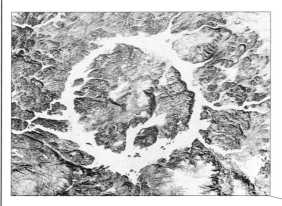

CRATERS ON EARTH
Impact craters are found on every continent on Earth, but they are most common in parts of Australia, Europe, and North America. This is not because more have fallen there, but because the surface of these areas has changed so little that craters have been preserved. The smallest are metres across, the largest on land is 140 km. Most were formed more than 50 million years ago.

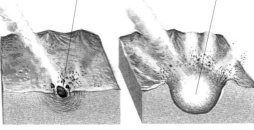

MANICOUAGAN CRATER
Astronauts orbiting Earth can make out the Manicouagan Crater, one of the largest impact craters in Canada. Two semicircular lakes form the outline, which is 100 km across.

METEOR CRATER
This huge, well-preserved crater in the Arizona Desert, USA, has been known since 1871. It was formed about 50,000 years ago when an iron meteorite about 30 m wide struck Earth. The crater measures 1.2 km across and its rim rises 45 m above the surrounding desert.

METEOR CRATER, ARIZONA, USA

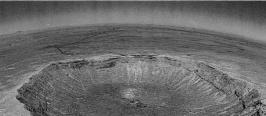

TUNGUSKA IMPACT

Space rocks do not have to hit Earth to have a devastating effect. On 30 June 1908 there was an explosion 6 km up in Earth's atmosphere, above the unpopulated Tunguska River region of Siberia. It was caused by the disintegration of a small piece of comet or asteroid. The blast uprooted trees in a 30-km area and was heard up to 1,000 km away.

SIZE OF TUNGUSKA IMPACT COMPARED TO NEW YORK CITY

SPACE ROCK DETECTION

Powerful telescopes are looking for space rocks that are following orbits that will bring them close to Earth. Telescopes such as those at the Kitt Peak Observatory in Arizona, USA, can detect objects as small as 1 km across.

HENBURY CRATERS

A cluster of 11 craters in northern Australia includes the smallest craters on Earth. The Henbury Crater Field covers an area measuring about 1 km from end to end. The craters are thought to have been formed by a meteorite that broke up in the atmosphere no more than 5,000 years ago. The smallest crater is 6 m across.

IMPACTS ON EARTH

- Earth and other young planets and moons were bombarded 4.6 billion to 3.8 billion years ago by space rocks that were left over from the formation of the Solar System.

- A mountain-sized rock hit Earth 65 million years ago and formed the 200-km Chicxulub Crater, now under the coastline of Mexico. Some people think the impact also led to the death of the dinosaurs.

- Impact craters are still occasionally formed on Earth. In February 1947, 23 tonnes of fragments fell in the Sikhote-Alin mountains, Siberia, and produced craters up to 26 m in diameter.

THE STARS

To the professional astronomer, the stars are part of a huge natural laboratory – one of enormous extremes. While an atomic physicist can test the behaviour of matter in a particle accelerator on Earth, an astrophysicist has access to the far more energetic conditions in the heart of a distant star, or close to a black hole. Light years away in the cosmos, the stars provide a test-bed for theories about the behaviour of matter that we cannot come close to on Earth. And they are much more besides. In a sense, the stars are alive: they are born, they live, and they die. Our local star, the Sun, is no exception. It is halfway through its 10 billion year life span, and it too will die – and with it, the Earth. But a star is a phoenix. From its ashes rises the next generation of stars and planets – and even the building blocks of life itself.

INSIDE THE SUN

OUR NEAREST STAR, THE SUN, is a huge globe of hot gas. It is 109 times the diameter of the Earth and has a mass 745 times greater than that of all the planets in the Solar System put together. Without the constant warming rays of the Sun there would be no life on Earth. The source of the Sun's heat is a nuclear furnace deep beneath its surface. It has been blazing for 4.6 billion years and will continue to burn for about the same time again.

SUN'S STRUCTURE

The Sun's energy is generated in the core, where it is so hot – 15 million °C – that atoms of gas are ripped apart, leaving just their bare nuclei, or centres. The energy travels through the radiative and convective zones to the surface, or photosphere, where it leaves the Sun, mostly as light and infrared radiation. On the way, it passes through the Sun's atmosphere, which extends millions of kilometres into space.

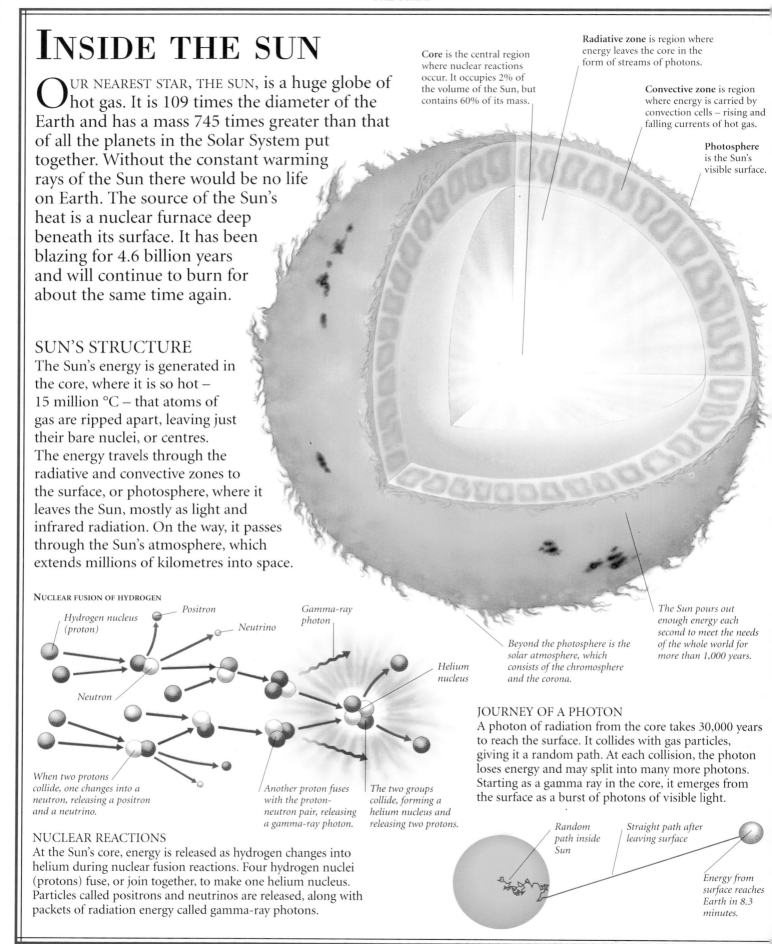

Core is the central region where nuclear reactions occur. It occupies 2% of the volume of the Sun, but contains 60% of its mass.

Radiative zone is region where energy leaves the core in the form of streams of photons.

Convective zone is region where energy is carried by convection cells – rising and falling currents of hot gas.

Photosphere is the Sun's visible surface.

The Sun pours out enough energy each second to meet the needs of the whole world for more than 1,000 years.

Beyond the photosphere is the solar atmosphere, which consists of the chromosphere and the corona.

NUCLEAR FUSION OF HYDROGEN

Hydrogen nucleus (proton)

Positron

Neutrino

Neutron

Gamma-ray photon

Helium nucleus

When two protons collide, one changes into a neutron, releasing a positron and a neutrino.

Another proton fuses with the proton-neutron pair, releasing a gamma-ray photon.

The two groups collide, forming a helium nucleus and releasing two protons.

NUCLEAR REACTIONS

At the Sun's core, energy is released as hydrogen changes into helium during nuclear fusion reactions. Four hydrogen nuclei (protons) fuse, or join together, to make one helium nucleus. Particles called positrons and neutrinos are released, along with packets of radiation energy called gamma-ray photons.

JOURNEY OF A PHOTON

A photon of radiation from the core takes 30,000 years to reach the surface. It collides with gas particles, giving it a random path. At each collision, the photon loses energy and may split into many more photons. Starting as a gamma ray in the core, it emerges from the surface as a burst of photons of visible light.

Random path inside Sun

Straight path after leaving surface

Energy from surface reaches Earth in 8.3 minutes.

Detectors sense flashes of light emitted when neutrinos pass through a tank of water.

SUDBURY NEUTRINO OBSERVATORY, ONTARIO, CANADA

SOLAR COMPOSITION

The Sun's outer layers are 73 per cent hydrogen, 25 per cent helium, and 2 per cent other elements. In the core, where more than 600 million tonnes of hydrogen are converted into helium every second, the amount of hydrogen is only about 34 per cent, while the amount of helium is about 64 per cent.

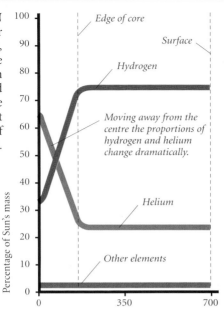

Moving away from the centre the proportions of hydrogen and helium change dramatically.

SOLAR NEUTRINOS

Neutrinos produced by nuclear reactions in the Sun's core travel out into space. Most of these ghostly particles pass through the Earth, but a few can be detected by neutrino telescopes. The Sudbury Neutrino Observatory, Canada, is 2 km underground to protect it from cosmic rays, which would affect its measurements. Astronomers are puzzled because they find less than half the number of neutrinos they expect.

SOLAR OSCILLATIONS

The photosphere – the Sun's surface – moves up and down in complex patterns of vibration. Most of these vibrations, or solar oscillations, are caused by sound waves generated below the surface in the convective zone and trapped inside the Sun. By carefully mapping the vibration patterns of the photosphere, scientists can work out the Sun's internal structure.

Area where the Sun's surface is rising.

Area where the surface is falling.

COMPUTERIZED IMAGE OF SOLAR OSCILLATION PATTERNS

Lines show shock waves around convection cell.

Shock waves spread outwards.

SUNQUAKES

Some solar oscillations may be caused by sunquakes. These are shock waves that spread out from the edges of turbulent circulations of hot gas called convection cells. The energy carried by the shock waves is equal to the energy that would be released by detonating 1.2 billion tonnes of high explosive.

VITAL STATISTICS

Distance from Earth	147.1 million km
Diameter	1.4 million km
Mass (Earth = 1)	330,000
Average density (water = 1)	1.41
Luminosity	390 quintillion megawatts
Average surface temperature	5,500°C
Core temperature	15 million °C
Rotation period	25.4 days (at equator)
Age	4.6 billion years

FIND OUT MORE

GAMMA-RAY ASTRONOMY 30 • UNUSUAL TELESCOPES 32
SUN'S SURFACE 156 • SUN'S ATMOSPHERE 158
PROPERTIES OF STARS 168 • LIFECYCLE OF STARS 170

EVOLUTION OF SOLAR THEORIES

• In the early 19th century, some scientists believed that the Sun was a vast lump of burning coal. Others thought that it was covered with volcanoes, or that it was kept hot by meteorites bombarding the surface.

SUN AS A MASS OF BURNING COAL

• In 1854, German physicist Hermann von Helmholtz (1821–94) proposed that the Sun was being heated as it shrank under its own weight.

• Scientists in the 1920s realized that nuclear reactions power the Sun.

• In 1938, German physicists Hans Bethe (1906–) and Carl von Weizsäcker (1912–) independently worked out how hydrogen converts into helium inside the Sun.

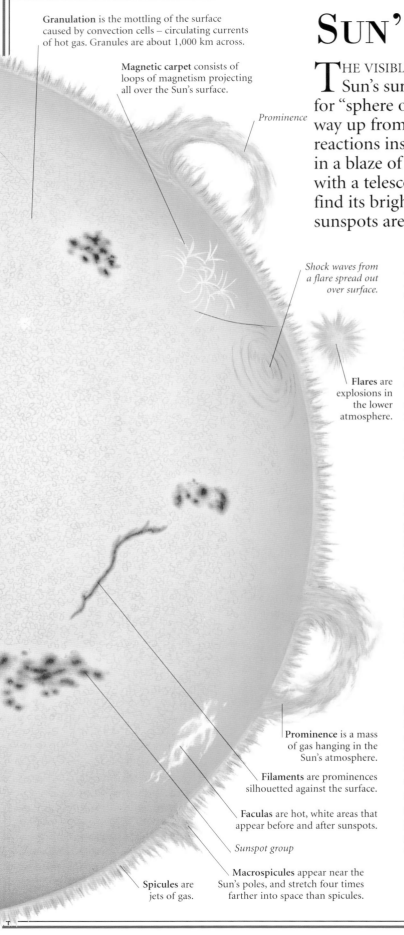

Granulation is the mottling of the surface caused by convection cells – circulating currents of hot gas. Granules are about 1,000 km across.

Magnetic carpet consists of loops of magnetism projecting all over the Sun's surface.

Prominence

Shock waves from a flare spread out over surface.

Flares are explosions in the lower atmosphere.

Prominence is a mass of gas hanging in the Sun's atmosphere.

Filaments are prominences silhouetted against the surface.

Faculas are hot, white areas that appear before and after sunspots.

Sunspot group

Spicules are jets of gas.

Macrospicules appear near the Sun's poles, and stretch four times farther into space than spicules.

SUN'S SURFACE

THE VISIBLE DISC OF THE SUN – what we think of as the Sun's surface – is called the photosphere (from the Greek for "sphere of light"). After thousands of years working its way up from the core, the energy released by nuclear reactions inside the Sun finally bursts from the photosphere in a blaze of light. When Galileo first examined the Sun with a telescope almost 400 years ago, he was amazed to find its bright surface speckled with dark markings. These sunspots are caused by magnetic fields inside the Sun.

PHOTOSPHERE

The photosphere is not solid like the Earth's surface, but a seething sea of glowing gas 500 km thick that marks the tops of currents of hot, opaque gas rising from the interior. At the photosphere, the gas becomes transparent, allowing light to escape into space. Temperatures range from 8,500°C at the bottom of the photosphere to 4,200°C at the top, with the average being about 5,500°C. By analysing light from the photosphere with a spectrograph, astronomers can tell that the Sun consists mainly of hydrogen and helium.

SUNSPOTS

Dark blotches, sunspots, periodically appear on the photosphere. They range from small spots known as pores, which are less than 1,000 km across, to clusters called sunspot groups that stretch for up to 100,000 km. Sunspots last from a few hours to many weeks.

Sunspot

Granulated surface

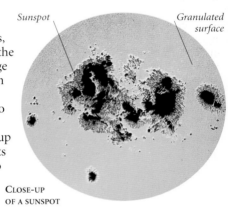

CLOSE-UP OF A SUNSPOT

SUNSPOT STRUCTURE

Sunspots are shallow depressions in the photosphere where strong magnetic fields stop currents of hot gas from reaching the Sun's surface. Sunspots are about 1,500°C cooler than the rest of the photosphere, and only look dark because of their brilliant surroundings.

Umbra is the dark, cooler centre of the sunspot.

Penumbra is the lighter, hotter area around the umbra.

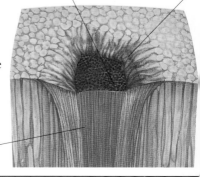

Cool region extends below photosphere.

SUNSPOT CYCLE

The overall number of sunspots rises and falls over an 11-year cycle. The first spots of each new cycle are seen near the poles. They gradually increase in number, appearing closer and closer to the equator until the cycle reaches its peak. The cycle may be caused by the way different parts of the Sun's surface rotate at different speeds, forcing bands of magnetic activity towards the equator.

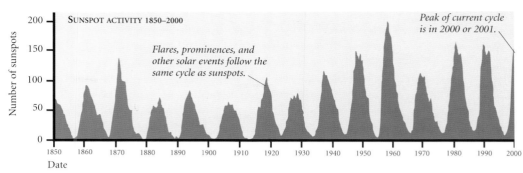

Peak of current cycle is in 2000 or 2001.

SUNSPOT ACTIVITY 1850–2000

Flares, prominences, and other solar events follow the same cycle as sunspots.

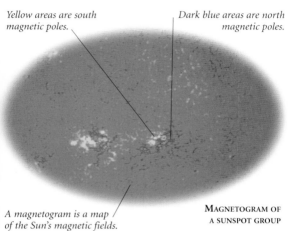

Yellow areas are south magnetic poles.

Dark blue areas are north magnetic poles.

A magnetogram is a map of the Sun's magnetic fields.

MAGNETOGRAM OF A SUNSPOT GROUP

MAGNETIC SUNSPOTS

Sunspots occur in areas of violent magnetic activity called active regions. The magnetic fields inside the Sun are wound up and twisted by the different speeds at which the Sun's surface rotates. Churning gas currents in the photosphere cause loops of magnetism to break through the surface and form sunspots. One end of each loop is a north magnetic pole, while the other end is a south magnetic pole.

EFFECT ON CLIMATE

Some scientists think that solar events may influence the Earth's climate, with periods of cooler weather linked to low solar activity. One such period was 1645–1715, when the Sun was almost spot-free, and the sunspot cycle seemed to have stopped. Northern Europe went through a period of unusually cold weather now known as the Little Ice Age.

People held "frost fairs" on frozen rivers.

RIVER THAMES, LONDON, DURING LITTLE ICE AGE

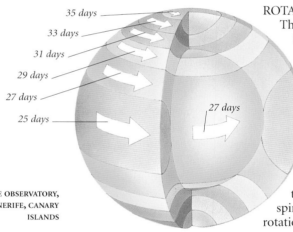

35 days
33 days
31 days
29 days
27 days
25 days
27 days

ROTATION SPEED

The Sun is a globe of gas, so it does not all rotate at the same speed as a solid object would. The Sun's equator makes one rotation roughly every 25 days, while areas near the poles turn once every 35 days. The way the Sun's surface oscillates, or vibrates, suggests that the inner part of the Sun spins like a solid ball, with a rotation period of 27 days.

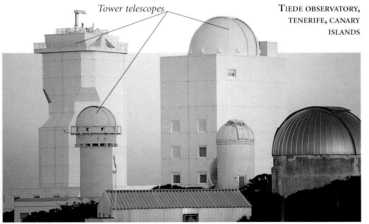

Tower telescopes

TIEDE OBSERVATORY, TENERIFE, CANARY ISLANDS

SOLAR TELESCOPES

A tower telescope is an optical telescope that tracks the Sun with a moving mirror (a heliostat) on top of a tower. The heliostat reflects light down a static, vertical shaft to measuring instruments at ground level. In a vacuum tower telescope, air is removed to stop the Sun's heat from stirring up air currents that may distort the image.

SOLAR OBSERVATORIES

Name	Location	Type	Observations
Big Bear Solar Observatory	USA	Optical	Active regions
GONG (Global Oscillation Network Group)	Six sites worldwide	Optical	Solar oscillations
Kamiokande Solar Observatory	Japan	Neutrino	Solar neutrinos
McMath-Pierce Solar Telescope	USA	Optical	Sunspots, spectra
Nobeyama Radioheliograph	Japan	Radio	Active regions
Sacramento Peak Observatory	USA	Optical	Corona
Sudbury Neutrino Observatory	Canada	Neutrino	Solar neutrinos
THÉMIS (Télescope Héliographique pour L'Étude du Magnétisme et des Instabilités Solaires)	Canary Islands	Optical	Magnetic fields, sunspots

FIND OUT MORE
ANALYSING LIGHT 18 • INSIDE THE SUN 154
SUN'S ATMOSPHERE 158 • PROPERTIES OF STARS 168
LIFECYCLE OF STARS 170 • DAYTIME ASTRONOMY 246

SUN'S ATMOSPHERE

THE OVERPOWERING BRILLIANCE OF THE PHOTOSPHERE – the Sun's surface – normally prevents us from seeing the faint, thin solar atmosphere. Only during total eclipses, when the Moon passes directly in front of the Sun, is the atmosphere clearly visible from Earth. The solar atmosphere consists of two main regions, the chromosphere and the corona. These regions are often rocked by enormous eruptions and explosions called prominences and flares. For reasons astronomers do not fully understand, the corona is hundreds of times hotter than the photosphere. As a result, the Sun's atmosphere is evaporating into space at the rate of a million tonnes every second.

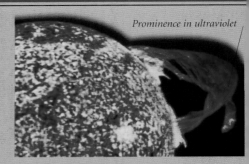
Prominence in ultraviolet

PROMINENCES
Huge clouds and sheets of gas, or prominences, can extend upwards from the chromosphere, stretching hundreds of thousands of kilometres into the corona. They are sculpted into vast loops or arches by magnetic fields over sunspot groups. The gas may splatter down into the photosphere as coronal rain or erupt into space.

CHROMOSPHERE
Just above the photosphere lies the chromosphere – a less dense layer of hydrogen and helium gas, mostly about 5,000 km thick. Nearest to the photosphere, the temperature is about 4,000°C, but it rises to more than 500,000°C at the top, where the chromosphere merges with the corona. Brush-like jets of gas, spicules, project from the chromosphere into the corona. They rise from the edges of huge convection cells, where hot gas from the Sun's interior rises and then sinks back beneath the surface.

This ultraviolet image of the chromosphere was taken by the SOHO spacecraft.

TOTAL ECLIPSE OF THE SUN

Chromosphere can be seen as a blotchy pink ring around the edge of the Moon during a total eclipse.

Hot hydrogen gas makes the chromosphere look pink in visible light

During a total eclipse, the dark disc of the Moon blots out the Sun, revealing the outer reaches of the solar atmosphere.

SOLAR SPACECRAFT

- **Ulysses** is a European Space Agency (ESA) craft launched by NASA in 1990 to study the solar wind. Its orbit takes it over the Sun's polar regions, where it detects high-speed particle streams that do not usually flow past the Earth.

SOHO

- **SOHO** (Solar and Heliospheric Observatory), launched in 1995, is a joint ESA-NASA craft for observing the corona and solar oscillations. It is stationed about 1.5 million km from the Earth.

TRACE

- **TRACE** (Transition Region and Coronal Explorer) is a NASA craft launched in 1998 to study the corona and the boundary between the chromosphere and the corona.

ULYSSES

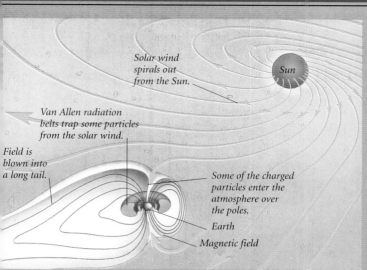

Solar wind spirals out from the Sun.

Van Allen radiation belts trap some particles from the solar wind.

Field is blown into a long tail.

Some of the charged particles enter the atmosphere over the poles.

Earth

Magnetic field

SOLAR WIND AND EARTH'S MAGNETIC FIELD

SOLAR WIND

Streaming out from the corona into space is the solar wind. It consists of particles, such as electrons and protons, and the magnetic fields and electric currents that they generate. The strength of the solar wind varies with solar activity. It affects a region called the heliosphere, which extends 15 billion km from the Sun. The solar wind passes the Earth at speeds of between 300 and 800 km/s. The Earth's magnetic field deflects most of the solar wind, but in the process the field is squeezed and drawn out into a long tail.

AURORA SEEN FROM SPACE

Auroras are striking displays of coloured lights that are sometimes seen over the Earth's magnetic poles. They occur when solar wind particles are trapped by the Earth's magnetic field and collide with molecules of air in the upper atmosphere.

Coronal condensation regions, the bright patches on this X-ray image, are places where hot gas is concentrated.

The photosphere appears as a dark disc because it is not hot enough to produce X-rays.

Density of corona is less than a trillionth the density of Earth's atmosphere.

Coronal holes – the dark patches – are low-density regions of the corona, from which high-speed streams of particles flow into the solar wind.

CORONA

Above the chromosphere and extending millions of kilometres into space is the corona – the outermost region of the Sun's atmosphere. Even though temperatures can rise to more than 3 million °C, the corona is very faint, because the gas is extremely thin. Bubbles containing billions of tonnes of gas sometimes erupt from the corona, sending shock waves out into the solar wind.

The eclipse shows up the corona as a milky-white halo, often displaying wisps, loops, and streamers.

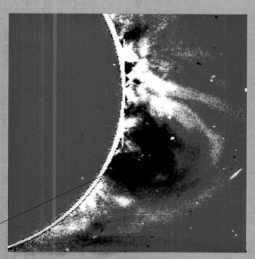

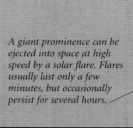

A giant prominence can be ejected into space at high speed by a solar flare. Flares usually last only a few minutes, but occasionally persist for several hours.

FLARES

Solar flares, violent explosions in the chromosphere above sunspot groups, are caused by a release of magnetic energy. They send out bursts of high-energy particles and radiation that can interfere with radio communications on Earth when they strike the ionosphere – the electrically charged layer of Earth's atmosphere. Flares can also endanger astronauts in space.

FIND OUT MORE

ULTRAVIOLET ASTRONOMY 26
X-RAY ASTRONOMY 28
ECLIPSES OF THE SUN 160

ECLIPSES OF THE SUN

IN ITS 27-DAY ORBIT OF THE EARTH, the Moon sometimes passes directly in front of the Sun and we see a solar eclipse. In one of the natural world's most eerie, beautiful spectacles, the dark circle of the Moon gradually creeps over the Sun. Between two and five solar eclipses are visible from somewhere on the Earth each year. Partial eclipses, when only a portion of the Sun is covered by the Moon, are visible over a wide area. Total eclipses, when the Sun is completely hidden, can be seen from only a narrow region of the Earth's surface.

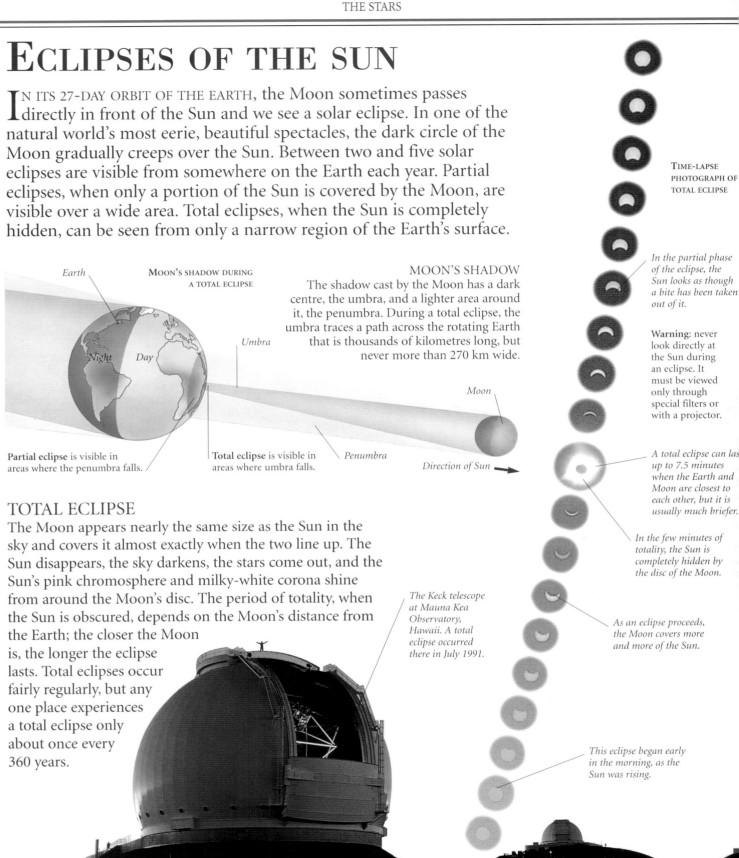

TIME-LAPSE PHOTOGRAPH OF TOTAL ECLIPSE

Earth

MOON'S SHADOW DURING A TOTAL ECLIPSE

Night Day

Umbra

Partial eclipse is visible in areas where the penumbra falls.

Total eclipse is visible in areas where umbra falls.

Penumbra

Moon

Direction of Sun →

MOON'S SHADOW
The shadow cast by the Moon has a dark centre, the umbra, and a lighter area around it, the penumbra. During a total eclipse, the umbra traces a path across the rotating Earth that is thousands of kilometres long, but never more than 270 km wide.

TOTAL ECLIPSE

The Moon appears nearly the same size as the Sun in the sky and covers it almost exactly when the two line up. The Sun disappears, the sky darkens, the stars come out, and the Sun's pink chromosphere and milky-white corona shine from around the Moon's disc. The period of totality, when the Sun is obscured, depends on the Moon's distance from the Earth; the closer the Moon is, the longer the eclipse lasts. Total eclipses occur fairly regularly, but any one place experiences a total eclipse only about once every 360 years.

In the partial phase of the eclipse, the Sun looks as though a bite has been taken out of it.

Warning: never look directly at the Sun during an eclipse. It must be viewed only through special filters or with a projector.

A total eclipse can last up to 7.5 minutes when the Earth and Moon are closest to each other, but it is usually much briefer.

In the few minutes of totality, the Sun is completely hidden by the disc of the Moon.

As an eclipse proceeds, the Moon covers more and more of the Sun.

The Keck telescope at Mauna Kea Observatory, Hawaii. A total eclipse occurred there in July 1991.

This eclipse began early in the morning, as the Sun was rising.

ANNULAR ECLIPSE

When the Moon is at its farthest from the Earth, it is not big enough in the sky to cover the Sun completely during an eclipse. Instead of a total eclipse, an annular eclipse occurs. When the Moon is exactly in front of the Sun, a bright ring of the Sun's photosphere is still visible around the edge of the Moon, like a ring of fire. Annular eclipses can last for more than 12 minutes.

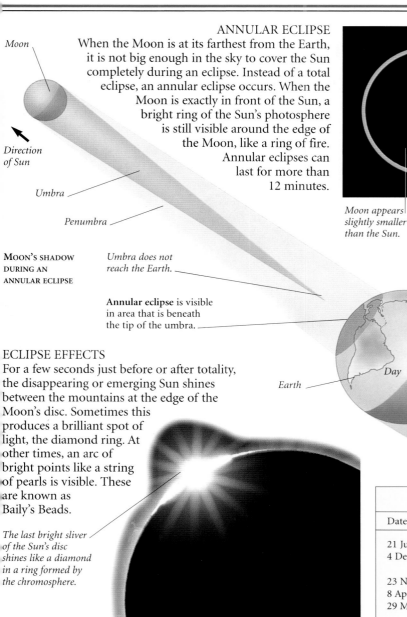

Moon

Direction of Sun

Umbra

Penumbra

MOON'S SHADOW DURING AN ANNULAR ECLIPSE

Umbra does not reach the Earth.

Annular eclipse is visible in area that is beneath the tip of the umbra.

Earth

Day   Night

Moon appears slightly smaller than the Sun.

A bright ring, or annulus, is seen around the Moon.

ECLIPSE EFFECTS

For a few seconds just before or after totality, the disappearing or emerging Sun shines between the mountains at the edge of the Moon's disc. Sometimes this produces a brilliant spot of light, the diamond ring. At other times, an arc of bright points like a string of pearls is visible. These are known as Baily's Beads.

The last bright sliver of the Sun's disc shines like a diamond in a ring formed by the chromosphere.

DIAMOND RING

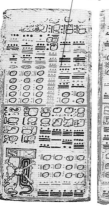
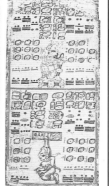

MAYAN ECLIPSE TABLES

Mayan astrologers made detailed calculations and produced these tables to predict when solar eclipses would occur.

PREDICTING ECLIPSES

Ancient peoples discovered that the Sun, Moon, and Earth return to roughly the same positions every 18 years and 11 days. This enabled them to forecast solar eclipses, which were important in many ancient religions. To the Maya of Central America, eclipses were omens of terrible events to come. Religious ceremonies were carried out to try to avert disaster.

TOTAL SOLAR ECLIPSES 2001–2010

Date	Maximum duration	Where visible
21 June 2001	4 minutes 57 seconds	South Atlantic, southern Africa
4 December 2002	2 minutes 4 seconds	Southern Africa, Indian Ocean, Australia
23 November 2003	1 minute 57 seconds	Antarctica
8 April 2005	42 seconds	Pacific, central America
29 March 2006	4 minutes 7 seconds	Atlantic, northern Africa, central Asia
1 August 2008	2 minutes 27 seconds	Greenland, Arctic, Russia, China
22 July 2009	6 minutes 39 seconds	India, China, Pacific
11 July 2010	5 minutes 20 seconds	South Pacific

Tracks show where total eclipses can be seen.

SCIENTIFIC ECLIPSE DISCOVERIES

• British astronomer Norman Lockyer (1836–1920) identified an unknown gas in the Sun's chromosphere during a total eclipse in 1868. He called it helium, from the Greek word *helios*, meaning Sun. Helium was not discovered on Earth until 1895.

• Arthur Eddington used a total eclipse in 1919 to prove Albert Einstein's idea that light from distant stars would be affected by the Sun's gravity. During the eclipse, he measured the positions of stars near the Sun in the sky, and showed that the Sun made their light bend. Einstein had predicted this in his theory of relativity.

MEASURE OF THE STARS

As we cannot yet travel outside the Solar System, we have to learn as much as we can about the stars by studying them at a distance. Astronomers can tell the brightness, colour, and temperature of a star by analysing the light it gives out. By splitting starlight into its constituent colours, they can find out what the stars are made of and how fast they are moving. And with accurate measurements of position, astronomers can predict where stars will wander through the sky thousands of years from now.

Hadar: magnitude 0.6, type B1

Mimosa: magnitude 1.3, type B0

Alpha Centauri (triple star): magnitude –0.3, types G2, K1, and M5

STARRY SKY

On a dark starry night, we can see perhaps 2,500 stars. To our eyes, they appear as little more than twinkling points of light. Some are brighter than others, some are grouped in clusters, and here and there a red or blue star stands out. It may seem hard to believe, but everything we understand about the stars has been learned by studying starlight. We know that they are suns and, like our Sun, they are powered by nuclear energy. We know how they are born, how they live their lives, and how they die. Astronomers classify stars according to their brightness (magnitude) and colour.

PANORAMIC VIEW OF THE SOUTHERN MILKY WAY

Coalsack Nebula

Alpha Muscae: magnitude 2.7, type B2

BRIGHTEST STARS

Name	Magnitude	Spectral type	Distance in ly
Sirius	–1.4 (double star)	A0, white dwarf	8.6
Canopus	–0.6	F0	310
Alpha Centauri	–0.3 (triple star)	G2, K1, M5	4.4
Arcturus	0.0	K2	36.8
Vega	0.0	A0	25.3
Capella	0.1 (double star)	G2, G6	42.2
Rigel	0.2	B8	800
Procyon	0.4 (double star)	F5, white dwarf	11.4
Achernar	0.5	B3	144
Betelgeuse	0.5 (variable star)	M2	400

FIND OUT MORE

ANALYSING LIGHT 18 • RADIATIONS FROM SPACE 20
INSIDE THE SUN 154 • HOW FAR ARE THE STARS 166
PROPERTIES OF STARS 168 • LIFECYCLE OF STARS 170

MAGNITUDE SCALE

Venus — –4
–3
Sirius (brightest star in the sky) — –2
–1
0
+1
Polaris — +2
+3
Faintest star visible to the naked eye — +4
+5
+6
+7
+8
Faintest star visible with binoculars — +9
+10
+11
+12
+13
+14
+15
+16
+17
+18
Faintest star visible on sky survey photographs — +19
+20
+21
+22

MAGNITUDE

Astronomers measure brightness in magnitudes. The smaller the magnitude number, the brighter the star. The very brightest stars have negative magnitudes. On a dark night, the faintest stars visible to the naked eye are about magnitude 6. Each step on the magnitude scale represents an increase or decrease in brightness of 2.5 times.

SPECTRAL TYPES

A star's colour depends on its temperature: the hottest stars are blue-white and the coolest are orange-red. Astronomers classify stars into seven spectral types: O, B, A, F, G, K, and M, where O is the hottest and M the coolest. Each spectral type has 10 subdivisions, numbered 0 to 9 (hotter to cooler). The Sun is type G2.

Type O (40,000–29,000°C)

Type B (28,000–9,700°C)

Type A (9,600–7,200°C)

Type F (7,100–5,800°C)

Type G (5,700–4,700°C)

Type K (4,600–3,300°C)

Type M (3,200–2,100°C)

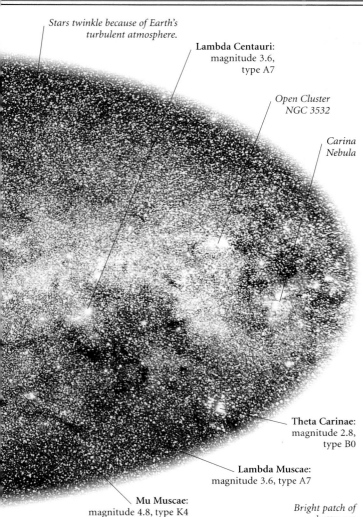

Stars twinkle because of Earth's turbulent atmosphere.

Lambda Centauri: magnitude 3.6, type A7

Open Cluster NGC 3532

Carina Nebula

Theta Carinae: magnitude 2.8, type B0

Lambda Muscae: magnitude 3.6, type A7

Mu Muscae: magnitude 4.8, type K4

SPECTRAL ANALYSIS

Light consists of electromagnetic waves of varying lengths. In spectral analysis, a spectrograph splits the light from a star into its different wavelengths, producing a band of colours called a spectrum. Elements in the star's atmosphere absorb light at some wavelengths, producing dark absorption lines on the spectrum. Each element gives a different pattern of lines, so by studying the lines on the spectrum, astronomers can tell what a star is made of.

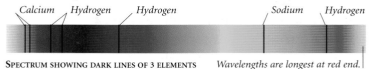

Calcium *Hydrogen* *Hydrogen* *Sodium* *Hydrogen*

SPECTRUM SHOWING DARK LINES OF 3 ELEMENTS *Wavelengths are longest at red end.*

DOPPLER SHIFT

The wavelengths of dark lines in a star's spectrum are affected by the star's motion. This is the Doppler effect. Motion towards the Earth shortens the wavelengths, shifting the lines towards the blue end of the spectrum (blue shift). Motion away from the Earth stretches the wavelengths and shifts the lines towards the red end of the spectrum (red shift). By measuring the changes in wavelength, astronomers can calculate the star's speed along the line of sight.

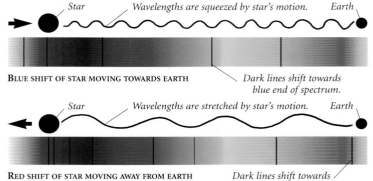

Star *Wavelengths are squeezed by star's motion.* *Earth*

BLUE SHIFT OF STAR MOVING TOWARDS EARTH *Dark lines shift towards blue end of spectrum.*

Star *Wavelengths are stretched by star's motion.* *Earth*

RED SHIFT OF STAR MOVING AWAY FROM EARTH *Dark lines shift towards red end of spectrum.*

SURFACE FEATURES

Even with large telescopes, most stars are too far away for astronomers to see markings on their surfaces. But with a few stars, it is possible to detect surface features. This image of the supergiant star Betelgeuse shows a bright patch, which may be hot gas rising to the surface.

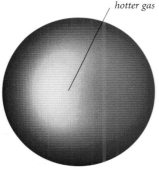

Bright patch of hotter gas

PROPER MOTION

Stars are so far away, we are not normally aware of their movement through space. But over time this movement, called proper motion, changes the shapes of constellations dramatically. Astronomers can work out a constellation's past and future shape by precisely measuring the positions of its stars over several years.

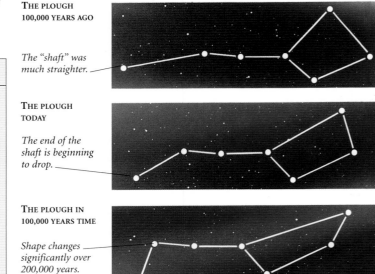

THE PLOUGH 100,000 YEARS AGO

The "shaft" was much straighter.

THE PLOUGH TODAY

The end of the shaft is beginning to drop.

THE PLOUGH IN 100,000 YEARS TIME

Shape changes significantly over 200,000 years.

UNDERSTANDING THE STARS

- The magnitude scale for measuring the brightness of stars was devised in 130 BC by Hipparchus of Nicaea.

- In 1718, Edmond Halley discovered proper motion when he noticed that stars recorded by Hipparchus in 129 BC had moved.

- Joseph von Fraunhofer used a spectroscope in 1814 to analyse light from the Sun. He found that the Sun's spectrum was crossed by many dark absorption lines.

- In 1868, William Huggins used the Doppler effect to find that Sirius was moving away from the Sun at 47 km/s.

VARIABLE STARS

THE STARS DO NOT SHINE as constantly as they appear to at first sight. Stars that vary in brightness are known as variable stars. In some variables, such as pulsating, eclipsing, and rotating ones, there is a regular pattern or period to their variation. Others, such as eruptive and cataclysmic variables, are more unpredictable in their behaviour. A star may vary because it gives out changing amounts of light, or because its light is obscured by shifting dust clouds or a companion star. By plotting graphs, or light curves, of the star's brightness, astronomers can work out why the brightness varies.

NOVA IN CONSTELLATION OF CYGNUS, 1975

CYGNUS AFTER THE NOVA

Position former nov

CATACLYSMIC VARIABLES

Stars that burst into brilliance when they undergo sudden, violent changes are cataclysmic variables. They include novas and supernovas. A nova occurs when a white dwarf in a double, or binary, star system pulls hydrogen gas off its companion. The gas builds up until there is a nuclear explosion. In 1975, a nova appeared in Cygnus, briefly making the binary star 40 million times brighter.

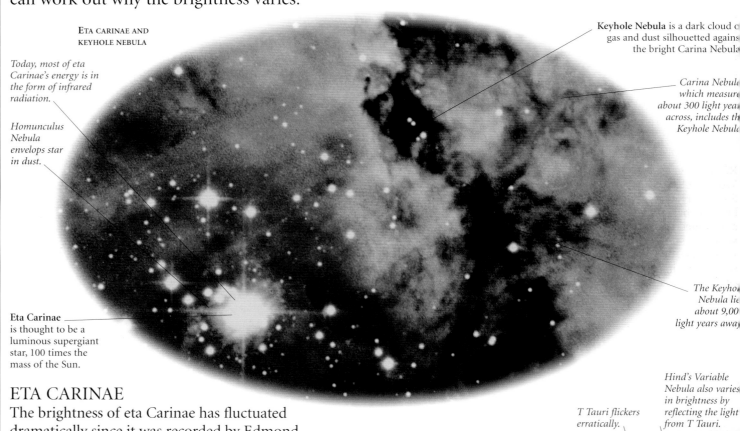

ETA CARINAE AND KEYHOLE NEBULA

Today, most of eta Carinae's energy is in the form of infrared radiation.

Homunculus Nebula envelops star in dust.

Eta Carinae is thought to be a luminous supergiant star, 100 times the mass of the Sun.

Keyhole Nebula is a dark cloud o gas and dust silhouetted agains the bright Carina Nebula

Carina Nebul which measure about 300 light yea across, includes th Keyhole Nebul

The Keyho Nebula lie about 9,00 light years awa

ETA CARINAE

The brightness of eta Carinae has fluctuated dramatically since it was recorded by Edmond Halley in 1677. By the middle of the 19th century, it had become the second brightest star in the sky at magnitude –0.8, but then suddenly plunged to below magnitude 6. Eta Carinae had thrown out a thick cloud of obscuring dust now known as the Homunculus Nebula. The shifting dust and the star's unstable outer layers account for the variations in its brightness. Eta Carinae is classed as an eruptive variable.

ERUPTIVE VARIABLES

Stars that brighten or fade with no regular pattern are called eruptive variables. Their brightness varies as violent changes occur in their outer atmospheres. Some puff out clouds of smoke that make them suddenly fade. Others, such as T Tauri, are young stars still shrinking to a stable size as stellar winds blow away the dust and gas from which they formed.

Hind's Variable Nebula also varies in brightness by reflecting the light from T Tauri.

T Tauri flickers erratically.

PULSATING VARIABLES

Towards the end of their lives, stars often pulsate, varying in brightness, temperature, and size. Mira stars (named after the star Mira) are red giants that pulsate over a period of up to 1,000 days. Cepheid variables (named after delta Cephei) are yellow supergiants that pulsate in a cycle that lasts 1 to 50 days.

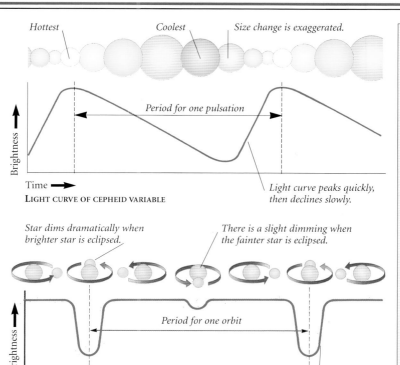

Hottest *Coolest* *Size change is exaggerated.*

Period for one pulsation

Brightness

Time ➔

LIGHT CURVE OF CEPHEID VARIABLE

Light curve peaks quickly, then declines slowly.

ECLIPSING VARIABLES

Some pairs of stars are so close to each other that they look like a single star. In addition, if their orbits are angled edge-on to the Earth, each star periodically passes in front of its companion and eclipses it. This reduces the total light reaching the Earth, so the star appears to fade.

Star dims dramatically when brighter star is eclipsed.

There is a slight dimming when the fainter star is eclipsed.

Period for one orbit

Brightness

Time ➔

LIGHT CURVE OF ECLIPSING VARIABLE

Light curve is steady, with sudden changes during eclipses.

ROTATING VARIABLES

Some stars vary because their surfaces are covered with spots similar to sunspots. As the stars rotate, different groups of spots come into view and the brightness changes. One such star is AB Doradus, a cool dwarf star about 65 light years from the Sun. It varies by up to 0.15 magnitudes over a period of 12.4 hours, the time it takes to complete one rotation.

Computerized images show half a rotation of the star.

STARSPOTS ON AB DORADUS

The more spots and the larger the area they cover, the dimmer the star.

Spots may be up to 1,000 times bigger than sunspots on the Sun.

Star dims when dark spots come into view.

IMPORTANT VARIABLE STARS

Star	Magnitude	Period (days)	Type
Algol	2.1–3.4	2.9	Eclipsing
Betelgeuse	0.0–1.3	2,100	Pulsating (semi-regular)
Cor Caroli A	2.84–2.96	5.5	Rotating
Delta Cephei	3.5–4.4	5.4	Pulsating (Cepheid)
Epsilon Aurigae	2.9–3.8	9,892	Eclipsing
Eta Carinae	−0.8–7.9	—	Eruptive
Mira	2.0–10.1	332	Pulsating (long period)
R Coronae Borealis	5.7–14.8	—	Eruptive (deep fades)
T Coronae Borealis	2.0–10.8	—	Cataclysmic (recurrent nova)

VARIABLE FIRSTS

• Chinese astronomers observed a nova near the star Antares in 1300 BC.

• In 134 BC, Hipparchus of Nicaea saw a nova in the constellation of Scorpius and was inspired to compile the first star catalogue.

• In 1596, German astronomer David Fabricius (1564–1617) noted a varying star, later named Mira by Polish astronomer Johannes Hevelius (1611–87).

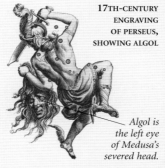

17TH-CENTURY ENGRAVING OF PERSEUS, SHOWING ALGOL

Algol is the left eye of Medusa's severed head.

• Italian astronomer and mathematician Geminiano Montanari (1633–87) noticed in 1669 that Algol varies in brightness. In 1782, Englishman John Goodricke (1764–86) proposed that Algol is an eclipsing binary.

• Goodricke discovered delta Cephei (the first Cepheid variable) in 1784. In 1912, Henrietta Leavitt discovered that the pulsation period of a Cepheid variable is related to its luminosity.

◉ OBSERVING ALGOL

Algol is an eclipsing variable in Perseus. Algol's eclipses last about 10 hours and dim the brightness by just over one magnitude. They occur every 2.9 days, and are easily viewed without a telescope. Perseus is best seen on autumn and winter evenings in the northern hemisphere.

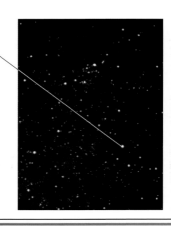

Algol

HOW FAR ARE THE STARS?

UNTIL 1838, ASTRONOMERS HAD LITTLE IDEA of the true size of the Universe. But in that year, Friedrich Bessel used a technique called the parallax method to make the first successful measurement of the distance to a star. Modern astronomers have many different ways of working out how far away an object is, but they all depend ultimately on the parallax method. Our knowledge of stellar distances was further revolutionized by the Hipparcos survey satellite, which used parallax to pinpoint many thousands of stars.

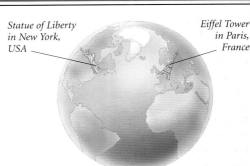

Statue of Liberty in New York, USA

Eiffel Tower in Paris, France

NEAREST STAR
The Sun's nearest neighbour is Proxima Centauri, one of the three stars that make up the Alpha Centauri system. It is 4.2 light years away. If the Sun were the size of a soccer ball, the distance to Proxima Centauri would be the same as the distance from Paris, France, to New York, USA.

HIPPARCOS SATELLITE

The European Space Agency launched its satellite Hipparcos in 1989. Located far above the disturbing effects of the Earth's atmosphere, Hipparcos spent three-and-a-half years measuring star positions. Its precision was so great that it could have picked out an astronaut standing on the Moon. From the data sent back, scientists calculated the parallaxes of 118,000 stars as faint as magnitude 12.5. Astronomers now have accurate distances to stars up to 500 light years from the Sun.

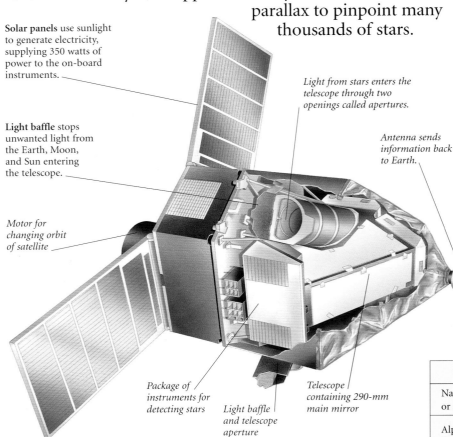

Solar panels use sunlight to generate electricity, supplying 350 watts of power to the on-board instruments.

Light baffle stops unwanted light from the Earth, Moon, and Sun entering the telescope.

Motor for changing orbit of satellite

Light from stars enters the telescope through two openings called apertures.

Antenna sends information back to Earth.

Package of instruments for detecting stars

Light baffle and telescope aperture

Telescope containing 290-mm main mirror

LIGHT YEARS AND PARSECS
Astronomers measure distances in light years and parsecs. One light year (ly) equals 9.5 trillion kilometres – the distance light would travel in one year. One parsec is equal to 3.26 ly, the distance at which a star shows a parallax angle of one arc second (1/3,600 of a degree).

NEAREST STARS AND STAR SYSTEMS			
Name of star or star system	Magnitude	Spectral type	Distance in ly
Alpha Centauri A, B, C	0.1, 1.4, 11.0	G2, K1, M5	4.4
Barnard's Star	9.5	M5	5.9
Lalande 21185	7.5	M2	8.3
Sirius A, B	−1.4, 8.5	A0, white dwarf	8.6
Ross 154	10.4	M4	9.7
Epsilon Eridani	3.7	K2	10.5
HD 217987	7.4	M2	10.7
Ross 128	11.1	M4	10.9
61 Cygni A, B	5.2, 6.1	K5, K7	11.4
Procyon	0.4, 10.7	F5, white dwarf	11.4

KEY STARS WITHIN 100 LY OF THE SUN

Stars not marked as giants or white dwarfs are main sequence stars.

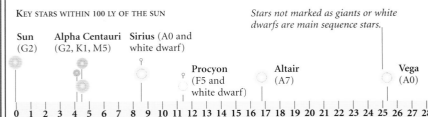

Sun (G2)

Alpha Centauri (G2, K1, M5)

Sirius (A0 and white dwarf)

Procyon (F5 and white dwarf)

Altair (A7)

Vega (A0)

Pollux (K0 giant)

Arcturus (K2 giant)

Capella (G6 and G2 giants)

0 1 2 3 4 5 6 7 8 9 10 11 12 13 14 15 16 17 18 19 20 21 22 23 24 25 26 27 28 29 30 31 32 33 34 35 36 37 38 39 40 41 42 43 44 45 46 47 48 49 5
Light years

0 1 2 3 4 5 6 7 8 9 10 11 12 13 14 15
Parsecs

PARALLAX METHOD

As the Earth orbits the Sun, the nearer stars seem to move from side to side against the background of more distant stars. The angle through which the star moves over a period of six months is called its parallax. Knowing this angle, astronomers can use simple geometry to calculate the star's distance. The smaller the parallax, the farther away the star. For stars more than a few hundred light years away, the parallax angle is too small to be measured.

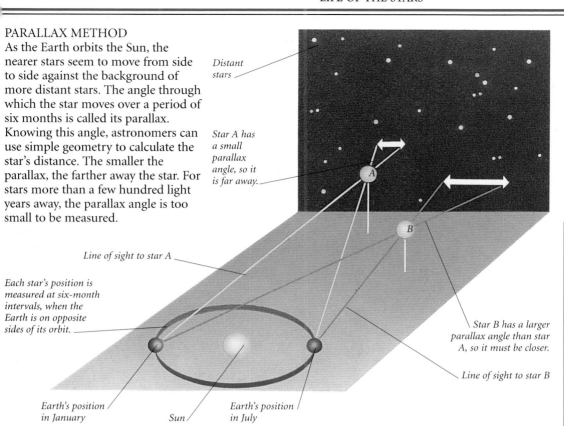

Distant stars

Star A has a small parallax angle, so it is far away.

Line of sight to star A

Each star's position is measured at six-month intervals, when the Earth is on opposite sides of its orbit.

Star B has a larger parallax angle than star A, so it must be closer.

Line of sight to star B

Earth's position in January

Sun

Earth's position in July

INVERSE SQUARE LAW

A more distant star looks dimmer than a nearby one of a similar luminosity. This is because its light spreads out over a larger area before it reaches Earth, making it appear fainter. The inverse square law states that a star's apparent brightness decreases with the square of its distance. For example, two stars of identical luminosity will differ in brightness by four times if one star is twice as far away as the other.

Star

The larger sphere has twice the radius of the smaller sphere.

Light from the star spreads over this area of the smaller sphere.

When the light reaches the larger sphere it is spread over four times the area (the square of the distance, or 2 x 2).

Aldebaran

Hyades

ALDEBARAN AND HYADES

Stars that seem close in the sky are not necessarily neighbours in space. The red giant star Aldebaran appears to be a member of the Hyades star cluster in Taurus. In fact, Aldebaran is much nearer to us than the cluster. It lies 65.1 light years from the Sun, compared with 150 light years for the Hyades.

◉ PARALLAX EXPERIMENT

Hold your two index fingers in front of you, one at arm's length and the other at half the distance. With one eye closed, rock your head from side to side. The nearer finger seems to move farther and faster than the more distant one. The amount of movement is a measure of the parallax. The farther your finger, the smaller the parallax.

STELLAR DISTANCES

PTOLEMY

● In AD 140, Ptolemy showed how the parallax method could be used to calculate the distance to the Moon.

● English physicist Robert Hooke (1635–1703) tried and failed to measure the parallax of a star in 1669.

● In 1838, Friedrich Bessel used the parallax method to measure the distance to the star 61 Cygni. Shortly after, Scottish astronomer Thomas Henderson (1798–1844) published the distance to alpha Centauri.

● In 1997, the European Space Agency published the Hipparcos star catalogue, which gives parallax distances to 118,000 stars.

FIND OUT MORE

HOW TELESCOPES WORK 14
MEASURE OF THE STARS 162
PROPERTIES OF STARS 168
CLUSTERS AND DOUBLES 174

Castor
(A2, A1, and M1)

Aldebaran
(K5 giant)

Regulus
(B7 and K1)

Alioth
(A0 giant)

Menkalinan
(A2 and A2)

Gacrux
(M4 giant)

Algol
(B8 and K0)

51 52 53 54 55 56 57 58 59 60 61 62 63 64 65 66 67 68 69 70 71 72 73 74 75 76 77 78 79 80 81 82 83 84 85 86 87 88 89 90 91 92 93 94 95 96 97 98 99 100

16 17 18 19 20 21 22 23 24 25 26 27 28 29 30

PROPERTIES OF STARS

HOW CAN WE FIND OUT what the stars are really like? Once we know the distance to a particular star, we can work out how bright the star is and begin to learn other things about it, such as its size, mass, and age. We find tiny white dwarfs about the size of the Earth and supergiants big enough to engulf much of our Solar System. Some stars are only a few million years old, while others are almost as ancient as the Universe itself. To sort out the different types of stars, astronomers draw a special graph called a Hertzsprung-Russell (H-R) diagram.

The apparent brightness of these stars depends both on their luminosity and on how far away they are.

LUMINOSITY AND ABSOLUTE MAGNITUDE
A star's real brightness, compared with the Sun, is called its visual luminosity: stars range from 100,000 times to 1/100,000 of the Sun's brightness. Astronomers also refer to luminosity in terms of a star's absolute magnitude, which is the magnitude the star would appear if it were 10 parsecs (32.6 light years) from the Earth.

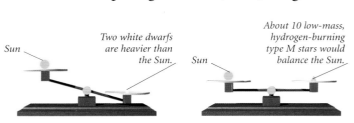

Sun

Two white dwarfs are heavier than the Sun.

Sun

About 10 low-mass, hydrogen-burning type M stars would balance the Sun.

Sun

Sun

A red giant has about the same mass as the Sun.

MASSES COMPARED
The masses of stars are not usually measured in kilograms or tonnes, but in relation to the mass of the Sun. The lightest stars are less than one-tenth of a solar mass, while the heaviest may be more than 50 solar masses. Like pebbles on a beach, there are uncountable small stars, but few really big ones.

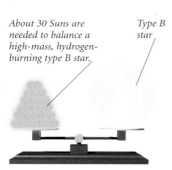

About 30 Suns are needed to balance a high-mass, hydrogen-burning type B star.

Type B star

AVERAGE SIZES OF STARS
Stars vary greatly in size, from supergiants 300 times the size of the Sun to neutron stars and black holes that are even smaller than the Earth.

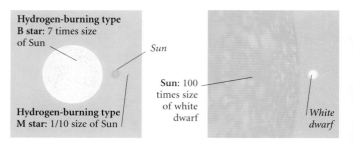

Supergiant: 10 times size of red giant

Red giant

Red giant: 30 times size of Sun

Sun

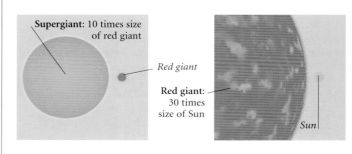

Hydrogen-burning type B star: 7 times size of Sun

Sun

Hydrogen-burning type M star: 1/10 size of Sun

Sun: 100 times size of white dwarf

White dwarf

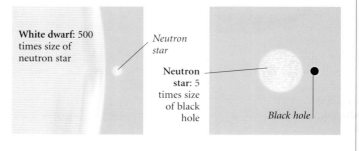

White dwarf: 500 times size of neutron star

Neutron star

Neutron star: 5 times size of black hole

Black hole

PLOTTING THE STARS

- In 1906, Ejnar Hertzsprung drew a diagram showing how stars could be classified into two groups, now called main sequence stars and giants.

- After Henry Russell produced a similar diagram in 1913, astronomers began to realize the importance of the Hertzsprung-Russell diagram in understanding stars.

RUSSELL'S 1913 DIAGRAM

FIND OUT MORE

HERTZSPRUNG-RUSSELL DIAGRAM

Astronomers plot stars on a graph, with spectral type along the bottom and visual luminosity up the side. Absolute magnitude and temperature may also be given. Each star has a place on this Hertzsprung-Russell diagram, according to what point it has reached in its life. Most stars fall into a band called the main sequence, while others fall into groups called giants, supergiants, and white dwarfs.

MAIN SEQUENCE STARS

The main sequence runs diagonally across the Hertzsprung-Russell diagram, from top left to bottom right. Main sequence stars burn hydrogen in nuclear reactions and change it into helium. Stars spend about 90 per cent of their lives on the main sequence, changing very little in luminosity or temperature while they are there. The Sun is a typical main sequence star.

Stars at the top of the main sequence are large, hot, blue, and massive.

Giants and supergiants are stars nearing the end of their lives. They have run out of hydrogen and are burning helium instead.

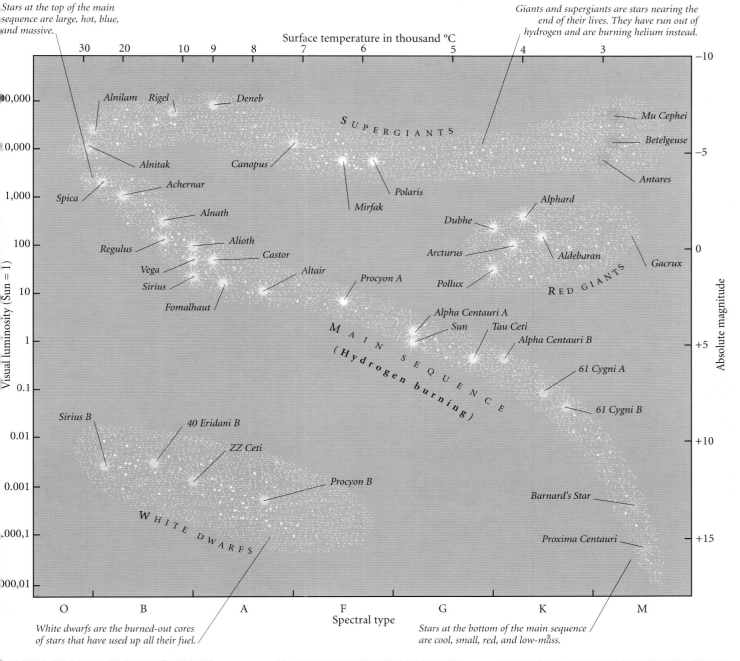

White dwarfs are the burned-out cores of stars that have used up all their fuel.

Stars at the bottom of the main sequence are cool, small, red, and low-mass.

MASSES OF MAIN SEQUENCE STARS

Stars lie on the main sequence in order of their mass, with the most massive at top left and the least massive at bottom right. Brown dwarfs are smaller bodies that do not appear on the main sequence, as they never get hot enough for nuclear reactions to start.

MAIN SEQUENCE LUMINOSITY

The luminosity of a main sequence star depends on its mass – the more massive the star, the greater its luminosity. The brightest stars are at the top of the main sequence, and the faintest stars are at the bottom.

LIFESPANS OF MAIN SEQUENCE STARS

The hot, bright stars at the top end of the main sequence will burn all their nuclear fuel within about a million years. Stars at the bottom end are shining so faintly that their hydrogen will last at least 100 billion years – longer than the current age of the Universe.

LIFECYCLE OF STARS

LIKE PEOPLE, STARS ARE BORN, live their lives, grow old, and die. Unlike people, their lives are measured in millions or even billions of years – too long for us to see them age. If a visitor from another planet could visit the Earth, he or she would see many kinds of people of different sizes and shapes. Our visitor might guess that the smallest creatures were newly born, and then try to work out how the different kinds of bigger people fitted into the human lifecycle. In a similar way, by studying the different types of star, astronomers are able to piece together the entire stellar lifecycle.

STELLAR EVOLUTION

A star begins its life as a shrinking clump of gas and dust called a protostar. It stops shrinking when nuclear fusion reactions start in its core. The first reactions fuse hydrogen to make helium. Later, helium is changed into carbon, oxygen, and – in the biggest stars – iron. Eventually, there is nothing left to burn and the star collapses. For a few massive stars, this results in a supernova explosion.

Nuclear reactions in the star produce heavier elements.

Star sheds material during the course of its life.

Clouds condense to form stars.

STAR

STAR FORMATION

MOLECULAR CLOUD

MASS LOSS

Gas and dust particle shed by stars join with interstellar material in gigantic molecular clouds

RAW MATERIALS
Stars are formed from the dust and hydrogen and helium gas of a molecular cloud. Inside the star, the hydrogen and helium are changed into heavier elements. Stars return some of their material back into space. This discarded material is then recycled to make new stars. The Sun and the Earth are made of material that was once inside a star.

1 Far out in space a cold, dark cloud of gas and dust starts to contract under the pull of its own gravity.

2 As the cloud shrinks and heats up, it breaks into smaller clumps, each of which will form a protostar.

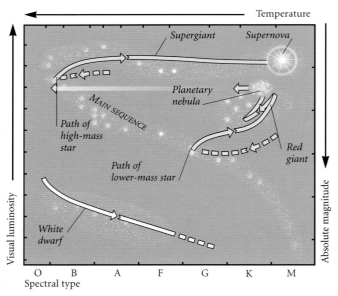

PROGRESS OF STARS
Stars of different masses evolve in different ways. This Hertzsprung-Russell diagram shows the lifecycles of two stars, one a lower-mass star like the Sun and the other 15 times more massive. The more massive the star, the shorter its life.

Temperature

Supergiant

Supernova

Planetary nebula

MAIN SEQUENCE

Path of high-mass star

Path of lower-mass star

Red giant

White dwarf

Visual luminosity

Absolute magnitude

O   B   A   F   G   K   M
Spectral type

LIFE ON THE MAIN SEQUENCE
Stars spend most of their lives on the main sequence of the Hertzsprung-Russell diagram, generating energy by nuclear reactions that steadily convert hydrogen into helium. As the hydrogen is gradually used, the star becomes slightly hotter and bigger.

7 As its hydrogen fuel runs out, the star expands to become a red supergiant.

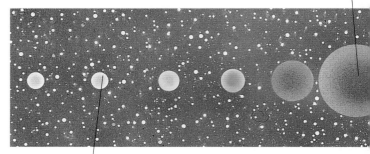

This "adult" blue-white star remains virtually unchanged for millions of years on the main sequence.

STAR DEATH
Stars heavier than eight times the mass of the swell and end their lives in a dramatic explos supernova, leaving only a tiny, dense remnan either a neutron star or a black hole.

SUN'S STORY

1 STEADY BURNER Most stars are not heavy enough to become supernovas. Stars like the Sun spend billions of years burning up their hydrogen on the main sequence before ending their lives in a quieter, less spectacular fashion.

2 SWELLING STAR When all the hydrogen is used, the Sun will swell to become a red giant, burning helium instead of hydrogen. When the helium runs out, the Sun will puff off its outer layers to form a planetary nebula.

3 WHITE DWARF The planetary nebula will disperse, leaving the Sun's core exposed. The core is a white dwarf – a small, dense ball of cinders with no nuclear fuel left. Over billions of years, it will cool and fade away.

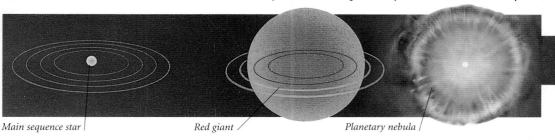

Main sequence star

Red giant

Planetary nebula

White dwarf

Star gradually fades.

3 Each protostar is shrouded in gas and dust, which flattens into a disc as the protostar spins.

4 Eventually, the contracting protostar bursts into life and strong jets of gas escape from either side of the disc.

5 Dust grains condense and stick together in the disc around the protostar, and may eventually form planets.

6 The young, fully formed star is now fusing hydrogen to make helium on the main sequence.

STARBIRTH

A molecular cloud may contract under the pull of its own gravity and split up into smaller clumps. These clumps warm up as they continue to shrink and grow more dense. Astronomers can detect radio waves and infrared radiation from the clumps before they are hot enough to emit light. Eventually they start to glow. At 10 million °C, nuclear reactions start and new stars are born.

10 Eventually, the iron core collapses and the star explodes as a brilliant supernova.

11 Most of the star's matter is blown away by the supernova. The star's collapsed core may survive as a neutron star or a black hole.

8 The core is now hotter. The star uses its helium to make carbon and oxygen.

9 Nuclear reactions produce heavier and heavier elements, until a core of iron builds up.

Neutron star is a dense ball of neutrons about 30 km in diameter.

Black hole is a collapsed object whose gravity is so strong that light cannot escape from it.

While the core heats up, the outer layers cool and glow red.

The exploding star shines brighter than a billion Suns.

WHERE STARS ARE BORN

EVEN THE MOST BRILLIANT STARS begin their lives hidden from view, deep within vast, dark swathes of gas and dust called molecular clouds. Some of these clouds are visible to the naked eye, showing up as silhouettes against the glowing band of the Milky Way. When newly hatched stars, known as protostars, start to shine, they light up and heat the cloud with the radiation they give out. Such a glowing cloud is called a nebula. As the stars shine, the rest of the dark cloud is squeezed by the powerful radiation, and it starts to collapse. Over millions of years, the whole cloud will turn into stars.

EVOLUTION OF YOUNG STARS
Newborn stars appear as glowing red objects on the right of the Hertzsprung-Russell diagram. They move to the left as they shrink and become hot enough to burn hydrogen on the main sequence.

HEART OF A NEBULA

The Orion Nebula is the star-forming region nearest to the Earth, about 1,500 light-years away in the direction of the constellation of Orion. The nebula is heated by ultraviolet radiation from a small cluster of young stars known as the Trapezium. Many more stars and protostars are concealed in the thick clouds of dust that surround the heart of the nebula. The Orion Nebula itself is burning its way through a much larger cloud (a giant molecular cloud) that may contain as much as 500,000 solar masses of dust and gas.

Radiation from nearby stars disperses thinner parts of the cloud.

Dense globules containing protostars become detached as parts of the cloud disperse.

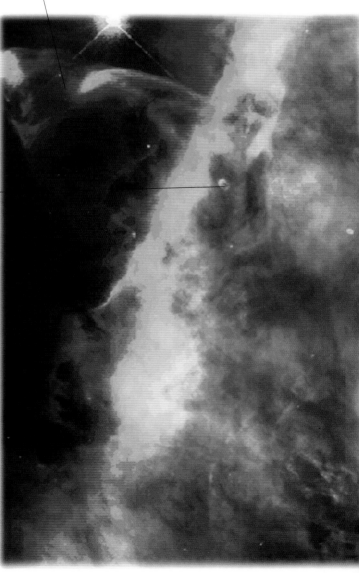

Infrared view reveals a bar-shaped area of newborn stars that cannot be seen in visible light.

The star-forming region will eventually spread into this dark cloud.

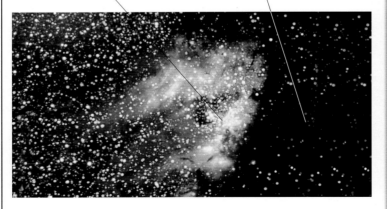

OMEGA NEBULA

Another well-known star-forming region is the Omega Nebula, about 5,000 light years away. Thick dust clouds block visible light from the inside of the nebula, but infrared light passes through the dust to reveal a mass of baby stars. Radiation from the new stars squeezes the dust clouds and triggers a new bout of star formation.

RECOGNIZING ORION NEBULA

- In 1656, Christiaan Huygens made the first drawing of the Orion Nebula. His sketch included a trapezium-shaped group of stars in the nebula's centre.

- In the 18th century, William Herschel described the Orion Nebula as "an unformed fiery mist, the chaotic material of future suns."

- In 1865, William Huggins studied the spectrum of light from the Orion Nebula and realized it was made of hot gas.

- In the 1960s, astronomers found bright infrared stars in the Orion Nebula and guessed that they were protostars buried in clouds of dust.

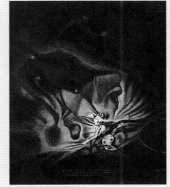

ORION NEBULA DRAWN BY LORD ROSSE OF PARSONSTOWN, IRELAND (1800–67)

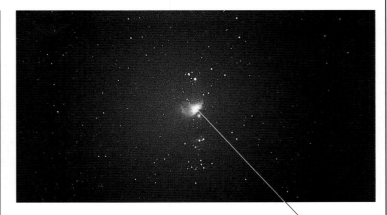

Orion Nebula lies just below the Belt of Orion.

OBSERVING ORION NEBULA

Several star-forming regions are bright enough to be seen with binoculars, appearing as misty patches against the sky. Brightest of all is the Orion Nebula. It is visible to the naked eye between November and March, and is easy to find, as it forms part of Orion's Sword.

PROTOSTAR GROUP

Astronomers have identified over 150 protostars within the Orion Nebula. The five protostars in this group are surrounded by the swirling discs of dust and gas out of which they formed. These discs are called protoplanetary discs, because planets may be forming inside them.

CLOSE-UP OF PROTOSTARS IN ORION NEBULA

In this false-colour image from the Hubble Space Telescope, hydrogen is green, oxygen is blue, and nitrogen is red.

Disc is thought to be 99% gas and 1% dust.

CLOSE-UP OF PROTOPLANETARY DISC

Disc is about 90 billion km across.

PROTOPLANETARY DISC

A new star is being hatched inside this small, dark disc of dust and gas. The protostar, which is only a few hundred thousand years old, has about one-fifth the mass of the Sun. The surrounding disc is seven-and-a-half times the diameter of Pluto's orbit and contains about seven times the mass of the Earth.

While nuclear reactions begin in the protostars, the discs may condense to form planets.

Stars of the Trapezium light up the nebula.

INTERESTING NEBULAS

Name	Constellation	Distance in light years	Diameter in light years
North America	Cygnus	1,500	50
Orion	Orion	1,600	30
Omega	Sagittarius	5,000	60
Lagoon	Sagittarius	5,200	150
Trifid	Sagittarius	5,200	40
Rosette	Monoceros	5,500	50
Eagle	Serpens	7,000	60
Carina	Carina	9,000	300
Tarantula	Dorado	160,000	800

FIND OUT MORE

INFRARED ASTRONOMY 22 • PROPERTIES OF STARS 168
LIFECYCLE OF STARS 170 • INTERSTELLAR MEDIUM 196

CLUSTERS AND DOUBLES

STARS ARE NOT BORN SINGLY BUT IN CLUTCHES. Everywhere we look we see stars tucked together in clusters or paired off. Open clusters – loose groupings of up to several hundred stars – are found all along the Milky Way's spiral arms. Clusters are important, because all their stars were born out of the same material at the same time. Astronomers study them to find out how stars evolve. Even seemingly solitary stars have surprises in store: when examined with a telescope, about half the stars in the sky prove to be doubles or multiples. Measuring the movements of such stars is the only reliable way to find the masses of stars.

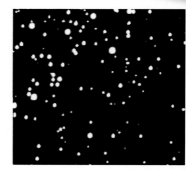

Pleione is the mother of the Pleiades.

Alcyone

Atlas is named after the father of the Pleiades.

The stars of the Pleiades look like a swarm of fireflies and are a prominent sight late in the year.

PLEIADES OPEN CLUSTER
Named after the Seven Sisters of Greek mythology, the Pleiades is the best-known open cluster. It contains about 100 stars, seven of which can be seen with the naked eye. The presence of several young, blue stars and the absence of red giants show that the cluster is about 78 million years old. Like all open clusters, it will eventually disperse as the stars drift away into space.

AGES OF CLUSTERS
Young clusters, such as NGC 2264, are full of short-lived, hot, blue stars. They are often found in or near the nebula from which they formed. The gas of the nebula has long dispersed from older clusters such as M67. Old clusters contain many red giants, which are stars that have used their hydrogen fuel and are nearing the end of their lives.

M67, A 3.2-BILLION-YEAR-OLD CLUSTER

NGC 2264, A 20-MILLION-YEAR-OLD CLUSTER

OPEN CLUSTERS

Name	Constellation	Age in millions of years	Distance in light years	Number of stars
Double Cluster (h and chi Persei)	Perseus	3.2 + 5.6	7,400	150 + 200
Jewel Box	Crux	7.1	7,600	100
NGC 2264	Monoceros	20	2,400	40
Butterfly Cluster	Scorpius	51	2,000	80
M47	Puppis	78	1,600	30
Pleiades	Taurus	78	375	100
M41	Canis Major	190	2,300	100
Praesepe	Cancer	660	520	50
Hyades	Taurus	660	150	200
M67	Cancer	3,200	2,600	200

Asterope

Taygeta

Maia

Celaeno

Electra

Streaks in the dust clouds are caused by interstellar magnetic fields.

Merope

Clouds of dust around the stars are lit up by starlight.

DOUBLE STARS

Two stars that are not really close may look as it they are paired if they lie along the same line of sight. These are optical pairs. Two stars bound together by the pull of their gravity form a true binary system. The stars orbit a shared point of balance determined by their masses. In a visual binary, two separate stars can be seen. In a spectroscopic binary, the stars are so close together that they appear as one. In some spectroscopic binaries, the stars pass in front of each other, so the brightness changes. These are called eclipsing binaries or eclipsing variables.

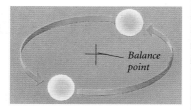

In a binary system with stars of equal mass, the balance point is in the middle.

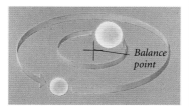

If one star in a binary system is more massive than the other, the balance point is closer to the heavier star.

INTERACTING BINARIES

Some binary systems are interacting: the stars are so close together that gas passes between them. In a semi-detached binary, one of the stars has swollen and is spilling gas on to the other. In a contact binary, the stars are touching each other and share a common outer atmosphere. Interacting binaries often appear as variable stars, and may also be strong sources of X-rays.

Stream of gas snatched from companion.

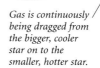

Swollen yellow star loses mass.

Gas is continuously being dragged from the bigger, cooler star on to the smaller, hotter star.

SEMI-DETACHED BINARY SYSTEM

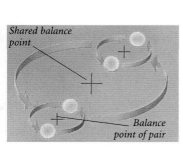

Shared balance point

Balance point of pair

In a double binary system, each star orbits its companion, and the two pairs orbit the same balance point.

MULTIPLE STARS

Sometimes three or more stars are grouped together in a multiple system. The stars are usually arranged in pairs, or as a pair orbited by a single star. One of the most famous multiple star systems, epsilon Lyrae, consists of two pairs of binary stars. Both pairs orbit the same central balance point.

● PRAESEPE

In the heart of the constellation of Cancer lies Praesepe (nicknamed the Beehive). This open cluster of about 50 stars can just be made out with the naked eye on a dark night, but is a fine sight through binoculars. The very old cluster M67 may be glimpsed a few degrees to the south of Praesepe.

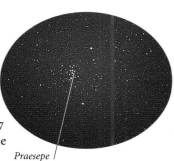

Praesepe

IMPORTANT MULTIPLE STARS

Name	Constellation	No of stars	Magnitudes
Albireo	Cygnus	2	3.1, 5.1
Almach	Andromeda	3	2.3, 5.5, 6.3
Alpha Centauri	Centaurus	3	0.0, 1.4, 11.0
Castor	Gemini	3	1.9, 2.9, 8.8
Trapezium	Orion	4	5.1, 6.7, 6.7, 7.9
Epsilon Lyrae	Lyra	4	5.0, 5.2, 5.5, 6.1
Sigma Orionis	Orion	5	4.0, 6.0, 6.5, 7.5, 10.3
15 Monocerotis	Monoceros	7+	4.7, 7.5, 7.7, 8.1, 8.2, 9.6, 9.6

FIND OUT MORE

GLOBULAR CLUSTERS

FEW SIGHTS IN THE SKY are more magnificent than a globular cluster. These tight-knit swarms of up to a million stars inhabit the lonely outer reaches of the Milky Way. Our Galaxy may contain as many as 200 of them, and other galaxies contain many more. As well as being beautiful, globular clusters are of great scientific importance. Their stars are among the oldest in the Galaxy and help astronomers to determine the age of the Universe. In recent years, astronomers have discovered younger globular clusters in other galaxies, and it now seems that some globulars are being formed even as we watch.

Stars in the centre of a globular cluster are packed about a million times more densely than the stars near the Sun.

47 TUCANAE GLOBULAR CLUSTER

WHAT GLOBULARS LOOK LIKE

Globular clusters, such as the stunning 47 Tucanae, are bigger and brighter than open clusters and contain about a thousand times more stars. While open clusters are irregular in shape, globulars are roughly spherical. Globulars measure about 100 light years in diameter and are bound tightly together by their own gravity. Open clusters have a bluish appearance because they contain hot, young stars, but globular clusters look yellowish because their stars are much cooler and older.

47 Tucanae is the second-brightest globular cluster in the sky.

Most globulars move in long, elliptical orbits around the galactic centre, journeying far out into the halo.

A few globulars orbit close to the bulge.

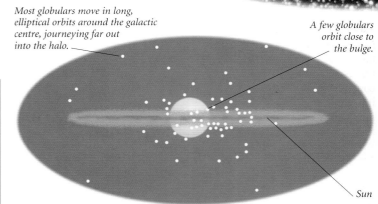

Sun

IMPORTANT GLOBULAR CLUSTERS

Name	Constellation	Distance in light years	Diameter in light years
M4	Scorpius	7,000	50
M22	Sagittarius	10,000	70
47 Tucanae	Tucana	15,000	140
Omega Centauri	Centaurus	17,000	180
M13 (Great Cluster)	Hercules	23,000	110
M92	Hercules	25,000	85
M5	Serpens	25,000	130
M15	Pegasus	31,000	110
M3	Canes Venatici	32,000	150
M2	Aquarius	37,000	140

FIND OUT MORE
PROPERTIES OF STARS 122 • VARIABLE STARS 164
HOW FAR ARE THE STARS 166 • CLUSTERS AND DOUBLES 174 • MILKY WAY 194

MAPPING GLOBULARS

Unlike open clusters, which are found only in the disc of the Milky Way, globular clusters occupy a spherical region around the Galaxy's central bulge. Astronomers find the distances to globulars by examining RR Lyrae stars within the clusters. RR Lyrae stars are a type of pulsating variable star. All RR Lyrae stars have the same luminosity, so astronomers can calculate how far away the globulars are by measuring the brightness of these stars.

47 Tucanae measures 140 light years across and has a mass of about a million Suns.

Globulars probably contain many white dwarfs, but they are too faint to see.

IDENTIFYING GLOBULARS

● In 1677, Edmond Halley recorded the globular Omega Centauri on a trip to the South Atlantic island of St Helena.

● In the 1830s, English astronomer John Herschel realized that Omega Centauri was made up of countless separate stars.

● In 1899, US astronomer Solon Bailey (1854–1931) discovered 85 pulsating RR Lyrae stars in the globular cluster M5.

● By using RR Lyrae and Cepheid stars to measure the distances to globular clusters, Harlow Shapley found in 1918 that globulars lie in a sphere whose centre marks the Galaxy's nucleus.

FORMATION OF GLOBULARS

Globulars are typically 10 billion years old. Astronomers used to think that globulars were created as their parent galaxies first started to form. But the Hubble Space Telescope has found much younger globulars, especially in galaxies that are colliding with each other. Some of our own globulars may have been brought to the Milky Way by smaller galaxies that collided with it in the past. Astronomers have also found a giant open cluster, R136, that is so big it may be in the process of becoming a globular.

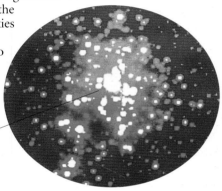

R136, in the Tarantula Nebula in the Large Magellanic Cloud, may become a globular cluster within 100 million years.

Most of the bright stars are giants.

At the core, about 1,000 stars are packed into each cubic light year.

👁 OMEGA CENTAURI

Most globular clusters are faint, but three can easily be seen with the naked eye: M13, 47 Tucanae, and Omega Centauri. Of these, Omega Centauri in the constellation of Centaurus is the brightest, because it is highly luminous and relatively close to the Earth. This slightly flattened cluster contains a million stars in a region 180 light years across.

FINDING THE AGE OF GLOBULARS

Astronomers can estimate the age of a globular cluster by plotting its stars on a Hertzsprung-Russell (H-R) diagram. This will show which of the main sequence stars have used up their hydrogen. The H-R diagram of a very old cluster shows no bright main sequence stars and many giants. Some globulars appear to be even older than the Universe – one of astronomy's unsolved mysteries.

Omega Centauri looks like a slightly fuzzy, bright star.

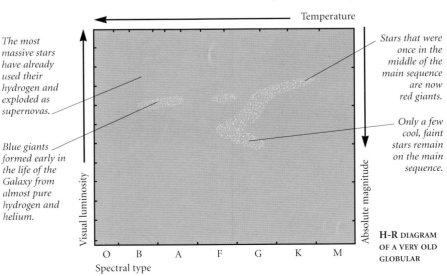

Temperature

The most massive stars have already used their hydrogen and exploded as supernovas.

Blue giants formed early in the life of the Galaxy from almost pure hydrogen and helium.

Stars that were once in the middle of the main sequence are now red giants.

Only a few cool, faint stars remain on the main sequence.

Visual luminosity

Absolute magnitude

O B A F G K M

Spectral type

H-R DIAGRAM OF A VERY OLD GLOBULAR

OTHER SOLAR SYSTEMS

IS OUR SOLAR SYSTEM UNIQUE IN THE UNIVERSE? Until recently, astronomers could only guess whether other stars are orbited by planetary systems. Extrasolar planets – those that orbit stars other than the Sun – are difficult to detect, because they are about one-billionth the brightness of their parent stars. But since 1995, astronomers using highly sensitive instruments have succeeded in discovering a number of extrasolar planets, and they expect to find many more in the years to come. A new generation of space telescopes is planned that will give us the first pictures of these planets.

WHAT ARE OTHER PLANETS LIKE?

Most planets detected so far are about the mass of Jupiter or even bigger. Astronomers believe they are gas giants like Jupiter and Saturn, rather than rocky planets like the Earth or Mars. Most of the planets are close to their parent stars, so they will be very hot. The biggest ones may even be brown dwarfs – bodies that do not quite have enough mass for nuclear reactions to start and turn them into stars.

EXTRASOLAR ORBITS

The diagram compares the orbits of the Earth and the first 10 extrasolar planets discovered, as if they were all orbiting the same parent star. Astronomers were surprised to find that most of these planets are much closer to their parent stars than the Earth is to the Sun. Some of them are even closer than Mercury. One explanation is that these planets formed farther away from their stars and then gradually spiralled inwards. Also surprising is that some of them are in much more elliptical orbits than the planets of our Solar System.

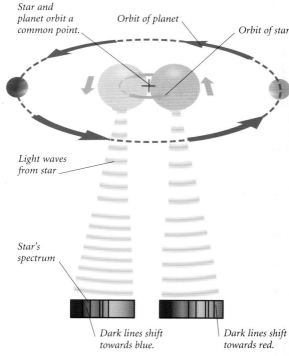

Star and planet orbit a common point. *Orbit of planet* *Orbit of star*

Light waves from star

Star's spectrum

Dark lines shift towards blue. *Dark lines shift towards red.*

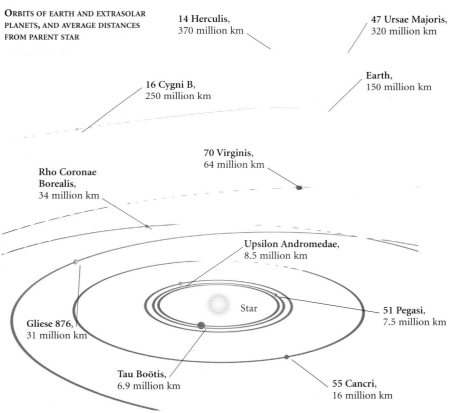

ORBITS OF EARTH AND EXTRASOLAR PLANETS, AND AVERAGE DISTANCES FROM PARENT STAR

14 Herculis, 370 million km

47 Ursae Majoris, 320 million km

16 Cygni B, 250 million km

Earth, 150 million km

70 Virginis, 64 million km

Rho Coronae Borealis, 34 million km

Upsilon Andromedae, 8.5 million km

Star

Gliese 876, 31 million km

51 Pegasi, 7.5 million km

Tau Boötis, 6.9 million km

55 Cancri, 16 million km

WOBBLING STARS

Extrasolar planets can be found by observing their gravitational effects on their parent stars. As a planet circles a star, its gravity pulls on the star, causing it to wobble slightly. Astronomers detect these wobbles by splitting the star's light into a spectrum. As the star wobbles towards us, its light waves are squeezed and the dark lines in the spectrum shift towards the blue end; as the star wobbles away, its light waves are stretched and the lines shift towards the red end.

FIRST 10 EXTRASOLAR PLANETS DISCOVERED

Name of parent star	Distance of parent star from Sun in ly	Year of planet's discovery	Minimum mass of planet (Earth = 1)	Time to orbit star in days
51 Pegasi	50	1995	150	4.2
55 Cancri	44	1996	270	14.6
47 Ursae Majoris	46	1996	890	1,090
Tau Boötis	49	1996	1,230	3.3
Upsilon Andromedae	54	1996	220	4.6
70 Virginis	59	1996	2,100	117
16 Cygni B	72	1996	480	804
Rho Coronae Borealis	55	1997	350	39.6
Gliese 876	15	1998	670	60.8
14 Herculis	55	1998	1,050	1,620

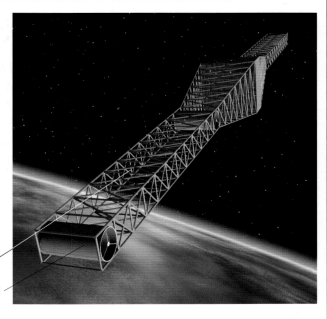

Telescope floats in space.

With four mirrors 6 m in diameter, the telescope will be able to detect very faint light coming from planets orbiting bright stars.

OTHER LOCATION METHODS

Extrasolar planets can also be detected by watching for a drop in brightness as a planet transits, or passes in front of, its parent star. The changing brightness of the star can be plotted on a graph called a light curve. Another proposal, called gravitational microlensing, is to watch for sudden brightenings as the planet's gravitational field acts like a lens and magnifies the light from a more distant star.

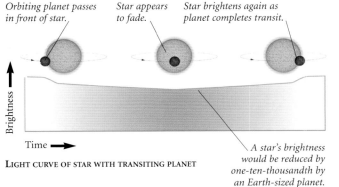

Orbiting planet passes in front of star. *Star appears to fade.* *Star brightens again as planet completes transit.*

Brightness

Time ➡

LIGHT CURVE OF STAR WITH TRANSITING PLANET

A star's brightness would be reduced by one-ten-thousandth by an Earth-sized planet.

PULSAR PLANETS

The pulsar PSR 1257+12 is orbited by at least three planets, each with a mass similar to that of the Earth. Another planet has been found around the pulsar PSR 1620-26. A pulsar forms when a star explodes as a supernova; how existing planets could survive such a cataclysmic event is a puzzle. One possibility is that the planets formed after the supernova, from the debris left by the explosion.

ARTIST'S IMPRESSION OF A PULSAR SEEN FROM ITS PLANET

TERRESTRIAL PLANET FINDER

NASA's planned Terrestrial Planet Finder will be a space telescope designed to investigate extrasolar planets. As it floats in deep space, beyond the orbit of Jupiter, it will search for new planets around the brightest 1,000 stars within 42 light years of the Solar System. It will be able to spot planets the size of the Earth and will measure the composition of their atmospheres by spectral analysis.

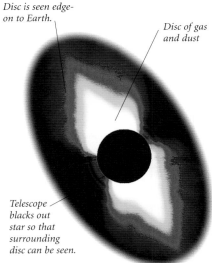

Disc is seen edge-on to Earth.

Disc of gas and dust

Telescope blacks out star so that surrounding disc can be seen.

BETA PICTORIS

Astronomers have discovered planets that are being formed around newborn stars. Beta Pictoris is a young star surrounded by a swirling disc of gas and dust. The disc is quite cool, but glows brightly at infrared wavelengths. Planets are probably forming within the disc, in the same way that the planets of our own Solar System formed around the young Sun.

SEARCHING FOR SOLAR SYSTEMS

- In 1964, US astronomer Peter van de Kamp (1901–95) claimed to have detected a planet in orbit around Barnard's Star, one of the stars nearest to the Sun. No one has been able to confirm its existence.

- In 1984, infrared emissions from the star Beta Pictoris were shown to be produced by a disc of gas and dust in which planets are forming.

- The first definite example of an extrasolar planet was found in orbit around the star 51 Pegasi in 1995.

FIND OUT MORE

RED GIANTS

STARS DO NOT LIVE FOREVER. A time comes when the supply of hydrogen dwindles and the nuclear reactions in the core die down. But instead of fading away, the star now balloons out to become a brilliant red giant maybe a hundred times its former diameter. More massive stars become powerful supergiants, bright enough to be seen across intergalactic space. This transformation happens because, deep within its core, the star has tapped a new source of energy, helium, that can keep it shining for a while longer.

INSIDE A RED GIANT

Just like any other star, the source of a red giant's heat is nuclear reactions in the core. With its supply of hydrogen almost gone, the core has shrunk to one-tenth of its former size, and is not much larger than the Earth. Enormous temperatures and pressures within this tiny core allow the star to produce energy by fusing helium to make heavier elements such as carbon and oxygen. On the outside of the core, a thin shell of hydrogen continues to make helium.

Convection cells carry heat from the core to the surface in rising and falling currents of hot gas. Some of the elements made in the core are carried to the surface as well.

INSIDE A RED GIANT STAR

Helium-burning inner shell at 100 million °C

Carbon and oxygen products of helium burning

Helium produced by main sequence hydrogen burning

Hydrogen continues to burn in a shell on the outside of the core.

Enlarged view of core region

Hotspot where a large current of hot gas reaches the surface. Hotspots can be detected on the surfaces of nearby red giants.

High-mass stars use up fuel rapidly, and become supergiants after only a few million years.

Instability strip is a region where stars pulsate and vary in brightness.

Temperature

RED GIANTS ON HERTZSPRUNG-RUSSELL DIAGRAM

MAIN SEQUENCE

Visual luminosity

Absolute magnitude

O B A F G K M
Spectral type

Supergiants

Red giants

Smaller stars burn their hydrogen fuel slowly, taking billions of years to become red giants.

EVOLUTION OF GIANT STARS

A star enters the giant phase when the hydrogen in its core runs out. As the star swells and cools, it moves away from the main sequence. Lower-mass stars brighten dramatically and move into the red giant region. High-mass stars remain about the same brightness but move into the supergiant region. The colour of a giant star depends on its surface temperature – supergiant stars can be blue (hottest), white, yellow, or red.

STELLAR WINDS

A giant star's outer atmosphere can drift out into space across many light years as a stellar wind. The Toby Jug Nebula is a cloud of gas and dust which has been blown out by the giant star at its heart.

SUPERGIANTS

Stars with more than eight times the mass of the Sun leave the main sequence to become supergiants. Like giants, their source of energy is the fusion of helium. Unlike giants, the carbon and oxygen produced can undergo further nuclear fusion, to make heavier elements.

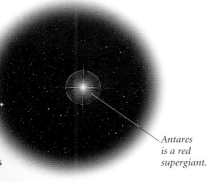

SUPERGIANT STAR ANTARES

Antares is a red supergiant.

SIZES OF RED GIANTS

Giant stars have a huge range of sizes. When it first leaves the main sequence, a typical star can swell up to 200 times the diameter of the Sun. Once helium burning starts, the star will settle down to between 10 and 100 times the diameter of the Sun. Supergiants can be even bigger and may exceed 1,000 times the Sun's diameter. One of the biggest stars of all, the red supergiant mu Cephei, is bigger than the orbit of Saturn.

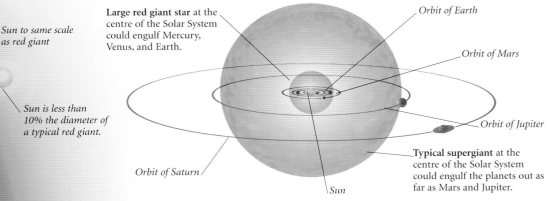

Sun to same scale as red giant

Sun is less than 10% the diameter of a typical red giant.

Large red giant star at the centre of the Solar System could engulf Mercury, Venus, and Earth.

Orbit of Earth

Orbit of Mars

Orbit of Jupiter

Orbit of Saturn

Sun

Typical supergiant at the centre of the Solar System could engulf the planets out as far as Mars and Jupiter.

Sooty grains of dust condense in the outer atmosphere of the star and are blown away on the stellar wind. The dust drifts away into interstellar space, where it can be formed into a new generation of stars.

VIEW FROM EARTH OF THE SUN AS A RED GIANT

FUTURE OF THE SUN

In about 5 billion years, the Sun's supply of hydrogen will run out. By this time, it will already be twice as bright as it is now. As it transforms into a red giant, it will expand enormously – perhaps engulfing Mercury – and shine 1000 times brighter than it does today. When helium fusion starts, the Sun will become more stable, and will settle down for a further 2 billion years as a giant star about 30 times its present diameter.

ANTARES AND NEARBY STARS IN SCORPIUS

👁 WHERE TO SEE RED GIANTS

Giants and supergiants are among the best-known stars in the sky. Bright giants include Arcturus in Boötes and Aldebaran in Taurus. Capella in Auriga is made up of two giants orbiting around each other. Supergiants include Canopus in Carina, Rigel and Betelgeuse in Orion, Antares in Scorpius, and Deneb in Cygnus. Mu Cephei, one of the biggest supergiants, is known as the Garnet Star because of its red colour.

GIANT STAR STATISTICS

Name	Magnitude	Spectral type	Distance in light years
Canopus	−0.6	F0 White supergiant	310
Arcturus	0.0	K2 Orange giant	37
Capella	0.1	G6 & G2 Yellow giants	42
Rigel	0.2	B8 Blue supergiant	800
Betelgeuse	0.5	M2 Red supergiant	400
Hadar	0.6	B1 Blue giant	530
Aldebaran	0.9	K5 Red giant	65
Antares	1.1	M1 Red supergiant	500
Pollux	1.2	K0 Orange giant	129
Deneb	1.2	A2 White supergiant	1,500
Mimosa	1.2	B0 Blue giant	350
Gacrux	1.6	M4 Red giant	88

FIND OUT MORE

PROPERTIES OF STARS 168 • LIFECYCLE OF STARS 170
PLANETARY NEBULAS 182 • SUPERNOVAS 184

PLANETARY NEBULAS

L IKE A FLOWER BURSTING INTO BLOOM, a planetary nebula unfolds into space. Another swollen red giant has died and puffed off its outer layers in an expanding cloud that will shine for tens of thousands of years. All stars with a mass up to eight times that of the Sun will end their lives in this way, their material spread out into delicate glowing rings and shells. The nebula will gradually fade and disappear, but at its heart is a white dwarf – the hot, dense remains of the star's core that, over billions of years, will cool and disappear.

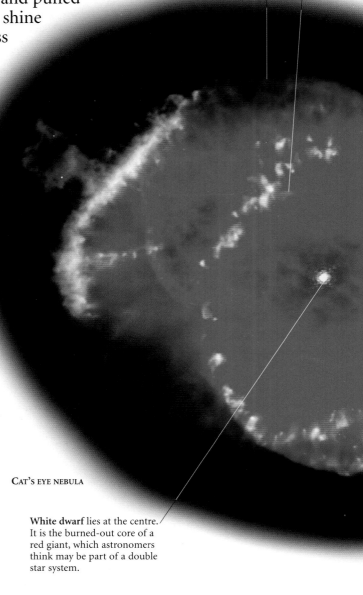

Outer lobes of older gas

Inner shell of recently ejected gas

CAT'S EYE NEBULA

White dwarf lies at the centre. It is the burned-out core of a red giant, which astronomers think may be part of a double star system.

CAT'S EYE NEBULA

When a red giant has no more helium fuel to burn, its core shrinks and the star expands once again. But this time the expansion is so sudden that the outer layers of the star lift off and blow away into space. The intensely hot core lights up the departing gas and creates a planetary nebula (given its name by William Herschel, who thought that the disc-like clouds looked like planets). Planetary nebulas last a few thousand years, and so are quite rare – only about 1,500 are known in the Milky Way Galaxy. The Cat's Eye Nebula is one of the most complex. It is about 1,000 years old.

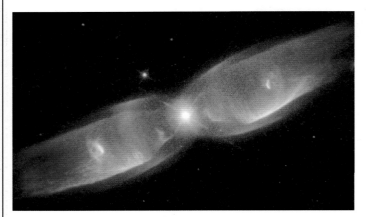

BUTTERFLY NEBULA

One of the most beautiful planetary nebulas is Minkowski 2-9, an example of a butterfly nebula. Astronomers believe that the white dwarf at its centre is pulling material off a larger companion star, creating a swirling disc of gas and dust. When the red giant blew off its outer layers, the disc deflected the material into two jets, streaming out at more than 300 km/s. The nebula lies about 2,100 light years from Earth in the constellation of Ophiuchus, and is about 1,200 years old.

👁 SPOTTING PLANETARY NEBULAS

Planetary nebulas are faint and often cannot be seen without a telescope. One of the easiest to find is the Ring Nebula in Lyra, to the southeast of Vega and east of Sheliak. It looks like a small, faint smoke ring and can be seen through a small telescope on a dark, moonless night.

RING NEBULA AND NEARBY STARS

Hydrogen makes up most of the material in the nebula. In this Hubble Space Telescope photograph, it is shown in red.

Heavier elements, such as oxygen and nitrogen, show up as green and blue areas.

Glowing nebula is made of gas blown off the star during its red giant phase. It is kept hot by the white dwarf in the middle.

WHITE DWARFS

At the centre of every planetary nebula is a tiny, hot star called a white dwarf. This is the burned-out core of the original red giant, rich in carbon and oxygen produced by the star's helium-burning reactions, and exposed now the outer layers have been removed. Because they are no longer producing energy, white dwarfs have collapsed down to a very small volume – a typical white dwarf has the mass of the Sun compressed into a volume about the size of the Earth. About 10% of all the stars in the Galaxy may be white dwarfs, but they are so faint that only the nearest ones can be seen.

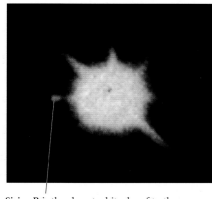

Sirius B is the closest white dwarf to the Sun. It is a tiny star in orbit around the bright star Sirius.

Planetary nebula phase

Supergiants

Red giants

Temperature

MAIN SEQUENCE

Visual luminosity

Absolute magnitude

O B A F G K M
Spectral type

White dwarf phase

Exposed core moves rapidly across diagram to become a white dwarf.

Planetary nebula forms as outer layers of star are lost.

EVOLUTION OF WHITE DWARFS

When a red giant puffs off its outer layers, the exposed core is seen as the bright central star in a planetary nebula, on the far left of the Hertzsprung-Russell diagram. The core is extremely hot, and appears as a bright point of light with a temperature as high as 100,000°C. As the core cools, it moves into the bottom left of the diagram as a white dwarf. It has no more nuclear fuel to burn and gradually cools, moving down and to the right as it fades away.

DENSITY OF A WHITE DWARF

White dwarf material is a million times more dense than water. This means that the gravitational field around a white dwarf is intense. A person standing on a white dwarf would weigh about 600 tonnes. A matchbox of white dwarf material would weigh as much as an elephant.

More massive white dwarf is smaller and denser.

Less massive white dwarf is larger.

CHANDRASEKHAR LIMIT

No white dwarf can have a mass greater than 1.4 times the mass of the Sun. This surprising discovery was made in 1930 by Subrahmanyan Chandrasekhar, who showed that the more massive a white dwarf is, the more it is crushed under its own gravity, and the smaller it is. If the core of the burnt-out star is heavier than 1.4 solar masses (the Chandrasekhar limit), it collapses to form a neutron star or a black hole.

NOTABLE PLANETARY NEBULAS

Name	Constellation	Distance in light years	Size in light years
Helix	Aquarius	450	1.0
Dumbbell	Vulpecula	1,000	1.5
Owl	Ursa Major	1,300	1.0
Bug	Scorpius	2,000	0.5
Ring	Lyra	2,000	1.5
Saturn	Aquarius	3,000	1.5
Clown	Gemini	3,000	0.5
Blinking Planetary	Cygnus	3,500	2.5
Little Dumbbell	Perseus	3,500	5.0
Cat's Eye	Draco	3,500	6.0

FIND OUT MORE

PROPERTIES OF STARS 168 • RED GIANTS 180
SUPERNOVAS 184 • NEUTRON STARS 186 • BLACK HOLES 188

SUPERNOVAS

THE MOST MASSIVE STARS OF ALL end their lives in a colossal explosion known as a supernova. The star erupts into space, and for a few days can outshine an entire galaxy. We can still see the glowing remains of shattered stars that blew up hundreds or thousands of years ago. Supernovas are rare – only two or three are expected in our Galaxy each century, and most of these will be hidden by interstellar dust. The last one seen in the Milky Way was in 1604, but astronomers have found many more in other galaxies.

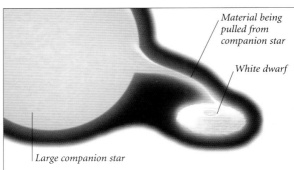

Material being pulled from companion star

White dwarf

Large companion star

OTHER KINDS OF SUPERNOVAS

An exploding supergiant is a Type II supernova – a Type Ia supernova is even more powerful. As a small, dense white dwarf star pulls gas from a larger companion star, it can increase its mass until it can no longer support itself and collapses, destroying itself in a huge explosion. Type Ia supernovas always reach the same brightness and can be used to measure the distance to faraway galaxies.

STAGES OF COLLAPSE

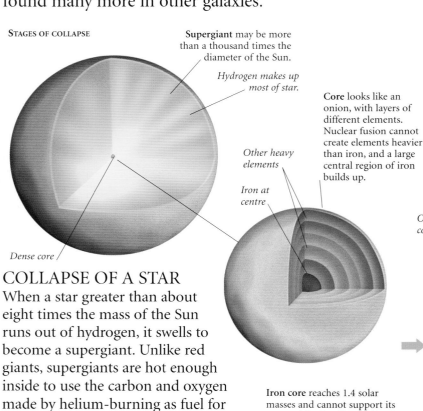

Supergiant may be more than a thousand times the diameter of the Sun.

Hydrogen makes up most of star.

Core looks like an onion, with layers of different elements. Nuclear fusion cannot create elements heavier than iron, and a large central region of iron builds up.

Other heavy elements

Iron at centre

Dense core

Outer layers of core collapse inward.

Subatomic neutrinos burst from iron at centre.

Shockwave from collapse tears through the star, creating an immense explosion. Heavy elements blown out into space help form the next generation of stars.

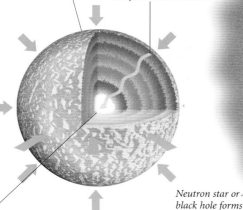

Iron core reaches 1.4 solar masses and cannot support its own weight. It collapses in on itself, setting off reactions that make elements heavier than iron.

Neutron star or black hole forms from collapsed core.

COLLAPSE OF A STAR

When a star greater than about eight times the mass of the Sun runs out of hydrogen, it swells to become a supergiant. Unlike red giants, supergiants are hot enough inside to use the carbon and oxygen made by helium-burning as fuel for making heavier elements. Supergiants can create elements as heavy as iron.

SUPERNOVA 1987A

The brightest supernova in Earth's skies for almost four centuries appeared on 23 February 1987 in the Large Magellanic Cloud, a small satellite galaxy of the Milky Way. Over 85 days, the star's brightness rose to magnitude 2.8, and it was easily visible without a telescope, but the supernova was surprisingly faint compared with those in distant galaxies. Astronomers also detected a burst of neutrinos from the collapse of the core three hours before the star began to brighten.

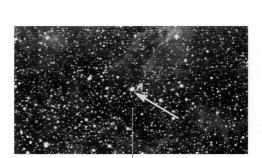

Three years before the explosion, the star that became Supernova 1987a was a barely visible blue supergiant known as Sanduleak −69°202. It originally had a mass about 20 times that of the Sun.

Supernova 1987A continued to brighten until 20 May, powered by radioactive elements created in the explosion. The original star's compact structure affected its maximum brightness.

SUPERNOVA REMNANTS

The remains of the exploded star are extremely hot, and continue to expand and glow for hundreds or thousands of years. About 150 supernova remnants are known. This X-ray image shows the remnant of the supernova that exploded in 1572 in Cassiopeia. The supernova bears the name of Tycho Brahe, who studied it in detail.

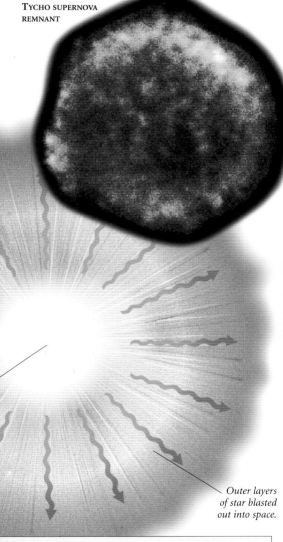

TYCHO SUPERNOVA REMNANT

Outer layers of star blasted out into space.

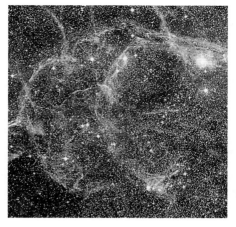

STELLAR REMAINS

The Vela supernova remnant is the remains of a star that exploded about 11,000 years ago. The centre is about 1,500 light years from the Sun. Material expanding at thousands of kilometres a second collided with gas lying in space, heating it and making it glow. The red light comes from hydrogen and the blue from oxygen. The hot glow of the Vela remnant can also be seen with X-ray telescopes.

1940 photograph of galaxy NGC 4725 in the constellation Coma Berenices

— Site of supernova

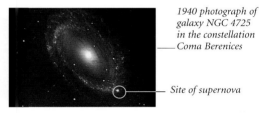

1941 photograph of the same area shows a brilliant supernova. Comparing such photos can reveal changes in the galaxy's stars.

SEARCHING FOR SUPERNOVAS

Astronomers cannot predict when a star will explode, and until recently supernovas were discovered only by accident. Professional astronomers today use automatic telescopes and computers to search hundreds of distant galaxies in one night. Amateur astronomers also play an important part in hunting for supernovas. Some use traditional photography, others use electronic cameras, while many just use their eyes and memory. They have discovered more than 130 supernovas since 1957, when the first amateur discovery of a supernova was made.

NOTABLE SUPERNOVAS

Year	Constellation	Magnitude	Distance in light years
185	Centaurus	–8	9,800
386	Sagittarius	1.5	16,000
393	Scorpius	0	34,000
1006	Lupus	–9.5	3,500
1054	Taurus	–5	6,500
1181	Cassiopeia	0	8,800
1572	Cassiopeia	–4	7,500
1604	Ophiuchus	–3	12,500
1987	Dorado	2.8	160,000

SUPERNOVA TIMELINE

• The first recorded sighting of a supernova was made in the 2nd century by Chinese astronomers.

• A bright supernova recorded by the Chinese in 1054 gave rise to the Crab Nebula in Taurus. It may also be shown in Native American wall paintings of the time.

• The last supernova observed in our galaxy was recorded by Johannes Kepler in 1604. At its brightest, it reached magnitude –3.

• The Crab Nebula was first recorded in Charles Messier's catalogue of 1771.

• In 1885, German astronomer Ernst Hartwig (1851–1923) discovered a bright new star in the Andromeda Galaxy – the first supernova to be seen in another galaxy.

• The term supernova was invented by Walter Baade and Fritz Zwicky in 1934.

• In 1942, the Crab Nebula was identified as the glowing remains of the 1054 supernova.

• In the 1950s, US astronomer William Fowler (1911–95) and Fred Hoyle explained how a supernova is created when a massive star runs out of fuel.

• Supernova 1987A in the Large Magellanic Cloud was the first nearby supernova to be studied with modern instruments.

NEUTRON STARS

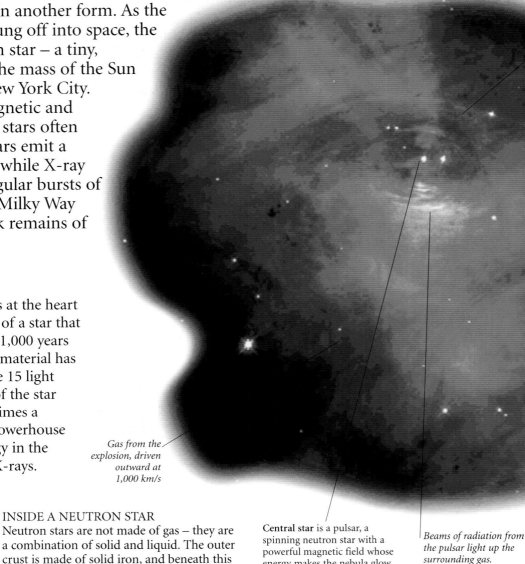

CRAB NEBULA

THE EXPLOSION OF A SUPERNOVA marks the death of a star, but also its rebirth in another form. As the outer parts of the star are flung off into space, the core collapses into a neutron star – a tiny, superdense object packing the mass of the Sun into an area smaller than New York City. Because of their intense magnetic and gravitational fields, neutron stars often become pulsars. Radio pulsars emit a regular beat of radio waves, while X-ray pulsars throw off equally regular bursts of high-energy radiation. The Milky Way may be strewn with the dark remains of these strange objects.

CRAB NEBULA

The best known neutron star lies at the heart of the Crab Nebula, the remains of a star that exploded as a supernova almost 1,000 years ago. Although most of the star's material has been flung over a region of space 15 light years across, the collapsed core of the star remains. Spinning furiously 30 times a second, the neutron star is the powerhouse of the nebula, pouring out energy in the form of light, radio waves, and X-rays.

Gas from the explosion, driven outward at 1,000 km/s

NEUTRON STAR INTERIOR

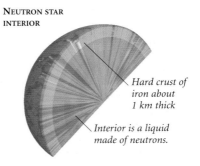

Hard crust of iron about 1 km thick

Interior is a liquid made of neutrons.

INSIDE A NEUTRON STAR

Neutron stars are not made of gas – they are a combination of solid and liquid. The outer crust is made of solid iron, and beneath this is a liquid made almost entirely of subatomic particles known as neutrons. When the core of the star collapsed, most of the atoms were crushed together, forcing electrons and protons to merge and make neutrons.

Central star is a pulsar, a spinning neutron star with a powerful magnetic field whose energy makes the nebula glow.

Beams of radiation from the pulsar light up the surrounding gas.

DENSITY OF A NEUTRON STAR

The neutrons in a neutron star are extremely small, and pack together very tightly. This makes neutron stars incredibly dense, with gravity so strong that a rocket would have to take off at half the speed of light to escape from the surface. A neutron star heavier than three solar masses will collapse under its own gravity to form a black hole.

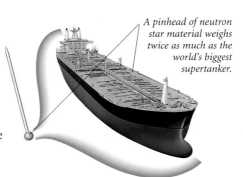

A pinhead of neutron star material weighs twice as much as the world's biggest supertanker.

NOTABLE PULSARS

Name	Period in seconds	Distance in ly	Comments
Millisecond	0.002	31,000	Shortest period
Black Widow	0.002	5,000	Binary pulsar
Crab	0.033	8,100	Formed in 1054
Binary	0.059	23,000	First binary found
Vela	0.089	1,500	Gamma ray source
PSR 1919+21	1.337	2,100	First radio pulsar
J1951+11	5.094	5,400	Longest period
Geminga	0.237	520	X-ray and gamma ray pulsar
Hercules X-1	1.24	15,000	X-ray pulsar
Centaurus X-3	4.84	25,000	First X-ray pulsar

FIND OUT MORE

X-RAY ASTRONOMY 28 • LIFECYCLE OF STARS 170
RED GIANTS 180 • SUPERNOVAS 184 • BLACK HOLES 188

PULSARS

Astronomers have discovered more than a thousand pulsars since the first one was found in 1967. Pulsars are strongly magnetic, spinning neutron stars which send out rhythmic bursts of radio waves. The fastest pulsar sends out a pulse 642 times a second, while the slowest pulses every 5.1 seconds. Most pulsars lie in our Milky Way Galaxy, but many have been found in globular clusters. Magnetars are a recently discovered type of neutron star with an even stronger magnetic field. They may be linked to some mysterious gamma-ray bursts from space.

Ripples spread out from the pulsar as its radio beams heat the as around them.

STRUCTURE OF A PULSAR

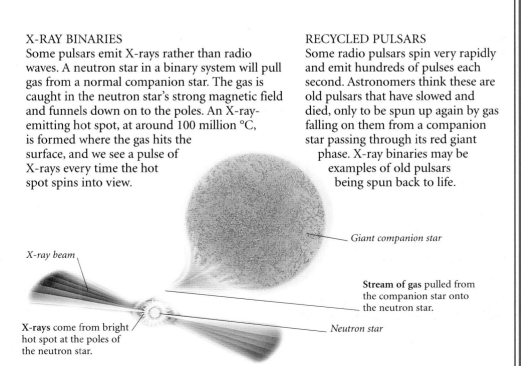

Rotation axis

Magnetic field

Neutron star

Beam of radio waves

Magnetic pole

Pulsar off

Pulsar on

Pulsar off

OPTICAL PULSARS
A few pulsars emit flashes of light as well as radio pulses. The pulsar in the Crab Nebula appears as a star which is flashing on and off 30 times a second. Another, in the Vela supernova remnant, flashes 11 times a second.

HOW PULSARS WORK
As it spins around, the neutron star sends out a radio beam from each of its magnetic poles. We detect a pulse of radio waves each time the beam sweeps past the Earth, similar to flashes from a lighthouse. The spinning neutron star gradually radiates away its energy and slows down. After a few million years it will be spinning too slowly to emit radio waves and will fade away.

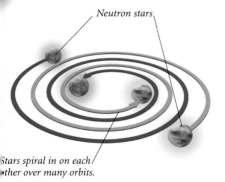

Neutron stars

Stars spiral in on each other over many orbits.

BINARY PULSARS
Often, pulsars are in orbit around other stars, in a system called a binary pulsar. The companion can be a normal star, a white dwarf, or a second neutron star. Astronomers have measured the pulsing behaviour in systems with two neutron stars, and have found that the neutron stars are slowly spiralling in towards each other. Eventually they will collide and may even form a black hole.

X-RAY BINARIES
Some pulsars emit X-rays rather than radio waves. A neutron star in a binary system will pull gas from a normal companion star. The gas is caught in the neutron star's strong magnetic field and funnels down on to the poles. An X-ray-emitting hot spot, at around 100 million °C, is formed where the gas hits the surface, and we see a pulse of X-rays every time the hot spot spins into view.

X-ray beam

X-rays come from bright hot spot at the poles of the neutron star.

RECYCLED PULSARS
Some radio pulsars spin very rapidly and emit hundreds of pulses each second. Astronomers think these are old pulsars that have slowed and died, only to be spun up again by gas falling on them from a companion star passing through its red giant phase. X-ray binaries may be examples of old pulsars being spun back to life.

Giant companion star

Stream of gas pulled from the companion star onto the neutron star.

Neutron star

BLACK HOLES

THE MOST BIZARRE OBJECTS in the Universe, black holes are aptly named – they emit no visible light at all. And yet, most black holes are the end state of the most brilliant objects in the cosmos: giant stars that go supernova. The supercompressed core that remains after the explosion has such strong gravity that even light cannot escape it – so the object is black. And as nothing can travel faster than light, anything that falls in is trapped forever – so it is also a hole in space. Tracking down black holes against the blackness of space is a great challenge, but astronomers are now convinced that they do exist.

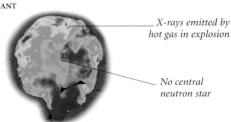

CYGNUS LOOP
SUPERNOVA REMNANT

X-rays emitted by hot gas in explosion

No central neutron star

FORMATION
When a supernova explodes, the star's core usually collapses to become a neutron star, but not always – this fiery supernova remnant shows no sign of a central neutron star. If the collapsing core is heavier than three solar masses, even densely packed neutrons cannot hold up against gravity, and the star collapses completely to become a black hole.

Streamer hits the gas orbiting the black hole, creating a bright hot spot.

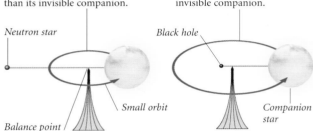

Small, slow orbit of visible star shows it is close to the balance point of the system, and that it must be heavier than its invisible companion.

Large, fast orbit of visible star shows it is farther from the balance point, and therefore lighter than its invisible companion.

Neutron star

Black hole

Small orbit

Balance point

Companion star

WEIGHING A BLACK HOLE
When astronomers find a star in orbit with an invisible companion, they can weigh the companion to discover whether it is a neutron star or a black hole. A neutron star can be no heavier than three solar masses, so anything more massive must be a black hole. Both objects orbit around the same balance point in the system, and the relative masses of the two stars can be found by looking at the position of this balance point. Astronomers find the mass of the visible star from its brightness and colour, and can then work out the mass of its companion.

DETECTION
Black holes can be detected only if they are close to another star. The hole's powerful gravity pulls streamers of gas off its companion at high speeds. The gas pours down toward the black hole, forming a spiral vortex around it called an accretion disc. Friction makes the swirling gas so hot that it glows fiercely – the hottest parts reach up to 100 million °C and emit X-rays.

Dust ring feeding accretion disc

Region of black hole

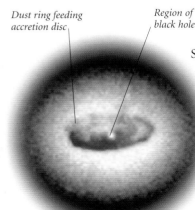

SUPERMASSIVE BLACK HOLES
Some black holes weigh in at millions or even billions of Suns. They lurk at the centres of galaxies, and were produced not by supernovas but by the collapse of huge gas clouds in the galaxy's past. Their immense gravity can attract dust and gas from large areas of space, forming massive accretion discs. These may appear dark, as in the galaxy NGC 4261, or shine brilliantly in quasars.

ACTIVE GALAXY NGC 4261

BLACK HOLE DATA

Name	Mass	Mass of companion star
MGROJ 1655-40	5.5 Suns	1.2 Suns
LMC X-3	6.5 Suns	20 Suns
J0422432	10 Suns	0.3 Suns
A0620-00	11 Suns	0.5 Suns
V404 Cygni	12 Suns	0.6 Suns
Cygnus X-1	16 Suns	30 Suns

Gas is torn away from the companion star by the black hole's powerful gravity.

Gas forms a long streamer, travelling faster the closer it gets to the black hole.

Close to the black hole, gas is heated to 100 million °C by the pull of the black hole's gravity.

Blue giant companion star

GINGA SATELLITE

X-rays emitted by superheated gas as it falls into the black hole

WILLIAM HERSCHEL TELESCOPE

Billion-tonne black hole only a million-billionth of a metre across

Black hole shrinks and loses mass through Hawking radiation.

Black hole finally disappears, exploding with a blast of gamma rays.

Particles generated by intense gravitational field cause a faint glow.

Gas forms a whirling vortex around the hole – the accretion disc.

Disc is dark and cold around edges. Black hole's gravity heats it until it glows nearer the centre.

SEARCHING FOR BLACK HOLES

Satellites in orbit first pinpoint outbursts of celestial X-rays. Then, telescopes on Earth search the same part of the sky for anything unusual. In 1991, for instance, the Japanese Ginga satellite and the William Herschel Telescope in the Canary Islands discovered a faint star being whirled around by an unseen companion weighing 12 solar masses. This object, V404 Cygni, does not emit radiation at other wavelengths, so it must be a black hole.

MINI BLACK HOLES

Some astronomers think that tiny black holes were created by the immense forces of the Big Bang. These black holes are the size of atoms but have masses up to billions of tonnes. Calculations by Stephen Hawking show that the intense gravity around a mini black hole can cause it to slowly release "Hawking radiation", which drains away its energy and mass. The mini black hole eventually disappears in a blast of gamma rays. If the theory is correct, mini black holes may be exploding at the present time.

INSIDE A BLACK HOLE

BLACK HOLES ARE PRISONS OF LIGHT, where gravity is so strong that nothing can escape. But they have even more bizarre effects: a black hole's gravity distorts space and time, and the laws of physics break down at its centre. No one can look inside a black hole, but mathematicians can explore them using Einstein's theory of gravity – general relativity. This shows strange effects at the edge of the black hole, and deep inside, where its matter has collapsed into a singularity – an infinitely small point of infinite density. Some calculations suggest that black holes could be gateways to other universes.

Shallow gravitational well

Sun makes a shallow gravitational well. Objects such as comets "roll" towards it at moderate speeds.

White dwarf, being denser, dents space more noticeably. Objects roll quickly towards it as they approach the steep slope.

Steeper gravitational well

GRAVITATIONAL WELL

According to Albert Einstein's theory of general relativity, gravity is not really a force between objects: it is a distortion of space itself. This is the best way to visualize the effects of gravity around a black hole. Einstein thought of space as being like a thin rubber sheet. If you place a heavy object, such as a billiard ball, on the sheet, it makes a dent. In the same way, the Sun warps the space around it, forming a gravitational well. The orbits of the planets are curved paths around this indentation. Denser stars make deeper gravitational wells, with steeper sides.

Very steep well

Neutron star – denser still than a white dwarf – creates a gravitational well with very steep sides. Objects rolling in reach half the speed of light.

Black hole makes such a steep dent that objects enter at the speed of light.

Objects approaching a black hole are deflected by steeply curved space.

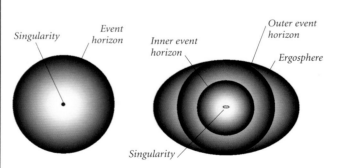

Singularity   *Event horizon*   *Inner event horizon*   *Outer event horizon*   *Ergosphere*

Singularity

STATIONARY BLACK HOLE   **SPINNING BLACK HOLE**

ANATOMY OF A BLACK HOLE

All black holes have the same basic structure. The singularity at the centre is surrounded by an invisible boundary called the event horizon: nothing can escape from inside it. The size of the event horizon is the Schwarzschild radius, named after the physicist who first realized its importance. A spinning black hole is more complex, with an ergosphere (a region like a cosmic whirlpool), an extra inner event horizon, and a singularity shaped like a ring.

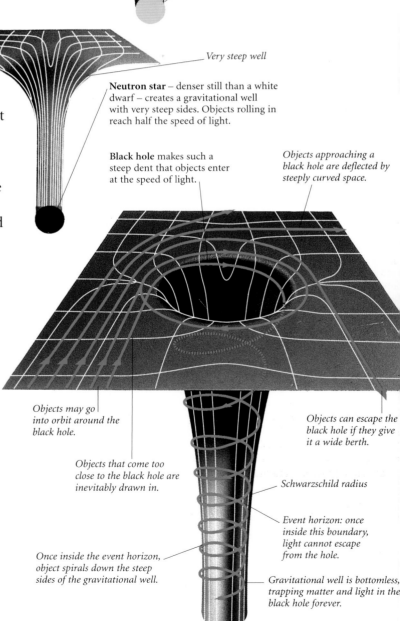

Objects may go into orbit around the black hole.

Objects can escape the black hole if they give it a wide berth.

Objects that come too close to the black hole are inevitably drawn in.

Schwarzschild radius

Event horizon: once inside this boundary, light cannot escape from the hole.

Once inside the event horizon, object spirals down the steep sides of the gravitational well.

Gravitational well is bottomless, trapping matter and light in the black hole forever.

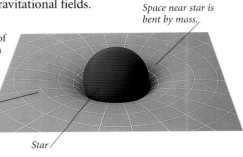
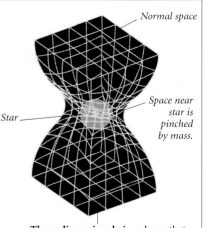
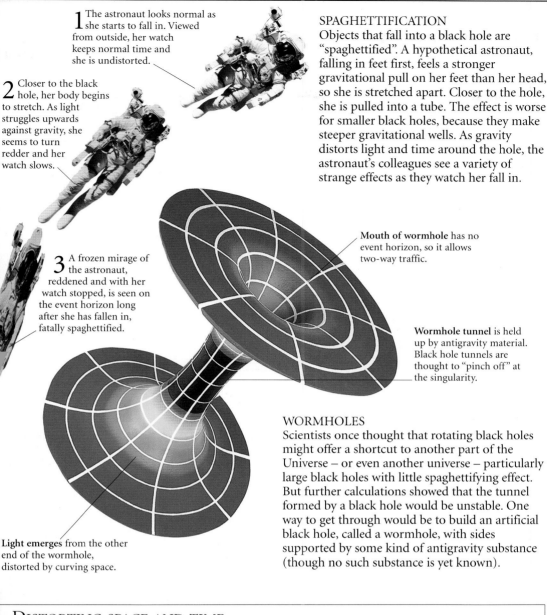

1 The astronaut looks normal as she starts to fall in. Viewed from outside, her watch keeps normal time and she is undistorted.

2 Closer to the black hole, her body begins to stretch. As light struggles upwards against gravity, she seems to turn redder and her watch slows.

3 A frozen mirage of the astronaut, reddened and with her watch stopped, is seen on the event horizon long after she has fallen in, fatally spaghettified.

Light emerges from the other end of the wormhole, distorted by curving space.

SPAGHETTIFICATION

Objects that fall into a black hole are "spaghettified". A hypothetical astronaut, falling in feet first, feels a stronger gravitational pull on her feet than her head, so she is stretched apart. Closer to the hole, she is pulled into a tube. The effect is worse for smaller black holes, because they make steeper gravitational wells. As gravity distorts light and time around the hole, the astronaut's colleagues see a variety of strange effects as they watch her fall in.

Mouth of wormhole has no event horizon, so it allows two-way traffic.

Wormhole tunnel is held up by antigravity material. Black hole tunnels are thought to "pinch off" at the singularity.

WORMHOLES

Scientists once thought that rotating black holes might offer a shortcut to another part of the Universe – or even another universe – particularly large black holes with little spaghettifying effect. But further calculations showed that the tunnel formed by a black hole would be unstable. One way to get through would be to build an artificial black hole, called a wormhole, with sides supported by some kind of antigravity substance (though no such substance is yet known).

DISTORTING SPACE AND TIME

The diagrams on these pages are a convenient simplification: they show space as two-dimensional, like a sheet, while in reality space has three dimensions. According to Einstein's theory of relativity, a massive object like a star distorts space. It is easier to show this effect in two dimensions, especially when it comes to the extreme distortion caused by a black hole. Time is an extra, fourth dimension: not shown here, it is also affected by strong gravitational fields.

Two-dimensional view of a massive body making a dent in space-time. The distortion is shown on gridlines that would lie in a flat plane if the star were absent.

Space near star is bent by mass.

Star

Normal space

Space near star is pinched by mass.

Star

Three-dimensional view shows that the star's gravity distorts space in a more complex way. Objects that would normally travel in straight lines are forced to follow the curved gridlines.

GALAXIES AND BEYOND

Cosmology – the study of the Universe on its largest scale – is the most challenging area in astronomy. It is also astronomy's newest field dating from a century ago. Until then, we were unaware of the extent of the Universe around us. First, came the discovery that our Sun is part of a Galaxy of 200 billion stars, and then that our Galaxy is just one of a hundred billion galaxies in the Universe. Next came the finding that all the galaxies are rushing away from one another, showing that our cosmos was once a more crowded place. Now astronomers know that the Universe began some 13 billion years ago in the Big Bang – but the future is still unknown. The biggest unanswered question, however, concerns life elsewhere in the Universe – is there anybody out there?

MILKY WAY

OUR HOME IN THE UNIVERSE is the Milky Way Galaxy. If you could look down on the Milky Way from above, the view would be rather like flying over a glittering city at night. The Sun is just one of the 200 billion stars that inhabit this space city. Mingled in with the stars are vast clouds of dust and gas, the material from which future stars will be made. In places, the clouds are pierced by brilliant nebulas in which stars have just formed. The Milky Way is a spinning, spiral-shaped galaxy 100,000 light years (ly) across, but only 2,000 ly thick. It started life billions of years ago as a vast, round cloud of gas that collapsed under the force of its own gravity, and was then flattened by its rotation into its present shape.

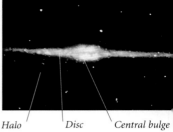

Halo   *Disc*   *Central bulge*

SHAPE OF THE MILKY WAY
Viewed from the side, the Galaxy is shaped like a flat disc with a bulge at its centre. Surrounding the disc is a huge spherical region called the halo, which marks the original extent of the Galaxy when it was a ball of gas. The halo contains globular star clusters and mysterious dark matter.

OVERHEAD VIEW OF THE MILKY WAY

The disc contains long, sweeping spiral arms.

In the outer reaches, there are large clouds of hydrogen gas.

Kepler's Supernova Remnant is the remains of a supernova observed by Johannes Kepler in 1604.

Most X-ray sources are discs of hot gas surrounding neutron stars or black holes.

One of the 5,000 molecular clouds in the Galaxy. The biggest ones are concentrated in the spiral arms.

Sagittarius Dwarf Galaxy is passing too close and being slowly ripped to pieces by the Milky Way's mighty gravitational forces.

Central galactic bulge contains many old, cool stars, red or yellow in colour, which give it a yellowish tinge.

Sagittarius Arm, the innermost of the major arms, stretches right around the Galaxy before fading out.

Spiral arms contain many hot, blue-white young stars, making them shine brightly.

OUTER ARM

SAGITTARIUS ARM

NORMA ARM

3 KILOPARSEC ARM

SCUTUM-CRUX ARM

SAGITTARIUS ARM

ORION ARM

PERSEUS ARM

SS 433

Cygnus X-1

Sun

NGC 3603

Carina Nebula

Crab Nebula

Cassiopeia A

STRUCTURE OF THE MILKY WAY

Mapping the objects in our Galaxy reveals its true shape. Two major spiral arms, and segments of others, wind around an elongated central bulge. Bright young stars, pinkly glowing nebulas of gas and dust, and dense, dark molecular clouds trace out the shape of the arms. By contrast, the central bulge contains little gas and mainly consists of old stars.

KEY TO MAP

- Star associations
- Hydrogen gas clouds
- Molecular clouds
- Nebulas
- X-ray sources and supernova remnants

Orion Arm, also called the Local Arm, is a major arm lying between the Perseus and Sagittarius Arms. Our Solar System lies at its inner edge.

Perseus Arm is the main outer arm. It is broad and ragged, and in places almost merges with the Orion Arm.

MILKY WAY THEORIES

- In about 500 BC, the ancient Greeks believed that the Milky Way was a stream of milk from the goddess Hera's breast. They called it *Kiklos Galaxias*, which means Milky Circle.

- Galileo, after looking through his tiny telescope in 1610, concluded that the Milky Way was made of "congeries [clumps] of innumerable stars grouped together in clusters".

- By plotting the distribution of selected stars in the sky, William Herschel discovered in 1785 that our Galaxy is lens-shaped.

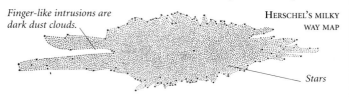

Finger-like intrusions are dark dust clouds.

HERSCHEL'S MILKY WAY MAP

Stars

- Between 1915 and 1920, Harlow Shapley established the true size and shape of the Milky Way by measuring distances to globular clusters, which mark the outer shell of our Galaxy.

◉ OBSERVING THE MILKY WAY

The Milky Way is especially bright from June to September, when the Earth's night-time side is turned towards the denser regions of the galactic centre. Because the Galaxy is relatively thin, and because we live inside it, the stars of the Milky Way appear as a band across the night sky. The dark rifts against this band are huge dust clouds that obscure the stars behind them.

HOW THE GALAXY SPINS

The Milky Way is not a single, solid object, so it does not all spin at the same rate. The rotation speed depends on gravity. At the sparsely populated outer edge, stars and other objects experience little pull and travel slowly around the Galaxy. In the central bulge, the stars are being pulled in all directions, so the average speed is again low. Objects in the dense regions halfway out feel the pull of billions of stars, and move through space at up to 250 km/s.

COMPARATIVE ROTATION SPEEDS IN THE MILKY WAY

200 km/s

250 km/s

240 km/s

220 km/s

The Sun, in the busy Orion Arm, is a fast-moving star.

ROTATION CURVE

The graph shows that objects about 20,000 ly from the centre travel round the Galaxy the fastest. Speeds level off towards the outer edge. Even though there are few stars there, the gravity of dark matter in the halo acts on them and keeps their speeds up.

Sun *Outer reaches of Galaxy*

Rotational speed (km/s)

260
240
220
200
180
160
140
120
100

0   10,000 20,000 30,000 40,000

Distance from centre (ly)

MAPPING THE GALAXY

Astronomers map the Galaxy using radio telescopes, which can penetrate the dust clouds that get in the way of optical telescopes. The key to mapping is to find the rotational speed of an object, which is done by measuring small changes in the length of the radio waves given out by the object as it moves. Astronomers know how fast the different parts of the Galaxy spin, so they use the object's rotational speed to calculate its distance from the Sun.

This tiny radio telescope, only 1.2 m across, mapped gas clouds in our Galaxy from the top of a building in the heart of New York City.

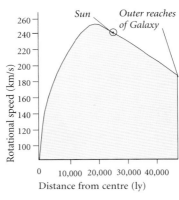

MILKY WAY DATA

Type of galaxy	Spiral (between Sb and SBc)
Luminosity	14 billion solar luminosities
Total mass (including dark matter)	1,000 billion solar masses
Mass in stars	200 billion solar masses
Mass in gas	20 billion solar masses
Mass in dust	200 million solar masses
Diameter	100,000 light years
Thickness of disc	2,000 light years
Thickness of central bulge	6,000 light years
Distance of Sun from centre	25,000 light years
Time for Sun to orbit centre	220 million years
Speed of Sun in orbit	240 km/s
Age of oldest star clusters	12 billion years
Number of globular clusters	140 known; total 200 (estimated)

FIND OUT MORE

RADIO ASTRONOMY 24 • INTERSTELLAR MEDIUM 196
OUR LOCAL NEIGHBOURHOOD 198 • PERSEUS ARM 200
SAGITTARIUS ARM 202 • HEART OF THE MILKY WAY 204
GALAXIES 210 • DARK MATTER 230

INTERSTELLAR MEDIUM

THE STARS DEFINE THE MILKY WAY'S shape and structure, but what lies between them is just as important. Space is not entirely empty: a volume about the size of a matchbox contains about half a dozen hydrogen atoms and the odd dust grain. Over the vast distances in space, these tiny amounts add up to 10 per cent of our Galaxy's mass. There is enough gas alone to make 20 billion stars like the Sun. This mixture of dust and gas – the interstellar medium – is always churning, giving birth to stars and absorbing some of their material when they die. The matter returned by a dying star is subtly different from that which made it, so the make-up of the interstellar medium is constantly evolving.

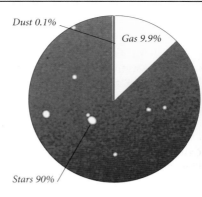

Dust 0.1%

Gas 9.9%

Stars 90%

GALACTIC COMPOSITION
Most of the Galaxy's visible mass is in the form of stars. Just 10 per cent is gas and dust, split equally between molecular clouds and the warm intercloud medium.

HORSEHEAD NEBULA IN ORION

Warm intercloud medium contains mainly hydrogen gas, which glows pink where it is most dense.

Invisible cosmic rays – mainly high-energy protons thrown out by supernovas – travel through the interstellar medium.

Alnitak is one of the stars forming Orion's Belt.

BETWEEN THE STARS

The interstellar medium is far from uniform. Most of the gas is spread out in what is called the warm intercloud medium, where "warm" is 8,000°C (hotter than the Sun). Throughout this are bubbles of thin gas, where temperatures exceed 1 million °C, created by the energy of supernovas or groups of young, hot stars. There are also cold clouds of hydrogen atoms – often curving, filament-like structures that outline the shells of ancient gas bubbles. Finally, there are very dark, dense clouds of molecules of gas and dust – molecular clouds – in which stars are born.

Dust clouds around young stars look blue because the stars' light is scattered by dust particles. The same happens to the Sun's rays in the Earth's atmosphere, which is why the sky is blue.

Horsehead Nebula is part of a dense molecular cloud. It is 4 light years from "nose" to "mane".

COSMIC DUST

Particles of cosmic dust are a type of soot that gets thrown off the surfaces of old, cool stars. These ice-covered particles measure less than a thousandth of a millimetre across and are made of graphite (as used in the "lead" in pencils) or minerals called silicates. They have an onion-like structure that is made up of concentric shells.

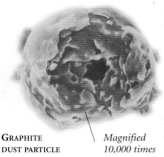

GRAPHITE DUST PARTICLE *Magnified 10,000 times*

NGC 3603 is the most massive nebula in the Galaxy visible to optical telescopes.

NGC 3576 forms part of the Carina complex of star formation.

DUST AND MAGNETISM

Cosmic dust particles spin around in space. Weak magnetic fields in the interstellar medium make the dust particles line up so that they spin at right angles to the direction of the magnetic fields. This is probably the cause of the striped effect behind the Horsehead Nebula.

Spinning particles

Lines of magnetic force

Dust particles line up with magnetic field.

EFFECTS OF DUST

Cosmic dust impedes the passage of light through space and has a dramatic effect on how we see the stars. For example, the nebulas NGC 3603 and NGC 3576 look rather like twins when viewed from the Earth. In fact, NGC 3603 is by far the more brilliant of the two. However, it appears comparatively faint to us because its brilliant light is dimmed and reddened by dust lying in front of it.

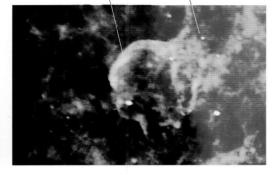

In this infrared image the Cygnus Loop is yellow-green.

Warm intercloud medium

Magnetic fields in space align dust particles and give the interstellar medium behind the Horsehead a striped appearance.

Molecular clouds are thick with dust, which blocks out the light from any newborn stars within the cloud.

HOT GAS BUBBLES

The hottest, but least dense, parts of the interstellar medium are gas bubbles such as the Cygnus Loop, which was created by a supernova more than 20,000 years ago. It is still being heated by the shock waves from the explosion.

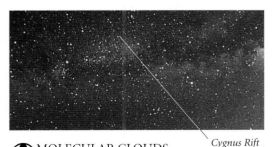

Cygnus Rift

◉ MOLECULAR CLOUDS

With the naked eye, a molecular cloud can be seen in the Cygnus region of the Milky Way. It is the starless gash down the centre – the Cygnus Rift – where a giant molecular cloud blocks out the light from the stars behind.

COSMIC CHEMISTRY

In dense molecular clouds, where the conditions are cool and undisturbed, atoms link up to form molecules. More than 80 molecules have been identified in space. Here are 10 of the best-known:

Name of molecule	Formula
Water	H_2O
Formaldehyde	CH_2O
Hydrogen cyanide	HCN
Formic acid	CH_2O_2
Hydrogen sulphide	H_2S
Cyanoacetylene	HC_3N
Ammonia	NH_3
Glycine	$C_2H_5NO_2$
Methanol	CH_3OH
Acrylonitrile	C_3H_3N

Chemical reactions inside molecular clouds can build up complex molecules from much simpler ones, such as the series of reactions that leads to the formation of methanol.

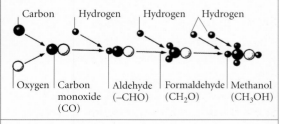

Carbon · Hydrogen · Hydrogen · Hydrogen

Oxygen · Carbon monoxide (CO) · Aldehyde (–CHO) · Formaldehyde (CH_2O) · Methanol (CH_3OH)

FIND OUT MORE

OUR LOCAL NEIGHBOURHOOD

THE PART OF THE MILKY WAY AROUND THE SUN is home to many of the most sensational sights in the night sky. This is not simply because they are relatively near to us: some regions, such as the spectacular star-forming complex in Orion, would be "tourist attractions" anywhere in the Galaxy. Our local neighbourhood covers 5,000 light years around the Sun. It includes the stars making up all the familiar constellations, such as Taurus, the Southern Cross, and, of course, Orion. It is mostly filled with the Orion or Local Arm, which was once thought to be a bridge between the Sagittarius and Perseus Arms, but is now known to be a spiral arm in its own right.

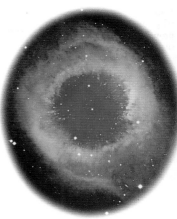

HELIX NEBULA
At 450 light years away, the Helix Nebula is the closest planetary nebula to the Sun. The Helix covers about half the area of the full Moon in the sky, although it is very faint. Its helix shape is probably the result of a red giant puffing off its outer layers on two separate occasions.

LOCATION OF MAP AREA IN MILKY WAY

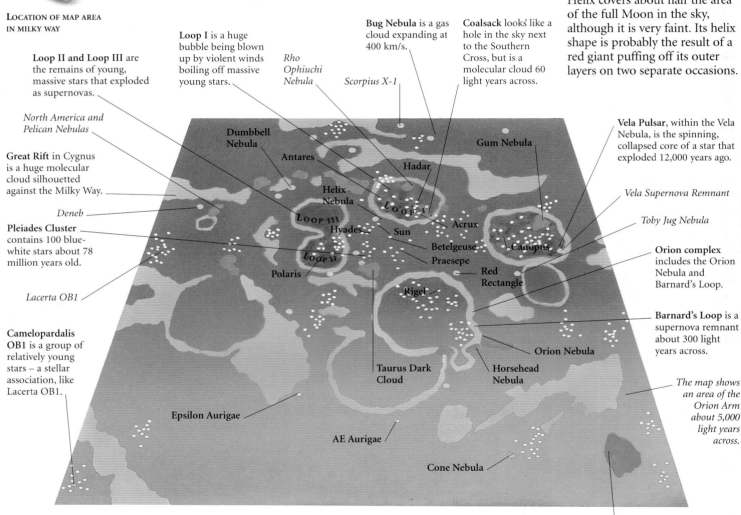

Loop II and Loop III are the remains of young, massive stars that exploded as supernovas.

Loop I is a huge bubble being blown up by violent winds boiling off massive young stars.

Rho Ophiuchi Nebula

Scorpius X-1

Bug Nebula is a gas cloud expanding at 400 km/s.

Coalsack looks like a hole in the sky next to the Southern Cross, but is a molecular cloud 60 light years across.

North America and Pelican Nebulas

Great Rift in Cygnus is a huge molecular cloud silhouetted against the Milky Way.

Deneb

Pleiades Cluster contains 100 blue-white stars about 78 million years old.

Lacerta OB1

Camelopardalis OB1 is a group of relatively young stars – a stellar association, like Lacerta OB1.

Dumbbell Nebula

Antares

Helix Nebula

LOOP III

Hyades

LOOP II

Polaris

LOOP I

Hadar

Sun

Acrux

Betelgeuse

Praesepe

Rigel

Red Rectangle

Gum Nebula

Canopus

Vela Pulsar, within the Vela Nebula, is the spinning, collapsed core of a star that exploded 12,000 years ago.

Vela Supernova Remnant

Toby Jug Nebula

Orion complex includes the Orion Nebula and Barnard's Loop.

Barnard's Loop is a supernova remnant about 300 light years across.

The map shows an area of the Orion Arm about 5,000 light years across.

Epsilon Aurigae

Taurus Dark Cloud

Horsehead Nebula

Orion Nebula

AE Aurigae

Cone Nebula

STRUCTURE OF THE ORION ARM
Starbirth dominates our neighbourhood, with "star factories" in the Orion complex and the North America and rho Ophiuchi Nebulas. Young stars abound, along with molecular clouds in which starbirth has yet to begin. There are also the remains of stars that died young.

KEY TO MAP
Hydrogen gas clouds
Molecular clouds
Interstellar bubbles
Nebulas
○ Star clusters and giant stars

Monoceros R2 contains a star that is 10,000 times brighter than the Sun. The star is obscured by dust, but it can be viewed through infrared telescopes.

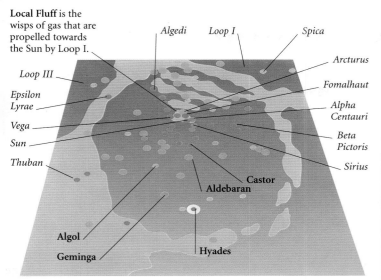

Local Fluff is the wisps of gas that are propelled towards the Sun by Loop I.

Algedi
Loop I
Spica
Arcturus
Loop III
Fomalhaut
Epsilon Lyrae
Alpha Centauri
Vega
Sun
Beta Pictoris
Thuban
Sirius
Castor
Aldebaran
Algol
Geminga
Hyades

THE LOCAL BUBBLE

The Sun sits in the Local Bubble, a barrel-shaped region of the Galaxy, 300 light years across, that is probably a supernova remnant. Although the gas in the bubble has a low density, its high temperature keeps the bubble inflated. It also contains several clouds of denser gas.

KEY TO MAP

Hydrogen gas clouds

Cool stars (K and M class)

Hot stars (A, F, and G class)

Very hot stars (O and B class)

Clusters

LOCAL ORION HIGHLIGHTS			
Name	Distance in ly	Type	Facts
Hyades	150	Star cluster	630 million years old
Canopus	310	Giant star	100,000 times brighter than the Sun
Betelgeuse	400	Red giant	Size equal to 400 Suns
Loop I	400	Hot bubble	700 ly across
Antares	500	Red giant	Name means "rival of Mars"
Praesepe	520	Star cluster	Nicknamed the "beehive"
Coalsack	550	Molecular cloud	Mass equal to 40,000 Suns
Rigel	800	Giant star	Blue-white star at 20,000°C
Red Rectangle	900	Red giant	Ejecting two flows of gas
Dumbbell Nebula	1,000	Planetary nebula	2 ly across
Vela Nebula	1,500	Supernova remnant	12,000 years old; contains a pulsar
Orion Nebula	1,600	Nebula	Contains 100 newborn stars
Horsehead Nebula	1,600	Molecular cloud	4 ly from "nose" to "mane"
Lacerta OB1	1,900	Star association	Under 30 million years old
Epsilon Aurigae	1,900	Double star	One star hidden in dark disc
AE Aurigae	1,900	Young star	Has "run away" from Orion Nebula
Cone Nebula	2,400	Nebula	Glowing gas with a dark "cone"
Cygnus Rift	2,400	Molecular cloud	1,500 ly long
Monoceros R2	2,600	Molecular cloud	Newborn stars hidden inside
Camelopardalis OB1	3,000	Star association	Stars are less than 10 million years old

FIND OUT MORE

MEASURE OF THE STARS 162 • PLANETARY NEBULAS 182 • SUPERNOVAS 184
MILKY WAY 194 • PERSEUS ARM 200 • SAGITTARIUS ARM 202

RHO OPHIUCHI COMPLEX

The rho Ophiuchi star-forming complex is one of the most colourful regions in the sky. The magenta colour comes from gas bombarded by ultraviolet radiation from young stars, while the blue is caused by dust grains scattering light rays. The real action – vigorous starbirth – is hidden behind a dark molecular cloud.

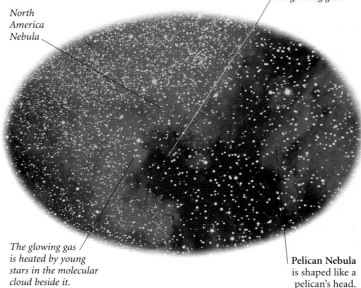

Dark cloud   Rho Ophiuchi star

Red giant star Antares is surrounded by a yellow nebula.

NORTH AMERICA NEBULA

When viewed through a telescope, it is easy to see how the North America Nebula got its name, as its shape amazingly mirrors that of the continent. The North America Nebula and its neighbour, the Pelican Nebula, are the visible parts of a vast, glowing nebula 100 light years across – six times bigger than the Orion Nebula.

The "Gulf of Mexico" is not a region of empty space, but a molecular cloud silhouetted against the glowing gas.

North America Nebula

The glowing gas is heated by young stars in the molecular cloud beside it.

Pelican Nebula is shaped like a pelican's head.

Aldebaran forms the point of the V-shape.

The stars in the Hyades Cluster form a V-shape in the sky.

👁 HYADES CLUSTER

The "head" of Taurus the Bull is traced out by the stars of the Hyades, while his red "eye" is marked by Aldebaran, a bright red giant star. The Hyades is the nearest star cluster to Earth, just 150 light years away. It lies at the centre of a supercluster of stars that envelops the Sun.

PERSEUS ARM

NOT UNTIL 1951 WERE ASTRONOMERS SURE that the Milky Way is a spiral galaxy. In that year, American astronomer William Morgan (1906–94) realized from the brightness of the stars in the constellations of Perseus, Cassiopeia, and Cepheus that they must all be at about the same distance. The graph he plotted showed that they lay in a band 5,000–8,000 light years away. He had discovered the Perseus Arm, the outermost main spiral arm. Being so close to the edge, it is vital to our understanding of the Galaxy because there are few bright stars or complicated structures behind it to clutter our view.

LOCATION OF MAP AREA IN MILKY WAY

Cluster h Persei

Cluster chi Persei

DOUBLE CLUSTER
The Double Cluster lies 7,000 light years away. The two open clusters (h and chi Persei) are 50 light years apart and each contains several thousand stars. They form the heart of a loose group, or association, of young stars 750 light years across.

Cassiopeia A is the tangled wreck of a dead star.

Tycho Brahe's Supernova Remnant is the remains of a white dwarf that collapsed when its companion star dumped too much gas on it.

Chi Persei and h Persei make up the Double Cluster. There are more stars in h Persei and they are older (5 million years) than those in chi Persei (3 million years).

In places, the Perseus Arm nearly merges with the Orion Arm.

NGC 7538 is a dark molecular cloud hiding a cluster of newly born stars. It contains enough matter to make 500,000 Suns.

IC 1795 is the biggest star-forming region in the Perseus Arm.

NGC 457 is a star cluster containing phi Cassiopeiae, a yellow supergiant that will one day explode as a supernova.

IC 1805 and IC 1848 form a double cluster, sparser and younger than h and chi Persei.

Sun

M36, M37, and M38 are young star clusters in the constellation of Auriga, lying just over 4,000 ly away.

Plaskett's Star is actually two stars very close together, weighing in at 51 and 43 times the Sun's mass.

M36

M38

M37

W3

h Persei

chi Persei

3C 58

IC 1805

IC 1848

Rosette Nebula

The map shows an area of the Perseus Arm about 8,500 ly across.

Crab Nebula

STRUCTURE OF THE PERSEUS ARM

The Perseus Arm is one of the Galaxy's main arms, but instead of wrapping itself all the way around the Galaxy, it is made up of a series of unconnected patches of young stars and nebulas. It also contains numerous supernova remnants – the corpses of dead stars – which gives it the feel of a stellar graveyard.

IC 443 nebula is a supernova remnant. Its expansion is compressing 1,000 solar masses of interstellar matter, which may one day form into stars.

KEY TO MAP

Nebulas

Molecular clouds

Star associations

Hydrogen gas clouds

Star clusters and giant stars

Pulsars and supernova remnants

The gases are spreading outwards at a speed of 1,500 km/s.

The curving filaments of the nebula look like a crab's pincers.

CRAB NEBULA

While most supernova remnants are spherical, the Crab Nebula consists of countless long filaments that stretch out across 15 light years of space. The ghostly blue glow inside the mass of filaments is synchrotron radiation produced by very fast-moving electrons. These electrons are generated by a central, rapidly spinning pulsar. The Crab Nebula Pulsar is only 25 km across, and yet its mass is greater than that of the Sun.

The radio waves come from electrons moving in strong magnetic fields.

The yellow and red areas show where the radio waves are most intense.

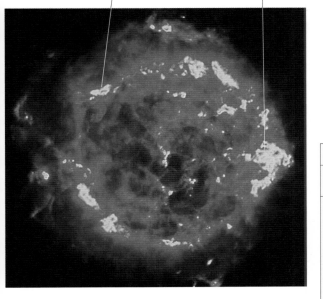

CASSIOPEIA A

The brightest radio source that can be observed from the Earth is Cassiopeia A – the remains of a star that exploded 300 years ago. This radio telescope view reveals it to be a shell of gases speeding outwards at 6,000 km/s. The bright, colour-coded parts are the dense, hot edges of the shell. Outside the shell, cooler gases in the interstellar medium are being swept up by the shell's expansion.

HISTORICAL SUPERNOVAS

- In about 1000 BC, a supernova inside the Gemini OB1 star association produced the nebula IC 443.

- Chinese astronomers saw a "guest star" exploding among the stars of Taurus in AD 1054. It was visible by day for three weeks, and at night for two years. Today, we call its remains the Crab Nebula.

- Tycho Brahe saw a new star (a supernova) in the constellation of Cassiopeia in 1572.

- In 1680, John Flamsteed logged a dim star as "3 Cassiopeiae" – possibly the star that exploded to create Cassiopeia A.

1572 Cassiopeia supernova

1603 STAR CHART SHOWING CASSIOPEIA CONSTELLATION

Young stars have already blown a hole as large as the famous Orion Nebula.

Rosette Nebula is found in the constellation of Monoceros.

ROSETTE NEBULA

Appearing bigger than the full Moon in the sky, the huge Rosette Nebula lies 5,500 light years away. It is gradually growing larger and fainter as the radiation and strong winds from young stars born at its centre blow away the gas that helped create them.

The stars at the centre form the open cluster NGC 2244.

MAJOR OBJECTS IN PERSEUS ARM

Name	Distance in light years	Type	Facts
M36	4,100	Open star cluster	20 million years old
M38	4,200	Open star cluster	Cross-shaped structure
M37	4,600	Open star cluster	300 million years old
Plaskett's Star	5,000	Double star	51 and 43 solar masses
Rosette Nebula	5,500	Nebula	100 light years across
W3	5,500	Molecular cloud	Huge starbirth complex
Crab Nebula	6,500	Supernova remnant	Contains active pulsar
Double Cluster	7,400	Open star clusters	3 and 5 million years old
Tycho's SNR	7,500	Supernova remnant	From supernova in 1572
3C 58	8,800	Supernova remnant	From supernova in 1181
Phi Cassiopeiae	9,400	Brilliant star	200,000 times brighter than the Sun
Cassiopeia A	10,000	Supernova remnant	Brightest radio source

FIND OUT MORE

RADIO ASTRONOMY 24 • CLUSTERS AND DOUBLES 174 • SUPERNOVAS 184
NEUTRON STARS 186 • MILKY WAY 194 • SAGITTARIUS ARM 202

SAGITTARIUS ARM

Lying between the Orion Arm and the galactic centre is the Sagittarius Arm, one of the Milky Way's two major spiral arms. It is a broad and sweeping arm that wraps itself around the entire Galaxy before beginning to peter out. The Sagittarius Arm is difficult to unravel from our position in the Orion Arm, because great swathes of dust block the view. Radio waves and infrared radiation can pass through the dust, but astronomers then find that objects in this busy region are often obscured because they lie along the same line of sight as other, nearer objects. Nevertheless, astronomers are discovering it to be full of strange and unusual features.

ETA CARINAE
At 5 million times brighter than the Sun, eta Carinae is one of the brightest stars known – and also one of the most unstable. This Hubble image shows it still cocooned in the dust it ejected when it flared up in 1843. It will probably explode as a supernova within a few thousand years.

LOCATION OF MAP AREA IN MILKY WAY

The map shows a section of the Sagittarius Arm approximately 12,000 ly across.

Millisecond Pulsar, spinning 642 times a second, rotates faster than any other pulsar. This may have been caused by a companion star dumping material onto it.

Eagle Nebula is named after a dusty, eagle-shaped silhouette superimposed on the glowing gas.

Omega Nebula is a blister of hot gas at one end of a dense molecular cloud 65 light years long.

SN 1006 is the wreck of a supernova in ad 1006 that shone so brightly that it cast shadows.

Jewel Box is a cluster of beautiful blue stars close to the Southern Cross in the sky. One star, kappa Crucis, has become a red giant.

Carina Nebula is home to the star HD 93129A, which is 5 million times brighter than the Sun.

Cygnus X-1 is a double star in which one of the stars is now a black hole.

Trifid Nebula

Lagoon Nebula

Black Widow Pulsar

V404 Cygni

FG Sagittae

Eta Carinae

Sun

KEY TO MAP

- Hydrogen gas clouds
- Nebulas
- Molecular clouds
- Star associations
- Pulsars and supernova remnants
- Star clusters

PSR 1919+21 was the first pulsar to be discovered. Its pulses seemed so artificial that its discoverers nicknamed it LGM–1, meaning Little Green Men–1.

Scorpius X-1, the first X-ray source to be discovered outside the Solar System, is a dead neutron star.

STRUCTURE OF THE SAGITTARIUS ARM

Great nebulas and dense molecular clouds dot the part of the arm that is closest to us. The Eagle, Omega, Trifid, and Lagoon Nebulas make up one enormous region of starbirth, with the giant Carina complex not far away. The region also has its share of star corpses, pulsars, and black holes. Closer to the galactic centre, molecular clouds dominate the arm.

BLACK HOLES IN CYGNUS

The Sagittarius Arm has its share of black holes, which astronomers can "weigh" if they lie in double-star systems. The masses of the two bodies involved dictate how they orbit one another. In V404 Cygni, the black hole is heavier than the star, so the balance point lies almost in the hole and the star swings around the hole. In Cygnus X-1, the star is heavier than the hole. The balance point lies inside the star and the hole orbits the star.

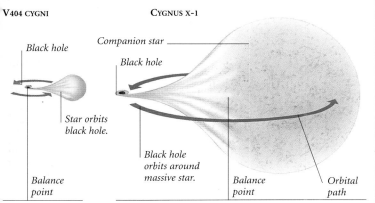

V404 CYGNI

Black hole

Star orbits black hole.

Balance point

CYGNUS X-1

Companion star

Black hole

Black hole orbits around massive star.

Balance point

Orbital path

KEY FEATURES IN SAGITTARIUS ARM

Name	Distance in ly	Type	Facts
Scorpius X-1	1,800	X-ray source	First X-ray source found outside Solar System
PSR 1919+21	2,100	Pulsar	First pulsar discovered
SN 1006	3,500	Supernova remnant	Left over from brightest supernova ever, in AD 1006
V404 Cygni	4,800	Black hole	8–15 solar masses
Black Widow	5,000	Pulsar	Devouring its neighbour
Omega Nebula	5,000	Nebula	Could form 1 million stars
Lagoon Nebula	5,200	Nebula	Stars are 2 million years old
Trifid Nebula	5,200	Nebula	Nicknamed for its dust bands
FG Sagittae	6,200	Unstable star	Shedding shells of gas
Eagle Nebula	7,000	Nebula	Stars 6 million years old
Cygnus X-1	7,500	Black hole	16 solar masses
Jewel Box	7,600	Star cluster	7 million years old
Eta Carinae	9,000	Variable star	Will explode as supernova
Kepler's SNR	12,500	Supernova remnant	Supernova seen in 1604 by Johannes Kepler
SS 433	18,000	Binary star	Jets emitted at 70,000 km/s
Binary Pulsar	23,000	Pulsar	In orbit around neutron star
NGC 3603	25,000	Nebula	Galaxy's most massive nebula
Millisecond Pulsar	31,000	Pulsar	Fastest-spinning pulsar

FIND OUT MORE

VARIABLE STARS 164 • NEUTRON STARS 186 • BLACK HOLES 188
MILKY WAY 194 • OUR LOCAL NEIGHBOURHOOD 198

TRIFID AND LAGOON NEBULAS

These two nebulas, more than 5,000 light years away, are among the most striking in the sky. The Trifid Nebula (top) gets its name, which means divided into three parts, because dark dust lanes split the nebula three ways. The nebula surrounds a compact cluster of stars whose radiation heats the hydrogen inside it until it glows pink. The Lagoon Nebula (bottom) envelops a cluster of stars about 2 million years old, many of which are so massive and bright that they can be seen with the naked eye.

BLACK WIDOW PULSAR

One of the most unusual pulsars is the Black Widow, named after a spider that devours its own mate. In this case, the pulsar's mate is a small companion star. Energy from the fast-spinning pulsar is heating the gas in the star and making it evaporate into space. The pulsar is now surrounded by a glowing cloud of gas seized from the companion star. Eventually, the entire star will have evaporated, destroyed by its pulsar neighbour.

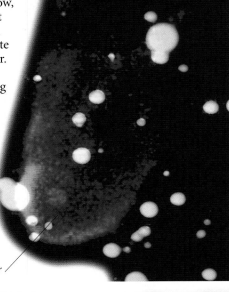

Gas cloud from companion star

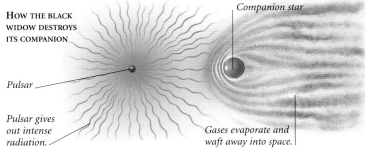

HOW THE BLACK WIDOW DESTROYS ITS COMPANION

Companion star

Pulsar

Pulsar gives out intense radiation.

Gases evaporate and waft away into space.

HEART OF THE MILKY WAY

THE CENTRE OF THE MILKY WAY is unlike any other part of the Galaxy. It is a bar-shaped bulge of old red and yellow stars with comparatively little gas. Until recently, what lay at the centre of this bulge was a mystery, because huge clouds of gas and dust block the view of optical telescopes. Now radio and infrared telescopes have revealed some of the amazing features that lie there, including rings or jets of gas moving at considerable speed, and areas of powerful magnetism. Towards the core, the temperature starts to climb. Together, these things indicate that the centre is a very disturbed and energetic place. The activity is stirred partly by a recent bout of star formation and partly by energy released by gas falling into a massive black hole.

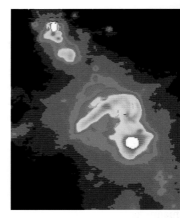

RADIO IMAGE OF CENTRE
This radio telescope view of the galactic centre covers an area about 450 light years across. Just below the centre of the image is the Sagittarius A complex (the bright white object), while the curved feature is the Arc, and at top left is the giant molecular cloud Sagittarius B2.

LOCATION OF MAP AREA IN MILKY WAY

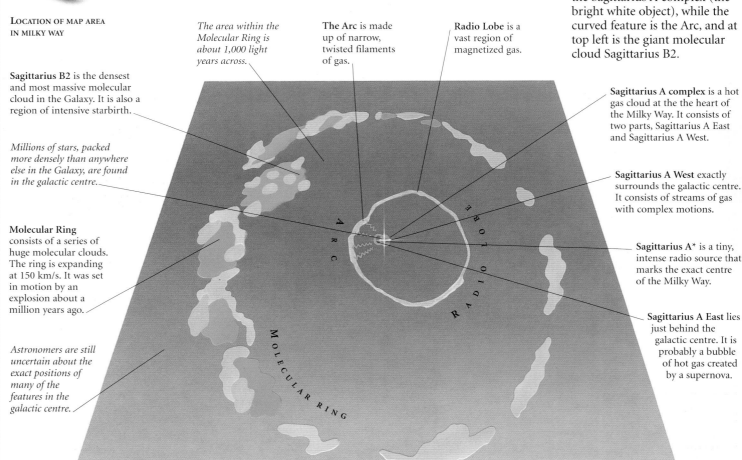

The area within the Molecular Ring is about 1,000 light years across.

The Arc is made up of narrow, twisted filaments of gas.

Radio Lobe is a vast region of magnetized gas.

Sagittarius B2 is the densest and most massive molecular cloud in the Galaxy. It is also a region of intensive starbirth.

Millions of stars, packed more densely than anywhere else in the Galaxy, are found in the galactic centre.

Molecular Ring consists of a series of huge molecular clouds. The ring is expanding at 150 km/s. It was set in motion by an explosion about a million years ago.

Astronomers are still uncertain about the exact positions of many of the features in the galactic centre.

Sagittarius A complex is a hot gas cloud at the the heart of the Milky Way. It consists of two parts, Sagittarius A East and Sagittarius A West.

Sagittarius A West exactly surrounds the galactic centre. It consists of streams of gas with complex motions.

Sagittarius A* is a tiny, intense radio source that marks the exact centre of the Milky Way.

Sagittarius A East lies just behind the galactic centre. It is probably a bubble of hot gas created by a supernova.

STRUCTURE OF THE GALACTIC CENTRE

The centre is the place where the Galaxy's biggest and heaviest objects congregate. At its core is a star cluster, many of whose members are red supergiants moving rapidly under the influence of strong gravity, and an intense radio source called Sagittarius A*. The high speed of the stars proves that Sagittarius A* is a massive black hole.

KEY TO MAP

Nebulas

Molecular clouds

Hydrogen gas clouds

MAGNETIC STRUCTURES

The innermost 100 light years are dominated by magnetic fields a thousand times stronger than those found elsewhere in the Milky Way. These are obvious in the filaments making up the Arc. This is part of the Radio Lobe, a vast region of magnetized gas in the shape of a chimney. Within this magnetized region are many strange objects unique to this part of the Galaxy, such as the Mouse. The origin of the magnetic fields is not known.

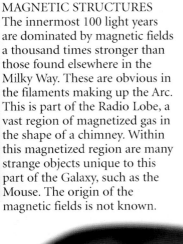

Tail is 100 light years long.

The Mouse is probably a neutron star speeding through space.

The Arc, which curves like a colossal solar prominence, consists of filaments of gas 150 light years long but only half a light year wide.

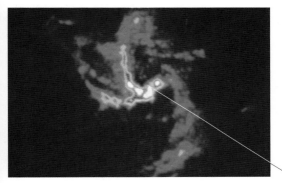

CENTRAL SPIRAL

The central 10 light years consist of three regions: Sagittarius A West, Sagittarius A★, and the central star cluster. Sagittarius A West looks like a tiny spiral galaxy, but the smaller spiral arms are streams of gas falling inwards, while the two main arms are parts of a tilted, spinning disc of hot gas. The rate at which the disc spins shows that the material inside it has a mass equal to 5 million Suns.

Sagittarius A★

Sagittarius A★

DISCOVERING THE CENTRE

- In 1918, Harlow Shapley calculated the Sun's position in the Galaxy and how far it is from the centre by measuring distances to globular clusters.

- After studying fast-moving gas clouds near the centre, Jan Oort proposed in 1957 that there must have been some sort of outburst there.

- In 1958, Josef Shklovski predicted that there is an "outstanding peculiarity" at the galactic centre.

- In the mid-1960s, scores of molecules were identified in the galactic centre, and the Molecular Ring was mapped.

- Infrared studies in the 1970s and 1980s revealed details about the central star cluster.

- In 1983, the USA's Very Large Array radio telescope discovered rotating gas in the Galaxy's central spiral.

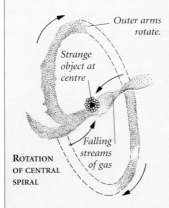

Outer arms rotate.

Strange object at centre

Falling streams of gas

ROTATION OF CENTRAL SPIRAL

- Astronomers discovered the Arc in 1984.

- Astronomers measuring stars' motion concluded in 1997 that there is a black hole of 2.5 million solar masses at the galactic centre.

CENTRAL GALACTIC FEATURES

Name	Distance from centre in ly	Facts
Sagittarius A★	0	Black hole equal to 2.5 million Suns
IRS 16	0.1	Blue star cluster
Sagittarius A West	10	Disc of hot gas
Circumnuclear disc	c.20	Reservoir of cooler gas
Sagittarius A East	30	Bubble of hot gas
Arc	100	Magnetic arc
Mouse	c.100	Neutron star with tail
Radio Lobe	c.300	Magnetized "chimney"
Great Annihilator	340	Black hole with jet
Sagittarius B2	400	Massive molecular cloud
Molecular Ring	500	Ring of molecular clouds

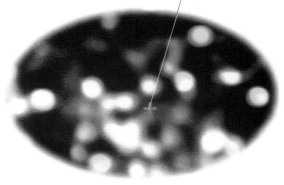

CENTRAL STAR CLUSTER

Within Sagittarius A West is the central star cluster, which contains 2.5 million stars. This infrared image shows stars in the innermost 2 light years. Right at the centre is Sagittarius A★, a black hole with a mass of 2.5 million Suns. It is not active at present, but it was once. If enough gas exists to "feed" it, it may become active again in the future.

MAGELLANIC CLOUDS

Just as the Earth's gravity holds the Moon in orbit so, on a vastly greater scale, the Milky Way Galaxy holds two large satellite galaxies in orbit around it. The Large and Small Magellanic Clouds orbit together on an elliptical path, taking over a billion years to travel once around. At present, the Magellanic Clouds are almost at their closest to us, and form a splendid spectacle in the southern sky. We can clearly see all the stars and gas clouds in these near neighbours, and the Magellanic Clouds have played a crucial role in helping astronomers to understand the properties of stars and galaxies.

LARGE MAGELLANIC CLOUD

The Milky Way's "little cousin", the Large Magellanic Cloud (LMC) contains roughly the same mix of stars and gas as our Galaxy, though it is only one-twentieth as massive. The LMC is too small to grow spectacular spiral arms like the Milky Way, but is more ordered than many smaller galaxies. Lying 160,000 light years away, the LMC is the nearest major galaxy to us – only the tiny Sagittarius Galaxy, currently being pulled apart by the Milky Way, is closer.

SUPERNOVA 1987A
On 23 February 1987, astronomers in Chile were amazed to see a new star in the Large Magellanic Cloud. Despite the galaxy's distance, this supernova could easily be seen by the naked eye for 10 months. At maximum brightness, it shone as brilliantly as 250 million Suns.

Site of Supernova 1987A

Tarantula Nebula is the biggest and brightest gas cloud in the LMC.

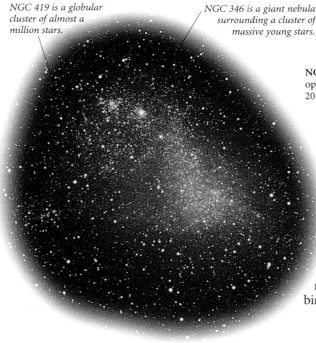

NGC 419 is a globular cluster of almost a million stars.

NGC 346 is a giant nebula surrounding a cluster of massive young stars.

NGC 2100 is a giant open star cluster only 20 million years old.

S Doradus is one of the LMC's brightest stars. It is variable, and can shine as brilliantly as 500,000 Suns.

Central bar of stars is 10,000 light years long.

SMALL MAGELLANIC CLOUD

Only a quarter as massive as its companion, the Small Magellanic Cloud (SMC) lies a little farther away, at 190,000 light years. Because of its small size, the SMC is being ripped apart by the gravity of the Milky Way, and is stretched into a peanut shape. The galaxy contains 2,000 star clusters, many created in a sudden burst of star birth 100 million years ago.

TARANTULA NEBULA

Named after the dreaded spider with hairy legs, the Tarantula is one of the biggest and brightest of all nebulas. Some 800 light years across, it is 50 times the size of the famous Orion Nebula in our Milky Way. If it were in the position of the Orion Nebula, the Tarantula would be bigger than the whole constellation of Orion and shine more brightly than the full Moon. This gas cloud is lit up by hot young stars: the cluster at its centre contains more than a hundred stars, each heavier than 50 Suns.

Faint spiral shape extends from this end of the central straight bar. Some astronomers call the LMC a "one-armed spiral".

LMC contains 6,500 star clusters.

Orbit tilted at 90° to the Milky Way

Orbit of Magellanic Clouds

Milky Way

Leading Arm

Magellanic Stream

Bridge

LMC

SMC

Dark dust clouds are less common in the LMC than in the Milky Way.

MAGELLANIC STREAM

Pulled by the Milky Way's mighty gravity, gas from the Magellanic Clouds has spilt out into space. A pool of gas, the Bridge, envelops both Clouds, while a long gas trail – the Magellanic Stream – has been left along the galaxies' elliptical orbits. Some gas – the Leading Arm – has even splashed ahead of the two galaxies.

◉ SPOTTING THE MAGELLANIC CLOUDS

The Clouds are easily seen from the Southern Hemisphere, and are highest in the sky during the spring. Look south on a moonless night, and they appear as two large hazy patches, like detached pieces of the Milky Way. Binoculars will show the Tarantula Nebula and the brightest clusters.

SMC   *LMC*

MAGELLANIC CLOUDS HISTORY

• The African Karanga tribe called the Clouds Famine and Plenty. Australian Aborigines thought the LMC was torn from the Milky Way.

FERDINAND MAGELLAN

• Ferdinand Magellan (c.1480–1521) was the first European to record the Clouds, during his voyage round the world, 1519–21.

• In 1908, Henrietta Leavitt recognized Cepheid variable stars in the SMC, allowing the first measurements of the distances to galaxies.

• The brightest supernova in 383 years appeared in the LMC in 1987.

FIND OUT MORE

SUPERNOVAS 184
MILKY WAY 194
LOCAL GROUP 208
GALAXIES 210
COLLIDING GALAXIES 212

EVOLUTION OF THE CLOUDS

The Magellanic Clouds orbit the Milky Way Galaxy once every 1.5 billion years, and with every close passage the gravity of our Galaxy tugs at their gas and stars. As a result, they are constantly evolving. The SMC is currently being pulled apart, and its stars will end up as part of the Milky Way. Eventually, the LMC will suffer the same fate.

500 million years ago: the Clouds head towards the Milky Way from their farthest point, 400,000 ly away.

250 million years ago: as the Clouds pass 150,000 ly from the Milky Way, gas and some stars are pulled out.

Today: the Clouds are heading outward again, with a stream of gas left behind, and the SMC starting to break up.

LOCAL GROUP

THE INFLUENCE OF THE MILKY WAY'S GRAVITY extends far beyond the Magellanic Clouds, attracting many small galaxies across greater distances. The cluster of galaxies formed around the Milky Way, with its nearest large neighbours the Andromeda and Triangulum Galaxies, is called the Local Group. It consists of roughly 30 galaxies scattered over about 5 million light years of space, the majority of them very small and faint. The Local Group is itself a member of the Local Supercluster – a collection of galaxy groups centred on the huge Virgo Cluster, around 50 million light years away.

ELLIPTICAL GALAXIES
About half of the Local Group galaxies are ellipticals, including NGC 205 – one of Andromeda's satellites. Ellipticals are uniform balls of old red stars that have no gas to fuel further starbirth, unlike the gas-rich irregular galaxies. The smallest, "dwarf ellipticals" are so faint that astronomers cannot see them in more distant galaxy clusters.

ELLIPTICAL NGC 205

Spiral arms containing younger stars   *M32*   *Central bulge of older stars*   *NGC 205*

ANDROMEDA GALAXY
At 2.5 million light years away, the Andromeda Galaxy is the most distant object visible to the naked eye. It is the largest galaxy in the Local Group and, with 400 billion stars, one of the biggest spirals known – half as wide again as the Milky Way. However, our Galaxy would look very much like this if viewed from afar, even down to having two prominent companions – M32 and NGC 205. Unfortunately, we look at the Andromeda Galaxy almost edge-on, which makes its spiral structure difficult to see.

GALACTIC NEIGHBOURHOOD
The galaxies in our corner of the Universe cluster together around the Andromeda and Milky Way Galaxies. These are the most massive galaxies in the Local Group, and their strong gravity allows them to gather smaller satellite galaxies around them. Other, more distant galaxies are also held into the group by gravity. Big spiral galaxies like our own and Andromeda are the exception in the Local Group: the vast majority of its members are dwarf elliptical and dwarf irregular galaxies.

— Pegasus

Triangulum

IC 1613

WLM

Dwarf galaxies are so faint they would be undetectable in a more distant galaxy cluster.

Mapped in three dimensions, the galaxies of the Local Group divide clearly into two main clumps.

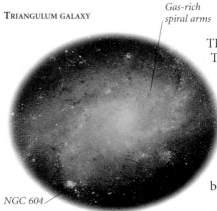

TRIANGULUM GALAXY

Gas-rich spiral arms

TRIANGULUM GALAXY
The third largest galaxy in the Local Group, Triangulum, has just one-tenth the stars of Andromeda, and is only half the size of the Milky Way. Like the other major members of the Local Group, the Triangulum is a spiral galaxy. It contains many huge and bright nebulas, one of which, NGC 604, is among the biggest regions of starbirth known.

NGC 604

CENTRAL REGION OF THE LOCAL GROUP

Irregular galaxies contain many young blue stars and star-forming nebulas.

IC10

IRREGULAR GALAXY NGC 6822

IRREGULAR GALAXIES

Many Local Group galaxies are small and irregular. Like spirals, they contain nebulas where stars are forming, but they have no real structure. NGC 6822 and Andromeda were the first galaxies to have their distances measured, using Cepheid variable stars, in 1923. This proved that separate galaxies existed beyond our own.

And III

Andromeda Galaxy is surrounded by the Triangulum spiral galaxy, and the small ellipticals M32 and NGC 205.

NGC 185

NGC 147

Gravity is pulling Andromeda and the Milky Way together. Eventually, all the Local Group galaxies will merge into a single supergalaxy.

And II

SagDIG

NGC 6822

Sagittarius

Milky Way's satellites include the Magellanic Clouds, the Sagittarius dwarf, and several dwarf ellipticals.

Ursa Minor

Draco

Sextans

Leo II

Leo I

Fornax

Sculptor

Large Magellanic Cloud (LMC)

Small Magellanic Cloud (SMC)

Carina

◉ SPOTTING THE ANDROMEDA GALAXY
The Andromeda Galaxy is visible on autumn evenings in the northern hemisphere. Look south to locate the large, barren Square of Pegasus. To the top left is a line of stars – find the third, and look a little way above it. In really dark, clear skies, you can see the galaxy as a misty oval about the size of the full Moon.

ANDROMEDA REGION

LOCAL GROUP GALAXIES

Name	Distance in light years	Diameter in light years	Luminosity in millions of Suns	Type
Milky Way	0	100,000	14,000	Spiral
Sagittarius	78,000	15,000	30	Elliptical
LMC	160,000	30,000	2,000	Irregular
SMC	190,000	20,000	250	Irregular
Ursa Minor	225,000	1,000	0.3	Elliptical
Draco	248,000	500	0.3	Elliptical
Sculptor	250,000	1,000	1.5	Elliptical
Carina	280,000	500	0.4	Elliptical
Sextans	290,000	1,000	0.8	Elliptical
Fornax	430,000	3,000	20	Elliptical
Leo II	750,000	500	1	Elliptical
Leo I	880,000	1,000	10	Elliptical
Phoenix	1,270,000	1,000	0.8	Irregular
NGC 6822	1,750,000	8,000	300	Irregular
And II	1,910,000	2,000	5	Elliptical
NGC 147	1,920,000	10,000	80	Elliptical
NGC 185	2,000,000	6,000	110	Elliptical
Andromeda	2,500,000	150,000	40,000	Spiral
M32	2,500,000	5,000	300	Elliptical
NGC 205	2,500,000	10,000	250	Elliptical
Triangulum	2,500,000	40,000	4,000	Spiral
IC 1613	2,500,000	12,000	80	Irregular
LGS 3	2,500,000	1,000	0.6	Irregular
And I	2,570,000	2,000	5	Elliptical
And III	2,570,000	3,000	1	Elliptical
EGB0427+63	2,600,000	1,000	0.8	Elliptical
Tucana	2,900,000	500	0.6	Elliptical
WLM	3,000,000	7,000	30	Irregular
SagDIG	3,700,000	5,000	2	Irregular
IC 10	4,000,000	6,000	1,000	Irregular
Pegasus	5,800,000	7,000	50	Irregular

FIND OUT MORE

MILKY WAY 194 • MAGELLANIC CLOUDS 206
GALAXIES 210 • COLLIDING GALAXIES 212
CLUSTERS OF GALAXIES 214 • SCALE OF THE UNIVERSE 218

GALAXIES

ONCE KNOWN AS ISLAND UNIVERSES, galaxies are vast spinning collections of stars, gas, and dust. Everywhere we look we see countless billions of these celestial cities, ranging in size from fewer than a million stars to a trillion or more, and from tens to hundreds of thousands of light years across. Some are simple ovals packed with elderly stars, while others, like our own Milky Way, are graceful, rotating spirals with trailing arms of young stars and glowing gas. All galaxies are held together by their own gravity, but astronomers still puzzle over why galaxies are the shape they are.

Malin 1 is the largest known galaxy in the Universe, 800 million light years away.

LARGEST GALAXIES
Astronomers have discovered new types of galaxy, so faint they have been overlooked until recently. These ghostly galaxies contain few stars but a lot of gas. Some of them are many times the size of the Milky Way.

GALAXY CLASSIFICATION
Galaxies vary widely in size, mass, and brightness, but astronomers classify them into just a few main types. The three main groups are ellipticals, spirals, and barred spirals. These groups are then subdivided further. Other galaxies are irregular, with no obvious structure. Different types of galaxy may form, depending on the speed of the galaxy's rotation and the rate of star formation. Spiral galaxies are all about the same size, but ellipticals can be both the largest and the smallest galaxies.

GALAXY NGC 3379: TYPE E0 **GALAXY M32: TYPE E2** **GALAXY M59: TYPE E5**

ELLIPTICALS
More than half of all galaxies are ball-shaped collections of old stars, with no sign of spiral arms or a disc. Ellipticals have very little dust and gas, and no stars are being born inside them. They vary a lot in mass – some of the smallest and largest galaxies are ellipticals. Ellipticals are denoted by E followed by a number. E0 galaxies are almost circular, while E7 galaxies are flattened ovals.

Lenticular galaxies (type S0) are a group of galaxies that seems to bridge the gap between ellipticals and spirals. Lenticulars have a central bulge of older stars and a disc of younger ones, but no spiral arms.

GALAXY STATISTICS

Name	Constellation	Type	Distance in millions of ly
M105	Leo	E0	38
M32	Andromeda	E2	2.5
M59	Virgo	E5	50
Sombrero	Virgo	Sa	50
NGC 2841	Ursa Major	Sb	33
Andromeda	Andromeda	Sb	2.5
Pinwheel	Ursa Major	Sc	20
Triangulum	Triangulum	Sc	2.5
Whirlpool	Canes Venatici	Sc	20
NGC 2859	Leo Minor	SBa	72
NGC 5850	Virgo	SBb	100
NGC 7479	Pegasus	SBc	110
M82	Ursa Major	Irr	12
Large Mag. Cloud	Dorado	Irr	0.16

Bright regions are areas of starbirth.

IRREGULAR GALAXY M82

IRREGULARS
Some galaxies cannot be classed as ellipticals, spirals, or barred spirals. Irregular galaxies (type Irr) have no regular shape and are rich in gas and dust. The Magellanic Clouds, the two companion galaxies of the Milky Way, are irregulars. The galaxy M82, which is going through a massive burst of star formation, is also classed as irregular.

Astronomers once thought that M82 was an exploding galaxy.

SPIRALS

Galaxies such as the Milky Way are spiral in shape, like a catherine wheel. An elliptical central hub of old stars is surrounded by a flat disc of stars containing two or more spiral arms. The arms are rich in young stars, bright nebulas, gas and dust. Spiral galaxies are denoted by S followed by a small letter a, b, c, or d. Sa galaxies have a large hub and tightly wound arms, while Sd galaxies have a small hub and very loose arms. About one-third of all galaxies are spirals or barred spirals.

GALAXY M101: TYPE **Sc**

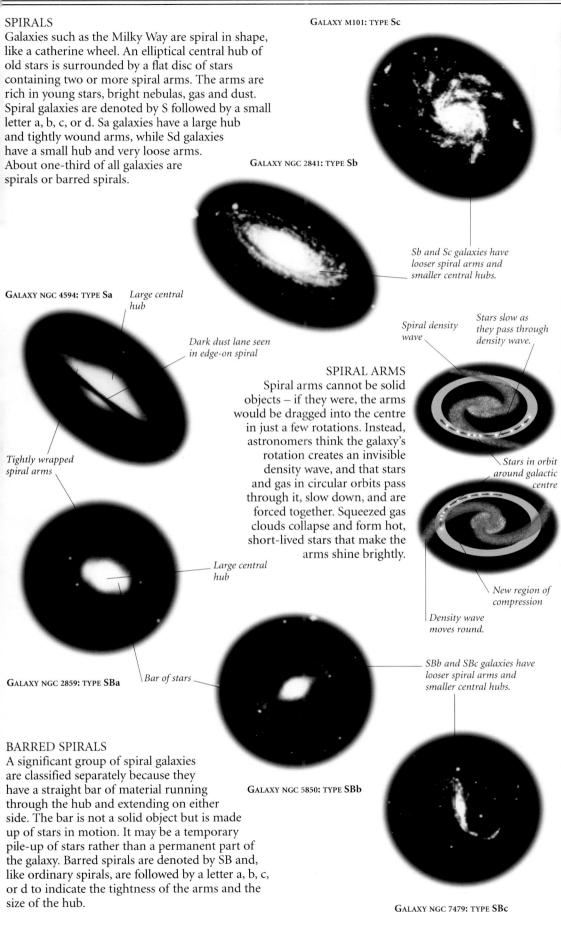

GALAXY NGC 2841: TYPE **Sb**

GALAXY NGC 4594: TYPE **Sa**

Large central hub

Dark dust lane seen in edge-on spiral

Tightly wrapped spiral arms

Sb and Sc galaxies have looser spiral arms and smaller central hubs.

SIDE-ON SPIRAL
Spiral galaxies are flattened discs. When we see one edge-on, the disc looks like a miniature Milky Way with the hub bulging out on either side. In NGC 891, a dark band of dust is visible against the background stars.

GALAXY HISTORY

● Persian astronomer Al-Sufi viewed the Andromeda Nebula as early as AD 964.

● In 1755, German philosopher Immanuel Kant (1724–1804) proposed that nebulas were distant island universes of stars.

● William Herschel completed a survey of 2,500 nebulas in 1802, but astronomers still did not know what they were.

SPIRAL NEBULA DRAWN BY ROSSE

● In 1845, William Parsons, Earl of Rosse, found spiral structures in some nebulas.

● In 1924, Edwin Hubble proved that some nebulas lay beyond the Milky Way and were galaxies in their own right. He also devised a galaxy classification scheme.

FIND OUT MORE

SPIRAL ARMS

Spiral arms cannot be solid objects – if they were, the arms would be dragged into the centre in just a few rotations. Instead, astronomers think the galaxy's rotation creates an invisible density wave, and that stars and gas in circular orbits pass through it, slow down, and are forced together. Squeezed gas clouds collapse and form hot, short-lived stars that make the arms shine brightly.

Spiral density wave

Stars slow as they pass through density wave.

Stars in orbit around galactic centre

New region of compression

Density wave moves round.

GALAXY NGC 2859: TYPE **SBa**

Large central hub

Bar of stars

GALAXY NGC 5850: TYPE **SBb**

SBb and SBc galaxies have looser spiral arms and smaller central hubs.

BARRED SPIRALS

A significant group of spiral galaxies are classified separately because they have a straight bar of material running through the hub and extending on either side. The bar is not a solid object but is made up of stars in motion. It may be a temporary pile-up of stars rather than a permanent part of the galaxy. Barred spirals are denoted by SB and, like ordinary spirals, are followed by a letter a, b, c, or d to indicate the tightness of the arms and the size of the hub.

GALAXY NGC 7479: TYPE **SBc**

COLLIDING GALAXIES

IT IS THE BIGGEST, MOST SPECTACULAR pile-up of all: two speeding galaxies, each made of a hundred billion stars, smashing together at a million kilometres per hour. Giant clouds of gas in the galaxies crash together in a blaze of fireworks, spawning thousands of hot new stars. One sign of a past cosmic collision is a starburst – a sudden spurt of star formation in an ordinary-looking galaxy. Colliding galaxies often merge to make a bigger galaxy. Eventually, most galaxies will merge with their neighbours, and the Universe will consist of a smaller number of much bigger galaxies.

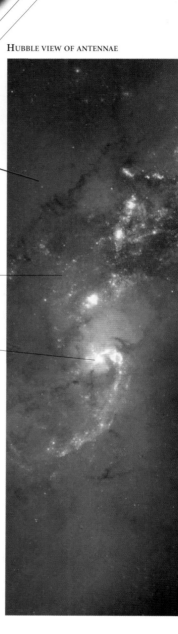

Stars in the Antennae stretch over half a million light years.

NGC 4039

NGC 4038

HUBBLE VIEW OF ANTENNAE

WIDE VIEW OF ANTENNAE GALAXIES

Both galaxies were typical spirals before the collision.

Hubble Space Telescope close-up of the central regions reveals the turmoil as giant gas clouds collide.

Dust and gas from spiral arms have fallen into the cores of both galaxies, making the stars here appear redder.

CARTWHEEL GALAXY

A spectacular example of a direct hit between two galaxies, the Cartwheel was once a normal spiral, like our Milky Way. About 300 million years ago, a smaller galaxy sped through its centre. The impact triggered a burst of star formation, producing the ring of young blue stars.

Ring could easily contain the entire Milky Way.

Central region is choked with dust, hiding giant clusters of young stars.

Gas and dust spread out in ripples from direct hit on core, creating a starburst.

INTERACTING GALAXIES

When galaxies collide, the interaction is much more complex than two billiard balls bumping together. Each galaxy is held together only by gravity, and the collision causes a tug of war as each galaxy pulls at the other's material. In the centre, gas clouds crash together, while at the edge, stars are flung out into space. In galaxies NGC 4038 and 4039, the collision has formed a pair of long curved streamers of stars, resembling an insect's antennae.

CLOSE ENCOUNTER

A simulation reveals how the Antennae may have formed. The computer is not powerful enough to simulate all the billions of stars in the two galaxies, so each galaxy is represented by only 350 stars, revolving around a massive central point. As the two galaxies approach and orbit one another, the computer calculates how these stars respond to the complex gravitational tug of war.

NGC 4038   *NGC 4039*

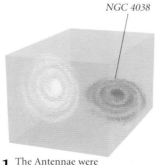

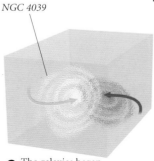

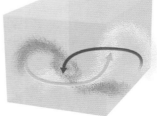

1 The Antennae were two separate spiral galaxies 1.2 billion years ago.

2 The galaxies began to smash into each other 900 million years ago.

3 The galaxies became distorted as they span round each other 600 million years ago.

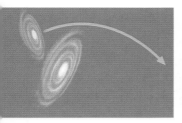

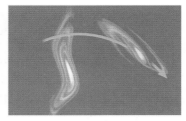

300 MILLION YEARS AGO

200 MILLION YEARS AGO

100 MILLION YEARS AGO

TODAY

GLANCING BLOW

About 300 million years ago, the Whirlpool galaxy had a near-miss with a smaller galaxy. In this computer simulation, we are seeing the collision from one side. As a smaller galaxy brushed the edge of its disc, the more massive Whirlpool escaped relatively unharmed. However, the collision wreaked havoc on the smaller galaxy, as the Whirlpool's gravity tore out stars to form a temporary bridge between the two.

Blue regions are clusters of star formation triggered by the collision. Some contain a million hot, young blue stars.

Collision has created more than a thousand new star clusters.

Hot stars, less than 10 million years old, show that the collision took place very recently.

Fate of the Milky Way: in 5 billion years time, our Galaxy will smash into the Andromeda Galaxy, perhaps forming a system like the Antennae.

False-colour image combines optical and radio observations.

Blue regions are gas.

WHIRLPOOL GALAXY

Telescopes today reveal that the Whirlpool appears to have a smaller galaxy dangling from one spiral arm. This is the galaxy that struck the Whirlpool hundreds of millions of years ago, and now lies some distance beyond it. The gravity of the passing galaxy has stirred up the gas and stars in the Whirlpool, producing the unusually prominent spiral pattern that gives rise to its name.

Red reveals strong magnetism.

Green shows stars.

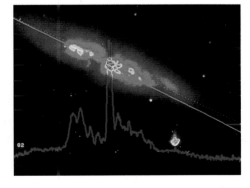

STARBURST GALAXY

A starburst galaxy is usually the aftermath of a galactic collision in which the galaxy's gas clouds are squeezed together, triggering a sudden burst of star formation. Discovered in 1983 by the Infrared Astronomical Satellite, starburst galaxies are filled with hot young stars – seen as red spots in this infrared view of M82 (a galaxy in Ursa Major). The graph shows the energy given out by different regions of the galaxy.

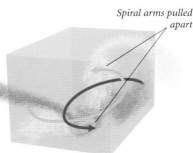

Spiral arms pulled apart

4 By 300 million years ago, stars from the spiral arms had been flung out of both galaxies.

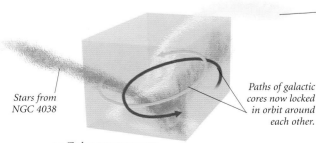

Stars from NGC 4038

5 Today, two streamers of ejected stars extend far beyond the original galaxies.

Stars from NGC 4039

Paths of galactic cores now locked in orbit around each other.

CLUSTERS OF GALAXIES

GALAXIES ARE NOT SOLITARY OBJECTS. They gather together in groups that range from pairs to clusters containing thousands of galaxies. Some clusters are regular in shape – they are roughly spherical and contain mainly elliptical galaxies. Others are irregular sprawls dominated by spiral galaxies. Astronomers believe clusters grow by merging with each other, and that irregular clusters have merged more recently than regular ones. Hot gas from the galaxies gathers in the middle of the cluster and gives off X-rays that can be detected from Earth, showing up the form of the cluster even more clearly. Clusters themselves are grouped into even bigger superclusters – the largest structures in the Universe.

NGC 4473
Type E4

NGC 4461
Type Sa

Arp 120
Type Sa

Virgo Cluster is dominated by spiral galaxies – some other clusters contain mainly ellipticals.

NGC 4425
Type Sb

VIRGO CLUSTER

Our galaxy, the Milky Way, is a member of a cluster of about 30 mostly small and faint galaxies known as the Local Group. The nearest large cluster is the Virgo Cluster, which lies 50 million light years away towards the constellation of Virgo. It is an irregular cluster of more than 2,000 galaxies that has been known for two centuries – William and Caroline Herschel catalogued 300 "nebulas" in this part of the sky during the 1780s and 1790s. Although the Virgo Cluster is dominated by three giant elliptical galaxies, most of its brighter members are spirals.

IMPORTANT CLUSTERS OF GALAXIES

Name	Distance in millions of light years	Size in millions of light years	Gas temperature (million °C)
Virgo	50	11	30
Fornax	70	8	–
Centaurus	140	5	45
Cancer	210	11	–
Perseus	240	17	75
Coma	290	20	95
Hercules	490	15	45
Abell 2256	760	10	85
Corona Borealis	940	8	100
Gemini	1,000	9	–

X-RAY PHOTO OF CENTRE OF VIRGO CLUSTER

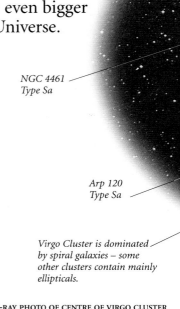

X-RAY PHOTO OF CENTRE OF ABELL 2256

HOT GAS IN CLUSTERS

Observations from X-ray satellites show that galaxy clusters are filled with hot gas at temperatures of up to 100 million °C. The gas comes from the galaxies, and forms pools in the centre of clusters. This X-ray image of the Virgo Cluster reveals a cloud of hot gas more massive than all the galaxies in the cluster put together.

CLUSTER EVOLUTION

Clusters form from mergers of smaller groups of galaxies. An X-ray picture of gas in the Abell 2256 Cluster shows a bright spot to the right of centre caused as another group of galaxies is absorbed into the cluster. In clusters that are no longer swallowing groups, the gas is more evenly spread throughout the cluster.

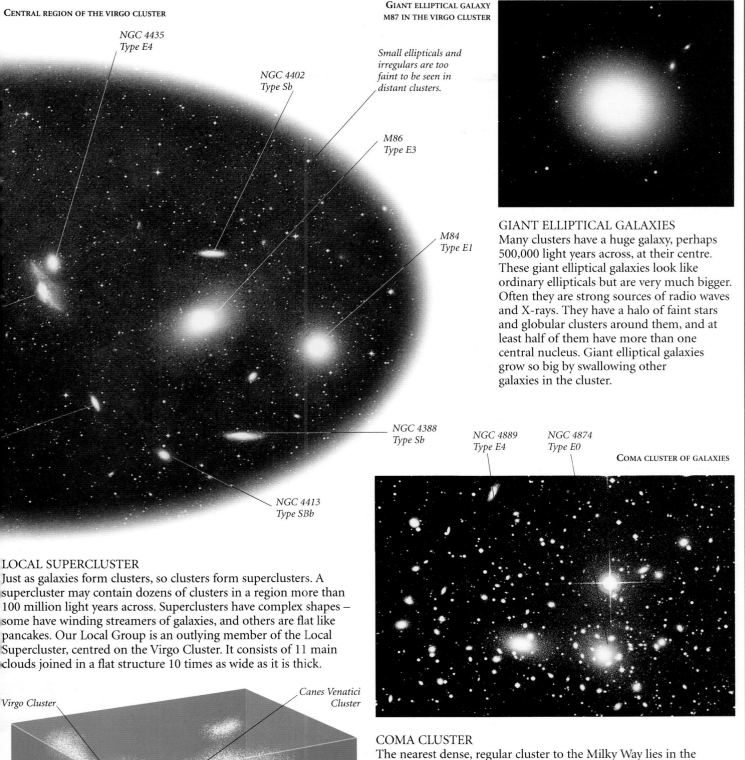

CENTRAL REGION OF THE VIRGO CLUSTER

NGC 4435
Type E4

NGC 4402
Type Sb

Small ellipticals and irregulars are too faint to be seen in distant clusters.

M86
Type E3

M84
Type E1

NGC 4388
Type Sb

NGC 4413
Type SBb

GIANT ELLIPTICAL GALAXY M87 IN THE VIRGO CLUSTER

GIANT ELLIPTICAL GALAXIES

Many clusters have a huge galaxy, perhaps 500,000 light years across, at their centre. These giant elliptical galaxies look like ordinary ellipticals but are very much bigger. Often they are strong sources of radio waves and X-rays. They have a halo of faint stars and globular clusters around them, and at least half of them have more than one central nucleus. Giant elliptical galaxies grow so big by swallowing other galaxies in the cluster.

NGC 4889
Type E4

NGC 4874
Type E0

COMA CLUSTER OF GALAXIES

LOCAL SUPERCLUSTER

Just as galaxies form clusters, so clusters form superclusters. A supercluster may contain dozens of clusters in a region more than 100 million light years across. Superclusters have complex shapes – some have winding streamers of galaxies, and others are flat like pancakes. Our Local Group is an outlying member of the Local Supercluster, centred on the Virgo Cluster. It consists of 11 main clouds joined in a flat structure 10 times as wide as it is thick.

Virgo Cluster

Canes Venatici Cluster

Crater Cluster

Leo Cluster

Local Group is falling towards centre of Supercluster at 250 km/s.

COMA CLUSTER

The nearest dense, regular cluster to the Milky Way lies in the constellation of Coma Berenices. The Coma Cluster contains more than 3,000 galaxies and is about 300 million light years away. It consists mainly of elliptical and lenticular galaxies. Unlike the sprawling Virgo Cluster, Coma is compact and rounded with a smooth, nearly spherical distribution of hot gas. The cluster appears to have two clumps, each centred on a giant elliptical galaxy. It is possible that the Coma Cluster is the result of a merger long ago between two clusters of about the same size. The Coma Cluster is itself at the centre of the Coma Supercluster.

ACTIVE GALAXIES

A SMALL NUMBER OF GALAXIES are different from all the rest, pouring out huge amounts of energy from a tiny region at their centres not much bigger than the Solar System. These so-called active galaxies, which include quasars, radio galaxies, Seyfert galaxies, and blazars, are all members of the same family of objects. Though they are related, what we see depends on how far away the galaxy is and the angle at which we are viewing it.

INSIDE AN ACTIVE GALAXY

All active galaxies share many common features, but only radio galaxies show all aspects of these complex structures. From a distance, the most obvious features are the radio-emitting jets emerging from either side of the galaxy, and billowing out into vast clouds. Closer in, at the heart of the galaxy, lies a doughnut-shaped ring of dust and gas, heated until it glows brilliantly. At the heart of each one is a supermassive black hole that generates enough power to outshine the Sun by a trillion times.

Jet emits radio waves and sometimes visible light.

Huge gas lobe emits radio waves.

Galaxy

Central region

CENTRAL DUST RING

The central region of an active galaxy consists of an intense source of energy at the core, hidden by a doughnut-shaped ring of dust and gas. The ring is dark on the outside, but glows brightly on the inner edge, where it absorbs radiation from the core. The jets emerge from either side of the centre of this ring.

Inner edge of gas and dust cloud is hot and rotates rapidly.

Core

Energy from core heats the inside of the ring, making it glow.

Black hole swallows gas falling into it.

Outer edge of gas and dust cloud is cool and slow-moving.

RADIO LOBES

Jets of hot gas are blown out of the galaxy's centre across hundreds of thousands of light years. Where they encounter intergalactic gas clouds, they billow out into huge radio-emitting lobes.

Jet wavers as it runs into other particles.

Magnetic field funnels charged particles around the black hole. Those travelling at very high speeds can escape.

ACTIVE GALAXIES			
Name	Constellation	Type	Distance in millions of light years
Centaurus A	Centaurus	Radio	15
M77	Cetus	Seyfert	45
NGC 1566	Dorado	Seyfert	50
M87	Virgo	Radio	50
NGC 4151	Canes Venatici	Seyfert	65
Cygnus A	Cygnus	Radio	740
BL Lacertae	Lacerta	Blazar	900
PKS 2349-01	Pisces	Quasar	1,500
3C 273	Virgo	Quasar	2,100
OJ 287	Cancer	Blazar	3,800
3C 48	Triangulum	Quasar	4,500
3C 279	Virgo	Blazar	5,800
3C 368	Ophiuchus	Radio	8,400

INSIDE THE CORE

At the heart of the galaxy is a huge black hole perhaps a billion times the mass of the Sun. This is the galaxy's power source or engine, fuelled by infalling interstellar gas. As it is sucked into the hole, the gas forms a spinning accretion disc. Electrically charged particles released as the gas heats up are caught up in an intense magnetic field, and escape at the poles to form the jets.

Jet contains charged particles and magnetic fields.

Jets are travelling close to the speed of light as they leave the core.

Gas from just a single star, shredded by the black hole's gravity, can fuel even the most luminous galaxy for a year.

Central part of disc is hot enough to emit X-rays.

Outer edge of accretion disc is fed by disrupted stars and interstellar gas.

Accretion disc is made of interstellar gas and the remains of stars.

Quasar PKS 2349-01: Hubble photograph of this quasar, 1.5 billion light years away, reveals a faint galaxy surrounding the brilliant central engine.

Seyfert galaxy NGC 1566 lies 50 million light years away, and is a dimmer version of a quasar.

Radio galaxy 3C 368: blue lines over this image show the intensity of the galaxy's radio emissions.

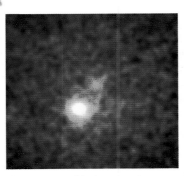

Blazar 3C 279: this Compton Gamma Ray Observatory image shows high-energy radiation from the blazar's core.

QUASARS

Quasars are among the most powerful objects in the Universe, but are so far away that they look like faint stars. They emit radio waves, X-rays, and infrared, as well as light, and sometimes have visible jets. Quasars are the brilliant cores of remote galaxies, with the dust ring tilted to reveal radiation emitted by the accretion disc.

SEYFERT GALAXIES

About one in 10 big spiral galaxies has a very bright spot of light at its centre. This is a Seyfert galaxy, and may be a less powerful version of a quasar, with a smaller black hole in its core. Some astronomers think that all large spiral galaxies, including the Milky Way, may become Seyferts at some time.

RADIO GALAXIES

Radio galaxies are some of the largest objects in the sky. One or two jets shoot out for thousands of light years from the centre, feeding streams of gas into huge clouds on either side of the galaxy. In a radio galaxy the central dust ring is seen edge-on, so the core is hidden and the fainter jets become visible.

BLAZARS

Looking similar to quasars, blazars vary rapidly in brightness by as much as 100 times, showing changes from day to day. Blazars are believed to be active galaxies with jets pointed directly towards us. We are looking straight down the jet into the core and seeing light and other radiation from the accretion disc around the black hole.

HISTORY OF ACTIVE GALAXIES

• In 1943, US astronomer Carl Seyfert (1911–1960) noted a class of spiral galaxies with very bright cores – Seyfert galaxies.

• British physicist Stanley Hey (1909–), discovered an intense source of radio waves in Cygnus in 1946.

• In 1954, German-born US astronomers Walter Baade (1893–1960) and Rudolph Minkowski (1895–1976) found a faint, peculiar galaxy at the position of the Cygnus A radio source.

RADIO GALAXY CYGNUS A

• Dutch astronomer Maarten Schmidt (1929–) showed in 1963 that a faint star-like object found at the position of radio source 3C 273 lay far beyond our own Galaxy. This was the first quasar.

• In 1968, radio signals were detected from the strange object known as BL Lacertae, previously mistaken for a variable star. BL Lac became the prototype of the blazars.

• In the 1970s and 1980s, many astrophysicists helped to show how all these different types of active galaxy could be explained as ordinary galaxies with supermassive black holes at their centres.

SCALE OF THE UNIVERSE

THE UNIVERSE IS UNIMAGINABLY LARGE. The most distant galaxies are so far away that their light takes some 10 billion years to reach us, even though light rays travel so fast that they could go seven times round the world in a single second. Even astronomers cannot visualize these distances, but they can chart the Universe at different scales. They use a variety of methods to measure distances: some are appropriate for planets, others for stars or galaxies. Often astronomers build on the distances of nearer objects to push out farther, so each measurement becomes a step in a ladder of distances stretching across the Universe.

Dots represent galaxies: 1,059 galaxies appear on the map.

750 million light years

500 million light years

250 million light years

Milky Way

STICKMAN
The first map of galaxies beyond the Local Supercluster, out to a distance of 750 million light years, produced a figure that astronomers have nicknamed the "stickman". The man's arms and legs are long strips, or filaments, of galaxies, while the gaps between are huge areas of empty space – or voids.

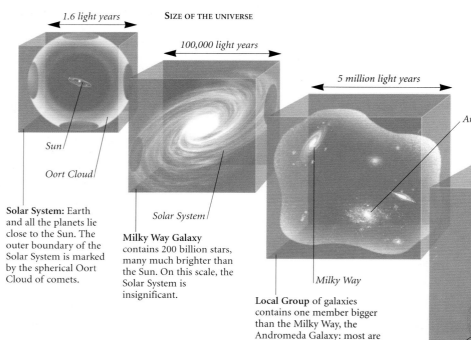

SIZE OF THE UNIVERSE

1.6 light years

100,000 light years

5 million light years

120 million light years

Sun

Oort Cloud

Solar System

Andromeda Galaxy

Milky Way

Solar System: Earth and all the planets lie close to the Sun. The outer boundary of the Solar System is marked by the spherical Oort Cloud of comets.

Milky Way Galaxy contains 200 billion stars, many much brighter than the Sun. On this scale, the Solar System is insignificant.

Local Group of galaxies contains one member bigger than the Milky Way, the Andromeda Galaxy: most are much smaller.

Local Group

Virgo Cluster

GEOGRAPHY OF THE UNIVERSE
To comprehend the immensity of space, astronomers can draw maps of the Universe at different scales, just as a geographer's maps can range from detailed streetplans to an atlas of the whole planet. In this sequence, the three-dimensional maps range from our backyard in space – the Solar System – to galaxies visible only with giant telescopes. The sizes are given in light years: 1 light year is the distance that a ray of light travels in one year, equivalent to 9.5 trillion km.

LOCAL SUPERCLUSTER
The Local Supercluster contains dozens of small galaxy clusters, including the Local Group, which lies near one edge. It is centred on the giant Virgo Cluster of galaxies, 50 million light years from the Milky Way.

NEARBY UNIVERSE
Superclusters of galaxies are strung together in vast filaments that can stretch across hundreds of millions of light years. They are separated by huge voids containing very few galaxies. These empty regions are often 100 million light years across.

DISTANCE MEASUREMENT

Astronomers use radar to measure the distance to planets, and parallax to measure the distances of stars. Neither method can be used outside the Milky Way. So researchers have built up a ladder of distances, finding the distance to nearby galaxies by comparing their stars to similar stars in the Milky Way, and then using the distances to these galaxies to find how far away other galaxies lie.

ROTATING SPIRAL GALAXY

Red shift on edge
moving away from Earth

Blue shift on edge
moving toward us

GALAXY ROTATION METHOD

By studying nearby galaxies with distances established from Cepheids, astronomers have found that a spiral galaxy's total brightness is related to the rate it is spinning. This rate can be established from the red and blue shifts on each side of the galaxy. Galaxies with the same rotation speeds can be used to measure distances up to a billion light years.

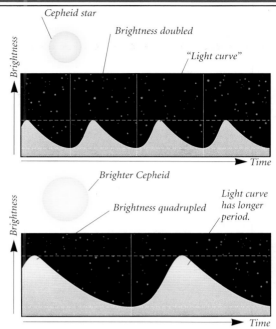

Cepheid star

Brightness doubled

"Light curve"

Brightness

Time

Brighter Cepheid

Light curve
has longer
period.

Brightness quadrupled

Brightness

Time

CEPHEID STANDARD CANDLES

If two stars generate the same amount of light but one appears dimmer, it must lie farther away. Astronomers use Cepheid variables to measure distance in this way, because the period of their brightness variations is dictated by their average brightness – the brighter the star, the longer the cycle. Astronomers find the true brightness of a Cepheid from the length of its cycle, and compare this to its apparent brightness to measure the distance to the galaxy in which it lies.

1 billion light years

Void

Local
Supercluster

Galaxy
filament

DISTANCES FROM SUPERNOVAS

Supernovas are exploding stars so brilliant that astronomers can spot them in galaxies billions of light years away. Astronomers identify different kinds of supernova from the way their light brightens, then fades. Type 1a supernovas always reach the same maximum brightness, so they form ideal standard candles – though they appear only once or twice a century in an average galaxy.

GROWING UNIVERSE

- Aristarchus realized the Universe was much bigger than the Earth in about 260 BC: his observations put the Sun 7 million km away from Earth.

MEDIEVAL IDEA OF THE UNIVERSE

- In 1619, Johannes Kepler proved the planets orbited the Sun, and that Saturn was nearly 10 times farther out than Earth.

- During the 1780s, William Herschel calculated the Milky Way was about 10,000 light years across – far bigger than generally believed, but only one-tenth of the actual figure.

- In 1918, Harlow Shapley proposed that the Milky Way constituted the entire Universe, with a diameter of 300,000 light years.

- Edwin Hubble, in 1923, found that the Andromeda Galaxy is a system separate from the Milky Way. It is now known to be 2.5 million light years away.

- In 1963, astronomers identified the first quasar, 3C 273, which lies 2 billion light years away.

- In 1995, the Hubble Space Telescope photographed galaxies 10 billion light years away.

EXPANDING UNIVERSE

Look deep into space, and something very odd seems to be going on. In every direction, distant clusters of galaxies are rushing away from us – and the farther a cluster lies, the quicker it is speeding away. It seems that our Milky Way is distinctly unpopular! In fact, every galaxy cluster is moving apart from every other one, just as raisins in a cake move apart when it is baked. The expansion of the Universe is very useful to astronomers: once they have measured the rate of expansion for nearby galaxies, they can use a galaxy's speed to find its distance.

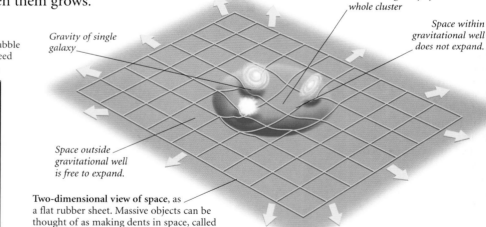

3 billion years ago: distances between galaxy clusters were 25% smaller than they are today.

75 million light years

Hercules Cluster

Perseus Cluster

Virgo Cluster

Coma Cluster

SPACE AROUND A CLUSTER

EXPANSION OF SPACE

Although the Universe is expanding, it is not expanding *into* anything. Instead, space itself is stretching, and carrying clusters of galaxies with it. Imagine space as a framework of rubber strips, with the clusters attached. As the framework expands, they are drawn apart. Every region of space is expanding at the same rate, so the further apart two clusters are, the more rapidly the space between them grows.

Combined gravity of whole cluster

Gravity of single galaxy

Space within gravitational well does not expand

Space outside gravitational well is free to expand.

Two-dimensional view of space, as a flat rubber sheet. Massive objects can be thought of as making dents in space, called gravitational wells.

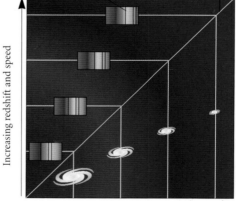

Dark lines formed by elements in galaxy absorbing light

Hubble's law: Edwin Hubble found that a galaxy's speed depends on its distance.

Increasing redshift and speed (vertical axis)

Increasing distance (horizontal axis)

REDSHIFTING GALAXIES

Astronomers measure a galaxy's speed by investigating dark lines visible in its spectrum. The position of these lines is affected by a galaxy's motion (the Doppler effect). If the galaxy is moving away, the lines are shifted towards redder, longer wavelengths (an effect known as redshift). The more the lines are redshifted, the higher the speed. More distant galaxies are speeding away more rapidly.

EXPANSION AND GRAVITY

It is not true to say that everything in the Universe is expanding. The Earth is not getting bigger; nor is the Solar System, or the Milky Way Galaxy. In fact, whole clusters of galaxies stay the same size, because they are held together by gravity. Only in the huge distances between clusters of galaxies does the expansion of space win out over the attractive force of gravity.

Galaxies in the Coma Cluster are not separating from one another, though the whole cluster is speeding away from us at 6,600 km/s.

Today: Each square in this imaginary framework of space is 100 million light years across. With every passing year, it grows larger by 0.01 light years.

100 million light years

2 billion years in the future: galaxy clusters are 15% farther apart than they are today.

Hercules Cluster

115 million light years

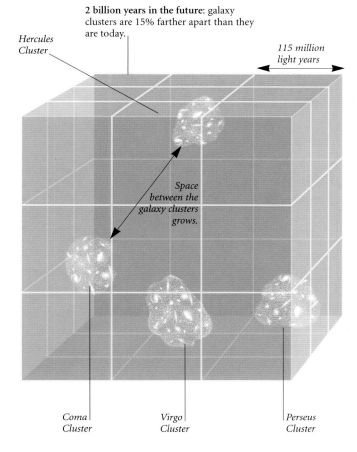

Space between the galaxy clusters grows.

Perseus Cluster

Milky Way

Virgo Cluster

Coma Cluster

Virgo Cluster

Perseus Cluster

UNDERSTANDING EXPANSION

- In 1917, US astronomer Vesto Melvin Slipher (1875–1969) announced the speeds of 25 galaxies: most were moving rapidly away.

- In 1929, Edwin Hubble calculated the Universe's rate of expansion (Hubble's constant) as 500 km/s per megaparsec (3.26 million light years) distance.

HUBBLE AT HIS TELESCOPE

- In 1948, the international team of Fred Hoyle, Hermann Bondi (1919–) and Tommy Gold (1920–) proposed that matter was created in the space between receding galaxies. This steady state theory was overthrown by the Big Bang theory in 1965.

- German-American astronomer Walter Baade (1893–1960) remeasured Hubble's Constant in 1952: it became 225 km/s/megaparsec.

- In 1963, Dutch-American astronomer Maarten Schmidt (1929–) used redshift to work out the distance to quasar 3C 273.

- Observations in 1998 by the Hubble Space Telescope gave Hubble's Constant as 73 km/s/megaparsec.

MEASURING REDSHIFTS

Many galaxies are so faint that it is difficult to detect them, let alone spread their light out into a spectrum that can reveal their redshifts and therefore their distances. This is one of the main reasons for building huge telescopes that can collect the maximum amount of light. Astronomers have also developed sensitive electronic spectrometers that measure the redshifts of many galaxies at the same time.

2dF spectrometer on the Anglo-Australian telescope is designed to take spectra of up to 400 distant galaxies at one time.

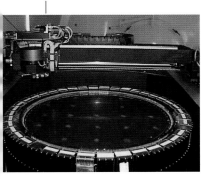

Brightest light from 3C 273 is colour-coded black.

Jet is a stream of high-speed electrons.

False-colour photograph shows levels of brightness as different colours.

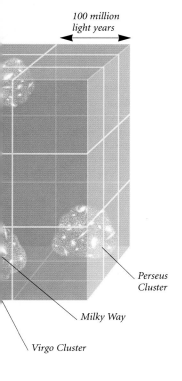

Spikes caused by telescope

DISCOVERY OF QUASARS

In the 1950s, astronomers discovered strange radio-emitting star-like objects with inexplicable lines in their spectra. Eventually, the lines in the brightest object, 3C 273, were recognized as those caused by hydrogen atoms, but shifted to the red by 16%. Using Hubble's law, this redshift means that 3C 273 must lie 2 billion light years away – so far off that it must be brighter than any galaxy. Today, we know that these quasi-stellar radio sources (quasars) are violent active galaxies.

BIG BANG

THE BIG BANG WAS THE BEGINNING of everything: time, space, and the building blocks of all the matter in the Universe. The great cosmic clock began ticking some 13 billion years ago in a fireball so concentrated that matter and antimatter were created spontaneously out of energy. At the instant of creation, the Universe was almost infinitely hot and dense. Then it began to expand and cool – and it is still expanding and cooling today.

Very hot, young Universe

Young galaxies were densely packed.

Gravity holds clusters of galaxies together.

The Universe today

Earliest possible date for Big Bang: 15 billion years ago

Most likely date for Big Bang: 13 billion years ago

Latest possible date for Big Bang: 11 billion years ago

EXPANSION REVERSED
The Universe is expanding – and so it stands to reason that, in the past, everything must have been closer together. If the motion of the galaxies we see today is reversed, it leads back to an instant around 13 billion years ago when they all occupied a single point. This was the origin of the explosion called the Big Bang.

Fuelled by the release of the strong force, the Universe suddenly inflates. It doubles its size every 10 quadrillion quintillionths of a second.

An instant after creation, the Universe is almost infinitely hot and expanding quite slowly.

Increasing time

Big Bang

BEFORE THE BIG BANG
There was no "before" the Big Bang, because time did not exist. Time and space have always been intimately linked in what Albert Einstein called a space-time continuum. Once time came into being, space could start to expand. Equally, once space had been created, time could begin to flow.

Undisturbed space-time, seen in an imaginary view from outside the Universe.

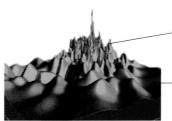

Peaks show space-time disturbances.

Turbulent space-time has peaks, each potentially a Big Bang that can create a Universe like ours.

INFLATION
Most astronomers believe the Big Bang was quite a small bang. Conditions in the early Universe turned energy directly into equal amounts of matter and antimatter – about a kilogram of material. Moments later, something vastly more dramatic happened: cosmic inflation. The Universe blew up, growing in size a hundred trillion quintillion quintillion times in a fraction of a second. Inflation released huge amounts of energy to create more matter, and shape the forces that control our Universe.

Matter and antimatter particles have the same mass, but their other properties are equal and opposite to each other.

The force of inflation works like antigravity, driving everything apart.

The temperature drops rapidly. It dips briefly to absolute zero immediately after inflation, before rising again.

FUNDAMENTAL FORCES

Four forces control the Universe today. Electromagnetism rules electricity and magnetism; the weak force governs how the stars shine; the strong force glues together the nuclei in atoms; and gravity keeps planets and stars in orbit. Early on, these four forces were united in a single superforce, but as the Universe expanded and cooled, they split off, one by one. When the strong force split away, it released the vast amounts of energy that fuelled inflation.

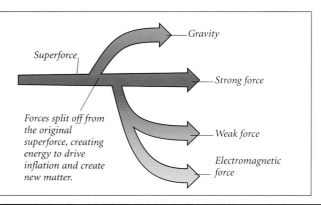

Gravity

Superforce

Strong force

Weak force

Electromagnetic force

Forces split off from the original superforce, creating energy to drive inflation and create new matter.

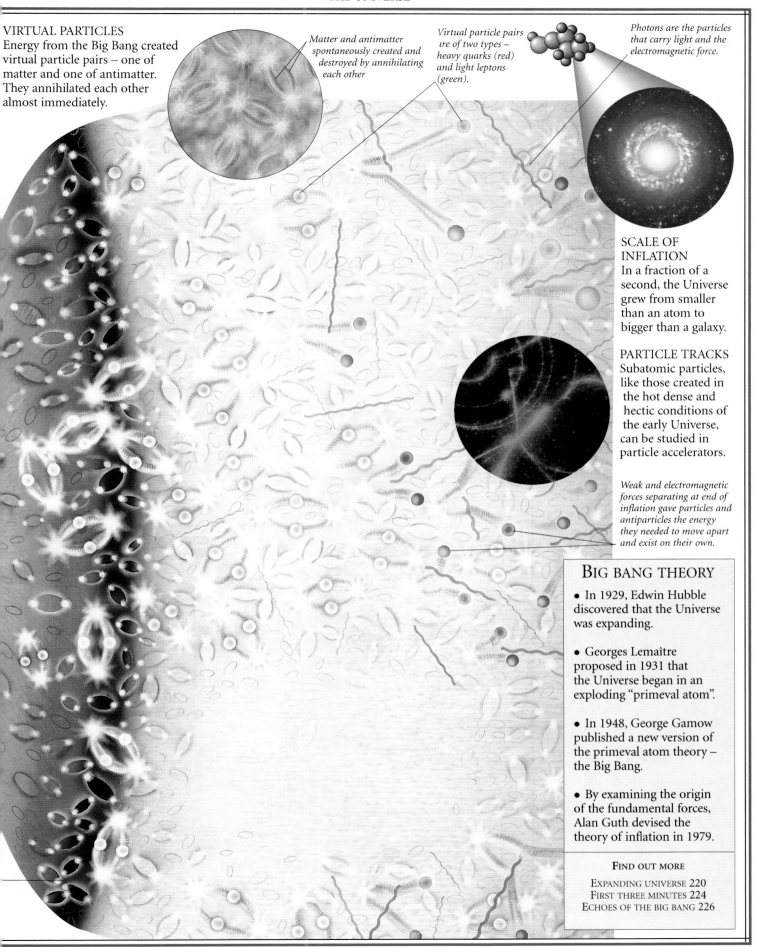

VIRTUAL PARTICLES
Energy from the Big Bang created virtual particle pairs – one of matter and one of antimatter. They annihilated each other almost immediately.

Matter and antimatter spontaneously created and destroyed by annihilating each other

Virtual particle pairs are of two types – heavy quarks (red) and light leptons (green).

Photons are the particles that carry light and the electromagnetic force.

SCALE OF INFLATION
In a fraction of a second, the Universe grew from smaller than an atom to bigger than a galaxy.

PARTICLE TRACKS
Subatomic particles, like those created in the hot dense and hectic conditions of the early Universe, can be studied in particle accelerators.

Weak and electromagnetic forces separating at end of inflation gave particles and antiparticles the energy they needed to move apart and exist on their own.

BIG BANG THEORY

- In 1929, Edwin Hubble discovered that the Universe was expanding.

- Georges Lemaître proposed in 1931 that the Universe began in an exploding "primeval atom".

- In 1948, George Gamow published a new version of the primeval atom theory – the Big Bang.

- By examining the origin of the fundamental forces, Alan Guth devised the theory of inflation in 1979.

FIND OUT MORE

FIRST THREE MINUTES

THE SEARINGLY HOT EARLY UNIVERSE at the end of inflation contained a huge range of subatomic particles – equally balanced in battalions of matter and antimatter. Most of these particles wiped each other out, but finally matter triumphed. As the Universe continued to expand and cool, construction, rather than destruction, could begin. Gradually, particles began to clump together in larger, more stable groups, and the thick soup of particles began to thin out. By the end of its third minute, the Universe had created the building blocks of all the matter around us today – the nuclei of the first three elements: hydrogen, helium, and lithium.

DARK MATTER
Huge clusters often contain thousands of brilliantly shining galaxies. But visible matter like this in the Universe is vastly exceeded by invisible, dark matter created after inflation. This dark matter probably consists of the numerous WIMPs and neutrinos that survived the first three minutes.

As particles and antiparticles annihilated each other, the intense radiation energy released created new particle-antiparticle pairs.

Quarks (red) and leptons (green) released during inflation

Exotic particles include X bosons, Higgs bosons, and WIMPS.

MATURING UNIVERSE
The early Universe was seething with exotic particles and antiparticles, some extremely shortlived. Quarks, leptons, and WIMPS, among others, cannoned around at temperatures of about 10,000 trillion trillion °C. Within three minutes, the temperature dropped to less than 1 billion °C and the Universe was a much calmer place with fewer, more stable particles.

Forces are carried between particles by W and Z bosons, gluons, photons, and gravitons.

ACCUMULATION OF MATTER
Inflation created equal amounts of matter and antimatter particles. The reason they did not annihilate each other completely, leaving an empty Universe, may be due to the X boson and its twin, the anti-X. These were the heaviest particles of all, and could be created only by the high energy of inflation. As the Universe cooled, both particles became unstable and decayed into lighter quarks and leptons. But, for every 100,000,000 quarks and leptons created, only 99,999,999 antiparticles emerged. This tiny imbalance resulted in all the matter in the Universe today.

X-BOSON DECAY

X boson

Anti-X

Particles / *Antiparticles* *Particles* \ *Antiparticles*

More particles than antiparticles

Particles

Antiparticles

SEARCHING FOR ANTIMATTER
An antimatter galaxy would look exactly like a normal one, except around its edge. Here, where antimatter meets normal matter from the rest of the Universe, there would be tell-tale flashes of energy as they annihilated each other – but so far, none has been detected.

PROTONS AND NEUTRONS

As the Universe cooled, gluons pulled quarks together in threes to form equal numbers of protons and neutrons. At the end of the first second, some neutrons started to decay into protons, and by the time the temperature had dropped to 900 million °C, there were seven protons to every neutron. The remaining neutrons rapidly bonded with protons to form the nuclei of atoms. By the end of the first three minutes, there were no free neutrons left.

Protons

Neutron

Free protons (hydrogen nuclei)

Neutron in helium nucleus

Quarks locked up in protons and neutrons

Leptons still moving freely

Photons carry radiation through thinned-out Universe.

COMPOSITION OF THE COSMOS

Detailed calculations predict that the ashes of the Big Bang – the elements created in the first three minutes – should have the proportions 77% hydrogen, 23% helium, and 0.000,000,1% lithium. Analysis of gas clouds such as the Eagle Nebula bears these figures out.

CREATING NUCLEI

Protons and neutrons started to form at about one second, and over the next three minutes they combined to form the nuclei of the lightest elements – mostly hydrogen and helium. Each element has a unique number of protons, but can have several isotopes with different numbers of neutrons. The Universe soon dropped below the temperature and density needed for this nuclear fusion, and no more elements were formed.

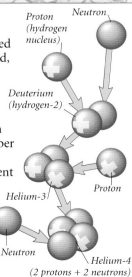

Proton (hydrogen nucleus)

Neutron

Deuterium (hydrogen-2)

Helium-3

Proton

Neutron

Helium-4 (2 protons + 2 neutrons)

ELEMENTARY PARTICLES

Many subatomic particles from the early Universe no longer exist, or have changed into other particles. The most important early particles are listed below.

Cosmic string: incredibly heavy strand of matter millions of light years long, predicted by theory.

 X boson: very heavy particle predicted by theory but as yet undetected.

 Higgs boson: a very heavy particle proposed by British physicist Peter Higgs.

WIMP: weakly interacting massive particle, thought to make up most of the Universe's dark matter.

W and Z bosons: particles similar to photons – but with mass – that carry the weak force.

 Quark: building block of protons and neutrons, found in six varieties.

 Lepton: particle sensitive to the weak force – electrons are the lightest type of lepton.

 Neutrino: low-mass, very common particle found in three types.

Gluon: transmits the strong force that joins quarks together.

Photon: massless particle carrying radiation and electromagnetism. The most common particle.

Graviton: particle thought to carry gravitational force.

ECHOES OF THE BIG BANG

AFTER ITS FRENETIC FIRST THREE MINUTES, when the first atomic nuclei were created, the Universe settled down. For a quarter of a million years, the ingredients of the cosmos stayed the same, but became increasingly dilute as the Universe continued to expand. Most of the energy was in the form of radiation, but the early cosmos was foggy – light could not travel far before bouncing off something. Then the fog lifted suddenly and space became transparent. Echoes of this event survive as a background radiation filling the sky.

PENZIAS, WILSON, AND THEIR ANTENNA

AFTERGLOW
In 1965, physicists Arno Penzias and Robert Wilson discovered a weak radio signal coming from every direction in the sky. This signal was equivalent to that emitted by an object at –270°C (3 degrees above absolute zero). The only possible source for this radiation was the dying heat of the Big Bang, cooled by the expansion of the Universe.

Slight temperature differences caused by dark-matter clumps show up in the background radiation.

At three minutes, matter is a mixture of atomic nuclei, electrons, and dark matter particles.

Time

Dark matter in the Universe, unaffected by radiation, begins to clump together under gravity.

As the Universe cools, heavier leptons decay into electrons. Normal matter is soon dominated by atomic nuclei and electrons.

Photons travel only short distances between collisions.

Electrons

Hydrogen nucleus

Helium nucleus

COOLING UNIVERSE
At three minutes, the cosmos was filled with photons of high-energy gamma radiation. As the Universe expanded and cooled, the radiation lost some of its energy, turning into X-rays, light, and finally heat radiation. The drop in temperature also affected particles, slowing down the electrons until they began to combine with the atomic nuclei to form the first atoms. These atoms did not interact with radiation, so light was finally able to travel in straight lines over long distances, and the Universe became transparent.

PHOTON SCATTERING
In the early Universe, photons of light were continuously interacting with atomic nuclei and electrons, so neither got anywhere. Photons would bounce off one particle, only to collide with another, then another. Light could never travel in a straight line and, as a result, the Universe was opaque.

"Last scattering surface": this division, formed 300,000 years after the Big Bang, separates the opaque from the transparent Universe. The heat radiation that forms the background radiation comes from this "surface".

BACKGROUND RADIATION RIPPLES

At first, the background radiation seemed to be uniform, but in 1992, the Cosmic Background Explorer (COBE) satellite detected ripples in it. These are regions that are slightly warmer or cooler than average. The blue patches in COBE's all-sky map are cooler places where radiation is trying to escape from strong gravity. They show the dark-matter clumps that "seeded" the formation of galaxies.

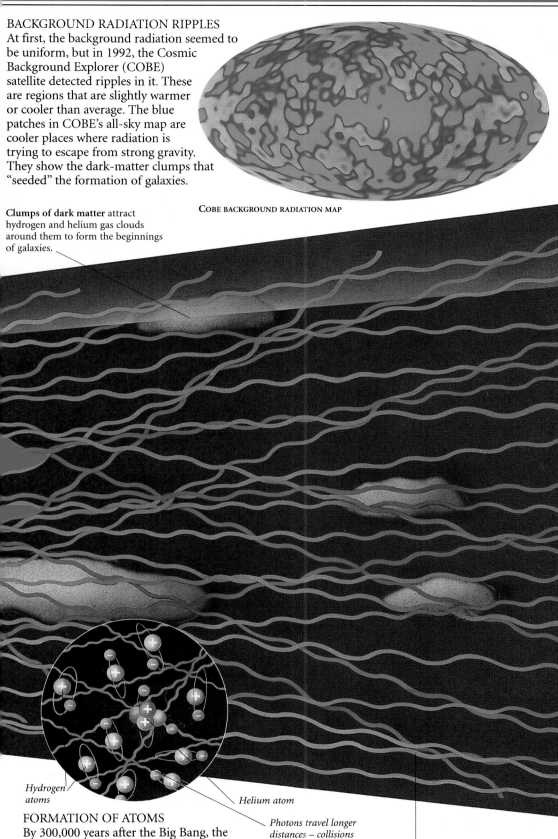

COBE BACKGROUND RADIATION MAP

Clumps of dark matter attract hydrogen and helium gas clouds around them to form the beginnings of galaxies.

Hydrogen atoms

Helium atom

Photons travel longer distances – collisions are rarer.

FORMATION OF ATOMS

By 300,000 years after the Big Bang, the temperature had dropped to 3,000°C. The negatively charged electrons had now slowed down so much that they could be pulled into orbit around the positively charged nuclei of hydrogen and helium, forming the first atoms.

Radiation from the "last scattering surface" continues to cool as the Universe expands, turning from light and heat to radio waves.

DETECTING THE ECHOES

• Walter Adams (1876–1956) working at Mount Wilson Observatory, discovered in 1938 that molecules in a star were being stimulated by external radiation at 2.3 degrees above absolute zero, Nobody realized the significance of this discovery at the time.

• In 1948, Ralph Alpher (1921–) and Robert Herman (1914–) predicted a relic radiation at 5 degrees above absolute zero from the Big Bang.

• Robert Dicke (1916–) began building a receiver to detect the background radiation in 1964.

• Penzias and Wilson discovered the background radiation in 1965. They published their discovery alongside a paper by Dicke explaining the origin of the radiation.

• In 1977, a NASA aircraft found that the background radiation is slightly hotter in one half of the sky – a result of the Doppler effect as the Earth moves through the Universe.

COBE SATELLITE

• In 1992, COBE discovered ripples in the background radiation.

GALAXY FORMATION

IN THE UNIVERSE TODAY, matter is clumped together into galaxies – but the Big Bang produced only a fog of gas spread more or less uniformly across the cosmos. One of the great mysteries of astronomy is how this gas was pulled together, condensing into individual galaxies. Did each galaxy form as a single object, or did they start small and grow? Why did some galaxies become beautiful spirals, with large reserves of gas, while others became ellipticals with all their gas tied up in stars? Why do galaxies lie in vast filaments, with empty voids in between? Astronomers are only now learning the answers.

HUBBLE DEEP FIELD

This image from the Hubble Space Telescope, taken in 1995, provided the first glimpse of galaxies being born, as the first stars began to shine. The Universe had just emerged from a period of darkness some 300,000 years after the Big Bang. Astronomers can use Hubble as a time machine, because light takes time to reach us: the most distant galaxies the telescope can detect are more than 10 billion light years away. Astronomers see them as they were over 10 billion years ago – just a couple of billion years after the Big Bang. To reveal these faint galaxies, Hubble collected light from the same spot of sky for 120 hours.

DARK AGE OF THE UNIVERSE
The Universe became transparent 300,000 years after the Big Bang. The brilliant light from the explosion turned into invisible infrared, and then into a background radiation of radio waves. The matter it left behind was cold and dark, unable to generate light, and the Universe went through a long period of darkness until the first stars began to shine. During this gloomy era, clumps of dark matter that had already formed began to attract the surrounding gas, laying the foundations of galaxies.

1 Gas shone brilliantly 300,000 years after the Big Bang, forming a patchwork of hotter (pink) and cooler (blue) regions. Then the Universe went dark.

Close-up from COBE background radiation map

Dots show distribution of gas.

2 The gravity of dark matter began to draw gas into a network of filaments about 3 million years later.

3 By the age of 300 million years, the Universe consisted of huge empty voids, surrounded by filaments of denser gas. As the gas pulled together into galaxies, the first generation of stars began to shine.

Filament

Void

Spiral galaxy forming from merger of two smaller galaxies, 5 billion light years away

Hubble Deep Field covers a tiny region of sky, about the size of a pinhead held at arm's length. It is located just above the familiar stars of the Plough.

Stars all lie in foreground, within the Milky Way.

Spiral galaxy similar to the Milky Way, 6 billion light years away

FIRST STARS

The first stars were made almost entirely of hydrogen and helium, the gases from the Big Bang. During their short lives, they created new elements such as carbon and oxygen, and threw them out into space in supernova explosions, to be incorporated in a second generation of stars and planets. Apart from hydrogen, helium, and a small amount of lithium, all the other elements in the Universe today were made by stars.

First stars formed from dense regions of gas where clouds collided.

Small irregular galaxy appears large because it is "only" 1 billion light years away.

1 Milky Way probably formed from thousands of small gas clouds pulled together by dark matter.

Globular clusters and stars near the galaxy's centre date from this time.

Small galaxies merging into a larger galaxy, 8 billion light years away

Cross-section of quasar – accretion disc around a black hole

Young galaxy, 10 billion light years away

The original Hubble image contains some 500 galaxies, but most are too faint to show up in this reproduction.

Milky Way today

GALAXY ORIGIN THEORIES

- In 1966, American physicist Jim Peebles (1935–) proposed the bottom-up theory, in which galaxies built up from smaller clouds.

- Soviet physicist Yakov Zeldovich (1914–87) put forward a top-down theory in 1969: primordial gas formed huge flat clouds that broke up into galaxies.

- The discovery of huge filaments of galaxies in 1981 provided support for the top-down theory.

- In 1995, the Hubble Deep Field showed mergers of small galaxies, supporting the bottom-up theory.

FIND OUT MORE

HUBBLE SPACE TELESCOPE 12 • COLLIDING GALAXIES 212
ACTIVE GALAXIES 216 • ECHOES OF THE BIG BANG 226
DARK MATTER 230

2 Dense gas in the galaxy's core collapsed to form a massive black hole, surrounded by a brilliant disc of gas – a quasar.

3 Twin beams of electrons from the quasar core billowed out to form invisible clouds of hot gas a million light years across.

BIRTH OF A GALAXY

The Hubble Deep Field shows that most galaxies formed from colliding clouds of gas. If the clouds were swirling around one another, the resulting galaxy was a rotating spiral with some gas left over. If the clouds were not rotating, then all their gas turned to stars, forming a gas-free ball of stars – an elliptical galaxy. Other ellipticals were late starters, formed when two galaxies collided at high speed.

Old stars

Black hole at core now quiet

Young stars and gas

CONTINUING FORMATION

Galaxy formation is still going on today, as small galaxies and gas clouds come together to build up larger galaxies. Often, a large galaxy will collide with and absorb a smaller galaxy. The giant elliptical radio galaxy Centaurus A has recently swallowed a spiral galaxy.

Dark band of gas and dust in Centaurus A, left over from the spiral galaxy it merged with

DARK MATTER

THE OBJECTS WE SEE IN THE COSMOS – planets, stars, gas clouds, and galaxies – make up only a small fraction of the total matter in the Universe. They are outnumbered some 30 times by invisible material, or dark matter, that cannot be spotted even with the most powerful telescopes. Astronomers know dark matter exists, however – its gravity pulls on stars, galaxies, and light rays as they cross the Universe. In fact, there are probably several types of dark matter, ranging from small stars to subatomic particles.

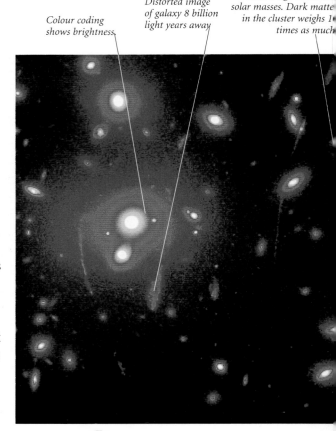

Colour coding shows brightness

Distorted image of galaxy 8 billion light years away

Galaxies in cluster Abel. 2218 weigh 50 trillion solar masses. Dark matter in the cluster weighs 1(times as much

COSMIC MIRAGE

Resembling strands of a cosmic spider's web, the luminous arcs in this Hubble image provide strong evidence for dark matter. Abell 2218, a cluster of galaxies 3 billion light years away, is acting as a gravitational lens. Its gravity is pulling at passing light rays from more distant galaxies, focusing them into bright curves. The gravity needed to focus light in this way is 10 times stronger than the visible galaxies can provide, so 90% of the cluster's mass must reside in invisible dark matter.

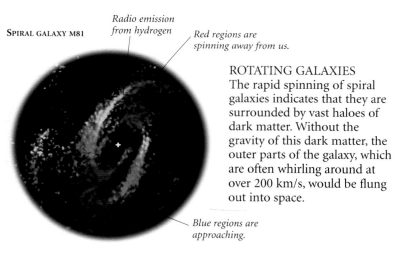

SPIRAL GALAXY M81

Radio emission from hydrogen

Red regions are spinning away from us.

Blue regions are approaching.

ROTATING GALAXIES
The rapid spinning of spiral galaxies indicates that they are surrounded by vast haloes of dark matter. Without the gravity of this dark matter, the outer parts of the galaxy, which are often whirling around at over 200 km/s, would be flung out into space.

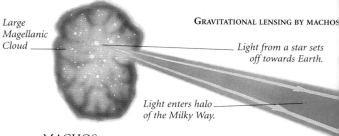

Large Magellanic Cloud

GRAVITATIONAL LENSING BY MACHOS

Light from a star sets off towards Earth.

Light enters halo of the Milky Way.

MACHOS
Ordinary matter may be compressed into small (planet-size) objects that are invisible, such as dim brown dwarfs (failed stars) or black holes. Most of these objects are believed to be in halos around galaxies, and are known as MACHOS – massive compact halo objects. Astronomers have detected some MACHOs by spotting the lensing effects their gravity has on light from stars in our neighbouring galaxy, the Large Magellanic Cloud.

SPEEDING GALAXIES
The first evidence for dark matter came from clusters of galaxies. In the 1930s, Fritz Zwicky found that these galaxies move so fast that the cluster should rapidly break up. Gravity from some unseen matter must be pulling them back. Later, astronomers found hot gas in clusters, also trapped by a strong gravitational pull.

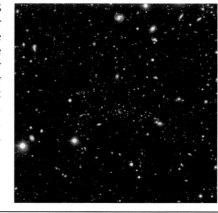

GALAXY CLUSTER CL0024+1654

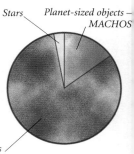

Stars

Planet-sized objects – MACHOS

TYPES OF DARK MATTER
According to the latest theories, 20% of the mass of the Universe consists of large objects (though only 3% shines as stars). The other 80% consists of subatomic particles such as WIMPs and neutrinos.

Subatomic particles – WIMPs and neutrinos

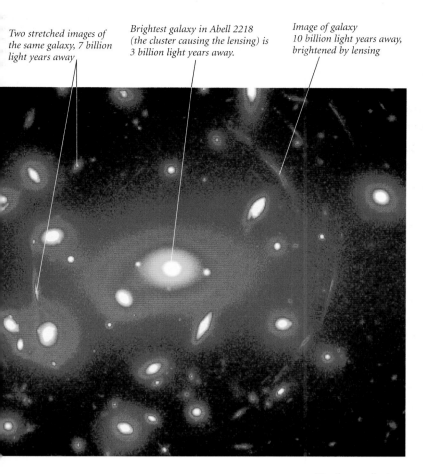

Two stretched images of the same galaxy, 7 billion light years away

Brightest galaxy in Abell 2218 (the cluster causing the lensing) is 3 billion light years away.

Image of galaxy 10 billion light years away, brightened by lensing

HOW LENSING WORKS

Einstein's theory of general relativity predicts that gravity can bend light. As light from a distant galaxy passes through a nearer cluster of galaxies on its way to Earth, the gravity of the cluster bends and focuses it. If the distant galaxy lies precisely behind the cluster's centre, it is distorted into a circle called an Einstein ring. Generally, though, the distant galaxy is off-centre, and only parts of the ring are seen, as circular arcs.

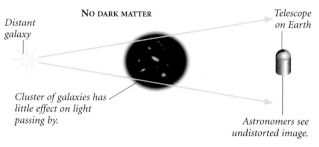

NO DARK MATTER

Distant galaxy

Telescope on Earth

Cluster of galaxies has little effect on light passing by.

Astronomers see undistorted image.

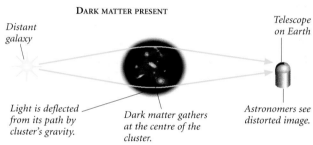

DARK MATTER PRESENT

Distant galaxy

Telescope on Earth

Light is deflected from its path by cluster's gravity.

Dark matter gathers at the centre of the cluster.

Astronomers see distorted image.

Gravity of MACHO is shown as a "gravitational well" in space.

Star (arrowed) at normal brightness

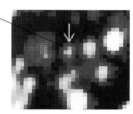

MACHO BRIGHTENING

As a MACHO moves in front of a distant star, its gravity focuses and brightens the star's light. Astronomers have found stars in the Large Magellanic Cloud occasionally brightening in just this way.

Light converges and brightens as it approaches Earth.

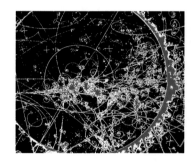

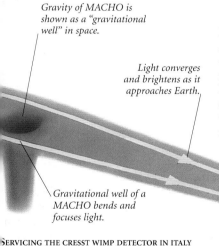

Gravitational well of a MACHO bends and focuses light.

Star temporarily brightened in 1993.

Telescope on Earth

NEUTRINOS

The Big Bang filled the Universe with neutrinos. Previously thought to have no mass, new experiments suggest that a neutrino actually has a mass 1/100,000 that of an electron – enough for these particles to account for a large proportion of all dark matter.

SERVICING THE CRESST WIMP DETECTOR IN ITALY

WIMPS

The Big Bang is thought to have created subatomic weakly interacting massive particles, or WIMPs. A WIMP is heavier than a hydrogen atom, and generally speeds straight through normal matter: if WIMPs make up most of the dark matter, then thousands are streaming through your body right now. Physicists are currently trying to discover whether WIMPs really exist.

FIND OUT MORE

RADIO ASTRONOMY 24
PROPERTIES OF STARS 168 • BLACK HOLES 188
CLUSTERS OF GALAXIES 214
FIRST THREE MINUTES 224 • SHAPE OF SPACE 232

SHAPE OF SPACE

SINCE THE DAWN OF TIME, people have thought of the Universe as a hollow sphere, with a centre and an edge. But astronomers today know that things are not this simple – the large-scale shape of the Universe is affected by the gravity of the matter within it, and by forces hidden in the structure of space itself. In fact, the Universe has no centre and no edge. The latest observations suggest that it extends forever in all directions, but we can see only part of this infinite cosmos – the "observable Universe".

CURVED SPACE

Einstein's theory of general relativity says that space is not just an empty vacuum – it is an invisible framework in which stars and galaxies are embedded. These large masses distort the framework, creating a "pinch" in the space around them. The three dimensions of ordinary space are distorted, and bent into a fourth dimension. Because this is so hard to visualize, scientists usually simplify things by showing a two-dimensional "rubber sheet" Universe bent into the third dimension by an object's mass.

3-D VIEW OF STAR'S GRAVITY

Three-dimensional model depicts empty space as an invisible framework of straight lines.

In reality, space bends into the fourth dimension, which cannot be represented here.

Where gravity bends space, parallel lines can meet.

A massive object such as a star distorts the structure of space. This distortion is felt as gravity.

Two-dimensional representation of space around a star shows empty space as a flat sheet.

2-D VIEW OF STAR'S GRAVITY

Distortion of space by the star's mass creates a "well", as if a heavy ball has been placed on the sheet.

Objects passing near the well "roll" towards it. This is seen as gravity.

The Universe was born infinite in size. However much it expands, it will always be infinitely large.

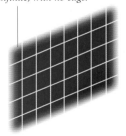

If there is just the right amount of matter, the Universe could be completely flat, and would be infinite, with no edge.

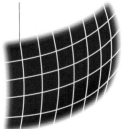

If there is a vast amount of matter, space could be bent back on itself by the gravity of the matter inside. It could even create a closed Universe.

If there is less matter, space could not only be infinite, with no edge. It could curve outward due to natural stretching forces within space itself.

FLAT SPACE　　**POSITIVELY CURVED SPACE**　　**NEGATIVELY CURVED SPACE**

WARPED UNIVERSE

On the biggest scale of all, the mass of the whole Universe can curve the space around it. The theory of general relativity predicts that the Universe can curve in one of three ways, depending on the density of matter within it. Using the rubber sheet model again, the Universe could be flat; it could curve inward to meet itself; or it might bend outward in a saddle shape.

STRETCHING SPACE

The mass of an object tends to bend space inward around it, but many astronomers now believe there is another force, hidden within empty space itself, that has the opposite effect, pushing space outward. This could explain recent observations that suggest the Universe matches the flat model. The hidden force, called the cosmological constant, was first proposed by Albert Einstein as part of his theory of general relativity, though he later called it his greatest blunder. The cosmological constant makes the space between objects in the Universe gradually stretch.

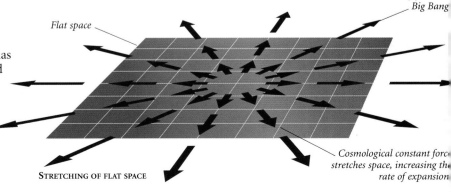

Space is already expanding as matter rushes away from the Big Bang

Flat space

Cosmological constant force stretches space, increasing the rate of expansion

STRETCHING OF FLAT SPACE

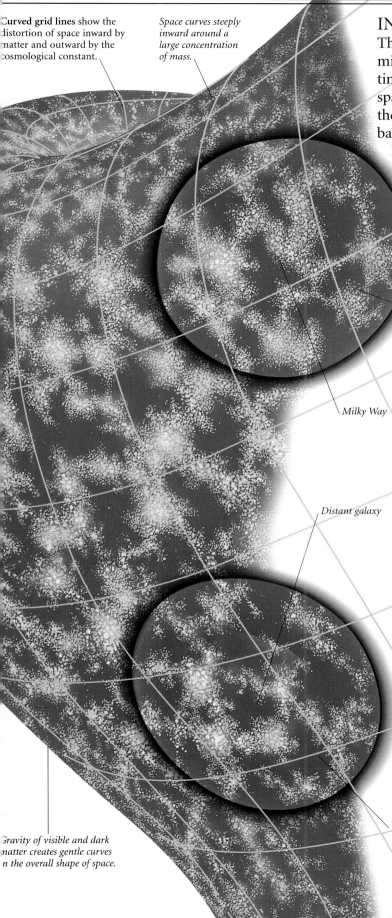

Curved grid lines show the distortion of space inward by matter and outward by the cosmological constant.

Space curves steeply inward around a large concentration of mass.

INFINITE UNIVERSE

This is the ultimate bird's-eye view: how the Universe might look to a superior being outside our space and time. The illustration represents the three dimensions of space in two dimensions. The Universe is expanding like the skin of an inflating balloon, and so, just like the balloon's surface, it has no edge and no centre. As we look into space, we appear to be at the centre of an "observable" Universe stretching for 13 billion light years in each direction, but there is nothing special about our place in the cosmos. Everything is relative, and our observable Universe is only a tiny patch in an infinite landscape.

Our observable Universe is centred on the Milky Way. It extends 13 billion light years in all directions – the maximum distance light can have travelled since the Big Bang took place.

Milky Way

Distant galaxy

Gravity of visible and dark matter creates gentle curves in the overall shape of space.

CLOSED UNIVERSE

If there is enough matter in the Universe, space may curve so much that it bends right back on itself, creating a closed universe. Astronauts exploring this universe would travel right around without finding an edge. The gravity of matter in a closed universe would eventually stop its expansion, and pull it back in to collapse in a Big Crunch. Astronomers have found that visible galaxies do not provide enough gravity to close our Universe, however, and recent measurements suggest there is not even enough dark matter – so it is unlikely that we live in a closed universe.

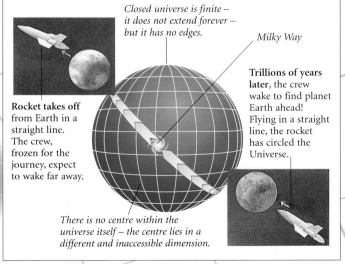

Closed universe is finite – it does not extend forever – but it has no edges.

Milky Way

Rocket takes off from Earth in a straight line. The crew, frozen for the journey, expect to wake far away.

Trillions of years later, the crew wake to find planet Earth ahead! Flying in a straight line, the rocket has circled the Universe.

There is no centre within the universe itself – the centre lies in a different and inaccessible dimension.

Observable universe for a distant galaxy is also 13 billion light years in radius. It does not overlap ours, so we cannot see this galaxy, and its inhabitants cannot see the Milky Way.

FAR FUTURE

LARGE TELESCOPES ARE TIME MACHINES – because light from distant galaxies takes billions of years to reach Earth, they show the Universe in the distant past. But astronomers can also predict the future of the cosmos. There are three possible fates for the Universe, depending on how much matter it contains. A dense Universe will eventually stop expanding and contract under the pull of its own gravity, while a nearly empty Universe will continue to expand forever. However, there is growing evidence for the third option: that our Universe is not just expanding at a constant speed, but is accelerating.

Closed Universe reaches maximum size, and begins to contract.

Universe expands

Big Bang

At boundary, expansion slows down, but does not reverse.

Closed Universe ends in Big Crunch.

Open Universe expands forever.

POSSIBLE FATES
The fate of the Universe depends on how much matter it contains. Too little, then it is an open universe that will expand forever. If there is enough mass to bend space around it, then it is a closed Universe that will eventually collapse. There may also be just enough matter to slow, but not reverse the expansion.

OPEN UNIVERSE
A Universe that is low in mass is open – it will continue to expand, and cool, forever. This sounds like immortality, but it is actually a slow, lingering death. Over trillions of years, all the stars in all the galaxies will eventually die: even the supermassive black holes in the centres of the galaxies will not last forever. Ultimately, our cosmos will be unimaginably cold and dark, home to just a tiny handful of subatomic particles.

2 After 10 trillion trillion years, the Milky Way has become a graveyard of star corpses spiralling into a central supermassive black hole.

OPEN UNIVERSE

UNIVERSE TODAY
Today, galaxies like the Milky Way are in their prime. Stars are being born, and there is plenty of gas and dust around to fuel starbirth in the future. The Milky Way's spiral arms are studded with glowing nebulas and hot, young, blue stars.

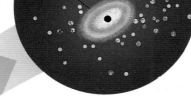

CLOSED UNIVERSE

Universe slows to a halt after several trillion trillion years. By this time our galaxy is long dead, with only a central black hole surrounded by the remains of stars.

Older stars in hub

1 A trillion years after the Big Bang, the Milky Way uses up all its gas and dust, so no new stars form. Even the longest-lived stars start to die, and the spiral arms disappear.

Starbirth in spiral arms

CLOSED UNIVERSE
If there is sufficient matter, the Universe is closed: expansion will stop and gravity will pull it back on itself, collapsing in a fiery collision, the Big Crunch. The countdown to the Big Crunch is like a reversed Big Bang – as matter packs together, the Universe heats up. Any remaining matter disintegrates into atoms, then into subatomic particles. Black holes alone are unaffected by the intense heat, and start to collide and join together. Finally, they form a single mega black hole that sucks in all remaining matter.

EVOLUTIONARY PATHS OF THE UNIVERSE

ACCELERATING UNIVERSE

Whatever the ultimate fate of the Universe is, gravity should be slowing it down – but recent observations suggest that the expansion could be accelerating. Distant galaxies seem to have travelled too far, too fast, since the Big Bang. Astronomers call the repulsive force driving the galaxies away the cosmological constant – it may be created by space itself slowly stretching.

SUPERNOVA 5 BILLION LIGHT YEARS AWAY

SUPERNOVA DISTANCES

Exploding stars called Type 1 supernovas always reach the same maximum brightness. By detecting these stars in galaxies, astronomers can calculate distances across the Universe. They find that the most distant galaxies are farther away than predicted by the Big Bang theory, and that the Universe's expansion must be accelerating.

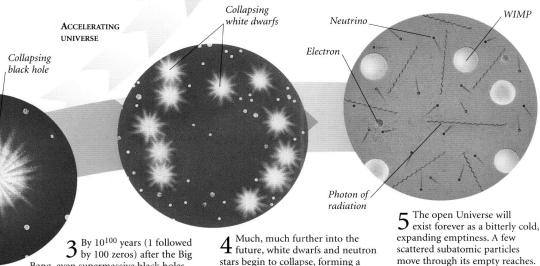

ACCELERATING UNIVERSE

Collapsing white dwarfs

Collapsing black hole

Neutrino

Electron

WIMP

Photon of radiation

3 By 10^{100} years (1 followed by 100 zeros) after the Big Bang, even supermassive black holes disappear in a burst of radiation. A few neutron stars and white dwarfs may survive.

4 Much, much further into the future, white dwarfs and neutron stars begin to collapse, forming a new generation of black holes. Eventually, these too disappear in a flash of radiation.

5 The open Universe will exist forever as a bitterly cold, expanding emptiness. A few scattered subatomic particles move through its empty reaches. All were created long ago in the Big Bang.

3 million years to the Big Crunch

100,000 years to the Big Crunch

Last three minutes

OSCILLATING UNIVERSE

Big Bang

Big Crunch

Universe expands again

Universe expands

Universe contracts

Galaxies merge as the Universe contracts. The background temperature rises to 20°C.

Background temperature of the Universe is hotter than the stars, so material in the stars boils off into space, and the Universe becomes a sea of atoms.

Supermassive black holes at the centres of galaxies merge. The Universe becomes so hot that the nuclei of atoms cannot stay together, and break up into subatomic particles that are swallowed by the black holes.

Finally, the entire Universe disappears into a single mega black hole – the Big Crunch.

NEW UNIVERSES

Some astronomers think that a Big Crunch might not be the ultimate end. They believe that the Universe oscillates – it expands, contracts, and is then reborn. They predict that a new expanding Universe could emerge from the final mega black hole. Because all matter is destroyed in the Big Crunch, the new universe would have completely different particles and laws of physics from the old one.

FATES OF THE UNIVERSE

● British physicist Lord Kelvin (1824–1907) and German physicist Rudolph Clausius (1822–88) independently suggested in the 1850s that the Universe would slowly die of cold.

● In 1922, Russian astronomer Alexandr Friedmann (1888–1925) calculated that the Universe has three possible fates.

● US physicist Howard M. Georgi (1947–) calculated in 1973 that the protons in white dwarfs and neutron stars may eventually decay, causing them to "evaporate".

● In 1974, Stephen Hawking predicted that black holes could vanish in a flash of radiation.

● British physicist Freeman J. Dyson (1923–) calculated in 1979 that white dwarfs and neutron stars eventually become black holes.

● New measurements made in 1997 showed that the Universe does not have enough mass to pull it back into a Big Crunch.

TELESCOPE USED TO INVESTIGATE THE FUTURE

● In 1998, several groups of astronomers measuring distances to supernovas in remote galaxies suggested that the Universe could be accelerating.

FIND OUT MORE

LIFE ON OTHER WORLDS

ONE OF THE MOST IMPORTANT astronomical questions must be: is there life out there? The odds are certainly in its favour – many planets are now being discovered around other stars, and there are billions of suitable parent stars in our Galaxy alone. We know that the building blocks of life – the elements carbon, hydrogen, and oxygen – are common in space. But would we recognize life if we found it? Alien lifeforms might look nothing like us – witness the incredible diversity of life on Earth.

ALTERNATIVE LIFE
Evolution can take strange routes. Arnold was designed by a biologist to show what intelligent life might now look like on Earth if different creatures had gained the upper hand 570 million years ago. The environment that led to Arnold was identical to the conditions that gave rise to humans.

ARNOLD – AN ALIEN FROM EARTH

PLANET URSA

The star 47 Ursae Majoris has a planet 2.8 times the mass of Jupiter – and it is likely to have several more. This illustration shows a hypothetical small, low-gravity planet – named Ursa – in the outer reaches of its planetary system, with some of the lifeforms that might have evolved there. These creatures grow high, curl up when cold, have big eyes to see in the dark, and have developed efficient ways of breathing in the thin air.

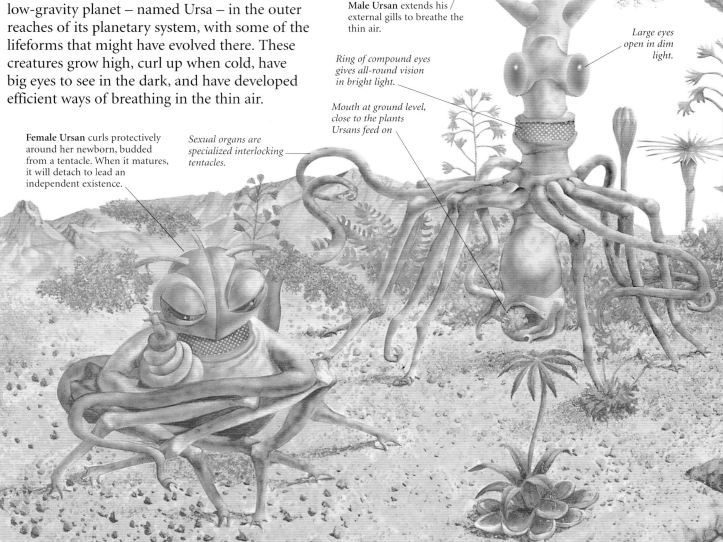

Male Ursan extends his external gills to breathe the thin air.

Ring of compound eyes gives all-round vision in bright light.

Large eyes open in dim light.

Mouth at ground level, close to the plants Ursans feed on

Female Ursan curls protectively around her newborn, budded from a tentacle. When it matures, it will detach to lead an independent existence.

Sexual organs are specialized interlocking tentacles.

REQUIREMENTS OF LIFE

Exactly how life arose from the basic chemicals that existed on the early Earth is a mystery, but a major factor must have been the right environment. These stromatolites in Western Australia are the unaltered descendants of the earliest life on our planet. Their environment shows the conditions needed for life: warmth, light, a suitable atmosphere, and water to aid the complex chemical reactions which life requires.

Stromatolites are layers of algae.

STROMATOLITES IN SHARK BAY, WESTERN AUSTRALIA

Ursan "tree"

Ursa's plants are purple instead of green, because they photosynthesize using a different form of chlorophyll. In the low gravity, plants grow tall.

Air on Ursa is very thin, so plants and animals both need large surfaces to absorb it.

Water is essential to life on Ursa, just as it is on Earth. Because water is very good at dissolving chemicals, it can bring them together in the complex chemical reactions needed for life.

Fish on Ursa are a similar shape to those on Earth, because the buoyancy of water, rather than gravity, dictates the form of their bodies.

PROBABILITY OF LIFE

If intelligent life, capable of communicating over interstellar distances, is to arise on a planet, then a variety of different conditions must be just right. Pioneering astronomer Frank Drake, who began investigating extraterrestrial intelligence in 1960, was the first to consider the different factors.

 ● Stars must be born at a reasonable rate to replace those that die. In our Galaxy, 10 are born every year.

 ● The star must have planets for life to exist on.

 ● A planet of the right size must exist at the right distance from the star, where it is neither too hot nor too cold.

 ● Life needs to emerge on the planet.

 ● Life on the planet needs to evolve into intelligent life – green slime is not capable of communicating its existence.

 ● The intelligent lifeforms must develop technology to communicate over interstellar distances.

 ● The lifeforms must learn not to destroy themselves with their technology.

 ● Natural disasters – comet and asteroid impacts, large volcanic eruptions – must be rare to give intelligence time to evolve.

The pessimistic view of each of the factors giving rise to intelligent life can lead to an estimate that there is just one civilization in the Galaxy – our own.

An optimistic assessment of each of the factors can lead to an estimate of 10 million civilizations in the Milky Way Galaxy at any one time.

FIND OUT MORE

LIVING WORLD 90
SEARCH FOR LIFE ON MARS 116
OTHER SOLAR SYSTEMS 178
ET INTELLIGENCE 238

EXTRATERRESTRIAL INTELLIGENCE

ONCE REGARDED AS ECCENTRIC, the search for extraterrestrial intelligence (SETI) has become widely respected. It involves many disciplines – astronomy, physics, chemistry, information technology, and biology. Most SETI scientists use radio telescopes to listen for artificial signals from space, while a few are looking for laser transmissions. Any deliberate message should come in some easily decoded form. We have already sent our own messages, but have yet to detect a signal from space.

Radio waves carry the Arecibo message. This radiation can travel at the speed of light through even the dustiest regions of space, and so is ideal for interstellar communications.

BIRTH OF SETI
In the 1950s, during the early days of radio astronomy, a young American called Frank Drake realized that radio telescopes were ideal tools to communicate with extraterrestrials. They could pick up signals – and, used in reverse, broadcast signals – right across the Galaxy. Drake was soon joined in his research by other astronomers. Their most ambitious proposal was Project Cyclops – a purpose-built array of 1,500 radio telescopes – but it was too expensive to get off the drawing board.

ARECIBO MESSAGE
In 1974, the Arecibo Radio Telescope in Puerto Rico sent a message to the stars. It consisted of 1,679 on-off pulses beamed towards globular cluster M13, a dense ball of stars 25,000 light years away. An intelligent alien would realize that 1,679 is made by multiplying the prime numbers 23 and 73. Arranging the pulses in a rectangle 23 columns wide and 73 rows deep creates a pictogram explaining the basis of life on Earth.

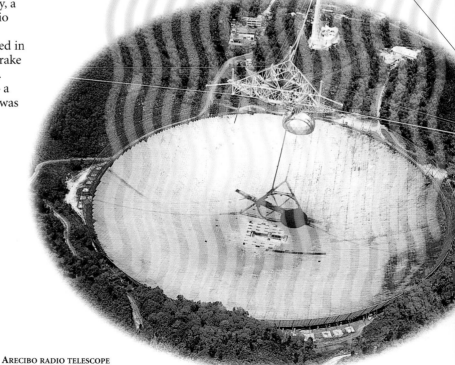

ARECIBO RADIO TELESCOPE

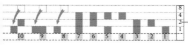

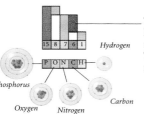

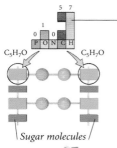

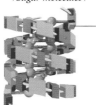

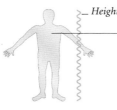

The first block shows the numbers 1 to 10 in binary code – the form of numbers used by computers.

The most important elements of life are hydrogen, carbon, nitrogen, oxygen, and phosphorus. This block picks out the atomic numbers of the five elements.

Hydrogen

Phosphorus

Oxygen   Nitrogen   Carbon

Proportions of the key elements in some important biological molecules are shown in this block. Sugar (C_5H_7O, coded green), phosphate (purple), and the nucleotides (orange) make up the structure of DNA, the molecule that forms the basis of life on Earth.

C_5H_7O C_5H_7O

Sugar molecules

Two twisted strands show the double-helix structure of DNA, the huge molecule that divides and replicates to pass on the blueprints of life. Alien lifeforms would almost certainly depend on a molecule like DNA to pass on genetic information.

Height of a human = 14 wavelengths of signal

Outline of a human being would probably be the most baffling image to an alien. It is flanked by numbers giving the world's population (left) and the human's height (right).

Solar System with its different bodies roughly to scale. The Earth is displaced to highlight it.

Arecibo radio telescope, with a sketch of how the radio waves carrying the message were beamed.

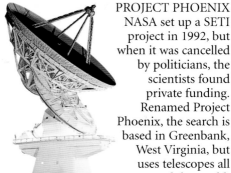

GREENBANK RADIO TELESCOPE

PROJECT PHOENIX

NASA set up a SETI project in 1992, but when it was cancelled by politicians, the scientists found private funding. Renamed Project Phoenix, the search is based in Greenbank, West Virginia, but uses telescopes all around the world.

CONTACT

When we do make contact with alien life, it will be the biggest news event of all time. Different groups of people – the military, religious communities, scientists, and politicians – will all respond in different ways according to their own agendas. Should we reply, or would it be too dangerous? Who will decide what to say?

SETI HITS THE HEADLINES

FUTURE SETI

Time is running out for SETI. Increasing electronic noise, from equipment such as mobile phones and microwave cookers, is drowning out any faint signals that might be coming from extraterrestrials. One way ahead could be a SETI base on the farside of the Moon, screened from Earthly interference. SETI scientists have even found a location: the 100-km crater Saha.

DEVELOPMENT OF SETI

- SETI began in 1959, when Giuseppe Cocconi (1914–) and Philip Morrison (1915–) published a paper, "Searching for Interstellar Communications", in the science journal *Nature*.

- In 1960, Frank Drake began Project OZMA – the first radio telescope search for artificial signals.

- NASA's Jupiter and Saturn probes Pioneer 10 and 11, launched in 1972 and 1973, each carried an engraved plaque with a primitive message from Earth – intended to be read by any extraterrestrials who might encounter the probes after they left the Solar System.

PIONEER PLAQUE

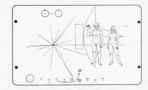

- In 1974, the Arecibo message was sent towards globular cluster M13.

- In 1977, a radio telescope in Ohio picked up the "Wow!" signal – the strongest-ever unidentified transmission. It was never found again.

- The two Voyager probes were launched in 1977, each carrying a gold-plated record encoded with sounds and images of Earth.

- In 1995, Project Phoenix began a new, systematic survey searching for extraterrestrial signals.

FIND OUT MORE

LUNAR SETI STATION

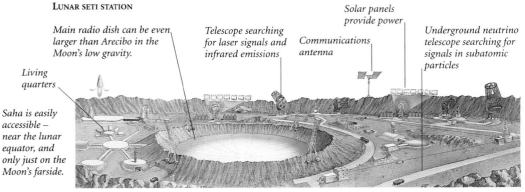

Main radio dish can be even larger than Arecibo in the Moon's low gravity.

Telescope searching for laser signals and infrared emissions

Communications antenna

Solar panels provide power

Underground neutrino telescope searching for signals in subatomic particles

Living quarters

Saha is easily accessible – near the lunar equator, and only just on the Moon's farside.

PRACTICAL STARGAZING

Astronomy is one of those very rare sciences in which you do not have to be a professional to take part. Even without binoculars or a telescope, an amateur astronomer can make a contribution – by observing meteors, for example. In fact, there is a long tradition of observing the sky for practical reasons, such as navigation, timekeeping, or calendar making. To get started in astronomy, it helps to learn your way around the sky and to be able to recognize the stars of different seasons. A pair of binoculars will reveal more, and even allow amateurs to make valuable observations such as monitoring variable stars. With a telescope, the sky literally is the limit. Some amateur telescopes today are more sophisticated than many of those used by professionals just a few years back.

SPINNING EARTH

WE OBSERVE THE UNIVERSE from the deck of a giant spaceship speeding through the cosmos. Spaceship Earth is not, however, an ideal observing platform. It spins all the time, so everything seems to move across the sky in the opposite direction – nothing stays in the same place. The solid Earth beneath us also blocks out much of the Universe: Europeans never see the Southern Cross, while the star Polaris is always hidden from Australians. What is visible in the sky depends on the time and a person's location. Conversely, observers can use what is visible in the sky to reveal time and location.

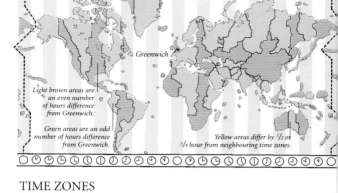

Light brown areas are an even number of hours difference from Greenwich.

Green areas are an odd number of hours difference from Greenwich.

Yellow areas differ by ¹/₂ or ³/₄ hour from neighbouring time zones.

TIME ZONES
As Earth spins, different places around the world face the Sun at different times, so that it may be dawn in the USA, noon in Europe, and sunset in Australia. The world is divided into 24 main time zones, each an hour apart. In any one zone, the Sun is at its highest in the sky at about noon local time.

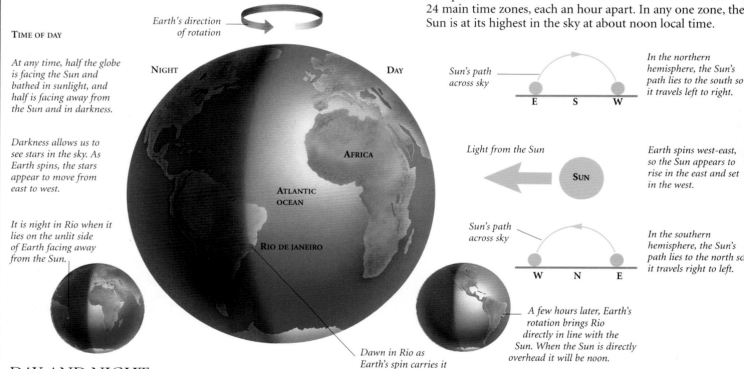

TIME OF DAY

Earth's direction of rotation

At any time, half the globe is facing the Sun and bathed in sunlight, and half is facing away from the Sun and in darkness.

Darkness allows us to see stars in the sky. As Earth spins, the stars appear to move from east to west.

It is night in Rio when it lies on the unlit side of Earth facing away from the Sun.

NIGHT

DAY

AFRICA

ATLANTIC OCEAN

RIO DE JANEIRO

Dawn in Rio as Earth's spin carries it round to face the Sun.

A few hours later, Earth's rotation brings Rio directly in line with the Sun. When the Sun is directly overhead it will be noon.

Sun's path across sky

E　S　W

In the northern hemisphere, the Sun's path lies to the south so it travels left to right.

Light from the Sun

SUN

Earth spins west-east, so the Sun appears to rise in the east and set in the west.

Sun's path across sky

W　N　E

In the southern hemisphere, the Sun's path lies to the north so it travels right to left.

DAY AND NIGHT
Earth rotates on its axis at a steady rate, carrying everyone from night into day, then back into night again. As the globe spins, so our view of the Universe changes. After one complete spin, Earth is facing the same direction, and the stars have returned to the same place in the sky – this takes 23 hours 56 minutes (a sidereal day). In this time, Earth has travelled 2.5 million km along its orbit of the Sun, and it has to rotate an extra 1° before the Sun is in the same place in the sky. This takes 4 minutes, so a day measured relative to the Sun (a solar day) is 24 hours long.

FINDING LONGITUDE
Longitude is the distance east or west of a north-south line that runs through Greenwich in England. Earth spins through 360° in 24 hours, so it turns by 15° in each hour. If the time in Greenwich (GMT, or Greenwich Mean Time) is 6 p.m., it must be 6 a.m. at 180° east. The Earth's spin helps navigators to find their longitude – provided they know the time at Greenwich.

Calculate longitude by multiplying difference in hours by 15.

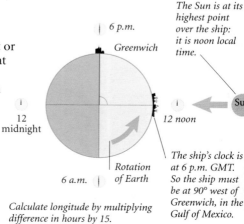

6 p.m.

Greenwich

12 midnight

12 noon

Rotation of Earth

6 a.m.

Sun

The Sun is at its highest point over the ship: it is noon local time.

The ship's clock is at 6 p.m. GMT. So the ship must be at 90° west of Greenwich, in the Gulf of Mexico.

POLARIS AND LATITUDE

In the northern hemisphere, the height of Polaris, or the Pole Star, in the sky varies according to latitude (distance north of the Equator). At the North Pole (latitude 90°N), Polaris is directly overhead (90° above the horizon), and at the Equator (latitude 0°), it is just visible on the horizon (0° above the horizon). At 60°N, it is 60° above the horizon, and at 45°N it is 45° above the horizon.

Star altitudes: Astronomers measure the height of a star above the horizon in degrees. From the horizon to overhead is 90°; a star halfway up in the sky is at 45°; one on the horizon is at 0°.

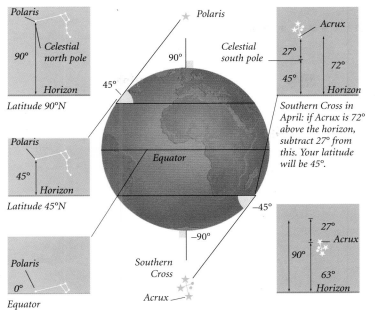

Latitude 90°N

Latitude 45°N

Equator

SOUTHERN LATITUDE

In the southern hemisphere there is no pole star, but the Southern Cross (Crux), which is 27° from the celestial south pole can act as a guide to finding latitude. It is easiest to use in April (when it appears upright in the sky) or in October (when it appears upside down). Work out the height of the star Acrux from the horizon. If the cross is upright, subtract 27° to find your latitude; if upside down, add 27°.

Southern Cross in April: if Acrux is 72° above the horizon, subtract 27° from this. Your latitude will be 45°.

Southern Cross in October: if Acrux is 63° above the horizon, add 27° to this. Your latitude will be 90°S.

SUNDIALS

The principle behind a sundial – literally a sun-clock – is that as Earth rotates, the Sun seems to move across the sky, and shadows move across the ground in the opposite direction. Every sundial has a stick called the gnomon. Its shadow falls onto a scale, which is marked with the hours of the day. A simple sundial can be made from everyday objects. Follow the instructions, starting from the top right.

1 For the gnomon, use a knitting needle or long skewer.

2 Find a glass jar with a screwtop lid.

The shadow of the gnomon on the paper strip will tell you the time.

3 Remove the lid from the jar. Pierce a hole in it so that the needle or skewer can slide through.

4 Fix a plastic putty ball on the needle. Screw the lid on the jar with the putty resting in the middle of the base of the jar.

5 Make a base from card folded into a triangle. Glue a strip of card across the slope to prevent the jar sliding down.

6 Cut a paper strip 25 mm wide and long enough to fit around the jar. Mark 24 equal lines and number from 1–24 from right to left in the northern hemisphere (left to right in the southern).

7 Stick the strip around the jar with clear tape. Put the jar on the base so that 12 faces directly down the slope, which must point north in the northern hemisphere or south in the southern.

Right angle (90°)

Angle equal to the latitude of the sundial's location.

This end of the base points north (south in the southern hemisphere).

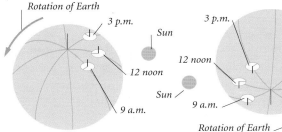

NORTHERN HEMISPHERE

Rotation of Earth

3 p.m.

12 noon

9 a.m.

Sun

SOUTHERN HEMISPHERE

3 p.m.

12 noon

9 a.m.

Sun

Rotation of Earth

The shadow on a sundial moves clockwise as the Earth rotates in the northern hemisphere.

The shadow on a sundial in the southern hemisphere rotates anticlockwise during the day.

SUNDIAL ACCURACY

The shadow of the gnomon tells the time to an accuracy of a few minutes. At some times of the year, however, the sundial can be several minutes fast or slow. This is because the Sun's apparent path in the sky is affected by changes in Earth's speed as it orbits around the Sun.

SUNDIAL ORIENTATION

A sundial is accurate only if the gnomon is parallel to the Earth's axis. The gnomon must therefore be carefully set up so that it is oriented in a north-south direction, and at an angle equal to your latitude. Sundials have other limitations. They cannot be used at night or when it is cloudy, and most cannot be adjusted for summer time.

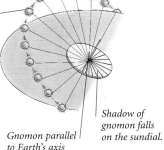

Sun's apparent path in the sky

Gnomon parallel to Earth's axis

Shadow of gnomon falls on the sundial.

FIND OUT MORE

EARTH'S ORBIT 244
MAPPING THE NIGHT SKY 250
STAR MAPS 252–261

EARTH'S ORBIT

As our planet spins on its axis, it is hurtling around the Sun at 100,000 km/h, providing ever-changing views of the Universe. During this orbit, the height of the Sun in our skies alters too, leading to the progression in weather from winter to summer, and back. By understanding Earth's orbit, astronomers can explain why some seasonal phenomena coincide with "signs in the sky" – for example, the annual flood of the River Nile just after the appearance of the star Sirius, which ancient Egyptians ascribed to the sky gods.

YEARS, SOLSTICES, AND EQUINOXES

Earth completes one orbit around the Sun in 365¼ days or one year. During this yearly trip, we look out in different directions in space, so that we see different stars as the year progresses. The Sun's path in the sky changes too, because the Earth's axis is not at right angles to its orbit: it is tilted away at an angle of 23.5°. The Sun is highest over the northern hemisphere on 21 June (giving the longest day, the solstice), and over the southern on 21 or 22 December. Halfway between at the equinoxes (about 21 March and 23 September), the Sun shines equally on both hemispheres.

JUNE TEMPERATURES

On this side of its orbit, the Earth's tilt leans the North Pole towards the Sun. In June, therefore, the Sun shines directly on the northern hemisphere, raising temperatures so that it is summer time. Sunlight hits the southern hemisphere at a slant, so it is spread out more thinly and delivers less heat. South of the Equator, the temperature drops to winter cold.

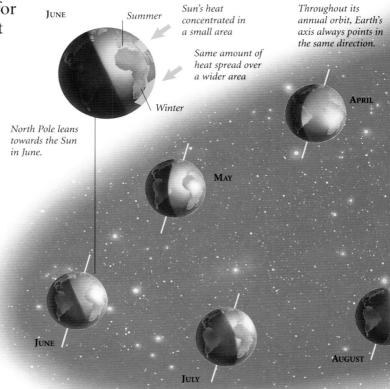

JUNE

Summer

Sun's heat concentrated in a small area

Same amount of heat spread over a wider area

Throughout its annual orbit, Earth's axis always points in the same direction.

APRIL

Winter

North Pole leans towards the Sun in June.

MAY

JUNE

AUGUST

JULY

As Earth speeds along its orbit, different stars are visible each month.

If Earth's axis were not tilted, day and night would always be of equal length, and there would be no seasons.

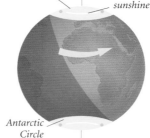

Arctic Circle

This area is in constant sunshine in June.

Antarctic Circle

MIDNIGHT SUN

In June, regions near the North Pole are tilted towards the Sun. Within the Arctic Circle (north of latitude 66°), the Sun is so high in the sky that it does not rise or set. It travels round and round the sky, moving downwards from its highest point at midday to its lowest point at 12 midnight. The same happens within the Antarctic in December.

Time-lapse photo of the midnight Sun in the Arctic Circle

| 9 P.M. | 10 P.M. | 11 P.M. | MIDNIGHT | 1 A.M. | 2 A.M. |

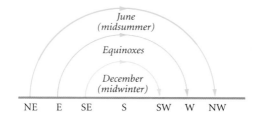

June (midsummer)

Equinoxes

December (midwinter)

NE   E   SE   S   SW   W   NW

SUN'S NORTHERN PATH

The Sun's path across the sky varies with Earth's orbit. In the northern hemisphere, the Sun passes high across the sky in the summer. At the equinoxes, its path is lower, while winter sees it at its lowest. Rising and setting points also change: east-west at the equinoxes, farther to the north in the summer, and more southerly in winter.

Shape of Earth's orbit (exaggerated)

January

July

Sun

ELLIPTICAL ORBIT
The average distance of the Earth from the Sun is 150 million km. But Earth follows an oval orbit, which brings it 5 million km closer to the Sun in January than it is in July. January is summer in the southern hemisphere, and southern summers are therefore very slightly warmer than northern summers.

Sun is 329,000 times more massive than Earth, so its powerful gravity keeps Earth in orbit.

South Pole leans towards the Sun in December.

LEAP YEAR
Every four years, an extra day is added to the year to keep the seasons in line. This is because during a complete orbit, Earth rotates 365¼ times. If our calendar had 365 days every year, each date would come earlier and earlier, and the seasons would end up in different months.

HOW THE SUN WOULD APPEAR IN TAURUS

JANUARY

DECEMBER

FEBRUARY

MARCH

DECEMBER

NOVEMBER

SUN

Winter

OCTOBER

Sun's heat spread thinly

Same amount of heat concentrated in a small area.

Summer

SEPTEMBER

September and March: at the two equinoxes, the Sun lies directly above Earth's Equator. Day and night are equal length – 12 hours each – everywhere.

SUN'S APPARENT PATH
As Earth moves around its orbit, the Sun appears to move among different stars. We cannot see this easily, because sunlight drowns out the background stars. If we could strip away the bright daytime sky, we would see the Sun against different star patterns – the constellations of the zodiac – in different months.

DECEMBER TEMPERATURES
In December, the South Pole tilts towards the Sun. Sunshine falls directly on the southern hemisphere, giving hot summer conditions, while the northern hemisphere experiences oblique sunshine. The two hemispheres have opposite seasons: summer in the south means winter in the north; southern autumn coincides with northern spring.

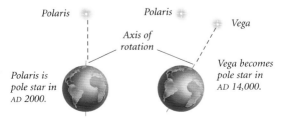

December (midsummer)

Equinoxes

June (midwinter)

SW   W   NW   N   NE   E   SE

PRECESSION
Earth's axis of rotation is not absolutely fixed: it swings around very gradually, like a spinning top about to fall over. At present, it points to Polaris. Over 26,000 years, the axis will slowly drift around the sky, pointing to different "pole stars", before once again pointing at Polaris. This effect, precession, is caused by the Moon's gravity pulling on the tilted Earth.

SUN'S SOUTHERN PATH
Midwinter in the southern hemisphere sees the Sun take its lowest path across the sky: it rises in the northeast and sets in the northwest. At the equinoxes, its path is higher and it rises in the east and sets in the west. During December, the Sun reaches its highest point, and is rising and setting in a more southerly direction.

Polaris

Polaris

Vega

Axis of rotation

Polaris is pole star in AD 2000.

Vega becomes pole star in AD 14,000.

EARTH'S ORBIT

● In 1543, Nicolas Copernicus proposed in *De Revolutionibus* that Earth travels around the Sun, contradicting previous teachings that everything revolved around Earth.

● In 1609, Johannes Kepler calculated that Earth's path around the Sun must be an ellipse, not a circle.

● In 1728, England's Astronomer Royal James Bradley (1693–1762) observed aberration – a seasonal shift in the direction of starlight caused by Earth's motion – which proved Earth is moving.

FIND OUT MORE

DAYTIME ASTRONOMY

ASTRONOMY CAN BE AS MUCH FUN by day as by night, because some celestial objects are bright enough to be seen even when the sky is not dark. The most obvious is the Sun – our own star, and the only one that can be seen in detail from the Earth. It is dangerous to observe the Sun directly, but projecting it onto a screen usually reveals plenty of ever-changing detail. The Sun's brightness makes it difficult to see fainter objects in the sky, but they are there. The Moon and some brighter planets are visible – there are even some advantages in observing the planets during the day rather than at night.

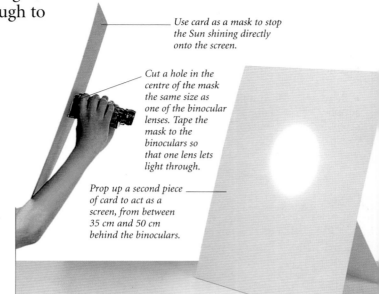

Use card as a mask to stop the Sun shining directly onto the screen.

Cut a hole in the centre of the mask the same size as one of the binocular lenses. Tape the mask to the binoculars so that one lens lets light through.

Prop up a second piece of card to act as a screen, from between 35 cm and 50 cm behind the binoculars.

OBSERVING THE SUN

One aspect of the Sun's activity is the change in sunspot patterns. To record these changes, draw a circle on a piece of paper every day and attach the paper to a screen. Project the Sun so that its disc fills the circle, and mark the positions of the sunspots and faculas where they appear on the screen.

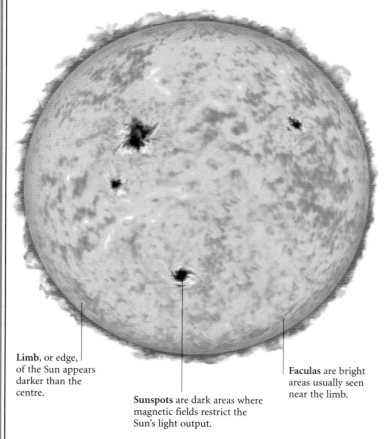

Limb, or edge, of the Sun appears darker than the centre.

Sunspots are dark areas where magnetic fields restrict the Sun's light output.

Faculas are bright areas usually seen near the limb.

SUN PROJECTION

To observe the Sun, project its image onto a piece of card, using binoculars or a telescope of less than 100 mm and a magnification of less than 30. Aim the instrument at the Sun, and turn and tilt it until a disc of light appears on the screen. Focus the instrument on the screen until the disc becomes a sharp-edged image of the Sun. To make the image bigger but fainter, move the screen farther away from the eyepiece.

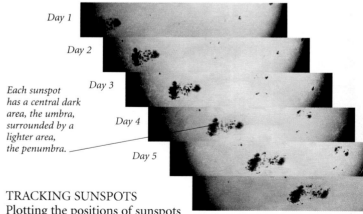

Day 1

Day 2

Day 3

Each sunspot has a central dark area, the umbra, surrounded by a lighter area, the penumbra.

Day 4

Day 5

Day 6

TRACKING SUNSPOTS

Plotting the positions of sunspots daily shows how they move across the face of the Sun. This is because the Sun rotates, just as the Earth does. Sometimes a sunspot goes right around and returns to the same position about 29 days later, but usually it changes over a few days and fades away. Big sunspots often appear in pairs, lined up roughly parallel with the Sun's equator.

WARNING

● Never look at the Sun with the naked eye, nor even anywhere close to it with binoculars or a telescope. Even a glimpse of the Sun can severely damage your eyesight.

● Use only the projection method to observe the Sun. If using a telescope, cap its finder so that no light shines through it.

● Be wary of the Sun filters that are often supplied with small telescopes, and which screw into the eyepiece. The Sun's heat can cause them to crack without warning.

PINHOLE PROJECTION

The Sun's image can be projected through a pinhole, though this is more suited to viewing partial eclipses than sunspots, which are usually too small to be seen. By increasing the distance between the screen and the pinhole to at least a metre, it is possible to get an image of the Sun from any shaped hole – even the holes in a cheese grater!

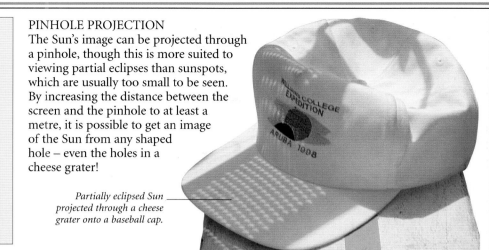

Partially eclipsed Sun projected through a cheese grater onto a baseball cap.

SUN BEFORE SUNSET

SUN REFLECTED OVER WATER

COLOUR OF THE SUN

The Sun is usually described as being yellow, but its true colour is pure white. The reason it looks yellow is that the human eye often glimpses the Sun when its light is dimmed by clouds, or when it is low in the sky just before sunset, which yellows its light. Reflections of the bright Sun on water, however, show clearly its real, pure-white colour.

STARS AND PLANETS

The brighter stars and planets can be seen in daylight through binoculars, but finding them can be quite difficult. Be careful not to look at the Sun by mistake. Telescopic observers of the planet Venus often prefer to look at it during the day or early evening. It is then higher in the sky and appears less dazzling than when it is dark.

DAYTIME MOON

The Moon is often easy to see in the daytime sky, particularly when it is at its brightest during its nearly full phase. Look for it in the afternoon in the east or southeast before full Moon (east or northeast in the southern hemisphere), and in the morning sky in the west or southwest after full Moon (west or northwest in the southern hemisphere). It will be higher in the sky during winter than during summer.

VENUS IN THE EVENING SKY

FIND OUT MORE

MOON 92
NEARSIDE OF THE MOON 100
VENUSIAN ATMOSPHERE 110
INSIDE THE SUN 154
SUN'S SURFACE 156
ECLIPSES OF THE SUN 160

PREPARING TO STARGAZE

THE SKY IS CLEAR, THE SUN HAS GONE DOWN, and the stars are beginning to come out. The scene is set for a good night's observing. This is the time to get prepared, because once outside there should be no need to come in for a forgotten pencil, or a pair of gloves. If the weather is cold, be prepared for it to become even colder. Put on warm clothes, not forgetting a warm hat. Plan carefully what to observe ahead of time. It is frustrating to miss seeing a particular favourite object while diverted by other activity in the sky. Learn how the stars and planets move through the sky.

ESSENTIAL EQUIPMENT
Good observers keep a record of what they have seen. Any notebook will do, but one with plain sheets will be better for drawing. For each observation, write down the time, date, year, and location, and describe the weather conditions, particularly any mist or cloud. Also note if the times are in summer time. Keep a record of any instruments used, such as binoculars or a telescope. To look at star maps or take notes, use a torch covered with red cellophane. This will give a reddish light that will not affect night vision.

GOOD VIEWING CONDITIONS
Some nights are good for looking at stars, while others are better for planets. Brilliantly clear evenings often have turbulent air. This spoils views of the Moon and planets, but is good for finding faint nebulas. Windless conditions are more suited to studying the Moon and planets, despite the mist that may form.

The fainter the stars visible, the better the "transparency".

NOTEBOOK

Before going outside to observe, organize the notebook into the categories of objects to be recorded.

CHECKLIST
- Warm clothing, including waterproof shoes
- Notebook and pen or pencil
- Accurate watch
- Red-covered torch
- Binoculars
- Something to sit on
- Books and star maps
- A small table (useful to put everything on)

RED-COVERED TORCH

Make a red torch by covering an ordinary torch with a piece of red cellophane held by an elastic band, or use a red bicycle lamp.

NORTH AND SOUTH
It is important to get one's bearings before observing. The Sun is due south at noon (north in the southern hemisphere), so note its position in relation to nearby objects such as trees that can be identified at night.

LIGHT POLLUTION
City lights spread their glow into the sky, causing light pollution that often drowns out the fainter stars. Town dwellers should choose a spot as far from lights as possible, and make sure that no lights shine directly into their eyes. If the Moon is full, even country dwellers will find it difficult to see faint objects.

STARGAZING TIPS

It can take up to 30 minutes for eyes to become properly accustomed to the dark and to get full night vision. Some types of light are particularly bad for night vision, such as fluorescent lights, and TV and computer screens, so try to avoid them before going outside to observe.

● Once outside, use only red light and try to persuade other family members not to switch on any distracting house lights.

● If outside lights are a problem, rig up a temporary light shield, such as a blanket draped over a stepladder.

ORION IN NORTHERN SKIES

Earth's rotation makes stars and planets appear to move across the sky at night. The constellation Orion, visible from November to March, is typical. It rises in the east where it appears tilted, then moves across the sky. It is highest when due south, then tilts the other way as it moves to set in the western horizon.

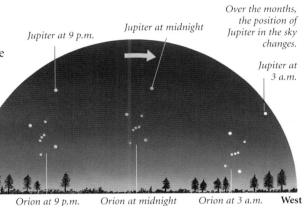

Jupiter at 9 p.m.
Jupiter at midnight
Over the months, the position of Jupiter in the sky changes.
Jupiter at 3 a.m.

East — *Orion at 9 p.m.* — *Orion at midnight* — *Orion at 3 a.m.* — **West**

South

ORION IN THE NORTHERN SKY

SIGNPOST IN THE SKY
When it is visible, Orion is a useful guide to directions in the sky. People in the southern hemisphere see it one way up while those in the northern hemisphere see it the other way around.

ORION IN THE SOUTHERN SKY

ORION IN SOUTHERN SKIES

In the southern hemisphere, Orion is also visible in November to March. Earth's rotation makes it appear to rise in the east and move across the sky, to reach its highest point when due north, and to set in the west. It appears to move right to left: the opposite to the motion seen in the northern hemisphere.

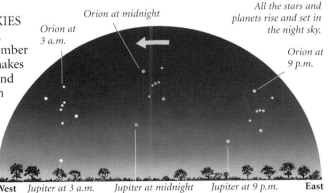

Orion at midnight
Orion at 3 a.m.
All the stars and planets rise and set in the night sky.
Orion at 9 p.m.

West — *Jupiter at 3 a.m.* — *Jupiter at midnight* — *Jupiter at 9 p.m.* — **East**

North

FINDING THE PLANETS
The planets, such as Saturn, can always be found close to the ecliptic – the Sun's path through the sky. If a bright star is not on a star map, it is probably a planet. Use the table to work out which one it is, remembering that Venus is visible only in the evening western sky and in the morning eastern sky.

SATURN IN THE NIGHT SKY

WHEN TO FIND THE PLANETS

Year	Planet	Month	Where to look
2000	Venus	Jan-March	Morning sky
		Oct-Dec	Evening sky
	Mars	Jan-April	Aquarius-Pisces
		Oct-Dec	Leo-Virgo
	Jupiter	Jan-April	Pisces-Aries
		July-Dec	Taurus
	Saturn	Jan-April	Aries
		July-Dec	Taurus
2001	Venus	Jan-March	Evening sky
		May-Nov	Morning sky
	Mars	Jan-Feb	Virgo-Libra
		Mar-Sept	Scorpius-Ophiuchus
		Oct-Dec	Sagittarius-Capricornus
	Jupiter	Jan-May	Taurus
		Aug-Dec	Gemini
	Saturn	Jan-May	Taurus
		July-Dec	Taurus
2002	Venus	April-Oct	Evening sky
		Dec	Morning sky
	Mars	Jan-Feb	Aquarius-Pisces
		Mar-May	Aries-Taurus
		Nov-Dec	Virgo-Libra
	Jupiter	Jan-June	Gemini
		Sept-Dec	Cancer-Leo
	Saturn	Jan-May	Taurus
		July-Dec	Taurus
2003	Venus	Jan-March	Morning sky
		Dec	Evening sky
	Mars	Jan-Feb	Libra-Ophiuchus
		Mar-May	Sagittarius-Capricornus
		June-Dec	Aquarius
	Jupiter	Jan-July	Cancer-Leo
		Sept-Dec	Leo
	Saturn	Jan-July	Taurus
		Aug-Dec	Gemini
2004	Venus	Jan-May	Evening sky
		July-Dec	Morning sky
	Mars	Jan-March	Pisces-Aries
		April-June	Taurus-Gemini
	Jupiter	Jan-Aug	Leo
		Oct-Dec	Virgo
	Saturn	Jan-June	Gemini
		Aug-Dec	Gemini
2005	Venus	July-Dec	Evening sky
	Mars	Jan-March	Scorpius-Sagittarius
		April-June	Capricornus-Aquarius
		July-Dec	Pisces-Aries
	Jupiter	Jan-Sept	Virgo
		Nov-Dec	Virgo-Libra
	Saturn	Jan-June	Gemini
		Aug-Dec	Cancer

FIND OUT MORE

SPINNING EARTH 242
MAPPING THE NIGHT SKY 250
STAR MAPS 252–261

MAPPING THE NIGHT SKY

STAR MAPS ARE USEFUL TO astronomers in much the same way that Earth maps are helpful to travellers on Earth. The sky even has a grid system, just like latitude and longitude on Earth, for measuring the positions of stars. There is, however, a way of getting to know the sky that has been in use for thousands of years, and that is to learn the constellations, or star patterns. Knowing where these groups of stars are will help turn the sky from a mass of stars into familiar ground.

CELESTIAL SPHERE

The stars stretch away in all directions, but for learning about the sky it is helpful to think of them as being on the inside of a great sphere, known as the celestial sphere, surrounding Earth. The celestial sphere has a north and south pole and an equator that are always above their counterparts on Earth. The sphere can also have grid lines, which are used to help astronomers plot the positions of the stars.

90°N latitude (North Pole)　　*45°N latitude (Mid-Europe)*

0° latitude (Equator)

45°S latitude (New Zealand)　　*90°S latitude (South Pole)*

STARS AT DIFFERENT LATITUDES
As Earth turns, the sky appears to move the opposite way. Except at the Poles, the stars rise and set at an angle that depends on the latitude of the observer. From the Equator, all of the sky is visible at one time or another, but at other latitudes part of it is always hidden.

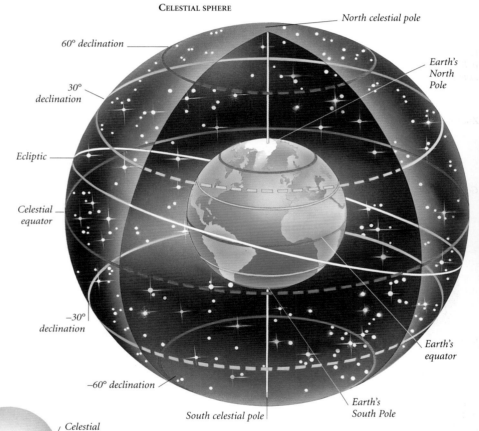

CELESTIAL SPHERE

North celestial pole

60° declination

30° declination

Ecliptic

Celestial equator

Earth's North Pole

−30° declination

−60° declination

Earth's equator

South celestial pole

Earth's South Pole

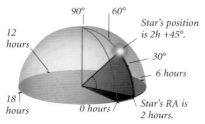

90°　60°

12 hours

Star's position is 2h +45°.

30°

6 hours

18 hours　*0 hours*

Star's RA is 2 hours.

CELESTIAL COORDINATES
Latitude in the sky is called declination (plus north of the equator and minus south of it). Its longitude is called right ascension (RA), and is measured in hours, minutes, and seconds.

Earth

Celestial equator

Ecliptic

ECLIPTIC
The Sun moves along a path in the sky known as the ecliptic. This path is inclined at an angle of 23° to the celestial equator. The paths of the Moon and planets lie close to the ecliptic.

STAR MAPS
The celestial sphere stretches in a curve all around us, but a map is flat. Plotting a curved surface on a flat map can mean that some star patterns become distorted. To keep this to a minimum, the sky is divided into pieces – somewhat like peeling an orange and pressing the individual segments flat.

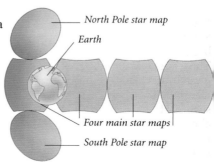

North Pole star map

Earth

Four main star maps

South Pole star map

CONSTELLATIONS

A distinctive pattern of stars is known as a constellation, and the entire sky is divided into 88 such groups. There is usually no real link between the individual stars of a pattern. In Cassiopeia, for instance, the five main stars are all at different distances, and none is near each other. The lines on star maps joining stars together are simply there to help the observer see the patterns.

CASSIOPEIA

TRUE POSITION OF STARS IN CASSIOPEIA

Gamma Cassiopeiae 615 light years

Epsilon Cassiopeiae 440 light years

Caph (beta Cassiopeiae) 54 light years

Schedar (alpha Cassiopeiae) 230 light years

Distances given for individual stars are distances from the Sun.

Ruchbah (delta Cassiopeiae) 100 light years

STARS IN A CONSTELLATION

The main stars of a constellation may have names, but they are also given Greek letters, starting with alpha for the brightest, through beta to omega for the fainter stars. When identifying an individual star, the name of the constellation is altered for reasons of grammar – alpha Cassiopeiae means "alpha of Cassiopeia".

The W shape of Cassiopeia as seen in the sky

ZODIAC CIRCLE

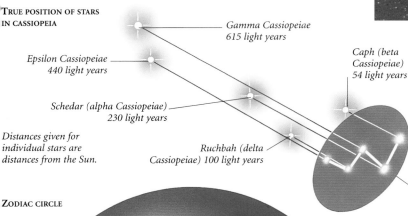

Taurus *Aries* *Pisces*

Gemini *Aquarius*

Cancer *Capricornus*

Leo *Sagittarius*

Virgo

Libra *Scorpius*

The Moon and several planets can move some distance on either side of the ecliptic.

ZODIAC

The constellations along the ecliptic are host to the Sun, Moon, and planets, and were regarded as special in ancient times. They are known as the zodiac, a name that comes from the Greek word for animals – most of the constellations are named after animals. Traditionally, there are 12 constellations in the zodiac.

As Earth orbits the Sun, the Sun appears to move through the constellations of the zodiac in turn.

VIEWING CONSTELLATIONS

Name	When	Where
Aries	November	90°N–60°S
Taurus	December	90°N–60°S
Gemini	January	90°N–60°S
Cancer	February	90°N–60°S
Leo	April	80°N–80°S
Virgo	May	80°N–90°S
Libra	June	70°N–90°S
Scorpius	July	50°N–90°S
Sagittarius	July	50°N–90°S
Capricornus	September	60°N–90°S
Aquarius	October	60°N–80°S
Pisces	November	90°N–60°S
Orion	January	70°N–80°S
Crux	April	25°N–90°S
Ursa Major	April	90°N–25°S
Centaurus	April	25°N–90°S

NAMING CONSTELLATIONS

Some constellation names date back for thousands of years. Those used today were mostly given by Greek astronomers and refer to mythological figures, such as Hercules, but there are also some practical modern names, particularly in the southern hemisphere.

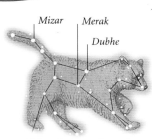

Mizar *Merak*

Dubhe

Ursa Major, the Great Bear, shows an unusual bear with a long tail, and also includes the well-known Plough pattern. The patterns of constellations rarely look much like their namesakes.

Alpha Centauri

Hadar

Centaurus is the creature from Greek myths who was half-man, half-horse. The constellation includes two bright stars, alpha Centauri and Hadar. Of all bright stars, alpha Centauri is the closest to Earth.

FIND OUT MORE

SPINNING EARTH 242
EARTH'S ORBIT 244
STAR MAPS 252–261

POLAR STAR MAPS

THESE MAPS SHOW STARS VISIBLE ALL YEAR in the northern and southern hemispheres. They also mark the position of interesting objects, such as star clusters and galaxies. To see what is visible, face north in the northern hemisphere and south in the southern, turning the map so that the observing month is at the top. This will show the sky at 10 p.m. (11 p.m. in summer time). If it is earlier, for each hour before 10 p.m., turn the map 1 hour clockwise in the northern hemisphere and anticlockwise in the southern.

NORTH POLAR HIGHLIGHTS
The seven main stars of Ursa Major make an easily recognized pattern, called the Plough. The stars Merak and Dubhe point towards Polaris, the Pole Star, which is in almost exactly the same position every night. Opposite the Plough from Polaris is the W-shape of Cassiopeia, with the stars of Perseus to one side. Between the two lies the beautiful Double Cluster.

The bright star Capella in Auriga consists of two yellow giant stars. They are so close together they appear as one.

Declination, the celestial equivalent of latitude on Earth, is shown by the circular grid lines. It is measured in degrees.

Right ascension (RA), the celestial equivalent of longitude on Earth, is shown by the straight grid lines coming from the centre. The sky has 24 hours of RA.

Two open star clusters, visible to the naked eye, make up the Double Cluster.

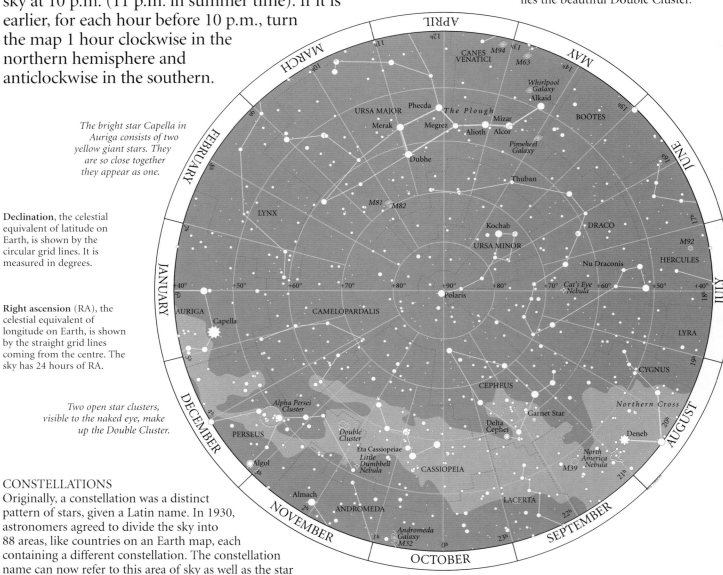

NORTH POLAR MAP

CONSTELLATIONS
Originally, a constellation was a distinct pattern of stars, given a Latin name. In 1930, astronomers agreed to divide the sky into 88 areas, like countries on an Earth map, each containing a different constellation. The constellation name can now refer to this area of sky as well as the star pattern it contains.

CIRCUMPOLAR STARS
Stars that never rise and set are called circumpolar. Even though they are always visible, their position in the sky is constantly changing – as the Earth rotates (by 15° each hour), the stars appear to move across the sky by the same amount. The circumpolar area of sky varies according to distance from the Equator. At the Poles, all stars are circumpolar; at the Equator, they all rise and set.

KEY TO THE STAR MAPS	
Magnitudes	⊙ Open cluster
-1 0 1 2 3 4 5 6	○ Globular cluster
Double stars	◻ Bright nebula
Milky Way	✛ Planetary nebula
Variable stars	☐ Supernova remnant
Constellation outline Constellation boundary	◉ Galaxy

SOUTH POLAR HIGHLIGHTS

The best-known feature of the southern sky is the Southern Cross, which is made up from the five brightest stars of Crux. Follow a line from Gacrux through Acrux to locate the south celestial pole, which is at the centre of the map. Two bright stars, alpha Centauri and Hadar, point towards the Southern Cross.

LOCATER

North polar map

South polar map

Crux is the smallest constellation in the sky but is one of the best known. Its main stars are on the flags of Australia and New Zealand.

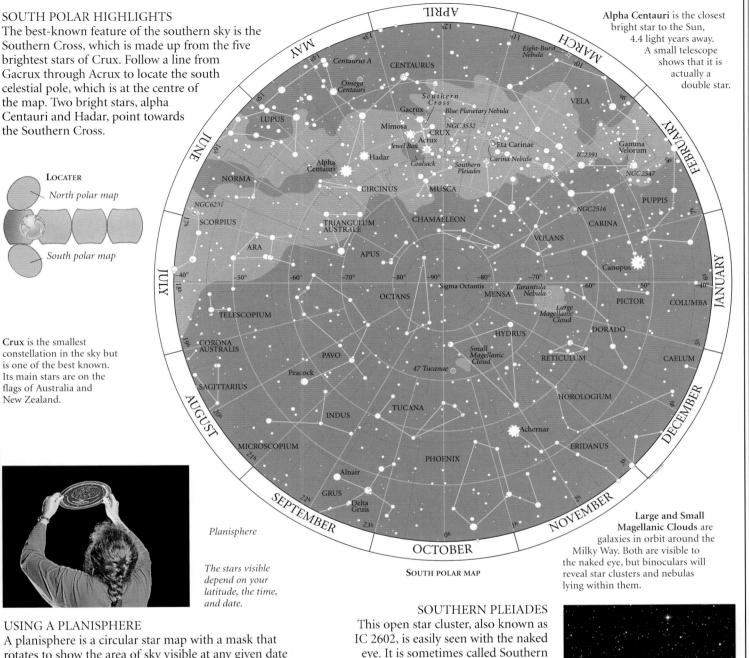

Planisphere

The stars visible depend on your latitude, the time, and date.

SOUTH POLAR MAP

Alpha Centauri is the closest bright star to the Sun, 4.4 light years away. A small telescope shows that it is actually a double star.

Large and Small Magellanic Clouds are galaxies in orbit around the Milky Way. Both are visible to the naked eye, but binoculars will reveal star clusters and nebulas lying within them.

USING A PLANISPHERE

A planisphere is a circular star map with a mask that rotates to show the area of sky visible at any given date or time. Held upside down over the head, it shows which stars will be visible at that moment. Planispheres are designed to work at specific latitudes, so find out your latitude before buying one.

SOUTHERN PLEIADES

This open star cluster, also known as IC 2602, is easily seen with the naked eye. It is sometimes called Southern Pleiades because of its similarity to the Pleiades cluster. It contains about 30 stars, eight of which are brighter than magnitude 6.

SCALE IN THE SKY

Hands are useful for measuring distances in the sky, and for comparing star maps with the real sky. A full circle, with you at the centre, is 360°. A finger at arm's length covers about 1° – twice the size of the Moon. A closed hand is about 10°, the width of the bowl of the Plough, while an open hand is the same width as the Square of Pegasus (16° to 20°).

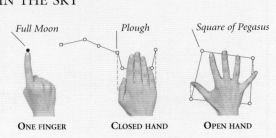

Full Moon *Plough* *Square of Pegasus*

ONE FINGER **CLOSED HAND** **OPEN HAND**

NORTHERN HEMISPHERE STAR MAPS JUNE TO NOVEMBER

The northern hemisphere maps show the stars with the observer facing south. Choose the map with the month in which you are observing. This will show the night sky as it appears at 10 p.m. (11 p.m. if summer time), with stars farther to the west visible earlier and those farther to the east visible later. The stars near the bottom of the map will be visible on the southern horizon, and those at the top will be almost overhead. The sky is shown for latitude 45° north: stars towards the bottom of the map will not be visible in more northerly latitudes.

The maps are designed to overlap. Stars at the edges are repeated on the next map. Stars at the top also appear on the outer edge of the north polar map, and those along the bottom on the south polar map. If joined together, they would form one continuous map.

Right ascension, the equivalent of longitude on Earth, is labelled in hours along the top and bottom.

Declination, the equivalent of latitude on Earth, is labelled in degrees on both edges.

Andromeda Galaxy is the most distant object usually visible to the naked eye. It is 2.5 million light years away from Earth. Find it by moving northeast from star to star, starting from Alpheratz.

M15 GLOBULAR CLUSTER
This cluster can be seen about 20° to the right of the bottom of the Square of Pegasus. In binoculars M15 looks hazy, but a telescope shows it to be ball-shaped.

KEY ON PAGE 252

SEPTEMBER TO NOVEMBER HIGHLIGHTS
The Square of Pegasus is the key pattern to look for. Its four stars, although not particularly bright are easy to find because there are few other stars around. Use the edges to point to Andromeda, which shares one star with the Square. Alpheratz the top left star of the Square, is actually in Andromeda. The right edge of the Square points down to Fomalhaut, and the diagonal from top left to lower right points to an arrow-shaped pattern of stars, the Water Jar, in Aquarius.

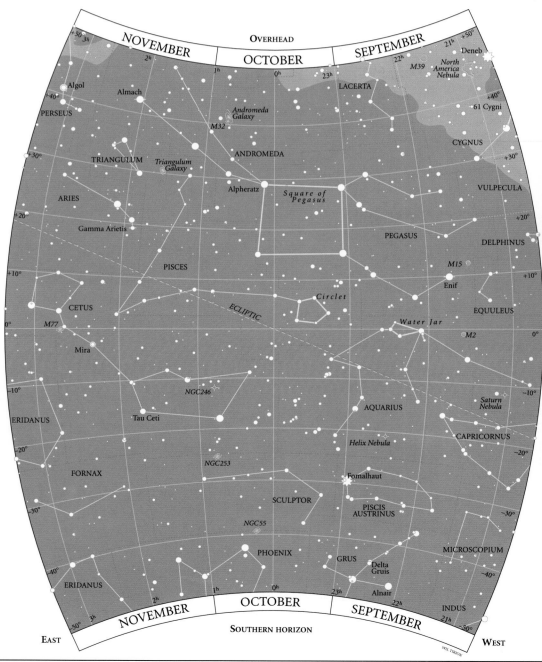

JUNE TO AUGUST HIGHLIGHTS

The Milky Way dominates the view, along with the Summer Triangle of Deneb, Vega, and Altair. Cygnus points along the Galaxy, while the dark band between Cygnus and Serpens, the Cygnus Rift, hides the stars beyond. Look for arrow-shaped Sagitta and Scutum; nearby is a bright patch of the Milky Way. To the south, the distinctive patterns of Scorpius and Sagittarius lie on either side of the Milky Way.

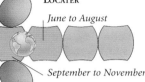

LOCATER

June to August

September to November

Dumbbell Nebula is the remains of a star that died thousands of years ago.

DUMBBELL NEBULA

Below Cygnus lies a small, faint planetary nebula. It is visible through binoculars, although its colours do not show up. In small telescopes its brightest parts look like a dumbbell.

WILD DUCK CLUSTER

This open star cluster, which is at the top of Scutum, is just visible with the naked eye. Binoculars show that it has a V-shape of stars that looks like a flight of ducks – hence its name.

Three bright stars from different constellations – Deneb in Cygnus, Vega in Lyra, and Altair in Aquila – make up the Summer Triangle.

Albireo is a double star that marks the head of Cygnus, the swan. In high-powered binoculars, its two stars have contrasting yellow and blue colours.

Eagle Nebula, just below Serpens Cauda, is visible as a hazy spot of light in binoculars. A medium-sized telescope reveals a dark shape within the nebula, which in photographs looks like an eagle flapping its wings.

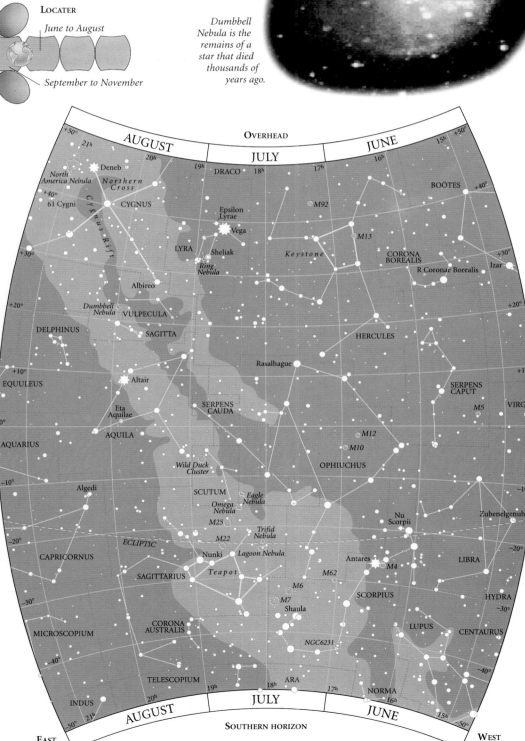

NORTHERN HEMISPHERE STAR MAPS DECEMBER TO MAY

IN WINTER, CONSTELLATIONS and stars are the main attractions because the Milky Way is faint. These include the brightest constellation, Orion, and the brightest star, Sirius. Most of the visible stars are in our own Local Arm of the Galaxy, which also contains several star nurseries that can be seen in close-up, such as the Orion Nebula. Star clusters are also common. By spring, the view shifts to looking sideways out of the Milky Way, and the great galaxy cluster in Virgo is on show.

MARCH TO MAY HIGHLIGHTS

The crouching lion of Leo is easy to spot. A curve of stars marks its head, also known as the Sickle. Following Leo to the southeast is Virgo, which is more difficult to pick out. Between Leo and Virgo is the Virgo Cluster of over 2,000 galaxies, although only a few are visible without a large telescope. Below Virgo is a small constellation, Corvus, with its four distinctive stars. Corvus is easy to find, even though the stars are not very bright.

BLACK EYE GALAXY
A spiral galaxy just below Coma Berenices, the Black Eye Galaxy has a dark dust lane near its centre. Small telescopes just show a little hazy oval of light, but large telescopes make it look like an eye, hence the name.

Arcturus, in Boötes, is a red giant and the fourth brightest star in the sky.

M65 and M66 galaxies are in Leo. They are easy to find as they are quite bright, and lie between two fairly bright stars. With a telescope, the galaxies look like tiny, hazy spindles.

Porrima in Virgo is a double star. From 2005 to 2007, the stars will be so close to each other that even with a telescope they will look like a single star. The next time this occurs will be in 2174.

KEY ON PAGE 252

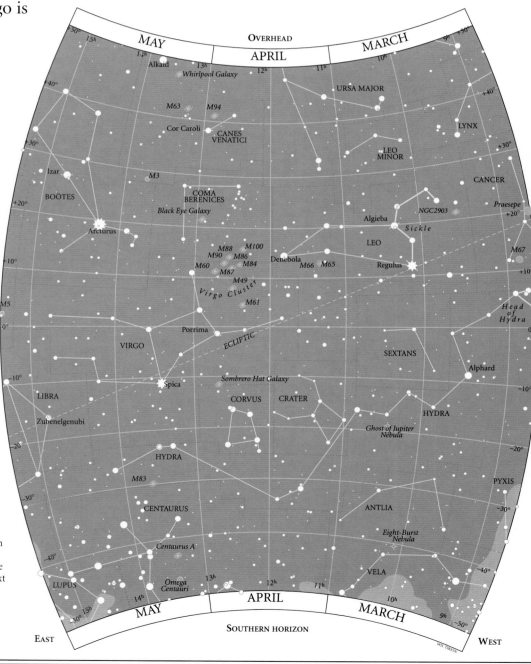

DECEMBER TO FEBRUARY HIGHLIGHTS

Orion the Hunter is the best signpost in the sky. The line of three stars that make up Orion's Belt point up towards Aldebaran in Taurus and, farther on, the Pleiades star cluster. Down, they point to Sirius in Canis Major. Betelgeuse, Sirius, and Procyon (in Canis Minor) are known as the Winter Triangle. A diagonal through Rigel and Betelgeuse leads to Gemini, while directly above Orion is Auriga, with the star clusters, M36 and M38.

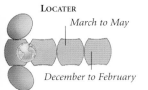

LOCATER

March to May

December to February

M36 is a compact cluster of about 60 stars, while there are about 100 stars scattered across a wider area in M38.

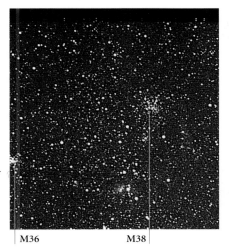

M36   **M38**

M36 AND M38 CLUSTERS

M36 is the brighter of the two open star clusters, both of which are visible with the naked eye. As M36 and M38 appear quite close, they can easily be mistaken for a comet at a casual glance.

PRAESEPE

An open star cluster in Cancer, Praesepe is visible with the naked eye on clear and dark nights. With binoculars, it is a splendid sight.

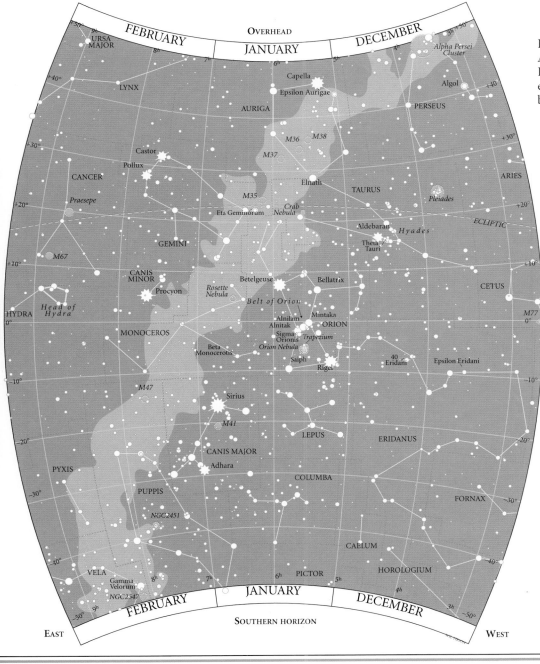

M35 CLUSTER

An open star cluster to the north of eta Geminorum, M35 is just visible with the naked eye. It is easy to spot with binoculars, which will show some of the brightest individual stars. The cluster contains about 120 stars.

Orion Nebula is the brightest nebula in the sky. It appears as a misty patch with the naked eye, but small telescopes show a group of four stars, the Trapezium, at its centre.

SOUTHERN HEMISPHERE STAR MAPS SEPTEMBER TO FEBRUARY

THE SOUTHERN HEMISPHERE MAPS show the stars when viewed looking north. Choose the map with the month in which you are observing. This will show the night sky as it appears at 10 p.m. (11 p.m. in summer time), with stars farther to the west visible earlier and those farther to the east later. Stars near the bottom of the map will be visible on the northern horizon, and those at the top will be almost overhead. The sky is shown for latitude 45° south: closer to the Equator, some stars from the north polar map will be visible on the northern horizon.

SEPTEMBER TO NOVEMBER HIGHLIGHTS

The brightest star in this part of the sky is Fomalhaut in Piscis Austrinus, the southern fish. The Square of Pegasus is in the northern sky. Use the edges and diagonals of the Square to locate Andromeda, Aquarius, Pisces, and Cetus. The constellation Pisces is occasionally enlivened by the appearance of a planet, although its stars are all faint.

The maps have been designed to overlap. Stars at the edges are repeated on the next map. Stars at the top also appear on the outer edge of the south polar map, and those along the bottom on the north polar map. If joined together, they would form one continuous map.

Right ascension, the equivalent of longitude on Earth, is labelled in hours along the top and bottom.

Declination, the equivalent of latitude, is labelled in degrees on both edges.

HELIX NEBULA

The largest, and closest, planetary nebula is the Helix Nebula in Aquarius. It can be seen in a very dark sky, using binoculars or a telescope. The red colour shows only in photographs.

Triangulum Galaxy, a misty patch about the size of the full Moon in the sky, can be seen with binoculars on a dark night. It is slightly farther away than the Andromeda Galaxy, which is to the northeast.

KEY ON PAGE 252

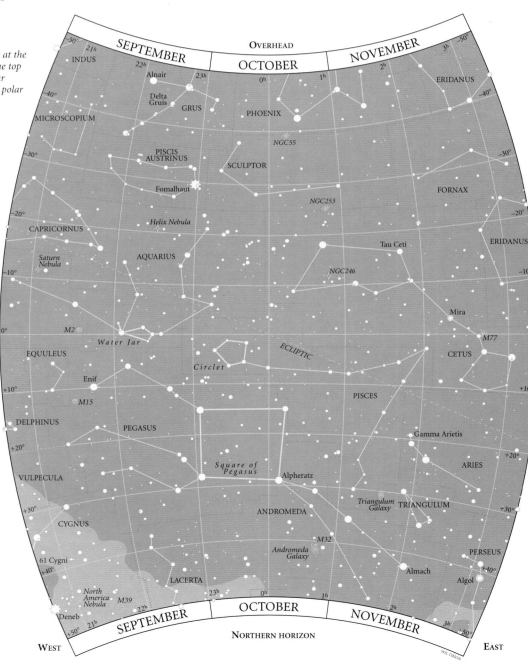

DECEMBER TO FEBRUARY HIGHLIGHTS

Orion acts as a signpost to many other constellations. The three stars of Orion's Belt point northeast to Sirius and Canis Major, and southwest towards Aldebaran in Taurus. Near Aldebaran is a V-shaped cluster of stars called the Hyades. The Pleiades, a little to the west, attracts the eye because there are few very bright stars near it.

M41 is about 2,300 light years away, and contains about 100 stars.

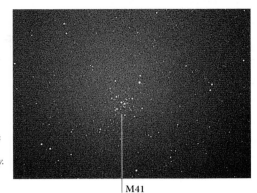

M41 CLUSTER

To the south of Sirius lies M41, an open star cluster just visible with the naked eye. Binoculars show that many of the stars seem to form chains. This is probably because, by chance, some stars lie almost along the same line of sight as more distant stars.

LOCATER

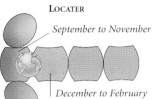

September to November

December to February

The Ancient Greeks observed M41, which is about the same size as the full Moon in the sky.

M41

Sirius is the brightest star in the sky and, at 8.6 light years away, one of the nearest. It is sometimes called the Dog Star because it is in the constellation of Canis Major, the great dog.

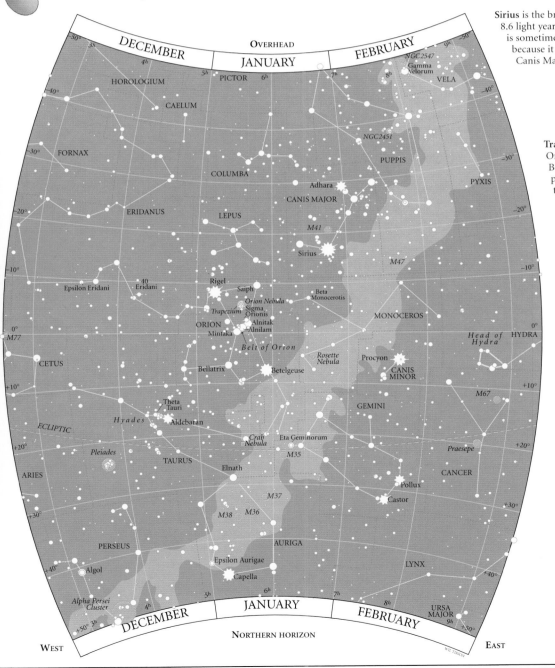

Trapezium is a multiple star in the Orion Nebula, just south of Orion's Belt. The nebula is visible as a misty patch with the naked eye. A telescope shows four stars in the shape of a trapezium that were recently born and are now illuminating the nebula.

Betelgeuse is a noticeable orange, while the other stars of Orion are mostly bluish. It is a red giant star, and varies slightly and unpredictably in brightness.

Crab Nebula in Taurus gets its name from its claw-like extensions. It is the remains of a brilliant supernova that appeared in 1054. Now all that can be seen with a telescope is a hazy blur.

FIND OUT MORE

SOUTHERN HEMISPHERE STAR MAPS MARCH TO AUGUST

IN THE EARLY PART OF THE YEAR the sky is rich in galaxies. The great Virgo Cluster of galaxies lies at right angles to the line of the Milky Way, so there is no dust from our own Galaxy to obscure the view. During May, the star clouds of the Milky Way start to appear low in the east, and then arch overhead in winter. Nebulas and star clusters are dotted along the Milky Way, many of them visible with binoculars.

MARCH TO MAY HIGHLIGHTS
There are three bright stars in this part of the sky – Arcturus in Boötes, Regulus in Leo, and Spica in Virgo. There are about 2,000 galaxies in Virgo, but only a few are visible in small telescopes, and even these can be hard to find because there are so few stars nearby to act as markers. The stars are so sparse at this time of the year that Alphard in Hydra was named "the solitary one" by the Arabs.

The centre of the hat is stars concentrated in the middle of the galaxy, and the rim is its spiral arm.

SOMBRERO HAT GALAXY
A spiral galaxy in Virgo, the Sombrero Hat Galaxy looks like a broad-brimmed Mexican hat in photographs. The dark line visible in a telescope is a dust lane, like the Cygnus Rift in the Milky Way.

M83 in Hydra is a spiral galaxy, which appears in small telescopes as a round hazy blur. With large telescopes, the spiral arms become visible.

M87, an elliptical galaxy, is near the centre of the Virgo Cluster. It is one of the largest galaxies known, but is not very spectacular in small telescopes as it lies 50 million light years away. It looks like a circular hazy spot, brighter in the middle.

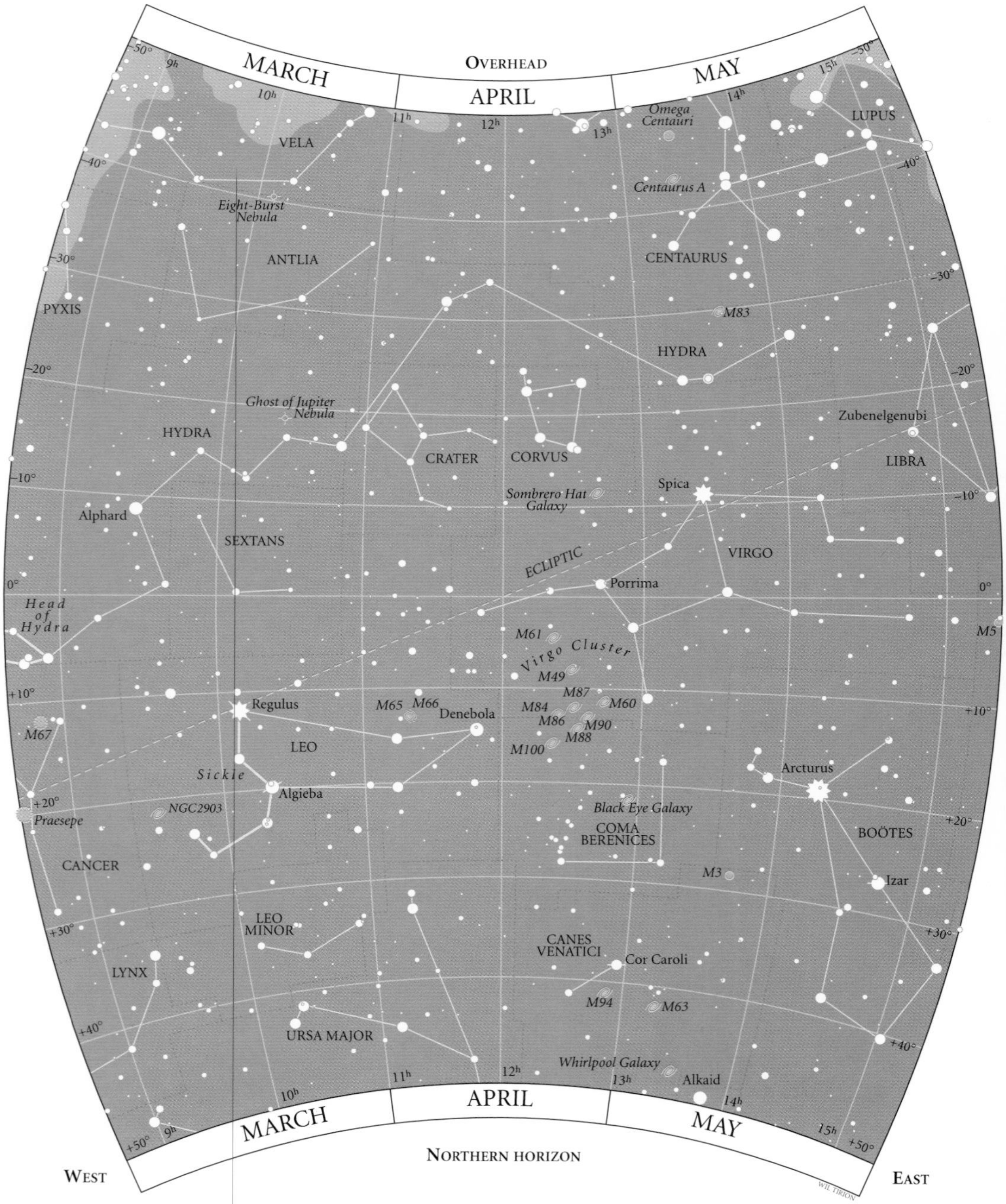

KEY ON PAGE 252

Star map labels:
MARCH OVERHEAD APRIL MAY
9h 10h 11h 12h 13h 14h 15h
VELA
Eight-Burst Nebula
ANTLIA
PYXIS
Ghost of Jupiter Nebula
HYDRA
CRATER CORVUS
Sombrero Hat Galaxy
ECLIPTIC
Porrima
VIRGO
Spica
SEXTANS
Alphard
Head of Hydra
M61
Virgo Cluster
M49
M65 M66 Denebola
M84 M87 M60
M86 M90
M88
M100
Regulus
LEO
Sickle
Algieba
NGC2903
Praesepe
CANCER
LEO MINOR
LYNX
URSA MAJOR
Omega Centauri
LUPUS
Centaurus A
CENTAURUS
M83
HYDRA
Zubenelgenubi
LIBRA
M5
Arcturus
Black Eye Galaxy
COMA BERENICES
M3
BOÖTES
Izar
CANES VENATICI
Cor Caroli
M94 M63
Whirlpool Galaxy
Alkaid
MARCH APRIL MAY
10h 11h 12h 13h 14h 15h
NORTHERN HORIZON
WEST EAST

JUNE TO AUGUST HIGHLIGHTS

The centre of the Milky Way lies in the direction of Sagittarius, but huge dust clouds block our view of it. Some of the stars of Sagittarius make a teapot shape – a bright part of the Milky Way looks like a wisp of steam coming from its spout. To the west of Sagittarius is Scorpius, with red Antares at the scorpion's heart and a curve of stars marking its tail. Many star explosions – novas and supernovas – have also been seen in these regions.

LOCATER

March to May

June to August

LAGOON NEBULA

One of the brightest nebulas in the Milky Way, the Lagoon Nebula is visible to the naked eye. It gets its name because telescopes show a curved dark area within it that looks like a desert island lagoon.

Lagoon Nebula, in the eastern part of Sagittarius, is 5,200 light years away.

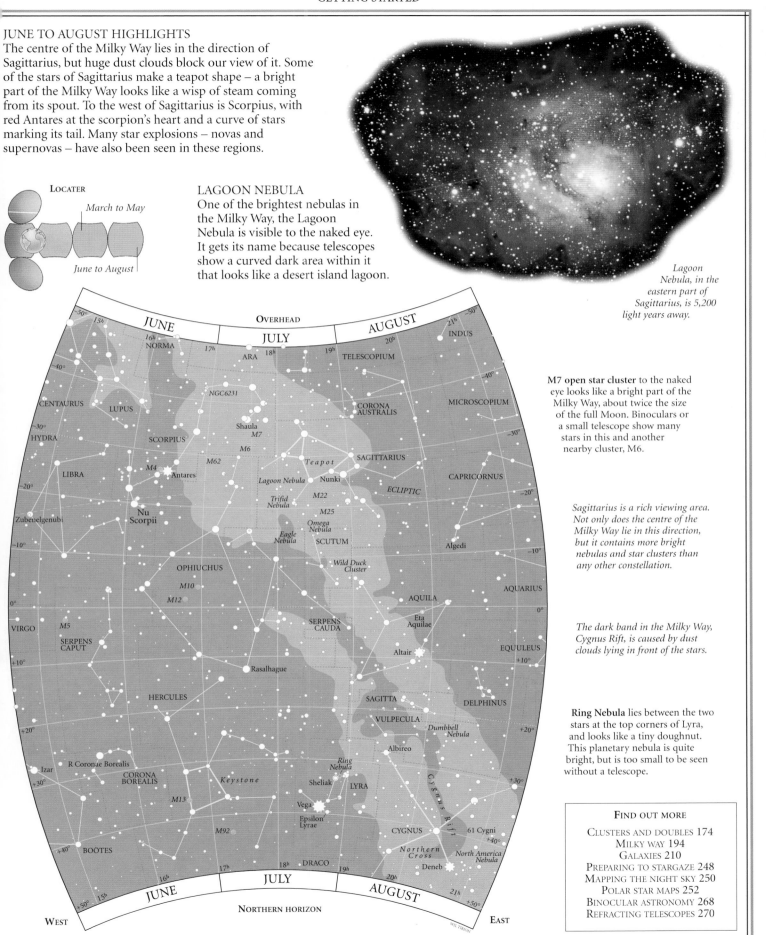

M7 open star cluster to the naked eye looks like a bright part of the Milky Way, about twice the size of the full Moon. Binoculars or a small telescope show many stars in this and another nearby cluster, M6.

Sagittarius is a rich viewing area. Not only does the centre of the Milky Way lie in this direction, but it contains more bright nebulas and star clusters than any other constellation.

The dark band in the Milky Way, Cygnus Rift, is caused by dust clouds lying in front of the stars.

Ring Nebula lies between the two stars at the top corners of Lyra, and looks like a tiny doughnut. This planetary nebula is quite bright, but is too small to be seen without a telescope.

ASTRONOMY UNAIDED

ONE OF THE PLEASURES in astronomy is simply looking up at the night sky with the naked eye. All that is needed is enthusiasm, patience, and the ability to identify the various celestial objects that can be seen there, both natural and artificial. In addition to the Moon, stars, and planets, there are other objects that appear briefly or occasionally and can be easily recognized. The important thing is to practise looking at them and record exactly what is visible. Experienced observers often see more than those who are just beginning.

CROWDED SKY

Most objects in the sky, including stars and planets, are recognizable by their appearance and movement, once you know what to look for. Study each new visible object carefully for telltale signs, such as changes of direction and speed, that will help with identification. Aircraft are common sights in many night skies, and are easy to distinguish from other objects. Listen for their sound to be certain of identification, but remember that the wind can carry sound away, and that the noise from a fast-moving plane often seems to come from far behind it.

Stars and planets rise and set slowly, and remain in almost the same position every night.

Aircraft have red and green wing lights, plus a white light in the centre, and move quickly across the sky.

Meteors are short streaks of light lasting a fraction of a second.

Lasers and searchlights can be seen for many kilometres. They can also reflect off thin cloud, as fast-moving spots of light.

Moon is seen in different positions from night to night.

Con-trails are trails left by aircraft, which catch the Sun after sunset. They may be slow moving if the plane is distant.

METEOR NEAR SIRIUS

METEOR WATCHING
Amateur observation of meteors makes an important contribution to astronomy. Individual watchers scan the sky for at least an hour, noting the time and direction from which the meteors appear. National and international organizations combine results to build an accurate picture of how meteor particles are distributed in space.

MILKY WAY
One of the most glorious sights visible to the naked eye is the Milky Way on a clear, dark night, well away from city lights. In the northern hemisphere, the area that runs through Sagittarius and Scorpius is spectacular. In the southern hemisphere, the stretch through Centaurus, Carina, and Vela has many bright stars.

MILKY WAY IN APRIL

MILKY WAY IN SEPTEMBER

Northern hemisphere: Milky Way is prominent in September, when Cygnus is overhead. In April only the faint Orion-Taurus area low in the west is visible.

Aircraft landing lights are bright and can reflect off thin cloud. They appear almost motionless for many minutes if the plane is approaching.

Bright comets are rare. When they do appear, they remain visible for a few days or weeks, staying in almost the same place from night to night.

Large satellites, such as the Space Shuttles, are brighter than most stars. They take a few minutes to cross the sky on a straight track.

Faint satellites may take 10 minutes or more to cross the sky, depending on their height.

Iridium (mobile phone) satellites have mirrored panels and flash brilliantly if sunlight catches them.

Venus can often be seen low at twilight. It rises and sets with the stars.

MOON WATCHING
Follow the Moon through its phases, starting with the crescent. As the month progresses, more and more details become visible. Make drawings of what can be seen, then identify the details using a Moon map.

NEARLY FULL MOON

WAXING CRESCENT MOON

HOW FAINT CAN YOU SEE?
The magnitude of the faintest star visible on a particular night is the limiting magnitude. This varies depending on whether it is misty or clear, a full or new Moon, and on the amount of light pollution. To estimate the limiting magnitude, use one of the maps below, go outside, and find the faintest star visible in the area shown.

The keys below give the magnitude of stars shown. Find the faintest visible to get limiting magnitude.

MAGNITUDE KEY	
A = 3.8	E = 5.3
B = 4.0	F = 5.9
C = 4.2	G = 6.2
D = 4.7	

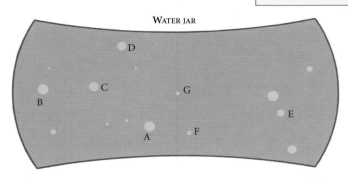

WATER JAR

July-December skies include the distinct pattern of stars in Aquarius known as the Water Jar. Locate the Water Jar in the sky between the Square of Pegasus and Fomalhaut (see maps on pages 254 and 258).

MAGNITUDE KEY	
A = 3.4	E = 5.4
B = 4.2	F = 6.0
C = 4.3	G = 6.2
D = 4.4	

HEAD OF HYDRA

January-June skies include the pattern of stars within Hydra known as the Head of Hydra. Locate Head of Hydra near Regulus in Leo (see maps on pages 256 and 260) and find the faintest star shown here that you can see. When observing, look slightly to one side of its position because the edge of the eye's field of view is more sensitive than the centre.

MILKY WAY IN JULY

MILKY WAY IN NOVEMBER

Southern hemisphere: July evenings are best, with the brightest parts of the Milky Way in Sagittarius and Scorpius overhead. By November, the Galaxy is quite hard to see.

FIND OUT MORE
NEARSIDE OF THE MOON 100
COMETS 142 • METEORS 144
MILKY WAY 194
STAR MAPS 252–261

AURORAS AND HALOES

Some of the most beautiful and colourful sights in the sky are glows and lights that may appear only rarely. Many of them, such as auroras, are produced in the Earth's atmosphere and are linked to astronomical objects like the Sun. Others, such as the zodiacal light, occur farther out in space. All these sights can be appreciated for themselves, but it is also useful for astronomers to be able to recognize them so that they can avoid confusing things happening in our own atmosphere with real astronomical events in space.

RAY

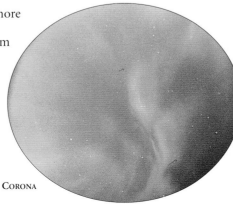

CORONA

AURORA

RAYS AND CORONAS
Auroras often appear as one or more rays of light, which look like searchlight beams shining up from the northern horizon in the northern hemisphere (or southern in the southern hemisphere). Occasionally, a large aurora can be seen overhead, with coloured rays appearing to stream down from high in the sky. This is known as a corona.

AURORAS
Coloured glows called auroras are common around the Earth's polar regions. They are caused by streams of particles from the Sun that are attracted by the magnetic poles – as the particles hit the Earth's upper atmosphere they cause atoms of gas to glow. Auroras can look like huge curtains hanging in the sky, slowly changing shape. Sometimes they are seen over a much wider area, particularly when sunspot activity is high.

Sun halo is visible as a huge circle surrounding the Sun. It sometimes has other arcs of light branching off.

SUNSET SKY SIGHTS

As sunlight passes through air, blue light is scattered in all directions, while yellow and red light pass through. This effect is exaggerated at sunrise or sunset when the Sun is low in the sky and its light passes through more of Earth's atmosphere. Sun pillars and sun dogs are caused by the Sun shining through layers of ice crystals in clouds.

Sun dogs occur when there is thin, high cloud. Bright, multicoloured patches appear either side of the Sun.

Sunset colours are mainly yellow, orange, and red as other colours are absorbed as they travel through the air.

DAYTIME SKY SIGHTS

Rainbow effects can be seen during the day even when there is no rain – in sun haloes, for example. Sun haloes can occur when there is a layer of thin, high cloud in the sky. High clouds are usually made up of ice crystals, even on hot days, because the air temperature at high altitudes is below freezing. As sunlight shines through the crystals, it splits into colours in the same way as sunlight shining on rain does.

Sun pillars occur when the Sun is near the horizon. Its light reflects off layers of ice crystals in clouds, forming a pillar above it.

Lunar halo is visible as a ring surrounding the Moon.

NOCTILUCENT CLOUDS

Noctilucent clouds are seen at latitudes above 50° looking towards the Poles in summer when the Sun is just below the horizon. They are made of ice crystals growing on dust from meteors and form so high up – 80 km – that they are visible at night.

Crepuscular rays occur in late twilight. They are caused by the Sun shining through gaps in clouds below the horizon.

NIGHT SKY SIGHTS

Lunar haloes, like Sun haloes, are caused by ice crystals in the atmosphere. Other kinds of glow originate beyond Earth, such as the zodiacal light. This is a faint cone of glowing light that extends along the ecliptic (the path of the Sun), caused by sunlight reflecting off dust particles in the Solar System.

Zodiacal light is sometimes seen in very clear skies for a short time after sunset in spring and before sunrise in autumn.

FIND OUT MORE

EARTH'S ATMOSPHERE 88
MOON 92
SUN'S SURFACE 156
SUN'S ATMOSPHERE 158
DAYTIME ASTRONOMY 246

PHOTOGRAPHING THE NIGHT SKY

PHOTOGRAPHY HAS BEEN IMPORTANT to astronomers ever since it was invented. Modern technology makes it easier than ever to take good colour pictures of the night sky. Photos can even show more detail than may be seen by the naked eye. This is because the camera's shutter can be left open for several minutes, allowing the film to collect more light and, therefore, more information. Fortunately, equipment need not be expensive, particularly if the camera is bought secondhand, and it is not necessary to use a telescope to take interesting photographs. The skill comes in knowing which film speed to use for which type of photograph, and how long the exposure should be.

Camera tripod holds the camera steady while a photograph is being taken. It also points the camera in the chosen direction during an exposure.

Cable release operates the shutter remotely. The flexible cable has a locking device that keeps the shutter open for a long time without the need to touch the camera.

CHOOSING A CAMERA

Single-lens reflex (SLR) cameras are the most useful cameras for photographing the night sky. The B setting is essential, because it allows the shutter to be kept open for long exposures of the film. The shutter should be mechanical: an electronically controlled one will drain the battery during long exposures. Avoid compact and digital cameras, which have a maximum exposure time of a fraction of a second – not long enough to record many astronomical objects.

Shutter button

Shutter speed control allows exposure times from 1/1000 second to 1 second, plus B setting for long exposures.

SLR CAMERA

Viewfinder looks through camera lens and shows image to be photographed.

Film rewind handle

Lens barrel

Aperture setting controls the light entering the camera.

Focusing ring alters focus position from nearby to infinity.

FILM SPEEDS (ISO)		
Subject	Speed	Exposure time
Camera on a fixed tripod		
Auroras	200–1600	10–60 seconds
Bright comets	400–1600	10–20 seconds
Constellations	400–1600	10 seconds
Meteors	200–1600	5–20 minutes
Moon close-ups	200–400	1/60 second
Star trails	50–200	5–60 minutes
Twilight sky	50–200	10–20 seconds
Motor-driven camera		
Comets and nebulas	200–1600	3–60 minutes
Constellations	50–1600	3–60 minutes
Milky Way	400–1600	3–5 minutes

USING A CAMERA

When taking sky photographs, set the focus on infinity and the aperture setting at its widest (the smallest number on the lens barrel, about 2.8 or 2.0). The sensitivity to light of a film is called its speed and is measured by an ISO rating. Slow films, rated about ISO 100, are less sensitive but give good colour and contrast; fast films (ISO 400–1600) are more sensitive but produce grainier pictures with less accurate colour.

FILM SPEED

Slow film is best for taking photographs at twilight that include the Moon or bright planets. Individual stars are too faint to be shown as points of light with slow film, but if the exposure is increased the Earth's rotation draws their images out into star trails. With fast film, it is possible to photograph stars with a short exposure time.

Moon and planets at twilight need an exposure time of 10–20 seconds at the widest aperture on slow film. This is enough to show bright planets and stars as points of light. Taking photos at twilight will make a more interesting picture because there will be some foreground detail.

Star trails result from a long exposure (from a few minutes to an hour) on slow or medium film. Fix the camera to a tripod and point it at the celestial pole. The stars will leave a trail of light on the film as the Earth rotates. Keep exposures short if there is light pollution.

Stars down to 6th magnitude will show as points of light, with no trailing, on fast film with a 10-second exposure. This is the best way to photograph the constellations.

USING A TELEPHOTO LENS

A standard camera lens has a focal length of about 50 mm, but telephoto lenses have longer focal lengths – often 135 mm or 200 mm – and give larger images. A camera with a telephoto lens fixed on a tripod is fine for photographing the Moon; it will also show star trails using exposures of only a few seconds. If the camera is attached to a telescope on a motorized equatorial mounting, long exposure times can be used to record faint objects, such as nebulas.

Focusing ring

Extending lens hood helps to reduce risk of dew forming on lens.

Telephoto lens

Heavy lenses are supported near the middle.

SLR camera body

Ball and socket head on tripod allows lens to be pointed in any direction.

Meteors appear suddenly in the sky. The best way to photograph them is to go out during a meteor shower, take long exposures on fast film, and hope that one will appear while the shutter is open.

Bright comets will show on fast film with a 10-second exposure. For fainter comets, stars, and nebulas, use an equatorial mounting which tracks the stars as they move across the sky.

FILM PROCESSING

Prints from colour film are often disappointing because automatic printing machines are not designed to give dark prints – they give a grey background. An operator may be able to override this, so try using a print shop with the machine on the premises, and explain what is needed. Or use slide film, which is not affected in the same way.

MACHINE-MADE PRINT OF STARS

MOON THROUGH TELEPHOTO LENS

The larger craters on the Moon become visible through a telephoto lens with a focal length of 200 mm or greater. The Moon is a sunlit environment, so use the same exposure as for a day scene, even when the surrounding sky is dark, to avoid the Moon appearing washed out.

MOON THROUGH 200-MM LENS

FIND OUT MORE

NEARSIDE OF THE MOON 100
COMETS 142
METEORS 144
SPINNING EARTH 242
MAPPING THE NIGHT SKY 250
STAR MAPS 252–261

BINOCULAR ASTRONOMY

BINOCULARS ARE MUCH more than the poor relations of telescopes. They show things that telescopes are not able to, and can be used to make serious observations. Above all, they are good value and convenient – even astronomers with large telescopes use them regularly. Binoculars are two low-magnification telescopes mounted side by side. For those who prefer to observe with both eyes rather than one, they are more comfortable to use than telescopes, and can give stunning views of the Milky Way, nebulas, and galaxies such as the Large Magellanic Cloud.

CHOOSING BINOCULARS

High magnification (power) binoculars are not needed for astronomy – those with a magnification of more than 10 magnify the user's movements to such a degree they can make viewing more difficult. Binoculars described as 10 x 50 magnify 10 times and have objective (main) lenses of 50 mm. Avoid zoom (variable power) binoculars – they have extra lenses that may cause distortion.

MAGNIFICATION

Binoculars will show stars in regions where none can be seen with the naked eye. This makes them useful even in cities where light pollution hides all but the brightest stars. The magnification of binoculars allows you to see star clusters, such as the Pleiades, in greater detail.

PLEIADES WITH THE NAKED EYE

PLEIADES WITH LOW- POWERED BINOCULARS

PLEIADES WITH HIGH-POWERED BINOCULARS

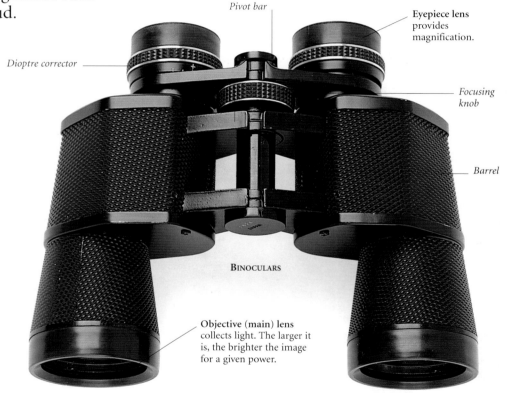

Pivot bar

Dioptre corrector

Eyepiece lens provides magnification.

Focusing knob

Barrel

BINOCULARS

Objective (main) lens collects light. The larger it is, the brighter the image for a given power.

ADJUSTING BINOCULARS

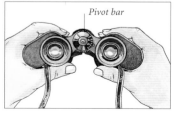

Pivot bar

FIT THE EYEPIECES
Adjust the separation of the eyepieces to match the eyes and note the reading on the scale on the pivot bar.

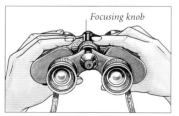

Focusing knob

FOCUS THE LEFT LENS
Choose a distant object and focus on it carefully, using the left side only, by turning the central focusing knob.

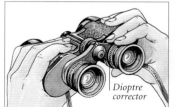

Dioptre corrector

FOCUS THE RIGHT LENS
Focus on the same object with the right side using the dioptre corrector to allow for differences between left and right eye.

TESTING BINOCULARS

It is possible to test binoculars during the day by viewing a distant object, such as a tall building, silhouetted against a bright sky. Adjust the binoculars, then look at the edges of the field of view for distortions and false colour. The more expensive the binoculars, the wider the field of view and the better the brightness. A good tip is to check a chosen model against the most expensive ones available before buying – it should be as close as possible in quality.

Distortion may affect the field of view and make stars near the edge appear blurred. If testing during the day, check that an object remains sharp from one side of the field of view to the other without refocusing.

False colour shows up as red and blue or green and pink edges of objects seen against a bright sky. Bad false colour, which may not appear too serious by day, will be very obvious when observing the Moon at night.

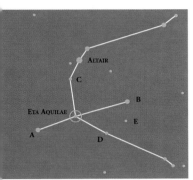

ETA AQUILAE AND NEARBY STARS

MAGNITUDE KEY

A = 3.2
B = 3.4
C = 3.7
D = 4.4
E = 4.5

OBSERVING VARIABLE STARS

Some stars vary in brightness, and many of these can best be observed using binoculars. Practise comparing the brightness of eta Aquilae with that of other stars nearby. Judge whether it is brighter or fainter, and by how much, then estimate its actual brightness using the figures given for the magnitudes of the comparison stars. Remember that brighter stars have lower numbers.

Observations over a week showed that eta Aquilae varied in brightness between 3.5 and 4.4.

WHAT TO LOOK FOR

Object	Type	Location	Best visible
Alpha Persei Cluster	Open cluster	Perseus	December
Andromeda	Galaxy	Andromeda	November
Carina Nebula	Nebula	Carina	April
Double Cluster	Open clusters	Perseus	November
Hyades	Open cluster	Taurus	December
Lagoon Nebula	Nebula	Sagittarius	August
Large Magellanic Cloud	Galaxy	Dorado	January
Moon	–	Ecliptic	All year
Omega Nebula	Nebula	Sagittarius	August
Orion Nebula	Nebula	Orion	January
Pleiades	Open cluster	Taurus	December
Praesepe	Open cluster	Cancer	March
Small Magellanic Cloud	Galaxy	Tucana	November
Triangulum	Galaxy	Triangulum	November

SEEING WITH BINOCULARS

The difference between viewing the Milky Way with the naked eye and through binoculars is striking. Binoculars show many more stars and other objects than can be seen unaided – even those that are only just visible to the naked eye, such as the Omega Nebula, become easy to observe. Practise using the binoculars by finding a bright nebula with both the naked eye and binoculars.

MILKY WAY, INCLUDING OMEGA NEBULA, WITH THE NAKED EYE

MILKY WAY, INCLUDING OMEGA NEBULA, WITH BINOCULARS

FIND OUT MORE

REFRACTING TELESCOPES

T HE SIMPLEST TELESCOPE is called a refracting telescope, or refractor. It has a large lens, the objective, at the top of its tube and a smaller lens, the eyepiece, through which a magnified image is seen. The key feature of any telescope is the size of its objective lens, the aperture. The larger the aperture, the better. Basic refractors give an upside-down view and need extra lenses to give an upright image. These lenses absorb precious light, so astronomers use a simple telescope giving an upside-down image. Refractors are ideal first telescopes but some are no more than toys. It is possible to make one, but this will have a limited use.

ACCESSORIES
Refractors are usually provided with a finder (a low-magnification telescope that helps aim the main instrument), several eyepieces giving different magnifications, and a star diagonal. The star diagonal turns the light through a right angle, and avoids the need to crouch on the ground while viewing. A Barlow lens is also often included – this multiplies the power of each eyepiece.

Dewcap is a hollow tube that helps to prevent dew from forming on the objective.

Objective is an achromatic lens with two separate components, one behind the other, to reduce false colour.

CHOOSING A REFRACTOR
The best type is one with a colour-corrected, or achromatic, objective. Avoid non-achromatic lenses. Telescopes with these lenses usually have a disc with a hole in it, behind the lens, to reduce the aperture in order to improve the image. False colour is reduced but the image is much dimmer and of little use for astronomy. Magnifications more than twice the telescope's aperture in millimetres also produce dim images.

Finder scope

Tripod

REFRACTING TELESCOPE

Eyepiece

Star diagonal

Altazimuth mount provides movement up and down (altitude) and from side to side (azimuth).

HOW A REFRACTOR WORKS
The objective collects and focuses incoming light to a point near the bottom. An eyepiece then magnifies the image. The distance from the objective to its focus point is called its focal length. The focal length divided by the focal length of the eyepiece (it is engraved on it) gives the power of magnification.

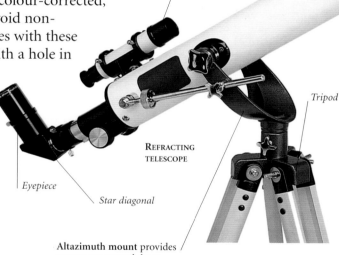

Objective lens

Incoming light

Focus point

Eyepiece

MOON THROUGH A 152-MM REFRACTOR

SATURN THROUGH A 152-MM REFRACTOR

SEEING THROUGH A REFRACTOR
All refractors suffer from false colour to some extent, but they give sharp images with good contrast between light and dark. This is because there is no obstruction in the light beam, and the light path is fully enclosed by the tube and objective. Refractors are particularly good for observing the Moon and planets, where it is important to see fine details. A refractor with an aperture as small as 60 mm will reveal the rings of Saturn.

MAKE A SIMPLE TELESCOPE

Making a telescope is easy if the right lenses are available for the objective and the eyepiece. For the objective, opticians may sell a single spectacle lens (ask for one with a power of +2 dioptres), or camera shops sell close-up lenses for SLR cameras. A lens from a broken pair of spectacles might do. Any simple convex lens will work if the objective has a longer focal length than the eyepiece. For the eyepiece, use a loupe – a magnifying glass with a short focal length; camera shops sell these, too.

WHAT TO LOOK FOR

Object	Type	Location	Best visible
Moon	–	Ecliptic	All year
Jupiter	Planet	Ecliptic	See p 249
Mars	Planet	Ecliptic	See p 249
Saturn	Planet	Ecliptic	See p 249
Venus	Planet	Ecliptic	See p 249
Albireo	Double star	Cygnus	September
47 Tucanae	Globular cluster	Tucana	November
Jewel Box Cluster	Open cluster	Crux	May
M13	Globular cluster	Hercules	July
Omega Centauri	Globular cluster	Centaurus	June
Wild Duck Cluster	Open cluster	Scutum	August

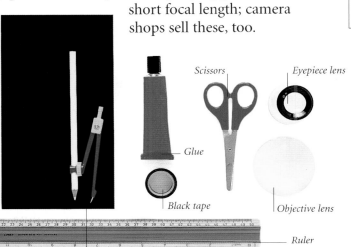

Scissors

Glue

Black tape

Eyepiece lens

Objective lens

Ruler

Black paper, compass, and white pencil

YOU WILL NEED
- Objective – convex lens with a focal length of about 50 cm
- Eyepiece – loupe or lens with a focal length of about 3 cm
- Thick black paper, about 50 x 50 cm
- Black tape
- Compass and white pencil to draw rings before cutting
- Scissors
- Large ruler or tape measure
- Glue

CUTTING OUT THE RINGS
Cut two rings from black paper, one 1 cm wide, with the same diameter as the objective, the second the same size as the first but with four tabs about 2.5 cm long.

PUTTING IT TOGETHER
Make two tubes, one for the objective (tube A) and one for the eyepiece (tube B). Tube B should have a slightly smaller diameter than tube A so that it can slide inside it to focus the telescope. Both should be 37.5 cm long or three-quarters the focal length of the objective. Check the focal length of the objective by focusing a streetlamp through the lens onto paper (the distance from the lens to the paper will be the focal length). Do not use the Sun for this – it can set fire to the paper.

Objective is glued to one side of the plain black ring. The other side of the ring is glued to the tabbed ring. Fold the tabs towards the objective and slide the assembly about 2.5 cm inside tube A. Glue tabs to the inside of the tube so that ends are level with the tube's end.

Black ring is inserted between the objective and tabbed ring.

Lens

Objective should be mounted at right angles to tube A.

Black ring with tabs holds the objective in position within tube A.

If using close-up camera lens, the untabbed black ring will not be needed because the lens will be set inside a ring.

Tube A

Tube B

Eyepiece loupe with circular frame is glued to tabs at the end of tube A. If another type of lens is used, adapt the design to fit.

Body is made of two tubes of rolled black paper. The diameter of the inside of tube A is the same as the diameter of the objective while tube B is slightly smaller.

Loupe used as an eyepiece

Assemble by cleaning the lens and then sliding tube B into tube A. Focus the telescope by sliding tube B inside tube A until the view is sharp.

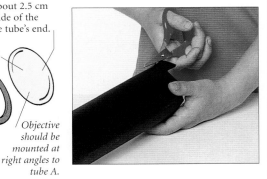

CUTTING OUT TABS
Cut out narrow tabs 2.5 cm long around one end of tube B. Bend them around the loupe, making sure that it is held centrally within the tube exactly at right angles to the tube. Glue the tabs to the loupe when it is in position.

FIND OUT MORE
HOW TELESCOPES WORK **14**
PREPARING TO STARGAZE **248**
STAR MAPS **252–261**

REFLECTING TELESCOPES

THE MOST COMMON type of telescope for astronomy is the reflecting telescope, or reflector. Reflectors use a mirror rather than a lens to focus light. Reasonably priced reflectors can be made in much larger sizes than refractors and they do not suffer from false colour. They do need more taking care of, however, and can give lower contrast images. Even so, almost all large telescopes are reflectors. They are quite simple to build, and some people buy the optical parts and make their own. At the expensive end of the scale, a telescope which combines both mirrors and lenses – a catadioptric – is increasing in popularity. This is often computer-controlled.

CHOOSING A REFLECTOR

Reflectors start in size with an aperture of about 100 mm, and a 150-mm telescope can give very good views of a wide range of objects. The cheapest design is called a Dobsonian. It has a simple tube and mounting and can give good results, but it is not very versatile. More expensive telescopes have equatorial mounts, which make it easier to follow objects as they move across the sky. Equatorial mounts are essential for taking photographs of faint objects.

DOBSONIAN REFLECTOR

Eyepiece

Formica ring enables the telescope to pivot up and down.

Dobsonian tube is made of cheap, light-weight material such as thick rolled cardboard.

Pivot system has a Formica surface that slips against a Teflon pad for low friction.

Altazimuth mount enables telescope to move easily by pushing and pulling tube to locate objects in the sky.

Main mirror is at bottom of the tube.

Pivot for side-to-side motion

Eyepiece

Incoming light

Focus point

Secondary (flat) mirror

Reflected light

Main (concave) mirror

HOW A REFLECTOR WORKS
The main mirror of a reflector is at the bottom of the tube. It has a dish-shaped surface that focuses the incoming light near the top of the tube. There, a flat mirror reflects the beam to the side of the tube where it can be magnified with an eyepiece. This optical design is called a Newtonian.

MARS THROUGH A 150-MM REFLECTING TELESCOPE

COMET LEVY THROUGH A 250-MM REFLECTING TELESCOPE

SEEING THROUGH A REFLECTING TELESCOPE
The eyepiece is situated on the side of the tube and the image is upside down. Reflectors are ideal for looking at faint objects, such as comets and nebulas, but they also give good views of the Moon and planets. Before it is used, the telescope must be allowed to cool to the outside temperature to avoid air currents inside the tube, which can cause shimmering.

CATADIOPTRIC TELESCOPES

Some telescopes combine mirrors with lenses to make a large telescope with a short tube, a sort of reflector/refractor. The most common design is the Schmidt-Cassegrain telescope, or the SCT. SCTs are popular because they have shorter tubes than Newtonians for a given aperture. Mountings are usually equatorial, which can be motorized to follow objects in the sky automatically. The enclosed tube means that mirrors stay clean for longer, and it also helps to prevent air currents, which affect the quality of image.

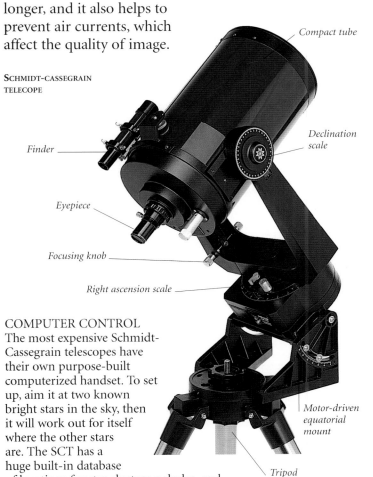

SCHMIDT-CASSEGRAIN TELECOPE

Compact tube

Finder

Declination scale

Eyepiece

Focusing knob

Right ascension scale

Motor-driven equatorial mount

Tripod

WHAT TO LOOK FOR			
Object	Type	Location	Best visible
Andromeda Galaxy	Galaxy	Andromeda	November
Black Eye Galaxy	Galaxy	Coma Berenices	May
Centaurus A Galaxy	Galaxy	Centaurus	May
Dumbbell Nebula	Planetary nebula	Vulpecula	September
Eight-Burst Nebula	Nebula	Vela	April
Lagoon Nebula	Nebula	Sagittarius	August
Little Dumbbell	Planetary nebula	Perseus	November
M65	Spiral galaxy	Leo	April
M81	Spiral galaxy	Ursa Major	March
NGC 253	Spiral galaxy	Sculptor	November
Omega Nebula	Nebula	Sagittarius	August
Ring Nebula	Planetary nebula	Lyra	August
Tarantula Nebula	Nebula	Dorado	January
Trifid Nebula	Nebula	Sagittarius	August
Whirlpool Galaxy	Galaxy	Canes Venatici	May

TARANTULA NEBULA

Reflectors are excellent for observing nebulas such as the Tarantula Nebula. The Tarantula is the brightest spot within the Large Magellanic Cloud, visible only from the southern hemisphere within the constellation of Dorado. Its colour is difficult to see because the eye is not sensitive to the nebula's deep red light, even using a large telescope.

COMPUTER CONTROL

The most expensive Schmidt-Cassegrain telescopes have their own purpose-built computerized handset. To set up, aim it at two known bright stars in the sky, then it will work out for itself where the other stars are. The SCT has a huge built-in database of locations for star clusters, nebulas, and galaxies and can point itself automatically at any object.

WHIRLPOOL GALAXY

This galaxy is in the northern constellation of Canes Venatici. The astronomer Lord Rosse (1800–67) first saw its spiral structure in 1845 using a 180-cm reflector, then the largest telescope in the world. With modern reflectors the spiral can be seen with telescopes of only 30 cm aperture.

HOW AN SCT WORKS

To keep the tube short, an SCT has a strongly curved mirror which would normally give poor images. A corrector lens at the top of the tube overcomes this problem. This lens also supports a secondary mirror that reflects the light back down through a hole in the main mirror, so the eyepiece looks up the tube, as in a refractor.

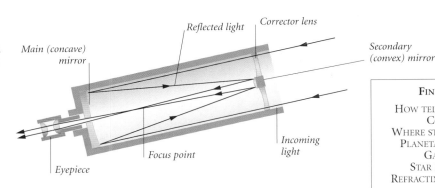

Reflected light

Corrector lens

Main (concave) mirror

Secondary (convex) mirror

Focus point

Incoming light

Eyepiece

FIND OUT MORE

HOW TELESCOPES WORK 14
COMETS 142
WHERE STARS ARE BORN 172
PLANETARY NEBULAS 182
GALAXIES 210
STAR MAPS 252–261
REFRACTING TELESCOPES 270

ASTRONOMICAL NAMES

ASTRONOMERS HAVE USED MANY DIFFERENT NAMES for stars and planets. In the early days, these names were based on local myths about the sky. As the science of astronomy developed, the same constellation patterns became recognized around the world, and more methodical systems were devised for naming individual objects. Today, the names given to newly discovered planetary features, stars, comets, and other objects in the sky are controlled by the International Astronomical Union (IAU).

PLANETS AND MOONS

The names of the planets come from figures in Greek and Roman legends. The Romans saw the characteristics of different gods in the five planets visible to the naked eye – fast-moving Mercury is named after the Messenger God, red Mars after the God of War, and stately Jupiter after the king of the Gods. The later planets followed this convention – Uranus was named after the father of the Gods, and distant Pluto after the God of the Underworld.

The names of moons are often associated with their parent planet – Phobos and Deimos were the sons of Mars in Greek myth, while Jupiter's moons are named after his various lovers. Pluto's lone moon, Charon, is named after the boatman who ferried dead souls across the River Styx, while all the moons of Uranus bear names from English literature. Surface features on planets and moons are also named according to specific themes – nearly all the features on Venus have female names while those on Callisto are from Norse myths.

NEBULAS AND OTHER OBJECTS

Some nebulas, galaxies, star clusters, and other distant objects have common names (such as the Pleiades), but all have catalogue numbers. The best-known catalogue is Messier's, which dates from 1784 when Charles Messier compiled a list of 103 fuzzy-looking objects and assigned each an M number (the Pleiades, for example, is M45). The Messier system was improved from the 1880s by John Dreyer, whose New General Catalogue (NGC) and Index Catalogues (IC) list more than 13,000 objects.

Some naming systems apply only to objects of a particular type. For example, quasar 3C 273 was the 273rd radio source found in the Third Cambridge (3C) Survey. Cygnus X-1 was the first X-ray source found in Cygnus, the Crab Pulsar is designated PSR 0531+21 by its coordinates, and Supernova 1987A was the first supernova observed in 1987.

EAGLE NEBULA (M16)

COMETS AND ASTEROIDS

Comets are the only astronomical objects named after their discoverers. The discovery of a comet can be reported by e-mail or telegram to the IAU. If two astronomers report the discovery at the same time, the comet bears both their names (as with Comet Hale-Bopp of 1997)

Once the comet's orbit has been determined, it is also given an official designation – Comet Hale-Bopp, for instance, was C/1995 O1 (the O indicates the two-week period of

1995 when it was found). The only exception to the naming rule is the most famous comet of all. Halley's Comet is named after the man who calculated its orbit, not its discoverer.

Asteroids are also unusual – they are the only objects that the discoverer has the right to name. Astronomical catalogues list asteroids by number and name – (1) Ceres, for example, indicates that it was the first to be discovered in 1801. More recently, asteroids have been given year and letter designations similar to those used for comets. The actual name, however, can be chosen by the discoverer (subject to control by the IAU), and asteroid names therefore include everything from ancient gods to modern pop stars.

CONSTELLATIONS

Constellations were originally patterns of bright stars in which ancient civilizations saw animals, people, and mythical beasts. About AD 150, Ptolemy created a list of 48 constellations, and later astronomers added to these to create the current list of 88. Constellations are now defined as areas of sky rather than as particular patterns of stars.

Name	Common Name	Genitive (possessive)	Size in square degrees
Andromeda	Andromeda	Andromedae	722
Antlia	Air Pump	Antliae	239
Apus	Bird of Paradise	Apodis	206
Aquarius	Water Carrier	Aquarii	980
Aquila	Eagle	Aquilae	652
Ara	Altar	Arae	237
Aries	Ram	Arietis	441
Auriga	Charioteer	Aurigae	657
Boötes	Herdsman	Boötis	907
Caelum	Chisel	Caeli	125
Camelopardalis	Giraffe	Camelopardalis	757
Cancer	Crab	Cancri	506
Canes Venatici	Hunting Dogs	Canun Venaticorum	465
Canis Major	Great Dog	Canis Majoris	380
Canis Minor	Little Dog	Canis Minoris	183
Capricornus	Sea Goat	Capricorni	414
Carina	Keel	Carinae	494
Cassiopeia	Cassiopeia	Cassiopeiae	598
Centaurus	Centaur	Centauri	1,060
Cepheus	Cepheus	Cephei	588
Cetus	Whale	Ceti	1,231
Chamaeleon	Chameleon	Chamaeleontis	132
Circinus	Compasses	Circini	93
Columba	Dove	Columbae	270
Coma Berenices	Berenice's Hair	Comae Berenicis	386
Corona Australis	Southern Crown	Coronae Australis	128
Corona Borealis	Northern Crown	Coronae Borealis	179
Corvus	Crow	Corvi	184
Crater	Cup	Crateris	282
Crux	Southern Cross	Crucis	68
Cygnus	Swan	Cygni	804
Delphinus	Dolphin	Delphini	189
Dorado	Swordfish	Doradus	179
Draco	Dragon	Draconis	1,083
Equuleus	Foal	Equulei	72
Eridanus	River	Eridani	1,138
Fornax	Furnace	Fornacis	398
Gemini	Twins	Geminorum	514
Grus	Crane	Gruis	366

Name	Common Name	Genitive	Size in square degrees
Hercules	Hercules	Herculis	1,225
Horologium	Clock	Horologii	249
Hydra	Water Snake	Hydrae	1,303
Hydrus	Little Water Snake	Hydri	243
Indus	Indian	Indi	294
Lacerta	Lizard	Lacertae	201
Leo	Lion	Leonis	947
Leo Minor	Little Lion	Leonis Minoris	232
Lepus	Hare	Leporis	290
Libra	Scales	Librae	538
Lupus	Wolf	Lupi	334
Lynx	Lynx	Lyncis	545
Lyra	Lyre	Lyrae	286
Mensa	Table Mountain	Mensae	153
Microscopium	Microscope	Microscopii	210
Monoceros	Unicorn	Monocerotis	482
Musca	Fly	Muscae	138
Norma	Level	Normae	165
Octans	Octant	Octantis	291
Ophiuchus	Serpent Bearer	Ophiuchi	948
Orion	Orion, Hunter	Orionis	594
Pavo	Peacock	Pavonis	378
Pegasus	Pegasus, Winged Horse	Pegasi	1,121
Perseus	Perseus	Persei	615
Phoenix	Phoenix	Phoenicis	469
Pictor	Painter's Easel	Pictoris	247
Pisces	Fishes	Piscium	889
Piscis Austrinus	Southern Fish	Piscis Austrini	245
Puppis	Stern	Puppis	673
Pyxis	Mariner's Compass	Pyxidis	221
Reticulum	Net	Reticuli	114
Sagitta	Arrow	Sagittae	80
Sagittarius	Archer	Sagittarii	867
Scorpius	Scorpion	Scorpii	497
Sculptor	Sculptor	Sculptoris	475
Scutum	Shield	Scuti	109
Serpens	Serpent	Serpentis	637
Sextans	Sextant	Sextantis	314
Taurus	Bull	Tauri	797
Telescopium	Telescope	Telescopii	252
Triangulum	Triangle	Trianguli	132
Triangulum Australe	Southern Triangle	Trianguli Australis	110
Tucana	Toucan	Tucanae	295
Ursa Major	Great Bear	Ursae Majoris	1,280
Ursa Minor	Little Bear	Ursae Minoris	256
Vela	Sails	Velorum	500
Virgo	Virgin	Virginis	1,294
Volans	Flying Fish	Volantis	141
Vulpecula	Fox	Vulpeculae	268

STAR NAMES

Over a hundred stars still bear the names they were given centuries ago. These names may describe the star, or link it to myth and legend. For example, Aldebaran is Arabic for "the follower" (because it follows the Pleiades) while Castor and Pollux are named after twins in Greek legend.

Astronomers today prefer a more systematic method of naming stars. The most popular is to give each star in a constellation a Greek letter to indicate its brightness. So for example, Sirius, the brightest star in Canis Major, is called alpha Canis Majoris (Canis Majoris is the Latin genitive, or possessive, form meaning "of Canis Major").

The invention of more powerful telescopes revealed millions of faint stars, and some astronomers set out to compile catalogues of all the stars above a certain magnitude. These catalogues are another way of referring to the stars. A bright star can have a proper name, a systematic name, and several catalogue numbers such as an SAO (Smithsonian Astrophysical Observatory) number and an HD (Henry Draper) number.

3000 BC — 1750

ASTRONOMY TIMELINE

3000 BC STONE ASTRONOMY Stonehenge, built about this time in southern England, is a giant astronomical calendar with stones aligned to the Sun and possibly the Moon. Many other ancient sites are thought to have astronomical significance, such as the Egyptian pyramids (c. 2600 BC) and buildings in China and Central and South America (1st century AD).

750 BC LUNAR CYCLE In Babylon, astronomers discover 18.6 year cycle in the rising and setting of the Moon. From this they create the first almanacs – tables of movements of the Sun, Moon, and planets for use in astrology. In 6th century Greece, this knowledge is used to predict eclipses.

380 BC EARTH-CENTRED VIEW Greek philosopher Plato founds a school of thought that will influence the next 2,000 years. This promotes the idea that everything in the Universe moves in harmony, and that the Sun, Moon, and planets move around Earth in perfect circles.

270 BC SUN-CENTRED VIEW Aristarchus of Samos proposes an alternative to the geocentric (Earth-centred) Universe. His heliocentric model places the Sun at its centre, with the Earth as just one planet orbiting around it. However, few people take the theory seriously – if the Earth is moving through space, then why do the stars not move through the sky?

164 BC HALLEY'S COMET The earliest recorded sighting of Halley's Comet is made by Babylonian astronomers. Their records of the comet's movements allow 20th century astronomers to predict accurately how the comet's orbit changes over the centuries.

AD 150 STAR CATALOGUE Ptolemy publishes his star catalogue, listing 48 constellations, and endorses the Earth-centred view of the Universe. His views go unquestioned for nearly 1,500 years, and are passed down to Arabic and medieval European astronomers in his book, *The Almagest.*

AD 928 ASTROLABE The earliest surviving astrolabe is made by Islamic craftsmen. Astrolabes are the most advanced instruments of their time. The precise measurement of the positions of stars and planets allows Arab astronomers to compile the most detailed almanacs and star atlases yet.

1054 SUPERNOVA Chinese astronomers record the sudden appearance of a bright star. Native American rock carvings also show the brilliant star close to the Moon. This star is the Crab supernova exploding.

1543 COPERNICAN SYSTEM Nicolaus Copernicus publishes his theory that the Earth goes around the Sun, in contradiction of the Church's teachings. However, he complicates his theory by retaining Plato's perfect circular orbits of the planets.

1577 TYCHO'S COMET A brilliant comet is observed by Tycho Brahe, who proves that it is travelling beyond the Earth's atmosphere and therefore provides the first evidence that the heavens can change.

1608 FIRST TELESCOPE Dutch spectacle-maker Hans Lippershey (c.1570–c.1619) invents the refracting telescope. The invention spreads rapidly across Europe, as scientists make their own instruments. Their discoveries begin a revolution in astronomy.

1609 KEPLER'S LAWS Johannes Kepler publishes his *New Astronomy.* In this and later works, he announces his three laws of planetary motion, replacing the circular orbits of Plato with elliptical ones. Almanacs based on his laws prove to be highly accurate.

1610 OBSERVATIONS Galileo Galilei publishes the findings of his observations with the telescope he built. These include spots on the Sun, craters on the Moon, and four satellites of Jupiter. Proving that not everything orbits Earth, he promotes the Copernican view of a Sun-centred Universe.

1655 TITAN As the power and quality of telescopes increases Christiaan Huygens studies Saturn and discovers its largest satellite, Titan. He also explains Saturn's appearance, suggesting the planet is surrounded by a thin ring.

1663 REFLECTOR Scottish astronomer James Gregory (1638–75) builds a reflecting telescope, using mirrors instead of lenses, to allow a larger aperture and reduce light loss. Within five years, Isaac Newton improves the design, creating the Newtonian telescope; other variations soon follow.

1687 THEORY OF GRAVITY Isaac Newton publishes his *Principia Mathematica,* establishing the theory of gravitation and laws of motion. The *Principia* explains Kepler's laws of planetary motion and allows astronomers to understand the forces acting between the Sun, the planets, and their moons.

1705 HALLEY'S COMET Edmond Halley calculates that the comets recorded at 76 year intervals from 1456 to 1682 are one and the same. He predicts that the comet will return again in 1758. When it reappears as expected, the comet is named in his honour.

1750–1905

1750 SOUTHERN SKIES French astronomer Nicolas de Lacaille (1713–62) sails to southern oceans and begins work compiling a catalogue of more than 10,000 stars in the southern sky. Although Halley and others have observed from the southern hemisphere before, Lacaille's star catalogue is the first comprehensive one of the southern sky.

1781 URANUS Amateur astronomer William Herschel discovers the planet Uranus, although he at first mistakes it for a comet. Uranus is the first planet to be discovered beyond Saturn (the most distant of the planets known since ancient times).

1784 MESSIER CATALOGUE Charles Messier publishes his catalogue of star clusters and nebulas. Messier draws up the list to prevent these objects being identified as comets. However, it soon becomes a standard reference for the study of star clusters and nebulas, and is still in use today.

1800 INFRARED RADIATION William Herschel splits sunlight through a prism and, with a thermometer, measures the energy given out by different colours; this is the first study of a star's spectrum. He notices a sudden increase in energy beyond the red end of the spectrum, discovering invisible infrared (heat) radiation and laying the foundations for spectroscopy.

1801 ASTEROIDS Italian astronomer Giuseppe Piazzi (1746–1826) discovers what appears to be a new planet orbiting between Mars and Jupiter, and names it Ceres. William Herschel proves it is a very small object – calculating it to be only 320 km in diameter – and not a planet. He proposes the name asteroid, and soon other similar bodies are being found. We now know that Ceres is 932 km in diameter – but still too small to be a planet.

1814 FRAUNHOFER LINES Joseph von Fraunhofer builds the first accurate spectrometer and uses it to study the spectrum of the Sun's light. He discovers and maps hundreds of fine dark lines crossing the solar spectrum. In 1859, these lines are linked to chemical elements in the Sun's atmosphere. Spectroscopy becomes the method for studying what the stars are made of.

1838 STELLAR PARALLAX Friedrich Bessel successfully uses the method of stellar parallax (the effect of the Earth's annual movement around the Sun) to calculate the distance to 61 Cygni: the first star other than the Sun to have its distance measured. Bessel has pioneered the truly accurate measurement of stellar positions, and the parallax technique establishes a framework for measuring the scale of the Universe.

1843 SUNSPOT CYCLE German amateur astronomer Heinrich Schwabe (1789–1875), who has been studying the Sun for the past 17 years, announces his discovery of a regular cycle in sunspot numbers – the first clue to the Sun's internal structure.

1845 LARGE TELESCOPES Irish astronomer the Earl of Rosse completes the first of the world's great telescopes, with a 180-cm mirror. He uses it to study and draw the structure of nebulas, and within a few months discovers the spiral structure of the Whirlpool Galaxy.

1845 ASTROPHOTOGRAPHY French physicists Jean Foucault (1819–68) and Armand Fizeau (1819–96) take the first detailed photographs of the Sun's surface through a telescope – the birth of scientific astrophotography. Within five years, astronomers produce the first detailed photographs of the Moon. Early film is not sensitive enough to image stars.

1846 NEPTUNE A new planet, called Neptune, is identified by German astronomer Johann Gottfried Galle (1812-1910). He is searching in the position suggested by Urbain Le Verrier. Le Verrier has calculated the position and size of the planet from the effects of its gravitational pull on the orbit of Uranus. An English mathematician John Couch Adams (1819–92) also made a similar calculation a year earlier.

1868 SUN'S COMPOSITION Astronomers notice a new bright emission line in the spectrum of the Sun's atmosphere during an eclipse. The emission line is caused by an element giving out light, and British astronomer Norman Lockyer (1836–1920) concludes that it is an element unknown on Earth. He calls it helium, which is from the Greek word for the Sun. Nearly 30 years later, helium is found on the Earth.

1872 SPECTRA OF STARS An American astronomer Henry Draper (1837–82) takes the first photograph of the spectrum of a star (Vega), showing absorption lines that reveal its chemical make-up. Astronomers begin to see that spectroscopy is the key to understanding how stars evolve. William Huggins uses absorption lines to measure the red shifts of stars, which give the first indication of how fast stars are moving.

1895 ROCKETS Konstantin Tsiolkovsky publishes his first article on the possibility of space flight. His greatest discovery is that a rocket, unlike other forms of propulsion, will work in a vacuum. He also outlines the principle of a multistage launch vehicle.

1901 SPECTRAL CATALOGUE A comprehensive survey of stars, the Henry Draper Catalogue, is published. In the catalogue, Annie Jump Cannon proposes a sequence of classifying stars by the absorption lines in their spectra, which is still in use today.

1905–1965

1906 STAR MAGNITUDE Ejnar Hertzsprung establishes the standard for measuring the true brightness of a star (its absolute magnitude). He shows that there is a relationship between colour and absolute magnitude for 90% of the stars in the Milky Way Galaxy. In 1913, Henry Russell publishes a diagram that shows this relationship. Although astronomers agree that the diagram shows the sequence in which stars evolve, they argue about which way the sequence progresses. Arthur Eddington finally settles the controversy in 1924.

1916 BLACK HOLES German physicist Karl Schwarzschild (1873–1916) uses Albert Einstein's theory of general relativity to lay the groundwork for black hole theory. He suggests that if any star collapses below a certain size, its gravity will be so strong that no form of radiation will escape from it.

1923 GALAXIES Edwin Hubble discovers a Cepheid variable star in the "Andromeda Nebula" and proves that Andromeda and other nebulas are galaxies far beyond our own. By 1925, he produces a classification system for galaxies.

1926 ROCKETS Robert Goddard launches the first rocket powered by liquid fuel. He also demonstrates that a rocket can work in a vacuum. His later rockets break the sound barrier for the first time.

1930 DWARF STARS By applying new ideas from subatomic physics, Subrahmanyan Chandrasekhar predicts that the atoms in a white dwarf star of more than 1.44 solar masses will disintegrate, causing the star to collapse violently. In 1933, Walter Baade and Fritz Zwicky describe the neutron star that results from this collapse, causing a supernova explosion.

1929 HUBBLE'S LAW Edwin Hubble discovers that the Universe is expanding and that the farther away a galaxy is, the faster it is moving away from us. Two years later, Georges Lemaître suggests that the expansion can be traced back to an initial "Big Bang".

1930 PLUTO Clyde Tombaugh discovers the planet Pluto at the Lowell Observatory in Flagstaffe, Arizona, USA. The planet is so faint and slow moving that he has to compare photos taken several nights apart.

1932 RADIO ASTRONOMY Karl Jansky detects the first radio waves coming from space. In 1942, radio waves from the Sun are detected. Seven years later radio astronomers identify the first distant sources – the Crab Nebula, and the galaxies Centaurus A and M87

1938 STELLAR ENERGY German physicist Hans Bethe (1906–) explains how stars generate energy. He outlines a series of nuclear fusion reactions that turn hydrogen into helium and release enormous amounts of energy in a star's core. These reactions use the star's hydrogen very slowly, allowing it to burn for billions of years.

1944 V-2 ROCKET A team of German scientists led by Wernher von Braun develops the V-2, the first rocket-powered ballistic missile. Scientists and engineers from von Braun's team are captured at the end of World War II and are drafted into the American and Russian rocket programmes.

1948 HALE TELESCOPE The largest telescope in the world, with a 5.08 m mirror, is completed at Palomar Mountain in California. At the time, the telescope pushes single-mirror telescope technology to its limits – larger mirrors tend to bend under their own weight.

1957 SPACECRAFT Russia launches the first satellite, Sputnik 1, into orbit, beginning the Space Age. The USA launches its first satellite, Explorer 1, four months later.

1959 MOON PROBES Russia and the USA both launch space probes to the Moon, but NASA's Pioneer probes all fail. The Russian Luna programme is more successful. Luna 2 crash lands on the Moon's surface in September, and Luna 3 returns the first pictures of the Moon's farside in October.

1961 HUMANS IN SPACE Russia again takes the lead in the space race as Yuri Gagarin becomes the first person to orbit Earth in April. NASA astronaut Alan Shepard becomes the first American in space a month later, but does not go into orbit. John Glenn achieves this in early 1962.

1962 PLANETARY PROBE Mariner 2 becomes the first space probe to reach another planet, flying past Venus in December. NASA follows this with the successful Mariner 4 mission to Mars in 1965, and both the USA and Russia send many more probes to planets through the rest of the 1960s and 1970s.

1963 QUASARS Dutch-American astronomer Maarten Schmidt (1929–) measures the spectra of quasars, the mysterious star-like radio sources discovered in 1960. He establishes that quasars are active galaxies, and among the most distant objects in the Universe.

1965 BIG BANG Arno Penzias and Robert Wilson announce the discovery of a weak radio signal coming from all parts of the sky. Scientists work out that this must be emitted by an object at a temperature of –270°C. Soon it is recognized as the remnant of the very hot radiation from the Big Bang that created the Universe 13 billion years ago.

1965–2000

1966 LUNAR LANDINGS The Russian Luna 9 probe makes the first successful soft landing on the Moon in January, while the USA lands the far more complex Surveyor 1 in May. The Surveyor missions, which are follow-ups to NASA's Ranger series of crash landers, scout sites for possible manned landings.

1967 PULSARS Jocelyn Bell Burnell and Antony Hewish detect the first pulsar, an object emitting regular pulses of radio waves. Pulsars are eventually recognized as rapidly spinning neutron stars with intense magnetic fields – the remains of a supernova explosion.

1969 APOLLO 11 The USA wins the race for the Moon, as Neil Armstrong steps onto the lunar surface on 21 July. Apollo 11 is followed by five further landing missions, three carrying a sophisticated Lunar Rover vehicle.

1970 X-RAY ASTRONOMY The Uhuru satellite, designed to map the sky at X-ray wavelengths, is launched by NASA. The existence of X-rays from the Sun and a few other stars has already been found using rocket-launched experiments, but Uhuru charts more than 300 X-ray sources, including several possible black holes.

1971 SPACE STATIONS Russia launches its first space station, Salyut 1, into orbit. It is followed by a series of stations, culminating with Mir in 1986. A permanent platform in orbit allows cosmonauts to carry out serious research and to set a series of new duration records for spaceflight.

1975 PLANETARY VISIT The Russian probe Venera 9 lands on the surface of Venus and sends back the first pictures of its surface. The first probe to land on another planet, Venera 7 in 1970, had no camera. Both break down within an hour in the hostile atmosphere.

1976 VIKING PROBES Two NASA space probes arrive at Mars. Each Viking mission consists of an Orbiter, which photographs the planet from above, and a Lander, which touches down on the surface, analyses the rocks, and searches (unsuccessfully) for life.

1977 VOYAGERS NASA launches the two Voyager space probes to the outer planets. The Voyagers return scientific data and pictures from Jupiter and Saturn, and, before leaving the Solar System, Voyager 2 becomes the first probe to visit Uranus and Neptune.

1981 SPACE SHUTTLE Columbia, the first of NASA's reusable Space Shuttles, makes its maiden flight. Ten years in development, the shuttle will make space travel routine and eventually open the path for a new International Space Station.

1983 INFRARED ASTRONOMY The first infrared astronomy satellite, IRAS, is launched. It must be cooled to extremely low temperatures with liquid helium, and it operates for only 300 days before its supply of helium is exhausted. During this time it completes an infrared survey of 98% of the sky.

1986 CHALLENGER DISASTER NASA's space flight programme comes to a halt when the Space Shuttle Challenger explodes shortly after launch. A thorough inquiry and modifications to the rest of the fleet keep the shuttle on the ground for nearly three years.

1986 COMET PROBES The returning Halley's Comet is met by a fleet of five space probes from Russia, Japan, and Europe. The most ambitious is the European Space Agency's Giotto, which flies through the comet's coma and photographs the nucleus itself.

1990 MAGELLAN The Magellan probe, launched by NASA, arrives at Venus and spends three years mapping the planet with radar. Magellan is the first in a new wave of space probes including Galileo, which arrives in Jupiter in 1995, and Cassini, which is scheduled to arrive at Saturn in 2004.

1990 SPACE TELESCOPE The Hubble Space Telescope, the first large optical telescope in orbit, is launched using the Space Shuttle, but astronomers soon discover it is crippled by a problem with its mirror. A complex repair mission in 1993 allows the telescope to start producing spectacular images of distant stars, nebulas, and galaxies.

1992 COSMIC RIPPLES The Cosmic Background Explorer (COBE) satellite produces a detailed map of the background radiation remaining from the Big Bang. The map shows "ripples", caused by slight variations in the density of the early Universe – the seeds of galaxies and galaxy clusters.

1992 KECK TELESCOPE The 10-m Keck Telescope on Mauna Kea, Hawaii, is completed. The first of a revolutionary new wave of telescopes, the Keck's main mirror is made of 36 six-sided segments, with computers to control their alignment. New optical telescopes also make use of interferometry – improving resolution by combining images from separate telescopes.

1998 INTERNATIONAL SPACE STATION Construction work on a huge new space station begins. A joint venture between many countries, including former space rivals Russia and the USA, the space station will be the size of a football pitch when complete. It will house up to seven astronauts in orbit at any one time and act as a platform for microgravity research, astronomy, and further exploration of the Solar System.

BIOGRAPHIES

EDWIN (BUZZ) ALDRIN
born 1930

The American astronaut piloted the Lunar Module of Apollo 11 and on 21 July 1969 became the second man to walk on the Moon. Aldrin was an engineer by training, and an elder of the Presbyterian Church. In November 1966, he had made a record 5-hour space walk during the Gemini 12 mission.

ARISTARCHUS OF SAMOS
about 320–250 BC

Greek astronomer who, using geometry, measured the distance between the Sun and Moon. He used this to calculate that the Sun was 20 times farther away than the Moon (it is actually 400 times farther). He also suggested that because the Sun was seven times bigger than Earth (it is actually 109 times bigger), Earth must travel around the Sun. It was 18 centuries before this idea started to become accepted.

NEIL ARMSTRONG
born 1930

American Air Force test pilot who, as commander Apollo 11, was the first man to walk on the Moon on 21 July 1969. As he stepped on to the Moon he said "That's one small step for man, one giant leap for mankind". He left NASA in 1971 and became a university professor before going into business.

TYCHO BRAHE
1546–1601

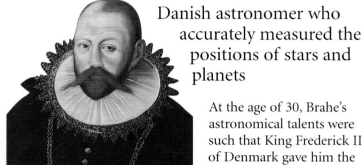

Danish astronomer who accurately measured the positions of stars and planets

At the age of 30, Brahe's astronomical talents were such that King Frederick II of Denmark gave him the Baltic island of Hven on which to build an observatory. Brahe's instruments were well made and accurate, and he measured the position of the Sun and planets against the stars for more than 20 years. Between 1572 and 1574, he recorded a new star – a supernova – in Cassiopeia, proving that the sky could change. He measured the distance to the great comet of 1577 and showed that it was farther away than the Moon, and that it had an elongated orbit which passed the planets. He moved to Prague in 1597 and recruited Johannes Kepler as his assistant. Kepler used Brahe's results to calculate the orbits of the planets.

GIOVANNI CASSINI
1625–1712

Italian astronomer who was the first to understand the nature of Saturn's rings

As professor of astronomy at the University of Bologna, Cassini measured the time it takes Jupiter, Venus, and Mars to spin once on their axes. He also discovered four of Saturn's satellites and a gap in that planet's rings. Cassini suggested that the rings were not solid but made of individual rocks. In 1669, he moved to France to help build and run the Paris Observatory. In Paris, he measured the distance between Earth and Mars and used this to calculate the Sun-Earth distance. However, he refused to accept that Earth went around the Sun or that gravity was universal. Both his son and grandson became directors of the Paris Observatory.

WALTER BAADE
1893–1960

Emigrating to the USA from Germany in 1931, Baade worked at Mount Wilson Observatory in California and in 1948 moved to nearby Palomar Observatory. In 1943 he discovered that the Universe contains two types of stars: very old ones containing few metals, and newer ones rich in metals. This also applied to the Cepheid variable stars, whose properties can be used to help calculate the size of the Universe. The Universe was then found to be twice as big as previously thought.

JOCELYN BELL BURNELL
born 1943

British astronomer who, as a research student at Cambridge, discovered pulsars. On 6 August 1967, while observing the rapid variations in signals from radio sources and looking for quasars, she discovered an unusual radio signal consisting of a rapid series of pulses that occurred precisely every 1.337 seconds. This turned out to be a pulsating neutron star (a pulsar), a star slightly more massive than the Sun but only a few kilometres in diameter.

FRIEDRICH BESSEL
1784–1846

German astronomer who supervised the construction of a new observatory at Königsberg and became its first director in 1813. He concentrated on measuring the exact positions of stars. In 1838 he observed the slight movement of the star 61 Cygni, movement he knew to be caused by viewing it when Earth is at opposite points on its orbit around the Sun. From this, he calculated that the star was 10.3 light years away. This was the first star to have its distance measured by parallax, and helped establish a scale for the Universe.

ANNIE JUMP CANNON
1863–1941

American astronomer who classified the spectra of more than 300,000 stars into a temperature sequence. She joined the staff of Harvard College Observatory in 1896 and stayed there until she retired in 1940. Her work was the foundation stone of the Henry Draper Catalogue of stellar spectra.

SUBRAHMANYAN CHANDRASEKHAR 1910–95

Indian-born astrophysicist who studied astronomy in Madras and England before moving to the USA in 1936. He received the 1983 Nobel Prize for Physics for his work on dying stars. Chandrasekhar realized that a white dwarf star with more than 1.4 times the Sun's mass could not stop shrinking: it would become a neutron star or a black hole.

ARTHUR C. CLARKE
born 1917

In 1945, this British science fiction writer suggested that a satellite in geostationary orbit – 35,800 km above Earth – would be useful for communications. One satellite above the Atlantic could be used to transmit TV and telephone signals between Europe and North America. The technology was not available then, but geostationary satellites are now commonplace.

NICOLAUS COPERNICUS
1473–1543

Polish astronomer, doctor, and priest who suggested that the Sun and not the Earth was at the centre of our planetary system

Copernicus studied mathematics and classics in Poland and law and astronomy in Italy. He returned to Poland in 1506 to become a Canon at Frauenberg Cathedral, a post he held until he died. His duties were light and he devoted most of his time to astronomy. By about 1513 he had realized that Earth was not at the centre of the Universe or even of the Solar System. Earth, which went around the Sun, was not special as had been thought, but merely one of a collection of planets. He was aware that his idea went against the teachings of the church, and his book *De Revolutionibus Orbium Coelestrium* was not published until he was on his deathbed.

ARTHUR EDDINGTON
1882–1944

English astronomer who showed how the physical characteristics inside a star can be calculated from its surface features

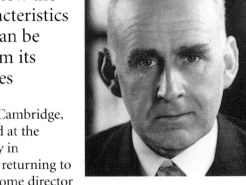

After studying at Cambridge, Eddington worked at the Royal Observatory in Greenwich before returning to Cambridge to become director of its Observatory for 31 years. Eddington produced a model of the interior of a star, discovered the relationship between a star's mass and its luminosity, stressed that nuclear fusion produced stellar energy, and measured how much a ray of light is bent by a gravitational field. He also calculated the mass of the Universe, arguing that constants, such as the velocity of light, depended on it. A skilful writer, he popularized both astronomy and Einstein's theory of general relativity.

FRANK DRAKE
born 1930

American radio astronomer who, in 1960, pioneered the use of radio telescopes to listen for signals from extraterrestrial life. In 1974 this project continued using the Arecibo radio telescope in Puerto Rico. Drake also devised an equation to estimate the number of communicating technological civilizations there might be in the Galaxy at any one time.

ERATOSTHENES OF CYRENE
about 273–192 BC

Greek scholar who calculated the size of Earth. Born in north Africa, Eratosthenes was educated in Athens and then became librarian at Alexandria in Egypt and the tutor of the son of King Ptolemy III of Egypt. He was, among other things, a skilled geographer who calculated the curvature of Earth. He did this by measuring the length of shadow cast by the Sun at two places 950 km apart. From this he estimated the circumference of Earth to be 46,500 km (it is actually 40,075 km at the Equator).

EUDOXUS OF CNIDUS
about 408–355 BC

A Greek astronomer and mathematician who constructed a model of the Solar System with Earth at its centre and the planets carried around Earth, supported on a series of transparent spheres. The spheres were nested inside each other, with the axis of each sphere attached to the inside of the surrounding sphere. His model was able to explain the motion of planets as viewed from Earth, but it did not account for the everyday changes that occur in the distances between Earth and individual planets. It was replaced after a few centuries.

JOHN FLAMSTEED
1646–1719

As England's first Astronomer Royal, Flamsteed was in charge of the new Royal Observatory at Greenwich near London, which opened in 1676. He used a mural arc and a sextant with telescopic sights, in conjunction with the new, accurate clocks that ran for a year, to produce a new catalogue of 3,000 stars. This was published after he died, in 1725, and the accuracy of the star positions was 15 times better than previous catalogues. Flamsteed also made detailed studies of the shape of the orbits of both the Moon and Earth.

JOSEPH VON FRAUNHOFER
1787–1826

A Bavarian glass and lens maker, Fraunhofer tried to make a lens that did not disperse light into its rainbow of colours. In 1814, while testing this lens, he noticed that the Sun's spectrum was crossed by numerous fine, dark lines. He measured the wavelengths of 324 of the 574 lines that he could see: they are now known as Fraunhofer lines. In the 1820s he found that light could be split into colours by passing it through a grating of fine slits, and that the splitting increased as the slits were moved closer together. Gratings are now used extensively in spectroscopy.

YURI GAGARIN
1934–68

On 12 April 1961, the Russian cosmonaut Gagarin became the first person to fly in space. The flight lasted one orbit of Earth; the Vostok 1 spaceship reached a height of 344 km. Gagarin was airborne for 108 minutes before the retrorockets slowed him down and he parachuted the last 7 km to the ground. He died in a plane crash while training to return to space.

ALBERT EINSTEIN
1879–1955

German-born American theoretical physicist whose theory of general relativity explains the evolution of the expanding Universe

Einstein received the Nobel Prize for Physics in 1921 for explaining how light is radiated in packets of energy called quanta, but he is best remembered for his theories of relativity. These showed that nothing could move faster than the velocity of light (c), that this velocity was constant, and that objects became more massive as they moved faster. Einstein found that mass (m) was equivalent to energy (E) according to his now famous equation $E = mc^2$. He also realized that gravitational fields can bend light beams and change their wavelengths. Einstein was a life-long pacifist and in 1933 moved to America to avoid Nazi persecution as a Jew. In 1952 he turned down the offer to be President of Israel.

GALILEO GALILEI
1564–1642

Italian mathematician, physicist, and astronomer who was the first to turn a telescope toward the heavens

As professor of mathematics at the Universities of Pisa and Padua, Galileo did much to disprove ancient Greek theories of physics. On learning of the invention of the telescope, he built one in 1609 and discovered that the Sun spun around every 25 days, the Moon was mountainous, Jupiter had four satellites, and Venus showed Moon-like phases. The Venus observations helped prove that the Sun and not Earth was at the centre of the Solar System. These revolutionary ideas, coupled with his belligerent nature and love of publicity, got him into trouble with the Church, and late in life he was tried by the Inquisition in Rome and placed under house arrest.

GEORGE GAMOW
1904–68

Ukrainian physicist who in 1933 defected to the USA. In 1948, with Ralph Alpher (1921–) and Hans Bethe (1906–), he showed how helium could be produced during the Big Bang from protons and neutrons, and how helium could combine with other nuclei to create elements. Gamow also predicted that the Universe would be filled with radiation remaining from the intense temperatures that existed during the Big Bang.

JOHN GLENN
born 1921

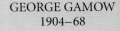

In 1962, Glenn was the first American to orbit Earth; he made three orbits during a 5-hour flight. After retiring from the space programme in 1964 he took up politics, and in 1974 was elected Senator in Ohio. In 1998, he became the world's oldest astronaut when he flew on a Space Shuttle mission.

ALAN GUTH
born 1947

American particle physicist who turned to cosmology. He devised the theory of inflation in 1979, in which he proposed that just after the Big Bang the Universe expanded from the size of a proton to the size of a grapefruit in a tiny fraction of a second. This both smoothed out space-time and made a Universe that looks the same in all directions.

GEORGE HALE
1868–1938

American astronomer who invented the spectroheliograph, an instrument that revealed the details of the Sun's surface. In 1904 he became the director of the Mount Wilson Observatory in California where, in 1908, he discovered that sunspots had magnetic fields, and then measured the strengths of these fields. Hale devoted much of his working life to raising funds for and organizing the building of large telescopes, including the great 5-metre telescope on Palomar Mountain in California, which was named the Hale Telescope in his honour.

JOHN HARRISON
1693–1776

Harrison, a British clockmaker, introduced a pendulum that did not change length as its temperature varied, and a ratchet that kept a clock going as it was being wound up. In the early 1730s he was given money to build a clock that worked accurately when on board a ship at sea. His final precision clocks enabled a ship's longitude to be measured when out of port, and Harrison received a £20,000 prize for this. Accurate clocks are very important in astronomy for measuring the position of stars in the sky.

STEPHEN HAWKING
born 1942

British theoretical physicist who, even though he suffers from a neuromotor disease, has spent his life studying the behaviour of matter close to a black hole. Astronomers used to think that nothing could escape from a black hole but Hawking showed that thermal radiation could be emitted. His *A Brief History of Time* is one of the best-selling science books ever.

ROBERT GODDARD
1882–1945

American inventor and rocket engineer who, in 1926, made and launched the world's first liquid-fuelled rocket

Goddard was a rocket pioneer whose work was mainly ignored by his own country. From an early age he was fascinated by the idea of space travel, and he carried out experiments at Clark University in Massachusetts, where he was a research student and, for 30 years, a lecturer in physics. In 1919, he published his theory of rocketry, not knowing of the theories of Konstantin Tsiolkovsky two decades earlier. In the 1930s he launched his first stabilized rocket. This had a liquid-fuel motor that used petrol and liquid oxygen, pumped into a combustion chamber. Its success attracted funding and Goddard went on to produce rockets with gyroscopic control and jet vanes.

EDMOND HALLEY
1656–1742

English astronomer and mathematician who proved that some comets were periodic and predicted when Halley's Comet would return

Halley did much of his research while working for the Royal Society. He was a close friend of Isaac Newton and, in the 1680s, helped him to prepare his book, *Principia*. In 1698 Halley became a captain in England's Royal Navy and sailed over the north and south Atlantic measuring the deviation of the magnetic compass and hoping to invent a mechanism for measuring longitude. Halley drew the first map of the southern sky, discovered that stars move, and realized that Earth was very old. He is best known for predicting that Halley's Comet returns to the Sun every 76 years. Later in life he became professor of mathematics at Oxford and England's second Astronomer Royal.

CAROLINE HERSCHEL
1750–1848

Born in Hanover, Germany, Caroline Herschel came to England in 1772 to collaborate with her brother William. She discovered eight comets between 1786 and 1797. In 1787, the British King granted her a salary to continue as assistant to her brother. She is remembered especially for her catalogue of 2,500 nebulas and star clusters.

EJNAR HERTZSPRUNG
1873–1967

Danish astronomer who devised a standard of stellar brightness, defined as the brightness stars would have if they were all 32.6 light years away. He noticed in 1906 that standard brightness was related to the temperature of a star. This was independently discovered in 1913 by Henry Russell. The graph plotting standard brightness against temperature, the Hertzsprung-Russell diagram, is a vital tool in the study of stellar evolution.

ANTONY HEWISH
born 1924

English radio astronomer who studied fluctuations in radio sources and the way in which the signals from two radio telescopes can be combined to mimic a dish as large as the distance between them. In 1967, together with his student Jocelyn Bell Burnell, he discovered pulsars. He was awarded a Nobel Prize for Physics jointly with Martin Ryle, in 1974.

HIPPARCHUS
about 190–120 BC

Greek astronomer remembered for inventing an improved theodolite with which he measured the position of 850 stars. He produced a catalogue of these, which was still in use 18 centuries later. He also classified the stars according to how bright they appeared in the sky. This system forms the basis for today's magnitude scale of stellar brightness. Earth's spin axis moves like a spinning top, and Hipparchus measured the rate at which the axis changed position, and the way in which the distance between Earth and the Sun varies throughout the year.

WILLIAM HUGGINS
1824–1910

Until 1854 this Englishman was a draper, but he then sold the family business to concentrate on observing the sky. He built his own private observatory in London and designed a telescope fitted with a spectroscope. Using this, he was able to study the composition of the Sun, Moon, planets, and stars and showed, in 1863, that the Universe is made of the same elements as exist on Earth. In 1868, he became the first astronomer to use the spectroscope to measure the speed with which stars are moving away from Earth. He also discovered that some nebulas are made of gas.

WILLIAM HERSCHEL
1738–1822

German-born astronomer who made superb reflecting telescopes and discovered Uranus

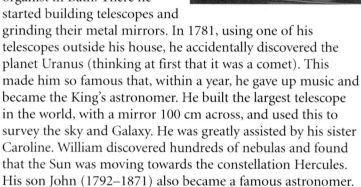

In 1757 Herschel moved from Hanover to England where he earned a living as a musician. In 1766 he was hired as an organist in Bath. There he started building telescopes and grinding their metal mirrors. In 1781, using one of his telescopes outside his house, he accidentally discovered the planet Uranus (thinking at first that it was a comet). This made him so famous that, within a year, he gave up music and became the King's astronomer. He built the largest telescope in the world, with a mirror 100 cm across, and used this to survey the sky and Galaxy. He was greatly assisted by his sister Caroline. William discovered hundreds of nebulas and found that the Sun was moving towards the constellation Hercules. His son John (1792–1871) also became a famous astronomer.

FRED HOYLE
born 1915

English astrophysicist who showed how stars could produce elements and who suggested that the Universe was in a steady state

Hoyle worked at the University of Cambridge in England, apart from 10 years at the Hale Observatory in California. At Hale, he collaborated with William Fowler (1911–95) and in 1957 they showed how elements such as lithium, carbon, oxygen, and iron could be created inside stars. When large stars eventually explode as supernovas, these elements are distributed into space and are recycled in second-generation stars. In 1948 Hoyle, with Thomas Gold and Hermann Bondi, introduced the steady state theory of the Universe. This theory lost ground after the discovery of the background radiation, the remnant of the Big Bang, in 1965.

CHRISTIAAN HUYGENS
1629–95

Huygens was a Dutch scientist who moved to Paris in 1666 and worked there for 15 years before returning home. He produced the best telescope of his time and a new form of telescope eyepiece. In 1655 he used these to observe Saturn and discovered a large satellite that later became known as Titan. He then discovered that the planet was surrounded by a ring. Huygens also invented the pendulum clock and proposed that light was a wave motion, like sound or water.

KARL JANSKY
1905–50

American radio engineer who was the father of radio astronomy. He set out to discover the source of interference in radio signals being used for ship-to-shore communications. He built a rotating radio aerial and receiver in 1932, and soon realized that the interference came from the constellation of Sagittarius. This is the densest part of the Milky Way, and Jansky was detecting radiation from electrons in the Galaxy's magnetic field.

SERGEI KOROLEV
1906–66

In 1931 this Russian engineer was a founding member of the Moscow Group for the Study of Rocket Propulsion. In World War II he was imprisoned by Stalin and put to work developing jet-assisted aircraft. After the war, he developed improved versions of captured German V-2 rockets and was responsible for the production of the first Russian inter-continental missile. He went on to design the Sputnik satellite, and the Vostok, Voskhod, and Soyuz crewed spacecraft.

PIERRE SIMON DE LAPLACE
1749–1827

French mathematician and astronomer who was a professor at the École Militaire in Paris. Starting in 1773, he spent 3 years explaining how the variations in the orbits of Jupiter and Saturn could be accounted for within Newton's laws of gravity. In 1796 he proposed that the Sun and Solar System were formed out of a gas cloud that rotated faster and faster as it shrank, and threw off rings of material as it got smaller. These rings then formed planets. This theory of the formation of the Solar System held until the end of the 19th century.

GEORGES LEMAÎTRE
1894–1966

Belgian physicist who became a priest in 1923 and then turned to cosmology. In 1931, Lemaître proposed that the Universe was once contained in a primeval atom about 30 times the size of the Sun. This exploded into space, scattering material that then condensed to form galaxies and stars. He suggested that the movement of galaxies could be used as indicators of the expansion of the Universe. This later developed into the Big Bang theory.

URBAIN LE VERRIER
1811–77

French astronomer who proved that the orbits of the planets were stable. In 1845 he become interested in the way that the orbits of planets are pulled slightly off course by the gravitational force of adjacent planets. He predicted the position of an unknown planet that was affecting Uranus. He gave his predictions to the German astronomer Johann Galle (1812–1910) who, in 1846, quickly found Neptune.

EDWIN HUBBLE
1889–1953

American astronomer who proved that the Universe contained a multitude of galaxies that were moving away from the Milky Way

Hubble studied law at Chicago and in England, but on returning to the USA he became an astronomer. At the Mount Wilson Observatory in California he used the new 2.5-m telescope to study nebulas. He identified two types: those in our own Galaxy and those beyond. In 1924, he realized that the distant ones were separate galaxies. He also found that the fainter and more distant the galaxy, the faster it was moving away from our own Galaxy. He classified the different types of galaxies but (incorrectly) suggested that one type evolved into another as they aged.

JOHANNES KEPLER
1571–1630

German astronomer who plotted the orbits of planets and realized that they were elliptical

Kepler worked out his three laws of planetary orbits – now known as Kepler's laws of motion – using data obtained by Tycho Brahe, whom he had assisted for the last few months of the Danish astronomer's life. Kepler was convinced that Brahe's observations were accurate, and persisted until he had calculated the orbits correctly. By 1609, Kepler had found that the orbits of planets were ellipses, not circles, and that the speed of a planet around its orbit was slower the farther away it was from the Sun. Kepler was a Lutheran and, because of religious persecution, had to move several times. In 1627 he published the Rudolphine Tables, which allowed astronomers to calculate the positions of planets, in the future, present, and past. Mistakenly, he suggested that planets emitted musical notes as they moved.

BERNARD LOVELL
born 1913

Lovell developed airborne radar for non-visual bombing raids during World War II. After the war, this Englishman pioneered radar observations of meteors at Manchester University. In 1949 he instigated funding for a 76-m radio telescope at Jodrell Bank near Manchester. Building started in 1951 and it was completed just in time to track the rocket of the first Russian satellite, Sputnik 1, in 1957. This attracted much needed funds. Lovell was director of the Jodrell Bank radio observatory for more than 30 years.

PERCIVAL LOWELL
1855–1916

After a brief career in the family cotton business and as a diplomat, this American mathematician set up an observatory in Flagstaff, Arizona. He concentrated on visual and photographic observations of Mars and became convinced that a system of canals existed on that planet. Lowell's books stressed that Mars might be an abode for life. In 1905, he erroneously predicted the position of a Planet X that he thought was affecting the orbits of Uranus and Neptune. Pluto – the ninth planet – was serendipitously discovered by Clyde Tombaugh, using Lowell's telescope, in 1930.

CHARLES MESSIER
1730–1817

Comets were the main interest of this French astronomer; he was the first deliberately to search for new comets, starting with the predicted appearance of Comet Halley in 1758–59. Messier discovered more than 15 new comets, earning him the nickname of the "comet ferret". He also compiled a list of 103 nebulas, star clusters, and galaxies so that he would not mistake them for comets. This list is still used: Andromeda Galaxy, for example, is Messier 31 or M31.

HERMANN OBERTH
1894–1989

With Robert Goddard and Konstantin Tsiolkovsky, Oberth was a founding father of astronautics, and his books The Rocket into Interplanetary Space (1923) and The Road to Space Travel (1929) are classics. Oberth experimented on rocket motors in the 1930s and, during World War II, developed the German V-2 rocket. In the late 1950s, he spent some time in the USA with his old assistant, Wernher von Braun, developing satellite launchers.

ERNST ÖPIK
1893–1985

This Estonian astronomer spent his early life working at the University of Tartu, but in 1948 moved to Northern Ireland, where he later became director of the Armagh Observatory. In 1932, he predicted that the Solar System was surrounded by a cloud of comets – a cloud that is now named after Jan Oort. Öpik's work on the way dust particles burn up as they enter Earth's atmosphere has been applied to the design of devices to protect spacecraft from heat as they re-enter the atmosphere .

HENRIETTA LEAVITT
1868–1921

American astronomer who studied Cepheid variable stars and discovered that the cycle of variation was related to their brightness

Leavitt worked at Harvard College Observatory in Massachusetts, measuring the brightness of star images on photographic plates. For many years, she studied Cepheid variables – stars that oscillate in brightness in regular cycles – in the Magellanic Clouds. In 1912, she confirmed that the longer the cycle, the brighter the star: so by determining the length of the cycle, a star's distance could be calculated from its apparent and real magnitude. This led to the discovery that the Magellanic Clouds were about 100,000 light years away and were small galaxies beyond our own Galaxy.

ISAAC NEWTON
1642–1727

English scientist who explained how gravity keeps the planets in orbit around the Sun and invented a reflecting telescope.

Newton became professor of mathematics at the University of Cambridge at the age of 26. He revolutionized the concept of gravity, and his theory brought together Kepler's laws of planetary motion and Galileo's laws of falling bodies. In the 1680s he suggested that gravity applied throughout the Universe and not just near the surface of Earth. In the 1660s he began to study the nature of light. He found that white light was made up of a rainbow-like spectrum of colours, which was revealed when the light passed through a prism or

a lens. He tried to make a telescope but, because of this effect, the images he saw had coloured edges. To overcome this, in 1668 he invented and built a reflecting telescope that used mirrors. His book, *Principia Mathematica*, published in 1687, is one of the most influential science books ever written.

ARNO PENZIAS
born 1933

A refugee from Nazi Germany, Penzias moved to the USA as a child. He became a radio engineer, joining Bell Telephone Laboratories in 1961. In 1965, while trying to trace a source of radio interference, Penzias and his colleague Robert Wilson found radio waves that came towards Earth from all directions. The source had a temperature of –270°C, and was what remained from the hot radiation produced by the Big Bang. In 1978, Penzias and Wilson received the 1978 Nobel Prize for Physics for their work.

VALERI POLIAKOV
born 1942

Russian doctor and cosmonaut who holds two world records: the most time spent in space and the longest single stay in space. He travelled aboard Soyuz TM-6 to the Mir orbiting space station on 29 August 1988 and stayed for 241 days. He returned to Mir on 8 January 1994, when he stayed for 438 days. He was participating in an unusual medical experiment: before the mission he had some of his bone marrow removed so that it could be compared with another sample of bone marrow taken when he returned after months of weightlessness.

MARTIN REES
born 1942

The major work of England's 15th Astronomer Royal has been carried out at the University of Cambridge where he has concentrated on the study of the centres of active galaxies and the way in which jets of gas from these galaxies interact with the surrounding interstellar medium. He has also written extensively on cosmology and the dark matter in the universe. Rees enthusiastically promotes the communication of science to the general public.

HENRY RUSSELL
1877–1957

An American who became professor of astronomy at Princeton in 1905, Russell studied multiple stars and the relationship between their orbits and masses. From his work on stellar distances, he was able to show that there was a main sequence of stars by plotting stellar luminosity against surface temperature on a graph. This became known as the Hertzsprung-Russell diagram because Ejnar Hertzsprung had plotted a similar graph in 1906. Russell incorrectly predicted that stars evolved by moving either up or down this sequence. In 1929 he suggested, correctly, that stars consist mainly of hydrogen.

JAN OORT
1900–92

Dutch astrophysicist who studied the Milky Way using radio waves, and proposed that the Solar System was surrounded by a cloud of comets

After studying at Groningen University, Oort moved to Leiden University where he became interested in the structure of our Galaxy. By 1927 he realized that the Sun was not at the centre of the Milky Way, and that the paths of nearby stars indicated that the galactic centre was 30,000 light years away, behind the constellation Sagittarius. He found that the Sun orbited the Milky Way every 200 million years and that the Galaxy's mass was 100 billion times that of the Sun. In 1951 he traced the shape of the galactic spiral arms by monitoring the radio waves emitted by the hydrogen between the stars. At about this time, he also suggested that the Sun was surrounded by a huge reservoir of comets that were occasionally disturbed by passing stars.

CECILIA PAYNE-GAPOSCHKIN
1900–79

British-born American astronomer who was the first to suggest that hydrogen and helium were the main constituents of the Universe

After attending lectures at Cambridge given by Sir Arthur Eddington, Cecilia Payne decided to become an astronomer. In 1923, she left England for Harvard College Observatory in Massachusetts to work with Harlow Shapley. After showing that the temperature of a star is related to its type or spectral class, she established that main sequence stars are made almost entirely of hydrogen and helium. In 1934 she married Sergei Gaposchkin: working together, they identified variable stars using photographic observations. She also studied very luminous stars, used today for measuring distances to the farthest galaxies. In 1956 she was awarded the Harvard Chair in Astronomy, and became the first female professor at Harvard.

CARL SAGAN
1934–96

American astronomer whose studies concentrated on the atmospheres of planets. In the 1960s he calculated that the surface of Venus was very hot as a result of a runaway greenhouse effect. He also researched the early atmosphere of Earth and experimented with ways in which life could be generated. Sagan was a well-known science popularizer, and in 1980 his television series, *Cosmos*, was viewed by millions of people around the world.

ALLAN SANDAGE
born 1926

American astronomer who worked at the Mount Wilson and Palomar Observatories in California, starting as an assistant of Edwin Hubble. In 1960, with Canadian astronomer Tom Matthews, he was the first to provide an optical identification of a quasar. In 1965, he discovered the first "radio-quiet" quasars. In fact, only 1 in 200 quasars emits radio waves. His measurements of the distances of galaxies indicate that the Universe is expanding rather slowly.

GIOVANNI SCHIAPARELLI
1835–1910

From 1860 to 1900, this Italian astronomer worked at the Brera Observatory in Milan. In 1862 he realized that the Perseid meteor shower was produced by the decay of Comet Swift-Tuttle, and that they both had the same orbit. He then turned to detailed observations of Mars, which he concluded had channels (canali) on its surface, some of which he thought were splitting into two. He incorrectly suggested that one face of Mercury was always pointing towards the Sun.

BERNHARD SCHMIDT
1879–1935

Born in Estonia, Schmidt moved to Germany in 1900 to study engineering. He then made astronomical lenses and mirrors, eventually joining the staff of the Hamburg Observatory in 1926. Large reflecting telescopes can cover only a very small field of view, and Schmidt devised a telescope for the observatory that used a spherical mirror behind a thin correcting lens to produce a very sharp image over a large field of view. Many Schmidt telescopes have been used for mapping the sky.

HARLOW SHAPLEY
1885–1972

Starting work as a journalist, this American quickly turned to astronomy. While working at Mount Wilson Observatory in California, he used Cepheid variable stars to estimate the distance to globular star clusters. He used these clusters to plot the shape and size of the Milky Way Galaxy. Shapley moved to Harvard in 1921 and became famous for the debate he had with Heber Curtis (1872–1942), the Director of the Allegheny Observatory, USA, about whether the Universe consisted of one galaxy or a multitude. Shapley showed that galaxies are clustered into groups.

ALAN SHEPARD
1923–98

This US Navy test pilot was the first American in space. His suborbital hop on 5 May 1961 took him and his Mercury space capsule to a height of 180 km before it landed in the Atlantic Ocean 485 km down range from the launchpad at Cape Canaveral in Florida, USA. He returned to space in early 1971, when he commanded the Apollo 14 Moon mission.

PTOLEMY
about AD 90–168

Egyptian astronomer who published the astronomical ideas of the ancient Greeks in a book, *The Almagest*

The astronomical works of Ptolemy dominated scientific thought until the 17th century. His writing built on the works of Hipparchus and others. To these he added his own observations, made from a rooftop observatory.

Ptolemy thought that Earth was a perfect sphere at the centre of the Universe, surrounded by seven transparent spheres each of which carried a moving object. In order of speed across the sky (and supposed distance from Earth), these were Moon, Mercury, Venus, Sun, Mars, Jupiter, and Saturn. An eighth sphere contained the stars. He devised a mathematical system that could predict the movement of the planets. He also noted the latitude and longitude of many places on Earth; his maps were so good that Christopher Columbus used them.

MARTIN RYLE
1918–84

British radio astronomy pioneer who produced a catalogue of 5,000 radio sources

The son of a physician, Ryle worked on radar during World War II. Afterwards, he moved to Cambridge University where he perfected a technique of combining signals from different movable radio telescopes to create one high-resolution image of the object emitting radio waves. In the late 1940s, Ryle observed the Sun and mapped the regions that gave out radio waves. In the early 1950s he discovered that radio waves were being emitted by distant galaxies. In a series of detailed catalogues of radio sources, he showed that galaxies were closer together in the early Universe – strong evidence for the Big Bang. In 1974, Ryle and Antony Hewish were awarded the Nobel Prize for Physics.

JOSEF SHKLOVSKII
1916–85

Ukrainian astronomer who, in 1953, started the radio astronomy division of Russia's Astronomical Institute. He was among the first to suggest that spiralling electrons trapped in astronomical magnetic fields produced radio waves with a long wavelength called synchrotron radiation.

JILL TARTER
born 1944

Turning her back on the hunt for brown dwarf stars, this American astrophysicist became the first radio astronomer to start searching full-time for extraterrestrial intelligence in the early 1970s. As the chief scientist of Project Phoenix, she uses a multichannel analyser that takes the signal from large radio telescopes and then listens to many frequencies at the same time, searching for messages.

VALENTINA TERESHKOVA
born 1937

A former textile worker and amateur parachutist, this Russian cosmonaut was the first woman in space. In June 1963, she made 48 orbits of Earth on the Vostok 6 spacecraft in a 71-hour flight. Nineteen years passed before the next woman flew. Tereshkova married in 1963 and, after having a child, continued to train as a cosmonaut until 1969.

CLYDE TOMBAUGH
1906–1997

Born in Illinois, this American astronomer was too poor to attend university. Instead he joined the Lowell Observatory, in Flagstaff, Arizona in 1929 as an assistant. Percival Lowell had predicted the position of Planet X in 1905. To assist the search, Tombaugh built a machine that looked at two photographic plates taken of the same area of sky, a few hours apart, to see if anything had moved against the fixed background of stars. On 18 February 1930 he found Pluto. Uncertain as to whether Pluto was big enough to disturb the orbit of Uranus, he continued his search for another planet for eight years, but without success.

FRED WHIPPLE
born 1906

American astronomer who studied in California before moving to Harvard University in Massachusetts in 1931. Whipple became professor of astronomy at Harvard in 1950 and director of the Smithsonian Astrophysical Observatory in 1955. In addition to discovering six new comets, he suggested in 1951 that the heart of a comet was a large ball of snow and dust, the surface of which evaporated as it was heated in the inner Solar System. Whipple also studied the orbits of meteors and spacecraft, and worked out how the density and temperature of Earth's upper atmosphere affected their orbits.

KONSTANTIN TSIOLKOVSKY
1857–1935

Russian pioneer of the theory of space flight. Sputnik I was launched to commemorate the centenary of his birth

Tsiolkovsky produced theories of rocketry but did not have the resources to build a rocket. By 1898 he had produced a theory that showed how much fuel a rocket would use and how its velocity was related to the thrust of its engines. His book *Exploration of Cosmic Space by Means of Reaction Devices* (1903) contained designs of liquid hydrogen and liquid oxygen rockets very similar to those in use today. He also showed that multistage rockets would be needed to leave Earth's gravitational field and how these could be stacked one on top of another (as in the US Saturn V) or arranged side by side (as in the Russian space boosters).

WERNHER VON BRAUN
1912–77

German rocket engineer who developed the V-2 missile and the Saturn V Moon launcher

Von Braun's work on rocket engines in the 1930s led to his appointment as technical director of the rocket establishment in Peenemünde, where he developed the V-2, a liquid-fuelled rocket weapon, during World War II. Between 1942 and 1945, more than 5,000 V-2s were built.

After the war, the US Army selected von Braun for work in New Mexico, USA. There he designed the Redstone rocket, which in 1958 put Explorer 1, America's first satellite, into orbit, and in 1961 launched Alan Shepard on the first Mercury suborbital mission. In 1960 von Braun was put in charge of the Marshall Space Flight Center in Alabama, where he developed the Saturn rockets that were used to send men to the Moon in the Apollo programme.

ROBERT WILSON
born 1936

Born in Houston, Texas, in 1963 this American physicist joined Bell Telecommunication Laboratories in New Jersey. Working with Arno Penzias on reducing the radio noise in a horn-shaped radio antenna, in 1965 he discovered radio waves coming in all directions from a source which had a temperature of −270°C. This was what remained of the hot radiation produced by the Big Bang. Penzias and Wilson received the 1978 Nobel Prize for Physics for their work.

JOHN YOUNG
born 1930

American astronaut who trained as a test pilot in the navy. In 1965, he flew in Gemini 3, the first US two-man space mission. After flying in Gemini 10, in 1969 he made 31 lunar orbits in Apollo 10, the dress rehearsal for the first Moon landing. He was commander of the Apollo 16 mission in 1972, making three walks on the Moon. In April 1981 he was commander of the first Space Shuttle flight.

FRITZ ZWICKY
1898–1974

Swiss astrophysicist who in 1927 moved to the California Institute of Technology, USA. In 1934, he realized that supernova explosions were much more energetic than novas. He suggested that the supernova explosion destroyed most of the star, leaving only the central core, which appeared as a neutron star. He searched for supernovas but calculated that in any galaxy only one would appear every 400 years. Zwicky also studied clusters of galaxies and observed that, unlike the Universe as a whole, the clusters were not expanding.

GLOSSARY

Words in *italics* have their own entries in the glossary.

ABSOLUTE MAGNITUDE See *magnitude*.

ABSOLUTE ZERO The lowest possible temperature: –273°C.

ABSORPTION LINE A dark line in a *spectrum*, caused by *atoms* absorbing *radiation* of a certain *wavelength*. Astronomers use absorption lines to identify *elements* in *stars* and *galaxies*.

ACCRETION DISC A disc of material spiralling into a *black hole*.

ACTIVE GALAXY A *galaxy* with a *black hole* at its centre that is generating huge amounts of energy.

ANNIHILATION The destruction of a *subatomic particle* and its *antimatter* opposite when they meet.

ANTIMATTER *Matter* made of *subatomic particles* with equal and opposite properties to normal *matter*.

APERTURE The diameter of a telescope's main mirror or lens – a measure of the amount of *light* it can collect.

APHELION The point in an object's *orbit* at which it is farthest from the Sun.

APOGEE The farthest point from Earth reached by the Moon or an orbiting artificial *satellite*.

APPARENT MAGNITUDE See *magnitude*.

ARC SECOND A unit used by astronomers to measure the size or separation of objects in the sky. One arc second is equal to 1/3,600 *degrees*.

ASTEROID A chunk of rock or metal in space, varying from a few metres to more than 900 km across.

ASTROLABE An ancient astronomical instrument used to measure the position and movement of objects in the sky.

ASTRONOMICAL UNIT (AU) The average distance between the Earth and the Sun – 149.6 million km.

ATMOSPHERE A layer of gas held around a *planet* by its *gravity*. Also the outer layers of a *star*, beyond its *photosphere*.

ATOM The smallest part of an *element*, made up of three types of *subatomic particles* – protons, neutrons, and electrons.

AURORA Green and red glow seen in the sky near the polar regions, caused by particles from the Sun colliding with gases in Earth's *atmosphere*.

AXIS An imaginary line that passes through the centre of a *planet* or *star*, around which the object rotates.

BACKGROUND RADIATION A faint radio signal emitted by the entire sky – the remnant of *radiation* from the *Big Bang*.

BARRED SPIRAL GALAXY A *galaxy* with spiral arms linked to a central bulge by a straight bar of *stars* and gas.

BIG BANG The violent event that gave birth to the Universe about 13 billion years ago.

BILLION One thousand million.

BINARY SYSTEM A pair of *stars* in *orbit* around each other.

BLACK HOLE A collapsed object whose *gravity* is so strong that nothing – not even *light* – can escape it.

BLAZAR An *active galaxy* angled in such a way that when viewed from Earth we see *radiation* coming straight from its core.

BLUE SHIFT A shift in *spectral lines* towards the blue end of the *spectrum*. The shift, caused by the *Doppler effect,* indicates that the *radiation* is emitted by an object moving towards us.

BRIGHTNESS See *luminosity* and *magnitude*.

BROWN DWARF An object smaller than a *star* but larger than a *planet*. It produces heat, but no *light*.

CARBON One of the most common *elements* in the Universe, produced by stars. Carbon is the basis of all life.

CCD See *charge-coupled device*.

CELESTIAL OBJECT Any object seen in the sky, including *planets*, *stars*, and *galaxies*.

CELESTIAL SPHERE An imaginary sphere of sky that surrounds Earth and on which *celestial objects* appear to lie. Astronomers measure *star* positions according to their declination (latitude) and right ascension (longitude) on the celestial sphere.

CEPHEID VARIABLE A type of *variable star* that changes in brightness and size. The length of the cycle of change is linked to the *absolute magnitude* of the star. Astronomers use Cepheids to measure distances in space.

CHARGE-COUPLED DEVICE A light-sensitive electronic device used for generating images in modern telescopes.

CHROMOSPHERE The lower layer of the Sun's *atmosphere*. It shines pinkish-red, but can be seen only when the brighter *photosphere* is blocked out.

CIRCUMPOLAR STAR Any star that does not appear to set from an observer's location on Earth, but instead appears to circle the celestial pole.

CLUSTER See *star cluster* and *galaxy cluster*.

COMET A small object made of ice and rocky dust. When a comet nears the Sun, the Sun's heat melts the ice, creating a glowing head of gas with tails of dust and gas.

CONJUNCTION The point in the *orbit* of a *planet* when it appears directly in line with the Sun when viewed from Earth.

CONSTELLATION A pattern of *stars* in the sky, often named after a mythological person or creature. Astronomers define constellations as areas of sky, rather than individual stars.

CORONA The Sun's very hot upper *atmosphere*, visible as a pearly halo during a total solar *eclipse*.

COSMIC RAY A tiny, fast-moving electrically charged *particle* coming from space.

COSMOLOGICAL CONSTANT A hidden property of space, first proposed by Einstein, that may be stretching space itself and accelerating the expansion of the Universe.

COSMOS Another word for the Universe.

CRATER A saucer-shaped hole blasted in the surface of a *moon* or *planet* by the impact of a *meteorite*.

CRUST The rocky surface layer of a *planet* or *moon*.

DARK MATTER Invisible matter that is thought to make up 97% of the Universe's *mass*. Dark matter may include *brown dwarfs*, *WIMPs*, and *neutrinos*.

DEEP-SKY OBJECT A collective term for *nebulas*, *star clusters*, and *galaxies*.

DEGREE The basic unit for measuring angles – 1/360 of a full circle.

DOPPLER EFFECT The change in the *frequency* of waves (of sound or *radiation*) that reach an observer when the source is moving closer or farther away.

DOUBLE STAR See *binary system*.

DUST Microscopic grains in space that absorb starlight. The dust is "soot" from cool *stars*, and sometimes clumps together in huge dark clouds.

ECLIPSE An effect caused by one *celestial object* casting a shadow on another. A lunar eclipse happens when Earth's shadow falls on the Moon. A solar eclipse is when the Moon's shadow falls on Earth.

ECLIPSING BINARY A pair of *stars* in *orbit* around each other in such a way that the stars pass in front of and behind each other as seen from Earth.

ECLIPTIC An imaginary line around the sky along which the Sun appears to move in the sky through the year, and near which most of the *planets* are seen. In fact, this line is a projection of Earth's *orbit* around the Sun onto the sky.

ELECTROMAGNETIC RADIATION Waves of energy, carried by *photons*, that can travel through space and *matter*. It travels at the *speed of light*, and ranges from *gamma rays* (shortest *wavelength*) to *radio waves* (longest wavelength).

ELECTRON See *atom*.

ELEMENT Any of the basic substances of nature which cannot be broken down by chemical reactions. Each element has unique properties.

ELLIPTICAL GALAXY A *galaxy* with an oval or round shape, and no spiral arms. Elliptical galaxies are made mostly of old *stars*, and contain very little *dust* or gas.

ELLIPTICAL ORBIT An *orbit* in the shape of an elongated circle. All orbits are elliptical – a circle is just a special type of ellipse.

EMISSION LINE A bright line in a *spectrum* caused by *atoms* giving out energy of a certain *wavelength*. Emission lines often arise from hot gas in a *nebula*.

ESCAPE VELOCITY The speed at which one object must travel to escape another's *gravity*.

EYEPIECE A small lens placed at the viewing end of a *telescope*.

The eyepiece magnifies the image produced by the main mirror or lens.

EXTRASOLAR Not belonging to the Sun – outside the *Solar System*.

EXTRATERRESTRIAL Not belonging to the Earth.

FILAMENT A string of galaxy *superclusters* stretching across a huge expanse of space. Filaments are the largest structures in the Universe, and are separated by immense *voids*.

FLY-BY An encounter between a space probe and a *planet*, *comet*, or *asteroid*, in which the probe does not stop to orbit or land.

FOCAL LENGTH The distance between a lens or mirror and the point where the *light* rays it collects are brought into *focus*.

FOCUS The point in a telescope where *light* rays gathered by the main lens or mirror come together to form an image.

FREQUENCY The number of waves of *electromagnetic radiation* that pass a point every second.

GALAXY A body consisting of millions of *stars*, and gas and *dust* held together by *gravity* and separated from other galaxies by empty space.

GALAXY CLUSTER A group of *galaxies* held together by gravity.

GAMMA RAYS *Electromagnetic radiation* with very short *wavelengths* emitted by the most energetic objects in the Universe.

GAS GIANT A large planet that is made largely of a very deep, dense gaseous *atmosphere*.

GEOSTATIONARY ORBIT An *orbit* 35,880 km above the Equator in which a *satellite* takes the same time to circle Earth as Earth takes to spin on its *axis*. The satellite therefore appears to be fixed in the sky.

GIANT STAR A *star* that has reached the last stages of its evolution, has swollen in size, increased in brightness, and changed in colour. Sun-like stars become red giants; stars with more than 10 times the mass of the Sun become supergiants, which are the most *luminous* stars in the Universe.

GLOBULAR CLUSTER See *star cluster*.

GRAVITATIONAL LENSING Distortion of *light* from a distant object as it passes through a region of powerful *gravity*.

GRAVITATIONAL WELL The distortion of space and time caused by the *gravity* of a massive object such as a *star*.

GRAVITY Force of attraction between any objects with *mass*, such as the pull between Earth and the Moon.

GREENHOUSE EFFECT The rise in temperature caused by gases – such as carbon dioxide and *methane* – trapping the heat that a *planet's* surface should be reflecting back into space.

HALO The spherical region around a *spiral galaxy*, containing *dark matter* and globular *star clusters*.

HELIOSPHERE Space within 100 *astronomical units* of the Sun, where the *solar wind* still has an effect.

HELIUM The second lightest and second most common *element* in the Universe, produced in the *Big Bang* and by *nuclear fusion* in stars.

HERTZSPRUNG-RUSSELL DIAGRAM A diagram showing how a *star's* brightness and colour are related. Such a diagram shows that stars fall into just a few main types, and can be used to trace the lifecycle of stars.

HUBBLE CONSTANT A measure of the rate at which the *Universe* is expanding, measured in kilometres per second per million *parsecs*.

HYDROGEN The most common and lightest *element* in the Universe – the main component of *stars* and *galaxies*.

INFERIOR PLANET Any *planet* in the *Solar System* that orbits closer to the Sun than Earth.

INFLATION A period of rapid expansion occurring within less than a second of the *Big Bang*.

INFRARED Heat radiation – a type of *electromagnetic radiation* with *wavelengths* just longer than visible *light*.

INTERGALACTIC Between *galaxies*.

INTERSTELLAR Between *stars*.

INTERSTELLAR MEDIUM A *toms* and *molecules* in the space between the *stars*.

IONOSPHERE The electrically charged region of the Earth's atmosphere between 50 and 600 km above the surface.

IRREGULAR GALAXY A *galaxy* with no obvious shape. Irregular galaxies are generally small, full of gas, and contain a mix of young and old *stars*.

KUIPER BELT An area of the *Solar System* containing millions of icy, comet-like objects. It extends from the *orbit* of Neptune to the inner edge of the *Oort Cloud*.

LAVA Molten rock released from the interior of a *planet*.

LEPTON Any of three types of negatively charged *subatomic particles* created in the *Big Bang*; only the electron (see *atom*) still exists.

LIBRATION A wobble in the Moon's rotation that allows observers to see slightly more than half of its surface.

LIGHT *Electromagnetic radiation* with *wavelengths* that are visible to the human eye.

LIGHT POLLUTION A glow in the sky, caused by streetlights and atmospheric pollution, that blocks astronomers' view of faint objects.

LIGHT YEAR A standard unit of astronomical measurement, based on the distance light travels in one year – roughly 9.5 million million km.

LOCAL ARM Also Orion Arm – the spiral arm of the Milky Way Galaxy in which the Sun lies.

LOCAL GROUP The cluster of about 30 *galaxies* to which the *Milky Way* belongs.

LOW-EARTH ORBIT An orbit about 200 km above Earth's surface. Low-Earth orbits are used by the Space Shuttle, space stations, and many *satellites*.

LUMINOSITY The amount of energy given off by a *star* as *radiation* each second.

MAGNETIC FIELD Magnetism generated by a *planet*, *star*, or *galaxy*, that extends into space.

MAGNETOSPHERE The bubble around a *planet* where the *magnetic field* is strong enough to keep out the *solar wind*.

MAGNITUDE The brightness of a *celestial object*, expressed on a scale of numbers. Bright objects have low (sometimes negative) numbers; dim objects have high numbers. Apparent magnitude is a measure of brightness as seen from Earth; absolute magnitude is a measure of an object's real brightness.

MAIN SEQUENCE The region on the *Hertzsprung-Russell diagram* where most *stars* lie. Stars on the main sequence generate energy by nuclear reactions that convert *hydrogen* into *helium*.

MANTLE The rocky layer that lies between the *crust* and the *core* inside a *planet*.

MARE (PLURAL MARIA) A large, dark marking on the Moon, originally thought to be a lunar sea but now known to be huge depressions flooded with *lava*.

MASS A measure of the amount of *matter* in an object, and how it is affected by *gravity*.

MATTER Anything that has *mass* and occupies space.

METEOR A streak of light in the sky – also known as a shooting star – caused by a small *meteoroid* burning up as it enters Earth's *atmosphere*.

METEOROID Fragments of rock and dust from *asteroids* and *comets* that are found in space.

METEORITE A *meteoroid* fallen to the surface of a *planet* or *moon*. Where it hits the surface, it may form a *crater*.

METHANE A gas made of *carbon* and *hydrogen*.

MICROGRAVITY Very low *gravity*, as experienced in *orbit*. Microgravity is a more accurate term than zero gravity, because a spacecraft's movements are almost always creating gravity in one direction.

MICROMETRE One millionth of a metre.

MICROWAVE A type of *radio wave*, which has the shortest of the radio *wavelengths*.

MICROWAVE BACKGROUND See *background radiation*.

MILKY WAY The name of the *galaxy* in which we live. Also the pale band of *stars* running across the sky when we look along the plane of our Galaxy.

MOLECULAR CLOUD An *interstellar* cloud made up of molecules such as *hydrogen* and carbon monoxide.

MOLECULE A collection of *atoms* linked by chemical bonds so that they act as a single unit.

MOON A planet's natural *satellite*. Earth's satellite is called the Moon; those of other planets have unique names, such as Io, Jupiter's moon.

MULTIPLE STAR Three or more *stars* held in *orbit* around each other by *gravity*.

NAKED EYE Unassisted human eyesight. The term naked eye is used for any object that should be visible to an average observer in good conditions.

NANOMETRE One billionth of a metre.

NEBULA A cloud of gas and *dust* in space. Nebulas are visible when they reflect starlight or when they block out light coming from behind them. See also *planetary nebula*.

NEUTRINO An extremely common *subatomic particle* produced by *nuclear fusion* in *stars* and by the *Big Bang*. Neutrinos have a tiny *mass* and are very difficult to detect.

NEUTRON See *atom*.

NEUTRON STAR A collapsed *star* composed mainly of *neutrons* – the most common aftermath of a *supernova* explosion.

NITROGEN A gas that makes up 79% of Earth's *atmosphere*.

NOVA A *white dwarf* star in a *binary system* that pulls material off its companion *star*, collecting an *atmosphere*. When the atmosphere ignites, the resulting nova shines thousands of times brighter.

NUCLEAR FUSION The combination of *nuclei* of *atoms* to form heavier ones at very high temperatures and pressures. Nuclear fusion is the energy source of *stars*.

NUCLEUS (PLURAL NUCLEI) The central part of an *atom*, where nearly all its *mass* is contained. The nucleus is made up of protons and neutrons.

OCCULTATION The passing of one *celestial object* in front of another – for instance when the Moon blocks the view of a distant *star*.

OORT CLOUD A huge spherical cloud, about 1.6 light years wide, that surrounds the Sun and *planets*. It contains billions of *comets*.

OPEN CLUSTER See *star cluster*.

OPPOSITION The point in the *orbit* of a *planet* when it appears directly opposite the Sun for an observer on Earth. This is when the planet is best viewed.

OPTICAL LIGHT See *light*.

ORBIT The path of one object round another, more massive object in space. *Satellites*, *planets*, and *stars* are held in orbit by the pull of *gravity* of a more massive body.

ORBITAL PERIOD The time taken for one object to complete its *orbit* around another.

OXYGEN An *element* vital to the development of life, and widespread in the Universe. Oxygen makes up 20% of the Earth's *atmosphere*.

PARALLAX The shift in a nearby object's position against a more distant background when seen from two separate points. Astronomers use parallax from opposite sides of Earth's *orbit* to measure the distances of nearby *stars*.

PARSEC The distance at which a *star* or other object has a *parallax* of 1 *arc second*, equivalent to 3.26 *light years*.

PARTICLE See *subatomic particle*.

PAYLOAD The cargo carried into space by a launch vehicle or on an artificial *satellite*.

PENUMBRA The outer, lighter part of a *sunspot*. Also the lightest part of a *lunar eclipse* shadow, where the Moon lies only partially in Earth's shadow.

PHASE The size of the illuminated portion of a *planet* or *moon*, as seen from Earth.

PHOTON A particle of *electromagnetic radiation*. Photons are the most common particles in the Universe.

PHOTOSPHERE A *star's* visible surface, at which the star becomes transparent. This allows the star's *light* to blaze out into space.

PLANET A spherical object made of rock or gas that *orbits* a *star*. A planet does not produce its own *light*, but it reflects the light of the star. See also *brown dwarf*.

PLANETARY NEBULA The shell of gas puffed off by a *red giant* star before it becomes a *white dwarf*.

POLAR ORBIT A *satellite orbit* passing above or close to the Earth's poles.

POLE STAR The star Polaris, in the *constellation* Ursa Minor, around which the northern sky appears to rotate.

POSITRON The *antimatter* equivalent of an electron (see *atom*). It has the same *mass* as an electron, but a positive, rather than negative, charge.

PROMINENCE A huge arc of gas in the Sun's lower *corona*.

PROTON See *atom*.

PROTOSTAR A young *star* that has not yet started *nuclear fusion* in its core.

PULSAR A spinning *neutron star* that sends beams of *radiation* across space.

QUADRILLION One thousand million million.

QUARK A basic *subatomic particle*, created in the *Big Bang*. Three quarks combined can produce a proton or a neutron (see *atom*).

QUASAR A distant *active galaxy*, releasing enormous amounts of energy from a small central region. Quasars are some of the most distant galaxies in the Universe.

QUINTILLION One million million million.

RADAR The technique of bouncing *radio waves* off an object to measure its distance or map its surface.

RADIATION Energy released by an object in the form of *electromagnetic radiation*.

RADIO GALAXY An *active galaxy* that shines brightly at *radio wavelengths*. Most of its *radiation* comes from huge clouds on either side of the main galaxy.

RADIO WAVES *Electromagnetic radiation* with very long *wavelengths*, produced by gas clouds and energetic objects.

RED GIANT See *giant star*.

RED SHIFT A shift in *spectral lines* towards the red end of the *spectrum*. The shift, caused by the *Doppler effect*, indicates that the *radiation* is emitted by an object moving away from us.

RESOLVING POWER A measure of a *telescope's* ability to distinguish fine detail.

RETROGRADE MOTION An apparent backward movement of a *superior planet* in the sky, as the Earth overtakes it on its journey around the Sun.

SATELLITE Any object held in *orbit* around another object by its *gravity*, ranging from *moons* and artificial satellites in orbit around *planets* to small *galaxies* in orbit around larger ones.

SEYFERT GALAXY A *spiral galaxy* with an unusually bright centre – a type of *active galaxy*.

SOLAR FLARE A huge explosion above the surface of the Sun, caused as two loops of the Sun's *magnetic field* touch.

SOLAR SYSTEM Everything trapped by the Sun's *gravity*, from *planets* to *comets*. Other *stars* also have solar systems.

SOLAR WIND A stream of high-speed *particles* blowing away from the Sun.

SPECTRAL ANALYSIS The study of *spectral lines* to reveal information about the composition of a *star* or *galaxy*, or to find its *red shift*.

SPECTRAL LINES Bright or dark lines in the *spectrum* of a body emitting *radiation*. See also *absorption line* and *emission line*.

SPECTRAL TYPE A method of classifying *stars* according to their colour and surface temperature.

SPECTROSCOPE An instrument used for splitting starlight into

a *spectrum* and revealing *spectral lines* that tell astronomers about the composition of the Universe.

SPECTRUM (PLURAL SPECTRA) A band of *radiation* split up by different *wavelengths*. The rainbow is a spectrum produced by splitting *light*.

SPEED OF LIGHT A measure of how far a ray of light travels in one second – nearly 300,000 km. Nothing can travel faster than this speed.

SPIRAL GALAXY A *galaxy* with spiral arms emerging from a smooth central hub. Spiral galaxies have a mix of old and young *stars*, and are rich in star-forming gas and *dust*.

STAR A hot, massive, and luminous ball of gas that makes energy by *nuclear fusion*.

STARBURST GALAXY A *galaxy* that has undergone a sudden period of *star* formation, often as the result of colliding with another galaxy.

STAR CLUSTER A group of *stars* held together by *gravity*. Open clusters are loose groups of a few hundred young stars; globular clusters are dense balls containing many thousands of old stars.

STAR SYSTEM See *multiple star*.

STEADY STATE THEORY A now-discredited theory that the Universe has no beginning and no end, and will remain the same forever.

SUBATOMIC PARTICLE Any particle smaller than an *atom*. Protons, neutrons, and electrons are the main subatomic particles that make up atoms.

SUNSPOT A cool dark spot on the Sun's surface, created by the Sun's *magnetic field*, that stops the normal circulation of gases.

SUPERCLUSTER A group of *galaxy clusters* held together by *gravity*.

SUPERGIANT See *giant star*.

SUPERIOR PLANET Any *planet* whose orbital path is farther from the Sun than Earth's.

SUPERNOVA An enormous stellar explosion. Supernovas happen when a *supergiant* star runs out of fuel, or when a *white dwarf* explodes.

TIDAL FORCE A force on the surface of one object caused by a nearby object's *gravity*.

TRILLION One million million.

ULTRAVIOLET *Electromagnetic radiation* with a *wavelength* just shorter than visible *light*.

UMBRA The inner, darker region of a *sunspot*. Also the darkest part of a lunar *eclipse* shadow, where the Moon is completely eclipsed.

VAN ALLEN BELTS Regions of *radiation* around Earth, where Earth's *magnetic field* traps particles from the *solar wind*.

VARIABLE STAR A *star* that changes in brightness. Many variable stars also regularly change size.

VISIBLE LIGHT See *light*.

VOIDS Immense empty r egions of space, separating the *filaments* of galaxies.

WAVELENGTH The distance between the peaks or troughs in waves of *electromagnetic radiation*.

WEIGHTLESSNESS See *microgravity*.

WHITE DWARF The collapsed *core* of a Sun-like *star* that has stopped generating energy.

WIMP A "weakly interactive massive particle" created in the *Big Bang*. Most *dark matter* is thought to be made of WIMPs.

X-RAYS Radiation with a very short *wavelength* produced by hot gas clouds and *stars*, and around *black holes*.

ZERO GRAVITY See *microgravity*.

ZODIAC The 12 *constellations* through which the Sun, Moon, and *planets* appear to move.

N

O

PICTURE SOURCES

The publisher would like to thank the following for permission to use their photographs.

Abbreviations: r = right, l = left, t = top, c = center, b = bottom, a = above

AKG London: 9cb, 15tl, 281t, 282all, 288t Bryan & Cherry Alexander/Ann Hawthorne: 149cl Anglo Australian Observatory: 13tr, 14tr, 19bc, 164c, 174bl, 180br, 184bl, br, 197tr, 198tl, 209tl, 215tr, 221bl /David Malin: 208bl, 210tr, 217cla, 219br /Malin/Pasachoff/Caltech 1992: 201tl /Royal Observatory Edinburgh: 185tc, 196-7b, 214-5t Associated Press/Mikhail Metzel: 42bl /NASA TV: 64bl Astronomical Society of the Pacific, San Francisco, CA: 210br Aviation Picture Library: 51bc

Bell Laboratories: 25tr Philip Blanco (UCSC) & John Conway from observations made at the Very Large Array radio telescope (NRAO/AUI) New Mexico: 217cr The Boeing Company: 43cr, 70br Bridgeman Art Library: 285bl

Carnegie Institution of Washington, Observatories of the: 221cra 246br CERN: 223cr Bruce Coleman Ltd: 87bl Colorific: 143bc, 151tr Corbis UK Ltd: 17b, 47bc, 51tr, 57br, 58bl, 60br, 61tl, cl, br, 63br, 67b, 73tl, 75cb, 84-

5b, 88t, 91tl, 98b, 132tr, 141tr, 160b, 226t, 244bl Compton Gamma Ray Observatory: 217bl

Dr. Thomas Dame, Harvard-Smithsonian Center for Astrophysics: 195cb Emmanuel Davoust, Université Paul Sabatier, Observatoire Midi-Pyrenees, 14 Avenue Edouard Belin, 31400 Toulouse, France: 221cb

ESA: 41bl, 44cl, 54-5c, 66bl /CNES: 44-5t, 45cl, r /CNES/CSG: 45br /D. Ducros: 42c NES/CSG: 44cr /B. Paris: 44b European Southern Observatory: 176-7t Mary Evans Picture Library: 93cr, 117br, 144tr, 149br, 155br, 207tr, 219tr, 280br, 283bc, 284tr Eye Ubiquitous: 149bc

Vivien Fifield Picture Library: 283t Forward, Dr. Robert L., Hughes Aircraft Company/Art by Seichi Kiyohara: 74c, br

Galaxy Picture Library: 8br, 95cr, 101tr, 102clb, b, 105br, 111tr, 115c, cl, 121tr, 123cr, 127cr, 142bl, 143, 165br, 167c, 168tr, 173tr, c, cr, 175b, 177bl, 181bl, 182br, 197bc, 199br, bl, 209tr, 245tr, 247cl, cr, bl, br, 248t, cr, br, 249cl, cr, bl, 251tr, 253cl, cr, 254bl, 255tc, tr, 256l, 257tc, tr, cr, 258l, 259t, 260l, 262bl, 263tr, trb, 264cl, 265all, 267tl, tc, tr, cr, c, bca, bl, 268tl, cl, bl, 269tr, tc, bc, bl, 270br, 272bc, bl, 273cr, bra, 274cr, bl, /David Graham: 270bl /Palomar Sky Survey: 164br /Alistair Simmons: 264r /Paul Stephens: 100ca, 102clb, cb /Michael Strecker: 261tr Gemini 8m Telescope

Project: 14br Genesis Space Photo Library: 41cr /CSG: 44tr Isabella Gioia, Institute for Astronomy, 2700 Woodlawn Drive, Honolulu, HI 96822: 230bc

Robert Harding Picture Library: 87cra Harvard-Smithsonian Center for Astrophysics: 218tr Harvard University Archives: 287b Hencoup Enterprises: 19cl, 30t, 32br, 157tr, bl, 210cl, c, cr, 211bra, 236t, 247t, 287cl, 289cl /ESO: 4br /Hale Observatory: 185c, crb /Noel Murto & Ian Cooper: 206t /NRAO/AUI: 25br /Realm of the Nebula by Edwin Hubble: 211tl, cla, cl, clb, bca, br /Royer: 207cb Jim Henderson: 264b J.J. Hester & S.R. Kulkarni/California Institute of Technology, Pasadena: 203cr HMX Inc: 71cr Hughes Space and Communications Company: 40tr, bla, 41cl, 47tl, 48tr Hulton Getty: 281br, 283br, 285cr, 286b, 287t, 288bc, 289br

ICRR (Institute for Cosmic Ray Research) University of Tokyo: 33tr Image Select: 79br

D. Jewitt (University of Hawaii) & J. Luu (University of Leiden): 141bc

Ernest Orlando Lawrence, Berkeley National Laboratory, California: 155tl Lockheed Martin Corporation: 40bl Lowell Observatory: 138cla, clb Lucent Technologies Inc, 600 Mountain Avenue, Murray Hill, NJ 07974: 235br Lunar and

Planetary Institute, 3600 Bay Area Blvd, Houston, TX 77058-1113: 101cra, 103crb, 112tr

Matra Marconi Space: 56tl, 57cl **James Marks:** 145cr **Mullard Radio Astronomy Observatory**, University of Cambridge: 163c

NASA: 27ca, cb, 37br, 39br 42tr, 59bca, 60tr, 61cr, 64t, c, 65t, br, bl, 66bc, 68c, br, bl 68-9c, 69t, bc, 70-1c, 99tr, 100cl, 101cra, crb, 102tr, 128tr, 133cb, cba, 142br, 147cl, 148br, 150cl, 159tr, 210b, 239r /Carla Thomas: 71bl /GSFC: 27br, bl /Hubble Space Telescope: 139t, 228-9c /JPL: 72cr, 84t, 85cb, 98t, 112bl, 120b, 126c, 130br, bc, 137tl, 139c /JSC: 86t, bca /JSC/Pat Rawlings: 73br /Langley Research Center: 59cla /Marshall Space Flight Center: 67t **NASDA:** 41tl, tc **National Radio Astronomy Observatory**, Charlottesville, VA: 25tl **Natural History Museum Picture Library:** 99cr, 148bl, 149t **NOAA (National Oceanic and Atmospheric Administration):** 52tr, 53cra **NOAO:** 229bl **Nobeyama Radio Observatory**, National Astronomical Observatory of Japan: 24bl **NSSDC (National Space Science Data Center):** 100bc, 102cla, 103tl, tr, ca, b, 104bl, 106cl, bc, 107bc, 109clb, 112c, 113c, br

Orbital Sciences Corporation, Reston, VA: 40br, bra, 70bl

PA News Photo Library: 281bl /EPA: 239c **Patrick Air Force Base**, Cape Canaveral, FL: 40tl **Planet Earth Pictures:** 94bl, cl, 151c **Popperfoto:** 59bl

ROSAT/Max-Planck-Institut für Extraterrestrische Physik (MPE): 29cr, bc, 214br /GRO/Comptel Mission: 31tr /Levenson et al: 188tr /S. L. Snowden: 185cla, 214bc

Royal Astronomical Society Library: 116br, 165cr, 173tl, 195tl, 201tr, 286t **Royal Greenwich Observatory**, Cambridge: 18-19, 189cr /Simon Tulloch: 18bla **Royal Observatory Edinburgh:** 22br 280tr /photo by David Malin, AAO: 15tr, 174-5t, 196-7t, 199c, 201cr, 280t

Sachsische Landesbibliothek, Dresden: 161tr **SaVi: Satellite Visualisation software created at the Geometry Center**, University of Minnesota (www.geom.umn.edu/locate/SaVi); **Science Museum**, London: 15br **Science & Society Picture Library:** 168bl, 284cl **Science Photo Library:** 1, 2-3, 4tl, 6b, 7r, 8t, 10-11, 12bl, 13br, 22t, 23tr, tc, 26bl, 27t, 29cl, 30bl, 32-3t, 34-5, 38bl, r, 46bl, 47cl, 49tr, 50br, cb, 50-1c, 51c, 52c, crb, bl, 53bl, br, 54cl, 55tl, crb, bc, 56cl, tr, 58-9t, 59tc, br, 60tl, bl, bc, 61tr, c, 67cr, 68t, 69br, 70tl, 75tl, bl, br, 76-7, 81tr, 84cr, 89c, 90cl, bc, 91tr, 92tl, 93tl, 95tr, 101tl, 104tr, 107tr, 108tl, b, 109tl, cla, br, 110tr, cr, 111tl, cla, cr, cra, 113t, bc, 114bl, 116bl, 116-7t, 117tr, 118t, c, b, 119tl, tr, 120bl, 121tl, cr, br, 122t, 123tr, 124cl, bl, 125tc, br, 126br, 127tr, tl, cla, c, 129cl, 130tr, 131tl, 133t, c, 135cl, 140bl, 142-3tl, 144bca, 146b, 147cr, 149cr, 150b, 151tl, 152-3, 155c, 156-7cr, 157tl, 158tr, c, 158-9c, 159c, b, 161t, c, 162-3t, 168cr, 172bl, 174br, 178tr, 179br, 181t, cb, 182-3t, 194tr, 195tr, 197tl, c, 200tl, 201bl, 202tr, 203bl, 204tr, 205tr, cla, clb, bc, 206bl, 206-7c, 207tl, 208tr, cl,b, 213cr, bca, 215br, 219tl, 227t, 230bla, 230-1tc, 231c, cr, crb, 237tc, 238br, 239tr, 240-1, 280tl, 284br, 285tc, 287cr, 289t **SETI Institute/Seth Shostak:** 288cr **Shimizu Corporation**, Japan: 71bl **Space and Missile Systems Center**, Los Angeles Air Force Base, California, USA: 57t **Stanford University**, Visual Arts Service, California: 222cl, bl **Carole Stott:** 141cr, 145tr **Louis Strous**, New Jersey Institute of Technology & National Solar Observatory/ Sacramento Peak: 155bl, blc **STScI:** 8bl,

13cl, 128-9bc, 172-3b, 177cr, 182bl, 224br /Association of Universities for Research in Astronomy Inc: 223tr /J Bahcall (Institute for Advanced Study, Princeton): 217tl /Bruce Balick, University of Washinton, Vincent Icke, Leiden University, Netherlands, Garrelt Mellema, Stockholm University, NASA: 182bl /W. Baum (U.WA), NASA: 220bc /K. Borne (STScI), NASA: 212cl /W.N. Colley and E. Turner (Princeton University), J.A. Tyson (Bell Laboratories, Lucent Technologies) and NASA: 224t /H. Ford & L. Ferarese (JHU), NASA: 188b /Peter Garnavich, Harvard-Smithsonian Center for Astrophysics, the High-z Supernova Search Team and NASA: 235t /J. Hester & P. Scowen (Arizona State University) & NASA: 186-7t, 225bl /M. Longair (Cavendish Laboratory), NASA: 217clb /Brad Whitmore (STScI) & NASA: 212-3c /R. Williams (STScI), NASA: 228-9c **Tony Stone Images:** 87cl Sygma: 56br

Gérard Therin (www.astrosurf.com/therin): 122c **TRH Pictures:** 51cr 56bl, 57bl

USGS: 107ca **University of California/Lick Observatory:** 9tl, 164tr, tl 183tr, 187tl, tlc, tlr **University of Florida**, Department of Astronomy: 83ca **University of Oxford**, Department of Physics: 231bl

WIYN Observatory/Blair Savage, Chris Howk (University of Wisconsin) N.A. Sharp (NOAO)/AURA/NSF: 211tr

X-Ray Astronomy Group at the Department of Physics & Astronomy, University of Leicester, UK: 189ca

Additional photos by Andy Crawford, Steve Gorton, Glenn I. Huss, Colin Keates, and James Stevenson.

ILLUSTRATORS

David Ashby: 169c, 170bl, 172tr, 177br, 180bl, 183cl, 288-303

Julian Baum: 82-83, 96-97tc, 105tl, 128bl, 130-131c, 132bl, 134c, 138b, 168

Rick Blakely Art Studio: 36cr, cl, bl, 37cr, 39c, 56-57b, 62ct, 64cr, 65cr, 70bc, 72b, 74-75c, 242-243, 242br, 243tc, 244cl, 245cr, br, 270cr, 272cr, 273bc

Peter Bull Studio: 12-13c, 14-15c, 15bl, bc, 17c, 18bc, 19bl, 20-21, 22-23, 23bc, 24-25, 25c, 26-27, 28tr, br, 29t, 30-31b, 30br, 31b, 32bl, 33b, 46cr, 48br, c, bc, 49bl, br, 53c, 57bc, 60-61c, 71tl, 78-79c, 83cr, 85cr, c, 86bc, 94tr, br, 95tl, 95bl, 108tr, 109cr, 110bl, 111bl, 123c, 124bc, 126b, 131c, 133bc, 135bc, 137cr, bl, 139bl, 140bc, 141cr, 142bc, 144c, bc, 145cr,

146c, 147t, b, 150c, 151c, 154c, l, br, 155tr, 156cl, 157tr, br, 158tr, br, 159tl, 160cl, 161tl, 163br, 165ct, 166tr, l, b, 167l, 170tr, 176cl, 180-181, 184-185c, 195tr, 207tc, b, 212-213b, 213tr, 215bl, 216c, 217tr, cr, br, 218-219c, 220-221t, 220c, 249ct, cb, 250tr, bc, br, 251tl, 252tl, 255tl, 257tl, 258tl, 260tl, 269cl

Roy Flooks: 74c, 242cl, 244-245c, 244cl, 245cr, 245bc

Martyn Foote: 14bc, 15cl, tr, 18bl, 19tr, cr, 20-21b, 21r, 22-23bc, 24t, 24-25cb, 26-27bc, 28c, bc, bl, 30bc, 181tr, 183br, 184tr, 186tr, 187tr, cr, bl, 188bl, 208-209c, 211cr, 212tr, 219tc, 223tr, 225r, br, b, 228t, 230br, 231bc, tr, cr, 232t, c, l, cl, cb, b, 233br, 234-235c, 237r, 238cl, r

Ray Grinaway: 91ct, cc,cb, 90c, 90-91c

Aziz Khan: 194c, 198c, 199tl, 200c, 202c, 204c

James Marks: 89tl, 128cr, 129cl, 149r

Coral Mula: 268br

Robin Scagell: 262-263cb, cr

Roger Stewart: 36-37c, 64-65c

Wil Tirion: 252c, bc, 253cr, 254r, 255bl, 256r, 257bl, 258r, 259bl, 260r, 261bl.

With thanks for additional illustrations to Lynn Chadwick, Luciano Corbella, Brian Delf, Mike Dunning, Martyn Foote, and Mark Franklin

ACKNOWLEDGEMENTS

Dorling Kindersley would like to thank:

Jack Challoner for additional editorial consultancy

Hilary Bird for compiling the index

Wil Tirion for assistance in preparing the star maps

Sarah Johnson for downloading web images

Jo Earl for additional design assistance

Sally Hamilton, **Lee Thompson**, and **Fergus Muir** for additional picture research

Mathew Birch, **Andrew O'Brien**, and **Almudina Diaz** for additional DTP assistance

Omissions Every effort has been made to trace the copyright holders and we apologize in advance for any unintentional omissions. We would be pleased to insert the appropriate acknowledgements in any subsequent edition of this publication.